Bel

FOOD FOR FIFTY

Grace Shugart

Professor Emeritus of Dietetics, Restaurant
and Institutional Management;
formerly Head of Department
KANSAS STATE UNIVERSITY

Mary Molt

Administrative Dietitian, Housing and Food Service;
Instructor of Dietetics, Restaurant
and Institutional Management
KANSAS STATE UNIVERSITY

Maxine Wilson

Professor Emeritus of Restaurant, Hotel
and Institutional Management
PURDUE UNIVERSITY

FOOD FOR FIFTY

7th EDITION

Macmillan Publishing Company
New York

Collier Macmillan Publishers
London

Copyright © 1986, by Macmillan Publishing Company,
a division of Macmillan, Inc.

Copyright © 1961, 1971, 1979, 1985, by John Wiley & Sons, Inc.

Copyright © 1937, 1941, 1950, by Sina Faye Fowler
and Bessie Brooks West

All rights reserved. No part of this book may be
reproduced or transmitted in any form or by any means,
electronic or mechanical, including photocopying,
recording, or any information storage and retrieval system,
without permission in writing from the Publisher.

Macmillan Publishing Company
866 Third Avenue, New York, New York 10022
Collier Macmillan Canada, Inc.

Library of Congress Cataloging in Publication Data:

Shugart, Grace Severance, 1910–
   Food for fifty.

  Rev. ed. of: Food for fifty/Bessie Brooks West, Grace
Severance Shugart, Maxine Fay Wilson. 6th ed. c1979.
   Includes indexes.
   1. Quantity cookery.   2. Menus.   I. Molt, Mary K.
II. Wilson, Maxine Fay.   III. West, Bessie Brooks.
Food for fifty.   IV. Title.   V. Title: Food for 50.

TX820.S45   1985   641.5′7   84-13109
ISBN 0-02-411060-4

Printed in the United States of America

Printing 4 5 6 7   Year 6 7 8 9 0

ISBN 0-02-411060-4

In Memory of
BESSIE BROOKS WEST
A pioneer in food service administration, whose leadership was an inspiration to students and professional colleagues

Food for Fifty began in 1937 under the leadership of the late Bessie Brooks West. Her quest for quality food inspired the writing of the first edition and has remained a basic premise in the editions that followed. Mrs. West's contributions through the last 47 years have made possible the esteem in which *Food for Fifty* has been held.

Preface

The seventh edition of FOOD FOR FIFTY is designed, as were the previous six editions, to be used as a text by students in quantity food production and as a reference for persons engaged in food service management. This revised edition includes updated tables, new tested recipes, standardized yields, and simplified procedures.

The purpose of *Food for Fifty* is to provide basic information, recipes, and guidelines needed for planning and preparing food in quantity. The book is divided into four parts: general information, recipes, menu planning, and planning special meals and receptions. The general information section, considered by many users of the book to be a valuable reference, has been updated, expanded, and made simpler to use. The recipe section includes a variety of standardized recipes grouped by menu category, with a discussion of the procedures essential for production of quality food in quantity. The sections on menu planning and special meal service have been modified to be compatible with contemporary food services.

We wish to express our appreciation to the many individuals who have given freely of their time, knowledge, and ideas in the preparation of the seventh edition of *Food for Fifty*.

Grace Severance Shugart
Mary K. Molt
Maxine F. Wilson

Contents

Tables

PART ONE

GENERAL INFORMATION
How to Use Tables and Guides 3
Amounts of Food to Serve 50 4
Tables of Weights and Measures 21
Preparation and Serving Guides 33
Recipe Adjustment 42

PART TWO

RECIPES
Recipe Information 59

Appetizers 62

Beverages 67

Breads 80
Quick Breads 84
Yeast Breads 110

Desserts 135
Cakes, Frostings, and Fillings 135
Cookies 175
Pies 199
Puddings and Other Desserts 229

Eggs and Cheese 252

Fish 276

Meat 294

Pasta, Rice, and Cereals 346
Poultry 365
Salads and Salad Dressings 394
Sandwiches 447
Sauces 469
Meat and Vegetable Sauces 470
Dessert Sauces 487
Soups 493
Vegetables 520

PART THREE
MENU PLANNING

Factors Affecting Menu Planning 569
Menu Patterns and Cycles 571
Menu Planning Procedures 572
Menu Planning for Different Types of Food Services 575
Menu Planning Suggestions 582

PART FOUR
SPECIAL MEALS AND RECEPTIONS

Planning Responsibilities 595
Receptions and Teas 596
Coffees and Brunches 597
Buffet Dinners and Luncheons 599
Banquet Service 602

APPENDIX

Use of Herbs and Spices in Cooking 607
Glossary of Menu and Cooking Terms 609

Index 623

Tables

PART ONE GENERAL INFORMATION

TABLE 1.1	AMOUNTS OF FOOD TO SERVE 50	4
TABLE 1.2	APPROXIMATE YIELD IN THE PREPARATION OF FRESH FRUITS AND VEGETABLES	20
TABLE 1.3	FOOD WEIGHTS AND APPROXIMATE EQUIVALENTS IN MEASURE	21
TABLE 1.4	BASIC EQUIVALENTS IN MEASURES	29
TABLE 1.5	WEIGHT (1–16 OZ) AND MEASURE EQUIVALENTS FOR COMMONLY USED FOODS	30
TABLE 1.6	U.S. MEASURES OF WEIGHT AND METRIC EQUIVALENTS	32
TABLE 1.7	U.S. MEASURES OF VOLUME AND METRIC EQUIVALENTS	32
TABLE 1.8	TEMPERATURES AND TIMES USED IN BAKING	33
TABLE 1.9	TERMS FOR OVEN TEMPERATURES	34
TABLE 1.10	METRIC TEMPERATURE EQUIVALENTS	34
TABLE 1.11	TEMPERATURES AND TESTS FOR SYRUPS AND CANDIES	35
TABLE 1.12	DEEP-FAT FRYING TEMPERATURES	36
TABLE 1.13	COATINGS FOR DEEP-FAT FRIED FOODS	37
TABLE 1.14	DIPPER EQUIVALENTS	37
TABLE 1.15	LADLE EQUIVALENTS	38
TABLE 1.16	COMMON CAN SIZES	38
TABLE 1.17	SUBSTITUTING ONE CAN FOR ANOTHER SIZE	38
TABLE 1.18	INGREDIENT SUBSTITUTIONS	39
TABLE 1.19	PROPORTIONS OF INGREDIENTS	41
TABLE 1.20	GUIDE FOR ROUNDING OFF WEIGHTS AND MEASURES	44
TABLE 1.21	OUNCES AND DECIMAL EQUIVALENTS OF A POUND	45
TABLE 1.22	DIRECT READING TABLE FOR ADJUSTING WEIGHT INGREDIENTS OF RECIPES DIVISIBLE BY 25	47
TABLE 1.23	DIRECT READING MEASUREMENT TABLE FOR ADJUSTING RECIPES WITH INGREDIENT AMOUNTS GIVEN IN VOLUME MEASUREMENT AND DIVISIBLE BY 25	50
TABLE 1.24	DIRECT READING TABLE FOR INCREASING HOME SIZE RECIPES WITH INGREDIENT AMOUNTS GIVEN IN VOLUME MEASUREMENT AND DIVISIBLE BY 8	53

PART TWO RECIPES

TABLE 2.1	SCALING WEIGHTS AND YIELDS FOR CAKES	138
TABLE 2.2	SCALING WEIGHTS FOR FROSTINGS AND FILLINGS	139
TABLE 2.3	GUIDE FOR USING FROZEN FRUIT IN PIES AND COBBLERS	207
TABLE 2.4	GUIDE TO NATURAL CHEESES	254
TABLE 2.5	FISH BUYING AND COOKING GUIDE	279
TABLE 2.6	SUGGESTED METHODS OF COOKING FISH AND SHELLFISH	280

TABLE 2.7	TIMETABLE FOR ROASTING BEEF	**297**
TABLE 2.8	TIMETABLE FOR ROASTING LAMB AND VEAL	**298**
TABLE 2.9	TIMETABLE FOR ROASTING FRESH AND CURED PORK	**299**
TABLE 2.10	TIMETABLE FOR BROILING MEAT	**301**
TABLE 2.11	TIMETABLE FOR GRIDDLE BROILING MEAT	**301**
TABLE 2.12	TIMETABLE FOR BRAISING MEAT	**303**
TABLE 2.13	TIMETABLE FOR COOKING MEAT IN LIQUID	**303**
TABLE 2.14	COOKING METHODS FOR POULTRY	**366**
TABLE 2.15	ROASTING GUIDE FOR POULTRY	**370**
TABLE 2.16	TIMETABLE FOR BOILING OR STEAMING VEGETABLES	**522**

FOOD FOR FIFTY

PART ONE

GENERAL INFORMATION

General Information

Information in this section is presented as a guide for ordering food, adjusting recipes, and for the planning, preparation, and serving of food.

HOW TO USE TABLES AND GUIDES

Table 1.1 suggests amounts of food to purchase and prepare for 50 persons. The quantity of any item must be adjusted to the requirements of each group. Rarely is 50 the exact number to be served. The amounts given in this table are based on average servings, with the knowledge that an adjustment may be necessary to fit each situation. The size of portions may need to be increased, or because inexperienced employees find it difficult to obtain the exact number of portions indicated for a given quantity, a small increase in allowance for these items may be desirable. Table 1.2 is a guide for ordering fruits and vegetables.

Tables 1.3 through 1.5 are tables of weights and measures, intended as aids in converting ingredients in recipes from weight to measure. Tables 1.6 and 1.7 provide metric weight and measure equivalents.

Tables 1.8 through 1.19 include preparation and serving guides such as cooking temperatures (Tables 1.8 through 1.13), dipper and ladle equivalents (Tables 1.14 and 1.15), can sizes in Tables 1.16 and 1.17, and food equivalents, substitutions, and proportions in Tables 1.18 and 1.19. A guide for use of herbs and spices in cooking and a glossary of cooking and menu terms are found in the Appendix

Information on adjusting recipes begins on p. 42. Tables 1.20 and 1.21 include information on rounding off weights and measures, and changing pounds and ounces to decimal parts of a pound. Tables 1.22 through 1.24 are direct reading tables for adjusting yields of recipes. Table 1.22 is used when ingredient amounts in recipes are given in *weights* and portion yields are divisible by *25*. In Table 1.23, ingredients are stated in *volume* measurement and portions are divisible by *25*. Table 1.24 is especially useful when enlarging home-size recipes. Ingredients are in *volume* measurement and are in yields from *8* to *96*.

AMOUNTS OF FOOD TO SERVE 50

TABLE 1.1 AMOUNTS OF FOOD TO SERVE 50[a]

Food	Serving Portion	Amount for 50 Portions	Miscellaneous Information
Beverages			
Cider	4 oz (½ c)	2 gal	64 4-oz portions
Cocoa	6 oz (¾ c)	2½ gal	
Unsweetened powder		8 oz	
Instant mix		2½ lb	
Coffee	6 oz (¾ c)	2½ gal	
Regular or urn grind		1–1½ lb	
Freeze-dried		2 oz	
Instant		3 oz	20 tea cups water per oz
Lemonade	8 oz (1 c)	3 gal	48 8-oz portions
Frozen concentrate		3 32-oz cans	dilute 1:4 parts water
Orange juice, see Juices			
Punch	4 oz (½ c)	2–2½ gal	1 gal yields 32 4-oz portions
			2½ gal yields 50 4-oz portions plus 30 refills
Tea			
Hot	6 oz (¾ c)	2½ gal	
Bulk		2 oz	Amount may vary with quality of tea
Iced	8 oz (1 c)	3 gal	48 8-oz portions
1-oz bag		6 bags	6 1-oz bags make 3 gal
Instant		1–1½ oz	
Bread and Crackers			
Biscuits			
Baking powder	1 biscuit	4½ doz	
Dough, ready for baking		5 lb	
Mix		2½ lb	
Bread			
1-lb loaf	1 slice	3½ loaves	16 slices per loaf
1½-lb loaf	1 slice	2½ loaves	24 slices per loaf
2-lb pullman	1 slice	1½ loaves	36 slices per loaf
Breads, quick, 5 × 9 × 2¾-in. loaves	1 slice	4 loaves	16 slices per loaf
Coffee cake, 12 × 18 × 2 in.	3 × 2¼ in.	2 pans	Cut 4 × 8
Batter, ready to bake		5–6 lb per pan	

AMOUNTS OF FOOD TO SERVE 50

Food	Serving Portion	Amount for 50 Portions	Miscellaneous Information
Crackers			
Graham	2 crackers	1¾–2 lb	60–65 per lb
Saltines	4 crackers	1½ lb	150–160 per lb
Soda	2 crackers	1½–2 lb	65 per lb
Muffins	1 muffin	4½ doz	
Batter, ready to bake		5 lb	
Mix		3½ lb	
Pancakes	3½ oz	6½ qt batter	2 4-in. cakes
Mix		6 lb	
Rolls			
Breakfast, 3-oz	1 roll	4½ doz	
Dinner, 1½-oz	1 roll	4½ doz	
Frozen dough		10 lb	
Mix		5 lb	
Toast			
French	2 slices	7 lb bread	
Buttered or cinnamon	2 slices	7 lb bread	
Waffles	3 oz	6 qt batter	1 waffle
Cereals			
Barley, for soup		14–16 oz	For 3 gal soup
Cream of wheat	⅔ c	2 lb	2 gal cooked
Hominy grits	⅔ c	2 lb	2 gal cooked
Prepared cereal, flakes, crisp	1 oz (½–¾ c)	3 lb	
Rice	½ c	3–4 lb	6–8 qt cooked
Rolled oats	⅔ c	2 lb	2 gal cooked
see also PASTA			
Dairy Products			
Butter or margarine			
For sandwiches		1 lb	To butter 100 slices
For table	1–2 pats	1–1½ lb	
For vegetables	½–1 t	4–8 oz	
Cheese, cheddar	1–1½ oz	3–5 lb	For sandwich or with cold cuts
Sandwich slices, Cheddar or Swiss	1 oz	3¼ lb	
Cottage	2 oz (No. 20 dipper)	6½ lb	For salad or side dish
Cream	½ oz	2 lb	For salad or garnish
Dessert (cream, blue, camembert)	1 oz	3 lb	
Cream			
Coffee		1–1½ qt	
Whipping	2 T	1½ pt	1½ qt whipped

6 GENERAL INFORMATION

TABLE 1.1 (Continued)

Food	Serving Portion	Amount for 50 Portions	Miscellaneous Information
Ice cream, bulk	No. 12 dipper	2 gal	Dish or sundae
	No. 16 dipper	1½ gal	With cake or cookie
	No. 20 dipper	1¼ gal	For à la mode
Milk			
Fluid	8 oz (1 c)	3 gal	
Nonfat dry	8 oz (1 c)	3 lb	4 oz (1⅓ c) dry milk per qt of water. Volume may vary with brand.
Nondairy creamer	1 t	3 oz	
Sherbet	No. 20 dipper	1¼ gal	
Whipped topping mix			
Dry	2 T	5 oz	
Frozen	2 T	18 oz (1½ qt)	
Liquid	2 T	1½ pt	1½ qt whipped
Desserts			
Cakes			
Angel food	1 oz	3–4 cakes	12–14 cuts per cake
Pound or loaf, 5 × 9-in	3 oz	4 loaves	
Sheet, 12 × 18 × 2-in. batter, ready to bake	3 × 2¼ in.	2 pans 4–5 lb	Cut 4 × 8
sheet, 18 × 26 × 2-in. batter, ready to bake	3 × 2½ in.	1 pan 8–10 lb	Cut 6 × 10
Cake mixes			
Angel food		4 lb	
Chocolate, white, yellow		5 lb	
Pies, 8 in.	⅙ pie	8 pies	Cut 6 pieces per pie
Filling			
Chiffon	3 c per pie	6 qt	
Cream or custard	3 c per pie	6 qt	
Fruit	3 c (1 lb 8 oz per pie)	6 qt (10–12 lb)	
Meringue	4 oz per pie	2 lb	
Pastry			
1 crust	5 oz per pie	2 lb 8 oz	
2 crust	9 oz per pie	4 lb 8 oz	

AMOUNTS OF FOOD TO SERVE 50

Food	Serving Portion	Amount for 50 Portions	Miscellaneous Information
Pies, 9 in.	⅛ pie	6 pies	Cut 8 pieces per pie
Filling			
Chiffon	3¾ c per pie	6 qt	
Cream or custard	3¾ c per pie	6 qt	
Fruit	3¾–4 c (1 lb 14 oz)	6 qt (10–12 lb)	
Meringue	5–6 oz per pie	2–2¼ lb	
Pastry			
1 crust	8 oz per pie	3 lb	
2 crust	13 oz per pie	5 lb	
Puddings	½ c (4 oz)	6¼ qt	No. 10 dipper
Toppings, sauce	2–3 T	2–3 qt	

Eggs

Food	Serving Portion	Amount for 50 Portions	Miscellaneous Information
Eggs			
In shell	1 egg	4½ doz	
Fresh or frozen, whole	1 egg	5 lb (2½ qt)	

Fish and Shellfish

Food	Serving Portion	Amount for 50 Portions	Miscellaneous Information
Fish			
Fillets and steaks, 4 per lb	3 oz	14–16 lb	1 lb AP = 0.70 lb cooked fish
Whole, dressed	3 oz	40 lb	1 lb AP = 0.27 lb cooked fish
Oysters, shucked	3–4 oz	1½–2 gal	1 lb AP = 0.38 lb cooked oysters
Scallops, frozen, to fry	3 oz	10–12 lb	
Shrimp			
Raw, in shell	2 oz	12½ lb	1 lb AP = 0.54 lb cooked shrimp
	3 oz	18–20 lb	
Raw, peeled and cleaned	3 oz	16 lb	1 lb peeled = 0.62 lb cooked shrimp
Cooked, peeled and cleaned	3 oz	10 lb	1 lb AP = 1.00 lb cooked shrimp

Fruits

Food	Serving Portion	Amount for 50 Portions	Miscellaneous Information
Canned			
For pies, see Desserts, p. 6.			
For salad or dessert	3–4 oz (½ c)	2–2½ No. 10 cans	For fruits such as peach or pear halves, and sliced pineapple, depends on count per can

TABLE 1.1 *(Continued)*

Food	Serving Portion	Amount for 50 Portions	Miscellaneous Information
Dried			
Apricots or peaches	3 oz	4½ lb	
Prunes, with pits	4–5 prunes	6 lb	Size 30–40
Fresh			
Apples	1 apple	½ box	Size 113
8 8-in. pies	⅙ pie	16 lb AP	1 lb AP = 0.91 lb ready to cook or serve raw with peels; 0.78 lb pared, cooked
Salad or dessert	3–3½ oz	15 lb AP	
Apricots	2	9 lb AP	Medium size 12 per lb
Avocado	½	25 avocados	Medium size 2 per lb
Salad	3 slices	12 avocados	1 lb AP = 0.67 lb ready to serve raw
Bananas	1	16 lb AP	Small, 5–6 in.
8 8-in. pies	⅙ pie	5 lb AP	1 lb AP = 0.65 lb ready to serve raw
Salad	3 oz	10 lb AP	Medium, 7–8 in., 3 per lb
Blueberries	4 oz	12–14 lb AP	1 lb AP = 0.96 lb ready to serve raw
Cherries, sweet	3 oz	10 lb AP	1 lb AP = 0.98 lb ready to serve with pits; 0.84 lb pitted
Cranberries, for sauce	¼ c	4 lb AP	1 lb AP = 0.95 lb ready to cook
Fruit cup (mixed fruits)	3 oz (⅓ c)	9 lb (6 qt)	
Grapefruit	½	25 fruit	64 to 80 size
Salad	5 sections	21 fruit	12 sections per fruit 1 lb AP = 0.52 lb ready to serve raw
Grapes, seedless	4 oz	15 lb AP	1 lb AP = 0.97 lb ready to serve raw
With seeds			1 lb AP = 0.89 lb raw seeded
Kiwi fruit	1 slice	6–8 fruit	For garnish
Lemons			
For tea or fish	⅙ lemon	8–10 lemons	Medium, size 165
For lemonade	8-oz glass	3 doz	Medium, size 165
Limes			
Garnish	1 wedge	12 limes	4 wedges per lime
Limeade	8-oz glass	4½ doz	

AMOUNTS OF FOOD TO SERVE 50

Food	Serving Portion	Amount for 50 Portions	Miscellaneous Information
Mangoes, cubed or sliced	½ c	12½ lb AP	1 lb AP = 0.69 lb ready to serve raw
Melon			
Cantaloupe	½ melon	25 melons	
Fruit cup		5 melons	1 lb AP = 0.52 lb ready to serve raw
Salad slices		6 melons	
Casaba, honeydew, or persian	⅛ melon	7 melons	1 lb AP = 0.46 lb ready to serve raw
Watermelon	12–16 oz	38–50 lb AP	1 lb AP = 0.57 lb fruit without rind
Nectarines	1 nectarine (5 oz)	15–16 lb AP	1 lb AP = 0.91 lb ready to serve raw
Oranges	1 orange	½ box	Size 113
Juice	4 oz (½ c)	6¼ qt	16–18 doz size 113
Sections	5 sections	18 oranges	Size 150; 1 lb AP = 0.40 lb ready to serve, without membrane
Peaches	1 peach (4–5 oz)	12–15 lb AP	
Diced or sliced	½ c	20 lb AP	1 lb AP = 0.76 lb ready to cook or serve raw
Pears	1 pear (5–6 oz)	17–19 lb AP	1 lb AP = 0.92 lb ready to cook or serve raw, unpared; 0.78 lb pared
Salad	3 slices	15–17 lb AP	8–10 slices per pear
Pineapple, cubed	½ c	24 lb AP (6 pineapples)	1 lb AP = 0.54 lb ready to serve raw
Plums, Italian or purple	2 plums	12½ lb AP	Medium size, 8 per lb; 1 lb AP = 0.94 lb ready to cook or serve raw
Rhubarb, 8 8-in. pies	⅙ pie	12 lb AP	1 lb AP = 0.86 lb ready to cook
Sauce	½ c	14 lb AP	
Strawberries	4 oz	14 lb AP	1 lb AP = 0.88 lb ready to serve raw
Garnish	1 berry	1 qt AP	1 qt AP = about 1.32 lb ready to serve raw

10 GENERAL INFORMATION

TABLE 1.1 (Continued)

Food	Serving Portion	Amount for 50 Portions	Miscellaneous Information
Shortcake	¾ c	8 qt AP	
Sundaes	½–¾ c	6–8 qt AP	
Frozen			
For pies, see DESSERTS			
For salad or dessert	4 oz (½ c)	13–15 lb	
For topping	1½ oz	5 lb	
Juices			
Fruit or vegetable	4 oz (½ c)	6¼ qt	
	6 oz (¾ c)	9½ qt	
Canned	4 oz	4 46-oz cans	
	6 oz	7 46-oz cans	
Frozen	4 oz	4–5 12-oz cans	Dilute 1:3 parts water
		2 32-oz cans	Dilute 1:3 parts water
	6 oz	7 12-oz cans	Dilute 1:3 parts water
		3 32-oz cans	Dilute 1:3 parts water
Meat			
Beef			
Brisket, corned, boneless	3 oz EP	25–30 lb AP	1 lb AP = 0.42 lb cooked lean meat
Brisket, fresh, boneless	3 oz EP	25–30 lb AP	1 lb AP = 0.46 lb cooked lean meat
Cubed, 1-in., for stew	3 oz EP	12–15 lb AP	1 lb AP = 0.56 lb cooked lean meat
Ground, no more than 30% fat	3 oz EP	13–15 lb AP	1 lb AP = 0.70 lb cooked meat
Heart	3 oz EP	20–24 lb AP	1 lb AP = 0.44 lb cooked heart
Liver	3 oz EP	12–13 lb AP	1 lb AP = 0.70 cooked liver
Roast			
Chuck, pot roast, boneless	3 oz EP	16–18 lb AP	1 lb AP = 0.60 lb lean cooked meat
With bone	3 oz EP	20–22 lb AP	1 lb AP = 0.45 lb cooked lean meat
Rib			
Standing	6 oz EP	45–50 lb AP	Bone in, oven prepared
Ribeye	3 oz EP	12–15 lb AP	1 lb AP = 0.70 lb lean cooked meat
Round, boneless	3 oz EP	16–18 lb AP	1 lb AP = 0.61 lb cooked lean meat

Food	Serving Portion	Amount for 50 Portions	Miscellaneous Information
Rump, boneless	3 oz EP	16–18 lb AP	1 lb AP = 0.62 lb cooked lean meat
Sirloin, boneless, trimmed	3 oz EP	16–18 lb AP	1 lb AP = 0.61 lb cooked lean meat
Short ribs, trimmed	3 oz EP	38–40 lb AP	1 lb AP = 0.25 lb cooked meat
Steaks			
Cubed, 4 per lb	3 oz EP	13 lb AP	
Flank, 4 per lb	3 oz EP	13 lb AP	1 lb AP = 0.67 lb cooked lean meat
Loin strip	8 oz AP	25 lb AP	Short cut, bone in
Round, boneless, 3 per lb	3½ oz EP	18–20 lb AP	1 lb AP = 0.59 lb cooked lean meat
Sirloin, boneless	3½ oz EP	14–16 lb AP	1 lb AP = 0.75 lb cooked lean meat
Tenderloin, trimmed	4 oz EP	14 lb AP	1 lb AP = 0.90 lb cooked lean meat
T-bone	8 oz AP	25 lb AP	
	12 oz AP	36–38 lb AP	
Lamb			
Chops, rib, 4 per lb	2 each	25 lb AP	1 lb AP = 0.46 lb cooked lean meat
Roast, leg, boneless	3 oz EP	15 lb AP	1 lb AP = 0.61 lb cooked lean meat
With bone	3 oz EP	22 lb AP	1 lb AP = 0.45 lb cooked lean meat
Pork, fresh			
Chops, loin, with bone, 3 per lb	1 chop	17 lb AP	1 lb AP = 0.41 lb cooked lean meat
Cutlets, 3 or 4 per lb	3–3½ oz EP	12–15 lb AP	1 lb AP = 0.75 lb cooked meat
Roast, loin, boneless	3 oz EP	18–20 lb AP	1 lb AP = 0.54 lb cooked lean meat
With bone	3 oz EP	22–24 lb AP	1 lb AP = 0.41 lb cooked lean meat
Fresh ham, whole boneless	3 oz EP	18–20 lb AP	1 lb AP = 0.53 lb cooked lean meat
With bone	3 oz EP	20–22 lb AP	1 lb AP = 0.46 lb cooked lean meat
Shoulder, Boston butt, boneless	3 oz EP	18–20 lb AP	1 lb AP = 0.54 lb cooked lean meat
With bone	3 oz EP	19–21 lb AP	1 lb AP = 0.50 lb cooked lean meat
Shoulder Picnic, boneless	3 oz EP	20–22 lb AP	1 lb AP = 0.46 lb cooked lean meat

12 GENERAL INFORMATION

TABLE 1.1 *(Continued)*

Food	Serving Portion	Amount for 50 Portions	Miscellaneous Information
With bone	3 oz EP	25 lb AP	1 lb AP = 0.38 lb cooked lean meat
Sausage, bulk	2-oz pattie	12½–15 lb AP	1 lb AP = 0.47 lb cooked lean meat
Links, 12–16 per lb	2 links	7–8 lb AP	1 lb AP = 0.47 lb cooked lean meat
Spareribs	8–12 oz AP	25–40 lb AP	1 lb AP = 0.39 lb cooked meat
Pork, Cured			
Bacon, sliced,			
Hotel pack	2 slices	4–5 lb	24 slices per lb
Sliced	2 slices	5–6 lb	17–20 slices per lb
Canadian	2 slices (2 oz)	10 lb	16 slices per lb
Ham, boneless	3 oz EP	15 lb AP	1 lb AP = 0.63 lb cooked lean meat
With bone	3 oz EP	18–20 lb AP	1 lb AP = 0.53 lb cooked lean meat
Fully cooked, ready to eat	3 oz EP	15 lb AP	
Pullman, canned	3 oz EP	12–15 lb AP	1 lb AP = 0.64 lb cooked lean meat
Shoulder, Boston butt, boneless	3 oz EP	16 lb AP	1 lb AP = 0.60 lb lean meat
Shoulder, picnic, boneless	3 oz EP	18 lb AP	1 lb AP = 0.53 lb cooked lean meat
Variety and Luncheon Meats			
Braunschweiger	2 oz	7 lb	
Frankfurters			
8 per lb	2 franks	12½ lb	
10 per lb	2 franks	10 lb	
Knockwurst	3 oz	10 lb	
Sliced luncheon meat	1 oz	3¼ lb	16 slices per lb
Veal			
Cubed, 1-in. for stew	2 oz EP	12–15 lb AP	1 lb AP = 0.65 lb cooked lean meat
Cutlets, 3 or 4 per lb	3–3½ oz EP	12½–15 lb AP	1 lb AP = 0.80 lb cooked lean meat
Ground	3–4 oz EP	15 lb AP	1 lb AP = 0.73 lb cooked lean meat
Liver, calves	3–4 oz EP	15–18 lb AP	1 lb AP = 0.70 lb cooked liver
Roast, leg, boneless	3 oz EP	15–18 lb AP	1 lb AP = 0.61 lb cooked lean meat
Shoulder, boneless	3 oz EP	18 lb AP	1 lb AP = 0.59 lb cooked lean meat

AMOUNTS OF FOOD TO SERVE 50

Food	Serving Portion	Amount for 50 Portions	Miscellaneous Information
Pasta			
Macaroni, noodles, and spaghetti	4 oz	4½–5 lb dry	12 lb cooked
In casseroles	1½–2½ oz	2–3 lb dry	5–7½ lb cooked
Poultry			
Chicken, fryers			
Parts			
½ breast	5 oz AP	15–16 lb AP	1 lb AP = 0.66 lb cooked chicken
1 drumstick and thigh	6 oz AP	19–20 lb AP	
1 drumstick	3 oz AP	10 lb AP	1 lb AP = 0.49 lb cooked chicken
1 thigh	3 oz AP	10–11 lb	1 lb AP = 0.50 lb cooked chicken
2 wings	5 oz AP	15 lb	1 lb AP = 0.34 lb cooked chicken
Whole	¼ fryer	13 fryers	2½–3 lb each
	½ fryer	25 fryers	1¾–2 lb each
Whole, for stewing	2 oz cooked chicken	18–20 lb AP	1 lb AP = 0.36 lb cooked chicken without skin, neck, or giblets; 0.41 lb with neck meat and giblets.
Canned, boned			1 lb AP = 0.88 lb EP
Boned, solid pack			1 lb AP = 0.93 lb EP
Boned, with broth			1 lb AP = 0.78 lb EP
Frozen, cubed			1 lb AP = 0.98 lb EP
Turkey, dressed, whole for roasting	3 oz EP	35–40 lb AP	1 lb AP = 0.53 lb cooked turkey with skin, without neck and giblets; without skin 0.47 lb
Boneless roll, raw	3–4 oz EP	16–18 lb AP	1 lb AP = 0.66 lb cooked turkey meat
Boneless roll, cooked	3–4 oz EP	12–15 lb AP	1 lb AP = 0.92 lb cooked turkey meat
Breasts, whole, raw	3 oz EP	19 lb AP	1 lb AP = 0.64 lb turkey meat with skin; 0.57 lb without skin

14 GENERAL INFORMATION

TABLE 1.1 *(Continued)*

Food	Serving Portion	Amount for 50 Portions	Miscellaneous Information
Leg quarters	3 oz EP	19 lb AP	1 lb AP = 0.53 lb cooked turkey; without skin 0.48 lb
Turkey ham, cooked	1½ oz	5 lb	
Turkey, cooked, cubed	1½–2 oz	5–6 lb EP (18–20 lb AP)	3¾–4½ qt
Canned, see chicken			
Relishes			
Catsup	1 oz	½ No. 10 can	1 No. 10 can = about 12 c
	1 oz	5 14-oz bottles	
Olives, green, whole	3	2 qt	88–90 per qt
Ripe, whole or pitted	3	1½ qt	120–150 per qt
Pickles, dill, whole	1 pickle	2½ qt	
Dill or sweet, sliced	1 oz	2¼ qt	
Pickle relish	1 oz	2 qt	1 gal = about 58 oz drained
Salads and Salad Dressings			
Salads			
Bulky vegetable	1 c	3 gal	
Fish or meat	⅔ c	2 gal	
Fruit	⅓ c	4¼ qt	
Gelatin	½ c	1 12 × 20 × 2-in. pan	24-oz pkg flavored gelatin, 1 gal liquid
potato	½ c	6¼ qt	
Dressings			
Mixed in salad			
French, thin	2 t	2–3 c	
Mayonnaise	1 T	1 qt	
Self-service			
Thousand Island or roquefort	1–2 T	1½–2 qt	
French	2 t	1 qt	
Sauces			
Gravy	3–4 T	3–4 qt	
Meat accompaniment	2 T	2 qt	
Pudding	2–3 T	2–3 qt	
Vegetable	2–3 T	2–3 qt	

AMOUNTS OF FOOD TO SERVE 50

Food	Serving Portion	Amount for 50 Portions	Miscellaneous Information
Soups			
Soup			
First course	⅔ c	2 gal	
Main course	1 c	3¼ gal	
Soup			
Concentrated	1 c	5 46-oz cans	
Dehydrated		1½ lb	For 3 gal soup
Soup base, paste		8 oz	For 2½ gal soup
Sugars, Jellies, Sweets, Nuts			
Candies, small	2 each	1 lb	
Honey	2 T	5 lb (2 qt)	
Jam or jelly	1 T	2–3 lb	
Marshmallows	3	1–1½ lb	
Nuts, mixed	1½ T	1–1½ lb	
Sugar, cubes	1–2 cubes	1½ lb	
granulated	1½ t	12 oz	
Syrup	¼ c	3 qt	
Toppings for dessert	2 T	1½–2 qt	
Vegetables			
Canned	2½ oz	2 No. 10 cans	Most vegetables yield 60–70 oz drained weight
Dried			
Dehydrated potatoes			
Diced or sliced	3–4 oz EP	2–2½ lb AP	
Instant for mashing	4 oz EP	2–2¼ lb AP	
Dried beans	4 oz EP	5–6 lb AP	
Split peas or lentils	4 oz EP	4 lb AP	
Fresh			
Alfalfa sprouts	2 T EP	1 lb AP	
Asparagus	3 oz EP	18–20 lb AP	1 lb AP = 0.53 lb ready to cook; 0.50 lb cooked
Beans, green or wax	3 oz EP	10–12 lb AP	1 lb AP = 0.88 lb ready to cook
Bean sprouts	2 T EP	12 oz AP	
Beets, topped	3 oz EP	12–14 lb AP	1 lb AP = 0.77 lb peeled; 0.73 lb cooked slices
Broccoli	3 oz EP	16–20 lb AP	1 lb AP = 0.81 lb ready to cook
Brussels sprouts	3 oz EP	12–14 lb AP	1 lb AP = 0.76 lb ready to cook

TABLE 1.1 *(Continued)*

Food	Serving Portion	Amount for 50 Portions	Miscellaneous Information
Cabbage			
Green	1 wedge or 3 oz EP shredded	12–14 lb AP	1 lb AP = 0.89 lb ready to cook or serve raw
Red, chopped or shredded	2 oz EP	10 lb AP	1 lb AP = 0.64 lb ready to cook or serve raw
Carrots, without tops	3 oz EP	14–16 lb AP	1 lb AP = 0.70 lb ready to cook or serve raw; 0.60 lb cooked
Strips for relish	3 strips 4 × ½ in.	4–5 lb	
Cauliflower	3 oz EP	16–18 lb AP	1 lb AP = 0.62 lb ready to cook or serve raw; 0.61 lb cooked
Salad pieces	¼ c	8 lb AP	1 medium head = about 6 c (50–75) flowerets
Celery,			
sliced	3 oz EP	12 lb AP	1 lb AP = 0.83 lb ready to cook or serve raw; 0.74 lb cooked
Sticks for relishes	4 sticks 4 × ½ in.	4–5 lb AP	
Celery cabbage	2 oz EP	9 lb AP	1 lb AP = 0.93 lb ready to serve raw
Corn, on cob	1 ear	5 doz (25 lb with husks)	1 lb AP = 0.33 lb edible portion cooked
Cucumbers	1½ oz EP	5–6 lb AP	1 lb AP = 0.84 lb ready to serve raw pared
Eggplant	3 oz EP	12–15 lb AP	1 lb AP = 0.81 lb ready to cook
Endive, escarole	½ c	8–10 lb AP	1 lb AP = 0.78 lb ready to serve
Lettuce			
Head, wedges	⅙ head	8–10 heads	
Broken, for salad	1 c (2½ oz)	9 lb AP	1 lb AP = 0.76 lb ready to serve
Garnish	1 leaf	4–5 lb AP	

AMOUNTS OF FOOD TO SERVE 50

Food	Serving Portion	Amount for 50 Portions	Miscellaneous Information
Leaf, for garnish	1 leaf	3–4 lb AP	1 lb AP = 0.66 lb ready to serve
Bibb	2½ oz EP	9 lb	
Romaine, for salad	2½ oz EP	9 lb AP	1 lb AP = 0.64 lb ready to serve
Mushrooms, sliced	3 oz EP	12 lb AP	1 lb AP = 0.98 ready to serve raw or cook; 0.22 lb cooked
For sauce	1 oz EP	3–4 lb AP	
Onions			
Green, chopped for salad	¼ c (with tops)	3½–4 lb AP	1 lb AP = 0.83 lb ready to serve raw with tops; 0.37 lb without tops
Mature	2 oz EP	7–8 lb AP	1 lb AP = 0.88 lb ready to serve raw or cook; 0.78 lb cooked
Whole, to bake	1 medium	12–15 lb AP	
Parsley, for garnish or seasoning		2 lb AP	
Parsnips	3 oz EP	12–15 lb AP	1 lb AP = 0.83 lb ready to cook
Peppers, green, strips	3 strips	4–5 lb AP	1 lb AP = 0.80 lb ready to cook or serve raw; 0.73 lb cooked
Chopped for salads	½ oz	1–2 lb AP	
Potatoes, sweet, or yams to bake	1 potato (4½–5 oz)	18–20 lb AP	1 lb AP = 0.61 lb baked, without skins
Candied	4 oz EP	20–25 lb AP	1 lb AP = 0.80 lb peeled, ready to cook
Mashed	4 oz EP	18 lb AP	
Potatoes, white, baked	1 potato	17–25 lb AP	1 lb AP = 0.74 lb baked potato without skins
Mashed	4 oz (½ c)	15 lb AP	1 lb AP = 0.81 lb ready to cook pared

TABLE 1.1 (Continued)

Food	Serving Portion	Amount for 50 Portions	Miscellaneous Information
Steamed	4 oz (1 potato)	16–17 lb AP	
French fried	4–5 oz EP	16–20 lb AP	1 lb AP = 0.81 lb ready to cook
Radishes, without tops, for relishes	2 oz EP	6 lb AP	1 lb AP = 0.94 lb ready to serve raw
Spinach	3 oz EP	12 lb AP	1 lb AP = 0.88 lb ready to cook or serve raw
For salad	1 oz EP	4–5 lb AP	
Squash, summer, yellow	3 oz EP	10 lb AP	1 lb AP = 0.95 lb ready to cook; 0.83 lb cooked
Zucchini	3 oz EP	10 lb AP	1 lb AP = 0.94 lb ready to cook; 0.86 lb cooked
Squash, winter, acorn	½ squash	20–25 lb AP	1 lb AP = 0.87 lb ready to cook in skin
Butternut	3 oz EP	12 lb AP	1 lb AP = 0.84 lb ready to cook pared
Hubbard, baked	2½-in. square	20–25 lb	
Mashed	3 oz EP	15 lb AP	1 lb AP = 0.64 lb ready to cook pared
Tomatoes	1 small	20 lb AP	
Sliced, salad	3 slices	15 lb AP	1 lb AP = 0.90 lb ready to cook or serve raw
Diced	½ c	10 lb AP	
Cherry, salad	1 oz EP	4 lb AP	1 lb AP = 0.97 lb stemmed
Turnips	3 oz EP	12–15 lb AP	1 lb AP = 0.79 lb ready to cook or serve raw; 0.78 lb cooked
Watercress	1½ oz EP	4–5 lb AP	
Frozen			
Asparagus spears	3 oz	10 lb	
Beans, cut green or lima	3 oz	10 lb	
Broccoli	3 oz	10 lb	
Brussels sprouts	3 oz	10 lb	

AMOUNTS OF FOOD TO SERVE 50

Food	Serving Portion	Amount for 50 Portions	Miscellaneous Information
Cauliflower	3 oz	10 lb	
Corn, whole kernel	3 oz	10 lb	
Peas	3 oz	10 lb	
Potatoes			
French fried	4 oz	12–13 lb	
Hashed brown	4 oz	12–13 lb	
Spinach	3 oz	10 lb	
Miscellaneous			
Ice			
For water glasses	3–4 oz	10–12 lb	
For punch bowl		10 lb	
Potato chips	1 oz	3 lb	

[a] Abbreviations used: AP, = as purchased; EP, edible portion. For Metric equivalents, see Tables 1.6 and 1.7. Yield information from *Food Buying Guide*, USDA Program Aid 1257, revised October 1981.

TABLE 1.2 APPROXIMATE YIELD IN THE PREPARATION OF FRESH FRUITS AND VEGETABLES[a]

Weight of Ready To Cook or Ready To Serve Raw from 1 lb as Purchased				
	lb		lb
Apples	0.78	Lettuce, head	0.76
Asparagus	0.53	Lettuce, leaf	0.66
Avocado	0.67	Lettuce, romaine	0.64
Bananas	0.65	Mangoes	0.69
Beans, green or wax	0.88	Mushrooms	0.98
Beans, lima	0.44	Nectarines	0.91
Beets	0.77	Okra	0.87
Blueberries	0.96	Onions, mature	0.88
Broccoli	0.81	Orange, sections	0.40
Brussels sprouts	0.76	Parsnips	0.83
Cabbage, green	0.87	Peaches	0.76
Cabbage, red	0.64	Pears, served pared	0.78
Cantaloupe, served without rind	0.52	Peas, green	0.38
		Peppers, green	0.80
Carrots	0.70	Pineapple	0.54
Cauliflower	0.62	Plums	0.94
Celery	0.83	Potatoes, sweet	0.80
Chard, Swiss	0.92	Potatoes, white	0.81
Cherries, pitted	0.87	Radishes, without tops	0.94
Chicory	0.89	Rhubarb, without leaves	0.86
Collards, leaves	0.57	Rutabagas	0.85
Collards, leaves and stems	0.74	Spinach, partly trimmed	0.88
Cranberries	0.95	Squash, acorn	0.87
Cucumber, pared	0.84	Squash, butternut	0.84
Eggplant	0.81	Squash, Hubbard	0.64
Endive, escarole	0.78	Squash, summer	0.95
Grapefruit, sections	0.52	Squash, zucchini	0.94
Grapes, seedless	0.97	Strawberries	0.88
Honeydew melon, served without rind	0.46	Tomatoes	0.99
		Turnips, without tops	0.79
Kale	0.67	Watermelon	0.57

[a] Adapted from *Food Buying Guide for School Food Service*, U.S. Dept. Agriculture PA 1257, Washington, D.C., 1980.

How to Use This Table:
To determine the amount of fruits or vegetables to yield the amount stated in a recipe as EP or as ready to cook in the Timetable for Boiling or Steaming Fresh Vegetables, p. 522:

Divide the weight of ready to cook or EP desired by the figure given in this table. For example, the recipe for Mashed Potatoes, p. 551, calls for 12 lb EP potatoes. To change the 12 lb EP to AP, divide 12 lb by 0.81, the ready to cook weight from 1 lb AP.

12 lb EP ÷ 0.81 lb = 14.8 or 15 lb to purchase

TABLES OF WEIGHTS AND MEASURES

TABLE 1.3 FOOD WEIGHTS AND APPROXIMATE EQUIVALENTS IN MEASURE

Food	Weight[a]	Approximate Measure[a]
Alfalfa sprouts	1 lb	6 c
Allspice	1 oz	4½ T
Almonds, blanched	1 lb	3 c
Apples, canned, pie pack	1 lb	2 c
Apples, fresh AP[b]	1 lb	3–4 medium (113)
Apples, fresh, pared and sliced	1 lb	1 qt
Apples, pared and diced, 1½-in. cubes	1 lb	3½ c
Applesauce	1 lb	2 c
Apricots, canned, halves, without juice	1 lb	2 c or 12–20 halves
Apricots, canned, pie pack	1 lb	2 c
Apricots, dried AP	1 lb	3 c
Apricots, dried, cooked, without juice	1 lb	4½–5 c
Apricots, fresh	1 lb	5–8 apricots
Asparagus, canned, cuts	1 lb	2½ c
Asparagus, canned tips, drained	1 lb	16–20 stalks
Asparagus, fresh	1 lb	16–20 stalks
Avocado	1 lb	2 medium
Bacon, cooked	1 lb	85–95 slices
Bacon, uncooked	1 lb	14–25 slices
Bacon, uncooked, diced	1 lb	2¼ c
Baking powder	1 oz	2⅓ T
Baking powder	1 lb	2⅓ c
Baking soda	1 oz	2⅓ T
Baking soda	1 lb	2⅓ c
Bananas AP	1 lb	3 medium
Bananas, diced	1 lb	2½–3 c
Bananas, mashed	1 lb	2 c
Barley, pearl	1 lb	2 c
Basil, sweet	1 oz	1 c
Beans, baked	1 lb	2 c
Beans, garbanzo, canned	1 lb	2½ c
Beans, garbanzo or Great Northern, dried, AP	1 lb	2½ c
Beans, green, cut, cooked	1 lb	3½ c
Beans, kidney, dried AP	1 lb	2½ c
Beans, kidney, dried, 1 lb AP, after cooking	2 lb 6 oz	6–7 c
Beans, lima, dried AP	1 lb	2½ c
Beans, lima, dried, 1 lb AP, after cooking	2 lb 9 oz	6 c
Beans, lima, fresh or canned	1 lb	2 c
Beans, navy, dried AP	1 lb	2¼ c
Beans, navy, dried, 1 lb AP, after cooking	2 lb 3 oz	5½–6 c
Beans, pinto, dried AP	1 lb	2⅜ c

TABLE 1.3 *(Continued)*

Food	Weight[a]	Approximate Measure[a]
Bean sprouts, canned	1 lb	1 qt
Bean sprouts, fresh	1 lb	2 qt
Beef, dried, solid pack	1 lb	3¾ c
Beef, cooked, diced	1 lb	3 c
Beef, ground, raw	1 lb	2 c
Beets, fresh, medium	1 lb	3–4 beets
Beets, cooked, diced or sliced	1 lb	2½–2¾ c
Blackberries, fresh	1 lb	3½ c
Blackberries or boysenberries, pie pack	1 lb	2½ c
Blackeyed peas, dried	1 lb	2¾ c
Blueberries, fresh	1 lb	3½ c
Blueberries, canned	1 lb	2¼ c
Bran, all bran	1 lb	2 qt
Bran flakes	1 lb	3 qt
Bread, loaf	1 lb	16–18 slices, ½ in. each
Bread, sandwich	2 lb	36–40 slices, thin
Bread, soft, broken	1 lb	2½ qt
Bread, dry, broken	1 lb	8–9 c
Bread, fresh	1 lb	8 oz dry crumbs
Bread crumbs, dry, ground	1 lb	4 c
Bread crumbs, soft	1 lb	2 qt
Brussels sprouts AP	1 lb	1 qt
Butter	1 lb	2 c
Buttermilk, dry	1 oz	⅓ c
Buttermilk, dry	1 lb	5⅓ c
Cabbage, raw, shredded EP[c]	1 lb	1 qt lightly packed
Cabbage, AP, shredded, cooked	1 lb	1½ c
Cake crumbs, soft	1 lb	6 c
Cake mix	1 lb	4 c
Cantaloupe	3 lb	1 melon, 6-in. diameter
Caraway seed	1 oz	4 T
Carrots, fresh	1 lb	4–5 medium
Carrots, diced, cooked	1 lb	3 c
Carrots, diced, raw	1 lb	3–3¼ c
Carrots, ground, raw EP	1 lb	3 c
Catsup	1 lb	2 c
Cauliflower, head	12 oz	1 small
Cayenne pepper	1 oz	3 T
Celery, diced EP	1 lb	1 qt
Celery, diced	1–2 bunches	1 qt
Celery cabbage, shredded	1 lb	6 c
Celery flakes, dried	1 oz	1⅓ c

TABLES OF WEIGHTS AND MEASURES 23

Food	Weight[a]	Approximate Measure[a]
Celery salt	1 oz	2 T
Celery seed	1 oz	4 T
Cheese, cheddar or Swiss, shredded	1 lb	4 c
Cheese, cottage	1 lb	2 c
Cheese, loaf, slices	1 lb	16–20 slices
Cheese, parmesan or romano, grated	1 lb	5⅔ c
Cheese, Philadelphia cream	1 lb	2 c
Cherries, glacé	1 lb	96 cherries or 2½ c
Cherries, maraschino, drained	1 lb	50–60 cherries
Cherries, red, pie pack, drained	1 lb	2½ c
Cherries, Royal Anne, drained	1 lb	2¼ c
Chicken, ready to cook	4–4½ lb	1 qt cooked, diced
Chicken, cooked, cubed	1 lb	3 c
Chili powder	1 oz	4 T
Chili sauce	1 lb	1⅓ c
Chives, freeze-dried	1 oz	2⅞ c
Chives, frozen	1 oz	⅓ c
Chocolate, baking	1 lb	16 squares
Chocolate chips	1 lb	3 c
Chocolate, grated	1 lb	3½ c
Chocolate, melted	1 lb	2 c (scant)
Chocolate wafers	1 lb	4 c crumbs
Cinnamon, ground	1 oz	4 T
Cinnamon, ground	1 lb	4 c
Cinnamon, stick	1 oz	10 pieces
Citron, dried, chopped	1 lb	2½ c
Cloves, ground	1 oz	4 T
Cloves, whole	1 oz	5 T
Cocoa	1 lb	4½ c
Coconut, flaked	1 lb	4⅔ c
Coconut, shredded	1 lb	5 c
Coffee, ground coarse	1 lb	5–5½ c
Coffee, instant	1 oz	½ c
Corn, canned	1 lb	1¾–2 c
Cornflakes	1 lb	1 qt
Cornmeal, coarse	1 lb	3 c
Cornmeal, 1 lb AP, dry, after cooking	6 lb	3 qt
Cornstarch	1 oz	3½ T
Cornstarch	1 lb	3½ c
Corn syrup	1 lb	1⅓ c
Crabmeat, flaked	1 lb	3½ c
Crab in shell	1 lb	½ c cooked meat
Cracked wheat	1 lb	3½ c
Crackers, graham	1 lb	60–65 crackers
Crackers, 2⅝ × 2⅝ in.	1 lb	65 crackers
Crackers, saltines, 2 × 2 in.	1 lb	150–160 crackers

TABLE 1.3 *(Continued)*

Food	Weight[a]	Approximate Measure[a]
Cracker crumbs, medium fine	1 lb	5–6 c
Cranberries, raw	1 lb	4 c
Cranberries, cooked	1 lb	2 c
Cranberries, sauce, jellied	1 lb	2 c
Cream of tartar	1 oz	3 T
Cream of wheat or farina, quick, AP	1 lb	2⅔ c
Cream of wheat or farina, 1 lb AP, after cooking	8 lb	1 gal
Cream, cultured sour	1 lb	2 c
Cream, whipping	1 pt	1 qt, whipped
Cucumbers	1 lb	2–3 large
Cucumbers, diced EP	1 lb	3 c
Cucumbers, sliced	1 lb	50–60 slices
Cumin, ground	1 oz	4 T
Currants, dried	1 lb	3 c
Curry powder	1 oz	4 T
Dates, pitted	1 lb	2½ c
Eggplant	1 lb	8 slices 4 × ½ in.
Eggplant	1 lb	1 qt diced
Eggs, whole, in shell[d]	1 lb	8 large eggs
Eggs, shelled, fresh or frozen, whole	1 lb	2 c (9–11 eggs)
Eggs, shelled, fresh or frozen, whites	1 lb	2 c (16–20 eggs)
Eggs, shelled, fresh or frozen, yolks	1 lb	2 c (20–26 eggs)
Eggs, hard-cooked, chopped	1 lb	2⅔ c
Eggs, hard-cooked, chopped	1 doz	3½ c
Eggs, dried, whole	1 lb	5⅓ c
Eggs, dried, whites	1 lb	5 c
Eggs, dried, yolks	1 lb	5⅔ c
Fennel seed	1 oz	4 T
Figs, dry, cut fine	1 lb	2½ c
Flour, all-purpose	1 lb	4 c
Flour, cake or pastry	1 lb	4¾ c
Flour, rye	1 lb	5 c
Flour, white, bread	1 lb	4 c
Flour, whole wheat	1 lb	3¾ c
Garlic	1 oz	8 large cloves
Garlic, minced	1 oz	2⅔ T
Garlic powder	1 oz	4 T
Garlic salt	1 oz	4 t
Gelatin, granulated	1 oz	4 T
Gelatin, granulated	1 lb	3 c
Gelatin, prepared, flavored	1 lb	2½ c
Ginger, ground	1 oz	4 T
Ginger, ground	1 lb	4¼ c
Ginger, candied, chopped	1 oz	2 T

Food	*Weight*[a]	*Approximate Measure*[a]
Grapefruit, medium	1 lb	1 grapefruit, 10–12 sections, ⅔ c juice
Grapenuts	1 lb	4 c
Grapes, cut, seeded EP	1 lb	2¾ c
Grapes, on stem	1 lb	1 qt
Ham, cooked, diced	1 lb	3 c
Ham, cooked, ground	1 lb	2 c
Hominy, coarse	1 lb	2½ c
Hominy grits, dry	1 lb	3 c
Hominy grits, 1 lb AP, after cooking	6½ lb	3¼ qt
Honey	1 lb	1⅓ c
Horseradish, prepared	1 oz	2 T
Ice cream	4½–6 lb	1 gal
Jam	1 lb	1⅓ c
Jelly	1 lb	1½ c
Lard	1 lb	2 c
Lemons, size 165	1 lb	4–5 lemons, ¾ c juice
Lemon juice	1 lb	2 c (8–10 lemons)
Lemon peel, fresh	1 lemon	3 T
	1 oz	4 T
Lettuce, average head	2 lb	1 head
Lettuce, shredded	1 lb	6–8 c
Lettuce, leaf	1 lb	25–30 salad garnishes
Limes, fresh	1 lb	⅞ c juice
Macaroni, 1-in. pieces, dry	1 lb	4 c
Macaroni, 1 lb AP, after cooking	2¾–3 lb	1¾ qt
Macaroni, cooked	1 lb	2¾ c
Margarine	1 lb	2 c
Marshmallows (1¼ in.)	1 lb	80–90
Marshmallows, miniature 10 miniature = 1 regular	1 lb	8 c
Mayonnaise	1 lb	2 c (scant)
Meat, cooked, chopped	1 lb	2 c
Milk, fluid, whole	1 lb 1 oz	2 c
Milk, evaporated	1 lb	1¾ c
Milk, sweetened condensed	1 lb	1½ c
Milk, nonfat, dry	1 lb	5⅓ c
Milk, nonfat, dry	1 oz	⅓ c
Mincemeat	1 lb	2 c
Molasses	1 lb	1⅓ c
Mushrooms, fresh	1 lb	6¾ c
Mushrooms, canned	1 lb	2 c
Mustard, ground, dry	1 oz	4 T
Mustard, ground, dry	1 lb	4½ c

TABLE 1.3 *(Continued)*

Food	Weight[a]	Approximate Measure[a]
Mustard, prepared	1 oz	2 T
Mustard seed	1 oz	2½ T
Noodles, cooked	1 lb	2¼ c
Noodles, 1 lb AP, after cooking	2½–3 lb	1½–2 qt
Nutmeats	1 lb	3½ c
Nutmeg, ground	1 oz	3½ T
Oats, rolled, quick, AP	1 lb	6 c
Oats, rolled, 1 lb AP, after cooking	2½ lb	4 qt
Oil, vegetable	1 lb	2–2⅛ c
Olives, green, small size 180–200, 1 qt		109–116 olives
Olives, ripe, small size 120–150, 1 qt		152 olives
Olives, AP	1 lb	⅔ c chopped
Onions, mature AP	1 lb	4–5 medium
Onions, fresh, chopped	1 lb	2–3 c
Onions, dehydrated, chopped	1 lb	5–6 c
Onions, dehydrated	1 lb	8 lb raw (equivalent)
Onion soup mix, dry	1 oz	2⅔ T
Onion soup mix, dry	1 lb	2⅔ c
Oranges, medium	1 lb	3–4 oranges, 10–11 sections each, 1 c juice
Oranges	1 lb	2 c bite-size pieces
Orange peel, fresh	1 medium orange	4 T grated peel
	1 oz	4 T
Orange juice, frozen	6 oz	3 c reconstituted
Orange juice, frozen	32 oz	4 qt reconstituted
Oregano, ground	1 oz	5 T
Oregano, leaf	1 oz	¾ c
Oysters, shucked	1 lb	2 c
Paprika	1 oz	4 T
Parsley, coarsely chopped	1 oz	1 c
Parsley flakes, dry	1 oz	1⅓ c
Parsnips, AP	1 lb	4
Peaches, fresh, AP	1 lb	4 medium
Peaches, canned, sliced, drained	1 lb	2 c
Peanuts, shelled	1 lb	3¼ c
Peanut butter	1 lb	1¾ c
Pears, fresh, AP	1 lb	3–4
Pears, canned, drained, diced	1 lb	2½ c
Pears, halves, large, drained	1 lb 14 oz	1 qt (9 halves)
Peas, in pod, AP	1 lb	1 c shelled
Peas, cooked, drained	1¼ lb	2–2½ c
Peas, dried, split AP	1 lb	2⅓ c

TABLES OF WEIGHTS AND MEASURES

Food	Weight[a]	Approximate Measure[a]
Peas, dried, 1 lb, after cooking	2½ lb	5½ c
Pecans, shelled	1 lb	3½ c
Pepper, ground	1 oz	4 T
Pepper, ground	1 lb	4 c
Peppercorns	1 oz	6 T
Peppers, green	1 lb	2–3
Peppers, green, chopped	1 lb	3 c
Peppers, green, dried flakes	1 oz	¾ c
Pickle relish	1 lb	2 c
Pickles, chopped	1 lb	3 c
Pickles, halves, 3 in.	1 lb	3 c or 36 halves
Pimiento, chopped	1 lb	2½ c
Pineapple, fresh	2–4 lb	1 pineapple 2–4 c cubed
Pineapple, canned, crushed	1 lb	1¾ c
Pineapple, canned, slices, drained	1 lb	8–12 slices
Pineapple, canned, tidbits	1 lb	2 c
Poppy seed	1 oz	3 T
Potatoes, white, AP	1 lb	3 medium
Potatoes, cooked	1 lb	2½ c
Potatoes, dehydrated, flakes	1 lb	5 c
Potatoes, dehydrated, granules	1 lb	2¼ c
Potatoes, dehydrated, slices	1 lb	9⅔ c
Potatoes, sweet	1 lb	3 medium
Potatoes, sweet, cooked	1 lb	2 c
Potato chips	1 lb	4–5 qt
Poultry seasoning, ground	1 oz	4 T
Prunes, dried, size 30/40, AP	1 lb	2½ c
Prunes, dried, 1 lb AP, after cooking	2 lb	3–4 c
Prunes, cooked, pitted	1 lb	3¼ c
Pudding mix, dry, instant	1 lb	2½ c
Pudding mix, dry, regular	1 lb	2⅔ c
Pumpkin, cooked	1 lb	2½ c
Raisins, AP	1 lb	3 c
Raisins, 1 lb AP, after cooking	1 lb 12 oz	1 qt
Raspberries, fresh, AP	1 lb	3⅜ c
Rhubarb, raw, 1-in. pieces	1 lb	4 c
Rhubarb, 1 lb EP, after cooking		2½ c
Rice, brown AP	1 lb	2½ c
Rice, converted, AP	1 lb	2½ c
Rice, 1 lb AP, after cooking	4 lb	2 qt
Rice, precooked, AP	1 lb	4½ c
Rice, regular, AP	1 lb	2⅓ c
Rice cereal, crisp	1 lb	4 qt
Rice, puffed	1 oz	1⅔ c
Rosemary leaves	1 oz	1 c

TABLE 1.3 (Continued)

Food	Weight[a]	Approximate Measure[a]
Rutabagas, raw, cubed, EP	1 lb	3⅓ c
Sage, finely ground	1 oz	8 T
Sage, rubbed	1 oz	⅔ c
Salad dressing, cooked	1 lb	2 c
Salmon, canned	1 lb	2 c
Salt	1 oz	1½ T
Salt	1 lb	1½ c
Sausage, bulk, AP	1 lb	2 c
Sausages, link, small	1 lb	16–17
Sauerkraut	1 lb	3 c packed
Sesame seed	1 oz	3 T
Sherbet	6 lb	1 gal
Shortening, hydrogenated fat	1 lb	2¼ c
Shrimp, cleaned, cooked, peeled	1 lb	3¼ c
Soda, baking	1 oz	2⅓ T
Spaghetti, cooked	1 lb	2⅔ c
Spaghetti, 1 lb AP, after cooking	2½–3 lb	1½–2 qt
Spinach, raw	1 lb	5 qt lightly packed
Spinach, 1 lb raw EP, after cooking	13 oz	2¾ c
Spinach, canned or frozen	1 lb	2 c
Squash, Hubbard, cooked	1 lb	2 c
Starch, waxy maize	1 oz	3 T
Strawberries, fresh, AP	1 lb	3 c
Strawberries, frozen, sliced, with syrup	1 lb	2¼ c
Suet, ground	1 lb	3¾ c
Sugar, brown, lightly packed	1 lb	3 c
Sugar, brown, solid pack	1 lb	2 c
Sugar, cubes	1 lb	96 cubes
Sugar, granulated	1 lb	2–2⅛ c
Sugar, powdered, XXXX sifted	1 lb	3 c
Tapioca, quick cooking	1 lb	3 c
Tapioca, pearl	1 lb	2¾ c
Tapioca, 1 lb AP, after cooking		7½ c
Tarragon, leaf	1 oz	1 c
Tea, bulk	1 lb	6 c
Tea, instant	1 oz	½ c
Thyme, leaves	1 oz	½ c
Tomatoes, canned	1 lb	2 c
Tomatoes, fresh	1 lb	3–4 medium
Tomatoes, fresh, diced	1 lb	2¼ c
Turkey, AP, dressed weight	14 lb	11–12 c diced, cooked meat
Turnips, AP	1 lb	2–3
Tuna, canned	1 lb	2 c
Vanilla and other extracts	1 oz	2 T

Food	Weight[a]	Approximate Measure[a]
Vinegar	1 lb	2 c
Walnuts, English, shelled	1 lb	3½ c
Water	1 lb	2 c
Watercress, EP	1 oz	½ c
Watermelon	1 lb	1-in. slice, 6-in. diameter
Wheat, puffed	1 lb	32 c
Wheat, shredded	1 lb	15–16 biscuits
Whipped topping, liquid	1 lb	2 c
Yeast, dry	¼ oz	1 envelope (2½ t)
Yeast, dry	1 oz	3 T + 1 t

[a] For metric equivalents, see Tables 1.6 and 1.7.
[b] AP denotes "as purchased."
[c] EP denotes "edible portion."
[d] One case (30 doz) eggs weighs approximately 41–43 lb and yields approximately 35 lb liquid whole eggs.

TABLE 1.4 BASIC EQUIVALENTS IN MEASURES AND WEIGHTS

Equivalents		Abbreviations
1 T = 3 t	bu	bushel
⅛ c = 2 T in liquids, 1 fl oz	c	cup
¼ c = 4 T	fl oz	fluid ounce
⅓ c = 5 T + 1 t	gal	gallon
½ c = 8 T in liquids, 4 fl oz	g	gram
⅔ c = 10 T + 2 t	kg	kilogram
¾ c = 12 T	L	liter
1 c = 16 T in liquids, 8 fl oz	lb	pound
1 pt = 2 c	mL	milliliter
1 qt = 2 pt = 4 c	pk	peck
1 gal = 4 qt	pt	pint
1 lb = 16 oz	T	tablespoon
1 pk = 8 qt, approximately 12½ lb	t	teaspoon
1 bu = 4 pk, approximately 50 lb		
1 mL = ⅕ t		
1 L = 1.06 qt		
1 g = 0.035 oz		
1 kg = 2.2 lb		

TABLE 1.5 WEIGHT (1–16 oz) AND APPROXIMATE MEASURE EQUIVALENTS FOR COMMONLY USED FOODS

Food Item	1 oz	2 oz	3 oz	4 oz	5 oz	6 oz	7 oz	8 oz
Baking powder	2⅓ T	¼ c +1 t	⅓ c +2 T	½ c +1 T	¾ c	¾ c +2 T	1 c +1 t	1 c +3 T
Bread crumbs, dry	¼ c	½ c	¾ c	1 c	1¼ c	1½ c	1¾ c	2 c
Butter or margarine	2 T	¼ c	⅓ c + 2 t	½ c	½ c + 2 T	¾ c	¾ c + 2 T	1 c
Celery, chopped	¼ c	½ c	¾ c	1 c	1¼ c	1½ c	1¾ c	2 c
Cornstarch	3½ T	⅓ c + 2 T	⅔ c	¾ c + 2 T	1 c + 2 T	1¼ c + 1 T	1½ c + 1 T	1¾ c
Eggs, whole, whites or yolks, fresh or frozen	2 T	¼ c	⅓ c + 2 t	½ c	½ c + 2 T	¾ c	¾ c + 2 T	1 c
Flour, all purpose	¼ c	½ c	¾ c	1 c	1¼ c	1½ c	1¾ c	2 c
Milk, nonfat dry	¼ c	½ c	¾ c	1 c	1¼ c	1½ c	1¾ c	2 c
Nutmeats	3½ T	⅓ c + 2 T	⅔ c	¾ c + 2 T	1 c + 2 T	1¼ c + 1 T	1½ c + 1 T	1¾ c
Onion, chopped	2 T	¼ c	⅓ c + 2 t	½ c	½ c + 2 T	¾ c	¾ c + 2 T	1 c
Salt	1½ T	3 T	¼ c + 1½ t	⅓ c + 2 t	⅓ c + 2 T	½ c + 1 T	⅔ c	¾ c
Shortening, hydrogenated fat	2 T + 1 t	¼ c + 2 t	⅓ c + 2 T	½ c + 1 T	⅔ c + 1 T	¾ c + 2 T	1 c	1 c + 2 T
Soda	2⅓ T	¼ c + 1 t	⅓ c + 2 T	½ c + 1 T	¾ c	¾ c + 2 T	1 c + 1 t	1 c + 3 T
Sugar, brown, light pack	3 T	⅓ c + 2 t	½ c + 1 T	¾ c	¾ c + 3 T	1 c + 2 T	1¼ c + 1 T	1½ c
Sugar, granulated	2 T	¼ c	⅓ c + 2 t	½ c	½ c + 2 T	¾ c	¾ c + 2 T	1 c
Sugar, powdered	3 T	⅓ c + 2 t	½ c + 1 t	¾ c	¾ c + 3 T	1 c + 2 T	1¼ c + 1 T	1½ c
Yeast, dry	3 T + 1 t	⅓ c + 1 T	½ c + 2 T	¾ c + 1 T	1 c + 2 t	1¼ c	1½ c	1⅔ c

Food Item	*9 oz*	*10 oz*	*11 oz*	*12 oz*	*13 oz*	*14 oz*	*15 oz*	*16 oz*
Baking powder	1¼ c +1 T	1½ c	1½ c +2 T	1¾ c	1¾ c +2 T	2 c +1 T	2 c +3 T	2⅓ c
Bread crumbs, dry	2¼ c	2½ c	2¾ c	3 c	3¼ c	3½ c	3¾ c	4 c
Butter or margarine	1 c + 2 T	1¼ c	1⅓ c + 1 T	1½ c	1½ c + 2 T	1¾ c	1¾ c + 2 T	2 c
Celery, chopped	2¼ c	2½ c	2¾ c	3 c	3¼ c	3½ c	3¾ c	4 c
Cornstarch	2 c	2 c + 3 T	2⅓ c + 2 T	2½ c + 2 T	2¾ c + 2 T	3 c + 1 T	3¼ c + 1½t	3½ c
Eggs, whole, whites or yolks, fresh or frozen	1 c + 2 T	1¼ c	1⅓ c + 1 T	1½ c	1½ c + 2 T	1¾ c	1¾ c + 2 T	2 c
Flour, all purpose	2¼ c	2½ c	2¾ c	3 c	3¼ c	3½ c	3¾ c	4 c
Milk, nonfat dry	2¼ c	2½ c	2¾ c	3 c	3¼ c	3½ c	3¾ c	4 c
Nutmeats	2 c	2 c + 3 T	2⅓ c + 2 T	2½ c + 2 T	2¾ c + 2 T	3 c + 1 T	3¼ c + 1½t	3½ c
Onion, chopped	1 c + 2 T	1¼ c	1⅓ c + 1 T	1½ c	1½ c + 2 T	1¾ c	1¾ c + 2 T	2 c
Salt	¾ c + 2 T	¾ c + 3 T	1 c + 1 T	1 c + 2 T	1¼ c	1¼ c + 1 T	1⅓ c + 1 T	1½ c
Shortening, hydrogenated fat	1¼ c	1⅓ c + 1 T	1½ c + 1 T	1⅔ c	1¾ c + 1 T	2 c	2 c + 2 T	2¼ c
Soda	1¼ c + 1 T	1½ c	1½ c + 2 T	1¾ c	1¾ c + 2 T	2 c + 1 T	2 c + 3 T	2⅓ c
Sugar, brown, light pack	1⅔ c	1¾ c + 2 T	2 c + 1 T	2¼ c	2⅓ c + 2 T	2½ c + 2 T	2¾ c + 1 T	3 c
Sugar, granulated	1 c + 2 T	1¼ c	1⅓ c + 1 T	1½ c	1½ c + 2 T	1¾ c	1¾ c + 2 T	2 c
Sugar, powdered	1⅔ c	1¾ c + 2 T	2 c + 1 T	2¼ c	2⅓ c + 2 T	2½ c + 2 T	2¾ c + 1 T	3 c
Yeast, dry	1¾ c + 2 T	2 c + 1 T	2¼ c + 1 T	2½ c	2⅔ c + 1 T	2¾ c + 3 T	3 c + 2T	3⅓ c

32   GENERAL INFORMATION

TABLE 1.6   U.S. MEASURES OF WEIGHT AND METRIC EQUIVALENTS[a]

U.S. Weight	Metric	U.S. Weight	Metric	U.S. Weight	Metric
1 oz	28 g[b]	1 lb	454 g	2 lb	908 g
1½ oz	43 g	1 lb 1 oz[c]	482 g	2 lb 4 oz	1.02 kg
2 oz	57 g	1 lb 2 oz	510 g	2 lb 8 oz	1.14 kg
2½ oz	70 g	1 lb 3 oz	539 g	2 lb 12 oz	1.25 kg
3 oz	85 g	1 lb 4 oz	567 g	3 lb	1.36 kg
3½ oz	100 g	1 lb 5 oz	595 g	3 lb 4 oz	1.47 kg
4 oz (¼ lb)	114 g	1 lb 6 oz	624 g	3 lb 8 oz	1.59 kg
5 oz	142 g	1 lb 7 oz	652 g	3 lb 12 oz	1.70 kg
6 oz	170 g	1 lb 8 oz	680 g	4 lb	1.81 kg
7 oz	198 g	1 lb 9 oz	709 g	4 lb 4 oz	1.93 kg
8 oz (½ lb)	227 g	1 lb 10 oz	737 g	4 lb 8 oz	2.04 kg
9 oz	255 g	1 lb 11 oz	765 g	4 lb 12 oz	2.15 kg
10 oz	284 g	1 lb 12 oz	794 g	5 lb	2.27 kg
11 oz	312 g	1 lb 13 oz	822 g	6 lb	2.72 kg
12 oz (¾ lb)	340 g	1 lb 14 oz	851 g	7 lb	3.18 kg
13 oz	369 g	1 lb 15 oz	879 g	8 lb	3.63 kg
14 oz	397 g			9 lb	-4.08 kg
15 oz	425 g			10 lb	4.54 kg

[a] Basic figures used to calculate metric weights are: 1 oz = 28.35 g; 1 lb = 453.59 g. Resulting figures were rounded to nearest gram and to 2 decimals for kilograms.

[b] To change grams to kilograms, move decimal 3 places to left; e.g., 28 g = 0.028 kg.

[c] Abbreviations used: oz, ounce; lb, pound; g, gram; kg, kilogram.

TABLE 1.7   U.S. MEASURES OF VOLUME AND METRIC EQUIVALENTS[a]

U.S. Measure	Metric	U.S. Measure	Metric
1 t[b]	5 mL	1 qt	¼ gal	0.95 L
1 T	15 mL	1½ qt		1.42 L
¼ c (4 T)	60 mL	2 qt	½ gal	1.89 L
⅓ c	80 mL	3 qt	¾ gal	2.84 L
½ c (8 T)	120 mL	3½ qt		3.31 L
⅔ c	160 mL	4 qt	1 gal	3.79 L
¾ c (12 T)	180 mL	6 qt	1½ gal	5.68 L
1 c (16 T) ¼ qt	240 mL	8 qt	2 gal	7.57 L
2 c 1 pt	480 mL	10 qt	2½ gal	9.46 L
4 c 1 qt	950 mL	12 qt	3 gal	11.36 L

[a] Basic figures used to calculate metric volume are: 1 T = 14.8 mL rounded to 15 mL; 1 c = 237 mL rounded to 240 mL; 1 qt = 0.95 L (4 × 237 mL divided by 1000).

[b] Abbreviations used: t, teaspoon; T, tablespoon; c, cup; pt, pint; qt, quart; gal, gallon; mL, milliliter; L, liter.

PREPARATION AND SERVING GUIDES

TABLE 1.8 TEMPERATURES AND TIMES USED IN BAKING

Type of Product	Approximate Time Required for Baking[a] (minutes)	Oven Temperature °F	°C[b]
Bread			
Biscuits	10–15	425–450	220–230
Corn bread	30–40	400–425	205–220
Cream puffs	40–60	375	190
Muffins	20–25	400–425	205–220
Popovers	60	375	190
Quick loaf bread	60–75	350–375	175–190
Yeast bread	30–40	400	205
Yeast rolls			
Plain	15–25	400–425	205–220
Sweet	20–30	375	190
Cakes, with fat			
Cup	15–25	350–375	175–190
Layer	20–35	350–375	175–190
Loaf	45–60	350	175
Cakes, without fat			
Angel food and sponge	30–45	350–375	175–190
Cookies			
Drop	8–15	350–400	175–205
Rolled	8–10	375	190
Egg, meat, milk, cheese dishes			
Cheese soufflé (baked in pan of hot water)	30–60	350	175
Custard, plain, corn, other (baked in pan of hot water)	30–60	350	175
Macaroni and cheese	25–30	350	175
Meat loaf	60–90	300	150
Meat pie	25–30	400	205
Rice pudding (raw rice)	120–180	300	150
Scalloped potatoes	60	350	175
Pastry			
1-crust pie (custard type)	30–40	400–425	205–220
Meringue on cooked filling in preheated shell	12–15 or	350	175
	4–4½	425	205
Shell only	10–12	450	230
2-crust pies and uncooked filling in prebaked shell	45–55	400–425	205–220
2-crust pies with cooked filling	30–45	425–450	220–230

[a] For convection ovens follow time and temperature recommendations of manufacturer or decrease time and temperature 10%.

[b] Metric temperatures were obtained by using the following formula: 5/9 of °F after subtracting 32. Resulting figures were rounded to a functional temperature.

33

34 GENERAL INFORMATION

TABLE 1.9 TERMS FOR OVEN TEMPERATURES

Term	Temperature °F	°C[a]
Very slow	250–275	121–135
Slow	300–325	150–165
Moderate	350–375	175–190
Hot	400–425	205–220
Very hot (quick)	450–475	230–245
Extremely hot	500–525	260–275

[a] Metric temperatures were obtained by using the following formula: 5/9 of °F after subtracting 32. Resulting figures were rounded to a functional temperature.

TABLE 1.10 METRIC TEMPERATURE EQUIVALENTS[a]

°F	°C	°F	°C	°F	°C	°F	°C
32	0	200	95	300	150	400	205
100	38	212	100	310	155	425	220
105	40	220	105	320	160	450	230
110	43	225	107	324	162	475	245
115	46	230	110	325	165	500	260
120	49	234	112	330	166	525	275
125	52	238	114	335	168	550	290
130	55	240	115	338	170	575	300
140	60	244	118	340	171	600	315
150	65	248	120	350	175		
160	70	250	121	360	180		
170	75	260	125	365	182		
175	80	266	130	370	185		
180	82	270	132	375	190		
185	85	275	135	380	195		
190	88	290	143	390	200		
195	90						

[a] Temperatures in this edition of *Food for Fifty* are given in Fahrenheit and Celsius (Centigrade). To convert from °F to °C, the following formula was used: °F − 32 × 5/9 = °C. Some temperatures were rounded to numbers that would be functional in ovens and other equipment.

TABLE 1.11 TEMPERATURES AND TESTS FOR SYRUPS AND CANDIES

Product	Temperature of Syrup at Sea Level (Indicating Concentration Desired)[a] °F	°C	Test	Description of Test
Syrup	230–234	110–112	Thread	Syrup spins a 2-in. thread when dropped from fork or spoon.
Fondant Fudge Penoche	234–240	112–115	Soft ball	When dropped into very cold water, syrup forms a soft ball that flattens on removal from water.
Caramels	244–248	118–120	Firm ball	When dropped into very cold water, syrup forms a firm ball that does not flatten on removal from water.
Divinity Marshmallows Popcorn balls	250–266	121–130	Hard ball	When dropped into very cold water, syrup forms a ball that is hard enough to hold its shape, yet plastic.
Butterscotch Taffies	270–290	132–143	Soft crack	When dropped into very cold water, syrup separates into threads that are hard, but not brittle.
Brittle Glacé	300–310	150–155	Hard crack	When dropped into very cold water, syrup separates into threads that are hard and brittle.
Barley sugar	320	160	Clear liquid	Sugar liquefies.
Caramel	338	170	Brown liquid	Liquid becomes brown.

[a] Cook syrup about 1°C lower than temperature at sea level for each increase of 900 ft in elevation, or 1°F lower than temperature at sea level for each increase of 500 ft in elevation.

TABLE 1.12 DEEP-FAT FRYING TEMPERATURES

Type of Product	Preparation[a]	Temperature[b] °F	Temperature[b] °C	Frying Time[c] (minutes)
Bananas	Batter, See p. 37	375	190	1–3
Cauliflower, pre-cooked	See p. 540	370	185	3–5
Cheese balls	See p. 269	360	180	2–3
Chicken, disjointed,				
1½–2 lb fryers	Light coating or egg and crumb [b]	325	165	10–12
2–2½ lb fryers	Light coating or egg and crumb	325	165	12–15
Chicken, half				
1½–2 lb fryers	Light coating or egg and crumb	325	165	12–15
Croquettes (all previously cooked foods)		360–375	180–190	2–5
Cutlets, ½ in. thick	Eggs and crumb	325–350	165–175	5–8
Doughnuts	See p. 102	360–375	180–190	3–5
Eggplant	See p. 545	370	185	5–7
Fish fillets	Egg and crumb	375	190	4–6
Fish sticks	Egg and crumb	375	190	3–4
French toast	See p. 107	360	180	3–4
Fritters	See p. 109	370–380	185–195	2–5
Onion rings	Batter	350	175	3–4
Oysters	Egg and crumb	375	190	2–4
Potatoes, ½ in.	See p. 550			
Complete fry		365	182	6–8
Blanching		360	180	3–5
Browning		375	190	2–3
Frozen, fat blanched		375	190	2–3
Sandwiches	See p. 462	350–360	175–180	3–4
Scallops	Egg and crumb	360–375	180–190	3–4
Shrimp	Batter or egg and crumb	360–375	180–190	3–5
Zucchini	See p. 545	370	185	4–6

Note: Use fat with a high smoking temperature. Filter fat regularly, at least once a day or more often if fryer is in constant use. The breakdown of fat may be caused by using the fat for too long a period, cooking product at too high a temperature, failure to filter the fat regularly, or salting the food over the fryer.

[a] See p. 37 for light coating, egg and crumb, and batter.

[b] If food is frozen, use lower temperatures listed and allow additional cooking time. At high altitudes, the lower boiling point of water in foods requires lowering of temperatures for deep-fat frying.

[c] The exact frying time will vary with the equipment used, size and temperature of the food pieces, and the amount of food placed in the fryer at one time. If the fryer is overloaded, foods may become grease-soaked.

TABLE 1.13 COATINGS FOR DEEP-FAT FRIED FOODS

Ingredient	Light Coating	Egg and Crumb	Batter
Eggs[a]		3	6
Milk[b]	1 c	1 c	2 c
Flour, all-purpose	1 lb	8 oz (optional)	12 oz
Salt	2 t	1 t	2 t
Bread crumbs, fine		12 oz	
Baking powder			2 t
Shortening, melted, or cooking oil			3 T
Seasonings	As desired		

[a] For soft mixtures, such as egg cutlets, increase eggs to 6.

[b] Water may be substituted for milk, except for batter.

Light Coating. Dip prepared food in milk. Dredge with seasoned flour.

Egg and Crumb. Dip prepared food in flour (may omit), then in mixture of beaten egg and milk. Drain. Roll in crumbs to cover. (See Fig. 2.20, p. 368.)

Batter. Combine flour, salt, and baking powder. Add milk, beaten eggs, and shortening. Dip prepared foods in batter.

TABLE 1.14 DIPPER EQUIVALENTS

Dipper Number[a]	Approximate Measure	Approximate Weight	Suggested Use
6	10 T (⅔ c)	6 oz	Entrée salads
8	8 T (½ c)	4–5 oz	Entrées
10	6 T (⅜ c)	3–4 oz	Desserts, meat patties
12	5 T (⅓ c)	2½–3 oz	Croquettes, vegetables, muffins, desserts, salads
16	4 T (¼ c)	2–2¼ oz	Muffins, desserts, croquettes
20	3⅕ T	1¾–2 oz	Muffins, cup cakes, sauces, sandwich fillings
24	2⅔ T	1½–1¾ oz	Cream puffs
30	2⅕ T	1–1½ oz	Large drop cookies
40	1½ T	¾ oz	Drop cookies
60	1 T	½ oz	Small drop cookies, garnishes
100	Scant 2 t		Tea cookies

Note: These measurements are based on level dippers. If a rounded dipper is used, the measure and weight are closer to those of the next larger dipper.

[a] Portions per quart.

TABLE 1.15 LADLE EQUIVALENTS

Approximate Measure	Approximate Weight	Suggested Use
⅛ c	1 oz	Sauces, salad dressings
¼ c	2 oz	Gravies, some sauces
½ c	4 oz	Stews, creamed dishes
¾ c	6 oz	Stews, creamed dishes
1 c	8 oz	Soup

Note: These measurements are based on level ladles. If a rounded ladle is used, the measure is closer to that of the next larger ladle.

TABLE 1.16 COMMON CAN SIZES

Can Size (Industry Term)	Approximate Net Weight or Fluid Measure	Approximate Cups per Can	Number of Portions	Principal Products
No. 10	6 lb–7 lb 5 oz	12–13	25	Institutional size for fruits, vegetables
No. 3 Cyl	46 fl oz or 51 oz	5¾	10–12	Fruit and vegetable juices, condensed soups
No. 2½	26–30 oz	3½	5–7	Fruits, some vegetables
No. 2	18 fl oz or 20 oz	2½	5	Juices, fruits, ready-to-serve soups
No. 303	1 lb	2	4	Fruits, vegetables, ready-to-serve soups
No. 300	14–16 oz	1¾	3–4	Some fruits and meat products
No. 1 (Picnic)	10½–12 oz	1¼	2–3	Condensed soups
8 oz	8 oz	1	2	Ready-to-serve soups, fruits, vegetables

Note: See Tables 1.6 and 1.7 for metric equivalents.

TABLE 1.17 SUBSTITUTING ONE CAN FOR ANOTHER SIZE

	Approximate Equivalent
1 No. 10 can	7 No. 303 (1-lb) cans
	5 No. 2 (1-lb 4-oz) cans
	4 No. 2½ (1-lb 13-oz) cans
	2 No. 3 (46-to 50-oz) cans

TABLE 1.18 INGREDIENT SUBSTITUTIONS (APPROXIMATE)

Recipe Item	Amount	Substitute Ingredient
Baking powder	1 t[a]	¼ t baking soda + ½ t cream of tartar ¼ t baking soda + ½ c buttermilk or sour milk (to replace ½ c of the liquid)
Butter	1 lb	14 oz hydrogenated shortening + 1 t salt 14 oz lard + 1 t salt 14 oz (1 ⅜ c) oil + 1 t salt
Buttermilk	1 c	1 T lemon juice or vinegar + enough whole milk to make 1 c (let stand 5 minutes before using) or 1 c unflavored yogurt
Celery, fresh, chopped	8 oz	4 oz celery flakes, dry
Chocolate	1 oz (1 square)	3 T cocoa + 1 T (½ oz) fat
Cocoa	3 T	1 oz chocolate. Reduce fat in recipe by 1 T.
Cornstarch (thickening)	1 T 1 oz 1 T 1 oz	2 T flour, all-purpose 2 oz flour, all-purpose 2 t waxy maize starch ¾ oz waxy maize starch
Cream 18–20% 36–40%	 1 c 1 c	 ⅞ c milk + 3 T fat ¾ c milk + ⅓ c fat
Flour, all-purpose	1 c	1½ c bread flour 1 c + 2 T cake flour 1 c rye flour 1 c whole wheat flour ⅞ c cornmeal 1 c rolled oats
Flour, cake	1 c	1 c less 2 T all-purpose flour
Flour (thickening)	1 T 1 oz	½–¾ T cornstarch or waxy maize starch 1 T quick-cooking tapioca 3½ whole eggs (5½ oz) 7 egg yolks (4½ oz) 1⅓ oz quick-cooking tapioca ⅔ oz cornstarch ½ oz waxy maize starch ¾ oz bread crumbs
Garlic	1 medium clove	⅛ t garlic powder ½ t garlic, minced, dry ½ t garlic salt
Green peppers, fresh, chopped	8 oz	1 oz green pepper flakes, dry
Honey	1 c	1¼ c granulated sugar + ¼ c liquid

TABLE 1.18 (Continued)

Recipe Item	Amount	Substitute Ingredient
Milk, fluid, whole	1 c	1 oz (1/3 c) nonfat dry milk + water to make 1 c + 1 T fat (optional)
		1/2 c evaporated milk + 1/2 c water
	1 qt	4 oz (1 1/3 c) nonfat dry milk + water to make 1 qt + 1 1/4 oz fat (optional)
Milk, sour[b]	1 c	1 T vinegar or lemon juice + sweet milk to make 1 c
Onions, fresh chopped	8 oz	1 oz dry onions, chopped or minced[c]
Parsley, fresh, chopped	8 oz	3 oz parsley flakes, dry
Soup stock	1 gal	3 oz concentrated soup base + 1 gal water (commercial products may vary in strength; follow manufacturer's directions)
Tapioca, quick-cooking	1 T	1 T all-purpose flour (for thickening)
Yeast, active dry	1/4 oz (1 pkg)	1 cake compressed
	1 oz	2 oz compressed

[a] For metric equivalents, see Tables 1.6 and 1.7.

[b] To substitute buttermilk or sour milk for sweet milk, add 1/2 t baking soda and decrease baking powder by 2 t per cup of milk.

[c] Rehydrate onions unless they are to be used in a recipe in which there is a large volume of liquid. To rehydrate, cover onions with water, using 1 1/2 times the volume of onions; let stand 20–30 minutes.

TABLE 1.19 PROPORTIONS OF INGREDIENTS

Function	Ingredient	Relative Proportion
Leavening agents	Baking powder	1½–2 T to 1 lb flour
	Baking soda	2 t to 1 qt sour milk or molasses
	Yeast	½–1 envelope dry (⅛–¼ oz) to 1 lb flour (varies with ingredients and time allowed)
Seasonings	Salt	1–2 t to 1 lb flour
		1¼ t to 1 lb meat
		2 t to 1 qt water (for cereal)
		2½ t to 1 pt liquid (for rolls)
Thickening agents	Eggs	4–6 whole eggs to 1 qt milk
		8–12 egg yolks to 1 qt milk
		8–12 egg whites to 1 qt milk
	Flour	½ oz to 1 qt liquid—very thin sauce (cream soups, starchy vegetables)
		1 oz to 1 qt liquid—thin sauce (cream soups, nonstarchy vegetables)
		2 oz to 1 qt liquid—medium sauce (creamed foods, gravy)
		3–4 oz to 1 qt liquid—thick sauce (soufflés)
		4–5 oz to 1 qt liquid—very thick sauce (croquettes)
		1 lb to 1 qt liquid—pour batter (popovers)
		2 lb to 1 qt liquid—drop batter (cake muffins)
		3 lb to 1 qt liquid—soft dough (biscuits, rolls)
		4 lb to 1 qt liquid—stiff dough (pastry, cookies, noodles)
	Gelatin	2 T to 1 qt liquid—plain jellies (gelatin and fruit juices)
		2 T to 1 qt liquid—whips (gelatin and fruit juices whipped)
		3 T to 1 qt liquid—fruit jellies (gelatin, fruit juices, and chopped fruit)
		3 T to 1 qt liquid—vegetable jellies (gelatin, liquid, and chopped vegetables)
		3 T to 1 qt liquid—sponges (gelatin, fruit juice, and beaten egg whites)
		4 T to 1 qt liquid—Bavarian cream (gelatin, fruit juice, fruit pulp, and whipped cream)

RECIPE ADJUSTMENT

Adjusting recipes to meet the needs of individual food services is often necessary. Recipes may need to be standardized for either weights or measures, or policies may require yields different from the recipes in this book. In either case, recipe adjustment is simplified by using the following procedures for converting from weight to measure and increasing and decreasing recipe yields.

CONVERTING FROM WEIGHT TO MEASURE

Quantities of most dry ingredients in recipes in this book are given by weight in ounces and pounds and in metric grams and kilograms. However, if accurate scales are not available or if scales do not have gradations for weighing small amounts, the weights of ingredients may need to be converted to measures. The following tables will be helpful.

Table 1.3	Food Weights and Approximate Equivalents in Measure (p. 21)
Table 1.4	Basic Equivalents in Measures and Weights (p. 29)
Table 1.5	Weight (1–16 oz) and Measure Equivalents for Commonly Used Foods (p. 30)
Table 1.20	A Guide for Rounding off Weights and Measures (p. 44)
Table 1.21	Ounces and Decimal Equivalents of a Pound (p. 45)

Example: To convert ingredients in Plain Muffins (p. 86): Turn to Table 1.3 (p. 21). Change 2 lb 8 oz (2½ lb) flour to measure by multiplying by 4 c. The resulting 10 c would be equivalent to 2½ qt (p. 30). By referring to Table 1.5, the 2 oz baking powder, 6 oz sugar, and 8 oz shortening may be converted quickly by finding the amount in the appropriate columns. The same information is included in the longer table (p. 21), but for conversion of small amounts of commonly used foods, Table 1.5 is useful.

INCREASING AND DECREASING RECIPE YIELDS

It may be necessary to change the recipe yields in this book to meet the needs of individual situations. Recipes may be increased to batch sizes compatible with equipment to be used in preparation, such as mixers and steam-jacketed kettles, or consistent with pan sizes. Recipes may also need adjustment as portion sizes are increased or decreased or purchase units for ingredients change.

Factor Method A direct reading table (Table 1.22, p.47) provides information for adjusting yields when ingredients are given in weights. It requires a minimum of calculation, but its use is limited to desired yields that can be divided by 25.

If adjusting to a yield not divisible by 25, or if closer portion control is desired, the factor method may be useful. To use this method:

Step 1. Divide the desired yield by the known yield of the recipe being adjusted to obtain a basic FACTOR. For example, to increase a recipe that yields 50 portions to 125 portions, divide 125 by 50 for a FACTOR of 2.5.

Step 2. Wherever possible, convert ingredients to weight. If amounts of some ingredients are too small to convert to weight, leave them in measure.

Step 3. Multiply the amount of each ingredient in the original recipe by the FACTOR. To work with decimal parts of a pound instead of ounces for this multiplication, Table 1.21 will be helpful.

Step 4. Multiply the original total weight of ingredients by the FACTOR. Multiply the pounds and ounces separately and then combine them.

Step 5. Add together the new weights of all ingredients for the adjusted recipe. If the answers in Steps 4 and 5 are not the same, check the calculations.

Step 6. Change weights of any ingredients that can be more easily measured than weighed to measure.

Step 7. Check all amounts and use Table 1.20 for rounding off unnecessary fractions to simplify weights or measures as far as accuracy permits.

Percentage Method* The percentage method of recipe adjustment often is desirable, especially for large volume production where batch sizes may vary greatly. Once the ingredient percentage has been established, it remains constant for all future adjustments. Recipe increases and decreases are made by multiplying the percentage of each ingredient by the total weight desired. Checking ingredients for proper recipe balance is possible, as the percentage of each ingredient is available. Some computer recipe systems use the percentage method of recipe adjustment. To use this method:

Step 1. Convert all ingredients from measure or pounds and ounces to pounds and tenths of a pound. (See Tables 1.3, 1.21.) Make desired equivalent ingredient substitutions such as frozen whole eggs for fresh eggs, nonfat dry milk and water for liquid milk. Use edible portion (EP) weights when a difference exists between EP and as purchased (AP) weights. (See Table 1.1.) Piece meats and other meats in entrée recipes that do not require the meat to be cooked prior to combining with other ingredients are calculated on AP weight. Examples: pork chops, meat loaf, salisbury steak.

Step 2. Total the weight of ingredients in the recipe after each ingredient has been converted to EP weight.

Step 3. Calculate the percentage of each ingredient in relation to the total weight.

Formula: $\dfrac{\text{individual ingredient weight}}{\text{total weight}}$ = percentage of each ingredient.

Sum of percents should total 100%.

*McManis, H., and Molt, M. (1978). *Recipe Standardization and Percentage Method of Adjustment*, National Association of College and University Food Services Journal.

Step 4. Check the ratio of ingredients. Standards have been established for ingredient proportions of many items. The ingredients should be in proper balance before going further.

Step 5. Establish the weight needed to give the desired number of servings. The weight will be determined by portion size multiplied by the desired number of servings to be prepared. This weight may need to be adjusted because of pan sizes and/or equipment capacity.

Step 6. Handling loss must be added to the weight needed, and it may vary from 1 to 10%, depending on the product. Like items produce predictable losses and with some experimentation can be assigned accurately.

Formula for incorporating handling loss:

$$\text{Total weight needed} = \frac{\text{desired yield}}{100\% - \text{assigned handling loss }\%}.$$

For example, plain cake has a handling loss of approximately 2%, and 72 lb of batter is needed to make 9 18 × 26 × 2-in. pans. To determine the total amount of batter to be made, divide 72 lb by 98% (100% − 2% handling loss). Using this formula, a recipe calculated for 73.47 lb of batter is needed.

Step 7. Multiply each ingredient percentage by the total weight to give the exact amount of each ingredient needed. Once the percentages of a recipe have been established, any number of servings can be calculated and the ratio of ingredients to the total will remain the same.

Step 8. Unless scales are calibrated to read in pounds and tenths of a pound, convert to pounds and ounces (Table 1.21) or to measure (Table 1.3).

TABLE 1.20 GUIDE FOR ROUNDING OFF WEIGHTS AND MEASURES

Item	If the Total Amount of An Ingredient Is	Round it to
Weights		
	Less than 2 oz	Measure unless weight is ¼-, ½-, ¾-oz amounts
	2–10 oz	Closest ¼ oz or convert to measure
	More than 10 oz but less than 2 lb 8 oz	Closest ½ oz
	2 lb 8 oz–5 lb	Closest full ounce
	More than 5 lb	Closest ¼ lb
Measures		
	Less than 1 T	Closest ⅛ t
	More than 1 T but less than 3 T	Closest ¼ t
	3 T–½ c	Closest ½ t or convert to weight
	More than ½ c but less than ¾ c	Closest full teaspoon or convert to weight
	More than ¾ c but less than 2 c	Closest full tablespoon or convert to weight
	2 c–2 qt	Nearest ¼ c
	More than 2 qt but less than 4 qt	Nearest ½ c

Item	If the Total Amount of An Ingredient Is	Round it to
	1–2 gal	Nearest full cup or ¼ qt
	More than 2 gal but less than 10 gal	Nearest full quart
	More than 10 gal but less than 20 gal	Closest ½ gal
	Over 20 gal	Closest full gallon

Note: This table is intended to aid in rounding fractions and complex measurements into amounts that are as simple as possible to weigh or measure while maintaining the accuracy needed for quality control.

TABLE 1.21 OUNCES AND DECIMAL EQUIVALENTS OF A POUND

Ounces	Decimal Part of a Pound	Ounces	Decimal Part of a Pound
¼	0.016	8¼	0.516
½	0.031	8½	0.531
¾	0.047	8¾	0.547
1	0.063	9	0.563
1¼	0.078	9¼	0.578
1½	0.094	9½	0.594
1¾	0.109	9¾	0.609
2	0.125	10	0.625
2¼	0.141	10¼	0.641
2½	0.156	10½	0.656
2¾	0.172	10¾	0.672
3	0.188	11	0.688
3¼	0.203	11¼	0.703
3½	0.219	11½	0.719
3¾	0.234	11¾	0.734
4	0.250	12	0.750
4¼	0.266	12¼	0.766
4½	0.281	12½	0.781
4¾	0.297	12¾	0.797
5	0.313	13	0.813
5¼	0.328	13¼	0.828
5½	0.344	13½	0.844
5¾	0.359	13¾	0.859
6	0.375	14	0.875
6¼	0.391	14¼	0.891
6½	0.406	14½	0.906
6¾	0.422	14¾	0.922
7	0.438	15	0.938
7¼	0.453	15¼	0.953
7½	0.469	15½	0.969
7¾	0.484	15¾	0.984
8	0.500	16	1.000

Note: This table is useful when increasing or decreasing recipes. The multiplication or division of pounds and ounces is simplified if the ounces are converted to decimal parts of a pound. For example, when multiplying 1 lb 9 oz by 3, first change the 9 oz to 0.563 lb, by using the table. Thus, the 1 lb 9 oz becomes 1.563 lb which multiplied by 3 is 4.683 lb or 4 lb 11 oz.

DIRECTIONS FOR USING TABLES 1.22 AND 1.23:
DIRECT READING MEASUREMENT TABLES

Tables 1.22 and 1.23, which follow, are used in the same manner but for different types of ingredients. Table 1.22 is used for converting weighed ingredients using recipe yields that are divisible by 25. Table 1.23 is used for converting volume measures of ingredients using recipe yields that are divisible by 25.

Abbreviations Used in the Charts	Equivalents Helpful in Using the Charts
oz ounce	3 t = 1 T
# pound	4 T = ¼ c
t teaspoon	5 T + 1 t = ⅓ c
T tablespoon	8 T = ½ c
c cup	10 T + 2 t = ⅔ c
qt quart	12 T = ¾ c
gal gallon	16 T = 1 c
(r) slightly rounded	4 c = 1 qt
(s) scant	4 qt = 1 gal
* amounts cannot be weighed accurately without introducing errors	

Instructions for using direct reading measurement tables:

1. Locate the column that corresponds to the original yield of the recipe to be adjusted. For example, assume the original recipe yields 100 portions. Locate the "100" column across the top of the chart on Table 1.22.

2. Go down this column to the amount of the ingredient required (or to the closest number to that figure) in the recipe to be adjusted. If the recipe for 100 portions requires 21 lb of ground beef, for example, go down the column headed 100 to the figure "21."

3. Then go across the page, in line with that amount, to the column that is headed to correspond with the yield desired. For example, if only 75 portions are desired, begin with the 21 lb figure in the "100" column and slide across to the column headed "75" and read that figure. It indicates 15 lb 12 oz of ground beef would be required to make 75 portions with this recipe.

4. Record this figure as the amount of the ingredient required for the new yield of the recipe. Repeat steps 1, 2, and 3 for each ingredient in the original recipe to obtain the adjusted ingredient weight needed for the new yield. Follow the same procedure using Table 1.23 in adjusting ingredient amounts indicated in volume measures. Yields can be either increased or decreased in this manner.

5. If two columns need to be combined to obtain the desired yield, follow steps 1 through 4 and add together the amounts given in the two columns to obtain the amount required for the adjusted yield. For example, to find the amount

of ground beef for 225 portions of our hypothetical recipe, locate the figures in columns headed "200" and "25" and add them together. In this example it would be 42 lb + 5 lb 4 oz, so the required total for ground beef would be 47 lb 4 oz.

6. The figures given in these tables are given in exact weights including fractional ounces. After making yield adjustments for every ingredient, refer to Table 1.20 for rounding off fractional amounts, which are not of sufficient proportion to change product quality.

TABLE 1.22 DIRECT-READING TABLE FOR ADJUSTING WEIGHT INGREDIENTS OF RECIPES DIVISIBLE BY 25.[a]

25	50	75	100	200	300	400	500
*	*	*	¼ oz	½ oz	¾ oz	1 oz	1¼ oz
*	*	*	½ oz	1 oz	1½ oz	2 oz	2½ oz
*	*	*	¾ oz	1½ oz	2¼ oz	3 oz	3¾ oz
¼ oz	½ oz	¾ oz	1 oz	2 oz	3 oz	4 oz	5 oz
*	*	*	1¼ oz	2½ oz	3¾ oz	5 oz	6¼ oz
*	¾ oz	*	1½ oz	3 oz	4½ oz	6 oz	7½ oz
*	*	*	1¾ oz	3½ oz	5¼ oz	7 oz	8¾ oz
½ oz	1 oz	1½ oz	2 oz	4 oz	6 oz	8 oz	10 oz
*	*	1¾ oz	2¼ oz	4½ oz	6¾ oz	9 oz	11¼ oz
*	1¼ oz	2 oz	2½ oz	5 oz	7½ oz	10 oz	12½ oz
*	*	2 oz	2¾ oz	5½ oz	8¼ oz	11 oz	13¾ oz
¾ oz	1½ oz	2¼ oz	3 oz	6 oz	9 oz	12 oz	15 oz
*	*	2½ oz	3¼ oz	6½ oz	9¾ oz	13 oz	1# ¼ oz
*	1¾ oz	2¾ oz	3½ oz	7 oz	10½ oz	14 oz	1# 1½ oz
1 oz	2 oz	2¾ oz	3¾ oz	7½ oz	11¼ oz	15 oz	1# 2¾ oz
1 oz	2 oz	3 oz	4 oz	8 oz	12 oz	1#	1# 4 oz
1 oz	2¼ oz	3¼ oz	4¼ oz	8½ oz	12¾ oz	1# 1 oz	1# 5¼ oz
*	2½ oz	3½ oz	4½ oz	9 oz	13½ oz	1# 2 oz	1# 6½ oz
*	2½ oz	3½ oz	4¾ oz	9½ oz	14¼ oz	1# 3 oz	1# 7¾ oz
1¼ oz	2½ oz	3¾ oz	5 oz	10 oz	15 oz	1# 1 oz	1# 9 oz
*	2¾ oz	4¼ oz	5½ oz	11 oz	1# ½ oz	1# 6 oz	1# 11½ oz
1½ oz	3 oz	4½ oz	6 oz	12 oz	1# 2 oz	1# 8 oz	1# 14 oz
*	3¼ oz	4¾ oz	6½ oz	13 oz	1# 3½ oz	1# 10 oz	2# ½ oz
1¾ oz	3½ oz	5¼ oz	7 oz	14 oz	1# 5 oz	1# 12 oz	2# 3 oz
2 oz	3¾ oz	5¾ oz	7½ oz	15 oz	1# 6½ oz	1# 14 oz	2# 5½ oz
2 oz	4 oz	6 oz	8 oz	1#	1# 8 oz	2#	2# 8 oz
2¼ oz	4¼ oz	6½ oz	8½ oz	1# 1 oz	1# 9½ oz	2# 2 oz	2# 10½ oz
2¼ oz	4½ oz	6¾ oz	9 oz	1# 2 oz	1# 11 oz	2# 4 oz	2# 13 oz
2½ oz	4¾ oz	7¼ oz	9½ oz	1# 3 oz	1# 12½ oz	2# 6 oz	2# 15½ oz
2½ oz	5 oz	7½ oz	10 oz	1# 4 oz	1# 14 oz	2# 8 oz	3# 2 oz
2¾ oz	5½ oz	8¼ oz	11 oz	1# 6 oz	2# 1 oz	2# 12 oz	3# 7 oz
3 oz	6 oz	9 oz	12 oz	1# 8 oz	2# 4 oz	3#	3# 12 oz
3¼ oz	6½ oz	9¾ oz	13 oz	1# 10 oz	2# 7 oz	3# 4 oz	4# 1 oz

TABLE 1.22 (Continued)

25	50	75	100	200	300	400	500
3½ oz	7 oz	10½ oz	14 oz	1# 12 oz	2# 10 oz	3# 8 oz	4# 6 oz
3¾ oz	7½ oz	11¼ oz	15 oz	1# 14 oz	2# 13 oz	3# 12 oz	4# 11 oz
4 oz	8 oz	12 oz	1#	2#	3#	4#	5#
4½ oz	9 oz	13½ oz	1# 2 oz	2# 4 oz	3# 6 oz	4# 8 oz	5# 10 oz
5 oz	10 oz	15 oz	1# 4 oz	2# 8 oz	3# 12 oz	5#	6# 4 oz
5½ oz	11 oz	1# ½ oz	1# 6 oz	2# 12 oz	4# 2 oz	5# 8 oz	6# 14 oz
6 oz	12 oz	1# 2 oz	1# 8 oz	3#	4# 8 oz	6#	7# 8 oz
6½ oz	13 oz	1# 3½ oz	1# 10 oz	3# 4 oz	4# 14 oz	6# 8 oz	8# 2 oz
7 oz	14 oz	1# 5 oz	1# 12 oz	3# 8 oz	5# 4 oz	7#	8# 12 oz
7½ oz	15 oz	1# 6½ oz	1# 14 oz	3# 12 oz	5# 10 oz	7# 8 oz	9# 6 oz
8 oz	1#	1# 8 oz	2#	4#	6#	8#	10#
8½ oz	1# 1 oz	1# 9½ oz	2# 2 oz	4# 4 oz	6# 6 oz	8# 8 oz	10# 10 oz
9 oz	1# 2 oz	1# 11 oz	2# 4 oz	4# 8 oz	6# 12 oz	9#	11# 4 oz
9½ oz	1# 3 oz	1# 12½ oz	2# 6 oz	4# 12 oz	7# 2 oz	9# 8 oz	11# 14 oz
10 oz	1# 4 oz	1# 14 oz	2# 8 oz	5#	7# 8 oz	10#	12# 8 oz
11 oz	1# 6 oz	2# 1 oz	2# 12 oz	5# 8 oz	8# 4 oz	11#	13# 12 oz
12 oz	1# 8 oz	2# 4 oz	3#	6#	9#	12#	15#
13 oz	1# 10 oz	2# 7 oz	3# 4 oz	6# 8 oz	9# 12 oz	13#	16# 4 oz
14 oz	1# 12 oz	2# 10 oz	3# 8 oz	7#	10# 8 oz	14#	17# 8 oz
15 oz	1# 14 oz	2# 13 oz	3# 12 oz	7# 8 oz	11# 4 oz	15#	18# 12 oz
1#	2#	3#	4#	8#	12#	16#	20#
1# 1 oz	2# 2 oz	3# 3 oz	4# 4 oz	8# 8 oz	12# 12 oz	17#	21# 4 oz
1# 2 oz	2# 4 oz	3# 6 oz	4# 8 oz	9#	13# 8 oz	18#	22# 8 oz
1# 3 oz	2# 6 oz	3# 9 oz	4# 12 oz	9# 8 oz	14# 4 oz	19#	23# 12 oz
1# 4 oz	2# 8 oz	3# 12 oz	5#	10#	15#	20#	25#
1# 5 oz	2# 10 oz	3# 15 oz	5# 4 oz	10# 8 oz	15# 12 oz	21#	26# 4 oz
1# 6 oz	2# 12 oz	4# 2 oz	5# 8 oz	11#	16# 8 oz	22#	27# 8 oz
1# 7 oz	2# 14 oz	4# 5 oz	5# 12 oz	11# 8 oz	17# 4 oz	23#	28# 12 oz
1# 8 oz	3#	4# 8 oz	6#	12#	18#	24#	30#
1# 10 oz	3# 4 oz	4# 14 oz	6# 8 oz	13#	19# 8 oz	26#	32# 8 oz
1# 12 oz	3# 8 oz	5# 4 oz	7#	14#	21#	28#	35#
1# 14 oz	3# 12 oz	5# 10 oz	7# 8 oz	15#	22# 8 oz	30#	37# 8 oz
2#	4#	6#	8#	16#	24#	32#	40#
2# 2 oz	4# 4 oz	6# 6 oz	8# 8 oz	17#	25# 8 oz	34#	42# 8 oz
2# 4 oz	4# 8 oz	6# 12 oz	9 #	18#	27#	36#	45#
2# 6 oz	4# 12 oz	7# 2 oz	9# 8 oz	19#	28# 8 oz	38#	47# 8 oz
2# 8 oz	5#	7# 8 oz	10#	20#	30#	40#	50#
2# 12 oz	5# 8 oz	8# 4 oz	11#	22#	33#	44#	55#
3#	6#	9#	12#	24#	36#	48#	60#
3# 4 oz	6# 8 oz	9# 12 oz	13#	26#	39#	52#	65#
3# 8 oz	7#	10# 8 oz	14#	28#	42#	56#	70#
3# 12 oz	7# 8 oz	11# 4 oz	15#	30#	45#	60#	75#

25	50	75	100	200	300	400	500
4#	8#	12#	16#	32#	48#	64#	80#
4# 4 oz	8# 8 oz	12# 12 oz	17#	34#	51#	68#	85#
4# 8 oz	9#	13# 8 oz	18#	36#	54#	72#	90#
4# 12 oz	9# 8 oz	14# 2 oz	19#	38#	57#	76#	95#
5#	10#	15#	20#	40#	60#	80#	100#
5# 4 oz	10# 8 oz	15# 12 oz	21#	42#	63#	84#	105#
5# 8 oz	11#	16# 8 oz	22#	44#	66#	88#	110#
5# 12 oz	11# 8 oz	17# 4 oz	23#	46#	69#	92#	115#
6#	12#	18#	24#	48#	72#	96#	120#
6# 4 oz	12# 8 oz	18# 12 oz	25#	50#	75#	100#	125#
7# 8 oz	15#	22# 8 oz	30#	60#	90#	120#	150#
8# 12 oz	17# 8 oz	26# 4 oz	35#	70#	105#	140#	175#
10#	20#	30#	40#	80#	120#	160#	200#
11# 4 oz	22# 8 oz	33# 12 oz	45#	90#	135#	180#	225#
12# 8 oz	25#	37# 8 oz	50#	100#	150#	200#	250#

[a] Used with permission from *Quantity Food Preparation: Standardizing Recipes and Controlling Ingredients*. Copyright 1983 by The American Dietetic Association, Chicago Il.

To be used with Table 1.23, which is similarly constructed for volume measures.

TABLE 1.23 DIRECT READING MEASUREMENT TABLE FOR ADJUSTING RECIPES WITH INGREDIENT AMOUNTS GIVEN IN VOLUME MEASUREMENT AND DIVISIBLE BY 25

25	*50*	*75*	*100*	*200*	*300*	*400*	*500*
¼ t	½ t	¾ t	1 t	2 t	1 T	1 T + 1 t	1 T + 2 t
¼ t(r)	½ t(r)	1 t(s)	1¼ t	2½ t	1 T + ¾ t	1 T + 2 t	2 T + ¼ t
¼ t + ⅛ t	¾ t	1 t + ⅛ t	1½ t	1 T	1½ T	2 T	2½ T
½ t(s)	¾ t(r)	1¼ t(r)	1¾ t	1 T + ½ t	1 T + 2¼ t	2 T + 1 t	2 T + 2¾
½ t	1 t	1½ t	2 t	1 T + 1 t	2 T	2 T + 2 t	3 T + 1 t
½ t(r)	1 t + ⅛ t	1¾ t(s)	2¼ t	1½ T	2 T + ¾ t	3 T	3 T + 2¼
½ t + ⅛ t	1¼ t	2 t(s)	2½ t	1 T + 2 t	2½ T	3 T + 1 t	4 T + ½ t
¾ t(s)	1¼ t + ⅛ t	2 t(r)	2¾ t	1 T + 2½ t	2 T + 2¼ t	3 T + 2 t	4 T + 1¾
¾ t	1½ t	2¼ t	1 T	2 T	3 T	¼ c	5 T
1 t + ⅛ t	2¼ t	1 T + ¼ t + ⅛ t	1½ T	3 T	¼ c + 1½ t	⅓ c + 2 t	¼ c + 3½ T
1½ t	1 T	1½ T	2 T	¼ c	¼ c + 2 T	½ c	½ c + 2 T
1¾ t + ⅛ t	1 T + ¾ t	1 T + 2½ t + ⅛ t	2½ T	¼ c + 1 T	¼ c + 3½ T	½ c + 2 T	¾ c + ½ T
2¼ t	1½ T	2 T + ¾ t	3 T	⅓ c + 2 t	½ c + 1 T	¾ c	¾ c + 3 T
2¼ t + ⅛ t	1 T + 2¼ t	2 T + 1½ t + ⅛ t	3½ T	¼ c + 3 T	½ c + 2½ T	¾ c + 2 T	1 c + 1½
1 T	2 T	3 T	¼ c	½ c	¾ c	1 c	1¼ c
1 T + 1 t	2 T + 2 t	¼ c	⅓ c	⅔ c	1 c	1⅓ c	1⅔ c
2 T	¼ c	¼ c + 2 T	½ c	1 c	1½ c	2 c	2½ c
2 T + 2 t	⅓ c	½ c	⅔ c	1⅓ c	2 c	2⅔ c	3⅓ c
3 T	6 T	½ c + 1 T	¾ c	1½ c	2¼ c	3 c	3¾ c
¼ c	½ c	¾ c	1 c	2 c	3 c	1 qt	1¼ qt
¼ c + 1 T	½ c + 2 T	¾ c + 3 T	1¼ c	2½ c	3¾ c	1¼ qt	1½ qt + ¼ c
⅓ c	⅔ c	1 c	1⅓ c	2⅔ c	1 qt	1¼ qt + ⅓ c	1½ qt + ⅔ c
⅓ c + 2 t	¾ c	1 c + 2 T	1½ c	3 c	1 qt + ½ c	1½ qt	1¾ qt + ½ c
6 T + 2 t	¾ c + 4 t	1¼ c	1⅔ c	3⅓ c	1¼ qt	1½ qt + ⅔ c	2 qt + ⅓ c
¼ c + 3 T	¾ c + 2 T	1¼ c + 1 T	1¾ c	3½ c	1¼ qt + ¼ c	1¾ qt	2 qt + ¾ c
½ c	1 c	1½ c	2 c	1 qt	1½ qt	2 qt	2½ qt
½ c + 1 T	1 c + 2 T	1½ c + 3 T	2¼ c	1 qt + ½ c	1½ qt + ¾ c	2¼ qt	2¾ qt + ¼ c
½ c + 4 t	1 c + 2 T + 2 t	1¾ c	2⅓ c	1 qt + ⅔ c	1¾ qt	2¼ qt + ⅓ c	2¾ qt + ⅔ c

TABLE 1.23 (Continued)

25	50	75	100	200	300	400	500
c + 2 T	1¼ c	1¾ c + 2 T	2½ c	1¼ qt	1¾ qt + ½ c	2½ qt	3 qt + 1½ c
c	1⅓ c	2 c	2⅔ c	1¼ qt + ⅓ c	2 qt	2½ qt + ⅔ c	3 qt + 1⅓ c
c + 3 T	1¼ c + 2 T	2 c + 1 T	2¾ c	1¼ qt + ½ c	2 qt + ¼ c	2¾ qt	3¼ qt + ¾ c
c	1½ c	2¼ c	3 c	1½ qt	2¼ qt	3 qt	3¾ qt
c + 1 T	1½ c + 2 T	2¼ c + 3 T	3¼ c	1½ qt + ½ c	2¼ qt + ¾ c	3¼ qt	1 gal + ¼ c
c + 4 t	1⅔ c	2½ c	3⅓ c	1½ qt + ⅔ c	2½ qt	3¼ qt + ⅓ c	1 gal + ⅔ c
c + 2 T	1¾ c	2½ c + 2 T	3½ c	1¾ qt	2½ qt + ½ c	3½ qt	1 gal + 1½ c
c + 2T + 2½t	1¾ c + 4 t	2¾ c + ½ t	3⅔ c	1¾ qt + ⅓ c	2¾ qt	3½ qt + ⅔ c	1 gal + 1⅔ c
c + 3 T	1¾ c + 2 T	2¾ c + 1 T	3¾ c	1¾ qt + ½ c	3 qt + ¼ c	1 gal	1 gal + 3¾ c
c	2 c	3 c	1 qt	2 qt	3 qt	1 gal	1¼ gal
¼ c	2½ c	3¾ c	1¼ qt	2½ qt	3¾ qt	1¼ gal	1½ gal + 1 c
½ c	3 c	1 qt + ½ c	1½ qt	3 qt	1 gal + 2 c	1½ gal	1¾ gal + 2 c
¾ c	3½ c	1¼ qt + ¼ c	1¾ qt	3½ qt	1¼ gal + 1 c	1¾ gal	2 gal + 3 c
c	1 qt	1½ qt	2 qt	1 gal	1½ gal	2 gal	2½ gal
¼ c	1 qt + ½ c	1½ qt + ¾ c	2¼ qt	1 gal + 2 c	1½ gal + 3 c	2¼ gal	2¾ gal + 1 c
½ c	1¼ qt	1¾ qt + ½ c	2½ qt	1¼ gal	1¾ gal + 2 c	2½ gal	3 gal + 2 c
¾ c	1¼ qt + ½ c	2 qt + ¼ c	2¾ qt	1¼ gal + 2 c	2 gal + 1 c	2¾ gal	3¼ gal + 3 c
c	1½ qt	2¼ qt	3 qt	1½ gal	2¼ gal	3 gal	3¾ gal
¼ c	1½ qt + ½ c	2¼ qt + ¾ c	3¼ qt	1½ gal + 2 c	2¼ gal + 3 c	3¼ gal	4 gal + 1 c
½ c	1¾ qt	2½ qt + ½ c	3½ qt	1¾ gal	2½ gal + 2 c	3½ gal	4¼ gal + 2 c
¾ c	1¾ qt + ½ c	2¾ qt + ¼ c	3¾ qt	1¾ gal + 2 c	2¾ gal + 1 c	3¾ gal	4½ gal + 3 c
qt	2 qt	3 qt	1 gal	2 gal	3 gal	4 gal	5 gal

TABLE 1.23 (Continued)

25	50	75	100	200	300	400	5
1¼ qt	2½ qt	3¾ qt	1¼ gal	2½ gal	3¾ gal	5 gal	6¼ gal
1½ qt	3 qt	1 gal + 2 c	1½ gal	3 gal	4½ gal	6 gal	7½ gal
1¾ qt	3½ qt	1¼ gal + 1 c	1¾ gal	3½ gal	5¼ gal	7 gal	8¾ gal
2 qt	1 gal	1½ gal	2 gal	4 gal	6 gal	8 gal	10 gal
2¼ qt	1 gal + 2 c	1½ gal + 3 c	2¼ gal	4½ gal	6¾ gal	9 gal	11¼ ga
2½ qt	1¼ gal	1¾ gal + 2 c	2½ gal	5 gal	7½ gal	10 gal	12½ ga
2¾ qt	1¼ gal + 2 c	2 gal + 1 c	2¾ gal	5½ gal	8¼ gal	11 gal	13¾ ga
3 qt	1½ gal	2¼ gal	3 gal	6 gal	9 gal	12 gal	15 gal
3 qt + 1 c	1½ gal + 2 c	2¼ gal + 3 c	3¼ gal	6½ gal	9¾ gal	13 gal	16¼ ga
3½ qt	1¾ gal	2½ gal + 2 c	3½ gal	7 gal	10½ gal	14 gal	17½ ga
3½ qt + 1 c	1¾ gal + 2 c	2¾ gal + 1 c	3¾ gal	7½ gal	11¼ gal	15 gal	18¾ ga
1 gal	2 gal	3 gal	4 gal	8 gal	12 gal	16 gal	20 gal
1 gal + 1 c	2 gal + 2 c	3 gal + 3 c	4¼ gal	8½ gal	12¾ gal	17 gal	21¼ ga
1 gal + 2 c	2¼ gal	3¼ gal + 2 c	4½ gal	9 gal	13½ gal	18 gal	22½ ga
1 gal + 3 c	2¼ gal + 2 c	3½ gal + 1 c	4¾ gal	9½ gal	14¼ gal	19 gal	23¾ ga
1¼ gal	2½ gal	3¾ gal	5 gal	10 gal	15 gal	20 gal	25 gal
1¼ gal + 1 c	2½ gal + 2 c	3¾ gal + 3 c	5¼ gal	10½ gal	15¾ gal	21 gal	26¼ ga
1¼ gal + 2 c	2¾ gal	4 gal + 2 c	5½ gal	11 gal	16½ gal	22 gal	27½ g
1¼ gal + 3 c	2¾ gal + 2 c	4¼ gal + 1 c	5¾ gal	11½ gal	17¼ gal	23 gal	28¾ ga
1½ gal	3 gal	4½ gal	6 gal	12 gal	18 gal	24 gal	30 gal
1½ gal + 1c	3 gal + 2 c	4½ gal + 3 c	6¼ gal	12½ gal	18¾ gal	25 gal	31¼ g
1½ gal + 2 c	3¼ gal	4¾ gal + 2 c	6½ gal	13 gal	19½ gal	26 gal	32½ g
1½ gal + 3 c	3¼ gal + 2 c	5 gal + 1 c	6¾ gal	13½ gal	20¼ gal	27 gal	33¾ ga
1¾ gal	3½ gal	5¼ gal	7 gal	14 gal	21 gal	28 gal	35 gal

[a] (To be used with Table 1.22 which is similarly constructed for weight measures.) Used with permission Quantity Food Preparation: Standardizing Recipes and Controlling Ingredients. Copyright 1983 by American Dietetic Association, Chicago, Illinois.

RECIPE ADJUSTMENT 53

Directions for Using Table 1.24

	Basic Information	
Abbreviations in Table	Measuring Spoons	Equivalents
t = teaspoon	1 T	3 t = 1 T 12 T = ¾ c
T = tablespoon	1 t	4 T = ¼ c 16 T = 1 c
c = cup	½ t	5 T + 1 t = ⅓ c 4 c = 1 qt
qt = quart	¼ t	8 T = ½ c 4 qt = 1 gal
gal = gallon	for ¾ t combine	10 T + 2 t = ⅔ c
(b) = too small for accurate measure; use caution	½ t + ¼ t for ⅛ t use half of the ¼ t	
(r) = slightly rounded		
(s) = scant		

Table 1.24 is useful when enlarging small quantity recipes. Instructions for using this table are as follows:

1. Locate column that corresponds to the yield of the recipe to be increased. For example, if the recipe yields 8 portions use the figures in the first column under the heading 8.

2. Locate the ingredient amount for each ingredient to be adjusted. Example: the original recipe of 8 portions calls for 1 T sugar. Find 1 T in the column marked 8.

3. Locate the amount on the same line under the heading for the desired yield. Example: To increase the original recipe for 8 servings to 24, locate under the 24 column heading the number on the same line with the 1 T in the 8 column. In the case of 1 T sugar for 8 portions the enlarged amount is 3 T.

4. Repeat this procedure for each ingredient in the recipe. Refer to Table 1.20 for "rounding off" awkward fractions and complicated measurements.

54 GENERAL INFORMATION

TABLE 1.24 DIRECT-READING TABLE FOR INCREASING HOME-SIZE RECIPES WITH INGREDI
AMOUNTS GIVEN IN VOLUME MEASUREMENT (PORTION YIELDS DIVISIBLE BY 8)

8	16	24	32	48	64	96
(b)	(b)	⅛ t	⅛ t(r)	¼ t	¼ t(r)	½ t
(b)	⅛ t(r)	¼ t	¼ t(r)	½ t	¾ t(s)	1 t
¼ t(s)	¼ t(r)	½ t	¾ t(s)	1 t	1¼ t(r)	2 t
¼ t	½ t	¾ t	1 t	1½ t	2 t	1 T
¼ t(r)	¾ t(s)	1 t	1¼ t(r)	2 t	2¾ t(s)	1 T + 1 t
½ t(s)	¾ t(r)	1¼ t	1¾ t(s)	2½ t	1 T + ¼ t	1 T + 2 t
½ t	1 t	1½ t	2 t	1 T	1 T + 1 t	2 T
½ t(r)	1¼ t(s)	1¾ t	2¼ t(r)	1 T + ½ t	1 T + 1¾ t	2 T + 1 t
¾ t(s)	1¼ t(r)	2 t	2¾ t(r)	1 T + 1 t	1 T + 2¼ t	2 T + 2 t
¾ t	1½ t	2¼ t	1 T	1 T + 1½ t	2 T	3 T
¾ t(r)	1¾ t(s)	2½ t	1 T + ¼ t(r)	1 T + 2 t	2 T + ¾ t	3 T + 1 t
1 t(s)	1¾ t(r)	2¾ t	1 T + ¾ t(s)	1 T + 2½ t	2 T + 1¼ t	3 T + 2 t
1 t	2 t	1 T	1 T + 1 t	2 T	2 T + 2 t	¼ c
1½ t	1 T	1½ T	2 T	3 T	¼ c	⅓ c + 2
2 t	1 T + 1 t	2 T	2 T + 2 t	¼ c	⅓ c	½ c
2½ t	1 T + 2 t	2½ T	3 T + 1 t	¼ c + 1 T	⅓ c + 4 t	½ c + 2
1 T	2 T	3 T	¼ c	⅓ c + 2 t	½ c	¾ c
1 T + ½ t	2 T + 1 t	3½ T	¼ c + 2 t	¼ c + 3 T	½ c + 4 t	¾ c + 2
1 T + 1 t	2 T + 2 t	¼ c	⅓ c	½ c	⅔ c	1 c
1 T + 2¼ t	3 T + 2¾ t	⅓ c	¼ c + 3 T	⅔ c	¾ c + 2 T	1⅓ c
2 T + 2 t	⅓ c	½ c	⅔ c	1 c	1⅓ c	2 c
3 T + 1¾ t	⅓ c + 5 t	⅔ c	¾ c + 2 T	1⅓ c	1¾ c	2⅔ c
¼ c	½ c	¾ c	1 c	1½ c	2 c	3 c
⅓ c	⅔ c	1 c	1⅓ c	2 c	2⅔ c	1 qt
⅓ c + 4 t	¾ c + 4 t	1¼ c	1⅔ c	2½ c	3⅓ c	1¼ qt
⅓ c + 5¼ t	⅔ c + 3½ T	1⅓ c	1¾ c + 1¼ t	2⅔ c	3½ + 2½ t	1¼ qt +
½ c	1 c	1½ c	2 c	3 c	1 qt	1½ qt
½ c + 2¼ t	1 c + 5¼ t	1⅔ c	2 c + 3½ T	3⅓ c	4¼ c + 3 T	1½ qt +
½ c + 4 t	1 c + 3 T	1¾ c	2⅓ c	3½ c	1 qt + ⅔ c	1¾ qt
⅔ c	1⅓ c	2 c	2⅔ c	1 qt	1¼ qt + ⅓ c	2 qt
¾ c	1½ c	2¼ c	3 c	1 qt + ½ c	1½ qt	2¼ qt
¾ c + 1¼ t	1½ c + 2¾ t	2⅓ c	3 c + 2 T	1 qt + ⅔ c	1½ qt + ¼ c	2¼ qt +
¾ c + 4 t	1⅔ c	2½ c	3⅓ c	1¼ qt	1½ qt + ⅔ c	2½ qt
⅔ c + 3½ T	1¾ c + 1¼ t	2⅔ c	3½ c + 1 T	1¼ qt + ⅓ c	1¾ qt + 2 T	2½ qt +
⅔ c + ¼ c	1¾ c + 4 t	2¾ c	3⅔ c	1¼ qt + ½ c	1¾ qt + ⅓ c	2¾ qt
1 c	2 c	3 c	1 qt	1½ qt	2 qt	3 qt
1 c + 4 t	2 c + 2½ T	3¼ c	1 qt + ⅓ c	1½ qt + ½ c	2 qt + ⅔ c	3¼ qt
1 c + 5¼ t	2 c + 3½ T	3⅓ c	4¼ c + 3 T	1½ qt + ⅔ c	2 qt + ¾ c + 2 T	3¼ qt +
1 c + 2 T + 2 t	2¼ c + 4 t	3½ c	1 qt + ⅔ c	1¾ qt	2¼ qt + ⅓ c	3½ qt
1 c + 3½ T	2¼ c + 3 T	3⅔ c	4¾ c + 2 T	1¾ qt + ⅓ c	2¼ qt + ¾ c	3 qt + 2

RECIPE ADJUSTMENT 55

	8	16	24	32	48	64	96
c	2½ c	3¾ c	1¼ qt	1¾ qt + ½ c	2½ qt	3 qt + 3 c
c	2⅔ c	1 qt	1¼ qt + ⅓ c	2 qt	2¾ qt + ⅓ c	1 gal
c	3⅓ c	1¼ qt	1½ qt + ⅔ c	2½ qt	3¼ qt + ⅓ c	1¼ gal
	1 qt	1½ qt	2 qt	3 qt	1 gal	1½ gal
c	1 qt + ⅔ c	1¾ qt	2¼ qt + ⅓ c	3½ qt	1 gal + 2⅔ c	1¾ gal
c	1¼ qt + ⅓ c	2 qt	2½ qt + ⅔ c	1 gal	1¼ gal + 1⅓ c	2 gal
	1½ qt	2¼ qt	3 qt	1 gal + 2 c	1½ gal	2¼ gal
c	1½ qt + ⅔ c	2½ qt	3¼ qt + ⅓ c	1¼ gal	1½ gal + 2⅔ c	2½ gal
c	1¾ qt + ⅓ c	2¾ qt	3½ qt + ⅔ c	1¼ gal + 2 c	1¾ gal + 1⅓ c	2¾ gal
t	2 qt	3 qt	1 gal	1½ gal	2 gal	3 gal
t + ⅓ c	2 qt + ⅔ c	3¼ qt	1 gal + 1⅓ c	1½ gal + 2 c	2 gal + 2⅔ c	3¼ gal
t + ⅔ c	2¼ qt + ⅓ c	3½ qt	1 gal + 2⅔ c	1¾ gal	2¼ gal + 1⅓ c	3½ gal
qt	2½ qt	3¾ qt	1¼ gal	1¾ gal + 2 c	2½ gal	3¾ gal
qt + ⅓ c	2½ qt + ⅔ c	1 gal	1¼ gal + 1⅓ c	2 gal	2½ gal + 2⅔ c	4 gal
qt + ⅔ c	3¼ qt + ⅓ c	1¼ gal	1½ gal + 2⅔ c	2½ gal	3¼ gal + 1⅓ c	5 gal
t	1 gal	1½ gal	2 gal	3 gal	4 gal	6 gal

PART TWO

RECIPES

Recipe Information

YIELD

The recipes in this book provide servings for 50 people unless otherwise stated. It is recognized that many factors affect the probable yield; portioning probably is the most important. Yield also may be incorrect if an ingredient weighing error or a recipe increasing or decreasing calculation error exist.

A pan 12 × 20 in. has been indicated for many recipes because it is a standard counter pan size. For baked dessert and bread products, either a 12 × 18 in. or 18 × 26 in. pan is specified, as they are standard aluminumware sizes and are better than stainless steel for baking.

For products that are cut into servings, the yield may be adjusted slightly for ease of cutting. Many standard-sized baking or counter pans will yield from 24 to 32 servings per pan. The recipes in this case are generally calculated for 48 or 64 servings. Yield adjustment can be made by cutting the servings into sizes that will yield the desired number of portions. Some food services may wish to adjust yield based on the clientele to be served.

INGREDIENTS

In most cases, the type of ingredient used in testing the recipes has been specified; for example, granulated, brown, or powdered sugar; all-purpose or cake flour. High ratio and/or hydrogenated shortenings were used in cake and pastry recipes; margarine or butter in cookies, some quick breads, and most sauce recipes. Solid fats such as margarine, butter, and hydrogenated fats were used interchangeably in recipes that specify "fat." Unsaturated fat, including corn and vegetable oil, was used in recipes that specify salad oil. Sodium-aluminum–sulfate-type baking powder (double acting) and active dry yeast were used for leavening.

Fresh shell eggs, weighing approximately 2 oz (57 g), were used in the preparation of the recipes and are specified by both number and weight. In many food services, frozen eggs are used, in which case the eggs are weighed or measured. If the eggs are to be measured, the number and weight may easily be converted to volume by referring to Table 1.3.

Nonfat dry milk is indicated in some recipes, but in those calling for whole milk, dry milk may be substituted (see p. 40).

WEIGHTS AND MEASURES

Quantities in the recipes are given in both U.S. and metric measurements, but metric weights and measures were not included in most of the tables in Part One. To convert these amounts to metric, Tables 1.6 and 1.7 will be useful.

Most dry ingredients weighing more than 1 oz (28 g) are given by weight in ounces (oz) and pounds (lb) and in metric grams (g) up to 1000 g and in kilograms (kg) for 1000 g and over. Weights given are for foods as purchased (AP) unless stated otherwise.

All liquids are indicated by measure. Metric measures are in milliliters (mL) up to 950 mL and in liters (L) beyond that; although in some cases, small amounts of liquids have been given in weight (grams) for ease of measuring.

Metric measurements used in this book were determined by mathematical formula (see p. 32). This approach is a *soft* conversion as opposed to a *hard* conversion, which requires standardized metric modules and which will require new measuring devices. The soft conversion was used in this edition because of the uncertainty about standardization of measuring devices, particularly for measuring volume.

When using the metric weights and measures in this book, some quantities may need to be rounded off to a measurable amount or to the scale marking of the metric measure. For example, 1 qt in the recipes has been converted to 0.95 L, which would be difficult to measure. In some recipes this could be rounded to 1 L without affecting the final product; in some, the other ingredients would need changing also. Recipes in which quantities have been changed should be tested in 50 portions before enlarging. The metric measurements were not rounded off in this book because many food services enlarge the recipes to yields of more than 50 portions. In this case, it would be more accurate to round off the figures after the recipe has been enlarged.

Accurate weighing and measuring of ingredients are essential for a satisfactory product. Weighing ingredients, when possible, is recommended, since it is more accurate. Reliable scales are essential. A table model scale, 15- to 20-lb capacity, with ¼- to ½-oz gradations, or a 10-kg metric scale is suitable for weighing ingredients for 50 portions.

When measuring, use standard measuring equipment and make measurements level. Use the largest appropriate measure to reduce the possibility of error and to save time. For example, use a 1-gal measure once instead of a 1-qt measure four times. (Flour is the exception. Use measure no larger than 1 qt for flour.)

COOKING TIME AND TEMPERATURE

The cooking time given in each recipe is based on the size of pan indicated and the amount of food in the pan. If a smaller or larger pan is used, the cooking time should be adjusted accordingly. The number of pans placed in the oven at one time also may affect the length of baking time; the larger the number of pans, the longer the cooking time. In convection ovens, the time and temperature should be reduced by 10%.

Temperatures are given both in Fahrenheit (°F) and Celsius (°C). Celsius temperatures were determined by the conversion formula on p. 34, then rounded off to a functional number.

ABBREVIATIONS USED IN RECIPES

AP	as purchased	in.	inch
c	cup	kg	kilogram
°C	degrees Celsius	L	liter
doz	dozen	lb	pound
EP	edible portion	mL	milliliter
°F	degrees Fahrenheit	oz	ounce
f.d.	few drops	psi	pounds per square inch
f.g.	few grains	pt	pint
fl oz	fluid ounce	qt	quart
g	gram	t	teaspoon
gal	gallon	T	tablespoon

Appetizers

Appetizers are served preceding a meal and include an array of light foods that whet rather than satisfy the appetite. They may be served informally away from the dining table or as a first course at the table. Popular are parties that feature beverages and an assortment of appetizers with or without a dessert table as a finale. Appetizers in this case need to be substantial and varied and satisfy the appetite for the duration of the gathering. In either case the appetizers should be attractive in appearance, pleasing in flavor, and tastefully displayed.

Selections for appetizers may be from one or more of the following categories. *Hors d'oeuvres* are attractive hot and cold finger foods that may include crisp fresh fruits and vegetables, pickles, olives, cheese, fish, sausages, deviled eggs, or a combination of these. Hot or cold *dips* are accompaniments to fruits, vegetables, or crackers. They should be complementary to the foods being served with them. *Canapés* are made by spreading a well-seasoned mixture of eggs, cheese, fish, or meat on a canapé base. Bases include toasted or untoasted bread slices cut into various shapes, crackers, chips, tiny biscuits, or puff pastry shells. Fruit and nut breads add interest to many canapé mixtures. *Cocktails* are made of pieces of fruit, fruit or vegetable juices, and carbonated or alcoholic beverages. They may be made also of seafood such as oysters, shrimp, crab, or lobster and served with a highly seasoned sauce. *Soup* appetizers are light and delicate and generally served as a first course at the dining table. Hot or cold broth or cream soups may be served and should complement the remainder of the meal.

Appetizer suggestions follow.

HORS D'OEUVRES

HOT

Hot Cheese Balls. Prepare small cheese balls using recipe on p. 269. Serve hot on cocktail picks.

Cheese Olive Puffs. Blend 1 lb. grated sharp cheese with 8 oz soft butter or margarine. Add 8 oz flour, 1 t salt, and 2 t paprika. Mix. Wrap 1 t cheese mixture around each of 100 stuffed olives. Arrange on a baking sheet and bake 10 minutes at 400°F. May be frozen. To prepare frozen puffs, bake 15 minutes.

Sausage Balls. Form 2 lb sausage into 100 1-in. balls and place on baking sheets. Bake at 350°F for 15 minutes. Drain on paper towels. Combine 1 lb sharp cheddar cheese, softened or grated, 8 oz margarine or butter, softened, 12 oz flour, ½ t salt, and 2 t paprika. Wrap 2 T (No. 70 dipper) of dough around each sausage ball. (Freeze at this point if desired.) Place on ungreased baking sheet. Bake at 350°F for 12-15 minutes.

Sauerkraut Balls. Cook 8 oz ground pork sausage until lightly browned. Add 8 oz ground cooked ham, 8 oz ground cooked corned beef, ½ c finely chopped onion, and 1 t finely chopped parsley; continue to cook, stirring frequently, until hot. Mix 2 c flour, 1 t salt, and 1 t dry mustard and add to meat mixture, stirring constantly. Add 2 c milk and continue to cook over low heat until mixture is thickened. Stir in 6 c firmly packed sauerkraut, drained and finely chopped. Chill mixture. Form into balls, using a No. 70 dipper. Roll in flour, dip in egg and milk mixture, and then roll in bread crumbs. Refrigerate until ready to use. Fry in deep fat at 350°F until golden brown.

COLD

Apple-Cheese. Core and cut crisp tart red apples into wedges. Dip in fruit juice to prevent discoloration. Spread with Roquefort cheese softened with cream, and spear each wedge with a toothpick. Arrange sections close together in a circle around a whole red apple.

Carrot Curls. Cut long, paper-thin slices. Roll each strip around finger, fasten with toothpick, and chill in ice water for several hours.

Cheese Cubes. Cut cheddar, Swiss, Edam, or other hard or semihard cheese into cubes. Spear with a toothpick and arrange on a tray or in a grapefruit or fresh red apple.

Cherry Tomatoes. Select uniform firm cherry tomatoes; wash, chill, and serve whole; or marinate in French Dressing (p. 442) or Vegetable Marinade (p. 486) for several hours.

Deviled Eggs. Prepare deviled eggs (p. 268). Garnish with paprika, pimiento, or anchovy.

Fruit Chunks. Cut fresh fruit into chunks. May serve with a dip.

Ginger-Cheese Balls. Combine 8 oz cream cheese, 2½ oz crumbled Roquefort cheese, 2 T candied ginger, shredded, and 2-4 T cream. Mix well. Chill thoroughly. Make into small balls. Roll in chopped pecans.

Ham-Cheese Wedges. Spread 6 thin slices of pullman ham or luncheon meat with softened cream cheese and stack. Chill, cut into small wedges. Spear with cocktail picks.

Marinated Mushrooms. See p. 414.

Party Cheese Ball. Combine 8 oz cream cheese, 12 oz Blue cheese, 1 lb shredded sharp Cheddar cheese, 3 T onion juice, and f.d. Worcestershire sauce. Add 3 T finely cut candied ginger if desired. Mix until smooth and shape into a ball. Cover with chopped pecans and chill. Serve in center of plate surrounded by crisp assorted crackers. Cheese mixture may be formed into a long roll, wrapped in waxed paper, and chilled several hours. Slice and serve on crackers.

Salmon Log. Drain and flake 2 lb salmon, removing skin and bones. Combine salmon with 1 lb cream cheese softened, 2 T lemon juice, ¼ c grated onion, 2 t prepared horseradish, ½ t salt, 2 t liquid smoke seasoning. Chill several hours. Combine 1 c chopped walnuts and ½ c snipped parsley. Shape salmon mixture into 16 × 2-in. log; roll in nut−parsley mixture. Chill. Serve with crackers.

Shrimp. Marinate cooked shrimp in Italian Dressing (p. 442).

Strawberries. Arrange whole, perfect strawberries, with stems, around a bowl of powdered sugar or sour cream.

Stuffed Celery. Cut prepared celery into 3-in. lengths and stuff with cream cheese dip or with pimiento cheese.

Vegetable Relishes. Cut carrots, green pepper, zucchini, cucumber, turnips, or celery into sticks, circles, or slices, and separate cauliflower into flowerets. Crisp vegetables relishes may be served with a cold dip.

DIPS

HOT

Chili Con Queso. Melt 2 lb processed yellow cheese. Add 2 large onions, minced, 1 lb drained chopped canned tomatoes, 2 garlic cloves, minced, 6 oz drained and mashed green chili peppers, and 2 T Worcestershire sauce. A f.d. of hot pepper sauce may be added.

Hot Clam and Cheese. Sauté two small finely minced onions and ½ green pepper finely chopped in 6 T margarine. Add 1 lb drained clams (reserve liquid). Melt 2 lb processed American cheese. Add ¼ c catsup, ¼ c Worcestershire sauce, and ½ t cayenne pepper. Combine with onion−clam mixture. Add clam juice as necessary for dipping consistency. Serve with corn chips.

COLD

Avocado Dip. Mash 4 ripe avocados and blend with 2 c cultured sour cream, ½ t salt, 2 t onion juice, and ¼ c prepared horseradish.

Cheddar Cheese Dip. Blend 8 oz grated sharp Cheddar cheese, 1 T minced green onion, 1 c mayonnaise, and ½ t salt. Just before serving, add ½ c chopped crisp bacon. Garnish with ½ c chopped toasted almonds. Serve with crisp crackers.

Clam Dip. Combine 8 oz canned minced clams, 1 c cottage cheese, 8 oz cream cheese, 2½ oz Blue cheese, 2 t lemon juice, 1½ t Worcestershire sauce, ½ t salt, and f.d. Tabasco sauce. Thin with clam juice or cream. Blend well. Serve with crisp crackers, potato or corn chips.

Cream Cheese Dip. Blend 3 oz cream cheese, 2 oz crumbled Roquefort cheese, 1 t onion juice, ⅛ t pepper, ⅛ t salt, f.d. Tabasco sauce, and 2 T cream: ¼ c chopped pecans may be added. Serve with potato chips or pretzels.

Guacamole Dip. Mash 2 ripe avocados; add 1 T lemon or lime juice, ½ t salt, 1 T finely grated onion, ½ t chili powder, and 1 ripe tomato, peeled and mashed. Mix well. Spread ¼ c mayonnaise over top of mixture in a thin layer to prevent discoloration. Serve with chips or melba toast.

CANAPÉ SPREADS AND FILLINGS

Avocado–Shrimp. Mash 2 soft avocados; season with 1 T lemon juice, 1 T minced onion, and f.g. salt. Spread on crackers or canapé bases and top each with small whole shrimp.

Cheese, Hot. Combine 4 oz sharp grated Cheddar cheese, ⅛ t salt, and f.g. cayenne. Spread on toasted canapé base. Sprinkle with sesame seeds. Toast and serve hot.

Cheese–Mushroom. Sauté 4 oz canned mushrooms, drained, in 4 T margarine or butter. Add ¼ c heavy cream, f.d. onion juice, salt, pepper, and ¾ c grated Cheddar cheese. Mash to a paste. Spread toasted bread rounds with creamed butter and then cheese–mushroom mixture. Garnish with grated cheese and thinly sliced olives.

Miniature Puffs. Prepare Cream Puffs (p. 240) and drop on baking sheets by No. 100 dipper or by level teaspoonful. Bake. Combine 8 oz cream cheese, 4½ oz canned deviled ham, 1 t grated onion, 1 T horseradish, ½ t Worcestershire sauce, and ¼ t pepper. Blend until smooth. Fill each puff with cheese mixture.

Cheese Wafers. Blend 4 oz grated sharp Cheddar cheese and 8 oz margarine or butter. Add ½ t Worcestershire sauce, 6 oz flour, ½ t salt, and f.g. cayenne pepper, and mix thoroughly. Form into 1-in roll. Wrap in waxed paper and chill for several hours. Slice in ¼-in. slices and bake on ungreased baking sheet for 12–15 minutes at 375°F.

Chicken or Ham Spread. Combine 2 c chicken or ham, finely chopped, with creamed margarine or butter seasoned with ½ t curry powder or chutney. Spread on canapé bases. Garnish with watercress and/or paprika.

Liver Paté. Mash 8 oz liverwurst; add 1 t lemon juice, ½ t Worcestershire sauce, and cream to moisten. Spread on canapé bases. Garnish with outside border of riced hard-cooked egg yolk mixed with mayonnaise to moisten and season, and an inside border of finely chopped hard-cooked egg whites. Sprinkle with chopped parsley.

COCKTAILS

FRUIT
Grapefruit, Broiled. Cut grapefruit in halves and remove centers and seeds. Cut fruit from skin with a sharp knife. Add 1 t margarine or butter and 1 oz sugar to each center. Broil under a broiler or in a hot oven until fruit turns a golden brown.

Honeydew Melon. Combine chilled fresh pineapple chunks with honeydew melon balls, seedless grapes, and a small amount of grenadine syrup. Garnish with kiwi, lemon or lime wedges, blueberries, or strawberries.

Melon Cup. Cut small round balls or wedges from heart of ripe watermelon, cantaloupe, or honeydew melon, or use a combination of the three. Chill thoroughly. Cover with chilled ginger ale.

Pineapple–Strawberry Cup. Cube fresh pineapple and combine with whole fresh strawberries.

Strawberries. Arrange a few green leaves on each plate. Form a mound of powdered sugar in the center. Around the sugar arrange large unhulled strawberries.

SEAFOOD
Crab Meat. Line cocktail glasses with lettuce. Fill with alternate layers of crabmeat, chopped celery, or diced avocado and Cocktail Sauce (p. 483).

Shrimp. Line cocktail glasses with lettuce. Add cooked shrimp, either whole or cut into pieces, depending on size. Serve with Cocktail Sauce (p. 483).

Shrimp–Avocado–Grapefruit. Arrange avocado wedges, grapefruit sections, and shrimp in lettuce-lined cocktail glasses. Serve with Cocktail Sauce (p. 483).

SOUPS
Bouillon. Chicken, Beef, Tomato.   See recipes on pp. 496.

French Onion. See recipe on p. 505.

Gazpacho. See recipe on p. 518.

Vichyssoise. See recipe on p. 519.

Beverages

COFFEE

The type of coffee-making equipment used in a food service determines the method of preparation and the grind of coffee needed. The urn is used when large quantities of coffee are needed, as on a rapidly moving cafeteria line. Where the service is spread over a longer period, coffee may be prepared in small batches in a drip or vacuum coffee maker. The equipment selected should be one that makes a clear, rich brew, that holds the coffee at a consistent temperature, and that provides the quantity needed at an appropriate speed with a minimum of labor. Regardless of the method used, certain precautions should be observed.

1. Select a blend of coffee that is well liked by the clientele. The grind should be suitable for the equipment to be used.

2. Use fresh coffee. After coffee is ground, it deteriorates rapidly. Large amounts should not be accumulated. Coffee should be protected from exposure to heat, moisture, and air. Coffee not needed for immediate use may be stored in the refrigerator or freezer.

3. Use a proportion of water to coffee that makes a brew of the strength preferred by the clientele. A proportion of 2½ gal (9.46 L) of water per pound of coffee makes a brew of commonly accepted strength. Use 3 gal (11.36 L) when a milder flavor is preferred. See p. 69 for coffee recipes.

4. Measure coffee accurately. The number of servings per pound of coffee varies with the quality of the coffee bean, equipment used, and cup size. A pound (454 g) of high-quality coffee properly made should yield about 50 6-oz portions. Many food services purchase coffee in premeasured packages.

5. Have the water freshly drawn, accurately measured, and just brought to a boiling temperature.

6. Hold coffee at a temperature of 185 – 190°F (85 – 88°C) and do not allow it to boil.

7. Serve coffee very hot. The consumer often judges a food service by the quality of its coffee, and temperature is important to its acceptance.

8. Clean the urn or other equipment immediately after each use, following instructions that come with the equipment.

TEA

Tea is made by the process of infusion, in which boiling water is poured over tea leaves or tea bags and the mixture is allowed to stand until the desired concentration is reached. A stainless-steel or earthenware container is preferable for brewing tea. Use freshly drawn cold water, heated just to the boiling point.

For iced tea, make the brew stronger than for tea that is to be served hot. This is to compensate for the melting of the ice that is added at serving time. Keep the tea at room temperature because cloudiness develops in tea that is refrigerated.

PUNCH

Punch may be made easily from frozen or canned juices in various combinations. Lemonade (p. 74) or Foundation Fruit Punch (p. 75) makes a good base for many other fruit drinks by adding fresh, frozen, canned, or powdered juices of the desired flavor.

The amount of sugar needed varies with the sugar concentration of the juices and individual preference. A recipe for a simple syrup for sweetening punch is given on p. 75. If time does not permit making the syrup, add the sugar directly to the punch and stir until sugar is dissolved.

Most punch is served iced, but may be served hot if desired. Ingredients for making punch should be refrigerated and the chilled ingredients combined well in advance of serving time. If ginger ale or other carbonated beverage is to be used, it should be chilled and added just before serving. If served from a bowl, the punch may be kept cold by adding ice cubes or ring molds of ice. Ring molds made with lemonade will accent the flavor of other juices and will not dilute the flavor of the punch. To add color, arrange alternate slices of orange, lemon, and unstemmed strawberries or cherries to the molds. Sprigs of mint may be added as a garnish. Add water to fill the mold ¾ full and freeze. Unmold the ring and place upside down in the punch bowl. To make decorative ice cubes, fill ice cube trays with pastel-colored water or fruit juice. Add a red cherry to each ice cube section before freezing for additional color.

The amount of punch or iced beverage to prepare depends on the size of the punch cup or glass, on the number of guests to be served, and whether second servings will be offered. Service from a punch bowl will require slightly more punch than if it is to be poured from a pitcher for individual service. It is always desirable to have on hand and chilled, unopened cans of the main punch ingredients to facilitate serving a larger crowd than anticipated.

Most recipes in this book were developed for 2–2½ gal (7.57–9.46 L) of punch. Each gallon (3.79 L) will yield 32 ½-c (120-mL) portions. Punch cups vary in size from 3 oz (75 mL) to 6 oz (180 mL), so it is important that the size be considered in determining the correct amount of punch to prepare.

BEVERAGE RECIPES

COFFEE

Yield: 50 portions
2½ gal (9.46 L)
Portion: 6 oz (¾ c/180 mL)

Amount Metric	U.S.	Ingredient	Procedure
454 g	1 lb	Coffee	Use proper blend and grind for coffee maker used. Use method recommended by manufacturer of coffee maker.
9.46 L	2½ gal	Water	

Note: The amount of water will vary with the brand of coffee and the strength preferred.

Variations:
1. **Iced Coffee.** Make double-strength coffee. Pour over ice in glasses. Coffee may be cooled to room temperature but should not be refrigerated.
2. **Instant Coffee.** Use 3 oz (85 g) instant coffee or 2 oz (57 g) freeze-dried to 2½ gal (9.46 L) boiling water. Dissolve the coffee in a small amount of boiling water and add to the remaining hot water. Keep hot just below the boiling point.

STEEPED COFFEE

Yield: 50 portions
2½ gal (9.46 L)
Portion: 6 oz (¾ c/180 mL)

Amount Metric	U.S.	Ingredient	Procedure
454 g	1 lb	Coffee, regular grind	Tie coffee loosely in a cloth bag.
9.46 L	2½ gal	Water, cold	Immerse bag in water. Heat to boiling point. Boil 3 minutes or until of desired strength. Remove coffee bag. Cover and hold over low heat to keep at serving temperature.

Note: For an extra clear brew, beat an egg and 1 c (240 mL) water together and stir into coffee until dampened. Then proceed as above.

HOT TEA

Yield: 50 portions
2½ gal (9.46 L)
Portion: 6 oz (¾ c/180 mL)

Amount		Ingredient	Procedure
Metric	U.S.		
2 28-g	2 1-oz	Tea bags	Place tea bags in a stainless-steel, enamel, or earthen-ware container.
9.46 L	2½ gal	Water, boiling	Add water. Steep for 3 minutes. Remove bags.

Notes:
1. If bulk tea is used, tie loosely in a bag.
2. The amount of tea to be used will vary with the quality.
3. ¾–1 oz (21–28 g) instant tea may be used in place of the tea bags. The exact amount will vary according to the strength desired.

SPICED TEA

Yield: 48 portions
1½ gal (5.68 L)
Portion: 4 oz (½ c/120 mL)

Amount		Ingredient	Procedure
Metric	U.S.		
5.68 L	1½ gal	Water, boiling	Mix all ingredients except tea.
680 g	1 lb 8 oz	Sugar, granulated	
60 mL	¼ c	Lemon juice and 1 rind, grated	Simmer 20 minutes. Strain.
240 mL	1 c	Orange juice and 1 rind, grated	
8 g	4 t	Cloves, whole	
8	8	Cinnamon sticks	
1 28-g	1 1-oz	Tea bag	Add tea bag and let steep 5 minutes. Remove tea bag. Serve hot.

Variation: **Russian Tea.** Use only 1¼ gal (4.73 L) water. Add 1 qt (0.95 L) grape juice when adding other juice.

ICED TEA

Yield: 48 portions
3 gal (11.36 L)
Portion: 8 oz (1 c/240 mL)

Amount Metric	U.S.	Ingredient	Procedure
6 28-g	6 1-oz	Tea bags	Place tea bags in stainless-steel, earthenware or enamel container.
3.79 L	1 gal	Water, boiling	Add boiling water. Steep 4–6 minutes.
7.57 L	2 gal	Water, cold	Remove bags. Pour hot tea into cold water.
4.54–6.8 kg	10–15 lb	Ice, chipped or cubed	Fill 12-oz (360-mL) glasses with ice. Pour tea over ice just before serving.

Notes:
1. Always pour the hot tea concentrate into the cold water. Do not refrigerate or ice the tea prior to service. Cloudiness develops in tea that has been refrigerated.
2. 1–1½ oz (28–43 g) instant tea may be used in place of the tea bags.
3. Six to seven lemons may be cut in eighths to serve with the tea.

COCOA

Yield: 50 portions
2½ gal (9.46 L)
Portion: 6 oz (¾ c/180 mL)

Amount		Ingredient	Procedure
Metric	U.S.		
680 g	1 lb 8 oz	Sugar, granulated	Mix dry ingredients.
227 g	8 oz	Cocoa	
3 g	½ t	Salt	
0.95 L	1 qt	Water	Add water and mix until smooth. Boil approximately 3 minutes or to form a thin syrup.
8.52 L	2¼ gal	Milk	Heat milk. Add syrup. Just before serving, add vanilla and beat well with a wire whip.
5 mL	1 t	Vanilla	

Notes:
1. A marshmallow or 1 t whipped cream may be added to each cup if desired.
2. Cocoa syrup may be made in amounts larger than this recipe and stored in the refrigerator. To serve, add 1 qt (0.95 L) cocoa syrup to each 2 gal (7.57 L) of hot milk.

Variations:
1. **Hot Chocolate.** Substitute 10 oz (284 g) chocolate for cocoa.
2. **Instant Hot Cocoa.** Dissolve 2½ lb (1.14 kg) instant cocoa powder in 2 gal (7.57 L) boiling water.

FRENCH CHOCOLATE

Yield: 64 portions
3 gal (11.36 L)
Portion: 6 oz (¾ c/180 mL)

Amount		Ingredient	Procedure
Metric	U.S.		
510 g	1 lb 2 oz	Chocolate, baking, unsweetened	Combine chocolate and water.
720 mL	3 c	Water, cold	Cook over direct heat about 5 minutes, stirring constantly. Remove from heat. Beat with a wire whip until smooth.
1.14 kg	2 lb 8 oz	Sugar, granulated	Add sugar and salt to chocolate mixture. Return to heat. Cook over hot water 20–30 minutes or until thick. Chill.
3 g	½ t	Salt	
840 mL	3½ c	Cream, whipping	Whip cream. Fold into cold chocolate mixture.
9.46 L	2½ gal	Milk	Heat milk to scalding. To serve, place 1 rounded T chocolate mixture in each serving cup. Add hot milk to fill cup. Stir well to blend. Serve immediately.

Notes.
1. The milk must be kept very hot during the serving period.
2. The chocolate mixture may be stored for 24 hours in the refrigerator.

LEMONADE

Yield: 48 portions
3 gal (11.36 L)
Portion: 8 oz (1 c/240 mL)

Amount Metric	U.S.	Ingredient	Procedure
1.18 L	1¼ qt	Lemon juice (approx. 30 lemons)	Mix lemon juice and sugar.
1.14 kg	2 lb 8 oz	Sugar, granulated	
8.52 L	2¼ gal	Water, cold	Add water. Stir until sugar is dissolved. Chill.

Notes:
1. Three 6-oz (177-mL) cans undiluted frozen lemon juice may be substituted for fresh lemon juice. Increase water to 2½ gal (9.46 L).
2. Three 32-oz (0.95-L) cans frozen lemonade concentrate, diluted 1:4 parts water will yield 60 1-c (240-mL) portions.
3. Lemonade makes a good base for fruit punch.

GINGER ALE FRUIT PUNCH

Yield: 96 portions
3 gal (11.36 L)
Portion: 4 oz (½ c/120 mL)

Amount Metric	U.S.	Ingredient	Procedure
1.36 kg	3 lb	Sugar, granulated	Mix sugar and water.
0.95 L	1 qt	Water	Bring to boil. Cool.
1.42 L	1½ qt	Lemon juice	Combine juices and water.
1.42 L	1½ qt	Orange juice	
0.95 L	1 qt	Pineapple juice	Add sugar syrup. Chill.
3.79 L	1 gal	Water	
1.89 L	2 qt	Ginger ale, chilled	Add ginger ale just before serving.

Note: Lime, orange, lemon, or raspberry sherbet may be added to the punch just before serving.

SIMPLE SYRUP

Yield: 2 qt (1.89 L)

Amount		Ingredient	Procedure
Metric	U.S.		
908 g	2 lb	Sugar, granulated	Mix sugar and water. Boil
0.95 L	1 qt	Water	for 3 minutes.

Notes:
1. For a thicker syrup, increase sugar to 2½ lb (1.14 kg) and add 1 T (15 mL) corn syrup.
2. May be kept on hand for use in beverages or where recipe specifies simple syrup.

FOUNDATION FRUIT PUNCH

Yield: 80 portions
2½ gal (9.46 L)
Portion: 4 oz (½ c/120 mL)

Amount		Ingredient	Procedure
Metric	U.S.		
1.14 kg	2 lb 8 oz	Sugar, granulated	Mix sugar and water.
0.95 L	1 qt	Water	Bring to boil. Cool.
720 mL	3 c (2 12-oz cans)	Orange juice, frozen, undiluted	Combine juices and water.
720 mL	3 c (2 12-oz cans)	Lemon juice, frozen, undiluted	Add sugar syrup. Chill.
5.68 L	1½ gal	Water, cold	

Notes:
1. If time does not permit making and cooling syrup, the sugar may be added to the cold punch and stirred until dissolved. Increase cold water to 1¾ gal (6.62 L).
2. Ginger ale may be substituted for part or all of water. Chill and add just before serving.

Variations:
1. **Golden Punch.** Reduce orange and lemon juice to 1 12-oz (355-mL) cans each. Add 2 46-oz (1.36-L) cans pineapple juice.
2. **Sparkling Grape Punch.** Reduce orange and lemon juice to 1 12-oz (355-mL) can each. Add 2 12-oz (355-mL) cans frozen grape juice. Just before serving, add 2 20-oz (600-mL) bottles of ginger ale.

SPARKLING APRICOT-PINEAPPLE PUNCH

Yield: 80 portions
2½ gal (9.46 L)
Portion: 4 oz (½ c/120 mL)

Amount Metric	U.S.	Ingredient	Procedure
2.84 L	3 qt (2 46-oz cans)	Apricot nectar	Combine juices and water. Chill.
2.84 L	3 qt (2 46-oz cans)	Pineapple juice unsweetened	
360 mL	1½ c	Lemon or lime juice, frozen, undiluted	
1.89 L	2 qt	Water	
1.89 L	2 qt	Ginger ale, chilled	Add ginger ale just before serving.

RHUBARB PUNCH

Yield: 48 portions
1½ gal (5.68 L)
Portion: 4 oz (½ c/120 mL)

Amount Metric	U.S.	Ingredient	Procedure
4.54 kg	10 lb	Rhubarb, fresh	Wash and trim rhubarb. Cut into 1-in. pieces.
3.79 L	1 gal	Water	Add water and sugar. Cook below boiling point until soft. Strain. There should be 1¼ gal (4.73 L) juice. Chill.
1.81 – 2.27 kg	4–5 lb	Sugar, granulated	
480 mL	2 c	Pineapple juice	Add chilled pineapple juice and ginger ale just before serving.
830 mL	1 28-oz bottle	Ginger ale	

BANANA PUNCH

Yield: 64 portions
2 gal (7.57 L)
Portion: 4 oz (½ c/120 mL)

Amount Metric	U.S.	Ingredient	Procedure
908 g	2 lb	Sugar, granulated	Mix sugar and water.
1.42 L	1½ qt	Water, hot	Boil for 3 minutes. Cool.
360 mL	1½ c (1 12-oz can)	Orange juice, frozen, undiluted	Combine juices, fruits, and water.
180 mL	¾ c (1 6-oz can)	Lemon juice, frozen, undiluted	Add cooled sugar syrup. Chill.
0.95 L	1 qt	Water, cold	
2.84 L	3 qt (1 No. 10 can)	Pineapple, crushed	
6	6 medium	Bananas, ripe, mashed	
0.95 L	1 qt	Ginger ale, chilled	Add ginger ale just before serving.

Notes:
1. Mixture may be frozen before ginger ale is added and held for use later.
2. 2 46-oz (1.36-L) cans of unsweetened pineapple juice and 1 12-oz (355-mL) can lemonade may be substituted for the crushed pineapple and lemon juice.

Variation: **Banana Slush Punch.** Mix and freeze juices, syrup, and mashed bananas. To serve, fill glass about half full of partially frozen slush and add chilled ginger ale.

CRANBERRY PUNCH

Yield: 80 portions
2½ gal (9.46 L)
Portion: 4 oz (½ c/120 mL)

Amount Metric	U.S.	Ingredient	Procedure
2.84 L	3 qt	Cranberry juice	Mix juices and water. Chill.
2.84 L	3 qt (2 46-oz cans)	Pineapple juice	
0.95 L	1 qt (1 32-oz can)	Lemonade, frozen, undiluted	
0.95 L	1 qt	Water, cold	
2.5 L	3 28-oz bottles	Ginger ale, chilled	Add ginger ale just before serving.

WASSAIL BOWL

Yield: 80 portions
2½ gal (9.46 L)
Portion: 4 oz (½ c/120 mL)

Amount Metric	U.S.	Ingredient	Procedure
1.14 kg	2 lb 8 oz	Sugar, granulated	Mix sugar, water, and spices. Boil 10 minutes. Cover and let stand 1 hour in a warm place. Strain.
2.37 L	2½ qt	Water	
8 g	1½ t	Cloves, whole	
10	10	Cinnamon sticks	
10	10	Allspice berries	
57 g	2 oz	Crystallized ginger, chopped	
1.89 L	2 qt	Orange juice, strained	When ready to serve, add juices and cider. Heat quickly to boiling point. Pour over crabapples or small oranges studded with cloves, in a punch bowl. If using a glass bowl, temper by filling with warm water to prevent cracking when hot punch is poured in.
1.18 L	1¼ qt	Lemon juice, strained	
4.73 L	5 qt	Apple cider	
6–10	6–10	Crabapples or small oranges	
		Cloves, whole	

TOMATO JUICE COCKTAIL

Yield: 72 portions
2¼ gal (8.52 L)
Portion: 4 oz (½ c/120 mL)

Amount Metric	U.S.	Ingredient	Procedure
8 L	8½ qt (6 46-oz cans)	Tomato juice	Mix all ingredients. Chill.
180 mL	¾ c	Lemon juice	
45 mL	3 T	Worcestershire sauce	
3 mL	½ t	Tabasco sauce	
45 g	3 T	Celery salt	

Variation: **Sauerkraut Juice Cocktail.** Omit the seasonings and substitute 2 qt (1.89 L) sauerkraut juice for 2 qt (1.89 L) tomato juice.

HOT SPICED TOMATO JUICE

Yield: 64 portions
2 gal (7.57 L)
Portion: 4 oz (½ c/120 mL)

Amount		Ingredient	Procedure
Metric	U.S.		
4 L	4¼ qt (3 46-oz cans)	Tomato juice	Add onions and seasonings to tomato juice.
227 g	8 oz	Onion, chopped	Mix.
3	3	Bay leaves	Boil gently about 15 minutes.
12	12	Cloves, whole	
38 g	2 T	Salt	Strain.
14 g	1 T	Mustard, dry	
6	6	Celery stalks, cut	
3.79 L	1 gal	Consommé	Add consomme and reheat. Serve hot.

Note: 2 50-oz (1.48-L) cans condensed beef or chicken consommé, diluted with 2 qt (1.89 L) water, may be used.

SPICED CIDER

Yield: 80 portions
2½ gal (9.46 L)
Portion: 4 oz (½ c/120 mL)

Amount		Ingredient	Procedure
Metric	U.S.		
10	10	Cinnamon sticks	Tie cinnamon, cloves, and allspice loosely in a cheesecloth bag.
14 g	2½ T	Cloves, whole	
14 g	2½ T	Allspice berries	
9.46 L	2½ gal	Cider	Add spice bag, sugar, and other seasonings to cider. Bring slowly to the boiling point. Boil about 15 minutes. Remove spices. Serve hot or chilled.
340 g	12 oz	Sugar, brown	
3 g	½ t	Mace	
5 g	1 t	Salt	
f.g.	f.g.	Cayenne	

Variation: **Cider Punch.** Omit spices. Substitute 1 qt (0.95 L) reconstituted frozen orange juice and 1 qt (0.95 L) pineapple juice for an equal amount of cider. Garnish with thin slices of orange.

Breads

QUICK BREADS

Basic ingredients in all quick breads are flour, a liquid, a leavening agent, flavorings, and usually fat and eggs. The type and quantity of each of these ingredients and their interaction affect the characteristics of the finished product. They may be classified, according to the proportion of flour to liquid, as pour batters (pancakes, waffles, popovers, crepes); drop batter (muffins, pan breads, loaf breads); and soft dough (biscuits).

Quick breads are leavened by baking powder, soda, or steam, which act quickly, thus enabling them to be baked at once. If a double-acting baking powder is used, quick breads may be mixed at one time, refrigerated, and then baked as needed during the serving period. A variety of quick breads may be made from basic biscuit and muffin recipes by adding fruits, nuts, and other flavorings.

Quick bread mixes can be prepared by sifting together the dry ingredients, which generally include nonfat dry milk, and then cutting in the shortening. Such a mix may be made on days when the work load is light and stored for periods up to 6 weeks without refrigeration or longer in the refrigerator. Many food services use some type of commercial mix, and the decision to purchase these or to make their own depends on the amount of skilled labor available, food inventories, and the cost and quality of the mix.

METHODS OF MIXING

Ingredients for most quick breads are combined by the muffin or biscuit method, although the cake method is used for some loaf breads. Most quick bread ingredients should be mixed only to blend, with as little handling as possible.

Muffin Method   This method is used for muffins, pancakes, waffles, and popovers. Mix the dry ingredients in a mixer bowl. Combine beaten eggs, milk, and melted or liquid fat and add to dry ingredients all at once. Mix at low speed only enough to dampen the dry ingredients. The mixture will be lumpy. If dry milk is used, add it to the dry ingredients. Excess mixing causes gluten to develop and carbon dioxide to be lost, resulting in the formation of long "tunnels" in the baked product. Effects of overmixing are less evident in rich muffins and loaf breads that contain a higher proportion of fat and sugar, or when the batter is made with cake or pastry flour. Dip the batter into pans carefully to avoid additional mixing.

Biscuit Method Combine dry ingredients in a mixer bowl. Cut in the fat with the flat paddle attachment. Add liquid and mix to form a soft dough. Knead dough lightly 15−20 strokes to develop the gluten; this results in a biscuit that has good volume and a crumb that peels off in flakes. Overkneading, however, produces a biscuit that is compact and less tender.

Conventional and Dough-Batter Methods These methods, described on p. 135, may be used successfully for coffee cakes, loaf breads, and rich muffins.

YEAST BREADS

INGREDIENTS

An understanding of the functions of the main ingredients used in yeast-raised doughs is essential to the production of good bread and rolls.

Flour Flour used for baking must contain enough protein to make an elastic framework of gluten that will stretch and hold the gas bubbles formed as the dough ferments. Bread flour, made from hard wheat, contains more protein than other flour and is used by bakers who make large quantities of bread. All-purpose flour is milled from a blend of hard and soft wheats and contains enough protein to provide the gluten essential to make good rolls and yeast bread specialties of most food services. An all-purpose flour was used in testing these recipes. Whole wheat, rye, and other specialty flours add variety to breads. They should be combined with white flour, since they do not have enough gluten to effect proper bread structure.

Yeast Either compressed or active dry yeast may be used in yeast doughs. When substituting active dry for compressed yeast, only 50% by weight is required. Active dry yeast does not require refrigeration and remains active a reasonable length of time in cool dry storage. Compressed yeast is perishable and must be held under refrigeration (30 to 34°F/−1 to 1°C) and storage is limited to not more than 2 weeks. It may be frozen to extend its keeping time, but must be used immediately after defrosting.

Compressed yeast is softened in lukewarm water (95°F/35°C). Active dry yeast is softened in warm water (105−110°F/40−43°C) or may be mixed with the dry ingredients. In this method the yeast is blended with a portion of the flour, the sugar, salt, and dry milk solids if used. The liquid ingredients may be heated to very warm (120°F/49°C). The yeast can withstand the higher temperature because of protection provided by flour particles.

Yeast grows best between 80 and 85°F (27 and 29°C). Dough should be kept in this temperature range during fermentation and should be near 80°F (27°C) when mixing is completed. A moderate increase in the amount of yeast speeds up fermentaton, but too much gives the bread a yeasty flavor. There is on the market now a quick-rising dry yeast that reduces proofing time by about half.

Liquid The liquid used for yeast breads generally is milk or water, although potato water and fruit juice also may be used. Milk improves the nutritive value of the bread and tends to delay its staling. Liquid used for bread should be lukewarm (95°F/35°C) for compressed yeast, warm (105–110°F/40–43°C) if active dry yeast is used, or very warm (120°F/49°C) if the dry yeast is mixed with the flour and other dry ingredients. If fresh fluid milk is used, it is scalded to stop enzyme action that may produce undesirable flavors, then cooled to the desired temperature. Nonfat dry milk is used extensively in quantity baking and may be mixed with the dry ingredients or reconstituted and used in liquid form. The nutritive value of the bread may be increased by the addition of extra quantities of dry milk. Evaporated milk may be used also in bread making and generally is diluted with an equal amount of water.

Other Ingredients Although used in small quantities, other ingredients influence the quality of the finished product. *Salt* is added mainly for flavor, but does help to control the rate of fermentation. *Sugar,* a ready source of food for the yeast, accelerates the action of the yeast. Although the addition of a small amount of sugar makes the dough rise faster, too much sugar tends to slow the action of the yeast. If the dough is to be refrigerated or frozen, the amount of sugar is increased slightly. Granulated sugar generally is used for bread making, but honey, corn syrup, brown sugar, or molasses also are used, especially in dark whole grain bread, sweet rolls, or coffee cake. *Fat* is added to improve flavor, tenderness, browning, and keeping quality. Fat in large amounts, or if added directly to the yeast, will slow its action. *Eggs* are added for flavor and also to help form a framework.

MIXING THE DOUGH
Mixing and kneading are essential in developing a good gluten network. Kneading is accomplished by continuing the mixing process beyond the point of combining. In a mixer, use a dough hook or flat beater attachment. The mixing speed and exact length of time will be determined by the type of mixer, the mixer attachment used, and the amount of dough. Add the last part of the flour gradually to determine if the full amount is needed. It may be necessary to use more or less flour than the recipe specifies. The dough should be soft but not sticky. Dough for rolls is softer than that for plain bread. Soft dough makes a lighter and more tender product than a stiff dough. Mix the dough only until it leaves the sides and bottom of the bowl and small blisters appear on the surface of the dough.

FERMENTATION OF DOUGH
Fermentation begins when the dough is mixed and continues until the yeast is killed by the heat of the oven. Set the dough in a warm place (80–85°F/27–29°C), free from drafts, to ferment. The length of the fermentation period depends on the amount of yeast added, the strength of the flour, the amount of sugar added,

and the temperature. Temperatures above 140°F (60°C) will destroy the yeast. Usually 1½ hours are required for the dough to double its bulk the first time.

After the dough has doubled, punch down to its original bulk by placing the hand in the center of the dough and folding edges to the center, then turning over the ball of dough. Punching forces out excess carbon dioxide and incorporates oxygen, which allows the yeast cells to grow more rapidly. The yeast cells are more uniformly distributed, producing an even-textured product with a fine grain. After the dough has been punched down, it must be handled lightly to avoid breaking the small air cells that have been formed. If the dough is made with bread flour, usually it is allowed to rise a second time before shaping, although if the dough has been made with all-purpose flour, the second rising may be omitted.

The dough may be retarded at any point during the fermentation process by chilling the dough. The dough may also be allowed to rise first, scaled into rolls, and then refrigerated. The baking process may be halted at a time when the rising is complete and before browning occurs, as in brown-and-serve rolls.

SHAPING AND BAKING

When the dough has doubled in bulk and been punched down, divide it into 3–4 lb (1.36–1.81 kg) balls and allow it to rest for 10–15 minutes, then shape into loaves or rolls of the desired size. (See pp. 110 for recipes and directions for shaping.)

Let the panned bread or rolls rise (proof) at 90–100°F (32–38°C) until double in bulk. Dough that has not risen long enough makes a small, compact product. Dough that has risen too long tends to have an open, crumbly texture and reduced volume.

Bake bread at 375–400°F (190–205°C). The bread is done when tapping the crust produces a hollow sound. Remove bread from the pans immediately and place on a wire rack to prevent steaming and softening of the crust. Cool the loaves uncovered, and brush the tops with fat if a soft crust is desired. If time does not permit bread to rise fully, the temperature of the oven may be lower for a brief period to permit the dough to rise. The best volume is obtained if fully risen dough is put into a hot oven. The heat of the oven causes a rapid expansion of the gas in the dough. Long baking thickens the crust. Desirable yeast breads are golden brown and well shaped, with a thin, tender crust. The texture will be even, moist, light, and tender with a medium-fine grain.

Bake rolls from plain bread dough quickly in a 400°F (205°C) oven. Rich doughs are baked at lower temperatures (350–375°F/175–190°C) to prevent excessive browning of the crust. Roll doughs may be refrigerated and portions of the dough baked at intervals. Storage time should be limited to less than a week to prevent crust formation.

FREEZING YEAST DOUGHS AND BREADS

Yeast doughs can be frozen up to 6 weeks either before or after shaping. Sugar and yeast usually are increased slightly in doughs to be retarded or frozen. If the dough is to be frozen before shaping, divide it into pieces, flatten on baking sheets for quick freezing and defrosting, cover, and place in the freezer. If rolls are to be shaped before freezing, place on greased baking sheets or in muffin pans, cover, and freeze. When completely frozen, the rolls may be removed from the pans and stored in freezer bags. Allow time for thawing and rising (about 6 hours for bread and 2 hours for rolls).

To freeze baked bread and rolls, allow to cool to room temperature, then wrap and freeze. Frozen baked products should be allowed to return to room temperature, then placed in a warm oven for about 3 minutes or in a microwave oven for the length of time recommended by the manufacturer.

QUICK BREAD RECIPES

BAKING POWDER BISCUITS

Oven: 425°F (220°C)
Bake: 15 minutes

Yield: 100 2½-in. biscuits
130 2-in. biscuits

Metric	U.S.	Ingredient	Procedure
2.27 kg 142 g 38 g	5 lb 5 oz 2 T	Flour, all-purpose Baking powder Salt	Combine dry ingredients in mixer bowl. Blend on low speed, using flat beater, for 10 seconds.
567 g	1 lb 4 oz	Shortening, hydrogenated	Add shortening to flour mixture. Mix on low speed for 1 minute. Stop and scrape sides and bottom of bowl. Mix 1 minute longer. The mixture will be crumbly.
1.66 L	1¾ qt	Milk	Add milk. Mix on low speed to form a soft dough, about 30 seconds. Do not overmix. Dough should be as soft as can be handled.

1. Place one half of dough on lightly floured board or table. Knead lightly 15–20 times.
2. Roll to ¾-in. thickness. Cut with a 2½-in. (or 2-in.) cutter; or cut into 2-in. squares with a knife.

3. Place on baking sheets ½ in. apart for crusty biscuits, just touching for softer biscuits. Repeat, using remaining dough.
4. Bake at 425°F (220°C) for 15 minutes, or until golden brown.
5. Biscuits may be held 2–3 hours in the refrigerator until time to bake.

Note: 7 oz (198 g) nonfat dry milk and 1¾ qt (1.66 L) water may be substituted for fluid milk. Combine dry milk with other dry ingredients. Increase shortening to 1 lb 6 oz (624 g).

Variations:
1. **Buttermilk Biscuits.** Substitute cultured buttermilk (or 7 oz/198 g dried buttermilk and 1¾ qt/1.66 L water) for milk. Add 1 T (12 g) baking soda to dry ingredients.
2. **Butterscotch Biscuits.** Divide dough into 8 parts. Roll each part into a rectangle ¼ in. thick. Spread with melted margarine or butter and brown sugar. Roll the dough as for jelly roll. Cut off slices ¾ in. thick. Bake at 375°F (190°C) for 15 minutes.
3. **Cheese Biscuits.** Reduce shortening to 1 lb (454 g) and add 1 lb (454 g) dry grated cheese.
4. **Cinnamon Biscuits.** Proceed as for Butterscotch Biscuits. Spread with a mixture of 1 lb (454 g) sugar, 2 oz (57 g) cinnamon, and 1 lb (454 g) raisins.
5. **Drop Biscuits.** Increase milk to 2 qt (1.89 L). Drop by spoon or No. 30 dipper onto greased baking sheets.
6. **Orange Biscuits.** Proceed as for Butterscotch Biscuits. Spread with orange marmalade.
7. **Raisin Biscuits.** Reduce shortening to 14 oz (397 g) and use ½ c (120 mL) less milk; add 4 whole eggs, 3 T (45 mL) grated orange rind, 8 oz (227 g) sugar, and 8 oz (227 g) chopped raisins.
8. **Scotch Scones.** Add 10 oz (284 g) sugar and 7 oz (198 g) currants to dry ingredients. Add 5 eggs, beaten, mixed with the milk. Cut dough in squares and then cut diagonally to form triangles. Brush lightly with milk.
9. **Shortcake.** Increase shortening to 1 lb 12 oz (794 g). Add 8 oz (227 g) sugar.
10. **Whole Wheat Biscuits.** Substitute 2 lb (908 g) whole wheat flour for 2 lb (908 g) white flour.

PLAIN MUFFINS

Oven: 400°F (205°C)
Bake: 25 minutes

Yield: 5 doz

Amount		Ingredient	Procedure
Metric	U.S.		
1.14 kg	2 lb 8 oz	Flour, all-purpose	Combine dry ingredients mixer bowl.
57 g	2 oz	Baking powder	
19 g	1 T	Salt	Blend, using flat beater, on low speed for 10 seconds.
170 g	6 oz	Sugar, granulated	
4 (198 g)	4 (7 oz)	Eggs, beaten	Combine eggs, milk, and melted shortening.
1.42 L	1½ qt	Milk	
227 g	8 oz	Shortening, melted, cooled to room temperature	
			Add liquids to dry ingredients. Mix on low speed only long enough to blend, about 15 seconds. Batter still will be lumpy.
			Measure with No. 20 dipper into well-greased muffin pans, about ⅔ full. Batter should be dipped all at once with as little handling as possible, but may be refrigerated for 24 hours and baked as needed.
			Bake at 400°F (205°C) for 20–25 minutes, or until golden brown.
			Remove muffins from pans as soon as baked.

Notes:

1. 6 oz (170 g) nonfat dry milk and 1½ qt (1.42 L) water may be substituted for fluid milk. Combine dry milk with other dry ingredients. Increase fat to 9 oz (255 g).
2. No. 24 dipper yields 6½ doz muffins.

Variations:
1. **Apricot Muffins.** Add 1 lb (454 g) drained, chopped, cooked apricots to the liquid ingredients.
2. **Bacon Muffins.** Substitute 10 oz (284 g) chopped bacon, slightly cooked, and bacon fat for the shortening in the recipe.
3. **Blueberry Muffins.** Carefully fold 1 lb (454 g) well-drained blueberries into the batter. Increase sugar to 10 oz (284 g).
4. **Cherry Muffins.** Add 1 lb (454 g) well-drained, cooked cherries to liquid.
5. **Cornmeal Muffins.** Substitute 1 lb (454 g) white cornmeal for 1 lb (454 g) flour.
6. **Cranberry Muffins.** Sprinkle 4 oz (114 g) sugar over 1 lb (454 g) chopped raw cranberries. Fold into batter.
7. **Currant Muffins.** Add 8 oz (227 g) chopped currants.
8. **Date Muffins.** Add 1 lb (454 g) chopped dates.
9. **Jelly Muffins.** Drop ¼ – ½ t jelly on top of each muffin when placed in oven.
10. **Nut Muffins.** Add 10 oz (284 g) chopped nuts.
11. **Raisin–Nut Muffins.** Add 6 oz (170 g) chopped nuts and 6 oz (170 g) chopped raisins.
12. **Spiced Muffins.** Add 1½ t (3 g) cinnamon, 1 t (2 g) ginger, and ½ t (1 g) allspice to dry ingredients.
13. **Whole Wheat Muffins.** Substitute 12 oz (340 g) whole wheat flour for 12 oz (340 g) white flour. Add ¼ c (60 mL) molasses.

FRENCH BREAKFAST PUFFS

Oven: 350°F (175°C) Yield: 5 doz
Bake: 20–25 minutes

Amount Metric	U.S.	Ingredient	Procedure
510 g	1 lb 2 oz	Margarine or butter	Cream margarine and sugar on medium speed until light and fluffy.
737 g	1 lb 10 oz	Sugar, granulated	
6 (284 g)	6 (10 oz)	Eggs	Add eggs. Blend on low speed, then beat on medium speed for 3–5 minutes.
1.14 kg	2 lb 8 oz	Flour, all-purpose	Combine dry ingredients.
47 g	2½ T	Baking powder	
19 g	1 T	Salt	
4 g	1½ t	Nutmeg	
85 g	3 oz	Nonfat dry milk	
800 mL	3⅓ c	Water	Add dry ingredients and water alternately, on low speed, to creamed mixture. Measure into greased muffin pans with No. 20 dipper. Bake at 350°F (175°C) for 20–25 minutes.
567 g	1 lb 4 oz	Margarine or butter	Melt margarine.
737 g	1 lb 10 oz	Sugar, granulated	Mix sugar and cinnamon. When muffins are baked, remove from pans. Roll in melted margarine or butter, then in sugar-cinnamon mixture.
14 g	2 T	Cinnamon	

Note: For special occasions, dip batter with No. 40 dipper into small (1½-in.) muffin pans.

Variations:
1. **Apple–Nut Muffins.** Add 1 lb (454 g) chopped apples and 8 oz (227 g) chopped nuts.
2. **Plain Cake Muffins.** Delete nutmeg. Do not roll in sugar and cinnamon.

ALL-BRAN MUFFINS

Oven: 400°F (205°C)
Bake: 20 minutes
Yield: 5 doz

Metric	U.S.	Ingredient	Procedure
454 g 1.42 L 680 g	1 lb 1½ qt 1 lb 8 oz (2 c)	All-bran cereal Water Molasses	Combine cereal, water, and molasses in mixer bowl. Let stand 15 minutes.
4 (198 g) 120 mL	4 (7 oz) ½ c	Eggs Salad oil	Combine eggs and oil. Add to bran mixture. Mix on medium speed for 30 seconds.
454 g 9 g 16 g 142 g	1 lb 1½ t 4 t 5 oz	Flour, all-purpose Salt Baking soda Nonfat dry milk	Blend dry ingredients. Add all at once to bran-egg mixture. Mix on low speed only to blend, about 15 seconds. Do not overmix. Measure with No. 20 dipper into greased muffin pans. Bake at 400°F (205°C) for 20 minutes.

Note: 1 lb 8 oz (680 g) chopped dates, raisins, or nuts may be added for variety.

OATMEAL MUFFINS

Oven: 400°F (205°C)
Bake: 15–20 minutes
Yield: 5 doz

Amount Metric	Amount U.S.	Ingredient	Procedure
397 g	14 oz	Rolled oats	Combine rolled oats and buttermilk in mixer bowl. Let stand 1 hour.
1.18 L	1¼ qt	Buttermilk	
5 (255 g)	5 (9 oz)	Eggs, beaten	Combine eggs, sugar, and shortening.
567 g	1 lb 4 oz	Sugar, brown	Add to rolled oat mixture. Mix 30 seconds. Scrape down bowl.
454 g	1 lb	Shortening, melted, cooled	
567 g	1 lb 4 oz	Flour, all-purpose	Combine dry ingredients. Add to rolled oat mixture. Mix on low speed only until dry ingredients are moistened, about 15 seconds. Measure with No. 20 dipper into well-greased muffin pans (⅔ full). Bake at 400°F (205°C) for 15–20 minutes.
25 g	5 t	Baking powder	
12 g	2½ t	Salt	
10 g	2½ t	Baking soda	

Notes:
1. 4 oz (114 g) dry buttermilk and 1¼ qt (1.18 L) water may be substituted for liquid buttermilk.
2. No. 24 dipper yields 7 doz muffins.

BLUEBERRY COFFEE CAKE

Oven: 350°F (175°C)
Bake: 45 minutes
Yield: 64 portions
2 pans 12 × 18 × 2 in.
Portion: 3 × 2¼ in.

Amount Metric	Amount U.S.	Ingredient	Procedure
227 g	8 oz	Sugar, brown	Combine sugars, flour, cinnamon, and margarine. Mix on low speed to a coarse crumb consistency. Set aside.
114 g	4 oz	Sugar, granulated	
114 g	4 oz	Flour, all-purpose	
4 g	2 t	Cinnamon	
170 g	6 oz	Margarine or butter, soft	

QUICK BREAD RECIPES

Amount			
Metric	U.S.	Ingredient	Procedure
340 g 1.02 kg	12 oz 2 lb 4 oz	Shortening Sugar, granulated	Cream shortening and sugar on medium speed about 10 minutes.
6 (312 g)	6 (11 oz)	Eggs	Add eggs and continue mixing, about 5 minutes.
1.36 kg 57 g 19 g	3 lb 2 oz 1 T	Flour, all-purpose Baking powder Salt	Combine flour, baking powder, and salt.
720 mL	3 c	Milk	Add dry ingredients alternately with milk to creamed mixture. Mix on low speed 3 minutes. Scrape down bowl. Mix on medium speed 10 seconds.
680 g	1 lb 8 oz	Blueberries	Carefully fold frozen blueberries or well-drained and rinsed canned blueberries into batter. (Berries may be sprinkled on top of batter.) Scale into 2 greased 12 × 18 × 2-in. baking pans, 4 lb 14 oz (2.21 kg) per pan. Crumble topping mixture evenly over top of batter, 10 oz (284 g) per pan. Bake at 350°F (175°C) for 45 minutes. Cut 4 × 8.

Notes:
1. May be baked in 1 18 × 26 × 2-in. pan. Cut 6 × 10 for 60 3 × 2½-in. portions.
2. 3 oz (85 g) nonfat dry milk and 3 c (720 mL) water may be substituted for fluid milk. Add dry milk to other dry ingredients. Increase shortening to 13 oz (369 g).
3. After cake is baked, thin Powdered Sugar Glaze (p. 170) may be drizzled in a fine stream over the top to form an irregular design.

COFFEE CAKE

Oven: 350°F (175°C)
Bake: 25 minutes
Yield: 64 portions
2 pans 12 × 18 × 2 in.
Portion: 3 × 2¼ in.

Metric	U.S.	Ingredient	Procedure
284 g	10 oz	Margarine or butter	Mix until crumbly. Set aside.
567 g	1 lb 4 oz	Sugar, granulated	
85 g	3 oz	Flour, all-purpose	
28 g	1 oz	Cinnamon	
8 g	1½ t	Salt	
1.53 kg	3 lb 6 oz	Flour, all-purpose	Combine dry ingredients in mixer bowl.
57 g	2 oz	Baking powder	
908 g	2 lb	Sugar, granulated	
32 g	1⅔ T	Salt	
6 (312 g)	6 (11 oz)	Eggs, beaten	Combine eggs and milk. Add to dry ingredients. Mix on low speed until dry ingredients are just moistened.
1.18 L	1¼ qt	Milk	
737 g	1 lb 10 oz	Shortening, melted, cooled	Add melted shortening and mix on low speed for 1 minute. Scale into 2 greased 12 × 18 × 2-in. baking pans, 4 lb 2 oz (1.87 kg) per pan. Sprinkle with topping mixture, 1 lb (454 g) per pan. Bake at 350°F (175°C) for 25 minutes or until done. Cut 4 × 8.

Notes:

1. May be baked in 1 18 × 26 × 2-in. pan. Cut 6 × 10 for 60 portions 3 × 2½ in.

2. 5 oz (142 g) nonfat dry milk and 1¼ qt (1.18 L) water may be substituted for the fluid milk. Combine dry milk with other dry ingredients. Increase shortening to 1 lb 12 oz (794 g).

3. If used for breakfast, may be mixed and panned the day before. Refrigerate until morning, then bake.

BISHOP'S BREAD

Oven: 350°F (175°C)
Bake: 30 minutes

Yield: 64 portions
2 pans 12 × 18 × 2 in.
Portion: 3 × 2¼ in.

Amount Metric	U.S.	Ingredient	Procedure
397 g 1.25 kg	14 oz 2 lb 12 oz	Shortening Sugar, brown	Cream shortening and sugar on medium speed for 5 minutes.
1.14 kg 12 g 7 g	2 lb 8 oz 2 t 1 T	Flour, all-purpose Salt Cinnamon	Mix flour, salt, and cinnamon. Add to creamed mixture. Blend. Remove 2½ c (12 oz/340 g) of the mixture to sprinkle on top later.
454 g 20 g 8 g	1 lb 4 t 2 t	Flour, all-purpose Baking powder Baking soda	Mix flour, baking powder, and soda.
4 (198 g) 1.18 L	4 (7 oz) 1¼ qt	Eggs, beaten Buttermilk	Combine eggs and buttermilk. Add alternately with flour, baking powder, and soda to creamed mixture. Scrape down bowl. Mix on low speed about 30 seconds. (Batter will not be smooth.) Scale into 2 greased 12 × 18 × 2-in. baking pans, 4 lb 10 oz (2.1 kg) per pan. Sprinkle with mixture reserved from second step, 1¼ c (6 oz/170 g) per pan. Bake at 350°F (175°C) for 25–30 minutes. Cut 4 × 8.

Notes:
1. May be baked in 1 18 × 26 × 2-in. pan. Cut 6 × 10 for 60 portions 3 × 2½ in.
2. 5 oz (142 g) of dry buttermilk and 1¼ qt (1.18 L) water may be substituted for fluid buttermilk.

CORN BREAD

Oven: 350°F (175°C)
Bake: 35 minutes

Yield: 64 portions
2 pans 12 × 18 × 2 in.
Portion: 3 × 2¼ in.

Amount		Ingredient	Procedure
Metric	U.S.		
992 g	2 lb 3 oz	Cornmeal	Combine dry ingredients in mixer bowl.
1.05 kg	2 lb 5 oz	Flour, all-purpose	Blend on low speed.
100 g	3½ oz	Baking powder	
47 g	2½ T	Salt	
284 g	10 oz	Sugar, granulated	
9 (454 g)	9 (1 lb)	Eggs, beaten	Combine eggs, milk, and shortening.
1.66 L	1¾ qt	Milk	Add to dry ingredients. Mix on low speed only until dry ingredients are moistened.
284 g	10 oz	Shortening, melted, cooled	Scale into 2 greased 12 × 18 × 2-in. baking pans, 5 lb (2.27 kg) per pan.
			Bake at 350°F (175°C) for 35 minutes.
			Cut 4 × 8.

Notes:

1. May be baked in 1 18 × 26 × 2-in pan. Cut 6 × 10 for 60 portions 3 × 2½ in.

2. May be baked in corn stick or muffin pans. Reduce baking time to 15–20 minutes.

3. 7 oz (198 g) nonfat dry milk and 1¾ qt (1.66 L) water may be substituted for fluid milk. Mix dry milk with other dry ingredients. Increase shortening to 11 oz (312 g).

SPOON BREAD

Oven: 350°F (175°C)
Bake: 1 hour

Yield: 50 portions
2 pans 12 × 20 × 2 in.
Portion: 4 oz (114 g)

Amount Metric	U.S.	Ingredient	Procedure
5.44 L	5¾ qt	Milk	Scald milk.
794 g 28 g	1 lb 12 oz 1 oz (1½ T)	Cornmeal Salt	Add cornmeal and salt, stirring briskly with a wire whip. Cook 10 minutes or until thick.
25 (1.25 kg)	25 (2 lb 12 oz)	Eggs	Beat eggs. Add slowly to cornmeal mixture, while stirring.
170 g	6 oz	Margarine or butter, melted	Add margarine and baking powder. Stir to blend.
57 g	2 oz	Baking powder	Pour into 2 greased 12 × 20 × 2-in. baking pans, 8 lb (3.63 kg) per pan. Place in pans of hot water. Bake at 350°F (175°C) for 45–60 minutes or until set. Serve at once.

Note: Serve with crisp bacon, Creamed Chicken (p. 376) or Creamed Ham (p. 342).

BOSTON BROWN BREAD

Steam pressure: 5 lb
    Steam: 1¼–1½ hours
Yield: 64 portions
    8 round loaves 3¼ × 4½ in.
Portion: ½-in. slice

Amount Metric	Amount U.S.	Ingredient	Procedure
454 g	1 lb	Cornmeal	Combine dry ingredients in mixer bowl. Blend on low speed 10 seconds.
340 g	12 oz	Flour, whole wheat	
340 g	12 oz	Flour, all-purpose	
28 g	1½ T	Salt	
18 g	1½ T	Baking soda	
1.42 L	1½ qt	Buttermilk	Blend buttermilk and molasses. Add all at once to dry ingredients. Mix on low speed only until ingredients are blended. Fill 8 greased cans 3¼ × 4½ in. ¾ full. Cover tightly with aluminum foil. Steam for 1¼–1½ hours. Cut 8 slices per loaf.
540 mL	2¼ c	Molasses	

Notes:
1. May be baked as loaves. Add 3 T (45 mL) melted fat. Bake at 375°F (190°C) for 1 hour.
2. 12 oz (340 g) raisins may be added.

BANANA NUT BREAD

Oven: 350°F (175°C)
Bake: 50 minutes

Yield: 64 portions
    4 loaves 5 × 9 in.
Portion: ½-in. slice

Amount Metric	U.S.	Ingredient	Procedure
284 g	10 oz	Margarine	Cream margarine and sugar on medium speed for 5 minutes.
737 g	1 lb 10 oz	Sugar, granulated	
5 (255 g)	5 (9 oz)	Eggs	Add eggs to creamed mixture. Beat 2 minutes.
737 g	1 lb 10 oz	Bananas, mashed	Add bananas. Beat 1 minute.
908 g	2 lb	Flour, all-purpose	Combine dry ingredients and nuts.
56 g	4 T	Baking powder	
12 g	2 t	Salt	
2 g	½ t	Baking soda	
227 g	8 oz	Nuts, chopped	
180 mL	¾ c	Milk	Add dry ingredients and milk to creamed mixture. Mix on low speed 1 minute. Divide batter into 4 greased 5 × 9 × 2¾-in. loaf pans, approximately 2 lb (908 g) per pan. Bake at 350°F (175°C) for 50 minutes. Cut 16 slices per loaf.

CRANBERRY NUT BREAD

Oven: 350°F (175°C)
Bake: 50 minutes

Yield: 80 portions
5 loaves 5 × 9 in.
Portion: ½-in. slice

Amount Metric	Amount U.S.	Ingredient	Procedure
567 g	1 lb 4 oz	Cranberries, raw	Wash and sort cranberries.
198 g	7 oz	Orange rind	Coarsely grind cranberries and orange rind.
1.14 kg	2 lb 8 oz	Flour, all-purpose	Combine dry ingredients in mixer bowl. Blend on low speed for 10 seconds.
1.02 kg	2 lb 4 oz	Sugar, granulated	
28 g	1 oz	Baking powder	
12 g	2 t	Salt	
8 g	2 t	Baking soda	
5 (255 g)	5 (9 oz)	Eggs, beaten	Combine and add to dry ingredients. Mix on low speed only until dry ingredients are moistened.
360 mL	1½ c	Orange juice	
900 mL	3¾ c	Water	
120 mL	½ c	Salad oil	
454 g	1 lb	Nuts, chopped	Add nuts and cranberry mixture. Mix on low speed until blended. (Batter still may be lumpy.) Divide batter into 5 greased 5 × 9 × 2¾-in. loaf pans, approximately 2 lb (908 g) per pan. Bake at 350°F (175°C) for about 50 minutes. Cut 16 slices per loaf.

DATE-NUT BREAD

Oven: 350°F (175°C)
Bake: 50 minutes

Yield: 64 portions
    4 loaves 5 × 9 in.
Portion: ½-in. slice

Amount			
Metric	U.S.	Ingredient	Procedure
680 g 18 g 780 mL	1 lb 8 oz 1½ T 3¼ c	Dates, chopped Baking soda Water, boiling	Add water and soda to dates. Let stand 20 minutes.
85 g 794 g	3 oz 1 lb 12 oz	Shortening Sugar, granulated	Cream shortening and sugar on medium speed for 5 minutes.
4 (198 g) 23 mL	4 (7 oz) 1½ T	Eggs Vanilla	Add eggs and vanilla. Mix on medium speed for 2 minutes.
908 g 9 g 227 g	2 lb 1½ t 8 oz	Flour, all-purpose Salt Nuts, chopped	Combine flour, salt, and nuts. Add alternately with dates to creamed mixture. Divide batter into 4 greased 5 × 9 × 2¾-in. loaf pans, approximately 2 lb (908 g) per pan. Bake at 350°F (175°C) for about 50 minutes. Cut 16 slices per loaf.

NUT BREAD

Oven: 350°F (175°C)
Bake: 50 minutes

Yield: 80 portions
5 loaves 5 × 9 in.
Portion: ½-in. slice

Amount		Ingredient	Procedure
Metric	U.S.		
1.36 kg	3 lb	Flour, all-purpose	Combine dry ingredients and nuts in mixer bowl. Mix on low speed until blended.
28 g	1 oz	Baking powder	
19 g	1 T	Salt	
680 g	1 lb 8 oz	Sugar, granulated	
454 g	1 lb	Nuts, chopped	
6 (312 g)	6 (11 oz)	Eggs, beaten	Combine eggs, milk, and shortening. Add to dry ingredients. Mix on low speed only until blended. Divide batter into 5 greased 5 × 9 × 2¾-in. loaf pans, approximately 1 lb 14 oz (851 g) per pan. Bake at 350°F (175°C) for about 50 minutes. Cut 16 slices per loaf.
1.42 L	1½ qt	Milk	
114 g	4 oz	Shortening, melted, cooled	

Note: 5 oz (142 g) nonfat dry milk and 1½ qt (1.42) water may be substituted for fluid milk. Combine dry milk with other dry ingredients. Increase shortening to 6 oz (170 g).

PUMPKIN BREAD

Oven: 350°F (175°C)
Bake: 50 minutes

Yield: 80 portions
5 loaves 5 × 9 in.
Portion: ½-in. slice

Amount		Ingredient	Procedure
Metric	U.S.		
1.25 kg	2 lb 12 oz	Sugar, granulated	Combine sugar, oil, pumpkin, and eggs in mixer bowl. Cream on medium speed 10 minutes. Scrape down bowl and paddle.
480 mL	2 c	Salad oil	
1.08 kg	2 lb 6 oz	Pumpkin, canned	
9 (425 g)	9 (15 oz)	Eggs	
964 g	2 lb 2 oz	Flour, all-purpose	Combine dry ingredients.
16 g	4 t	Baking soda	
10 g	2 t	Baking powder	
19 g	1 T	Salt	
7 g	1 T	Cinnamon	
2 g	1 t	Nutmeg	
300 mL	1¼ c	Water	Add dry ingredients and water alternately to creamed mixture. Mix 3 minutes on low speed. Scrape down bowl. Scale into 5 greased 5 × 9 × 2¾-in. loaf pans, 1 lb 15 oz (879 g) per pan. Bake at 350°F (175°C) 50 minutes or until done. Cool 30 minutes before removing from pans. Cut 16 slices per loaf.

Note: 8 oz (227 g) chopped nuts or raisins may be added.

CAKE DOUGHNUTS

Deep-fat fryer: 375°F (190°C)
Fry: 3–4 minutes
Yield: 8 doz doughnuts

Amount		Ingredient	Procedure
Metric	U.S.		
6 (284 g)	6 (10 oz)	Eggs	Beat eggs.
567 g	1 lb 4 oz	Sugar, granulated	Add sugar and melted shortening. Mix on medium speed about 10 minutes.
85 g	3 oz	Shortening, melted, cooled	
1.47 kg	3 lb 4 oz	Flour, all-purpose	Combine dry ingredients.
85 g	3 oz	Baking powder	
15 g	2½ t	Salt	
4 g	2 t	Nutmeg	
¼ t	¼ t	Ginger	
6 g	1 T	Orange rind, grated	
0.95 L	1 qt	Milk	Add dry ingredients and milk alternately to egg mixture. Mix to form a soft dough. Add more flour if dough is too soft to handle. Chill. Roll to ⅜-in. thickness on floured board or table. Cut with 2½-in. doughnut cutter. Fry in deep fat for 3–4 minutes.
227 g	8 oz	Sugar, granulated	Sprinkle with sugar when partially cool.

Note: 4 oz (114 g) nonfat dry milk and 1 qt (0.95 L) water may be substituted for fluid milk. Increase shortening to 4 oz (114 g).

Variation: **Chocolate Doughnuts.** Substitute 2 oz (57 g) cocoa for 2 oz (57 g) flour.

WAFFLES

Yield: 6 qt (5.68 L) batter
50–60 waffles

Amount			
Metric	U.S.	Ingredient	Procedure
1.36 kg	3 lb	Flour, all-purpose	Combine dry ingredients in mixer bowl. Blend on low speed for 10 seconds.
85 g	3 oz	Baking powder	
38 g	2 T	Salt	
114 g	4 oz	Sugar, granulated	
18 (312 g)	18 (11 oz)	Egg yolks	Combine egg yolks, milk, and melted shortening. Add to dry ingredients. Mix on low speed just enough to moisten dry ingredients.
2.13 L	2¼ qt	Milk	
454 g	1 lb	Shortening, melted, cooled	
18 (595 g)	18 (1 lb 5 oz)	Egg whites	Beat egg whites until stiff but not dry. Fold into batter. Use No. 10 dipper to place batter on preheated waffle iron. Bake about 4 minutes.

Note: 10 oz (284 g) nonfat dry milk and 2¼ qt (2.13 L) water may be substituted for fluid milk. Mix dry milk with dry ingredients. Increase shortening to 1 lb 2 oz (510 g).

Variations:
1. **Bacon Waffles.** Add 1 lb (454 g) chopped bacon slightly cooked, and substitute bacon fat for the shortening in recipe.
2. **Cornmeal Waffles.** Substitute 12 oz (340 g) fine cornmeal for 8 oz (227 g) flour.
3. **Pecan Waffles.** Add 6 oz (170 g) chopped pecans.

PANCAKE MIX

Yield: 12 lb (5.44 kg) mix

Amount Metric	Amount U.S.	Ingredient	Procedure
4.08 kg	9 lb	Flour, all-purpose	Combine ingredients in mixer bowl. Blend well, using flat beater or whip. Store in covered container.
227 g	8 oz	Baking powder	
76 g	¼ c	Salt	
680 g	1 lb 8 oz	Sugar, granulated	
680 g	1 lb 8 oz	Nonfat dry milk	

Variation: **Buttermilk Pancake Mix.** Substitute 1 lb 8 oz (680 g) dry buttermilk for nonfat dry milk and add 2 T (24 g) baking soda.

TABLE FOR USING PANCAKE MIX

Ingredient	30 cakes	50 cakes	100 cakes	200 cakes
Mix	2 lb (908 g)	3 lb (1.36 kg)	6 lb (2.72 kg)	12 lb (5.44 kg)
Eggs, beaten	4 (7 oz)	6 (10 oz)	12 (1 lb 5 oz)	24 (2 lb 10 oz)
Water	1 qt (0.95 L)	1½ qt (1.42 L)	3 qt (2.84 L)	1½ gal (5.68 L)
Shortening, melted	4 oz (114 g)	6 oz (170 g)	12 oz (340 g)	1 lb 8 oz (680 g)

Note: To use mix, weigh appropriate amount as given in the table. Add beaten eggs, water, and cooled melted fat. Stir only until mix is dampened. Place on hot griddle with No. 16 dipper. Bake until cake is full of bubbles. Turn and finish baking.

PANCAKES

Yield: 7 qt batter
100 cakes 4-in. diameter

Amount Metric	U.S.	Ingredient	Procedure
2.04 kg	4 lb 8 oz	Flour, all-purpose	Combine dry ingredients in mixer bowl until well blended.
114 g	4 oz	Baking powder	
38 g	2 T	Salt	
340 g	12 oz	Sugar, granulated	
12 (595 g)	12 (1 lb 5 oz)	Eggs	Beat eggs until light.
3.31 L	3½ qt	Milk	Add milk and melted shortening to eggs.
340 g	12 oz	Shortening, melted, cooled; or salad oil	
			Add egg mixture to dry ingredients. Mix on low speed 30 seconds.
			If batter is thicker than desired, thin with milk.
			Use No. 16 dipper to place batter on griddle preheated to 350°F (175°C).
			Bake until surface of cake is full of bubbles. Turn and finish baking.

Note: 14 oz (397 g) nonfat dry milk and 3½ qt (3.31 L) water may be substituted for the fluid milk. Add dry milk to other dry ingredients. Increase shortening to 1 lb (454 g).

Variations:
1. **Apple Pancakes.** Add 1 lb (454 g) cooked chopped apples and 1 t (2 g) cinnamon or nutmeg.
2. **Blueberry Pancakes.** Add 1 lb (454 g) well-drained and rinsed (or frozen) blueberries to batter after cakes are mixed. Handle carefully to avoid mashing berries.
3. **Buttermilk Pancakes.** Substitute buttermilk for milk. Add 1 T (12 g) baking soda to dry ingredients. 14 oz (397 g) dry buttermilk and 3½ qt (3.31 L) water may be substituted for fluid buttermilk. Add dry buttermilk and soda to other dry ingredients. Increase shortening to 1 lb (454 g).
4. **Pecan Pancakes.** Add 1 lb (454 g) chopped pecans.

CRÉPES

Yield: 100 crêpes
5 qt (4.73 L) batter
Portion: 2 crêpes

Amount		Ingredient	Procedure
Metric	U.S.		
1.14 kg	2 lb 8 oz	Flour, all-purpose	Combine flour and salt in mixer bowl.
28 g	1½ T	Salt	
24 (1.19 kg)	24 (2 lb 10 oz)	Eggs	Beat eggs until fluffy.
2.37 L	2½ qt	Milk	Add milk and margarine to eggs.
57 g	2 oz	Margarine or butter, melted	Add to flour and mix until smooth. Batter will be thinner than pancake batter.
			Drop on lightly greased hot griddle with a No. 24 dipper (1½ oz/43 g).
			Brown lightly on both sides. Crêpes will roll more easily if they are not overcooked.
			Stack, with layers of waxed paper between, until ready to use.

Notes:
1. Crêpes may be folded or rolled around desired filling. (See recipe for Chicken Crêpes, p. 378.)
2. If used for dessert crêpes, add 3 T (42 g) sugar to dry ingredients. Fill with fruit filling.

FRENCH TOAST

Yield: 50 slices

Metric	U.S.	Ingredient	Procedure
24 (1.19 kg)	24 (2 lb 10 oz)	Eggs	Beat eggs.
1.42 L	1½ qt	Milk	Add milk, salt, and sugar to eggs. Mix well.
19 g	1 T	Salt	
114 g	4 oz	Sugar, granulated	
50	50	Bread slices, day-old	Dip bread into egg mixture. Do not let bread soak in it. Fry in deep fat at 360°F (180°C) or on a well-greased griddle until golden brown. Sprinkle with powdered sugar to serve.

Note: Unsliced bread may be sliced double thickness, cut into triangles, or left whole, dipped in egg mixture or in thin batter (p. 37), and fried in deep fat. Sprinkle with powdered sugar.

Variation: **Cinnamon French Toast.** Add 1 t (2 g) cinnamon to egg mixture.

DUMPLINGS

Steam pressure: 5 lb
Steam: 12–15 minutes

Yield: 100 dumplings
Portion: 2 dumplings

Amount		Ingredient	Procedure
Metric	U.S.		
1.14 kg	2 lb 8 oz	Flour, all-purpose	Combine dry ingredients in mixer bowl. Mix on low speed until blended.
85 g	3 oz (6 T)	Baking powder	
38 g	2 T	Salt	
6 (312 g)	6 (11 oz)	Eggs	Beat eggs. Combine with milk.
1.32 L	5½ c	Milk	Add to dry ingredients. Mix on low speed only until blended.
			Drop batter, using No. 24 dipper, on trays. Do not cover trays. Steam for 12–15 minutes.

Notes:

1. 5 oz (142 g) nonfat dry milk and 5½ c water may be substituted for the fluid milk. Add dry milk to other dry ingredients.
2. Serve with meat stew or stewed chicken. Mixture may be dropped onto hot meat mixture in counter pans and steamed.

Variation: **Spaetzles (Egg Dumplings).** Use 1 lb 4 oz (567 g) flour, 1 t (5 g) baking powder, 1½ t (9 g) salt, 6 eggs, and 3 c (720 mL) milk. Mix as above. Drop small bits of dough or press through a colander into 3 gal (11.26 L) hot soup. Cook approximately 5 minutes. Soup must be very hot to cook dumplings.

FRITTERS

Deep-fat fryer: 375°F (190°C)
Fry: 4–6 minutes
Yield: 100 fritters
Portion: 2 fritters

Amount Metric	U.S.	Ingredient	Procedure
1.81 kg	4 lb	Flour, all-purpose	Combine dry ingredients in mixer bowl. Blend on low speed for 10 seconds.
19 g	1 T	Salt	
114 g	4 oz	Baking powder	
57 g	2 oz	Sugar, granulated	
12 (340 g)	12 (1 lb 5 oz)	Eggs, beaten	Combine eggs, milk, and melted shortening.
1.89 L	2 qt	Milk	Add to dry ingredients. Mix only enough to moisten dry ingredients.
170 g	6 oz	Shortening, melted	Measure with No. 30 dipper into hot deep fat. Fry 4–6 minutes.

Notes:
1. Serve with syrup.
2. 8 oz (227 g) nonfat dry milk and 2 qt (1.89 L) water may be substituted for fluid milk. Add dry milk to other dry ingredients.

Variations:
1. **Apple Fritters.** Add 1 lb (454 g) raw apple, peeled and finely chopped.
2. **Banana Fritters.** Reduce flour to 2 lb (908 g). Dip quartered bananas into batter. Fry.
3. **Corn Fritters.** Add 2 qt (1.89 L) whole kernel corn, drained.
4. **Deep-Fat Fried Bananas.** Cut bananas into 2-in. pieces. Sprinkle with lemon juice and powdered sugar. Let stand 30 minutes. Dip in egg batter (p. 37) and fry for 1–3 minutes.
5. **Fruit Fritters.** Add 1 qt (0.95 L) drained fruit: peach, pineapple, or other fruit.

YEAST BREAD RECIPES

WHITE BREAD

Oven: 400°F (205°C)   Yield: 16 1½-lb loaves
Bake: 35–40 minutes

Amount Metric	U.S.	Ingredient	Procedure
142 g	5 oz	Yeast, active dry	Soften yeast in warm water. Let stand 10 minutes.
720 mL	3 c	Water, warm (110°F/43°C)	
284 g	10 oz	Sugar, granulated	Combine sugar, salt, dry milk, water, and shortening. Add softened yeast. Using dough hook, mix on medium speed until blended.
142 g	5 oz	Salt	
397 g	14 oz	Nonfat dry milk	
3.79 L	1 gal	Water, lukewarm	
340 g	12 oz	Shortening, melted	
6.8 kg	15 lb	Flour, all-purpose	Add flour. Mix on low speed about 10 minutes or until dough is smooth and elastic and small blisters appear on surface.

1. Let rise in a warm place (80°F/27°C) approximately 2 hours, or until double in bulk.
2. Punch down dough. Shape into 16 loaves, 1 lb 8 oz (680 g) each. (See Fig. 2.1.) Place in greased 5 × 9 × 2¾-in. loaf pans.
3. Let rise approximately 1½ hours, or until double in bulk.
4. Bake at 400°F (205°C) for 30–40 minutes or until loaves are golden brown and sound hollow when tapped (Fig. 2.2).
5. Brush tops of loaves with melted margarine or butter.

Notes:
1. The dough temperature should be about 80°F (27°C) when mixed.
2. Mixing may be simplified by combining dry yeast with sugar, salt, dry milk, and 2 lb (908 g) of the flour. Mix thoroughly. In mixer bowl, combine very warm water (120°F/49°C) and shortening. Blend on low speed. Add yeast–flour mixture while mixing on low speed. Add remaining flour gradually, mixing until a smooth, elastic dough is formed.
3. 1¼ gal (4.73 L) fresh milk may be substituted for the water and dry milk. Scald milk, combine with sugar, salt, and shortening. Let cool to lukewarm.
4. Shortening may be increased to 1 lb (454 g) and sugar to 2 oz (57 g) if a richer dough is desired.
5. A variety of shapes may be made from dough (Fig. 2.3).

See page 113 for variations.

YEAST BREAD RECIPES **111**

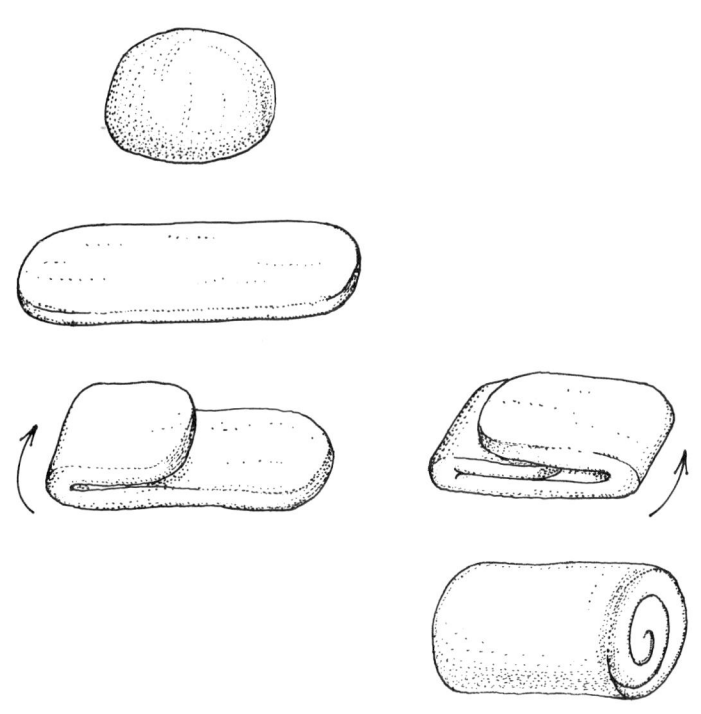

Figure 2.1 Shaping bread loaves.

Figure 2.2 Baked bread loaves, showing evenly browned top and sides. Courtesy of American Institute of Baking.

Figure 2.3 Basic bread or roll dough is shaped easily into a variety of products. Courtesy of Nabisco Brands, Inc., makers of Fleischmann's Yeast.

Variations:
1. **Butter Slices.** Divide dough into thirds. Roll ⅓ in. thick. Cut with 3-in. biscuit cutter or shape into long rolls and cut into slices. Dip in melted margarine or butter. Stand pieces on edge in 5 × 9-in. loaf pans (8 pieces per pan). Let rise and bake.
2. **Cinnamon Bread.** After dough has been divided and scaled into loaves, roll each into a rectangular sheet. Brush with melted margarine or shortening; sprinkle generously with cinnamon and sugar. Roll as for jelly roll. Seal edge of dough and place in greased loaf pan sealed edge down. Sprinkle top with cinnamon and sugar.
3. **French Bread.** Reduce dry milk to 8 oz (227 g) and shortening to 4 oz (114 g). Scale 1 lb 8 oz (680 g) dough for each loaf. Roll to 15 × 2-in. rectangle. Start at long side and roll dough tightly. Seal dough at the ends. Taper ends. Place 4 loaves seam-side down on each greased 18 × 26 × 1-in. baking sheet. (Cornmeal may be sprinkled on pan, if desired.) Let rise until double in bulk. Tops may be slashed diagonally ¼-in. deep with a sharp knife. Brush tops and sides of loaves with mixture of 2 egg whites and 2 T (30 mL) water. Bake at 375° (190°C) for 20 minutes.
4. **Raisin Bread.** Add 3 lb (1.36 kg) raisins to dough after mixing.
5. **Whole Wheat Bread.** Substitute whole wheat flour for ½ of white flour.

OATMEAL BREAD

Oven: 375°F (190°C)
Bake: 40–50 minutes
Yield: 5 1½-lb (680-g) loaves

Metric	U.S.	Ingredient	Procedure
35 g	1¼ oz	Yeast, active dry	Combine yeast, water, and sugar. Let stand 10 minutes.
240 mL	1 c	Water, warm (110°F/43°C)	
10 g	2 t	Sugar, granulated	
720 mL	3 c	Water, hot	Combine in mixer bowl, using dough hook.
170 g	6 oz	Rolled oats	
240 mL	1 c	Molasses	
170 g	6 oz	Shortening	
38 g	2 T	Salt	
1.64 kg	3 lb 10 oz	Flour, all-purpose	Add enough flour to mixture in mixer bowl to make a smooth, thin batter.
4 (198 g)	4 (7 oz)	Eggs	Add eggs and yeast mixture to batter. Mix 15 minutes on medium speed. Add remaining flour in small amounts, on low speed to make a soft dough. Let rest 10 minutes. Knead on low speed for 10 minutes or until smooth. Let rise until double in bulk.

| Amount | | Ingredient | Procedure |
Metric	U.S.	Ingredient	Procedure
114 g	4 oz	Rolled oats	Coat each greased loaf pan with ¼ c (60 mL) rolled oats. Punch down dough. Scale 1 lb 8 oz (680 g) dough for each pan and shape into loaf. Place in 5 × 9 × 2¾-in. loaf pan.
2 (57 g) 15 mL	2 (2 oz) 1 T	Egg whites Water	Combine egg whites and water. Brush loaves with egg mixture. Sprinkle with rolled oats. Let rise until double in bulk. Bake at 375°F (190°C) for 40–50 minutes.

ENGLISH MUFFIN BREAD

Oven: 375°F (190°C)
Bake: 40–50 minutes
Yield: 5 1½-lb (680-g) loaves

Amount Metric	U.S.	Ingredient	Procedure
600 mL	2¼ c	Water, hot	Combine water and oil in mixer bowl.
360 mL	1½ c	Salad oil	
908 g	2 lb	Flour, all-purpose	Add flour, sugar, salt, and eggs to water–oil mixture.
170 g	6 oz	Sugar, granulated	
57 g	2 oz	Salt	
6 (284 g)	6 (10 oz)	Eggs, beaten	
43 g	1¼ oz	Yeast, active dry	Dissolve yeast in warm water.
300 mL	1¼ c	Water, warm (110°F/43°C)	Add to flour mixture. Mix on medium speed 2 minutes.
908 g	2 lb	Flour, all-purpose	Add enough remaining flour to make a stiff batter. Cover and let rise until light and double in bulk. Punch down dough.
57 g	2 oz	Cornmeal	Grease 5 5 × 9 × 2¾-in loaf pans. Sprinkle with cornmeal. Scale 1 lb 8 oz (680 g) dough per pan. Shape and place in pans. Sprinkle with cornmeal. Cover. Let rise until double in bulk. Bake at 375°F (190°C) for 40–50 minutes or until loaf sounds hollow when tapped lightly.

SWEDISH RYE BREAD

Oven: 375°F (190°C)
Bake: 40–50 minutes
Yield: 5 1½-lb (680-g) loaves

Amount		Ingredient	Procedure
Metric	U.S.		
14 g	½ oz	Yeast, active dry	Combine yeast, water, and brown sugar. Let stand 10 minutes.
60 mL	¼ c	Water, warm (110°F/43°C)	
14 g	1 T	Sugar, brown	
1.18 L	1¼ qt	Water, warm	Combine in mixer bowl.
28 g	1 oz	Salt	
57 g	2 oz	Sugar, brown	
240 mL	1 c	Molasses	
240 mL	1 c	Vegetable oil	
1.36–1.59 kg	3–3 lb 8 oz	Flour, all-purpose	Combine flours. Add enough to mixture in mixer bowl to make a thin smooth batter. Add yeast mixture. Mix on high speed for 5 minutes. Reduce mixer speed. Add remaining flour in small amounts to make a soft dough that pulls itself from sides of bowl. Mix until smooth, about 10 minutes, or until small blisters appear on the surface. Let rise until double in bulk. Shape into 5 loaves, 1 lb 8 oz (680 g) each. Place in 5 × 9 × 2¾-in. loaf pans. Let rise until double. Bake at 375°F (190°C) 40–50 minutes or until bread sounds hollow when tapped lightly.
454 g	1 lb	Flour, rye	

Variations:
1. **Caraway Rye Bread.** Add 1 T (15 mL) caraway seeds to dough.
2. **Rye Rolls.** Shape into 1½-oz (43-g) rolls. Yield: 7 doz.

NORWEGIAN CHRISTMAS BREAD

Oven: 350°F (175°C)
Bake: 40 minutes
Yield: 6 loaves 5 × 9 in.

Amount		Ingredient	Procedure
Metric	U.S.		
0.95 L	1 qt	Milk, scalded	Combine milk, sugar, salt, and cardamom seed in mixer bowl. Cool to lukewarm.
454 g	1 lb	Sugar, granulated	
12 g	2 t	Salt	
5 mL	1 t	Cardamom seed, crushed	
43 g	1½ oz	Yeast, active dry	Soften yeast in water and add to milk mixture.
240 mL	1 c	Water, warm (110°F/43°C)	
680 g	1 lb 8 oz	Flour, all-purpose	Add flour and margarine. Mix to form a batter. Let stand 15 minutes.
454 g	1 lb	Margarine or butter, soft	
794 g	1 lb 12 oz (or more)	Flour, all-purpose	Slice cherries and dust with some of the flour. Add cherries, pecans, and remainder of flour to batter. Mix until a smooth dough is formed. Cover and let rise until double in bulk. Punch down gently. Turn onto lightly floured board. Divide into 6 loaves, 1 lb 8 oz (680 g) each, and shape. Let rise until almost double in bulk, about 40 minutes. Bake at 350°F (175°C) for 40 minutes. Cut 12–14 slices per loaf.
340 g	12 oz	Candied cherries (red and green)	
170 g	6 oz	Pecans, chopped fine	

Notes:

1. 4 oz (114 g) nonfat dry milk and 1 qt (0.95 L) water may be substituted for fluid milk. Add dry milk to first portion of flour.

2. Candied mixed fruits may be substituted for candied cherries.

QUICK ROLL DOUGH

Oven: 400°F (205°C)
Bake: 15–20 minutes
Yield: 10 doz rolls

Amount Metric	U.S.	Ingredient	Procedure
57 g	2 oz	Yeast, active dry	Soften yeast in warm water in mixer bowl.
1.89 L	2 qt	Water, warm (110°F/43°C)	
12 (595 g)	12 (1 lb 5 oz)	Eggs, beaten	Add eggs and melted shortening.
227 g	8 oz	Shortening, melted	
3.29 kg	7 lb 4 oz (variable)	Flour, all-purpose	Combine dry ingredients. Add to yeast mixture.
198 g	7 oz	Nonfat dry milk	Mix on low speed until dough is smooth and elastic and leaves sides of bowl, 15–20 minutes.
227 g	8 oz	Sugar, granulated	
57 g	2 oz (3 T)	Salt	

Divide dough into 10 equal portions (approximately 1½ lb/680 g each). Let rest 10 minutes.

Work one portion at a time. This will be a rather soft dough. Shape into 1½-oz (43-g) rolls and place on greased baking sheets. Let rise until double in bulk, about 45 minutes. Bake at 400°F (205°C) for 15–20 minutes. Brush with melted margarine or butter if desired.

Note: Mixing may be simplified by combining dry yeast with sugar, salt, dry milk, and 2 lb (908 g) of the flour. Add very warm water (120°F/49°C) and melted fat to beaten eggs. Mix. Add remaining flour gradually, mixing until a smooth, elastic dough is formed.

Variations: See Variations for Basic Roll Dough, pp. 120.

BASIC ROLL DOUGH

Oven: 400°F (205°C)
Bake: 15–25 minutes

Yield: 8 doz rolls
Portion: 1½ oz (43 g)

Amount Metric	U.S.	Ingredient	Procedure
43 g	1½ oz	Yeast, active dry	Soften yeast in warm water.
240 mL	1 c	Water, warm (110°F/43°C)	
1.18 L	1¼ qt	Water, hot	Place hot water, dry milk, sugar, salt, and shortening in mixer bowl. Mix thoroughly, using dough hook, until shortening is softened.
142 g	5 oz	Nonfat dry milk	
114 g	4 oz	Sugar, granulated	
57 g	2 oz (3 T)	Salt	
170 g	6 oz	Shortening	
4 (198 g)	4 (7 oz)	Eggs, beaten	Add eggs and softened yeast.
2.15 kg	4 lb 12 oz (variable)	Flour, all-purpose	Add flour to make a moderately soft dough. Mix on low speed until smooth and satiny and small blisters appear on surface.

1. Turn into lightly greased bowl, turn over to grease top. Cover. Let rise in warm place (80°F/27°C) until double in bulk.
2. Punch down. Divide into thirds for ease in handling. Shape into 1½-oz (43-g) rolls or into desired shapes. (See Variations.)
3. Let rise until double in bulk.
4. Bake at 400°F (205°C) for 15–25 minutes or until golden brown.

Notes:
1. Mixing may be simplified by combining dry yeast with sugar, salt, dry milk, and 2 lb (908 g) of the flour. Mix thoroughly. In mixer bowl combine 1½ qt (1.42 L) very warm water (120°F/49°C), shortening, and beaten eggs. Blend on low speed. Add remaining flour gradually, mixing until a smooth, elastic dough is formed.
2. 3–4 hours are required for mixing and rising. For a quicker rising dough, increase yeast to 2 oz (57 g).
3. 1¼ qt (1.18 L) fluid milk may be used in place of nonfat dry milk and hot water. Scald milk, then add sugar, salt, and shortening, and cool to lukewarm.

Variations:
1. **Bowknots.** Roll 1½-oz (43-g) portions of dough into strips 9 in. long. Tie loosely into a single knot. (See Fig. 2.4.)
2. **Braids.** Roll dough ¼ in. thick and cut in strips 6 in. long and ½ in. wide. Cross 3 strips in the middle and braid from center to end. Press ends together and fold under.

3. **Butterhorns.** Proceed as for crescents, but do not form crescent shape.
4. **Caramel Crowns.** Increase sugar in dough to 9 oz (255 g). Scale dough into balls 1½ oz (43 g) each. Drop into mixture of 1 lb 4 oz (567 g) sugar and 3 T (21 g) cinnamon to coat balls. Arrange 18 balls into each of 5 greased tube pans, into which 2 oz (57 g) pecans, halves or coarsely chopped, have been placed. The pan should be about ⅓ full. Let rise until double in bulk. Bake at 350°F (175°C) for 30 minutes. Immediately loosen from pan with a spatula. Invert pans to remove. Cool. Serve irregular-side up. Garnish with maraschino cherries.
5. **Cloverleaf Rolls.** Pinch off small balls of dough. Fit into greased muffin pans, allowing 3 balls for each roll. (See Fig. 2.5.)
6. **Crescents.** Weigh dough into 12-oz (340-g) portions. Roll each into a circle ⅛ in. thick and 8 in. in diameter. Cut into 12 triangles, brush top with melted margarine or butter. Beginning at base, roll each triangle, keeping point in middle of roll and bringing ends toward each other to form a crescent shape. Place on greased baking sheets 1½ in. apart. (See Fig. 2.6.)
7. **Dinner or Pan Rolls.** Shape dough into small balls, place on well-greased baking sheets. Cover. Let rise until light. Brush with mixture made of egg yolk and milk—1 egg yolk to 1 T (15 mL) milk. (See Fig. 2.7.)
8. **Fan Tan or Butterflake Rolls.** Weigh dough into 12-oz (340-g) pieces. Roll out into very thin rectangular sheet. Brush with melted margarine or butter. Cut in strips about 1 in. wide. Pile 6 or 7 strips together. Cut 1½-in. pieces and place on end in greased muffin pans.

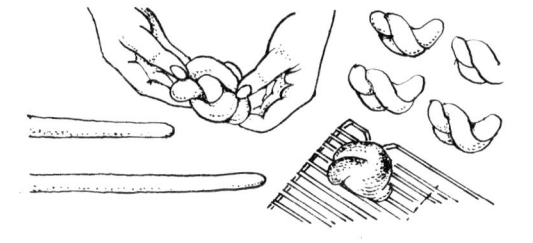

Figure 2.4 Shaping Bowknot Rolls.

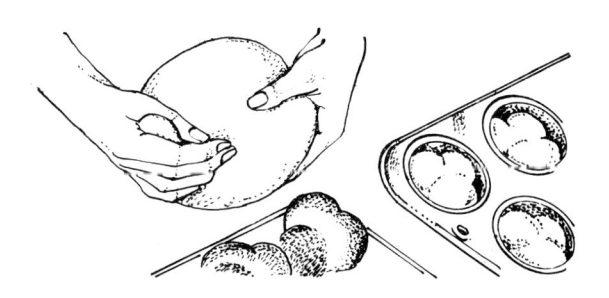

Figure 2.5 Shaping Cloverleaf Rolls.

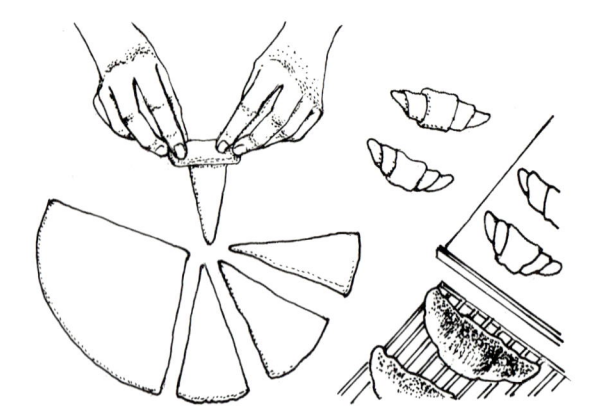

Figure 2.6 Shaping Crescent Rolls.

Figure 2.7 Shaping Dinner or Pan Rolls.

9. **Half-and-Half Rolls.** Proceed as for Twin Rolls. Use 1 round plain dough and 1 round whole wheat dough for each roll.
10. **Hamburger Buns.** Divide dough into 2 portions. Roll each piece of dough into a strip 1½ in. in diameter. Cut strips into pieces approximately 2½ oz (70 g) each. Round the pieces into balls. Place balls in rows on greased baking sheet 1½–2 in. apart. Let stand 10–15 minutes, flatten to desired thickness with fingers, rolling pin, or another baking sheet.
11. **Hot Cross Buns.** Divide dough into thirds. Roll ½ in. thick. Cut rounds 3 in. in diameter. Brush top with beaten egg. Score top of bun to make cross before baking, or after baking, make a cross on top with frosting. (See p. 129 for Variation.)
12. **Hot Dog Buns.** Divide dough into 2 portions. Roll each piece of dough into a strip 1½ in. in diameter. Cut strips of dough into pieces approximately 2½ oz (70 g) each. Round pieces of dough; roll into pieces approximately 4½ in. long. Place in rows on greased baking sheets ½ in. apart.

13. **Parkerhouse Rolls.** Divide dough into thirds. Roll to ⅓ in. thickness. Cut rounds 2–2½ in. in diameter or form 1½-oz (43-g) balls. Allow balls to stand for 10 minutes, then elongate with rolling pin. Crease middle of each roll with dull edge of knife. Brush with melted margarine or butter, fold over, and press together with palm of hand. (See Fig. 2.8.)
14. **Popcorn Rolls.** Shape dough into 1½-oz (43-g) balls. Place on greased baking sheets. Snip top of each ball twice with scissors.
15. **Poppy Seed Rolls.** (a) Proceed as for Twists. Substitute poppy seeds for sugar and cinnamon. (b) Proceed as for Cinnamon Rolls. Substitute poppy seed for sugar, cinnamon, and raisins.
16. **Ribbon Rolls.** Weigh dough into 12-oz (340-g) pieces. Roll ¼ in. thick. Spread with melted margarine or butter. Place on top of this a layer of whole wheat dough rolled to the same thickness. Repeat, using the contrasting dough until 5 layers thick. Cut with a 1½-in. cutter. Place in greased muffin pans with cut surface down.
17. **Rosettes.** Follow directions for Bowknots. After tying, bring one end through center and the other over the side.
18. **Sesame Rolls.** Proceed as for Twin Rolls. Brush tops with melted margarine or butter and sprinkle with sesame seeds.
19. **Twin Rolls.** Weigh dough into 12-oz (340-g) pieces. Roll ⅝ in. thick. Cut rounds 1 in. in diameter. Brush with melted margarine or butter. Place on end in well-greased muffin pans, allowing 2 rounds for each roll.
20. **Twists.** Weigh dough into 12-oz (340-g) pieces. Roll ⅓ in. thick, spread with melted margarine or butter, sugar, and cinnamon. Cut into strips ⅓ × 8 in., bring both ends together, and twist dough.
21. **Whole Wheat Rolls.** Substitute 2 lb 6 oz (1.08 kg) whole wheat flour for 2 lb 6 oz (1.08 kg) white flour. Proceed as for Basic Roll Dough.

Figure 2.8 Shaping Parkerhouse Rolls.

REFRIGERATOR ROLLS

Oven: 400°F (205°C)
Bake: 15–20 minutes
Yield: 8 doz rolls

Metric	U.S.	Ingredient	Procedure
340 g	12 oz	Sugar, granulated	Place, sugar, shortening, and potatoes in mixer bowl.
340 g	12 oz	Shortening	
57 g	2 oz	Salt	
360 mL	1½ c	Mashed potatoes, hot	
1.18 L	1¼ qt	Milk, scalded	Add milk. Mix to blend. Cool to lukewarm.
28 g	1 oz	Yeast, active dry	Soften yeast in warm water.
240 mL	1 c	Water, warm (110°F/43°C)	
6 g	1½ t	Baking soda	Add softened yeast, soda, and baking powder to milk mixture.
14 g	1 T	Baking powder	
1.81 kg	4 lb	Flour, all-purpose	Add just enough of the flour to make a stiff batter. Let rise 15 minutes. Add remaining flour or enough to make a stiff dough. Mix until dough is smooth. Place in a greased container. Grease top. Cover and place in the refrigerator for 24 hours. Remove dough from refrigerator and shape into rolls, 1½ oz (43 g) each. Let rise 1–1½ hours or until light. Bake at 400°F (205°C) for 15–20 minutes.

Note: 5 oz (142 g) nonfat dry milk and 1¼ qt (1.18 L) water may be substituted for fluid milk. Mix dry milk with soda, baking powder, and part of flour.

Variations: See variations for Basic Roll Dough, pp. 120.

BUTTER BUNS

Oven: 400°F (205°C)　　　　　　　　　　　　　　　　Yield: 9–10 doz buns
Bake: 15–20 minutes

Amount			
Metric	U.S.	Ingredient	Procedure
720 mL	3 c	Milk, scalded	Combine scalded milk, margarine, sugar, and salt in mixer bowl. Cool to lukewarm.
680 g	1 lb 8 oz	Margarine or butter	
454 g	1 lb	Sugar, granulated	
28 g	1 oz	Salt	
57 g	2 oz	Yeast, active dry	Soften yeast in warm water.
240 mL	1 c	Water, warm (110°F/43°C)	
12 (794 g)	12 (1 lb 5 oz)	Eggs	Beat eggs and yolks. Add eggs, lemon extract, and yeast to milk mixture.
16 (284 g)	16 (10 oz)	Egg yolks	
20 mL	4 t	Lemon extract	
2.04 kg	4 lb 8 oz	Flour, all-purpose	Add flour. Mix thoroughly. Let rise until double in bulk. Use No. 30 dipper to fill greased muffin pans. Let rise 1 hour. Bake at 400°F (205°C) for 15–20 minutes.

Note: 3 oz (85 g) nonfat dry milk and 3 c (720 mL) water may be substituted for the fluid milk. Combine dry milk with the flour. Increase margarine to 1 lb 9 oz (709 g).

RAISED MUFFINS

Oven: 350°F (175°C)   Yield: 8 doz
Bake: 20 minutes

Metric	U.S.	Ingredient	Procedure
255 g	9 oz	Shortening	Place shortening, sugar, and salt in mixer bowl.
340 g	12 oz	Sugar, granulated	
57 g	2 oz	Salt	
1.42 L	1½ qt	Milk, scalded	Add milk. Mix on low speed until blended. Cool to lukewarm.
43 g	1½ oz	Yeast, active dry	Soften yeast in warm water.
360 mL	1½ c	Water, warm (110°F/43°C)	
12 (595 g)	12 (1 lb 5 oz)	Eggs, beaten	Add eggs and softened yeast to milk mixture.
908 g	2 lb	Flour, all-purpose	Add flour. Beat on medium speed for 10 minutes. Let rise in warm place for 1½ hours.
1.25 kg	2 lb 12 oz (variable)	Flour, all-purpose	Add remaining flour. Beat until batter is smooth. Use No. 20 dipper to fill greased muffin pans. Let rise until double in bulk (about 1 hour). Bake at 350°F (175°C) for 20 minutes.

Note: 6 oz (170 g) nonfat dry milk and 1½ qt (1.42 L) water may be substituted for the fluid milk. Combine dry milk with the first portion of flour.

HERBED TOMATO BUNS

Oven: 375°F (190°C)
Bake: 15–18 minutes
Yield: 64 buns

Metric	U.S.	Ingredient	Procedure
14 g	1 T	Sugar, brown	Combine sugar, yeast, and water in mixing bowl. Let stand 10 minutes.
57 g	2 oz	Yeast, active dry	
240 mL	1 c	Water, warm (110°F/43°C)	
28 g	1 oz	Sugar, brown	Combine in mixer bowl. Mix with dough hook until shortening is softened.
28 g	1 oz	Salt	
114 g	4 oz	Shortening	
85 g	3 oz	Nonfat dry milk	
300 mL	1¼ c	Water, hot	
340 g	12 oz	Flour, all-purpose	Add flour. Mix to a smooth batter.
595 g	1 lb 5 oz	Tomatoes, canned, diced, drained	Finely chop tomatoes. Add to mixture in mixer bowl.
5 (227 g)	5 (8 oz)	Eggs	Add eggs, seasonings, and yeast mixture. Mix 15 minutes on medium speed.
2 g	2 t	Thyme, powdered	
1 g	1½ t	Basil leaves	
1.59 kg	3 lb 8 oz	Flour, all-purpose	Add flour gradually to make a soft dough that pulls itself away from sides of bowl.
			Let rise until double in bulk. Punch down. Shape into buns, 2 oz (57 g) each. Place 3 × 5 on greased bun sheets. Press down to make a flat round bun. Let rise. Bake at 375°F (190°C) for 15–18 minutes.

Note: To make loaves, scale 1 lb 8 oz (680 g) dough, shape and place in greased 5 × 9 × 2¾-in. loaf pans. Bake at 375°F (190°C) for 35–45 minutes or until golden brown and loaves sound hollow when tapped lightly.

BASIC SWEET ROLL DOUGH

Oven: 375°F (190°C)
Bake: 20–25 minutes
Yield: 8 doz rolls
Portion: 2 oz (57 g)

Amount Metric	U.S.	Ingredient	Procedure
57 g	2 oz	Yeast, active dry	Soften yeast in warm water.
360 mL	1½ c	Water, warm (110°F/43°C)	
720 mL	3 c	Water, hot	Combine hot water, dry milk, sugar, shortening, and salt in mixer bowl. Mix, using dough hook, until shortening is softened. Cool to lukewarm.
114 g	3 oz	Nonfat dry milk	
454 g	1 lb	Sugar, granulated	
454 g	1 lb	Shortening	
57 g	2 oz	Salt	
9 (454 g)	9 (1 lb)	Eggs, beaten	Add eggs and yeast to mixture in bowl. Blend.
2.27–2.72 kg	5–6 lb (variable)	Flour, all-purpose	Add flour gradually on low speed. Mix on medium speed to a smooth dough, 5–6 minutes. Do not overmix. Dough should be moderately soft.

1. The dough temperature just after mixing should be 78–82°F (26–28°C).
2. Place in lightly greased bowl. Grease top of dough, cover, and let rise in warm place until double in bulk, about 2 hours.
3. Punch down and let rise again, about 1 hour.
4. Punch down and divide into portions for rolls. Let rest 10 minutes.
5. Scale about 2 oz (57 g) per roll. Shape (see Variations) and let rise until rolls are almost double in bulk, about 45 minutes.
6. Bake at 375°F (190°C) for 20–25 minutes.

Notes:
1. Mixing may be simplified by combining dry yeast with sugar, salt, dry milk, and 2 lb (908 g) of the flour. Mix thoroughly. Combine eggs, very warm water (120°F/49°C), and melted shortening. Add yeast–flour mixture on low speed. Add remaining flour gradually, mixing until a smooth, elastic dough is formed.
2. 3 c (720 mL) fluid milk may be used in place of nonfat dry milk and hot water. Scald milk, then add sugar, salt, and shortening, and cool to lukewarm.
3. For a quicker rising dough, increase yeast to 3 oz (85 g).

Variations:

1. **Cherry–Nut Rolls.** Add 1 t (2 g) nutmeg, 1 t (5 mL) lemon extract, 1 lb (454 g) chopped glacé cherries, and 1 lb (454 g) chopped pecans to dough. Shape into 1-oz (28-g) balls. When baked, cover with glaze made of orange juice and powdered sugar.

2. **Coffee Cake.** Scale 4 lb (1.81 kg) dough, roll out to size of sheet pan. Cover top of dough with melted margarine or butter and topping (see p. 133). Fruit fillings may be used also.

3. **Crullers.** Roll dough ⅓ in. thick. Cut into strips ⅓ × 8 in. Bring 2 ends together and twist dough. Let rise, then fry in deep fat. Frost with Powdered Sugar Glaze (p. 170) or dip in fine granulated sugar.

4. **Danish Pastry.** Roll a 5-lb (2.27-kg) piece of dough into a rectangular shape about ¼ in. thick. Start at one edge and cover completely ⅔ of the dough with small pieces of hard butter, margarine, or special Danish pastry shortening. The latter is stable at bake shop temperature and is easier to use than butter or margarine. Use 2–5 oz (57–142 g) per lb (454 g) of dough. Fold the unbuttered ⅓ portion of dough over an equal portion of buttered dough. Fold the remaining ⅓ buttered dough over the top to make 3 layers of dough separated by a layer of fat. Roll out dough ¼ in. thick. This completes the first roll. Repeat folding and rolling two or more times. Do not allow the fat to become soft while working with the dough. Let dough rest 45 minutes. Make into desired shapes.

5. **Hot Cross Buns.** Add to dough 8 oz (227 g) chopped glacé cherries, 8 oz (227 g) raisins, 2 T (14 g) cinnamon, ¼ t cloves, and ¼ t nutmeg. Shape into round buns, 1 oz (28 g) per bun. When baked, make a cross on top with powdered sugar frosting.

6. **Kolaches.** Add 2 T (12 g) grated lemon peel to dough. Shape dough into 1-oz (28-g) balls. Place on lightly greased baking sheet. Let rise until light. Press down center to make cavity and fill with 1 t (5 g) filling. Brush with melted margarine or butter and sprinkle with chopped nuts. Suggested fillings: chopped cooked prunes and dried apricots cooked with sugar and cinnamon; poppy seed mixed with sugar and milk; apricot or peach marmalade.

7. **Long Johns.** Roll out dough to a thickness of ½ in. Cut dough into rectangular pieces ½ × 4 in. Let rise until double in bulk. Fry in deep fat.

8. **Swedish Braids.** Add to dough 1 lb (454 g) chopped candied fruit cake mix, 8 oz (227 g) pecans, and ½ t cardamom seed. Weigh dough into 1¾ lb (794 g) portions and braid. Place on greased sheet pans, 4 per pan. When baked, brush with Powdered Sugar Glaze (p. 170) made with milk in place of water.

CINNAMON ROLLS

Oven: 375°F (190°C)
Bake: 20–25 minutes

Yield: 7–8 doz rolls

Amount Metric	U.S.	Ingredient	Procedure
4.54 kg	10 lb (1 recipe)	Basic Roll Dough (p. 120) or Basic Sweet Roll Dough (p. 128)	Let dough rise until double in bulk. Divide dough into 8 portions, 1 lb 4 oz (567 g) each. Roll each portion into rectangular sheet 9 × 14 × 1/3 in.
340 g	12 oz	Margarine or butter, melted	Spread each sheet with melted margarine.
908 g 21 g	2 lb 3 T	Sugar, granulated Cinnamon	Combine sugar and cinnamon. Sprinkle 6 oz (170 g) over each sheet. Roll as for jelly roll (see Fig. 2.9). Cut into 1-in. slices. Place cut-side down on greased baking sheets (2 doz rolls, 1½ oz/43 g each, per 18 × 26 × 1-in. pan) or in muffin pans. Let rise until double in bulk, about 45 minutes. Bake at 375°F (190°C) for 20–25 minutes. After removing from oven, spread tops with Powdered Sugar Glaze (p. 170) made with milk in place of water.

Variations:
1. **Butterfly Rolls.** Cut rolled dough into 2-in. slices. Press each roll across center parallel to the cut side, with the back of a large knife handle. Press or flatten out the folds of each end. Place on greased baking sheets 1½ in. apart.

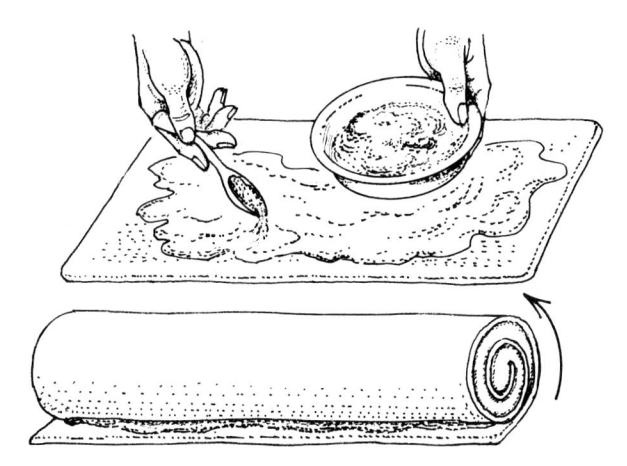

Figure 2.9 Preparing Cinnamon Rolls.

2. **Butterscotch Rolls.** Use brown sugar and omit cinnamon, if desired. Cream 8 oz (227 g) margarine or butter, 1½ lb (680 g) brown sugar, and 1 t (6 g) salt. Gradually add 1 c (240 mL) water, blending thoroughly. Spread 10 oz (284 g) mixture over each of 4 greased 18 × 26 × 1-in. baking sheets or spread 1 T (15 g) mixture into each greased muffin pan cup. Place rolls cut-side down in pans.

3. **Cinnamon–Raisin Rolls.** Use brown sugar in place of granulated sugar and add 8 oz (227 g) raisins to filling.

4. **Double Cinnamon Buns.** Proceed as for Butterfly Rolls. Roll sheet of dough from both sides to form a double roll.

5. **Glazed Marmalade Rolls.** Omit cinnamon. Dip cut slices in additional melted margarine or butter and sugar. When baked, glaze with orange marmalade mixed with powdered sugar until of a consistency to spread. Apricot marmalade, strawberry jam, or other preserves may be used for the glaze.

6. **Honey Rolls.** Substitute honey filling for sugar and cinnamon. Whip 1 lb (454 g) margarine or butter and 1 lb (454 g) honey until light and fluffy.

7. **Orange Rolls.** Omit cinnamon. Spread with mixture of 1½ lb (680 g) sugar and 1 c (240 mL) grated orange rind. When baked, brush with glaze made of powdered sugar and orange juice. If desired, use a filling made by creaming 1 lb (454 g) margarine or butter, 2 T (12 g) grated orange rind, 2 lb (908 g) sugar, and ¾ c (180 mL) undiluted frozen orange concentrate. Spread on dough.

8. **Pecan Rolls.** Chop 1 lb 8 oz (680 g) pecans. Sprinkle 8 oz (227 g) over bottom of each of 3 12 × 18 × 2-in. baking pans. Combine 2 lb (908 g) margarine, 2 T (14 g) cinnamon, ⅓ c (80 mL) corn syrup, ⅓ c (80 mL) water, and 2 lb 8 oz (1.14 kg) brown sugar. Cook over medium heat until margarine melts. Pour over chopped nuts, 1 lb 12 oz (794 g) per pan. Place rolls cut-side down on mixture.

9. **Sugared Snails.** Proceed as for Butterfly Rolls, rolling dough thinner before adding sugar filling. Cut rolled dough into slices ¾ in. thick. Dip cut surface of each roll in granulated sugar. Place on greased baking sheets ½ in. apart, with sugared side up. Allow to stand 10–15 minutes, then flatten before baking.

FRUIT COFFEE RINGS

Oven: 350°F (175°C)
Bake: 30 minutes
Yield: 8 rings

Metric	U.S.	Ingredient	Procedure
4.54 kg	10 lb (1 recipe)	Basic Roll Dough (p. 120) or Basic Sweet Roll Dough (p. 128)	Let dough rise until double in bulk. Divide dough into 1½-lb (680-g) portions. Roll out each portion into a rectangular strip 9 × 14 × ⅓ in.
1.89 L	2 qt	Filling (See below)	Spread each strip with 1 c (240 mL) filling. Roll as for cinnamon rolls. Arrange in ring mold or 10-in. tube pan. Cut slashes in dough with scissors about 1 in. apart. Let rise until double in bulk. Bake at 350°F (175°C) for 25–30 minutes. Brush with Powdered Sugar Glaze (p. 170).

Note: Nuts, raisins, or other fruits may be added to yeast dough and shaped in a variety of products (Figs. 2.10 and 2.11).

Suggested Fillings:
1. **Apricot Ring.** Use 2 qt (1.89 L) Apricot Filling (p. 172) or apricot preserves.
2. **Cranberry Ring.** Use 2 qt (1.89 L) Cranberry Filling (p. 172).
3. **Fig Ring.** Use 2 qt (1.89 L) Fig Filling (p. 172).
4. **Honey Ring.** Whip 1 lb (454 g) margarine or butter and 1 lb (454 g) honey until light and fluffy.
5. **Orange Ring.** Use 2 qt (1.89 L) orange marmalade.
6. **Prune–Date Ring.** Use 2 qt (1.89 L) Prune–Date Filling (p. 172).

FILLINGS OR TOPPINGS FOR COFFEE CAKE AND SWEET ROLLS

1. **Almond Filling.** Mix 1 lb (454 g) almond paste, 1 lb (454 g) sugar, 12 oz (340 g) margarine or butter, and 4 oz (114 g) flour. Add 2 eggs and beat until smooth.

2. **Butter Cinnamon Topping.** Cream 8 oz (227 g) butter or margarine, 1 lb (454 g) sugar, 3 T (21 g) cinnamon, and ½ t (3 g) salt. Add 4 beaten eggs and 3 oz (85 g) flour and blend.

3. **Butter Crunch Topping.** Blend 1 lb (454 g) sugar, 1 lb (454 g) butter or margarine, ½ t (3 g) salt, 3 oz (85 g) honey, and 2 lb (908 g) flour together to form a crumbly mixture.

4. **Crumb Topping.** Mix 8 oz (227 g) margarine or butter, 12 oz (340 g) sugar, ½ t cinnamon, and 12 oz (340 g) flour until crumbly. Add 4 oz (114 g) chopped nuts if desired.

Figure 2.10 Sweet roll or bread dough may be made into loaves and rolls in various shapes. Used by permission of Universal Foods, Red Star Yeast.

Figure 2.11 Nuts, raisins, or other fruits may be added to bread or sweet roll dough and shaped in a twist. Courtesy of Nabisco Brands, Inc., makers of Fleischman's Yeast.

Desserts

Cakes, Frostings, and Fillings

CAKES

Cakes may be classified according to two major types: butter or shortened cakes and foam or sponge cakes. A properly balanced formula, correct temperature of ingredients, accurate measurements, controlled mixing of ingredients, proper relationships of batter to pan, and correct oven temperature and baking time are essential to good cake making. Cake flour yields better volume and texture than all-purpose flour and was used in testing recipes in this section.

BUTTER OR SHORTENED CAKES

Butter or shortened cakes contain butter or other shortening and usually are leavened with baking powder or with baking soda and an acid. They may be mixed by one of the following methods:

Conventional Method of Mixing

1. Cream shortening and sugar on medium speed about 10 minutes, or until light and fluffy.
2. Add eggs and beat 3–5 minutes at high speed. Scrape down sides of bowl and beater.
3. Combine flour, leavening, and seasonings. Add alternately with the liquid to the creamed mixture.
4. Mix on low speed until thoroughly blended. Scrape down sides of bowl occasionally for even mixing.

Dough–Batter Method of Mixing

1. Cream flour, baking powder, and shortening on low speed for 2 minutes. Scrape bowl. Mix 3 minutes.
2. Add combined sugar, salt, and half the milk. Mix 2 minutes. Scrape bowl. Mix 3 minutes.

3. Combine egg, flavoring, and remaining milk. Add half to flour mixture. Mix 30 seconds. Scrape bowl. Mix 1 minute.
4. Add remaining egg mixture. Mix 1 minute. Scrape down bowl. Mix 2½ minutes.

This method requires less time and fewer utensils than the conventional method and yields a highly desirable product. See p. 144 for Plain Cake made by the dough-batter method.

Muffin Method of Mixing
1. Mix dry ingredients, including dry milk if used, in a mixer bowl.
2. Combine liquids (beaten eggs, milk or water, and melted shortening or oil).
3. Add liquids all at once to dry ingredients. Mix at low speed only enough to combine ingredients.

This method is quick and most successful when the cake is used soon after baking.

Pans for butter cakes should be greased and/or dusted with flour or lined with parchment paper. Sides of the pan should be left ungreased. A coating mixture may be prepared and brushed on the pans (p. 139).

Butter or shortened cakes usually are baked as sheet cakes because of ease of preparation and serving but may be baked in layers or as cup cakes. Layer cakes may be made by cutting 18 × 26-in. sheet cakes in half or layering 2 12 × 18-in. sheet cakes. (See Fig. 2.12 for layering and frosting a sheet cake.) Table 2.1 is a guide for scaling cake batter into various sizes of pans.

A variety of cakes may be made from a basic butter cake or white cake by using a variety of frostings and fillings. Suggested amounts are given in Table 2.2.

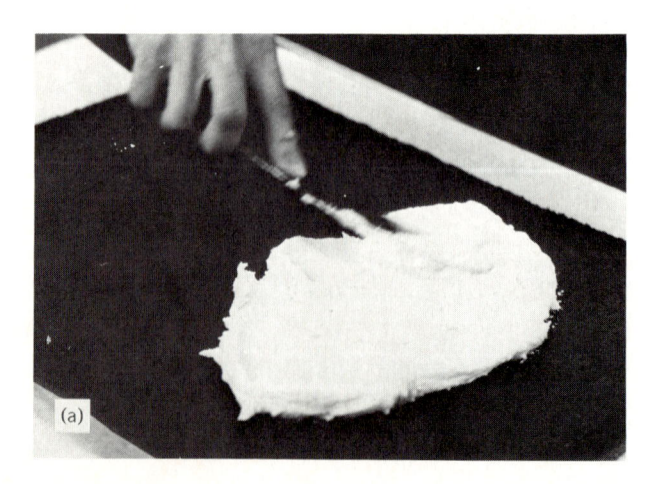

(a)

Figure 2.12 Layering and frosting a sheet cake. (a) Remove sheet cake from pan after loosening sides. Place top side down on inverted sheet pan. Spread frosting evenly over cake. (b) Carefully turn second cake onto frosted layer. (c) Remove parchment paper if used. (d) Frost top and sides of cake.

FOAM OR SPONGE CAKES

True sponge cakes are leavened chiefly by air incorporated in beaten eggs, although modified sponge cakes may have baking powder added. Foam cakes usually are baked in ungreased tube pans but may be baked in loaves. See Table 2.1 for batter weights.

Egg whites for angel food cakes should be at room temperature when beaten. Sugar is added gradually when whites are at the soft peak stage. Beating is continued until the whites are stiff but not dry. Flour and/or other ingredients are folded in carefully to minimize loss of air from the foam.

CAKE MIXES

Prepared cake mixes offer the food service a wide variety of products that can be produced with fewer and less skilled employees than cakes prepared "from scratch." However, care should be given to the selection of the mix, and the instructions for preparation should be carefully followed to assure high-quality products. The formulas in commercial mixes are balanced, and any deviation such as the substitution of milk for water or the addition of eggs can change the finished product. A dry cake mix may be prepared in the food service kitchen and stored for future use. The recipe for a master cake mix is given on p. 146.

FROSTINGS AND FILLINGS

The presentation of cakes may be varied by the use of different fillings and frostings. The amount to use will depend on the kind of cake to be frosted and the individual preferences of the patrons. Table 2.2 may serve as a guide.

TABLE 2.1 SCALING WEIGHTS AND YIELDS FOR CAKES

Pan Size	Approximate Weight per Pan	Yield	Type of Cake
12 × 18 × 2 in.	4–5 lb	5 × 6 (30 portions)	Butter, sheet
12 × 18 × 1 in.	2–2½ lb	6 × 8 (48 portions)	Butter, layer
12 × 18 × 1 in.	1¼–1½ lb	12 portions	Jelly roll
18 × 26 × 2 in.	8–10 lb	6 × 10 (60 portions)	Butter, sheet
9-in. round	20–32 oz	16 portions	Butter, layer
10-in. tube	28–40 oz	14 portions	Angel food, sponge
Cup cakes	1¾–2 oz each		Butter

Note: For metric equivalents, see Table 1.6.

TABLE 2.2 SCALING WEIGHTS FOR FROSTINGS AND FILLINGS

Pan Size	Approximate Weight per Pan
12 × 18 × 2 in.	3 c (1 lb 8 oz)
18 × 26 × 2 in.	1½ qt (3 lb)
9-in. layer	2 c (1 lb)
	¾ c in the middle
	1¼ c top and sides
10-in. tube	1½ c (12 oz)

Note: For metric equivalents see Tables 1.6 and 1.7.

CAKE RECIPES

COATING FOR BAKING PANS

Yield: 2 lb 12 oz (1.25 kg)

Metric	U.S.	Ingredient	Procedure
454 g	1 lb	Shortening	Mix shortening until creamy.
340 g	12 oz	Flour, all-purpose	Add flour gradually, whipping until smooth. Start on low mixer speed, then move to medium.
480 mL	2 c	Oil, cooking	Add oil very slowly and whip until light and frothy. Store at room temperature in tightly closed containers. Apply to pans with pastry brush. Use to grease cake pans or cookie sheets.

ANGEL FOOD CAKE

Oven: 350°F (175°C)
Bake: 50–55 minutes

Yield: 42 portions
3 10-in. cakes
Portion: 14 slices per cake

Amount		Ingredient	Procedure
Metric	U.S.		
1.14 kg (1.18 L)	2 lb 8 oz (5 c)	Egg whites, fresh or frozen, at room temperature	Beat on high speed for 1 minute, using whip attachment.
6 g 18 g	1 t 2 T	Salt Cream of tartar	Add salt and cream of tartar. Continue beating until egg whites are just stiff enough to hold shape.
680 g	1 lb 8 oz	Sugar, granulated	Add sugar slowly while beating on medium speed.
15 mL 5 mL	1 T 1 t	Vanilla Almond extract (optional)	Add flavorings. Continue beating on high speed for 2 minutes or until mixture will stand in stiff peaks.
340 g 340 g	12 oz 12 oz	Sugar, granulated Flour, cake	Mix sugar and flour. Sift 3 times. Gradually add to egg whites on low speed. Continue folding 2 minutes after last addition. Pour into 3 ungreased tube cake pans, 1 lb 12 oz (794 g) per pan. Bake at 350°F (175°C) for 50–55 minutes or at 400°F (205°C) for 35 minutes. Invert cake to cool.

Note: To mix by hand, remove bowl from machine and fold sugar–flour mixture into meringue with wire whip or spatula, adding 1 c (240 mL) at a time. Mix about 5 strokes after each addition.

Variations:
1. **Chocolate Angel Food Cake.** Substitute 1½ oz (43 g) cocoa for 1½ oz (43 g) flour.
2. **Frozen Filled Angel Food Cake.** Cut cake crosswise into 3 slices. Spread 1 pt (480 mL) softened strawberry ice cream on first layer and cover with cake slice. Spread second slice with 1 pt (480 mL) softened pistachio ice cream. Top with remaining slice. Frost top and sides with sweetened whipped cream (1 c/240 mL cream, 2 T/19 g powdered sugar, and ½ t/3 mL vanilla per cake). Cover with toasted coconut. Freeze. Remove from freezer 1 hour before serving. Other ice cream or sherbet may be used.
3. **Orange-Filled Angel Food Cake.** Cut cake crosswise into 3 slices. Spread Orange Filling (p. 174) between layers, and frost top and sides with Orange Frosting (p. 168).

YELLOW ANGEL FOOD (EGG YOLK SPONGE CAKE)

Oven: 350°F (175°C)
Bake: 30–45 minutes

Yield: 42 portions
3 10-in cakes
Portion: 14 per cake

Amount			
Metric	U.S.	Ingredient	Procedure
680 g	1 lb 8 oz (3 c)	Egg yolks	Beat egg yolks, using wire whip attachment.
480 mL	2 c	Water, boiling	Add water. Beat on high speed until light, about 5 minutes.
454 g	1 lb	Sugar, granulated	Sift sugar. Add to egg mixture gradually, beating on high speed while adding.
340 g 340 g	12 oz 12 oz	Flour, cake Sugar, granulated	Combine flour and sugar. Add on low speed to egg mixture.
284 g 21 g 6 g	10 oz 4½ t 1 t	Flour, cake Baking powder Salt	Mix flour, baking powder, and salt.
45 mL 15 mL	3 T 1 T	Lemon juice Lemon rind, grated	Gradually add on low speed dry ingredients alternately with lemon juice and rind to egg mixture.
15 mL 8 mL	1 T 1½ t	Vanilla Lemon extract	Add flavoring and continue mixing on low speed for 2 minutes. Pour into 3 ungreased tube cake pans, 1 lb 14 oz (850 g) per pan. Bake at 350°F (175°C) for 30–45 minutes. Immediately upon removal from oven, invert cakes to cool.

ORANGE CHIFFON CAKE

Oven: 350°F (175°C)
Bake: 45–50 minutes

Yield: 42 portions
3 10-in. cakes
Portion: 14 per cake

Metric	U.S.	Ingredient	Procedures
680 g	1 lb 8 oz	Flour, cake	Combine dry ingredients in mixer bowl. Blend for 10 seconds.
43 g	1½ oz (3 T)	Baking powder	
12 g	2 t	Salt	
539 g	1 lb 3 oz	Sugar, granulated	
454 g	1 lb (2 c)	Egg yolks, beaten	Combine egg yolks, salad oil, and water. Add to dry ingredients. Mix on medium speed until smooth.
360 mL	1½ c	Salad oil	
360 mL	1½ c	Water	
240 mL	1 c	Orange juice	Add orange juice and rind gradually. Mix well after each addition, but avoid overmixing.
12 g	2 T	Orange rind, grated	
567 g	1 lb 4 oz (2½ c)	Egg whites	Whip egg whites until foamy.
6 g	2 t	Cream of tartar	Add cream of tartar; continue beating until egg whites form soft peaks.
510 g	1 lb 2 oz	Sugar, granulated	Add sugar gradually and continue beating until very stiff. Fold gently into batter. Pour into 3 ungreased tube cake pans, 2 lb 8 oz (1.14 kg) per pan. Bake at 350°F (175°C) for 45–50 minutes. Immediately on removal from oven, invert cakes to cool.
1.42 L	1½ qt	Orange Frosting (p. 168)	When cake has cooled, remove from pan and frost.

Variations:
1. **Cocoa Chiffon Cake.** Omit orange juice and rind. Add 5 oz (142 g) cocoa to dry ingredients. Increase water to 2⅓ c (560 mL). Add 1 T (15 mL) vanilla.
2. **Walnut Chiffon Cake.** Omit orange juice and rind. Increase water to 2⅓ c (560 mL) and add 2 T (30 mL) vanilla and 12 oz (340 g) finely chopped walnuts. Frost with Burnt Butter Frosting (p. 165).

ORANGE CUPCAKES

Oven: 375°F (190°C)
Bake: 20–25 minutes
Yield: 4 doz

Amount Metric	U.S.	Ingredient	Procedure
198 g	7 oz	Raisins	Grind raisins. Set aside.
284 g	10 oz	Shortening	Cream shortening and sugar on medium speed for 10 minutes.
482 g	1 lb 1 oz	Sugar, granulated	
5 (227 g)	5 (8 oz)	Eggs	Add eggs and vanilla. Mix on medium speed until well blended.
15 mL	1 T	Vanilla	
3	3	Orange rinds, grated	Add orange rind and raisins to creamed mixture. Blend on low speed.
680 g	1 lb 8 oz	Flour, cake	Mix dry ingredients.
10 g	2¼ t	Baking soda	
43 g	1½ oz	Baking powder	
4 g	¾ t	Salt	
420 mL	1¾ c	Buttermilk	Add dry ingredients alternately with buttermilk on low speed to creamed mixture. Mix only until smooth. Measure with No. 30 dipper into greased muffin pans. Bake at 375°F (190°C) for 20–25 minutes.
170 g	6 oz	Sugar, granulated	Combine sugar and orange juice. While cakes are hot, brush with this mixture or frost with Orange Frosting (p. 168).
180 mL	¾ c	Orange juice	

Note: May be baked in loaves.

PLAIN CAKE

Oven: 350°F (175°C)
Bake: 40–45 minutes

Yield: 60 portions
2 pans 12 × 18 × 2 in.
Portion: 2½ × 3 in.

Amount		Ingredient	Procedure
Metric	U.S.		
1.05 kg	2 lb 5 oz	Flour, cake	Place flour, baking powder, and shortening in mixer bowl.
52 g	3¾ T	Baking powder	Mix on low speed 2 minutes, using flat beater.
454 g	1 lb	Shortening, hydrogenated	Scrape down bowl. Mix 3 minutes.
1.28 kg	2 lb 13 oz	Sugar, granulated	Combine sugar, salt, and milk. Add to flour mixture.
12 g	2 t	Salt	Mix on low speed 2 minutes.
480 mL	2 c	Milk	Scrape down bowl. Mix 3 minutes.
8 (397 g)	8 (14 oz)	Eggs	Combine eggs, milk, and vanilla.
600 mL	2½ c	Milk	Add half to flour mixture. Mix on low speed 30 seconds.
30 mL	2 T	Vanilla	Scrape down bowl. Mix 1 minute.
			Scrape down bowl. Mix 2½ minutes.
			Scale into 2 greased 12 × 18 × 2-in. baking pans, 4 lb 10 oz (2.1 kg) per pan.
			Bake at 350°F (175°C) 40–45 minutes.
			Cut 5 × 6.

Notes:
1. 4 oz (114 g) nonfat dry milk and 4½ c (1.06 L) water may be substituted for fluid milk. Add dry milk to flour mixture. Divide water as stated in recipe.
2. May be baked in 1 18 × 26 × 2-in. pan. Cut 6 × 10 for 60 portions.
3. For layer cakes, scale 1 lb 9 oz (709 g) batter into each of 6 9-in. layer cake pans.
4. For cupcakes, measure into muffin pans with No. 30 dipper. Yield 8½ doz.

Variations:
1. **Boston Cream Pie.** For 2 12 × 18-in. pies, scale batter into 4 pans, 2 lb 5 oz (1.05 kg) each. When baked, spread Custard Filling (p. 171) on 2 cakes, 3 lb 3 oz (1.45 kg) each. Place other cakes on top. Cover with Chocolate Glaze (p. 169) 1 lb (454 g) per cake. Cut 5 × 6.

    For 2 18 × 26-in. pies, scale 4 lb 10 oz (2.1 kg) into each of 2 pans. Use 6 lb 6 oz (2.89 kg) filling and 2 lb (908 g) Chocolate Glaze (p. 169). Cut 6 × 10.

    For 9-in. layers, scale batter into 8 pans, 1 lb 2 oz (510 g) per pan. Use ½ recipe Custard Filling (p. 171). Spread 1½ c (360 mL) on each of 4 layers. Use ½ recipe Chocolate Glaze (p. 169), spreading ½ c (120 mL) on each.

    Powdered sugar sifted over top of pies may be substituted for chocolate glaze.

2. **Cottage Pudding.** Cut cake into squares and serve with No. 20 dipper of fruit, lemon, nutmeg, or other sauce.

3. **Dutch Apple Cake.** After the cake batter is poured into baking pans, arrange 2½ lb (1.14 kg) pared sliced apples in rows over each pan. Sprinkle over top of each pan 4 oz (114 g) sugar and 1 t (2 g) cinnamon, mixed.

4. **Lazy Daisy Cake.** Mix 1 lb 2 oz (510 g) melted margarine or butter, 2 lb (908 g) brown sugar, 2 lb (908 g) coconut, and 1½ c (360 mL) half and half cream, or enough to moisten to consistency for spreading. Spread over baked cake, 3 lb (1.36 kg) per pan, and brown under broiler or in oven.

5. **Marble Cake.** Divide batter into 2 portions after mixing. To one portion add 3 T (27 g) cocoa, 3 t (6 g) cinnamon, and 1 t (2 g) nutmeg. Place batters alternately in cake pans; swirl with knife.

6. **Pineapple Upside Down Cake.** Mix 1 No. 10 can drained crushed pineapple (or tidbits), 8 oz (227 g) melted margarine or butter, 12 oz (340 g) brown sugar, and 8 oz (227 g) chopped nuts. Pour 4 lb 3 oz (1.9 kg) in each 12 × 18-in. pan. Pour cake batter over mixture. Apricots or peaches may be substituted for pineapple.

7. **Praline Cake.** Substitute chopped pecans for coconut in Lazy Daisy Cake.

MASTER CAKE MIX

Yield: 29 lb (13.15 kg) mix
7 cakes 12 × 18 × 2 in

Amount		Ingredient	Procedure
Metric	U.S.		
4.76 kg	10 lb 8 oz	Flour, cake	Mix flour, dry milk, baking powder, salt, and sugar on low speed 1 minute.
794 g	1 lb 12 oz	Nonfat dry milk	
227 g	8 oz	Baking powder, double acting	
57 g	2 oz	Salt	
2.38 kg	5 lb 4 oz	Sugar, granulated	
2.72 kg	6 lb	Sugar, granulated	Divide sugar into 2-lb (908-g) portions.
2.21 kg	4 lb 14 oz	Shortening, hydrogenated, emulsified	Cream shortening on medium speed using flat beater 3 minutes. Scrape down bowl and beater.
			Add 2 lb (908 g) sugar. Cream on medium speed 1 minute. Repeat until all sugar is added. Scrape down bowl and beater.
			Add 4 qt (3.79 L) blended dry ingredients. Mix on low speed 1 minute. Repeat once more. Lower bowl, add remaining dry ingredients. Blend on low speed 1 minute while slowly raising mixer bowl. Mix should resemble cornmeal in consistency. Store in tightly covered containers.

PLAIN CAKE (USING MASTER MIX)

Oven: 350°F (175°C)
Bake: 45 minutes
Yield: 60 portions
2 pans 12 × 18 × 2 in.
Portion: 2½ × 3 in.

Amount		Ingredient	Procedure
Metric	U.S.		
2.55 kg	5 lb 10 oz	Master Cake Mix (p. 146)	Place mix in mixer bowl. Add eggs, vanilla, and water. Mix on low speed 2 minutes. Scrape down bowl. Mix on medium speed 3 minutes. Scrape down bowl and beater.
9	9	Eggs, whole, frozen, or fresh	
(454 g)	(1 lb)		
20 mL	4 t	Vanilla	
480 mL	2 c	Water	
320 mL	1⅓ c	Water	Add water gradually, mixing on low speed 2 minutes. Scrape down bowl and mix on medium speed 1 minute. Scale batter into 2 lightly greased 12 × 18 × 2-in. baking pans, 4 lb (1.81 kg) per pan. Bake at 350°F (175°C) for 45 minutes. Cut 5 × 6.

Note: May be baked in 1 18 × 26 × 2-in. pan. Cut 6 × 10 for 60 portions.

Variations:
1. **Chocolate Cake.** Blend 5 oz (142 g) cocoa and 2 t (8 g) baking soda with mix.
2. **Spice Cake.** Blend 2 T (14 g) cinnamon, 1 T (8 g) nutmeg, 2 t (14 g) cloves, and 1½ t (3 g) allspice with cake mix.

See p. 115 for additional variations.

WHITE CAKE

Oven: 350°F (175°C)
Bake: 40–45 minutes
Yield: 60 portions
2 pans 12 × 18 × 2 in.
Portion: 2½ × 3 in.

Amount		Ingredient	Procedure
Metric	U.S.		
1.02 kg	2 lb 4 oz	Flour, cake	Mix flour, baking powder, and shortening on low speed for 2 minutes. Scrape down bowl. Mix 3 minutes.
43 g	1½ oz	Baking powder	
510 g	1 lb 2 oz	Shortening, hydrogenated	
1.02 kg	2 lb 4 oz	Sugar, granulated	Combine sugar, salt, and milk. Add to flour mixture. Mix on low speed 2 minutes. Scrape down bowl. Mix 3 minutes.
19 g	1 T	Salt	
480 mL	2 c	Milk	
12 (397 g)	12 (14 oz)	Egg whites	Combine egg whites, milk, and vanilla. Add half to mixture in bowl. Mix on low speed 30 seconds. Scrape down bowl. Mix 1 minute. Add remaining egg–milk mixture. Mix on low speed 1 minute. Scrape down bowl. Mix 2½ minutes. Scale into 2 greased 12 × 18 × 2-in. pans, 5 lb 7 oz (2.47 kg) per pan. Bake at 350°F (175°C) 40–45 minutes. Cut 5 × 6.
320 mL	1⅓ c	Milk	
30 mL	2 T	Vanilla	

Notes:
1. 3 oz (85 g) nonfat dry milk and 3⅓ c (800 mL) water may be substituted for fluid milk. Increase shortening to 1 lb 3 oz (539 g). Mix dry milk with flour.
2. May be baked in 1 18 × 26 × 2-in. pan. Cut 6 × 10 for 60 portions.
3. For 6 9-in. layer pans, scale 1 lb 6 oz (624 g) per pan.

Variations:
1. **Chocolate Chip Cake.** Add 12 oz (340 g) chocolate chips to batter.
2. **Coconut Lime Cake.** Scale into 6 9-in. layer cake pans. When baked, cool, then spread Lime Filling (p. 174) between layers. Frost with Fluffy Frosting (p. 165) or Ice Cream Frosting (p. 164). Sprinkle with toasted flaked coconut.
3. **Cup Cakes.** Use No. 20 dipper to portion into muffin pans or paper baking cups. Yield: 7 doz.
4. **Lady Baltimore Cake.** Bake cake in layers. Prepare 1 recipe Ice Cream Frosting (p. 164). To 1½ qt (1.42 L) frosting, add 1 t (5 mL) orange juice, 4 oz (114 g) macaroon crumbs, 5 oz (142 g) chopped almonds, and 6 oz (170 g) chopped raisins. Spread on bottom layers; place second layer on top and spread with filling. Frost tops and sides with remaining frosting.
5. **Poppy Seed Cake.** Add 6 oz (170 g) poppy seeds that have been soaked in part of the milk. Frost with Chocolate Frosting (p. 166).
6. **Silver White Cake.** Scale batter into 6 9-in. layer cake pans. When baked, cool then spread Lemon Filling (p. 174) between layers. Frost with Ice Cream Frosting (p. 164).
7. **Starburst Cake.** Bake in 2 12 × 18 × 2-in pans. While cake is warm, perforate top with a meat fork every half inch. Prepare 2 qt (1.89 L) flavored gelatin. Slowly pour 1 qt (0.95 L) over each cake. Cool and frost with Ice Cream Frosting (p. 164) or other white frosting.

BANANA CAKE

Oven: 350°F (175°C)
Bake: 25–30 minutes

Yield: 48 portions
3 2-layer cakes (9 in.)
Portion: 16 per cake

Amount Metric	U.S.	Ingredient	Procedure
454 g	1 lb	Shortening hydrogenated	Cream shortening, sugar, and vanilla on medium speed 10 minutes.
908 g	2 lb	Sugar, granulated	
15 mL	1 T	Vanilla	
908 g	2 lb (4 c)	Bananas, mashed	Add eggs and bananas to creamed mixture. Mix on medium speed 5 minutes.
8 (397 g)	8 (14 oz)	Eggs	
908 g	2 lb	Flour, cake	Combine dry ingredients.
7 g	1¼ t	Salt	
47 g	3⅓ T	Baking powder	
8 g	2 t	Baking soda	
240 mL	1 c	Buttermilk	Add dry ingredients alternately with buttermilk on low speed. Mix on medium speed 2–3 minutes. Scale into 6 greased 9-in. layer cake pans, 1 lb 6 oz (624 g) per pan. Bake at 350°F (175°C) 25–30 minutes. Cool. Remove from pans and frost. See Note 3 for suggested frostings.

Notes:
1. May be baked in 2 12 × 18 × 2-in. pans, scaled 4 lb 3 oz (1.9 kg) per pan. Cut 5 × 6.
2. For sheet cake, bake in 1 18 × 26 × 2-in. pan. Cut 6 × 10 for 60 portions.
3. Suggested frostings: Butter Cream Frosting (p. 167), Creamy Frosting (p. 167), or Cream Cheese Frosting (p. 167).

BURNT SUGAR CAKE

Oven: 375°F (190°C)
Bake: 35–40 minutes
Yield: 60 portions
2 pans 12 × 18 × 2 in.
Portion: 2½ × 3 in.

Amount			
Metric	U.S.	Ingredient	Procedure
454 g	1 lb	Shortening, hydrogenated	Cream shortening and sugar on medium speed for 10 minutes.
1.22 kg	2 lb 11 oz	Sugar, granulated	
8 (142 g)	8 (5 oz)	Egg yolks	Add egg yolks and mix 5 minutes.
480 mL	2 c	Milk	Combine liquids.
480 mL	2 c	Water	
160 mL	⅔ c	Burnt Sugar Syrup[a]	
20 mL	4 t	Vanilla	
964 g	2 lb 2 oz	Flour, cake	Combine dry ingredients. Add to creamed mixture alternately with liquids on low speed. Scrape down bowl. Mix 2 minutes.
38 g	2⅔ T	Baking powder	
7 g	1¼ t	Salt	
8 (255 g)	8 (9 oz)	Egg whites	Beat egg whites until they form soft peaks. Fold into batter on low speed. Pour into 2 greased 12 × 18 × 2-in. baking pans, 4 lb 8 oz (2.04 kg) per pan. Bake at 375°F (190°C) 35–40 minutes. Cool. Frost. See Note 2. Cut 5 × 6.

Notes:
1. May be baked in 1 18 × 26 × 2-in. pan; or in 8 9-in. layers, scaled 1 lb 2 oz (510 g) per pan.
2. Suggested frostings: Burnt Butter Frosting (p. 165), Butter Cream Frosting (p. 167), Cream Cheese Frosting (p. 167), Ice Cream Frosting (p. 164).

[a] **Burnt Sugar Syrup.** Place ⅓ c (80 mL) granulated sugar in pan and melt slowly, stirring constantly. Cook until light brown (caramelized), being careful not to scorch. Add ⅓ c (80 mL) boiling water. Cook slowly until a syrup is formed. For larger amounts, use 1 lb (454 g) sugar and 2 c (480 mL) boiling water.

CARROT CAKE

Oven: 325°F (165°C)
Bake: 45–60 minutes

Yield: 60 portions
2 pans 12 × 18 × 2 in.
Portion: 2½ × 3 in.

Amount		Ingredient	Procedure
Metric	U.S.		
1.08 kg	2 lb 6 oz	Sugar, granulated	Combine sugar, oil, and eggs.
600 mL	2½ c	Cooking oil	Beat 2 minutes on medium speed.
454 g	1 lb	Eggs	
794 g	1 lb 12 oz	Flour, all-purpose	Combine dry ingredients.
28 g	1 oz (1½ T)	Salt	Add to oil mixture and beat 1 minute.
19 g	⅔ oz (5 t)	Baking soda	
19 g	⅔ oz (3 T)	Cinnamon	
1.14 kg	2 lb 8 oz	Carrots, raw, grated	Add carrots and nuts. Mix until blended.
454 g	1 lb	Nuts, chopped	
			Pour batter into 2 12 × 18 × 2-in. pans, 5 lb (2.27 kg) per pan. Bake at 325°F (165°C) for 45–60 minutes. Cut 5 × 6.

Note: Frost with Cream Cheese Frosting (p. 167).

PINEAPPLE CASHEW CAKE

Oven: 350°F (175°C)
Bake: 25–30 minutes

Yield: 48 portions
3 2-layer cakes (9 in.)
Portion: 16 per cake

Amount			
Metric	U.S.	Ingredient	Procedure
510 g	1 lb 2 oz	Margarine or butter	Cream margarine, sugar, and vanilla on medium speed for 8 minutes.
850 g	1 lb 14 oz	Sugar, granulated	
15 mL	1 T	Vanilla	
10 (170 g)	10 (6 oz)	Egg yolks	Add egg yolks in 3 portions, while creaming. Mix 2 minutes.
850 g	1 lb 14 oz	Flour, cake	Combine flour, baking powder, and salt.
43 g	1½ oz	Baking powder	
8 g	1½ t	Salt	
540 mL	2¼ c	Milk	Add dry ingredients alternately with milk on low speed to creamed mixture.
454 g	1 lb	Pineapple, crushed, drained	Add pineapple. Mix on low speed only to blend.
10 (312 g)	10 (11 oz)	Egg whites	Beat egg whites on high speed until stiff but not dry. Fold into batter on low speed. Scale into 6 greased 9-in. layer cake pans, 1 lb 5 oz (595 g) per pan. Bake at 350°F (175°C) for 25–30 minutes.
1.89 L	2 qt	Pineapple Butter Frosting (p. 168)	When cool, remove from pans.
227 g	8 oz	Cashew nuts, toasted, coarsely chopped	Cover with frosting and sprinkle with toasted cashews.

Note: May be baked in 1 18 × 26 × 2-in. pan, cut 6 × 10 for 60 portions; or in 2 12 × 18 × 2-in. pans, scaled 4 lb (1.81 kg) per pan, and cut 5 × 6.

FUDGE CAKE

Oven: 350°F (175°C)
Bake: 25–30 minutes

Yield: 48 portions
      3 2-layer cakes (9 in.)
Portion: 16 per cake

Metric	U.S.	Ingredient	Procedure
340 g	12 oz	Shortening, hydrogenated	Cream shortening, sugar, and vanilla on medium speed for 10 minutes.
908 g	2 lb	Sugar, granulated	
15 mL	1 T	Vanilla	
6 (284 g)	6 (10 oz)	Eggs	Add eggs and mix on medium speed for 5 minutes.
142 g	5 oz	Cocoa	Mix cocoa and hot water.
360 mL	1½ c	Water, hot	
794 g	1 lb 12 oz	Flour, cake	Combine flour, salt, and soda.
6 g	1 t	Salt	
18 g	1½ T	Baking soda	
720 mL	3 c	Buttermilk	Add dry ingredients alternately with buttermilk and cocoa to creamed mixture on low speed. Scrape down bowl. Continue mixing until smooth and ingredients are mixed. Scale into 6 greased 9-in. layer cake pans, 1 lb 4 oz (567 g) per pan. Bake at 350°F (175°C) 25–30 minutes. Cool. Remove from pans and frost. See Note 2.

Notes:
1. For 12 × 18-in. layer cake, scale into 2 12 × 18 × 2-in. pans, 3 lb 13 oz (1.73 kg) per pan. When baked and cooled, frost one cake, then remove other cake from pan and place on top. Frost.
2. Suggested frosting: Chocolate Butter Cream Frosting (p. 166), Ice Cream Frosting (p. 164), Mocha Frosting (p. 169).

Variations:
1. **Chocolate Cup Cakes.** Portion with No. 20 dipper into muffin pans or paper liners. Yield: 5 doz.
2. **Chocolate Sheet Cake.** Bake in 1 18 × 26 × 2-in. baking pan. Cut 6 × 10 for 60 portions.

GERMAN SWEET CHOCOLATE CAKE

Oven: 350°F (175°C)
Bake: 40–45 minutes

Yield: 60 portions
2 pans 12 × 18 × 2 in.
Portion: 2½ × 3 in.

Amount Metric	U.S.	Ingredient	Procedure
284 g	10 oz	German sweet chocolate	Melt chocolate in water. Cool.
360 mL	1¼ c	Water, boiling	Add vanilla. Set aside.
13 mL	2½ t	Vanilla	
567 g	1 lb 4 oz	Shortening, hydrogenated	Cream shortening and sugar on medium speed for 10 minutes.
1.14 kg	2 lb 8 oz	Sugar, granulated	
10 (170 g)	10 (6 oz)	Egg yolks	Add egg yolks one at a time. Beat well after each addition. Add chocolate mixture and blend.
709 g	1 lb 9 oz	Flour, cake	Combine flour, salt, and soda.
7 g	1¼ t	Salt	
10 g	2½ t	Baking soda	
600 mL	2½ c	Buttermilk	Add dry ingredients alternately with buttermilk to creamed mixture. Mix on low speed until smooth. Scrape down bowl.
10 (312 g)	10 (11 oz)	Egg whites	Beat egg whites until stiff peaks form. Fold into batter on low speed. Do not overmix. Scale into 2 greased 12 × 18 × 2-in. baking pans, 4 lb 7 oz (2 kg) per pan. Bake at 350°F (175°C) for 40–45 minutes.
1.89 L	2 qt	Coconut Pecan Frosting (p. 166)	When cool, frost. Cut 5 × 6.

Notes:

1. May be baked in 1 18 × 26 × 2-in. pan. Cut 6 × 10 for 60 portions.
2. For 4 2-layer cakes, scale into 8 9-in. layer cake pans, 1 lb 1 oz (482 g) per pan. Cut 16 per cake for 64 portions.

CHOCOLATE ROLL

Oven: 325°F (165°C)
Bake: 20 minutes

Yield: 48 portions
4 pans 12 × 18 × 2 in.
Portion: 1-in. slices

Amount Metric	U.S.	Ingredient	Procedure
24 (397 g)	24 (14 oz)	Egg yolks	Beat yolks on high speed.
1.02 kg	2 lb 4 oz	Sugar, granulated	Add sugar and continue beating until mixture is lemon colored, thick, and fluffy.
340 g	12 oz	Chocolate, unsweetened, melted	Add chocolate and vanilla. Blend on low speed.
30 mL	2 T	Vanilla	
255 g	9 oz	Flour, cake	Combine flour, baking powder, and salt. Add to creamed mixture on low speed.
15 g	1 T	Baking powder	
9 g	1½ t	Salt	
24 (765 g)	24 (1 lb 11 oz)	Egg whites	Beat egg whites on high speed until they will form rounded peaks. Fold into cake mixture on low speed. Scale into 4 greased 12 × 18 × 2-in. pans lined with heavy waxed paper, 1 lb 7 oz (652 g) per pan. Bake at 325°F (165°C) for 20 minutes. When baked, remove from pans and quickly remove waxed paper. Trim edges if hard. Roll and let stand a few minutes. Unroll and spread with one of the fillings suggested below. Roll up securely. Cover with a thin layer of Chocolate Frosting (p. 169).

Note: Suggested fillings: Custard Filling (p. 171), Fluffy Frosting (p. 165), whipped cream, plain or flavored with peppermint.

Variation: **Ice Cream Roll.** Spread with a thick layer of softened vanilla ice cream. Roll up securely and wrap in waxed paper. Place in freezer for several hours before serving.

JELLY ROLL

Oven: 375°F (190°C)
Bake: 12 minutes

Yield: 48 portions
4 pans 12 × 18 × 2 in.
Portion: 1-in. slice

Metric	U.S.	Ingredient	Procedure
27 (1.36 kg)	27 (3 lb)	Eggs	Beat eggs on high speed for 1–2 minutes.
1.36 kg	3 lb	Sugar, granulated	Add sugar. Beat 10–15 minutes.
680 g 18 g 28 g 12 g	1 lb 8 oz 2 T 2 T 2 t	Flour, cake Cream of tartar Baking powder Salt	Mix dry ingredients. Fold on low speed into egg-sugar mixture.
15 mL	1 T	Vanilla	Add vanilla. Mix only to blend. Pour into 4 12 × 18 × 2-in. baking pans lined with heavy waxed paper, 1 lb 4 oz (567 g) per pan. Bake at 375°F (190°C) for 12 minutes. When baked, turn onto a cloth or heavy paper covered with powdered sugar (Fig. 2.13). Quickly remove waxed paper. Trim edges if hard. Immediately roll cakes tightly.
0.95 L 0.95 L	1 qt 1 qt	Jelly or Custard Filling (p. 171)	When cooled but not cold, unroll, spread with jelly or custard filling, 1 c (240 mL) per roll. Roll firmly and wrap with waxed paper until serving time.
454 g	1 lb	Sugar, powdered	Sprinkle top of each roll with 4 oz (114 g) powdered sugar. Slice each roll into 12 portions.

Note: May be baked in 2 18 × 26 × 1-in. pans, scaled 3 lb 12 oz (1.7 kg) per pan.

Variation: **Apricot Roll.** Cover cakes with Apricot Filling (p. 172) and roll. Cover outside with sweetened whipped cream or whipped topping and toasted coconut.

158 DESSERTS

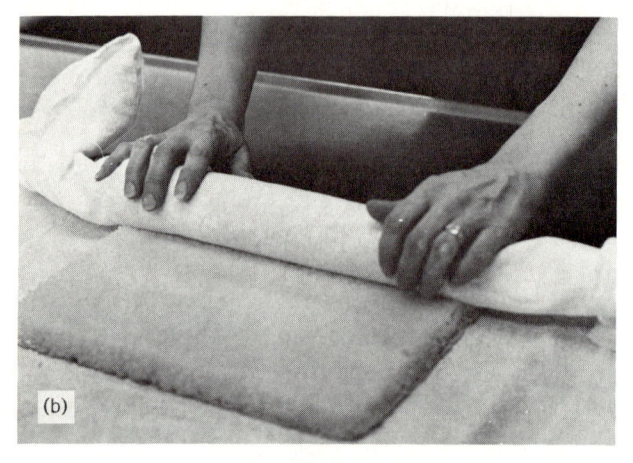

(a)

(b)

(c)

Figure 2.13 Rolling and filling Jelly Roll. (a) Turn baked cake onto a cloth sprinkled with powdered sugar. Remove waxed or parchment paper. (b) While still warm, roll tightly. (c) When cooled but not cold, unroll and spread with filling. (d) Roll firmly. (e) Sprinkle finished Jelly Roll with powdered sugar.

APPLESAUCE CAKE

Oven: 350°F (175°C)
Bake: 40–45 minutes

Yield: 60 portions
2 pans 12 × 18 × 2 in.
Portion: 2½ × 3 in.

Amount		Ingredient	Procedure
Metric	U.S.		
454 g	1 lb	Shortening, hydrogenated	Cream shortening and sugar on medium speed 10 minutes.
850 g	1 lb 14 oz	Sugar, granulated	
8 (397 g)	8 (14 oz)	Eggs	Add eggs to creamed mixture. Mix on medium speed 5 minutes.
794 g	1 lb 12 oz	Flour, cake	Combine dry ingredients.
35 g	2½ T	Baking powder	
10 g	1¾ t	Salt	
2 g	½ t	Baking soda	
5 g	2½ t	Cinnamon	
2 g	1 t	Cloves	
2 g	1 t	Nutmeg	
600 mL	2½ c	Water	Add dry ingredients alternately with water on low speed to creamed mixture.
600 mL	2½ c	Applesauce	Add remaining ingredients. Mix on low speed only to blend. Scale into 2 greased 12 × 18 × 2-in. baking pans, 5 lb (2.27 kg) per pan. Bake at 350°F (175°C) for 40–45 minutes. Cool and frost. See Note 3 for suggested frostings. Cut 5 × 6.
567 g	1 lb 4 oz	Raisins	
284 g	10 oz	Nuts, chopped	

Notes:
1. May be baked in 1 18 × 26 × 2-in. pan. Cut 6 × 10 for 60 portions.
2. This cake is too tender to bake in layers.
3. Suggested frostings: Ice Cream Frosting (p. 164), Fluffy Brown Sugar Frosting (p. 165), or Cream Cheese Frosting (p. 167).

FRUIT CAKE

Oven: 300°F (150°C)
Bake: 2½ hours

Yield: 64 portions
4 pans 5 × 9 in.
Portion: ½-in. slice

Amount		Ingredient	Procedure
Metric	U.S.		
227 g	8 oz	Shortening, hydrogenated	Cream shortening and sugar on medium speed for 8 minutes.
454 g	1 lb	Sugar, granulated	
4 (198 g)	4 (7 oz)	Eggs	Add eggs. Mix 5 minutes.
227 g	8 oz	Jelly	Add ingredients in order listed. Mix on low speed only until fruit is coated with flour mixture.
4 g	2 t	Cinnamon	
4 g	2 t	Cloves	
908 g	2 lb	Raisins	
454 g	1 lb	Currants	
454 g	1 lb	Dates, chopped	
227 g	8 oz	Nuts, chopped	
567 g	1 lb 4 oz	Flour, cake	
8 g	2 t	Baking soda	Dissolve soda in cold coffee. Add to other ingredients and mix until blended. Scale into 4 5 × 9-in. loaf pans lined with 2 layers of heavy waxed paper, 2 lb 3 oz (992 g) per pan. Bake at 300°F (150°C) for 2½ hours. Cut 16 slices per cake.
360 mL	1½ c	Coffee, brewed, cold	

Notes:
1. May be steamed for 4 hours.
2. Store in a container with a tight cover. Most fruit cakes mellow in flavor if kept about 2 weeks before using.

GINGERBREAD

Oven: 350°F (175°C)
Bake: 40 minutes

Yield: 60 portions
2 pans 12 × 18 × 2 in.
Portion: 2½ × 3 in.

Amount Metric	U.S.	Ingredient	Procedure
397 g	14 oz	Shortening, hydrogenated	Cream shortening and sugar on medium speed 10 minutes.
397 g	14 oz	Sugar, granulated	
840 mL	3½ c	Molasses or sorghum	Add molasses and mix on low speed until blended.
1.02 kg	2 lb 4 oz	Flour, cake	Combine dry ingredients.
24 g	2 T	Baking soda	
9 g	1½ t	Salt	
7 g	1 T	Cinnamon	
7 g	1 T	Cloves	
7 g	1 T	Ginger	
900 mL	3¾ c	Water, hot	Add dry ingredients alternately with water to creamed mixture.
7 (340 g)	7 (12 oz)	Eggs, beaten	Add eggs and mix on low speed 2 minutes. Scale into 2 greased 12 × 18 × 2-in. baking pans 4 lb 3 oz (1.9 kg) per pan. Bake at 350°F (175°C) for 40 minutes. Cut 5 × 6.

Notes:
1. May be baked in 1 18 × 26 × 2-in. pan. Cut 6 × 10 for 60 portions.
2. Sprinkle with powdered sugar and serve warm or serve with Lemon Sauce (p. 490).

Variations:
1. **Almond Meringue Gingerbread.** Cover baked gingerbread with meringue (p. 204). Sprinkle with almonds and brown in 375°F (190°C) oven.
2. **Ginger Muffins.** Measure into greased muffin pans with No. 20 dipper. Yield: 7 doz.
3. **Praline Gingerbread.** Combine 1 lb (454 g) margarine or butter, melted, 2 lb (908 g) brown sugar, 2 lb (908 g) chopped pecans, and 1½–2 c (360–480 mL) cream. Spread 2 lb 12 oz (794 g) mixture over each pan. Brown under broiler, or return to oven and heat until topping is slightly browned.

FROSTING AND FILLING RECIPES

BOILED FROSTING

Yield: 2 qt (1.89 L)

Amount Metric	Amount U.S.	Ingredient	Procedure
908 g 300 mL	2 lb 1¼ c	Sugar, granulated Water, hot	Combine sugar and water. Stir until sugar is dissolved. Boil without stirring to soft ball state (238°F/114°C).
4 (114 g)	4 (4 oz)	Egg whites	Beat egg whites on high speed until stiff but not dry.
15 mL	1 T	Vanilla	Gradually pour syrup over egg whites while beating. Continue beating until frosting is of consistency to spread. Add vanilla. Spread on cake at once.

Variations: See variations of Ice Cream Frosting, p. 164.

ICE CREAM FROSTING

Yield: 2½ qt (2.37 L)

Amount		Ingredient	Procedure
Metric	U.S.		
680 g	1 lb 8 oz	Sugar, granulated	Combine sugar and water. Boil without stirring to soft ball stage (238°F/ 114°C).
240 mL	1 c	Water, hot	
9 (284 g)	9 (10 oz)	Egg whites	Beat egg whites until frothy.
85 g	3 oz	Sugar, powdered, sifted	Add powdered sugar and beat on high speed to consistency of meringue. Add hot syrup slowly and continue beating until mixture is thick and creamy.
227 g	8 oz	Sugar, powdered, sifted	Add powdered sugar and vanilla. Beat until smooth. Add more sugar if necessary to make frosting hold its shape when spread.
15 mL	1 T	Vanilla	

Note: This frosting can be kept several days in a covered container in the refrigerator.

Variations:
1. **Bittersweet Frosting.** Melt 8 oz (227 g) bitter chocolate over water, gradually stir in 1½ oz (43 g) margarine or butter. When slightly cool, pour over white frosting to form a design.
2. **Candied Fruit Frosting.** Add 8 oz (227 g) chopped candied fruit.
3. **Chocolate Frosting.** Add 8 oz (227 g) melted chocolate.
4. **Coconut Frosting.** Frost cake, sprinkle with 4 oz (114 g) dry shredded coconut.
5. **Maple Nut Frosting.** Flavor with maple favoring; add 6 oz (170 g) chopped nuts.
6. **Maraschino Cherry Frosting.** Add 8 oz (227 g) chopped maraschino cherries.
7. **Peppermint Frosting.** Add 8 oz (227 g) finely crushed peppermint candy.

FLUFFY FROSTING

Yield: 2 qt (1.89 L)

Metric	U.S.	Ingredient	Procedure
567 g	1 lb 4 oz	Sugar, granulated	Boil sugar, water, syrup, and salt until mixture reaches the soft ball stage (238°F/114°C).
180 mL	¾ c	Water	
37 mL	2½ T	Corn syrup, white	
1 g	⅛ t	Salt	
5 (170 g)	5 (6 oz)	Egg whites	Beat egg whites on high speed until stiff but not dry.
8 mL	1½ t	Vanilla	Gradually add half of the hot syrup to egg whites, beating constantly. Cook remaining half of syrup until it forms a hard ball (250°F/121°C). Gradually add to first mixture. Beat on high speed until it holds its shape. Add vanilla.

Variation: **Fluffy Brown Sugar Frosting.** Substitute brown sugar for granulated sugar.

BURNT BUTTER FROSTING

Yield: 1¼ qt (1.18 L)

Metric	U.S.	Ingredient	Procedure
255 g	9 oz	Butter or margarine	Heat butter until golden brown.
680 g	1 lb 8 oz	Sugar, powdered	Add sugar to butter and blend.
15 mL	1 T	Vanilla	Add vanilla and water. Beat until of spreading consistency. Add more water if necessary.
120 mL	½ c	Water, hot	

Note: This amount will frost 8 doz 1½-in. cookies. If used for cake, increase by ¼.

CHOCOLATE BUTTER CREAM FROSTING

Yield: 2 qt (1.89 L)

Metric	U.S.	Ingredient	Procedure
680 g	1 lb 8 oz	Margarine or butter, soft	Cream margarine on medium speed until fluffy.
120 mL	½ c	Evaporated milk	Add milk and blend.
680 g	1 lb 8 oz	Sugar, powdered, sifted	Add sugar gradually. Mix on medium speed until smooth.
170 g	6 oz	Chocolate, unsweetened, melted	Add chocolate and vanilla. Beat on high speed until light and fluffy.
5 mL	1 t	Vanilla	

Note: Milk may be substituted for evaporated milk.

COCONUT–PECAN FROSTING

Yield: 2 qt (1.89 L)

Metric	U.S.	Ingredient	Procedure
480 mL	2 c	Evaporated milk	Combine milk, sugar, and margarine. Cook over hot water or in steam jacketed kettle until thickened.
454 g	1 lb	Sugar, granulated	
227 g	8 oz	Margarine or butter	
6 (114 g)	6 (4 oz)	Egg yolks	Beat egg yolks. Stir small amount of hot mixture into yolks, then stir into rest of hot mixture. Return to boiling point, stirring constantly. Turn off heat.
340 g	12 oz	Pecans, finely chopped	Add pecans, coconut, and vanilla. Cool, then beat well until thick enough to spread.
340 g	12 oz	Coconut, flaked	
10 mL	2 t	Vanilla	

CREAM CHEESE FROSTING

Yield: 1½ qt (1.42 L)

Amount		Ingredient	Procedure
Metric	U.S.		
2 227-g pkg	2 8-oz pkg	Cream cheese, softened	Blend cream cheese, margarine, and milk on medium speed until smooth.
85 g	3 oz	Margarine or butter	
60 mL	¼ c	Milk	
1.14 kg	2 lb 8 oz	Sugar, powdered, sifted	Add sugar gradually. Add vanilla. Beat until smooth and of spreading consistency.
15 mL	1 T	Vanilla	

Variation: **Orange Cheese Frosting.** Substitute 1 T (15 mL) orange juice and 1 T (15 mL) grated orange rind for vanilla.

CREAMY FROSTING

Yield: 1½ qt (1.42 L)

Amount		Ingredient	Procedure
Metric	U.S.		
340 g	12 oz	Margarine or butter	Cream margarine on medium speed 1 minute or until soft.
120 mL	½ c	Evaporated milk	Add remaining ingredients gradually. Whip on medium speed until mixture is smooth and creamy.
15 mL	1 T	Vanilla	
1.14 kg	2 lb 8 oz	Sugar, powdered, sifted	
12 g	2 t	Salt	

Note: Milk or cream may be substituted for evaporated milk.

Variations:
1. **Cocoa Frosting.** Increase liquid to 1¼ c (300 mL). Add 6 oz (170 g) cocoa sifted with the sugar.
2. **Lemon Butter Frosting.** Substitute ¼ c (60 mL) lemon juice for an equal amount of milk, and 1½ T (23 mL) grated lemon rind for the vanilla.
3. **Mocha Frosting.** Substitute cold coffee for liquid. Add 6 oz (170 g) cocoa sifted with the sugar.
4. **Orange Butter Frosting.** Substitute ½ c (120 mL) orange juice for an equal amount of milk, and 1 T (23 mL) grated orange rind for the vanilla.

ORANGE FROSTING

Yield: 1½ qt (1.42 L)

Amount Metric	U.S.	Ingredient	Procedure
227 g	8 oz	Margarine or butter	Cream margarine until fluffy.
1.14 kg	2 lb 8 oz	Sugar, powdered, sifted	Add sugar gradually on medium speed. Mix until creamy.
30 mL	2 T	Vanilla	Add remaining ingredients. Blend until smooth.
3 g	½ t	Salt	
60 mL	¼ c	Orange juice	
60 mL	¼ c	Lemon juice	
2 g	1 t	Orange rind, grated	

PINEAPPLE BUTTER FROSTING

Yield: 2½ qt (2.37 L)

Amount Metric	U.S.	Ingredient	Procedure
680 g	1 lb 8 oz	Margarine or butter	Mix margarine, sugar, and salt on medium speed until creamy.
1.36 kg	3 lb	Sugar, powdered	
3 g	½ t	Salt	
3 (57 g)	3 (2 oz)	Egg yolks	Add egg yolks. Whip on high speed until light and fluffy.
454 g	1 lb	Crushed pineapple	Drain pineapple. Add to creamed mixture. Blend on low speed. Refrigerate until ready to use.

Note: Use for Pineapple Cashew Cake (p. 153).

MOCHA FROSTING

Yield: 2 qt (1.89 L)

Amount			
Metric	U.S.	Ingredient	Procedure
360 mL	1½ c	Hot coffee, strong	Add coffee to margarine and cocoa. Mix on medium speed until blended.
85 g	3 oz	Margarine or butter, soft	
114 g	4 oz	Cocoa	
1.36 kg	3 lb	Sugar, powdered, sifted	Add sugar, salt, and vanilla. Mix until smooth. Add more sugar if necessary to make frosting hold its shape when spread.
3 mL	½ t	Salt	
3 mL	½ t	Vanilla	

Note: Instant coffee, 2 T (30 mL) dissolved in 1½ c (360 mL) hot water, may be used in place of brewed coffee.

CHOCOLATE GLAZE

Yield: 1 qt (0.95 L)

Amount			
Metric	U.S.	Ingredient	Procedure
114 g	4 oz	Chocolate, unsweetened	Melt chocolate and margarine over low heat.
85 g	3 oz	Margarine or butter	
595 g	1 lb 5 oz	Sugar, powdered, sifted	Gradually add sugar, vanilla, and boiling water. Beat until smooth. If needed, add a few drops boiling water to make spreading consistency.
15 mL	1 T	Vanilla	
120 mL	½ c	Water, boiling	

POWDERED SUGAR GLAZE

Yield: 1 qt (0.95 L)

Amount Metric	U.S.	Ingredient	Procedure
908 g	2 lb	Sugar, powdered, sifted	Gradually add water to sugar.
180 mL	¾ c	Water, boiling	Add vanilla. Beat until smooth.
10 mL	2 t	Vanilla	Thin, if necessary, to spread.

Note: Use for frosting baked rolls or products requiring a thin frosting.

ORNAMENTAL FROSTING

Yield: 1 qt (0.95 L)

Amount Metric	U.S.	Ingredient	Procedure
8 (255 g)	8 (9 oz)	Egg whites	Beat egg whites on high speed until stiff but not dry.
680 g	1 lb 8 oz	Sugar, powdered, sifted	Add sugar while mixing on low speed. Beat on high speed to consistency of heavy cream if used for frosting. If used for decorating with a pastry tube, beat until it will retain its shape when drawn to a point.

Notes:
1. This frosting dries quickly when exposed to air and should be covered with a damp cloth.
2. A teaspoon of lemon juice or vanilla may be added for flavoring if desired.

FROSTING AND FILLING RECIPES   **171**

CHOCOLATE CREAM FILLING

Yield: 3 qt (2.84 L)

Amount		Ingredient	Procedure
Metric	U.S.		
1.02 kg	2 lb 4 oz (3 12-oz pkg)	Chocolate chips	Combine chocolate chips, orange juice, and sugar.
240 mL	1 c	Orange juice or water	Melt over hot water.
227 g	8 oz	Sugar, granulated	Cool.
1.42 L	1½ qt	Cream, whipping	Whip cream until stiff. Fold into chocolate mixture.

Note: Use as filling for Orange Cream Puffs (p. 240).

Variation: **Chocolate Mousse.** Whip 10 egg whites to a soft peak and fold into chocolate–whipped cream mixture. Chill. May be frozen.

CUSTARD FILLING

Yield: 3 qt (6 lb/2.72 kg)

Amount		Ingredient	Procedure
Metric	U.S.		
170 g	6 oz	Cornstarch	Combine dry ingredients.
454 g	1 lb	Sugar, granulated	
3 g	½ t	Salt	
480 mL	2 c	Milk, cold	Add cold milk and stir until smooth.
2.37 L	2½ qt	Milk, hot	Add cold mixture to hot milk, stirring constantly. Cook over hot water until thick.
10 (454 g)	10 (1 lb)	Eggs	Beat eggs. Add gradually to thickened mixture. Cook 7 minutes.
10 mL	2 t	Vanilla	Remove from heat. Add vanilla. Cool.

Notes:
1. Use as a filling for cakes, Cream Puffs (p. 240), Chocolate Roll (p. 156), and Eclairs (p. 240).
2. To fill 3 9-in. layer cakes, use ⅓ recipe.

CRANBERRY FILLING

Yield: 2 qt (1.89 L)

Amount Metric	U.S.	Ingredient	Procedure
680 g	1 lb 8 oz	Cranberry Relish (p. 431)	Make relish.
1 No. 2 can 227 g 28 g	1 No. 2 can 8 oz ¼ c	Crushed pineapple Sugar, granulated Flour, all-purpose	Add pineapple, sugar, and flour. Cook until thick.
28 g	1 oz	Margarine or butter	Add margarine. Stir until blended.

Note: Use as filling for Cranberry Ring (p. 131).

FIG FILLING

Yield: 2 qt (1.89 L)

Amount Metric	U.S.	Ingredient	Procedure
908 g 480 mL	2 lb 2 c	Figs, dried Water	Chop figs and soak in water, then cook together.
454 g 114 g 3 g 240 mL	1 lb 4 oz ½ t 1 c	Sugar, granulated Flour, all-purpose Salt Lemon juice	Add sugar, flour, salt, and lemon juice. Cook to a paste.
454 g	1 lb	Margarine or butter	Blend margarine into hot mixture.

Variations:
1. **Apricot Filling.** Substitute 2 lb (908 g) dried apricots, cooked and chopped, for the figs. Reduce lemon juice to ½ c (120 mL).
2. **Prune–Date Filling.** Substitute 1 lb (454 g) cooked, pitted, and chopped prunes and 1 lb (454 g) chopped dates for the figs.

PRUNE FILLING

Yield: 1 qt (0.95 L)

Amount		Ingredient	Procedure
Metric	U.S.		
480 mL	2 c	Prunes, cooked, pitted, chopped	Add cream, margarine, and eggs to prunes.
240 mL	1 c	Cream, cultured sour	Heat over hot water.
57 g	2 oz	Margarine or butter	
4	4	Eggs, beaten	
(198 g)	(7 oz)		
454 g	1 lb	Sugar, granulated	Mix dry ingredients. Add to prune mixture.
3 g	½ t	Salt	
28 g	1 oz (¼ c)	Flour, all-purpose	Cook and stir over hot water until thick. Cool.

Note: 8 oz (227 g) chopped nuts may be added.

Variation: **Apricot Filling.** Substitute dried apricots for prunes.

DATE FILLING

Yield: 1½ qt (1.42 L)

Amount		Ingredient	Procedure
Metric	U.S.		
908 g	2 lb	Dates, pitted, chopped	Combine dates, water, and sugar. Cook until mixture is thick. Cool.
540 mL	2¼ c	Water	
340 g	12 oz	Sugar, granulated	Use as cake or cookie filling.

Note: 6 oz (170 g) jelly or ¼ c (60 mL) orange juice may be used in place of ¼ c (60 mL) of the water.

LEMON FILLING

Yield: 1 qt (0.95 L)

Metric	U.S.	Ingredient	Procedure
454 g 720 mL	1 lb 3 c	Sugar, granulated Water	Heat sugar and water to boiling point.
70 g 180 mL	2½ oz ¾ c	Cornstarch Water, cold	Blend cornstarch and cold water. Gradually add to boiling sugar and water. Cook until thickened and clear, stirring constantly.
4 (85 g)	4 (3 oz)	Egg yolks	Beat egg yolks. Blend into hot mixture. Cook 5–8 minutes while stirring.
4 g 4 g 120 mL 28 g	¾ t 2 t ½ c 1 oz (2 T)	Salt Lemon rind, grated Lemon juice Margarine or butter	Add remaining ingredients. Stir to blend. Cool.

Variations:
1. **Lime Filling.** Substitute fresh lime juice and rind for lemon juice and rind. Add a few drops of green food coloring.
2. **Orange Filling.** Substitute orange juice for water and orange rind for lemon rind. Reduce lemon juice to 3 T (45 mL).

Cookies

Cookies may be drop or bar cookies, made from a soft dough; or rolled, refrigerator, pressed, or molded cookies, made from a stiff dough. Almost all cookie dough may be made and stored in the refrigerator or freezer and used as needed.

Yields for drop cookie recipes in this section are calculated using a No. 40 dipper (Fig. 2.14). For a smaller cookie, use a No. 60 dipper. For jumbo-size cookies, use a No. 20 dipper. A smaller, tea-size cookie may be made with a No. 70 or No. 100 dipper or by dropping dough from the end of a teaspoon. Refrigerator cookies may be sliced with a meat slicer if they have been well chilled.

Bar cookies usually are baked on greased or silicone paper-lined 18 × 26 × 1-in. baking sheets or 12 × 18 × 2-in. pans. The 12 × 18-in. pans yield 30 2½ × 3-in. bars by cutting 5 × 6. The 18 × 26-in. pans may be cut 6 × 10 to yield 60 3 × 2-in. bars or 8 × 12 for 96 cookies.

Figure 2.14 Portioning cookie dough. Spacing on sheet pan will depend on type of cookie dough, size of cookie, and amount the dough will spread while baking.

COOKIE RECIPES

BUTTER TEA COOKIES

Oven: 375°F (190°C)
Bake: 10–12 minutes
Yield: 10 doz cookies

Metric	U.S.	Ingredient	Procedure
454 g	1 lb	Butter	Cream butter and sugar on medium speed for 5 minutes.
255 g	9 oz	Sugar, granulated	
6 (114 g)	6 (4 oz)	Egg yolks	Add egg yolks and vanilla. Mix on medium speed until blended.
15 mL	1 t	Vanilla	
567 g	1 lb 4 oz	Flour, all-purpose	Add flour and mix on low speed. Chill dough. Shape with cookie press onto ungreased baking sheets. Bake at 375°F (190°C) for 10–12 minutes.

Variation: **Thimble Cookies.** Roll dough into 1-in. balls. Dip in egg white and roll in finely chopped pecans. Bake 3 minutes at 325°F (150°C), then make indentation in center of cookies and fill with jelly. Bake 10–12 minutes longer.

BUTTERSCOTCH DROP COOKIES

Oven: 375°F (190°C)
Bake: 10–15 minutes
Yield: 8 doz cookies

Amount Metric	U.S.	Ingredient	Procedure
227 g	8 oz	Margarine or butter	Cream margarine and brown sugar on medium speed for 5 minutes.
454 g	1 lb	Sugar, brown	
4 (198 g)	4 (7 oz)	Eggs	Add eggs and vanilla. Mix on medium speed until well blended.
10 mL	2 t	Vanilla	
567 g	1 lb 4 oz	Flour, all-purpose	Combine dry ingredients.
5 g	1 t	Baking powder	
8 g	2 t	Baking soda	
6 g	1 t	Salt	
454 g	1 lb	Cultured sour cream	Add dry ingredients alternately with sour cream. Mix on low speed until blended.
227 g	8 oz	Walnuts, chopped	Add nuts. Mix until blended. Chill dough until firm. Drop on greased baking sheets with No. 40 dipper, ¾ oz (21 g) per cookie. Bake at 375°F (190°C) for 10–15 minutes. Cover with Burnt Butter Frosting (p. 165) while still warm.

Variations:

1. **Butterscotch Squares.** Spread batter in 12 × 18 × 2-in. pan. Bake at 325°F (165°C) for 25 minutes.
2. **Chocolate Drop Cookies.** Add 4 oz (114 g) chocolate, melted, to creamed mixture.

BUTTERSCOTCH REFRIGERATOR COOKIES

Oven: 375°F (190°C)
Bake: 8–10 minutes
Yield: 8 doz cookies

Amount Metric	U.S.	Ingredient	Procedure
227 g	8 oz	Margarine or butter	Cream fats and sugar on medium speed for 5 minutes.
227 g	8 oz	Shortening	
340 g	12 oz	Sugar, granulated	
454 g	1 lb	Sugar, brown	
4 (198 g)	4 (7 oz)	Eggs	Add eggs and vanilla. Mix on medium speed for 5 minutes.
10 mL	2 t	Vanilla	
908 g	2 lb	Flour, all-purpose	Combine dry ingredients.
6 g	2 t	Cream of tartar	
8 g	2 t	Baking soda	
227 g	8 oz	Dates, finely chopped	Add combined dry ingredients, dates and nuts. Mix on low speed until well blended. Place dough on waxed paper. Form into 3 2-lb (908-g) rolls, 2 in. in diameter. Wrap. Chill several hours. Slice cookies 1/8 in. thick. Place on ungreased baking sheets. Bake at 375°F (190°C) for 8–10 minutes.
227 g	8 oz	Nuts, chopped	

BUTTERSCOTCH PECAN COOKIES

Oven: 375°F (190°C)
Bake: 10–12 minutes
Yield: 10 doz cookies

Amount Metric	U.S.	Ingredient	Procedure
454 g	1 lb	Margarine or butter	Cream margarine and sugar on medium speed for 5 minutes.
908 g	2 lb	Sugar, brown	
4 (198 g)	4 (7 oz)	Eggs	Add eggs and vanilla. Mix on medium speed until well blended.
15 mL	1 T	Vanilla	
680 g	1 lb 8 oz	Flour, all-purpose	Add flour and pecans. Mix on low speed until blended. Drop onto greased baking sheets with No. 40 dipper, ¾ oz (21 g) per cookie. Bake at 375°F (190°C) 10–12 minutes.
454 g	1 lb	Pecans, chopped	

COCONUT MACAROONS

Oven: 325°F (165°C)
Bake: 15 minutes
Yield: 9 doz cookies

Amount Metric	U.S.	Ingredient	Procedure
8 (255 g)	8 (9 oz)	Egg whites	Beat egg whites and salt on high speed until foamy.
⅛ t	⅛ t	Salt	
340 g	12 oz	Sugar, granulated	Add sugars gradually. Add vanilla. Continue beating on high speed until stiff.
340 g	12 oz	Sugar, powdered	
10 mL	2 t	Vanilla	
624 g	1 lb 6 oz	Coconut, shredded	Carefully fold in coconut on low speed. Drop onto greased baking sheets with No. 60 dipper, ½ oz (14 g) each. Bake at 325°F (165°C) for 15 minutes.

CHOCOLATE CHIP COOKIES

Oven: 375°F (190°C) Yield: 10 doz cookies
Bake: 10−12 minutes

Amount		Ingredient	Procedure
Metric	*U.S.*		
340 g	12 oz	Margarine or butter	Cream margarine and
227 g	8 oz	Sugar, granulated	sugar on medium
227 g	8 oz	Sugar, brown	speed for 5 minutes or until sugars are dissolved.
4	4	Eggs	Add eggs and vanilla.
(198 g)	(7 oz)		beat until light and
10 mL	2 t	Vanilla	fluffy.
567 g	1 lb 4 oz	Flour, all-purpose	Combine dry ingredients.
12 g	2 t	Salt	Add on low speed to
8 g	2 t	Baking soda	creamed mixture.
454 g	1 lb	Nuts, coarsely chopped	Add nuts and chocolate chips. Mix until blended.
680 g	1 lb 8 oz	Chocolate chips	Drop on greased baking sheets with No. 40 dipper, ¾ oz (21 g) per cookie. Bake at 375°F (190°C) for 10−12 minutes.

Note: For jumbo cookies, use No. 20 dipper. Bake at 365°F (182°C) for 12−15 minutes.

CHOCOLATE TEA COOKIES

Oven: 350°F (175°C)
Bake: 6–10 minutes
Yield: 10 doz cookies

Metric	U.S.	Ingredient	Procedure
454 g	1 lb	Margarine or butter	Cream margarine and sugar on medium speed for 5 minutes.
340 g	12 oz	Sugar, granulated	
2 (114 g)	2 (4 oz)	Eggs	Add eggs and vanilla. Blend on medium speed for 5 minutes.
15 mL	1 T	Vanilla	
510 g	1 lb 2 oz	Flour, all-purpose	Combine dry ingredients. Add to creamed mixture and mix on low speed until blended. Chill dough. Shape with cookie press onto ungreased baking sheets. Bake at 350°F (175°C) for 6–10 minutes.
2 g	¼ t	Salt	
5 g	1 t	Baking powder	
28 g	1 oz (¼ c)	Cocoa	

CRISP GINGER COOKIES

Oven: 375°F (190°C)
Bake: 8–10 minutes
Yield: 8 doz cookies

Metric	U.S.	Ingredient	Procedure
240 mL	1 c	Molasses	Combine molasses and sugar. Boil 1 minute. Cool.
227 g	8 oz	Sugar, granulated	
227 g	8 oz	Shortening	Add shortening. Blend on medium speed.
2 (114 g)	2 (4 oz)	Eggs	Add eggs and mix well.
794 g	1 lb 12 oz (or more)	Flour, all-purpose	Combine dry ingredients. Add to molasses mixture. Mix on low speed until well blended. Form dough into a roll 2 in. in diameter. Chill thoroughly. Cut into 1/8-in. slices. Place on greased baking sheets. Bake at 375°F (190°C) for 8–10 minutes.
3 g	½ t	Salt	
4 g	1 t	Baking soda	
4 g	2 t	Ginger	

Note: Dough may be rolled and cut with cookie cutter.

DROP MOLASSES COOKIES

Oven: 350°F (175°C)
Bake: 8–10 minutes
Yield: 8 doz cookies

Metric	U.S.	Ingredient	Procedure
908 g	2 lb	Flour, all-purpose	Stir together flour, soda, and spices. Set aside.
32 g	2⅔ T	Baking soda	
28 g	¼ c	Cinnamon	
2 g	1 t	Cloves	
2 g	1 t	Nutmeg	
4 g	2 t	Ginger	
12 g	2 t	Salt	
680 g	1 lb 8 oz	Shortening, melted, cooled	Combine shortening and sugar. Beat until well blended.
908 g	2 lb	Sugar, granulated	
4 (198 g)	4 (7 oz)	Eggs	Add eggs, one at a time, beating well after each addition.
240 mL	1 c	Molasses	Gradually add molasses to egg–oil mixture. Gradually add dry ingredients, mixing well. Portion with No. 40 dipper onto lightly greased or silicone paper-lined baking pans. Bake at 350°F (175°C) for 8–10 minutes.

Note: Cookies will be soft in center.

OATMEAL CRISPIES

Oven: 350°F (175°C)
Bake: 12–15 minutes
Yield: 8 doz cookies

\ Amount			
Metric	U.S.	Ingredient	Procedure
340 g	12 oz	Flour, all-purpose	Combine flour, salt, and soda in mixer bowl.
12 g	2 t	Salt	
8 g	2 t	Baking soda	
454 g	1 lb	Shortening	Add shortening, sugars, eggs and vanilla. Mix on low speed about 5 minutes.
454 g	1 lb	Sugar, granulated	
454 g	1 lb	Sugar, brown	
4	4	Eggs	
(198 g)	(7 oz)		
10 mL	2 t	Vanilla	
454 g	1 lb	Rolled oats, quick, uncooked	Add rolled oats and nuts. Mix on low speed to blend.
227 g	8 oz	Nuts, chopped	
			Shape dough into 3 2-lb (908-g) rolls, 2 in. diameter. Wrap in waxed paper. Chill overnight.
			Cut into slices ¼ in. thick. Place 2 in. apart on ungreased baking sheets.
			Bake at 350°F (175°C) for 12–15 minutes.

Note: For smaller cookies form into 1½-in. roll and slice ⅛ in. thick. Yield: approximately 25 doz.

Variation: **Oatmeal Coconut Crispies.** Add 1 c (3½ oz/100 g) flaked coconut.

OATMEAL DROP COOKIES

Oven: 375°F (190°C)
Bake: 12–15 minutes
Yield: 10 doz cookies

Amount Metric	U.S.	Ingredient	Procedure
340 g	12 oz	Shortening	Cream shortening and sugar on medium speed for 5 minutes.
454 g	1 lb	Sugar, brown	
4 (198 g)	4 (7 oz)	Eggs	Add eggs and vanilla. Continue to cream until well mixed.
10 mL	2 t	Vanilla	
397 g	14 oz	Rolled oats, quick, uncooked	Add oats. Mix on low speed to blend.
454 g	1 lb	Flour, all-purpose	Combine dry ingredients.
20 g	4 t	Baking powder	
12 g	2 t	Salt	
4 g	1 t	Baking soda	
160 mL	⅔ c	Milk	Add dry ingredients and milk alternately. Mix on low speed until blended.
340 g	12 oz	Raisins, cooked, chopped	Add raisins. Mix only to blend. Drop onto greased baking sheets with No. 40 dipper, ¾ oz (21 g) per cookie. Bake at 375°F (190°C) for 12–15 minutes.

Note: For variety, add 1 lb (454 g) chopped nuts, chocolate chips, or coconut.

PEANUT COOKIES

Oven: 350°F (175°C)
Bake: 12–15 minutes
Yield: 9 doz cookies

Metric	U.S.	Ingredient	Procedure
340 g 227 g 454 g	12 oz 8 oz 1 lb	Margarine or butter Sugar, granulated Sugar, brown	Cream margarine and sugars on medium speed for 10 minutes.
4 (198 g) 10 mL	4 (7 oz) 2 t	Eggs Vanilla	Add eggs and vanilla and mix for 5 minutes.
340 g 4 g 6 g	12 oz 1 t 1 t	Flour, all-purpose Baking soda Salt	Combine dry ingredients. Add to creamed mixture.
284 g 454 g	10 oz 1 lb	Rolled oats Peanuts, salted	Add rolled oats and peanuts. Mix until blended. Drop onto greased baking sheets with No. 40 dipper, ¾ oz (21 g) per cookie. Bake at 350°F (175°C) for 12–15 minutes.

PEANUT BUTTER COOKIES

Oven: 375°F (190°C)
Bake: 8 minutes
Yield: 9 doz cookies

Amount Metric	U.S.	Ingredient	Procedure
454 g	1 lb	Margarine or butter	Cream margarine and sugars on medium speed for 5 minutes.
454 g	1 lb	Sugar, granulated	
284	10 oz	Sugar, brown	
4 (198 g)	4 (7 oz)	Eggs	Add eggs and vanilla. Continue beating until blended.
10 mL	2 t	Vanilla	
510 g	1 lb 2 oz	Peanut butter	Add peanut butter. Blend on low speed.
454 g	1 lb	Flour, all-purpose	Combine dry ingredients. Add to creamed mixture. Mix on low speed until well blended. Form into balls with No. 40 dipper (¾ oz/21 g) each. Place on ungreased baking sheets. Flatten with tines of a fork. Bake at 375°F (190°C) for 8 minutes.
8 g	2 t	Baking soda	
6 g	1 t	Salt	

SANDIES

Oven: 325°F (165°C)
Bake: 20 minutes
Yield: 8 doz cookies

Amount		Ingredient	Procedure
Metric	U.S.		
340 g	12 oz	Margarine or butter	Cream margarine, sugar, and vanilla on medium speed for 5 minutes.
85 g	3 oz	Sugar, granulated	
5 mL	1 t	Vanilla	
510 g	1 lb 2 oz	Flour, all-purpose	Add flour and salt. Mix on low speed until blended.
6 g	1 t	Salt	
15 mL	1 T	Water	Add water and pecans and blend. Chill dough. Shape into small balls ¾ in. in diameter. If mixture crumbles so it will not stick together, add a small amount of melted margarine. Place on lightly greased baking sheets. Bake at 325°F (165°C) until lightly browned, about 20 minutes.
227 g	8 oz	Pecans, finely chopped	
227 g	8 oz (approximate)	Sugar, powdered	Roll in powdered sugar while still hot.

Variation: **Frosty Date Balls.** Add 1 lb (454 g) chopped pitted dates.

SNICKERDOODLES

Oven: 375°F (190°C)
Bake: 8–10 minutes
Yield: 8 doz cookies

Amount		Ingredient	Procedure
Metric	U.S.		
454 g	1 lb	Margarine or butter	Cream margarine and sugar on medium speed for 5 minutes.
680 g	1 lb 8 oz	Sugar, granulated	
4 (198 g)	4 (7 oz)	Eggs	Add eggs. Mix thoroughly.
624 g	1 lb 6 oz	Flour, all-purpose	Mix dry ingredients. Add to creamed mixture. Mix on low speed until well blended.
12 g	4 t	Cream of tartar	
8 g	2 t	Baking soda	
3 g	½ t	Salt	
227 g	8 oz	Sugar, granulated	Combine sugar and cinnamon. Roll dough into 1-in balls or portion with No. 40 dipper. Roll in sugar–cinnamon mixture. Place 2 in. apart on ungreased baking sheets. Bake at 375°F (190°C) for 8–10 minutes or until lightly browned but still soft. These cookies puff up at first, then flatten out with crinkled tops.
35 g	5 T	Cinnamon	

DROP SUGAR COOKIES

Oven: 375°F (190°C)
Bake: 8–10 minutes
Yield: 8 doz cookies

Amount Metric	U.S.	Ingredient	Procedure
454 g	1 lb	Shortening	Cream fats and sugar, starting on low speed, progressing to medium, then high speed, 10–15 minutes.
510 g	1 lb 2 oz	Margarine or butter	
908 g	2 lb	Sugar, granulated	
20 mL	4 t	Vanilla	Add vanilla and eggs. Mix thoroughly.
3 (142 g)	3 (5 oz)	Eggs	
858 g	1 lb 14 oz	Flour, all-purpose	Combine dry ingredients. Add gradually to creamed mixture. Blend well. Portion with No. 40 dipper onto greased or silicone-lined baking pans. Bake at 375°F (190°C) for 8–10 minutes.
6 g	2 t	Cream of tartar	
11 g	2½ t	Baking soda	
3 g	½ t	Salt	

Notes:
1. Cookies will be soft in center.
2. For jumbo cookies, use No. 20 dipper.

ROLLED SUGAR COOKIES

Oven: 375°F (190°C)
Bake: 7 minutes
Yield: 10 doz 2-in. cookies

Amount		Ingredient	Procedure
Metric	U.S.		
454 g	1 lb	Margarine or butter	Cream margarine and sugar on medium speed for 5 minutes.
454 g	1 lb	Sugar, granulated	
4 (198 g)	4 (7 oz)	Eggs	Add eggs and vanilla. Blend on medium speed for 2 minutes.
15 mL	1 T	Vanilla	
680 g	1 lb 8 oz	Flour, all-purpose	Combine dry ingredients. Add to creamed mixture. Mix on low speed until blended. Roll dough ⅛ in. thick on board lightly dusted with a mixture of 1 c (240 mL) flour and ½ c (120 mL) sugar. Cut into desired shapes. Place on ungreased baking sheets. Bake at 375°F (190°C) for 7 minutes or until lightly browned.
12 g	2 t	Salt	
10 g	2 t	Baking powder	

Variations:

1. **Christmas Wreath Cookies.** Cut rolled dough with doughnut cutter. Brush with beaten egg and sprinkle with chopped nuts. Decorate with candied cherry rings and pieces of citron arranged to represent holly.

2. **Coconut Cookies.** Cut rolled dough with round cookie cutter. Brush with melted margarine or butter and sprinkle with shredded coconut, plain or tinted with food coloring.

3. **Filled Cookies.** Cut dough with round cutter. Cover half with Fig or Date Filling (pp. 172, 173). Brush edges with milk and cover with remaining cookies. Press edges together with tines of a fork.

4. **Pinwheel Cookies.** Divide dough into 2 portions. Add 2 oz (57 g) melted chocolate to 1 portion. Roll each portion into the same size sheet, ⅛ in. thick. Place chocolate dough over the white dough and press together. Roll as for jelly roll. Chill thoroughly. Cut into thin slices.

WHOLE WHEAT SUGAR COOKIES

Oven: 375°F (190°C)
Bake: 8–10 minutes

Yield: 8 doz cookies

Amount		Ingredient	Procedure
Metric	U.S.		
908 g	2 lb	Sugar, granulated	Cream sugar and margarine until light and fluffy.
454 g	1 lb	Margarine or butter	
4	4	Eggs	Add eggs, vanilla, and milk. Mix well.
(198 g)	(7 oz)		
20 mL	4 t	Vanilla	
120 mL	½ c	Milk	
680 g	1 lb 8 oz	Flour, whole wheat	Combine dry ingredients. Add gradually to creamed mixture. Blend well.
20 g	4 t	Baking powder	
8 g	2 t	Baking soda	
12 g	2 t	Salt	
5 g	2 t	Nutmeg	
32 g	4 T	Orange rind, grated	
114 g	4 oz	Sugar, granulated	Portion with No. 40 dipper onto greased or silicone paper-lined baking pans. Flatten slightly and sprinkle with sugar and cinnamon mixture. Bake at 375°F (190°C) for 8–10 minutes.
4 g	2 t	Cinnamon	

Note: Cookies will be soft in center.

BROWNIES

Oven: 325°F (165°C)
Bake: 20 minutes

Yield: 60 portions
2 pans 12 × 18 × 2 in.
Portion: 2½ × 3 in.

Amount Metric	U.S.	Ingredient	Procedure
15 (737 g)	15 (1 lb 10 oz)	Eggs	Beat eggs on high speed for 10 minutes.
1.02 kg 284 g 227 g 30 mL	2 lb 4 oz 10 oz 8 oz 2 T	Sugar, granulated Shortening, melted Margarine, melted Vanilla	Add sugar, fats, and vanilla. Mix on medium speed for 5 minutes.
397 g 284 g 10 g 3 g	14 oz 10 oz 2 t ½ t	Flour, cake Cocoa Baking powder Salt	Combine dry ingredients. Add to creamed mixture. Mix on low speed about 5 minutes.
340 g	12 oz	Nuts, chopped	Add nuts. Mix to blend. Scale into 2 greased 12 × 18 × 2-in. pans, 3 lb 8 oz (1.59 kg) per pan. Bake at 325°F (165°C) for 20 minutes. Should be soft to touch when done. Do not overbake. While warm, sprinkle with powdered sugar, or cool and cover with a thin layer of mocha or chocolate frosting if desired.

Notes:
1. 1 lb (454 g) unsweetened chocolate may be substituted for the cocoa. Melt and add to fat−sugar−egg mixture.
2. 2 lb (908 g) chopped dates may be added.
3. May be baked in 1 18 × 26 × 1-in. baking sheet.

BUTTERSCOTCH SQUARES

Oven: 325°F (165°C)
Bake: 25 minutes

Yield: 60 portions
2 pans 12 × 18 × 2 in.
Portion: 2½ × 3 in.

Amount Metric	U.S.	Ingredient	Procedure
454 g	1 lb	Margarine or butter	Cream margarine and sugar on medium speed for 5 minutes.
1.14 kg	2 lb 8 oz	Sugar, brown	
10 (454 g)	10 (1 lb)	Eggs	Add eggs, one at a time, and vanilla. Mix on low speed until blended.
15 mL	1 T	Vanilla	
680 g	1 lb 8 oz	Flour, all-purpose	Combine dry ingredients. Add to creamed mixture. Mix on low speed until blended.
28 g	2 T	Baking powder	
6 g	1 t	Salt	
340 g	12 oz	Nuts, chopped (optional)	Add nuts. Mix to blend. Spread mixture evenly in 2 greased 12 × 18 × 2-in. baking pans. Bake at 325°F (165°C) for 25 minutes. Cut 5 × 6.

Note: May be baked in 1 18 × 26 × 1-in. pan. Cut 6 × 10.

Variation: **Butterscotch Chocolate Chip Brownies.** Add 1 lb (454 g) chocolate chips.

COCONUT PECAN BARS

Oven: 350°F (175°C)
Bake: 30–35 minutes

Yield: 96 portions
2 pans 12 × 18 × 2 in.
Portion: 2 × 2¼ in.

Amount Metric	U.S.	Ingredient	Procedure
680 g	1 lb 8 oz	Margarine or butter	Blend margarine, brown sugar, and flour on low speed until mixture resembles coarse meal.
340 g	12 oz	Sugar, brown	
567 g	1 lb 4 oz	Flour, all-purpose	
			Press even layer of mixture into 2 12 × 18 × 2-in. pans, 1 lb 12 oz (794 g) per pan. Bake at 350°F (175°C) until light brown, 15–20 minutes.
8 (397 g)	8 (14 oz)	Eggs, beaten	Combine remaining ingredients to form topping.
114 g	4 oz	Flour, all-purpose	Spread over baked crust, 3 lb (1.36 kg) per pan.
14 g	1 T	Baking powder	Bake 20–25 minutes.
12 g	2 t	Salt	Frost with Orange Frosting (p. 168) if desired.
1.14 kg	2 lb 8 oz	Sugar, brown	Cut 6 × 8.
15 mL	1 T	Vanilla	
227 g	8 oz	Coconut, shredded or flaked	
340 g	12 oz	Pecans, chopped	

Note: May be baked in 1 18 × 26 × 1-in. pan.

Variation: **Dreamland Bars.** Reduce coconut to 4 oz (114 g). Increase pecans to 1 lb (454 g). Add 12 oz (340 g) maraschino cherries, chopped, 1 lb (454 g) chopped dates. Combine 2 oz (57 g) margarine or butter and 8 oz (227 g) powdered sugar. Spread over top. Bake.

DATE BARS

Oven: 350°F (175°C)
Bake: 25–30 minutes

Yield: 60 portions
2 pans 12 × 18 × 2 in.
Portion: 2½ × 3 in.

Amount Metric	U.S.	Ingredient	Procedure
12 (198 g)	12 (7 oz)	Egg yolks	Beat yolks on high speed until lemon colored.
908 g	2 lb	Sugar, granulated	Add sugar gradually and continue beating after each addition.
454 g 3 g 21 g	1 lb ½ t 1½ T	Flour, all-purpose Salt Baking powder	Combine flour, salt, and baking powder.
1.36 kg 454 g	3 lb 1 lb	Dates, chopped Nuts, chopped	Add dates and nuts to flour mixture. Combine with egg–sugar mixture.
12 (397 g)	12 (14 oz)	Egg whites	Beat egg whites on high speed until they form soft peaks. Fold into batter. Spread evenly in 2 greased 12 × 18 × 2-in. baking pans. Bake at 350°F (175°C) for 25–30 minutes.
170 g	6 oz	Sugar, powdered	Sift powdered sugar over top of warm baked bars. Cut 5 × 6.

Note: May be baked in 1 18 × 26 × 1-in. pan. Cut 6 × 10.

OATMEAL DATE BARS

Oven: 325°F (165°C)
Bake: 45 minutes

Yield: 96 portions
2 pans 12 × 18 × 2 in.
Portion: 2 × 2¼ in.

Amount		Ingredient	Procedure
Metric	U.S.		
737 g	1 lb 10 oz	Margarine or butter	Cream margarine and sugar on medium speed for 10 minutes.
1.25 kg	2 lb 12 oz	Sugar, brown	
908 g	2 lb	Flour, all-purpose	Combine dry ingredients. Add to creamed mixture. Mix on low speed until crumbly. Spread 2 lb 10 oz (1.19 kg) on each of 2 greased 12 × 18 × 2-in. baking pans. Pat down by hand to an even layer.
680 g	1 lb 8 oz	Rolled oats, quick, uncooked	
32 g	2⅔ T	Baking soda	
2.84 L	3 qt	Date Filling (p. 173)	Spread date filling over oatmeal mixture, 1½ qt (1.42 L) per pan. Cover with remainder of dough, 1 lb 4 oz (567 g) per pan. Bake at 325°F (165°C) for 45 minutes. Cut 6 × 8 into bars.

Notes:
1. May be baked in 1 18 × 26 × 1-in. pan. Cut 8 × 12.
2. Crushed pineapple or cooked dried apricots may be used in place of dates in the filling.

MARSHMALLOW SQUARES

Yield: 60 portions
2 pans 12 × 18 × 2 in.
Portion: 2½ × 3 in.

Amount		Ingredient	Procedure
Metric	U.S.		
454 g	1 lb	Margarine or butter	Melt margarine. Add marshmallows and vanilla. Stir until completely melted. Cook over low heat 3 minutes longer, stirring constantly. Remove from heat.
1.81 kg	4 lb	Marshmallows	
15 mL	1 T	Vanilla	
1.14 kg	2 lb 8 oz	Rice Krispies	Add Rice Krispies. Stir until well coated. Using buttered spatula, press mixture evenly into 2 greased 12 × 18 × 2-in pans, 3 lb 12 oz (1.7 kg) per pan. Cut while warm, 5 × 6.

Note: May be made in 1 18 × 26 × 1-in. pan. Cut 6 × 10.

Variations:
1. **Chocolate Marshmallow Squares.** Cover squares with a thin, rich chocolate frosting.
2. **Peanut Butter Squares.** Add 1 lb 2 oz (510 g) peanut butter to butter–marshmallow mixture. Proceed as above. Frost with Chocolate Glaze (p. 169).

Pies

A good pie should have a tender, flaky crust and a filling that will just hold its shape. The type of crust produced is partially determined by the method of combining the fat and flour. A flaky crust results when fat and flour are mixed until small lumps are formed throughout the mixture. A mealy crust results when fat and flour are mixed thoroughly.

Tenderness depends largely on the kind of flour and the amount of fat and water used. The tenderness of pastry increases with the proportion of fat; excess fat, however, may cause the crust to be too tender to remove from the pan. Excess water gives a less tender product, and overmixing after the water has been added or use of too much flour when rolling toughen pastry also.

A pie crust mix, made by cutting the fat into the flour and salt mixture, may be stored in the refrigerator for 4 to 6 weeks and used as needed by adding water to make fresh pie crusts. If freezer storage is adequate, crusts may be made and frozen unbaked until needed. Fruit pies can be made ahead and frozen.

PIE RECIPES

PASTRY

Yield: 50 lb (22.68 kg)

Amount Metric	U.S.	Ingredient	Procedure
11.34 kg	25 lb	Flour, all-purpose	Mix flour and shortening on low speed until fat particles are size of small peas, for a flaky crust. For a mealy crust, mixture should resemble cornmeal.
8.16 kg	18 lb	Shortening, hydrogenated	
3.55 L	3¾ qt	Water, cold	Add water and salt. Mix on low speed only until dough will hold together.
340 g	12 oz	Salt	

Notes:
1. For 8 8-in. one-crust pies, use 2 lb 8 oz (1.14 kg); for 8 two-crust pies, use 4 lb 8 oz (2.04 kg). See pp. 200, 201 for directions for making.
2. For 6 9-in. one-crust pies, use 3 lb (1.36 kg); for 6 two-crust pies, use 4 lb 14 oz (2.21 kg). See pp. 200, 201 for directions for making.

PASTRY FOR ONE-CRUST PIES

Yield: 2 lb 8 oz (1.14 kg)
8 8-in pies

Amount Metric	U.S.	Ingredient	Procedure
539 g 359 g	1 lb 3 oz 13 oz	Flour, all-purpose Shortening, hydrogenated	Mix flour and shortening on low speed for 1 minute, using pastry knife or flat beater. Scrape down sides of bowl and continue mixing until shortening is evenly distributed, 1–2 minutes.
180–240 mL 12 g	¾ –1 c 2½ t	Water, cold Salt	Dissolve salt in smaller amount of water (use reserved amount of water if needed). Add to flour mixture. Mix on low speed only until a dough is formed, about 40 seconds. Portion into 5-oz (142-g) balls.

Note: For 9-in. pies, divide into 8-oz (227-g) portions. To make a one-crust pie:

1. Roll dough into circle 2 in. larger than pie pan.
2. Fit pastry loosely into pan so that there are no air spaces between the crust and pan (Fig. 2.15).
3. Trim, allowing ½ in. extra to build up edge.
4. For custard-type pie, crimp edge, add filling, and bake according to recipe.
5. For cream or chiffon pies, fit pie crust over inside or outside of pie pans. Crimp edge and prick crust with fork.
6. Bake in a hot oven (425°F/220°C) for 10 minutes or until light brown. Cool. A second pan may be placed over the crust for the first part of baking, then removed and crust allowed to brown. The second pan helps to keep the crust in shape.
7. Fill baked crust with desired filling.

PASTRY FOR TWO-CRUST PIES

Yield: 4 lb 8 oz (2.04 kg)
8 8-in. pies

Amount		Ingredient	Procedure
Metric	U.S.		
908 g	2 lb	Flour, all-purpose	Mix flour and shortening on low speed for 1 minute, using pastry knife or flat beater. Scrape down sides of bowl and continue mixing until shortening is evenly distributed, 1–2 minutes.
680 g	1 lb 8 oz	Shortening, hydrogenated	
360–420 mL	1½–1¾ c	Walter, cold	Dissolve salt in smaller amount of water (use reserved amount if water is needed). Add to flour mixture. Mix on low speed only until a dough is formed, about 40 seconds. Portion into 5-oz (142-g) balls for bottom crust and 4-oz (114-g) balls for top crust.
28 g	1 oz (1½ T)	Salt	

Note: For 9-in. pies, portion into 8 oz (227 g) for bottom crust, 5 oz (142 g) for top crust.

To make a two-crust pie:
1. Roll each ball of dough into a circle. Place pastry for bottom crust in pie pans, easing into pans without stretching dough.
2. Trim off overhanging dough. If desired, leave ½ in. extra pastry around edge and fold over to make a pocket of pastry to prevent fruit juices from running out.
3. Add desired filling.
4. Moisten edge of bottom crust with water (Fig. 2.15).
5. Cover with top crust, in which slits or vents have been cut near the center to allow steam to escape.
6. Trim top pastry to extend ½ in. beyond edge of pan.
7. Fold edge of top pastry under edge of lower pastry, seal by pressing the two crusts together and fluting with fingertips.
8. If desired, brush top crusts with milk and sprinkle with sugar.
9. Bake as directed in recipe.

202 DESSERTS

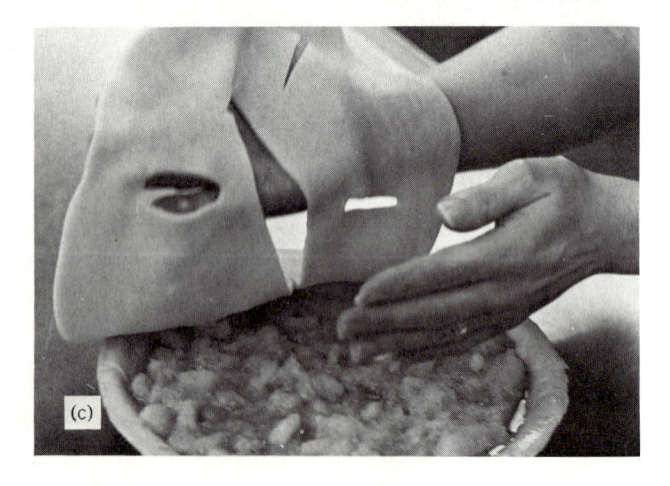

(a)

(b)

(c)

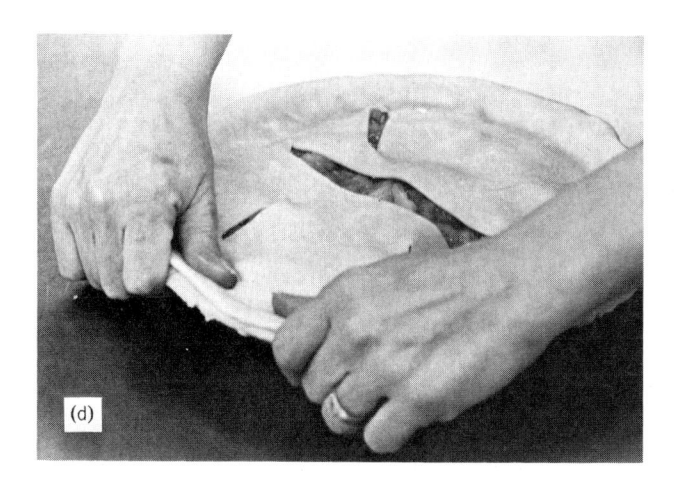

Figure 2.15 Pastry for one- or two-crust pies. (a) Preparing crust for a baked pie shell. Holes are made in shells that are to be baked before filling. (b) Moistening edge of crust for a two-crust pie. (c) Placing top crust on filled pie. (d) Pressing top crust to seal tightly. (e) Fluting edge of pie.

GRAHAM CRACKER CRUST

Oven: 375°F (190°C)
Bake: 5 minutes
Yield: 8 8-in. pie shells

Metric	U.S.	Ingredient	Procedure
595 g	1 lb 5 oz	Graham cracker crumbs	Mix all ingredients. Pat 5 oz (142 g) crumb mixture evenly into each pie pan. Bake at 375°F (190°C) for about 5 minutes.
284 g	10 oz	Sugar, granulated	
284 g	10 oz	Margarine or butter, melted	

Notes:
1. For 9-in. shells, 8 oz (227 g) per shell, make 1½ times the recipe.
2. Vanilla wafer crumbs may be substituted for graham cracker crumbs.
3. Crusts may be refrigerated several hours instead of baking.

MERINGUE FOR PIES

Oven: 375°F (190°C)
Bake: 12 minutes
Yield: Meringue for 8 8-in. pies

Metric	U.S.	Ingredient	Procedure
(16) 480 mL	16 (2 c)	Egg whites, room temperature	Add salt to egg whites. Whip past frothy stage, on high speed, approximately 1½ minutes.
3 g	½ t	Salt	
454 g	1 lb	Sugar, granulated	Add sugar gradually while beating. Beat until sugar has dissolved. The meringue should be stiff enough to hold peaks but not dry. Spread meringue on filled pies while filling is hot. It should touch all edges of the crust. Brown in oven at 375°F (190°C) for 10–12 minutes or until golden brown.

Note: For 8-in pies use 4 oz (114 g) per pie; for 9-in. pies use 5–6 oz (142–170 g) per pie.

MERINGUE SHELLS

Oven: 275°F (135°C)
Bake: 1 hour
Yield: 50 shells
Portion: 3 oz (85 g)

Amount		Ingredient	Procedure
Metric	U.S.		
28 (720 mL)	28 (3 c)	Egg whites	Add salt and cream of tartar to egg whites. Beat on high speed until frothy.
5 g	1 t	Salt	
3 g	1 t	Cream of tartar	
1.36 kg	3 lb	Sugar, granulated	Add sugar ½ c (120 mL) at a time, beating on high speed between each addition until sugar is dissolved and mixture will hold its shape, approximately 20–30 minutes. Place on greased and floured baking sheets with No. 10 dipper. Shape into nests with spoon or pastry tube. Bake at 275°F (135°C) for about 1 hour. Watch carefully the last 15–20 minutes to avoid overcooking. Meringues should be white, not brown. If overcooked, they are too brittle. Serve ice cream or fruit in center.

Variations:

1. **Angel Pie.** Place meringue in well-greased and floured pie pans, about 1¼ qt (1.18 l) per pan. Use spoon to build up sides. After baking, fill each shell with 3 c (720 mL) Cream Pie Filling (p. 216), Lemon Pie Filling (p. 220), or Chocolate Pie Filling (p. 217). Then top with a thin layer of whipped cream.

2. **Meringue Sticks.** Force mixture through pastry tube to form sticks. Sprinkle with chopped nuts. Bake.

3. **Meringue Torte.** Draw 6 10-in. circles on greased and floured baking sheets. Using pastry bag, fill in circles with meringue. Bake. Cover 3 meringues with sweetened whipped cream. Sprinkle with grated chocolate and chopped pecans. Top with another meringue. Cover with whipped cream, grated chocolate, or fruit such as pineapple, grapes, kiwi fruit. Refrigerate for 24 hours. Cut in wedges.

PIES MADE WITH FROZEN FRUIT

Oven: 400°F (205°C)
Bake: 30–40 minutes

Yield: 48 portions
8 8-in. pies
Portion: 6 per pie

Amount		Ingredient	Procedure
Metric	U.S.		
2.05 kg	4 lb 8 oz	Pastry for Two-Crust Pies (p. 201)	Divide pastry into 5-oz (142-g) balls for bottom crust, 4-oz (114-g) balls for top crust. Roll and place bottom crusts in 8 8-in. pie pans. (See p. 201).
4.54 kg	10 lb	Fruit, frozen	Thaw fruit.
See Table 2.3		Sugar, granulated	Measure juice. If necessary, add water to bring total liquid to 1½ – 2 qt (1.42 – 1.89 L) according to consistency desired. Heat to boiling point. Combine sugar, starch, and seasonings. Add to hot liquid, stirring with wire whip. Add seasonings. Pour over fruit. Mix carefully. Measure 3 c (720 mL) filling into each unbaked pie shell. Moisten edge of bottom crust with water. Cover with top crust in which slits have been made for steam to escape. Seal edge, trim and flute edges. (See p. 203.) Bake at 400°F (205°C) for 30–40 minutes or until fruit is done and crust is golden brown.
See Table 2.3		Cornstarch or waxy maize[a]	
See Table 2.3		Seasonings	

[a] Allow 2–3 oz (57–85 g) cornstarch or 2–2½ oz (57–70 g) waxy maize per qt (0.95 L) of liquid. Use of waxy maize or other waxy starch products results in a translucent soft gel through which the fruit shows clearly. The color is brighter and the gel is less opaque and less rigid, making it ideal for thickening fruit fillings. It is important to use a waxy starch if the pies are to be frozen.

TABLE 2.3   GUIDE FOR USING FROZEN FRUIT IN PIES OR COBBLERS (8 8-in. pies)

Fruit 10 lb (4.54 kg)	Sugar[a]	Thickening Cornstarch[a]	Waxy Maize[a]	Seasonings[b]
Apples	1 lb 12 oz (794 g)	3 oz (85 g)	2½ oz (70 g)	Salt, 1 t, nutmeg, 1 t, cinnamon, 1 T, butter, 2 oz (57 g)
Apricots	2–2½ lb (0.91–1.14 kg)	5½ oz (156 g)	4 oz (114 g)	Cinnamon, 2 t
Berries	2½–3½ lb (1.14–1.59 kg)	6½ oz (184 g)	5 oz (142 g)	Lemon juice, 2 T Salt, 1 t
Blueberries	3 lb (1.36 kg)	8 oz (227 g)	6 oz (170 g)	Salt, 1 t, butter 2 oz (57 g), lemon juice, 1½ c, cinnamon, 1 t
Blue plums	2–2½ lb (0.91–1.14 kg)	5½ oz (156 g)	4 oz (114 g)	Salt, 1 t, butter, 2 oz (57 g)
Cherries	2 lb (908 g)	7 oz (198 g)	5 oz (142 g)	Salt, 1 t
Gooseberries	6 lb (2.72 kg)	14 oz (397 g)	10 oz (284 g)	Salt, ½ t
Peaches	1 lb 6 oz (624 g)	5½ oz (156 g)	4 oz (114 g)	Butter, 1 oz, salt, 1 t, almond extract, ¼ t, 1 t cinnamon, 1 t nutmeg
Pineapple	2–2½ lb (0.91–1.14 kg)	5½ oz (156 g)	4 oz (114 g)	Salt, 1 t
Rhubarb	2 lb (908 g)	7 oz (198 g)	5 oz (142 g)	Salt, 1 t
Strawberries	2 lb (908 g)	12 oz (340 g)	8½ oz (240 g)	Lemon juice, ¾ c, red color, ¾ t

[a] The amount of sugar and cornstarch or waxy maize added to the fruit will vary according to the pack of the fruit and individual preferences of flavor and consistency. Frozen fruits packed without the addition of sugar are known as "dry pack." When sugar is added during the freezing process, the ratio is usually 3, 4, or 5 parts by weight of fruit to 1 part by weight of sugar. Use less thickening for cobblers.

[b] Metric equivalents: 1 t (5 mL), 1 T (15 mL), ¾ c (180 mL), 1½ c (360 mL).

PIES MADE WITH CANNED FRUIT

Oven: 400°F (205°C)
Bake: 30 minutes

Yield: 48 portions
8 8-in. pies
Portion: 6 per pie

Amount Metric	U.S.	Ingredient	Procedure
2.04 kg	4 lb 8 oz	Pastry for Two-Crust Pies (p. 201)	Divide pastry into 5-oz (142-g) balls for bottom crust, 4-oz (114-g) balls for top crusts. Roll and place bottom crusts in 8 8-in. pie pans. (See p. 201.)
1½ No. 10 cans	1½ No. 10 cans	Fruit, pie pack	Drain fruit. Measure liquid and add water to make 1½ qt (1.42 L). Bring 1 qt (0.95 L) of the liquid to boiling point.
170 g	6 oz	Cornstarch	Mix remaining 2 c (480 mL) liquid with cornstarch, then add gradually while stirring to hot liquid. Cook until thick and clear.
1.36 kg 19 g	3 lb 1 T	Sugar, granulated Salt	While still hot, add sugar and salt. Mix thoroughly and bring to boiling point. Add drained fruit and mix carefully to avoid breaking or mashing fruit. Cool slightly.

Amount		Ingredient	Procedure
Metric	U.S.		
			Measure 3 c (720 mL) filling into each unbaked pie shell. Moisten edge of bottom crust with water. Cover with top crust. Seal edge, trim, and flute edges. Bake at 400°F (205°C) for 30 minutes or until crust is browned.

Notes:

1. May be used for all canned fruit fillings, such as apricot, blackberry, cherry, gooseberry, peach, or raspberry (sugar variable).
2. For pies made with frozen fruit, see Table 2.3.
3. For 9-in. pies, use 2 No. 10 cans fruit, 3½ lb (1.59 kg) sugar (variable), 8 oz (227 g) cornstarch, and 1 oz (28 g) salt. Use 3½ c (840 mL) filling per pie.
4. Other thickening agents may be used, such as waxy maize (4½ oz/128 g) or tapioca (7½ oz/213 g). Cold-water starches also are available on the market.

FRESH APPLE PIE

Oven: 400°F (205°C)
Bake: 45 minutes

Yield: 48 portions
8 8-in. pies
Portion: 6 per pie

Amount Metric	U.S.	Ingredient	Procedure
2.04 kg	4 lb 8 oz	Pastry for Two-Crust Pies (p. 201)	Make pastry. Line 8 8-in. pie pans, 5 oz (142 g) per pan.
5.44 kg (6.8 kg AP)	12 lb (EP) (15 lb AP)	Apples, tart	Peel, core, and slice apples.
1.36 kg 114 g 7 g	3 lb 4 oz 1 T	Sugar, granulated Flour, all-purpose Cinnamon	Combine sugar, flour, and cinnamon. Add to apples and mix carefully.
227 g	8 oz	Margarine or butter, melted	Portion 2 lb (908 g) filling into each unbaked crust. Add 1 oz (28 g) margarine to each pie. Moisten edge of bottom crust. Cover with perforated top crust (4 oz/114 g). Seal edge, trim excess dough, and flute edges. (See p. 201.) Bake at 400°F (205°C) for 45 mintues or until apples are tender.

Notes:
1. Suggested apples are Jonathan, Granny Smith, and Winesap.
2. For apple pie made with canned or frozen fruit. (See pp. 207, 208.)

Variation: **Apple Crumb Pie.** Omit top crust. Sprinkle apples with Streusel Topping: Mix 1 lb (454 g) flour, 1 lb 10 oz (737 g) sugar, 2 oz (57 g) nonfat dry milk, and 1 t (6 g) salt. Cut in 10 oz (284 g) margarine or butter and add 6 oz (170 g) chopped pecans. Use 1 c (240 mL) per pie. Bake until apples are tender and topping is brown.

SOUR CREAM APPLE NUT PIE

Oven: 450°F (230°C), 350°F (175°C)
Bake: 65 minutes

Yield: 48 portions
8 8-in. pies
Portion: 6 per pie

Metric	U.S.	Ingredient	Procedure
1.14 kg	2 lb 8 oz	Pastry for One-Crust Pies (p. 200)	Make pastry. Line 8 8-in. pie pans, 5 oz (142 g) per pan.
1.25 kg 170 g 142 g 3 (142 g) 30 mL 6 g	2 lb 12 oz 6 oz 5 oz 3 (5 oz) 2 T 1 t	Cultured sour cream Sugar, granulated Flour, all-purpose Eggs Vanilla Salt	Combine and mix until thoroughly blended.
3.63 kg	8 lb	Apples, sliced, frozen, sugared	Combine apples and sour cream mixture, being careful not to break apples. Scale 1 lb 8 oz (680 g) filling into each unbaked crust. Bake at 450°F (230°C) for 10 minutes. Reduce temperature to 350°F (175°C) and continue baking until filling is slightly puffed and golden brown, about 40 minutes.

Topping

Metric	U.S.	Ingredient	Procedure
142 g 114 g 142 g 14 g	5 oz 4 oz 5 oz 2 T	Flour, all-purpose Sugar, brown Sugar, granulated Cinnamon	Combine.
142 g	5 oz	Margarine or butter	Add margarine to dry ingredients. Mix until crumbly.
227 g	8 oz	Walnuts, coarsely chopped	Add nuts. Mix in. Scale 3 oz (85 g) topping over each pie and bake 15 minutes.

RAISIN PIE

Oven: 400°F (205°C)
Bake: 30 minutes

Yield: 48 portions
8 8-in. pies
Portion: 6 per pie

Amount Metric	U.S.	Ingredient	Procedure
1.81 kg	4 lb	Raisins, washed	Simmer raisins until plump.
4.26 L	4½ qt	Water, hot	
1.02 kg	2 lb 4 oz	Sugar, granulated	Combine sugar, cornstarch, and salt. Cook until thickened. Remove from heat.
170 g	6 oz	Cornstarch	
10 g	2 t	Salt	
90 mL	6 T	Lemon juice	Add juice and margarine. Cool slightly.
85 g	3 oz	Margarine or butter	
2.04 kg	4 lb 8 oz	Pastry for Two-Crust Pies (p. 201)	Make pastry. Line 8 8-in. pie pans, 5 oz (142 g) per pan. Portion 3 c (720 mL) filling into each unbaked crust. Moisten edge of bottom crust. Cover with perforated top crust (4 oz/114 g). Seal edge, trim excess dough, and flute edges. (See p. 201). Bake at 400°F (205°C) for 30 minutes or until crust is golden brown.

Note: A superior product is obtained if 3 qt (2.84 L) cream is substituted for 3 qt (2.84 L) water.

Variation: **Dried Apricot Pie.** Use 5 lb (2.27 kg) dried apricots. Cover with hot water; let stand 1 hour. Cook slowly without stirring until tender. Combine 4 lb (1.81 kg) granulated sugar and 2½ oz (70 g) cornstarch. Mix with ½ c (120 mL) water. Add to fruit a few minutes before it is done. Continue cooking until juice is clear. Proceed as for Raisin Pie.

SOUR CREAM RAISIN PIE

Oven: 425°F (220°C) pastry,
       375°F (190°C) meringue
Bake: 10 minutes, 12 minutes

Yield: 48 portions
      8 8-in. pies
Portion: 6 per pie

_____Amount_____			
Metric	U.S.	Ingredient	Procedure
1.14 kg	2 lb 8 oz	Pastry for One-Crust Pies (p. 200)	Make pastry. Line 8 8-in. pie pans, 5 oz (142 g) per pan. Flute edges and prick crust with fork. Bake at 425°F (220°C) for 10 minutes or until light brown. Cool.
1.59 kg	3 lb 8 oz	Raisins, seedless	Steam raisins 3 minutes or simmer in small amount of water until raisins are plump.
2.37 L 1.25 kg 170 g 21 g 10 g 16 g	2½ qt 2 lb 12 oz 6 oz 3 T 1½ T 2 T	Cultured sour cream Sugar, granulated Flour, all-purpose Cinnamon Cloves Nutmeg	Mix sour cream, sugar, flour, and seasonings. Cook until thickened.
21 (369 g)	21 (13 oz)	Egg yolks	Beat egg yolks. Add to hot mixture, stirring with wire whip. Cook until thick.
			Add raisins. Pour into baked pie shells, 3 c (720 mL) per pie.
21 (680 g) 567 g 4 g	21 (1 lb 8 oz) 1 lb 4 oz ¾ t	Egg whites Sugar, granulated Salt	Prepare meringue (p. 204). Spread on pies, 5 oz (142 g) per pie. Bake at 375°F (190°C) for 12 minutes or until meringue is browned.

RHUBARB PIE

Oven: 400°F (205°C)
Bake: 35 minutes

Yield: 48 portions
8 8-in. pies
Portion: 6 per pie

Amount Metric	U.S.	Ingredient	Procedure
4.54 kg	10 lb (EP)	Rhubarb, fresh or frozen	If fresh rhubarb is used, wash and trim. Do not peel. Cut into ½-in. pieces.
170 g	6 oz	Tapioca	Combine and stir into rhubarb. Let stand 30 minutes.
2.5 kg	5 lb 8 oz	Sugar, granulated	
12 g	2 t	Salt	
45 mL	3 T	Orange rind, grated.	
2.04 kg	4 lb 8 oz	Pastry for Two-Crust Pies (p.201)	Make pastry. Line 8 8-in. pie pans, 5 oz (142 g) per pan. Portion 3 c (720 mL) filling into each unbaked crust. Distribute margarine over filling in each pie. Moisten edges with cold water. Cover with top crust or pastry strips. Press edges together. Bake at 400°F (205°C) for 35 minutes, or until crust is golden brown and fruit is tender.
142 g	5 oz	Margarine or butter, melted	

Note: 8 oz (227 g) cornstarch or 5 oz (142 g) waxy maize starch may be substituted for the tapioca.

RHUBARB CUSTARD PIE

Oven: 375°F (190°C)
Bake: 30–35 minutes

Yield: 48 portions
8 8-in. pies
Portion: 6 per pie

Amount Metric	U.S.	Ingredient	Procedure
1.14 kg	2 lb 8 oz	Pastry for One-Crust Pies (p. 200)	Make pastry. Line 8 8-in. pie pans, 5 oz (142 g) per pan. Flute edges.
3.4 kg (EP)	7 lb 8 oz (EP)	Rhubarb, fresh or frozen	If fresh rhubarb is used, wash and trim. Do not peel. Cut into ¼-in. pieces.
12 (595 g)	12 (1 lb 5 oz)	Eggs	Beat eggs. Add to rhubarb.
1.81 kg 227 g 6 g 4	4 lb 8 oz 1 t 4	Sugar, granulated Flour, all-purpose Salt Lemon rinds, grated	Mix dry ingredients. Add to rhubarb mixture.
			Portion 3 c (720 mL) filling into each unbaked crust. Bake at 375°F (190°C) for 30–35 minutes or until custard is set.

Notes:
1. May be topped with meringue (p. 204).
2. Unbaked pie may be covered with a top crust or a latticed top made of ⅛-in. pastry strips.

CREAM PIE

Oven: 425°F (220°C) pastry,
       375°F (190°C) meringue
Bake: 10 minutes, 12 minutes

Yield: 48 portions
      8 8-in. pies
Portion: 6 per pie

Amount (Metric)	Amount (U.S.)	Ingredient	Procedure
1.14 kg	2 lb 8 oz	Pastry for One-Crust Pies (p. 200)	Make pastry. Line 8 8-in. pie pans, 5 oz (142 g) per pan. Flute edges and prick crust with fork. Bake at 425°F (220°C) for 10 minutes or until light brown. Cool.
2.84 L	3 qt	Milk	Heat milk to boiling point.
312 g 1.02 kg 12 g 0.95 L	11 oz 2 lb 4 oz 2 t 1 qt	Cornstarch Sugar, granulated Salt Milk, cold	Mix cornstarch, sugar, and salt. Add cold milk and stir until smooth. Add to hot milk gradually, stirring briskly with a wire whip. Cook over hot water until smooth and thick, approximately 10 minutes.
16 (284 g)	16 (10 oz)	Egg yolks, beaten	Add, while stirring, a small amount of hot mixture to the egg yolks. Combine all ingredients, stirring constantly. Stir slowly and cook 5–10 minutes. Remove from heat.
114 g 30 mL	4 oz 2 T	Margarine or butter Vanilla	Add margarine and vanilla. Pour 3 c (720 mL) filling into each baked pie shell.

Amount		Ingredient	Procedure
Metric	U.S.		
16	16	Egg whites	Prepare meringue according to directions on page. 204. Cover each filled pie with 5 oz (142 g) meringue. Bake at 375°F (190°C) for 10–12 minutes or until meringue is golden brown.
(510 g)	(1 lb 2 oz)		
3 g	½ t	Salt	
454 g	1 lb	Sugar, granulated	

Variations:

1. **Banana Cream Pie.** Slice 1 large banana into each pie shell before adding cream filling.

2. **Chocolate Cream Pie.** Add 6 oz (170 g) cocoa and 3 oz (85 g) sugar. Omit 1 oz (28 g) cornstarch.

3. **Coconut Cream Pie.** Add 10 oz (284 g) toasted coconut to filling and sprinkle 2 oz (57 g) coconut over meringue.

4. **Date Cream Pie.** Add 3 lb (1.36 kg) chopped, pitted dates to cooked filling.

5. **Fruit Glazed Pie.** Use frozen blueberries, strawberries, or cherries. Thaw 6 lb (2.72 kg) frozen fruit and drain. Measure 1 qt (0.95 L) fruit syrup, adding water if needed to make that amount. Add slowly to a mixture of 4 oz (114 g) cornstarch, 6 oz (170 g) sugar, and ¾ c (180 mL) lemon juice. Cook until thick and clear. Cool slightly. Add drained fruit. Spread over cream pies.

6. **Fruit Tarts.** Substitute 2 qt (1.89 L) cream for equal quantity of milk. Fill baked individual pastry shells ⅓ full of cream pie filling; add fresh, canned, or frozen fruits. Cover with whipped cream.

7. **Nut Cream Pie.** Add ½ c (120 mL) chopped pecans or other nuts.

8. **Pineapple Cream Pie.** Add 3½ c (840 mL) crushed pineapple, drained, to cooked filling.

BUTTERSCOTCH CREAM PIE

Oven: 425°F (220°C) pastry,
      375°F (190°C) meringue
Bake: 10 minutes, 12 minutes

Yield: 48 portions
       8 8-in. pies
Portion: 6 per pie

Amount Metric	U.S.	Ingredient	Procedure
1.14 kg	2 lb 8 oz	Pastry for One-Crust Pies (p. 200)	Make pastry. Line 8 8-in. pie pans, 5 oz (142 g) per pan. Flute edges and prick crust with fork. Bake at 425°F (220°C) for 10 minutes or until light brown.
454 g 1.14 kg	1 lb 2 lb 8 oz	Margarine or butter Sugar, brown	Melt margarine. Stir in sugar. Cook over low heat to 220°F (105°C), stirring occasionally.
2.84 L	3 qt	Milk	Add milk slowly, while stirring. Stir until all sugar is dissolved. Heat mixture to boiling.
170 g 170 g 19 g	6 oz 6 oz 1 T	Cornstarch Flour, all-purpose Salt	Combine cornstarch, flour and salt.
0.95 L 5 (255 g) 10 (170 g)	1 qt 5 (9 oz) 10 (6 oz)	Milk, warm Eggs, whole Egg yolks	Combine milk and eggs. Add to cornstarch and flour and mix. Add to the hot mixture while stirring. Cook until thick. Remove from heat.
30 mL 114 g	2 T 4 oz	Vanilla Margarine or butter	Add vanilla and margarine. Partially cool. Fill baked pie shells, 3 c (720 mL) per pie.
16 (510 g) 3 g 454 g	16 (1 lb 2 oz) ½ t 1 lb	Egg whites Salt Sugar, granulated	Prepare meringue (p. 204). Cover each filled pie with 5 oz (142 g) meringue. Bake at 375°F (190°C) for 10–12 minutes, or until meringue is golden brown.

Note: Recipe may be used for pudding. Omit flour, increase cornstarch to 8 oz.

CUSTARD PIE

Oven: 450°F (230°C), 350°F (175°C)
Bake: 35 minutes

Yield: 48 portions
8 8-in. pies
Portion: 6 per pie

Amount Metric	U.S.	Ingredient	Procedure
1.14 kg	2 lb 8 oz	Pastry for One-Crust Pies (p. 200)	Make pastry. Line 8 8-in. pie pans, 5 oz (142 g) per pan. Flute edges.
24 (1.19 kg)	24 (2 lb 10 oz)	Eggs	Beat eggs slightly. Add sugar, salt, and vanilla. Mix.
680 g	1 lb 8 oz	Sugar, granulated	
6 g	1 t	Salt	
30 mL	2 T	Vanilla	
3.79 L	1 gal	Milk, scalded	Add hot milk, slowly at first, then more rapidly. Pour into unbaked pie shells, 3 c (720 mL) per pie.
5 g	2 t	Nutmeg	Sprinkle nutmeg over top. Bake at 450°F (230°C) for 15 minutes. Reduce heat to 350°F (175°C) and bake for 20 minutes or until a knife inserted halfway between the edge and center comes out clean.

Variation: **Coconut Custard Pie.** Add 1 lb (454 g) flaked coconut. Omit nutmeg.

LEMON PIE

Oven: 425°F (220°C) pastry,
   375°C (190°C) meringue
Bake: 10 minutes, 12 minutes

Yield: 48 portions
   8 8-in. pies
Portion: 6 per pie

Amount		Ingredient	Procedure
Metric	U.S.		
1.14 kg	2 lb 8 oz	Pastry for One-Crust Pies (p. 200)	Make pastry. Line 8 8-in. pie pans, 5 oz (142 g) per pan. Flute edges and prick crust with fork. Bake at 425°F (220°C) for 10 minutes or until light brown.
2.13 L 12 g 3	2¼ qt 2 t 3	Water Salt Lemon rinds, grated	Heat water, salt, and grated rind to boiling point.
1.59 kg 340 g 720 mL	3 lb 8 oz 12 oz 3 c	Sugar, granulated Cornstarch Water, cold	Mix sugar and cornstarch. Add cold water and stir until mixed. Add slowly to boiling water, stirring constantly. Cook until thickened and clear. Remove from heat.
360 mL	1½ c	Whole eggs or 16 yolks	Beat eggs. Add slowly to hot mixture, stirring constantly. Return to heat and cook about 5 minutes. Remove from heat.
85 g 360 mL	3 oz 1½ c	Margarine or butter Lemon juice	Add margarine and lemon juice. Blend. Pour into baked pie shells, 3 c (720 mL) per pie.
16 (510 g) 3 g 454 g	16 (1 lb 2 oz) ½ t 1 lb	Egg whites Salt Sugar, granulated	Prepare meringue according to directions on p. 204. Cover each pie with 5 oz (142 g) meringue. Bake at 375°F (190°C) for 10–12 minutes, or until meringue is golden brown.

PUMPKIN PIE

Oven: 450°F (230°C), 350°F (175°C)
Bake: 40 minutes

Yield: 48 portions
8 8-in. pies
Portion: 6 per pie

Amount			
Metric	U.S.	Ingredient	Procedure
1.14 kg	2 lb 8 oz	Pastry for One-Crust Pies (p. 200)	Make pastry. Line 8 8-in. pie pans, 5 oz (142 g) per pan. Flute edges.
14 (680 g)	14 (1 lb 8 oz)	Eggs, beaten	Combine eggs and pumpkin in mixer bowl.
2.37 L	2½ qt	Pumpkin (3 No. 2½ cans)	
794 g	1 lb 12 oz	Sugar, granulated	Combine sugars and seasonings. Add to pumpkin mixture.
284 g	10 oz	Sugar, brown	
3 g	1½ t	Ginger	
10 g	1½ T	Cinnamon	
19 g	1 T	Salt	
2.6 L	2¾ qt	Milk, hot	Add milk. Mix. Pour into unbaked pie shells, 3½ c (840 mL) per pie. Bake at 450°F (230°C) for 15 minutes. Reduce heat to 350°F (175°C) and bake for 30 minutes, or until a knife inserted halfway between the edge and center comes out clean.

Notes:
1. Undiluted evaporated milk may be used in place of fresh milk.
2. One pound (454 g) of chopped pecans may be sprinkled over tops of pies after 15 minutes of baking. Continue baking.

Variation: **Praline Pumpkin Pie.** Mix 12 oz (340 g) finely chopped pecans, 14 oz (397 g) brown sugar, and 8 oz (227 g) margarine or butter. Pat 4 oz (114 g) of mixture into each unbaked pie shell before pouring in filling.

PECAN PIE

Oven: 350°F (175°C)
Bake: 40 minutes

Yield: 48 portions
8 8-in. pies
Portion: 6 per pie

Amount Metric	U.S.	Ingredient	Procedure
1.14 kg	2 lb 8 oz	Pastry for One-Crust Pies (p. 200)	Make pastry. Line 8 8-in. pie pans, 5 oz (142 g) per pan. Flute edges.
1.81 kg 114 g 19 g	4 lb 4 oz 1 T	Sugar, granulated Margarine or butter Salt	Cream sugar, margarine, and salt on medium speed until fluffy.
24 (1.19 kg)	24 (2 lb 10 oz)	Eggs, beaten	Add eggs and mix well.
0.95 L 37 mL	1 qt 2½ T	Corn syrup, white Vanilla	Add corn syrup and vanilla. Blend thoroughly.
680 g	1 lb 8 oz	Pecan halves	Place 3 oz (85 g) pecans in unbaked pie shell. Pour egg–sugar mixture over pecans. Bake at 350°F (175°C) for 40 minutes, or until filling is set.

CHOCOLATE CHIFFON PIE

Oven: 425°F (220°C) pastry
Bake: 10 minutes

Yield: 48 portions
8 8-in. pies
Portion: 6 per pie

Amount Metric	U.S.	Ingredient	Procedure
1.14 kg	2 lb 8 oz	Pastry for One-Crust Pies (p. 200)	Make pastry. Line 8 8-in. pie pans, 5 oz (142 g) per pan. Flute edges and prick crust with a fork. Bake at 425°F (220°C) for 10 minutes or until light brown.
43 g 360 mL	1½ oz 1½ c	Gelatin, unflavored Water, cold	Sprinkle gelatin over water. Let stand 10 minutes.

PIE RECIPES

Amount		Ingredient	Procedure
Metric	U.S.		
227 g	8 oz	Chocolate, unsweetened	Melt chocolate. Add hot water slowly. Stir until mixed.
720 mL	3 c	Water, boiling	Add gelatin and stir until dissolved.
24 (454 g)	24 (1 lb)	Egg yolks, beaten	Combine egg yolks, sugar and salt. Cook until mixture begins to thicken.
680 g	1 lb 8 oz	Sugar, granulated	
9 g	1½ t	Salt	
30 mL	2 T	Vanilla	Add vanilla and chocolate mixture. Chill until mixture begins to congeal.
24 (794 g)	24 (1 lb 12 oz)	Egg whites	Beat egg whites until frothy. Gradually add sugar and beat at high speed until meringue will form soft peaks. Fold into chocolate mixture. Pour into baked pie shells, 3 c (720 mL) per pie. Refrigerate.
680 g	1 lb 8 oz	Sugar, granulated	
0.95 L	1 qt	Cream, whipping	Just before serving, whip cream. Add sugar. Spread 1 c (240 mL) over each pie.
57 g	¼ c	Sugar, granulated	

Note: Graham Cracker Crust (p. 204) may be used in place of pastry.

Variations:
1. **Chocolate Peppermint Chiffon Pie.** Cover pie with whipped cream to which 1 lb (454 g) crushed peppermint candy sticks has been added.
2. **Chocolate Refrigerator Dessert.** Use ⅔ recipe Chocolate Chiffon Pie. Spread 1 lb 12 oz (794 g) vanilla wafer crumbs over bottom of 12 × 20 × 2-in. pan. Pour in chocolate chiffon mixture and cover with 1 lb 12 oz (794 g) crumbs.
3. **Frozen Chocolate Chiffon Pie.** Fold in 3 c (720 mL) cream, whipped. Pile into pastry or graham cracker crust. Spread over tops of pies 1½ c (360 mL) cream, whipped, sweetened with 3 T (45 g) sugar. Freeze. Serve frozen.

LEMON CHIFFON PIE

Oven: 425°F (220°C) pastry
Bake: 10 minutes

Yield: 48 portions
8 8-in. pies
Portion: 6 per pie

Amount Metric	U.S.	Ingredient	Procedure
1.14 kg	2 lb 8 oz	Pastry for One-Crust Pies (p. 200)	Make pastry. Line 8 8-in. pie pans, 5 oz (142 g) per pan. Flute edges and prick crust with fork. Bake at 425°F (220°C) for 10 minutes or until light brown.
43 g 420 mL	1½ oz 1¾ c	Gelatin, unflavored Water, cold	Sprinkle gelatin over water. Let stand 10 minutes.
21 (369 g) 680 g 12 g 600 mL	21 (13 oz) 1 lb 8 oz 2 t 2½ c	Egg yolks Sugar, granulated Salt Lemon juice	Beat egg yolks. Add sugar, salt, and lemon juice. Cook over hot water until consistency of custard. Remove from heat. Add softened gelatin. Stir until dissolved.
12 g	2 T	Lemon rind, grated	Add lemon rind. Chill until mixture begins to congeal.
21 (680 g) 510 g	21 (1 lb 8 oz) 1 lb 2 oz	Egg whites Sugar, granulated	Beat egg whites until frothy. Gradually add sugar and beat until meringue will form soft peaks. Fold into lemon mixture. Pour into baked pie shells, 3 c (720 mL) per pie. Refrigerate.
0.95 L 57 g	1 qt ¼ c	Cream, whipping Sugar, granulated	Just before serving, whip cream. Add sugar. Spread 1 c (240 mL) over each pie.

Note: Graham Cracker Crust (p. 204) may be used in place of pastry.

Variations:
1. **Frozen Lemon Pie.** Increase sugar in custard to 2 lb (908 g). Delete sugar from meringue. Beat egg whites, fold into 2 qt (1.89 L) cream, whipped. Fold into chilled lemon mixture. Pour into Graham Cracker Crusts (p. 204). Freeze. Serve frozen.
2. **Lemon Refrigerator Dessert.** Crush 3 lb 8 oz (1.59 kg) vanilla wafers. Spread half of crumbs in bottom of 12 × 20 × 2-in. pan. Pour chiffon pie mixture over crumbs and cover with remaining crumbs.
3. **Orange Chiffon Pie.** Substitute 2 c (480 mL) orange juice for 2 c (480 mL) lemon juice. Substitute grated orange rind for lemon rind.

STRAWBERRY CHIFFON PIE

Oven: 425°F (220°C) pastry
Bake: 10 minutes

Yield: 48 portions
8 8-in. pies
Portion: 6 per pie

Amount		Ingredient	Procedure
Metric	U.S.		
1.14 kg	2 lb 8 oz	Pastry for One-Crust Pies (p. 200)	Make pastry. Line 8 8-in. pie pans, 5 oz (142 g) per pan. Flute edges and prick crust with fork. Bake at 425°F (220°C) 10 minutes or until light brown.
1.36 kg	3 lb	Strawberries, sliced, frozen	Drain strawberries. Reserve juice.
454 g	1 lb	Strawberry gelatin	Dissolve gelatin in boiling water.
0.95 L	1 qt	Water, boiling	
720 mL	3 c	Strawberry juice drained from berries	Add enough water to reserved strawberry juice to make 3 c (720 mL).
120 mL	½ c	Lemon juice	Combine lemon and strawberry juices. Add to gelatin mixture. Chill until partially set. Stir occasionally.
600 mL	2½ c	Whipped topping	Whip topping stiff but not dry. Whip gelatin mixture until soft peaks form. Fold in whipped topping.
8 (255 g)	8 (9 oz)	Egg whites	Add salt to egg whites. Beat until soft peaks form. Gradually add sugar. Beat until stiff peaks form. Fold into gelatin mixture. Fold strawberries into mixture. Portion 1 lb 4 oz (567 g) filling into each baked pie shell. Chill until firm.
6 g	1 t	Salt	
284 g	10 oz	Sugar, granulated	

FROZEN MOCHA ALMOND PIE

Yield: 48 portions
8 8-in. pies
Portion: 6 per pie

Amount		Ingredient	Procedure
Metric	U.S.		
1 recipe	1 recipe	Graham Cracker Crusts (p. 204)	Prepare 8 8-in. graham cracker crusts.
43 g 360 mL	1½ oz 1½ c	Gelatin Water, cold	Sprinkle gelatin over water. Let stand 10 minutes.
18 (312 g) 680 g 19 g 1.78 L	18 (11 oz) 1 lb 8 oz 1 T 7½ c	Egg yolks Sugar, granulated Salt Coffee, hot	Beat egg yolks. Add sugar, salt, and coffee. Cook over hot water until mixture coats spoon. Remove from heat. Add softened gelatin. Stir until dissolved. Chill until mixture is consistency of unbeaten egg whites.
18 (595 g) 4 g 680 g	18 (1 lb 5 oz) 1½ t 1 lb 8 oz	Egg whites Cream of tartar Sugar, granulated	Add cream of tartar to egg whites. Beat until frothy. Add sugar gradually and beat on high speed until consistency of meringue. Fold into gelatin mixture.
720 mL 454 g 30 mL	3 c 1 lb 2 T	Cream, whipping Almonds, toasted, chopped Vanilla	Whip cream. Fold cream, almonds, and vanilla into mixture. Pour into prepared crusts.
360 mL 57 g	1½ c ¼ c	Cream, whipping Sugar, granulated	Whip cream. Add sugar. Cover top of pies with whipped cream. Freeze. Remove from freezer 15–20 minutes before serving.

ICE CREAM PIE

Oven: 500°F (260°C)
Brown: 2–3 minutes

Yield: 48 portions
8 8-in. pies
Portion: 6 per pie

Amount		Ingredient	Procedure
Metric	U.S.		
1 recipe	1 recipe	Graham Cracker Crusts (p. 204)	Prepare 8 8-in. crusts.
7.57 L	2 gal	Vanilla ice cream	Soften ice cream. Dip into prepared crusts, using 1 qt (0.95 L) per pie. Freeze several hours.
24 (1.19 kg)	24 (2 lb 10 oz)	Egg whites	Add salt to egg whites. Beat until frothy.
4 g	¾ t	Salt	Add sugar gradually, beating at high speed until sugar has dissolved. Add vanilla. Cover pies with meringue, 8 oz (227 g) per pie. Brown quickly in oven at 500°F (260°C). Return to freezer if not served immediately.
680 g	1 lb 8 oz	Sugar, granulated	
8 mL	1½ t	Vanilla	
1.42 L	1½ qt	Chocolate Sauce (p. 488)	Serve with Chocolate Sauce or fresh strawberries.

Notes:
1. Pastry crust, baked, may be used in place of graham cracker crust.
2. Other flavors of ice cream may be used.

Variation: **Raspberry Alaska Pie.** Thicken 3 40-oz (1.14-kg) packages frozen raspberries with 2 oz (57 g) cornstarch. Make thin layers of thickened berries and ice cream in graham cracker crusts, using about half of the berries. Proceed as for Ice Cream Pie. Spoon remaining berries over individual servings of pie.

Puddings and Other Desserts

Recipes in this section include custards, puddings, fruit desserts, and gelatin and refrigerator desserts.

PUDDING AND OTHER DESSERT RECIPES

BUTTERSCOTCH PUDDING

Yield: 60 portions
7 qt (6.62 L)
Portion: ½ c (4 oz/114 g)

Amount Metric	U.S.	Ingredient	Procedure
2.84 L	3 qt	Milk	Heat milk to boiling point.
510 g	1 lb 2 oz	Flour, all-purpose	Mix flour, salt, sugar, and cold milk until smooth.
9 g	1½ t	Salt	
1.14 kg	2 lb 8 oz	Sugar, brown	Add gradually to hot milk.
1.42 L	1½ qt	Milk, cold	Cook and stir with wire whip until thickened.
18 (908 g)	18 (2 lb)	Eggs, beaten	Add eggs gradually to hot mixture, while stirring. Cook on medium heat about 10 minutes. Remove from heat.
15 mL	1 T	Vanilla	Add vanilla and margarine.
340 g	12 oz	Margarine or butter	Cover while cooling to prevent formation of film. Serve with No. 10 dipper.

CHOCOLATE PUDDING

Yield: 50 portions
6 qt (5.68 L)
Portion: ½ c (4 oz/114 g)

Amount Metric	U.S.	Ingredient	Procedure
3.79 L	1 gal	Milk	Heat milk to boiling point.
1.08 kg	2 lb 6 oz	Sugar, granulated	Mix dry ingredients.
170 g	6 oz	Flour, all-purpose	Add to hot milk gradually, while stirring briskly with a wire whip.
85 g	3 oz	Cornstarch	Cook until thickened, about 10 minutes, stirring occasionally.
6 g	1 t	Salt	Remove from heat.
227 g	8 oz	Cocoa	
227 g	8 oz	Margarine or butter	Add margarine and vanilla. Blend.
30 mL	2 T	Vanilla	Cover while cooling to prevent formation of film. Serve with No. 10 dipper.

TAPIOCA CREAM

Yield: 50 portions
6 qt (5.68 L)
Portion: ½ c (4 oz/114 g)

Amount			
Metric	U.S.	Ingredient	Procedure
3.79 L	1 gal	Milk	Heat milk to boiling point.
255 g	9 oz	Tapioca	Add tapioca gradually. Cook until clear, stirring frequently.
10 (170 g)	10 (6 oz)	Egg yolks, beaten	Mix egg yolks, sugar, and salt.
454 g	1 lb	Sugar, granulated	Add slowly to hot mixture, while stirring. Cook about 10 minutes. Remove from heat.
12 g	2 t	Salt	
10 (340 g)	10 (12 oz)	Egg whites	Beat egg whites until frothy.
114 g	4 oz	Sugar, granulated	Add sugar and beat on high speed to form a meringue. Fold egg whites and vanilla into tapioca mixture. Serve with No. 10 dipper.
30 mL	2 T	Vanilla	

Variation: **Fruit Tapioca Cream.** Add 1 qt (0.95 L) chopped canned peaches or crushed pineapple, drained. Add ½ t (3 mL) almond extract for peach tapioca.

VANILLA CREAM PUDDING

Yield: 50 portions
6 qt (5.68 L)
Portion: ½ c (4 oz/114 g)

Amount Metric	U.S.	Ingredient	Procedure
4.26 L	4½ qt	Milk	Heat milk to boiling point.
680 g 227 g 12 g	1 lb 8 oz 8 oz 2 t	Sugar, granulated Flour, all-purpose Salt	Mix sugar, flour, and salt.
720 mL	3 c	Milk, cold	Add cold milk to dry ingredients and stir until smooth. Add to hot milk gradually, stirring briskly with a wire whip. Cook over hot water until smooth and thick, approximately 10 minutes.
12 (595 g)	12 (1 lb 5 oz)	Eggs, beaten	Add, while stirring, a small amount of hot mixture to the beaten eggs. Add to remainder of hot mixture, stirring constantly. Stir slowly and cook about 5 minutes. Remove from heat.
30 mL 114 g	2 T 4 oz	Vanilla Margarine or butter	Add vanilla and margarine. Cover while cooling to prevent formation of film. Serve with No. 10 dipper.

Note: 5 oz (142 g) cornstarch may be substituted for flour.

Variations:

1. **Banana Cream Pudding.** Use ¾ recipe. Add 12 bananas, sliced, to cooled pudding.
2. **Chocolate Cream Pudding.** Add 6 oz (170 g) sugar and 8 oz (227 g) cocoa.
3. **Coconut Cream Pudding.** Add 8 oz (227 g) shredded coconut just before serving.
4. **Pineapple Cream Pudding.** Add 1 qt (0.95 L) crushed pineapple, well drained.

DATE PUDDING

Oven: 350°F (175°C)
Bake: 45 minutes

Yield: 48 portions
1 pan 12 × 20 × 2 in.
Portion: 3 oz (85 g)

Amount		Ingredient	Procedure
Metric	U.S.		
908 g	2 lb	Sugar, granulated	Combine in mixer bowl.
454 g	1 lb	Flour, all-purpose	Mix until blended.
43 g	1½ oz	Baking powder	
9 g	1½ t	Salt	
340 g	12 oz	Nuts, chopped	
1.02 kg	2 lb 4 oz	Dates, chopped	
540 mL	2¼ c	Milk	Add milk and blend. Pour into 1 well-greased 12 × 20 × 2-in. baking pan.
850 g	1 lb 14 oz	Sugar, brown	Mix sugar, margarine, and water. Pour over cake mixture. Do not stir. Bake at 350°F (175°C) for 45 minutes. Cool. Cut 6 × 8 for 48 portions or 6 × 9 for 54 portions. Serve with whipped cream or whipped topping.
57 g	2 oz	Margarine or butter	
2.13 L	2¼ qt	Water, boiling	

LEMON CAKE PUDDING

Oven: 350°F (175°C)
Bake: 1 hour

Yield: 60 portions
2 pans 12 × 20 × 2 in.
Portion: 2½ × 3 in.

Amount		Ingredient	Procedure
Metric	U.S.		
35 (624 g)	35 (1 lb 6 oz)	Egg yolks	Beat egg yolks, lemon juice, and margarine together until lemon colored.
1.18 L	5 c	Lemon juice	
85 g	3 oz	Margarine, softened	
2.72 kg	6 lb	Sugar, granulated	Combine sugar, flour, and salt.
539 g	1 lb 3 oz	Flour, all-purpose	
28 g	1 oz (1½ T)	Salt	
2.84 L	3 qt	Milk	Add dry ingredients and milk alternately to egg mixture.
27 (908 g)	27 (2 lb)	Egg whites	Beat egg whites until stiff. Blend into egg mixture, using low speed. Pour into 2 12 × 20 × 2-in. counter pans, 9 lb 8 oz (4.31 kg) per pan. Set filled pans in 2 other counter pans that have been filled half full of boiling water. Bake at 350°F (175°C) for 1 hour. Cut 5 × 6.

FUDGE PUDDING

Oven: 350°F (175°C)
Bake: 40–50 minutes

Yield: 64 portions
2 pans 12 × 18 × 2 in.
Portion: 3 oz (85 g)

Amount Metric	U.S.	Ingredient	Procedure
284 g	10 oz	Margarine or butter	Cream margarine on medium speed until light and fluffy.
908 g 60 mL	2 lb ¼ c	Sugar, granulated Vanilla	Add sugar and vanilla. Continue creaming for 10 minutes.
114 g	4 oz	Chocolate, unsweetened	Melt chocolate. Cool. Add to creamed mixture.
737 g 42 g 12 g	1 lb 10 oz 3 T 2 t	Flour, all-purpose Baking powder Salt	Combine flour, baking powder, and salt. Add to creamed mixture.
360 mL	1½ c	Milk	Add milk. Mix on low speed until smooth, about 2 minutes.
284 g	10 oz	Nuts, chopped	Add nuts. Mix until blended. Scale into 12 × 18 × 2-in. baking pans, 3 lb (1.36 kg) per pan.
908 g 908 g 114 g 12 g 40 g	2 lb 2 lb 4 oz 2 t 5 T	Sugar, granulated Sugar, brown Cocoa Salt Cornstarch	Combine sugars, cocoa, salt and cornstarch.
2.6 L	2¾ qt	Water, boiling	Add to sugar mixture. Mix thoroughly. Pour over batter in pans, 2 qt (1.89 L) per pan. Bake at 350°F (175°C) for 40–50 minutes. Pudding is done when cake layer springs back when touched lightly. Serve with whipped cream.

Note: Pudding separates into 2 layers when baked, a cake-like topping with chocolate sauce on the bottom. Serve with sauce on top.

CHEESE CAKE

Oven: 350°F (175°C)
Bake: 45 minutes

Yield: 48 portions
6 8-in. cakes
Portion: 8 per cake

Amount Metric	U.S.	Ingredient	Procedure
680 g	1 lb 8 oz	Graham cracker crumbs	Combine crumbs, sugar, and melted margarine.
340 g	12 oz	Sugar, granulated	Place 1 c (240 mL) crumb mixture into each of 6 8-in. pie pans or 6 6 × 6-in. square cake pans.
340 g	12 oz	Margarine or butter, melted	Press crumbs to sides and bottom of pans.
2.04 kg	4 lb 8 oz	Cream cheese	Let cheese stand until it reaches room temperature. Cream until smooth.
11 (539 g)	11 (1 lb 3 oz)	Eggs	Add eggs slowly to cream cheese, while beating.
510 g	1 lb 2 oz	Sugar, granulated	Add sugar and vanilla. Beat on high speed about 5 minutes.
30 mL	2 T	Vanilla	Place about 3 c (720 mL) filling in each shell. Bake at 350°F (175°C) for 30–35 minutes. Do not overbake.
1.18 L	1¼ qt	Cultured sour cream	Mix sour cream, sugar, and vanilla.
114 g	4 oz	Sugar, granulated	Spread 1 c (240 mL) topping on each cake.
8 mL	1½ t	Vanilla	
114 g	4 oz	Graham cracker crumbs	Sprinkle with a few graham cracker crumbs. Bake 10 minutes.

Variation: **Cheese Cake with Fruit Glaze.** Cover baked cheese cake with the following glaze. Thaw and drain 6 lb (2.72 kg) frozen strawberries, raspberries, or cherries. Measure 1 qt (0.95 L) fruit syrup, adding water if needed to make that amount. Add slowly to a mixture of 4 oz (114 g) cornstarch, 6 oz (170 g) sugar, and ¾ c (180 mL) lemon juice. Cook until thick and clear. Cool slightly. Add drained fruit. Spread over cheese cakes. Canned fruit pie fillings may be used for the glaze.

FLOATING ISLAND

Yield: 50 portions
6 qt (5.68 L)
Portion: ½ c (4 oz/114 g)

Amount			
Metric	U.S.	Ingredient	Procedure
4.26 L	4½ qt	Milk	Heat milk to boiling point.
454 g 114 g 3 g	1 lb 4 oz ½ t	Sugar, granulated Cornstarch Salt	Combine sugar, cornstarch and salt. Add gradually to hot milk, stirring briskly with wire whip. Cook over hot water or in heat-controlled kettle until slightly thickened.
24 (425 g) 30 mL	24 (15 oz) 2 T	Egg yolks, beaten Vanilla	Gradually stir egg yolks and vanilla into hot mixture. Continue cooking until thickened, about 5 minutes.
24 (794 g) 340 g	24 (1 lb 12 oz) 12 oz	Egg whites Sugar, granulated	Beat egg whites on high speed past the frothy stage, approximately 1½ minutes. Add sugar gradually, while beating. Beat until sugar has dissolved and mixture resembles meringue. Drop by spoonfuls onto hot water and bake at 375°F (190°C) until set.
			Cool custard slightly and pour into sherbet dishes; or dip, using a No. 10 dipper. Lift meringues from water with a fork and place on top of portioned custard. Add dash of nutmeg. Chill before serving.

BAKED CUSTARD

Oven: 325°F (165°C)
Bake: 40 minutes

Yield: 50 portions
Portion: 4 oz (114 g)

Amount Metric	U.S.	Ingredient	Procedure
20 (992 g)	20 (2 lb 3 oz)	Eggs	Beat eggs slightly. Add sugar, salt, cold milk, and vanilla. Mix on low speed only until blended.
567 g	1 lb 4 oz	Sugar, granulated	
3 g	½ t	Salt	
0.95 L	1 qt	Milk, cold	
30 mL	2 T	Vanilla	
3.79 L	1 gal	Milk	Scald milk. Add to egg mixture and blend. Pour into custard cups that have been arranged in baking pans.
5 g	2 t	Nutmeg	Sprinkle nutmeg over top. Pour hot water around cups. Bake at 325°F (165°C) for 40–45 minutes or until a knife inserted in custard comes out clean.

Note: Custard may be baked in a 12 × 20 × 2-in. pan set in a pan of hot water. Cut 5 × 8 for 40 portions.

Variations:
1. **Bread Pudding.** Pour liquid mixture over 1 lb (454 g) dry bread cubes and let stand until bread is softened. Add 1 lb (454 g) raisins if desired. Bake.
2. **Caramel Custard.** Add 1 c (240 mL) caramelized sugar (p. 151) slowly to scalded milk and stir carefully until melted.
3. **Rice Custard.** Use ½ custard recipe, adding 1 lb (454 g) rice (AP), cooked, 1 lb (454 g) raisins, and 3 oz (85 g) melted margarine or butter.

CHRISTMAS PUDDING

Steam pressure: 5–6 lb
Steam: 45–60 minutes
Yield: 50 portions
Portion: 3 oz (85 g)

Metric	U.S.	Ingredient	Procedure
567 g	1 lb 4 oz (EP)	Carrots, raw	Grate carrots and potatoes.
765 g	1 lb 11 oz (EP)	Potatoes, raw	
908 g	2 lb	Sugar, granulated	Blend sugar and margarine in mixer bowl.
454 g	1 lb	Margarine or butter	
567 g	1 lb 4 oz	Raisins	Add raisins, dates, and nuts to creamed mixture.
567 g	1 lb 4 oz	Dates, chopped	
340 g	12 oz	Nuts, chopped	
			Add carrots and potatoes. Mix on low speed until blended.
454 g	1 lb	Flour, all-purpose	Combine dry ingredients.
16 g	4 t	Baking soda	Add to fruit mixture. Mix on low speed until blended.
7 g	1 T	Cinnamon	
7 g	1 T	Cloves	
8 g	1 T	Nutmeg	Measure with No. 16 dipper into greased muffin pans.
1 g	¼ t	Salt	Cover each filled pan with an empty muffin pan. Steam for 45–60 minutes. Serve with Vanilla Sauce (p. 490) or Hard Sauce (p. 491).

Variation. **Flaming Pudding.** Dip sugar cube in lemon extract. Place on hot pudding and light just before serving.

CREAM PUFFS

Oven: 425°F (220°C); 325°F (165°C)
Bake: 45 minutes

Yield: 50 portions
Portion: 1 puff

Amount Metric	U.S.	Ingredient	Procedure
454 g 0.95 L	1 lb 1 qt	Margarine or butter Water, boiling	Melt margarine in boiling water.
539 g 6 g	1 lb 3 oz 1 t	Flour, all-purpose Salt	Add flour and salt all at once. Beat vigorously. Remove from heat as soon as mixture leaves sides of pan. Transfer to mixer bowl. Cool slightly.
16	16	Eggs	Add eggs one at a time, beating on high speed after each addition. Drop batter with No. 24 dipper onto greased baking sheets. Bake at 425°F (220°C) for 15 minutes. Reduce heat to 325°F (165°C) and bake 30 minutes longer.
			When ready to use, make a cut in top of each puff with a sharp knife. Fill with Custard Filling (p. 171), using a No. 16 dipper. Top with Chocolate Sauce (p. 488) if desired.

Variations:
1. **Butterscotch Cream Puffs.** Fill cream puffs with Butterscotch Pudding. (p. 229). Top with Butterscotch Sauce (p. 487) if desired.
2. **Eclairs.** Shape cream puff mixture with pastry tube into 4½-in. strips. Bake. Split lengthwise. Proceed as in directions for Cream Puffs.
3. **Ice Cream Puffs.** Fill puffs with vanilla ice cream and serve with Chocolate Sauce (p. 488).
4. **Orange Cream Puffs with Chocolate Filling.** Add ½ c (120 mL) grated orange rind and 10 oz (284 g) chopped almonds to cream puff mixture. Bake. Fill with Chocolate Cream Filling (p. 171) or Chocolate Pudding (p. 230).
5. **Puff Shells.** Make bite-size shells with pastry tube. Fill with chicken, fish, or ham salad. Yield: approximately 200 puffs.

ENGLISH TOFFEE DESSERT

Yield: 60 portions
2 pans 12 × 20 × 2-in.
Portion: 2½ × 3 in.

Amount			
Metric	U.S.	Ingredient	Procedure
992 g	2 lb 3 oz	Vanilla wafers, finely crushed	Mix crumbs, nuts, and margarine.
680 g	1 lb 8 oz	Nuts, finely chopped	Cover bottoms of 2 12 × 20 × 2-in. pans with
454 g	1 lb	Margarine or butter, melted	crumb mixture, 1 lb 8 oz (680 g) per pan.
794 g	1 lb 12 oz	Margarine or butter, soft	Cream margarine in mixer.
1.96 kg	4 lb 5 oz	Sugar, powdered	Add remaining
340 g	12 oz	Nonfat dry milk	ingredients except egg
340 g	12 oz	Chocolate, melted	whites. Beat on
23	23	Egg yolks	medium speed until
(397 g)	(14 oz)		smooth and fluffy,
60 mL	¼ c	Vanilla	about 15 minutes.
23	23	Egg whites	Beat egg whites until stiff but not dry. Fold into chocolate mixture on low speed. Pour over crumbs in pans, 4 lb 14 oz (2.21 kg) per pan. Sprinkle remaining crumbs over top, 12 oz (340 g) per pan. Refrigerate for 3–4 hours. Cut 5 × 6. Garnish with whipped cream if desired.
(737 g)	(1 lb 10 oz)		

Note: Graham cracker crumbs may be used in place of vanilla wafers.

PINEAPPLE BAVARIAN CREAM

Yield: 60 portions
2 pans 12 × 20 × 2 in.
Portion: 2½ × 3 in.

Amount Metric	U.S.	Ingredient	Procedure
85 g	3 oz	Gelatin, unflavored	Sprinkle gelatin over water. Let stand 10 minutes.
0.95 L	1 qt	Water, cold	
1 No. 10 can	1 No. 10 can	Pineapple, crushed	Heat pineapple and sugar to boiling point.
794 g	1 lb 12 oz	Sugar, granulated	
60 mL	¼ c	Lemon juice	Add gelatin to pineapple mixture. Stir until dissolved. Add lemon juice. Chill until mixture begins to congeal.
0.95 L	1 qt	Cream, whipping	Whip cream and fold into pineapple mixture. Pour into 50 individual molds or 2 12 × 20 × 2-in. pans. Cut 5 × 6.

Note: May be used for pie filling.

Variations:
1. **Apricot Bavarian Cream.** Substitute 3 lb/1.36 kg (AP) dried apricots, cooked, or 6 lb (2.72 kg) canned apricots, sieved, for the crushed pineapple. Fold 6 beaten egg whites into the whipped cream.
2. **Strawberry Bavarian Cream.** Substitute 6 lb (2.72 kg) fresh or frozen sliced strawberries for pineapple.

PINEAPPLE REFRIGERATOR DESSERT

Yield: 60 portions
2 pans 12 × 20 × 2 in.
Portion: 2½ × 3 in.

Amount			
Metric	U.S.	Ingredient	Procedure
1.81 kg	4 lb	Sugar, granulated	Cream sugar and margarine on medium speed for 5 minutes.
397 g	14 oz	Margarine or butter	
21	21	Egg yolks	Add egg yolks. Continue creaming until well blended.
(369 g)	(13 oz)		
1.66 L	1¾ qt	Pineapple, crushed	Add pineapple and cream.
240 mL	1 c	Cream, half and half	Cook over hot water until thick. Cool.
114 g	4 oz	Nuts, chopped	Add nuts and cherries.
114 g	4 oz	Maraschino cherries, chopped	
1.81 kg	4 lb	Vanilla wafers, crushed	Place a thin layer of crushed wafers in bottom of 2 12 × 20 × 2-in. pans. Fill pans with alternate thin layers of fruit mixture and crushed wafers. Refrigerate for 12 hours. Cut 5 × 6. Serve with whipped cream or whipped topping.

Note: Dry cake crumbs or sliced cake may be substituted for the wafers.

RUSSIAN CREAM

Yield: 50 portions
5 qt (4.73 L)
Portion: 4 oz (114 g)

Amount		Ingredient	Procedure
Metric	U.S.		
43 g	1½ oz (5 T)	Gelatin, unflavored	Sprinkle gelatin over cold water. Let stand 10 minutes.
1.18 L	1¼ qt	Water, cold	
1.42 L	1½ qt	Cream, half and half	Combine cream and sugar.
908 g	2 lb	Sugar, granulated	Heat until warm in steam-jacketed kettle or over hot water. Add softened gelatin. Stir until dissolved. Cool.
1.14 kg	2 lb 8 oz	Cultured sour cream	When mixture begins to thicken, fold in sour cream and vanilla, which have been beaten until smooth. Chill.
37 mL	2½ T	Vanilla	
2.27 kg	5 lb	Raspberries, frozen	Dip pudding with No. 12 dipper. Serve with No. 30 dipper of partially defrosted fruit.

JELLIED FRUIT CUP

Yield: 32 portions
1 pan 12 × 20 × 2 in.
Portion: 3 × 2½ in.

Amount		Ingredient	Procedure
Metric	U.S.		
680 g	1 lb 8 oz	Gelatin, flavored	Pour boiling water over gelatin. Stir until dissolved.
1.89 L	2 qt	Water, boiling	
1.89 L	2 qt	Fruit juice or water, cold	Add juice or water. Chill.
1.81 kg	4 lb	Fruit, drained	Arrange fruit in counter pan. When gelatin begins to congeal, pour over fruit. Refrigerate. Cut 4 × 8.

Note: For instructions on preparation of gelatin, see p. 422.

Suggested combinations:
1. Lemon gelatin, 2 lb (908 g) sliced peaches, 2 lb (908 g) mandarin oranges, 8 oz (227 g) maraschino cherries.
2. Lime gelatin, 2 lb (908 g) canned pear pieces, 2 lb (908 g) canned pineapple chunks.
3. Orange gelatin, 2 lb (908 g) orange sections, 1½ lb (680 g) canned pineapple chunks, 1½ lb (680 g) banana cubes.
4. Strawberry gelatin, 2 lb (908 g) frozen strawberries, 1 lb (454 g) sliced bananas, 1 lb (454 g) pineapple chunks.

APPLE BROWN BETTY

Oven: 350°F (175°C)
Bake: 1 hour

Yield: 64 portions
2 pans 12 × 20 × 2 in.
Portion: 3 × 2½ in.

Amount Metric	U.S.	Ingredient	Procedure
5.44 kg (4.54 kg EP)	12 lb (AP) (10 lb EP)	Apples, fresh	Pare, core, and slice apples.
908 g	2 lb	Cake or bread crumbs	Arrange apples and crumbs in layers in 2 greased 12 × 20 × 2-in. baking pans: 2 lb 8 oz (1.14 kg) apples; 8 oz (227 g) crumbs; 2 lb 8 oz (1.14 kg) apples; 8 oz (227 g) crumbs
680 g 2 g 1 g 1.89 L 30 mL	1 lb 8 oz 1 t ½ t 2 qt (or less) 2 T	Sugar, brown Cinnamon Nutmeg Water or fruit juice Lemon juice	Mix sugar, spices, water, and juice. Pour 1½ qt (1.42 L) over each pan.
227 g	8 oz	Margarine or butter, melted	Pour melted margarine over top. Bake at 350°F (175°C) for 1 hour or until apples are tender. Cut 4 × 8.

Notes:

1. Serve hot with Lemon Sauce (p. 490) or cold with whipped cream.
2. Ten pounds (4.54 kg) of canned or frozen apples may be used.
3. The amount of water will vary according to the dryness of the crumbs.
4. Graham cracker crumbs may be substituted for cake crumbs. 8 oz (227 g) nuts may be added.
5. Peaches, apricots, or rhubarb may be substituted for the apples.

APPLE CRISP

Oven: 350°F (175°C)
Bake: 45–50 minutes

Yield: 64 portions
2 pans 12 × 20 × 2 in.
Portion: 3 × 2½ in.

Amount Metric	U.S.	Ingredient	Procedure
6.8 kg (EP)	15 lb (EP)	Apples, sliced	Mix sugar and lemon juice with apples. Arrange in 2 greased 12 × 20 × 2-in. baking pans, 8 lb (3.63 kg) per pan.
340 g	12 oz	Sugar, granulated	
80 mL	⅓ c	Lemon juice	
567 g	1 lb 4 oz	Margarine or butter, soft	Combine remaining ingredients and mix until crumbly. Spread evenly over apples, 2 lb 4 oz (1.02 kg) per pan. Bake at 350°F (175°C) for 45–50 minutes. Serve with whipped cream, ice cream, or cheese. Cut 4 × 8.
340 g	12 oz	Flour, all-purpose	
340 g	12 oz	Rolled oats, quick, uncooked	
908 g	2 lb	Sugar, brown	

Notes:
1. Fresh, frozen, or canned apples may be used.
2. 1 t (2 g) cinnamon or nutmeg may be added to the topping.

Variations:
1. **Cheese Apple Crisp.** Add 8 oz (227 g) grated cheese to topping mixture.
2. **Cherry Crisp.** Substitute frozen pie cherries for apples. Increase granulated sugar to 1 lb (454 g). Add ½ t (3 mL) almond extract.
3. **Fresh Fruit Crisp.** Combine 3 lb (1.36 kg) sugar, 12 oz (340 g) flour, 1 T (8 g) nutmeg, and 1 T (7 g) cinnamon. Add to 15 lb (6.8 kg) fresh fruit, pared and sliced. Top with mixture of 2 lb 6 oz (1.08 kg) margarine or butter, 2 lb 8 oz (1.14 kg) brown sugar, and 2 lb 6 oz (1.08 kg) flour. Cream margarine, add brown sugar and flour, and mix until of dough consistency. Spread over fruit. Bake. Serve warm with cream.
4. **Peach Crisp.** Substitute sliced peaches for apples.

BAKED APPLES

Oven: 375°F (190°C)
Bake: 45 minutes
Yield: 50 apples

Amount Metric	U.S.	Ingredient	Procedure
50	50	Apples	Wash and core apples. Pare down about ¼ of the way from top. Place in baking pans, pared-side up.
1.36 kg	3 lb	Sugar, granulated	Mix sugar, water, salt, and cinnamon.
720 mL	3 c	Water, hot	Pour over apples.
6 g	1 t	Salt	Baste occasionally while cooking to glaze.
7 g	1 T	Cinnamon	Bake at 375°F (190°C) until tender when tested with a pointed knife, about 45 minutes.

Notes:
1. Use apples of uniform size, suitable for baking, such as Rome Beauty or Jonathan.
2. Amount of sugar will vary with tartness of apples.
3. ½ c (120 mL) red cinnamon candies may be substituted for cinnamon.
4. Apple centers may be filled with chopped dates, raisins, nuts, or mincemeat.
5. 3 oz (85 g) margarine or butter may be added to the syrup for flavor.

APPLE DUMPLINGS

Oven: 400°F (205°C)
Bake: 40–45 minutes
Yield: 50 portions
Portion: 1 dumpling

Amount Metric	U.S.	Ingredient	Procedure
2.27 kg	5 lb	Pastry (p. 199)	Roll to ⅛ in. thickness and cut into 5-in. squares.
5.44 kg	12 lb	Sliced apples, frozen	Place No. 16 dipper of apples in the center of each pastry square. Fold corners to center on top of fruit and seal edges together. Place in lightly greased baking pans. Prick top of dumplings.

PUDDING AND OTHER DESSERT RECIPES

Amount Metric	U.S.	Ingredient	Procedure
1.81 kg	4 lb	Sugar, granulated	Make syrup of sugar, hot water, margarine, and spices. Pour around dumplings.
1.89 L	2 qt	Water, hot	
454 g	1 lb	Margarine or butter	
4 g	2 t	Cinnamon	
5 g	2 t	Nutmeg	Bake at 400°F (205°C) until apples are tender and pastry is a golden brown, 40–45 minutes.

Notes:
1. Fresh or canned fruit may be used. The amount of sugar will vary with the type of fruit.
2. Pineapple juice may be substituted for part or all of the water.

Variation: **Apple Dumplings in Hot Butter Sauce.** Use 50 fresh apples (Jonathan or Winesap). Peel and core apples. Mix 1 lb 8 oz (680 g) sugar and 2 oz (57 g) cinnamon together. Increase pastry to 7 lb 8 oz (3.4 kg). Roll out and cut in squares large enough to cover whole apples. Brush with melted margarine or butter (4 oz/114 g). Place apple on a square, sprinkle with sugar–cinnamon mixture and completely cover apple with dough. Pierce several holes on outside of dough with fork. Place dumplings in baking pans. Pour sauce around dumplings and bake at 400°F (205°C) until apples are tender. Hot Butter Sauce: 2 lb 8 oz (1.14 kg) sugar, 12 oz (340 g) flour, ¾ t (4 g) salt, 4 oz (114 g) margarine or butter, and ⅓ c (80 mL) vanilla.

APPLESAUCE

Yield: 50 portions
Portion: ½ c (4 oz/114 g)

Amount Metric	U.S.	Ingredient	Procedure
6.8 kg	15 lb (AP)	Apples, tart	Pare and core apples. Cut into quarters. Add water. Cook slowly until soft.
0.95 L	1 qt	Water	
1.36 kg	3 lb	Sugar, granulated	Add sugar. Stir until sugar is dissolved. Serve with No. 12 dipper.

Notes:
1. Thin slices of lemon, lemon juice, or 1 t (2 g) cinnamon may be added.
2. Peaches or pears may be substituted for apples.
3. Apples may be cooked unpared.
4. Amount of sugar will vary with tartness of apples.

Variation: **Apple Compote.** Combine sugar and water and heat to boiling point. Add apples and cook until transparent.

FRUIT COBBLER

Oven: 425°F (220°C)
Bake: 30 minutes

Yield: 64 portions
2 pans 12 × 20 × 2 in.
Portion: 3 × 2½ in.

Amount Metric	U.S.	Ingredient	Procedure
2.37 L	2½ qt	Fruit juice	Heat juice to boiling point.
170 g 480 mL	6 oz 2 c	Cornstarch Water, cold	Mix cornstarch and water until smooth. Add to hot juice while stirring briskly with a wire whip. Cook until thickened.
1.14 kg 19 g	2 lb 8 oz 1 T	Sugar, granulated Salt	Add sugar and salt. Bring to boiling point.
4.54 kg	10 lb	Fruit, unsweetened or pie pack, drained	Add cooked, drained fruit. Mix carefully. Cool. Pour into 2 12 × 20 × 2 2-in. baking pans, 9 lb 6 oz (4.19 kg) per pan.
1.36 kg	3 lb	Pastry (p. 199)	Roll pastry to fit pans. Place on top of fruit. Seal edges to sides of pan. Perforate top. Bake at 425°F (220°C) for 30 minutes or until top is browned. Cut 4 × 8.

Notes:
1. The amount of sugar will vary with the tartness of the fruit.
2. Use cherries, berries, peaches, apricots, apples, plums, or other fruits.
3. For frozen fruit, see p. 207.

Variations:
1. **Fruit Slices.** Use 2 lb 12 oz (1.25 kg) pastry. Line an 18 × 26 × 2-in. baking sheet with 1½ lb (680 g) of the pastry. Add fruit filling prepared as for cobbler. Moisten edges of dough and cover with crust made of remaining pastry. Trim and seal edges and perforate top. Bake 1–1¼ hours at 400°F (205°C).
2. **Peach Cobbler with Hard Sauce.** Use 10 lb (4.54 kg) frozen sliced peaches, thawed, mixed with 1 lb (454 g) sugar, 1 t (2 g) nutmeg, 4 oz (114 g) flour, and 6 oz (170 g) margarine or butter, melted. Top with pastry crust and bake. Serve warm with hard sauce made with 8 oz (227 g) butter, whipped until fluffy with 1 lb (454 g) powdered sugar and ¼ c (60 mL) lemon juice.

OLD-FASHIONED STRAWBERRY SHORTCAKE

Oven: 375°F (190°C)
Bake: 15 minutes

Yield: 50 individual shortcakes
Portion: 1 shortcake
¾ c (6 oz/170 g) strawberries

Amount Metric	U.S.	Ingredient	Procedure
8.52 L 908 g	9 qt 2 lb (variable)	Strawberries, fresh Sugar, granulated	Wash, drain, and stem strawberries. Slice and sweeten. Adjust sugar according to sweetness of berries.
1.81 kg 142 g 38 g 595 g	4 lb 5 oz 2 T 1 lb 5 oz	Flour, all-purpose Baking powder Salt Sugar, granulated	Mix dry ingredients in mixer bowl.
908 g	2 lb	Butter or margarine	Cut butter into dry ingredients, using pastry blender or flat paddle. Mixture should have coarse, mealy consistency.
1.42 L	1½ qt	Milk	Stir milk quickly into flour mixture. Mix just enough to moisten. Drop dough with No. 20 dipper onto ungreased baking sheets. Place about 2 in. apart to allow for spreading. Bake at 375°F (190°C) for 12–15 minutes or until golden brown.
1.42 L	1½ qt	Cream, half and half	To serve, dip ¾ c (6 oz/170 g) strawberries over shortcake. Serve with cream if desired.

Note: For frozen strawberries, use 12 lb (5.44 kg). Portion ½ c (120 mL) over shortcake.

Eggs and Cheese

Eggs, cheese, and milk are basic ingredients in many quantity recipes, and their cookery requires carefully controlled temperatures and cooking times.

EGGS

MARKET FORMS

Fresh Eggs Federal quality standards classify fresh shell eggs as AA, A, and B. Grades AA and A are best for poaching, frying, and cooking in the shell because the yolks are firm, round, and high, and the thick white stands high around the yolk. Grade B eggs are suitable for use in baking and cost less than the higher grades. Eggs are graded also according to size, and the most readily available are extra large, large, and medium. Large eggs were used in testing recipes for this book. Fresh eggs deteriorate rapidly at room temperature and should be refrigerated and stored away from foods with strong odors.

Processed Eggs Although fresh shell eggs are used extensively for table service, processed eggs are convenient to use in quantity food preparation and eliminate the time-consuming task of breaking eggs. Whole eggs, whites, yolks, and various blends are available in liquid, frozen, and dried forms. Thawed frozen eggs and reconstituted dried eggs are highly perishable, and careful handling by the user is essential to prevent contamination.

Frozen Eggs These are usually made from high-quality eggs and are excellent for omelets, scrambled eggs, French toast, and in baking. They are pasteurized and are usually purchased in 30 lb (13.61 kg) cans. These require at least 2 days to thaw in the refrigerator. To speed thawing, the container may be placed in cold running water without submerging it. Use thawed eggs immediately, or refrigerate promptly in an airtight container and use within 24 hours.

Dried Eggs These are used primarily for baking. They should be stored in a cool, dry place where the temperature is not more than 50°F (10°C), preferably in the refrigerator. After opening a package, refrigerate any unused portion in a container with a close-fitting lid. Reconstitute only the amount needed at one time. Blend with water or combine with other dry ingredients in the recipe and add the amount of water needed to reconstitute. Use reconstituted eggs immediately, or refrigerate promptly in an airtight container and use within 1 hour.

A guide for substituting processed eggs for shell eggs is included in Table 1.3.

EGG COOKERY

The most important rule in egg cookery is to avoid high temperatures and long cooking times. Poached, soft- or hard-cooked, and scrambled eggs should be prepared as close to serving time as possible by batch cooking or cooking to order. If eggs must be held on a hot counter, they should be undercooked slightly to compensate for the additional heating that will occur. Directions for cooking eggs are given on p. 256.

For hard-cooked eggs, those that have been held a few days in the refrigerator will peel easier when cooked than will very fresh eggs. A greenish color sometimes appears on the yolks of hard-cooked eggs when the eggs have been overcooked or allowed to cool slowly in the cooking water. Cooking the eggs for the minimum length of time required to make them hard and cooling them in cold running water help to prevent this color formation.

CHEESE AND MILK

CHEESE COOKERY

Cheese used in cooking should be appropriate in flavor and texture to the item being prepared and should blend well with other ingredients. Aged natural cheese or process cheese blends more readily than green or unripened cheese. Process cheese is a blend of fresh and aged natural cheeses that have been melted, pasteurized, and mixed with an emulsifier. It has no rind or waste, is easy to slice, and melts readily but, during processing, it loses some of the characteristic flavor of natural cheese. For this reason, a natural cheese with a more pronounced flavor may be preferred for cheese sauce and as an addition to other cooked foods where a distinctive cheese flavor is desired.

Cheese to be combined with other ingredients usually is ground, shredded, or diced to expedite melting and blending. Cheese melts at 325°F (162°C), and baked dishes containing cheese should be cooked at a temperature no higher than 350°F (175°C). Excessive temperature and prolonged cooking cause cheese to toughen and become stringy and the fat to separate. When making cheese sauce, the cheese should be added after the white sauce is completely cooked and the mixture heated only enough to melt the cheese. When cheese is used as a topping, a thin layer of buttered bread crumbs will protect it from the heat and from becoming stringy.

Cheddar cheese, often called American cheese, leads all other types in amounts used in quantity food preparation. It is available in many forms and ranges in flavor from mild to very sharp. Other types of cheese are used for appetizers, sandwiches, salads, and with crackers and fruit for dessert. Table 2.4 lists some of the cheeses most often used in institution food services.

TABLE 2.4 GUIDE TO NATURAL CHEESES[a]

Type	Characteristics	Uses
Blue	Tangy, piquant flavor; semisoft, pasty sometimes crumbly texture; white interior marbled or streaked with blue veins of mold; resembles Roquefort	Appetizers, salad dressings, desserts
Brick	Mild to moderately sharp flavor, semisoft to medium firm, elastic texture; creamy white-to-yellow interior; brownish exterior	Appetizers, sandwiches, desserts
Brie	Mild to pungent flavor; soft, smooth texture; creamy yellow interior; edible thin brown and white crust	Appetizers, desserts
Camembert	Distinctive mild to tangy flavor; soft, smooth texture, almost fluid when fully ripened; creamy yellow interior; edible thin white or gray-white crust	Appetizers, desserts
Cheddar	Mild to very sharp flavor, smooth texture, firm to crumbly; light cream to orange	Appetizer, entrées, sauces, soups, sandwiches, salads, desserts
Colby	Mild to mellow flavor, similar to Cheddar; softer body and more open texture than Cheddar; light cream to orange	Sandwiches
Cottage	Mild, slightly acid flavor; soft open texture with tender curds of varying size; white to creamy white	Appetizers, salads
Cream	Delicate, slightly acid flavor; soft, smooth texture; white	Appetizers, salads, sandwiches, desserts
Edam	Mellow, nutlike, sometimes salty flavor; rather firm, rubbery texture; creamy yellow or medium yellow-orange interior; surface coated with red wax; usually shaped like a flattened ball	Appetizers, salads, sandwiches, desserts
Gouda	Mellow, nutlike, often slightly acid flavor; semisoft to firm, smooth texture, often containing small holes; creamy yellow or medium yellow-orange interior; usually has a red wax coating; usually shaped like a flattened ball	Appetizers, salads, sandwiches, desserts
Gruyere	Nutlike, salty flavor, similar to Swiss but sharper; firm, smooth texture with small holes or eyes; light yellow	Appetizers, desserts
Monterey jack	Very mild flavor, texture similar to Cheddar, light color	Sandwiches, cold plates
Mozzarella	Delicate, mild flavor; slightly firm, plastic texture; creamy white	Entrées, such as lasagna, sandwiches

Type	Characteristics	Uses
Parmesan	Sharp, distinctive flavor, very hard, granular texture; yellowish white	Grated for seasoning
Port du Salut	Mellow to robust flavor similar to Gouda; semisoft, smooth elastic texture; creamy white or yellow	Appetizers, desserts
Ricotta	Mild, sweet, nutlike flavor; soft, moist texture with loose curds (fresh Ricotta) or dry and suitable for grating	Salads, entrées, such as lasagna and ravioli, desserts
Romano	Very sharp, piquant flavor; very hard, granular texture; yellowish white interior; greenish black surface	Seasoning and general table use; grated for seasoning
Roquefort (imported)	Sharp, peppery, piquant flavor; semisoft pasty, sometimes crumbly texture; white interior streaked with blue-green veins of mold	Appetizers, salad dressings, desserts
Swiss	Mild, sweet, nutlike flavor; firm, smooth, elastic body with large round eyes; light yellow	Sandwiches, salads

[a] From U.S. Department of Agriculture, *Cheese in Family Meals*, Home and Garden Bulletin No. 112.

MILK COOKERY

Milk should be heated or cooked at a low temperature. At high temperatures the protein in milk coagulates into a film on top and a coating on the sides of the kettle that tends to scorch when milk is heated over direct heat. To prevent formation of this coating, milk should be heated over water, in a steamer, or in a steam jacketed kettle. Whipping the milk to form a foam or tightly covering the pan and heating the milk below boiling temperature helps to prevent formation of a top scum.

Curdling may be caused by holding the milk at high temperature or by the addition of foods containing acids and tannins. For example, the tannins in potatoes often cause curdling of the milk used in scalloped potatoes. Milk in combination with ham or with certain vegetables, such as asparagus, green beans, carrots, peas, or tomatoes, may curdle. Curdling may be lessened by limiting the salt used, adding the milk in the form of a white sauce, keeping the temperature below boiling, and shortening the cooking time. Danger of curdling in tomato soup may be lessened by adding the tomato to the milk, having both the milk and tomato hot when they are combined, or thickening either the milk or tomato juice before they are combined.

Dry milk is substituted extensively for fluid milk in quantity cooking because of the comparatively low cost of dry milk and its ease in handling and storage. It is available as whole, nonfat, and buttermilk. Nonfat dry milk is pure fresh milk from which only the fat and water have been removed. It has better keeping qualities than dry whole milk, although both should be kept dry and cool. There are on the market different types and kinds of nonfat dry milk of equal nutritional food value. Instant nonfat milk is the type that is readily reconstituted in liquid form. Whatever the type, it may be used in dry form or reconstituted as fluid milk. Once it has been reconstituted, it should be refrigerated immediately.

When dry milk is used in recipes that contain a large proportion of dry ingredients, such as bread, biscuits, and cakes, the only change in method would be to mix the unsifted dry milk with the other dry ingredients and use water in place of fluid milk. For best results, dry milk should be weighed, not measured. Package directions for reconstituting dry milk solids should be followed. A general guide is to use 3.5 oz (100 g) by weight, of instant or regular spray process nonfat dry milk plus 3¾ c (900 mL) water to make 1 qt (0.95 L) liquid milk; or 1 lb (454 g) plus 3¾ qt (3.55 L) water to make 1 gal (3.79 L). The same proportion is used for dry buttermilk. For some foods, additional fat (1.2 oz/35 g per quart/0.95 L of liquid) should be added. Additional amounts of nonfat dry milk may be added to some foods to supplement their nutritional value, although excessive amounts that affect palatability should not be used.

EGG RECIPES

PROCEDURE FOR COOKING EGGS

Method	Equipment	Procedure
Hard-or soft-cooked (in shell)	Kettle	1. Place room temperature eggs in wire baskets. Lower into kettle of boiling water. Simmer (do not boil), timing as follows: 　Soft-cooked　　　Hard-cooked 　3–5 minutes　　　10–15 minutes 2. Immerse hard-cooked eggs in cold water or serve immediately. Serve soft-cooked eggs immediately after cooking.
	Steamer	1. Place room temperature eggs in perforated counter pans: 3 doz per 12 × 20 × 2-in. pan. 2. Place in a preheated steamer and time as follows: 　Pressure　Soft-cooked　Hard-cooked 　5 lb　　　5–7 minutes　8–10 minutes 　15 lb　　　4–6 minutes　7–9 mintues 3. Immerse in cold water or serve immediately.

Method	Equipment	Procedure

Hard-cooked (out of shell)	Steamer	1. Crack room temperature eggs into a 12 × 20 × 2-in. solid, greased counter pan. Eggs should be thick enough in pans so whites come up to level of yolks (4 doz per pan).
		2. Place in preheated steamer and time as follows:
		    Pressure Hard-cooked
		    5 lb 6–8 minutes
		    15 lb 5–7 minutes
		3. Remove from steamer and drain off any accumulated condensate. Chop and cool.

Poached	Fry pan or kettle	1. Break eggs one at a time into sauce dishes. Carefully slide eggs into simmering water in fry pan or other shallow pan (Fig. 2.16). The addition of salt (1 T/19 g) or vinegar (2 t/10 mL) to the water increases the speed of coagulation and helps maintain shape. 2. Keep water at simmering (not boiling) temperature. Cook 5–7 minutes. 3. Remove eggs with slotted spoon.

	Steamer	1. Break eggs into water in 12 × 20 × 2-in. counter pans.
		2. Place eggs into preheated steamer and time as follows:
		    Pressure Soft-poached
		    5 lb 3–5 minutes
		    15 lb 2–4 minutes
		3. To serve, lift out of water into a warmed pan.

Fried	Skillet or griddle	1. Break eggs into sauce dishes. Slide carefully into hot fat in skillets or on griddle. 2. Cook over low heat until of desired hardness, 5–7 minutes.

258   EGGS AND CHEESE

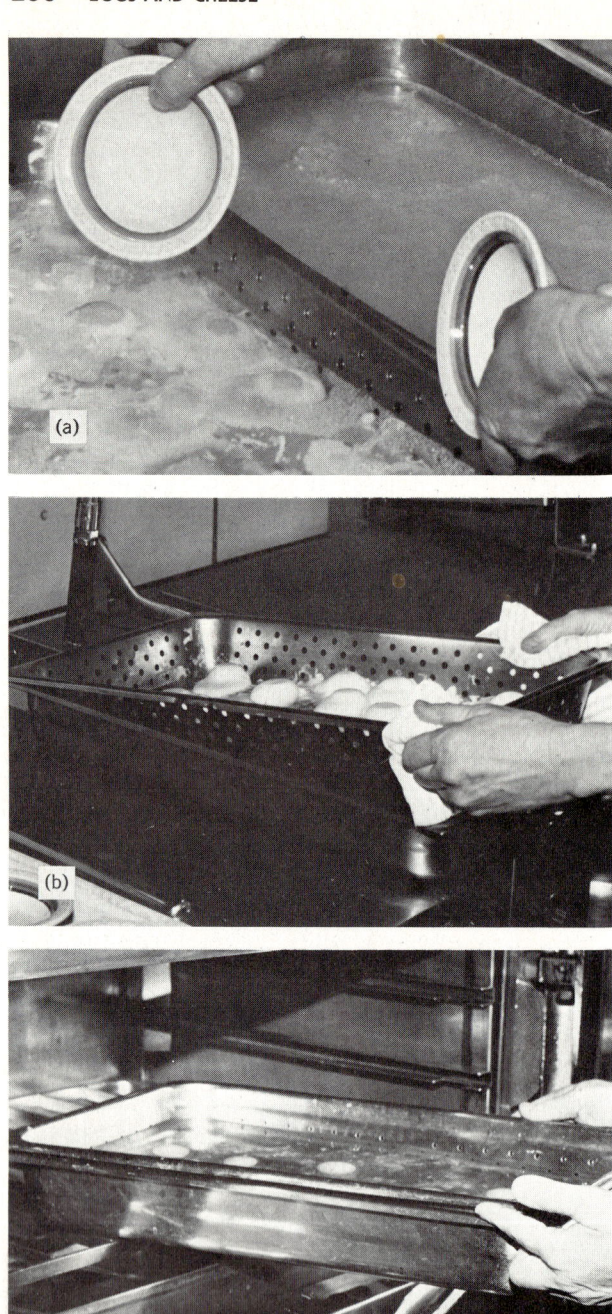

Figure 2.16   Poaching eggs. (a) Place perforated pan in simmering water. Carefully slide eggs individually into the water. In the picture a tilting fry pan is used. (b) Remove cooked eggs by lifting the pan from water and placing it into a solid counter pan to drain. (c) Eggs may be poached in a steamer. For timing, see Procedure for Cooking Eggs.

SCRAMBLED EGGS

Yield: 50 portions
Portion: 3 oz (85 g)

Amount		Ingredient	Procedure
Metric	U.S.		
75 (3.67 kg)	75 (8 lb 3 oz)	Eggs	Break eggs into mixer bowl. If using frozen eggs, defrost. Beat slightly on medium speed.
1.42 L 38 g	1½ qt 2 T	Milk Salt	Add milk and salt. Beat until blended.
227 g	8 oz	Margarine or butter	Melt margarine in skillet or steam-jacketed kettle. Pour in egg mixture. Cook over low heat, stirring occasionally, until of desired consistency. Eggs should be glossy. Serve with No. 10 dipper.

Notes:
1. **Steamer Method.** Melt 4 oz (144 g) margarine or butter in each of two steamer or counter pans. Pour egg mixture into pans. Steam for 6–8 minutes at 5-lb pressure until desired degree of hardness.
2. **Oven Method.** Melt 4 oz (114 g) margarine or butter in each of two counter or baking pans. Pour egg mixture into pans. Bake approximately 20 minutes at 350°F (175°C), stirring once after 10 minutes of baking.
3. Bacon fat may be used in place of margarine or butter.

Variations:
1. **Scrambled Eggs and Cheese.** Add 1 lb (454 g) grated Cheddar cheese.
2. **Scrambled Eggs and Chipped Beef.** Add 1 lb (454 g) chopped chipped beef. Reduce salt to 1 T (19 g) or less.
3. **Scrambled Eggs and Ham.** Add 1 lb 4 oz (567 g) chopped cooked ham. Reduce salt to 1 T (19 g) or less.

EGG AND SAUSAGE BAKE

Oven: 325°F (165°C)
Bake: 1 hour

Yield: 48 portions
2 pans 12 × 20 × 2 in.
Portion: 6 oz (170 g)

Amount Metric	U.S.	Ingredient	Procedure
1.14 kg	2 lb 8 oz	Bread, sliced	Remove crusts from bread. Cut in cubes. Cover bottoms of 2 greased 12 × 20 × 2-in. baking pans with bread cubes. Pans should be well covered.
4.08 kg	9 lb	Sausage, bulk	Brown sausage. Drain.
1.14 kg	2 lb 8 oz	Cheddar cheese, shredded	Spread cheese and sausage over bread cubes.
42 (2.04 kg) 2.84 L 10 g	42 (4 lb 8 oz) 3 qt 1½ T	Eggs Milk Mustard, dry	Beat eggs. Add milk and seasonings. Pour over mixture in pans, 2½ qt (2.37 L) per pan. Cover and refrigerate for 12 hours. Bake uncovered at 325°F (165°C) for 1 hour or until set. If browning too fast, cover with foil. Cut 4 × 6.

CREAMED EGGS

Yield: 50 portions
Portion: 5 oz (142 g)

Amount		Ingredient	Procedure
Metric	U.S.		
454 g	1 lb	Margarine or butter	Melt margarine. Add flour and seasonings.
227 g	8 oz	Flour, all-purpose	Stir until smooth.
28 g	1½ T	Salt	Add milk gradually,
¼ t	¼ t	Pepper, white	stirring constantly.
3.79 L	1 gal	Milk	Cook until thickened.
75	75	Eggs, hard-cooked (p. 256)	Peel eggs. Slice or quarter. When ready to serve, pour hot sauce over eggs. Mix carefully. Reheat to serving temperature.

Variations:
1. **Curried Eggs.** Substitute chicken broth for milk and add 2 T (14 g) curry powder. May be served with steamed rice or chow mein noodles.
2. **Eggs à la King.** Substitute Chicken Stock (p. 495) for milk and add 1 lb (454 g) mushrooms that have been sautéed, 12 oz (340 g) chopped green peppers, and 8 oz (227 g) chopped pimiento.
3. **Goldenrod Eggs.** Reserve 25 egg yolks to mash or rice, and sprinkle over top of creamed eggs. Serve on toast.
4. **Scotch Woodcock.** Add 1 lb (454 g) sharp Cheddar cheese to sauce. Cut eggs in half lengthwise and place in pans. Pour sauce over eggs. Cover with buttered crumbs. Bake until heated through and crumbs are brown.

CHINESE OMELET

Oven: 325°F (165°C)
Bake: 45 minutes

Yield: 48 portions
2 pans 12 × 20 × 2 in
Portion: 4 oz (114 g)

Metric	U.S.	Ingredient	Procedure
114 g	4 oz	Margarine or butter	Melt margarine. Add flour and salt. Stir until smooth.
57 g	2 oz	Flour, all-purpose	
6 g	1 t	Salt	
0.95 L	1 qt	Milk	Add milk gradually, stirring constantly. Cook until thickened.
454 g	1 lb	Cheddar cheese, sharp, shredded	Add cheese to white sauce. Stir until cheese is melted.
24 (425 g)	24 (15 oz)	Egg yolks	Beat egg yolks until light and fluffy. Add seasonings. Add to cheese sauce. Stir until smooth.
5 mL	1 t	Mustard, dry	
38 g	2 T	Salt	
2 g	1 t	Paprika	
908 g	2 lb (AP)	Rice	Cook rice according to directions on p. 358. Add to sauce.
2.37 L	2½ qt	Water	
24 g	4 t	Salt	
20 mL	4 t	Cooking oil	
24 (794 g)	24 (1 lb 12 oz)	Egg whites	Beat egg whites until they form soft peaks. Fold into rice mixture. Pour into 2 greased 12 × 20 × 2-in. pans, 7 lb (3.18 kg) per pan. Bake at 325°F (165°C) for 45 minutes or until set. Cut 4 × 6. Serve with Cheese Sauce (p. 471) or Tomato Sauce (p. 478).

POTATO OMELET

Oven: 325°F (165°C)
Bake: 1 hour

Yield: 56 portions
2 pans 12 × 20 × 2 in.
Portion: 6 oz (170 g)

Amount Metric	U.S.	Ingredient	Procedure
50	50	Bacon slices	Arrange bacon, slightly overlapping in baking pans. Cook in oven until crisp. Remove from pans.
4.08 kg	9 lb (EP)	Potatoes, cooked, diced	Brown potatoes slightly in bacon fat. Remove to 2 greased 12 × 20 × 2-in. baking pans, 4 lb 8 oz (2.04 kg) per pan.
36 (1.79 kg)	36 (3 lb 15 oz)	Eggs, beaten	Combine eggs, milk, and seasonings. Pour over potatoes. Bake at 325°F (165°C) for 1 hour. Serve as soon as removed from oven. Cut 4 × 7. Place a slice of crisp bacon on top of each serving.
57 g	2 oz	Salt	
2 g	1 t	Pepper	
f.g.	f.g.	Cayenne	
2.84 L	3 qt	Milk, hot	

Variation: **Potato–Ham Omelet.** Omit bacon. Add 4 lb (1.81 kg) diced cooked ham to potatoes. Reduce salt to 1 T (19 g).

BAKED OMELET

Oven: 325°F (165°C)
Bake: 45 minutes

Yield: 48 portions
2 pans 12 × 20 × 2 in.
Portion: 3 oz (85 g)

Amount		Ingredient	Procedure
Metric	U.S.		
340 g	12 oz	Margarine or butter	Melt margarine. Add flour and seasonings. Stir until smooth. Add milk gradually, stirring constantly. Cook until thick.
227 g	8 oz	Flour, all-purpose	
38 g	2 T	Salt	
1 g	½ t	Pepper, white	
2.84 L	3 qt	Milk	
24 (425 g)	24 (15 oz)	Egg yolks, beaten	Add egg yolks and mix well with a wire whip.
24 (794 g)	24 (1 lb 12 oz)	Egg whites	Beat egg whites until they form rounded peaks. Fold into egg yolk mixture. Pour into 2 greased 12 × 20 × 2-in. baking pans, 5 lb (2.27 kg) per pan. Set pans in pans of hot water. Bake at 325°F (165°C) for 45 minutes or until set. Cut 4 × 6.

Variations:

1. **Bacon Omelet.** Fry 1½ lb (680 g) diced bacon; substitute bacon fat for margarine in white sauce. Add diced bacon to egg mixture.
2. **Cheese Omelet.** Add 12 oz (340 g) grated cheese before placing pans in oven.
3. **Ham Omelet.** Add 3 lb (1.36 kg) finely diced cooked ham. Reduce salt to 1 T (19 g) or less.
4. **Jelly Omelet.** Spread 1 lb 6 oz (624 g) tart jelly over cooked omelet.
5. **Mushroom and Cheese Omelet.** Add 8 oz (227 g) grated cheese and 6 oz (170 g) sliced mushrooms.
6. **Spanish Omelet.** Add 8 oz (227 g) chopped green chilies to egg mixture. Serve with Spanish Sauce (p. 478).

QUICHE

Oven: 375°F (190°C)
Bake: 25–30 minutes

Yield: 48 portions
      12 8-in. quiches
Portion: 1/4 quiche

Amount Metric	U.S.	Ingredient	Procedure
794 g	1 lb 13 oz	Flour, all-purpose	Make pastry according to directions on p. 200. Line 12 8-in. pie pans with pastry, 5 oz (142 g) per pie. Partially bake shells at 375°F (190°C) for about 10 minutes.
19 g	1 T	Salt	
567 g	1 lb 4 oz	Shortening	
300 mL	1 1/4 c	Water, cold	
30 (1.47 kg)	30 (3 lb 4 oz)	Eggs	Beat eggs. Add cream, milk, and seasonings.
1.89 L	2 qt	Cream or half and half	
1.89 L	2 qt	Milk	
9 g	1 1/2 t	Salt	
1 g	1/2 t	Pepper, white	
1.14 kg	2 lb 4 oz	Swiss cheese, grated	Add cheese to egg mixture.
227 g	8 oz	Parmesan cheese, grated	
454 g	1 lb	Bacon, chopped, cooked, drained or Ham, finely diced	Sprinkle partially baked shells with bacon or ham, 2 oz (57 g) per pie. Pour egg mixture into shells, 3 c (720 mL) per pie. Bake until custard is set and lightly browned.

Note: One fourth quiche makes a generous serving. For 6 servings per pie, make 3/4 recipe.

Variations:

1. **Mushroom Quiche.** Delete bacon or ham and Parmesan cheese. Sprinkle 2 lb (908 g) sliced fresh mushrooms and 8 oz (227 g) finely chopped onions sautéed in margarine or butter over bottoms of shells.

2. **Seafood Quiche.** Use 3 lb (1.36 kg) flaked crab meat, shrimp pieces, or other seafood, 1 lb (454 g) sliced fresh mushrooms, and 12 oz (340 g) finely chopped onions sautéed in margarine or butter. Substitute 1 lb 8 oz (680 g) shredded Mozzarella cheese for Swiss and Parmesan cheeses.

3. **Swiss Spinach Quiche.** Delete bacon or ham and Parmesan cheese. Increase Swiss cheese to 6 lb (2.72 kg). Add 3 1/2 lb (1.59 kg) chopped spinach, well-drained. Add 1 t (2 g) nutmeg.

EGG CUTLETS

Deep-fat fryer: 375°F (190°C)
Fry: 3 minutes

Yield: 50 cutlets
Portion: 3 oz (85 g)

Amount Metric	U.S.	Ingredient	Procedure
340 g	12 oz	Margarine or butter, melted	Melt margarine. Add flour and salt. Stir until smooth.
284 g	10 oz	Flour, all-purpose	Add milk gradually, stirring constantly. Cook until very thick.
57 g	2 oz	Salt	
1.89 L	2 qt	Milk	
48	48	Eggs, hard-cooked (p. 256)	Peel eggs. Chop or grind coarsely. Add white sauce. Mix. Portion with No. 12 dipper onto greased sheet pans. Chill. Shape into cutlets. Chill.
6 (284 g)	6 (10 oz)	Eggs	Beat eggs. Combine with milk.
240 mL	1 c	Milk	Dip cutlets in egg mixture and roll in crumbs. Chill 2 hours. Fry in deep fat for 3 minutes.
340 g	12 oz	Bread crumbs	

Note: Cutlets may be baked. Place on greased baking sheets and bake at 350°F (175°C) for 1 hour.

Variation: **Chicken Cutlets.** Substitute finely chopped cooked chicken for hard-cooked eggs. Substitute 1 qt (0.95 L) Chicken Stock (p. 495) for 1 qt (0.95 L) of the milk.

EGG FOO YUNG

Yield: 50 portions
Portion: 4 oz (114 g) with 1½ oz (43 g) sauce

Amount		Ingredient	Procedure
Metric	U.S.		
454 g	1 lb	Mushrooms, canned	Drain and coarsely chop mushrooms and bean sprouts. Reserve liquid for use in final step.
1 No. 10 can	1 No. 10 can	Bean sprouts	
680 g	1 lb 8 oz	Onions, shredded	Combine onions and green peppers with mushrooms and bean sprouts. Fry in hot oil 2 minutes.
227 g	8 oz	Green peppers, shredded	
227 g	1 c	Cooking oil	
40 (1.81 kg)	40 (4 lb 6 oz)	Eggs, beaten	Combine eggs and ham. Add to vegetables and mix. Use No. 10 dipper to place mixture on preheated grill or frying pan. Brown on one side, fold in half. Serve with the following sauce.
454 g	1 lb	Ham, cooked, shredded	
57 g	2 oz	Cornstarch	Combine cornstarch and soy sauce into a smooth paste.
360 mL	1½ c	Soy sauce	
1.89 L	2 qt	Reserved vegetable juice or chicken stock	Add to vegetable juice, stirring with a wire whip. Cook until thickened.

Note: Roast pork, chicken, or bacon may be used in place of ham; green onions in place of shredded onions; and bamboo shoots and shredded water chestnuts in place of bean sprouts.

DEVILED EGGS

Yield: 50 portions
Portion: 2 halves

Amount Metric	U.S.	Ingredient	Procedure
50	50	Eggs, hard-cooked (p. 256)	Peel eggs. Cut in half lengthwise. Remove yolks to mixer bowl. Arrange whites in rows on a tray.
120 mL	½ c	Milk	Mash yolks, using flat beater. Add milk and mix until blended.
360 mL	1½ c	Mayonnaise or salad dressing	Add remaining ingredients and mix until smooth. Refill whites with mashed yolks, using approximately 1½ T for each half egg white. Sprinkle with paprika (optional).
19 g	1 T	Salt	
4 g	2 t	Mustard, dry	
120 mL	½ c	Vinegar	

Notes:
1. Pastry bag may be used to fill egg whites. Yolk mixture should be smooth and creamy. Use plain or rose tip.
2. 6 oz (170 g) finely chopped pimientos may be added to yolk mixture.

Variation: **Hot Stuffed Eggs.** To mashed egg yolks, add 3 oz (85 g) margarine or butter, melted, 2 t (12 g) salt, ⅛ t cayenne, 1 T (14 g) prepared mustard, and 1 lb (454 g) ham, minced. Arrange stuffed eggs in 2 12 × 20 × 2-in. baking pans. Cover with 1 gal (3.79 L) white sauce, 2 qt (1.89 L) per pan. Bake at 325°F (165°C) for 30 minutes. Sprinkle with chopped parsley.

CHEESE RECIPES

CHEESE BALLS

Deep-fat fryer: 360°F (180°C)
Fry: 2–3 minutes

Yield: 50 portions
150 balls
Portion: 3 balls

Amount		Ingredient	Procedure
Metric	U.S.		
4.08 kg	9 lb	Cheddar cheese, grated	Mix cheese, flour, salt, and cayenne.
227 g	8 oz	Flour, all-purpose	
38 g	2 T	Salt	
f.g.	f.g.	Cayenne	
48 (1.59 kg)	48 (3 lb 8 oz)	Egg whites	Beat egg whites until stiff. Fold into cheese mixture. Shape into balls 1–1¼ in. in diameter or dip with No. 30 dipper onto trays or baking sheets. Chill.
6 (284 g)	6 (10 oz)	Eggs	Beat eggs, add milk. Dip cheese balls in egg mixture, then roll in crumbs. Chill for several hours. Fry in deep fat for 2–3 minutes.
480 mL	2 c	Milk	
680 g	1 lb 8 oz	Bread crumbs	

Notes:
1. Serve 3 balls in center of hot buttered pineapple ring.
2. For serving as first-course accompaniment, use half the recipe and shape into balls ½–¾ in. in diameter. Yield: 150 balls
3. For 2 balls per portion, use No. 24 dipper. Yield: 40 portions.

CHEESE FONDUE

Oven: 350°F (175°C)
Bake: 50–60 minutes

Yield: 50 portions
2 pans 12 × 20 × 2 in.
Portion: 6 oz (170 g)

Amount Metric	U.S.	Ingredient	Procedure
4.26 L	4½ qt	Milk	Scald milk.
114 g	4 oz	Margarine or butter, melted	Add margarine and seasonings.
3 g	1½ t	Mustard, dry	
19 g	1 T	Salt	
f.g.	f.g.	Cayenne	
1.59 kg	3 lb 8 oz	Bread cubes, soft	Pour milk mixture over bread, 2¼ qt (2.13 L) per pan. Cool slightly.
2.04 kg	4 lb 8 oz	Cheddar cheese, shredded	Add cheese and egg yolks to bread mixture. Mix until blended.
24 (454 g)	24 (1 lb)	Egg yolks, beaten	
24 (794 g)	24 (1 lb 12 oz)	Egg whites	Beat egg whites until stiff. Fold into cheese mixture. Pour into 2 greased 12 × 20 × 2-in. pans, 10 lb (4.54 kg) per pan. Set pans in hot water. Bake at 350°F (175°C) for 50–60 minutes.

CHEESE SOUFFLÉ

Oven: 300°F (150°C)
Bake: 1 hour

Yield: 48 portions
2 pans 12 × 20 × 2 in.
Portion: 4 oz (114 g)

Amount		Ingredient	Procedure
Metric	U.S.		
567 g	1 lb 4 oz	Margarine or butter	Melt margarine. Add flour and salt. Stir until smooth. Add milk gradually, stirring constantly. Cook until thick.
284 g	10 oz	Flour, all-purpose	
6 g	1 t	Salt	
2.84 L	3 qt	Milk	
38 (680 g)	38 (1 lb 8 oz)	Egg yolks, beaten	Add egg yolks to white sauce, stirring constantly. Cook 2 minutes.
680 g	1 lb 8 oz	Cheddar cheese, shredded	Add cheese and stir until cheese is melted. Remove from heat.
38 (1.25 kg)	38 (2 lb 12 oz)	Egg whites	Add cream of tartar to egg whites. Beat until stiff, but not dry. Fold into cheese mixture. Pour 6 lb 12 oz (3.09 kg) into each of 2 12 × 20 × 2-in. baking pans greased only on the bottom. Bake at 300°F (150°C) for 55–60 minutes or until set. Cut 4 × 6.
5 g	2 t	Cream of tartar	

Note: Serve with Cheese Sauce (p. 471), Mushroom Sauce (p. 471), or Shrimp Sauce (p. 471).

Variation: **Mushroom Soufflé.** Add 1 lb (454 g) chopped mushrooms and 5 oz (142 g) chopped green peppers to uncooked mixture. Serve with Bechamel Sauce (p. 473).

CHEESE AND BROCCOLI STRATA

Oven: 325°F (165°C)
Bake: 1 hour

Yield: 56 portions
2 pans 12 × 20 × 2 in.
Portion: 8 oz (227 g)

Amount Metric	U.S.	Ingredient	Procedure
908 g	2 lb	Bread slices, dry	Cut bread into 1½-in. cubes. Set aside.
2.27 kg	5 lb	Broccoli cuts, frozen	Cook broccoli until tender.
908 g	2 lb	Cheddar cheese, shredded	Layer as follows in each pan: 8 oz (227 g) bread cubes 2 lb 8 oz (1.14 kg) broccoli 1 lb (454 g) cheese 8 oz (227 g) bread cubes
9 doz (5.44 kg) 3.79 L 57 g 85 g 8 mL	9 doz (12 lb) 1 gal 2 oz 6 T 1½ t	Eggs, beaten Milk Salt Mustard, prepared Tabasco sauce	Combine eggs, milk, and seasonings. Pour 1¼ gal (4.37 L) into each pan. Smooth down evenly.
			Sprinkle with paprika. Set each pan in another counter pan containing 3 c hot water. Bake uncovered at 325°F (165°C) until custard sets, about 1 hour. Cut 4 × 7.

Note: Baking time may be reduced if milk mixture is warmed to 140°F (60°C) before baking.

MACARONI AND CHEESE

Oven: 350°F (175°C)
Bake: 35 minutes

Yield: 48 portions
2 pans 12 × 20 × 2 in.
Portion: 8 oz (227 g)

Amount Metric	U.S.	Ingredient	Procedure
1.59 kg	3 lb 8 oz	Macaroni	Cook macaroni according to directions on p. 348. Drain.
13.25 L	3½ gal	Water, boiling	
38 g	2 T	Salt	
340 g	12 oz	Margarine or butter	Melt margarine. Stir in flour and salt. Add milk gradually, stirring constantly. Cook until thickened.
227 g	8 oz	Flour, all-purpose	
38 g	2 T	Salt	
3.79 L	1 gal	Milk, hot	
1.81 kg	4 lb	Cheddar cheese, sharp, shredded	Add cheese to sauce. Stir until cheese melts. Pour over macaroni and mix carefully. Scale into 2 greased 12 × 20 × 2-in. baking pans, 12 lb (5.44 kg) per pan.
454 g	1 lb	Bread crumbs	Mix crumbs and melted margarine. Sprinkle over macaroni and cheese, 8 oz (227 g) per pan. Bake at 350°F (175°C) for about 35 minutes.
170 g	6 oz	Margarine or butter, melted	

Variation: **Macaroni, Cheese, and Ham.** Add 3 lb (1.36 kg) chopped ham, 1 lb 8 oz (680 g) per pan.

EGGS AND CHEESE

NACHOS

Yield: 50 portions
Portion: 5 oz (142 g)

Amount Metric	Amount U.S.	Ingredient	Procedure
28 g	1 oz	Shortening	Sauté onions in shortening until tender.
85 g	3 oz	Onions, chopped	
170 g	6 oz	Green chile peppers, chopped	Add chilies and tomatoes to onions. Simmer for 15 minutes.
680 g	1 lb 8 oz	Tomatoes, diced, canned	
1.89 L	2 qt	Water	Add water, soup base, and seasonings. Bring to a boil. Reduce heat to medium.
28 g	1 oz	Chicken soup base	
7 g	1 T	Cumin	
4 g	2 t	Garlic powder	
3 kg	6 lb 10 oz	Processed cheese, shredded	Add cheese to hot mixture. Stir until melted.
85 g	3 oz	Cornstarch	Combine cornstarch and water to make a smooth paste. Add slowly to cheese mixture, stirring constantly. Cook and stir until mixture reaches desired thickness. Turn heat to low.
90 mL	3/8 c	Water	
1.81 kg	4 lb	Nacho chips	Place 12 nacho chips on dinner plate. Pour 4 oz (115 g) ladle of sauce over chips. Garnish with sliced jalapeño peppers.

Note: The sauce may be thinned with chicken broth.

WELSH RAREBIT

Yield: 50 portions
6½ qt (6.15 L)
Portion: ½ c (4 oz/114 g)

Amount Metric	U.S.	Ingredient	Procedure
284 g	10 oz	Margarine or butter	Melt margarine. Add flour and salt. Stir until smooth.
227 g	8 oz	Flour, all-purpose	
28 g	1 oz (1½ T)	Salt	Add milk gradually, stirring constantly. Cook until thickened.
3.79 L	1 gal	Milk	
2.27 kg	5 lb	Cheddar cheese, shredded or ground	Add cheese and seasonings. Cook over hot water until cheese is melted. Serve on toast or toasted buns.
14 g	2 T	Mustard, dry	
30 mL	2 T	Worcestershire sauce	
1 g	½ t	Pepper, white	

Variation: **Welsh Rarebit with Bacon.** Serve Rarebit over toast, with 2 slices cooked bacon and 2 slices fresh tomato.

FISH

PURCHASING AND STORAGE

MARKET FORMS OF FISH
Fish may be purchased fresh or frozen, and some are available canned. The most common market forms are *whole* or *round*, marketed just as they come from the water; *drawn*, entrails only removed; *dressed* or *pan dressed*, scaled and eviscerated; *steaks*, cross-section slices of the larger types of dressed fish; *fillets*, boneless sides of fish cut lengthwise; *butterfly fillets*, two sides of fish corresponding to two single fillets held together by uncut flesh; *fish sticks*, pieces of fish from fillet blocks cut into uniform sticks; and *portions*, cut from frozen fish blocks into uniform portions. Many kinds of fish are available breaded and ready to cook in various sizes and shapes.

The cost per edible pound in terms of both convenience and waste should be considered when deciding which form of fish to buy. Whole or round fish yield about 50% edible flesh after being eviscerated, scaled, and the head, tail, and fins removed; dressed fish yield 70%; steaks 90%; and fillets, sticks, and portions 100%. *Breaded* fish should contain at least 50% fish; *lightly breaded*, 65% fish.

MARKET FORMS OF SHELLFISH
Shellfish may be purchased fresh, frozen, and canned.

Clams   Clams are available alive in the shell; shucked, fresh or frozen; and canned, whole or chopped. Frozen clam strips are available for deep-fat frying.

Crabs   Crabs may be purchased alive, but most are marketed cooked and frozen in the shell, as crab legs or claws, or as frozen or canned crabmeat.

Lobsters   Northern lobsters are marketed alive in the shell and as cooked meat, fresh or frozen. A 1-lb (454 g) lobster will yield about 4 oz (114 g) cooked meat. Rock lobsters are marketed only as lobster tails, usually individually quick frozen (IQF).

Oysters   Oysters are marketed alive in the shell; shucked, fresh or frozen; and canned. Shucked oysters are in far greater demand in food services than those in the shell. Eastern oysters, which are larger and more readily available than the Olympia oysters, are graded according to the number per gallon. Small or standard oysters have 301–500 per gallon; medium or selects, 211–300; large or extra selects, 161–210; extra large or counts, 160 or less.

Scallops Scallops are always sold shucked and are available fresh, by the gallon or pound; and frozen, as individually quick frozen (IQF) or in 5-lb (2.27 kg) blocks. Large deep-sea scallops average 10–15 per pound; bay scallops are smaller, ranging from 32 to 40 per pound. Scallops also may be purchased breaded and ready to cook.

Shrimp Most shrimp are marketed frozen, although they are available canned and as fresh in some markets. Shrimp are marketed headless and are available as peeled and deveined, usually IQF; peeled, deveined, and cooked, usually IQF. Green shrimp, or raw shrimp in the shell, are marketed fresh only near the source of supply, and frozen. Shrimp also are available breaded. Shrimp are graded according to the number per pound, the higher the count the smaller the shrimp; for example, 20/25 means 20 to 25 per pound, usually considered large shrimp. Classification systems vary in different markets. The term *prawn* is sometimes used for large shrimp. Two pounds (908 g) of raw shrimp in the shells will yield about 1 lb (454 g) cooked, shelled, and deveined meat; about 1¼ lb (567 g) cooked shrimp in the shells are needed to yield 1 lb (454 g) of shelled meat.

STORAGE

Seafood is perishable and should be handled with great care during storage, thawing, preparation, cooking, and serving. Fresh fish and shellfish should be delivered packed in crushed ice and stored in the refrigerator at 35–40°F (1–4°C). Frozen seafood should be delivered hard frozen and stored in the freezer at 0°F (−18°C) or lower until it is removed for thawing and cooking. Neither fresh nor thawed fish or shellfish should be held longer than 1 day before cooking.

Frozen fish should be thawed in the refrigerator just prior to cooking. The thawing time will vary with the size and shape of the fish or package. Thawing time may be shortened by placing the wrapped packages under cold running water. Breaded fish portions and fish sticks should *not* be thawed before cooking. Frozen fillets and steaks may be cooked without thawing if additional cooking time is allowed. Fillets or steaks to be breaded or stuffed should be thawed.

COOKING METHODS

FISH

Fish by nature is tender and free of tough fibers that need to be softened by cooking and should be cooked only until the fish flakes easily when tested with a fork. Fish may be cooked in many ways, but the best method is determined by size, fat content, and flavor. Baking and broiling are suitable for fat fish. If lean fish is baked or broiled, fat is added to prevent dryness, and it often is baked in a sauce. Fish cooked in moist heat requires very little cooking time and usually is served with a sauce. Frying is suitable for all types, but those with firm flesh that will not break apart easily are best for deep-fat frying. Table 2.5 suggests cooking methods for specific types of fish. Table 2.6 lists cooking times and temperatures.

Baking Dip fish steaks or fillets in melted fat, then in flour. Season with salt, pepper, and/or herbs. Place a thin slice of lemon on each piece. Bake at 425°F (220°C) until lightly brown and tender, 20−25 minutes. Sprinkle with paprika or chopped parsley before serving. To bake whole fish for buffet display, wash and dry fish. Salt inside and out. Bake at 325°F (165°C) until fish flakes easily, about 2 hours for 12 lb (5.44 kg) and approximately 3 hours for a 20−24 lb (9.08−10.89 kg) fish. When done, gently remove skin, then garnish, being careful to arrange garnish so that fish can be cut and served easily.

Broiling Wipe fish fillets or steaks as dry as possible. Brush both sides with oil or melted margarine or butter. Season with salt and pepper and sprinkle with paprika. Lay fish on a pan covered with aluminum foil. Thick pieces of fish should be placed further from the heat than thinner pieces. Broil, turning skin-side up just long enough to crisp and brown. Serve with lemon, melted margarine or butter, and chopped parsley.

Frying Use small whole fish, fillets, or steaks. To pan fry, season with salt and pepper, roll in flour or cornmeal or a combination of both, and cook in a small amount of fat. Dip in egg and crumbs (p. 37) if fish is to be fried in deep fat. Fry 4−6 minutes at 375°F (190°C). Fried fish should be served at once, while crisp. If it must be held, arrange fish in counter pans and place uncovered in 250°F (121°C) oven until serving time. To oven fry, dip fish fillets, steaks, or small pan-dressed fish in salted milk; drain, and coat with fine dry bread crumbs. Place in shallow well-greased pans. Pour melted fat or oil over fish. Bake at 425°F (220°C) 10−15 minutes.

Poaching or Steaming Place fillets or thick slices of fish in a flat baking pan and cover with liquid. This may be acidulated water, court bouillon, fish stock, milk, or milk and water. Cover with parchment or oiled paper. Cook in a moderate oven (350°F/175°C) or in a steamer until fish loses its transparent appearance or until bones may be removed easily. Drain. Allow about 10 minutes per pound for cooking whole fish or 10 minutes for cooking fillets cut 4 to the pound. Avoid overcooking. Serve with a sauce.

Acidulated Water. Use 1 T (19 g) salt and 3 T (45 mL) lemon juice or vinegar for each quart (0.95 L) of water.

Court Bouillon. Add to 1 gal (3.79 L) of water ¾ c (180 mL) each of chopped carrots, chopped onion, and chopped celery; 3 T (57 g) salt, ½ c (120 mL) vinegar, 2 or 3 bay leaves, 6 peppercorns, 9 cloves, and 3 T (43 g) margarine or butter. Boil gently for 20−30 minutes. Strain to remove spices and vegetables.

TABLE 2.5 FISH BUYING AND COOKING GUIDE

Species	Fat or Lean	Usual Market Forms	Cooking Methods
Bass, sea	Lean	Fillets, steaks; whole pan-dressed	Fry, broil, bake
Bluefish	Fat	Fillets	Bake, poach, steam
Catfish	Lean	Whole, dressed; fillets	Fry
Cod	Lean	Fillets, steaks; breaded and precooked sticks, portions, sandwich squares	Bake, fry, broil
Flounder	Lean	Whole, pan-dressed; fillets; breaded and precooked portions	Fry, bake, broil
Grouper	Lean	Whole, steaks, fillets	Fry, bake, steam
Haddock	Lean	Whole, steaks, fillets; breaded and precooked sticks and portions	Bake, fry, steam
Halibut	Lean	Drawn, dressed, steaks	Broil, bake, fry
Mackerel	Fat	Whole, drawn; fillets	Broil, bake, poach, fry
Pike	Lean	Whole, dressed; fillets	Fry, bake
Perch	Lean	Whole, pan-dressed; fillets; breaded fillets and portions	Panfry, bake, deep-fat fry
Pollack	Lean	Fillets; breaded and precooked sticks and portions	Fry, broil, bake
Salmon	Fat	Dressed, steaks, fillets	Bake, poach, broil, panfry
Shad	Fat	Whole, drawn, fillets	Bake, poach, broil, fry
Snapper, Red	Lean	Dressed, fillets, portions	Bake, fry, broil
Sole	Lean	Whole, fillets	Bake, fry, broil, poach
Swordfish	Lean	Dressed, steaks	Broil, bake, poach
Trout, Lake	Fat	Whole, drawn, fillets	Bake, poach, panfry
Trout, Rainbow	Lean	Whole, dressed; boned and breaded fillets	Panfry, oven fry, broil, bake
Turbot	Lean	Fillets	Fry, bake
Whitefish	Fat	Whole, drawn, dressed, fillets	Bake, broil, poach
Whiting	Lean	Drawn, skinned; breaded and precooked portions and fillets	Deep-fat fry, broil, sauté, steam

TABLE 2.6 SUGGESTED METHODS OF COOKING FISH AND SHELLFISH[a]

Species	Approximate Weight[b] or Thickness	Baking Temperature[c]	Baking Min	Broiling Distance from Heat	Broiling Min	Boiling, Poaching or Steaming Method	Boiling, Poaching or Steaming Min	Deep-Fat Frying Temperature	Deep-Fat Frying Min	Panfrying Temperature	Panfrying Min
Fish											
Dressed	3–4 lb	350°F	40–60			Poach	10 per lb	325–350°F	4–6		
Pan-dressed	½–1 lb	350°F	25–30	3 in.	10–15	Poach	10	350–375°F	2–4	Moderate	10–15
Steaks	½–1¼ in.	350°F	25–35	3 in.	10–15	Poach	10	350–375°F	2–4	Moderate	10–15
Fillets		350°F	25–35	3 in.	8–15	Poach	10	350–375°F	2–4	Moderate	8–10
Portions	1–6 oz	350°F	30–40					350°F	4	Moderate	8–10
Sticks	¾–1¼ oz	400°F	15–20					350°F	3	Moderate	8–10
Shellfish											
Clams—live, shucked		450°F	12–15	4 in.	5–8	Steam	5–10	350°F	2–3	Moderate	4–5
Crabs—live, soft-shell				4 in.	8–10	Boil	10–15	375°F	2–4	Moderate	8–10
Lobsters—live	¾–1 lb	400°F	15–20	4 in.	12–15	Boil	15–20	350°F	2–4	Moderate	8–10
Spiny lobster tails—frozen	¼–½ lb	450°F	20–30	4 in.	8–12	Boil	10–15	350°F	3–5	Moderate	8–10
Oysters—live, shucked		450°F	12–15	4 in.	5–8	Steam	5–10	350°F	2–3	Moderate	4–5
Scallops—shucked		350°F	25–30	3 in.	6–8	Boil	3–4	350°F	2–3	Moderate	4–6
Shrimp											
Headless, raw						Boil	3–5				
Headless, raw, peeled		350°F	20–25	3 in.	8–10	Boil	3–5	350°F	2–3	Moderate	8–10

[a] From *How to Eye and Buy Seafood*, National Marine Fisheries Service, U.S. Department of Commerce
[b] Metric weight equivalents: see p. 32.
[c] Metric temperature equivalents: see p. 34.

SHELLFISH

Crabs Simmer hard-shelled crabs for 10–15 minutes in salted water. Cool rapidly in ice water. Break the shells apart and remove meat to be used in cooked dishes and salads. One 2-lb (908-g) crab yields about 12 oz (340 g) cooked body and leg meat. Soft-shelled crabs usually are parboiled, dipped in egg and crumbs (p. 37), pan fried or cooked in deep fat.

Lobsters To prepare frozen lobster tails, follow instructions on the package. Lobster meat, frozen or canned, may be used for salads and in cooked dishes. Live lobsters only are broiled or boiled.

Oysters Oysters are not ordinarily washed before using. If washing seems necessary, care should be taken to remove the oysters from the water quickly, so that they do not become soaked or waterlogged. They should be inspected and any bits of shell removed. Cook oysters just enough to heat through to keep oysters juicy and plump. Overcooking makes them shrunken and dry. To fry, dip oysters in egg and crumbs (p. 37) before frying.

Scallops To prepare fresh scallops, wash and remove any particles of shell. Drain. Dip in egg and crumbs (p. 37). Fry in deep fat at 350°F (175°C) 2–3 minutes.

Shrimp Raw or green shrimp should be washed carefully. Cover with water and bring to a boil. Let simmer 3 minutes in water to which has been added 1½ t salt to each quart, 2 bay leaves, and mixed spice. Drain. Remove shell and dark vein from the center back of each shrimp. To fry, dip peeled and cleaned raw or cooked shrimp in batter, or egg and crumb (p. 37). Fry in deep fat 3–5 minutes at 350–365°F (175–182°C). Breaded frozen shrimp may be cooked from their hard-frozen state.

FISH RECIPES

BAKED FISH FILLETS

Oven: 350°F (175°C)
Bake: 30 minutes

Yield: 50 portions
Portion: 5 oz (142 g)

Amount Metric	U.S.	Ingredient	Procedure
50	50	Fish fillets, 3 per lb	Dip fish in margarine.
454 g	1 lb	Margarine or butter, melted	
794 g	1 lb 12 oz	Bread crumbs	Combine bread crumbs, flour and seasonings. Dredge fish with mixture and place on greased baking pans. Bake at 350°F (175°C) for 20–30 minutes or until fish flakes easily.
284 g	10 oz	Flour, all-purpose	
19 g	1 T	Salt	
10 g	1½ T	Paprika	
19 g	1 T	Seasoned salt	
1 g	1 t	Marjoram	
2 g	1 t	Grated lemon rind	

Note: Fish portions or steaks may be substituted for fish fillets.

LEMON BAKED FISH

Oven: 350°F (175°C)
Bake: 30 minutes

Yield: 50 portions
Portion: 5 oz (142 g)

Amount Metric	U.S.	Ingredient	Procedure
50	50	Fish fillets, 3 per lb	Mix shortening, salt, pepper and lemon juice. Dip each fish portion into seasoned fat.
454 g	1 lb	Shortening, melted	
19 g	1 T	Salt	
2 g	1 t	Pepper, white	
120 mL	½ c	Lemon juice	
397 g	14 oz	Flour, all-purpose	Dredge fish with flour. Place close together in single layer in greased baking pans.
57 g	2 oz	Margarine or butter, melted	Mix margarine and milk and pour over fish. Bake at 350°F (175°C) for 20–30 minutes or until fish flakes easily.
180 mL	¾ c	Milk	

BREADED FISH FILLETS

Deep-fat fryer: 375°F (190°C)
Fry: 7–10 minutes
Yield: 50 portions
Portion: 5 oz (142 g)

Amount Metric	U.S.	Ingredient	Procedure
50	50	Fish fillets,[a] 5 oz	Dredge fish in mixture of flour, salt, and pepper.
227 g	8 oz	Flour, all-purpose	
19 g	1 T	Salt	
2 g	1 t	Pepper, white	
6 (312 g)	6 (11 oz)	Eggs, beaten	Combine eggs and milk.
480 mL	2 c	Milk	
567 g	1 lb 4 oz	Bread crumbs	Dip fish in egg mixture, then in crumbs. Fry in deep fat for 7–10 minutes or until fish is golden brown. Serve at once or place in uncovered counter pans in 250°F (120°C) oven until serving time.

[a] Suggested fish: flounder, sole, haddock, perch, grouper.

FILLET OF SOLE AMANDINE

Oven: 350°F (175°C)
Bake: 15–20 minutes
Yield: 50 portions
Portion: 5 oz (142 g)

\multicolumn{2}{c}{Amount}		
Metric	U.S.	Ingredient	Procedure
7.71 kg	17 lb	Fillet of sole, 3 per lb	Dredge fish in combined flour, salt, and pepper. Place in greased counter pans.
227 g	8 oz	Flour, all-purpose	
19 g	1 T	Salt	
2 g	1 t	Pepper, white	
680 g	1 lb 8 oz	Margarine or butter	Sauté onion and garlic in margarine.
114 g	4 oz	Onion, finely chopped	
1 clove	1 clove	Garlic, minced	
480 mL	2 c	Water	Combine. Add onion and garlic. Heat, but do not boil. Just before baking, pour sauce over fish, 1 c (240 mL) per pan.
360 mL	1½ c	Lemon juice	
19 g	1 T	Salt	
2 g	1 t	Pepper, white	
227 g	8 oz	Almonds, slivered	Sprinkle almonds over fish. Bake at 350°F (175°C) for 20–30 minutes.

Note: Other white fish, such as halibut, haddock, cod, or flounder, may be used.

DEVILED CRAB

Oven: 400°F (205°C)
Bake: 15 minutes
Yield: 50 portions
Portion: 3 oz (85 g)

Amount Metric	U.S.	Ingredient	Procedure
2.72 kg	6 lb	Crab meat	Separate crab meat into flakes.
5 (255 g)	5 (9 oz)	Eggs, beaten	Combine eggs, lemon juice, and seasonings. Add to crab meat. Mix lightly.
60 mL	4 T	Lemon juice	
28 g	1 oz (1½ T)	Salt	
4 g	2 t	Pepper	
f.g.	f.g.	Cayenne	
15 mL	1 T	Worcestershire sauce	
30 mL	2 T	Onion juice (optional)	
340 g	12 oz	Margarine or butter	Melt margarine. Add flour and mix until smooth. Add milk gradually, stirring constantly. Cook until thick.
227 g	8 oz	Flour, all-purpose	
1.89	2 qt	Milk	
8 g	1½ t	Mustard, prepared	Add mustard. Combine sauce and crab mixture. Mix lightly. Fill individual casseroles or shells.
227 g	8 oz	Bread crumbs	Sprinkle with buttered crumbs. Bake at 400°F (205°C) for 15 minutes.
114 g	4 oz	Margarine or butter, melted	

Variation: **Deviled Fish.** Use flaked white fish in place of crab meat.

SCALLOPED OYSTERS

Oven: 400°F (205°C)
Bake: 30 minutes

Yield: 50 portions
2 pans 12 × 20 × 2 in.
Portion: 5 oz (142 g)

Amount Metric	U.S.	Ingredient	Procedure
5.68 L	6 qt	Oysters	Drain oysters, saving liquor. Remove any pieces of shell.
2.84 L	3 qt	Cracker crumbs	Mix crumbs, margarine, and seasonings. Spread a third over bottoms of 2 greased 12 × 20 × 2-in. baking pans. Cover with half of the oysters; repeat with crumbs and oysters.
454 g	1 lb	Margarine or butter, melted	
28 g	1 oz (1½ T)	Salt	
1 g	½ t	Paprika	
1 g	½ t	Pepper, white	
0.95 L	1 qt	Milk or cream	Mix milk or cream and oyster liquor. Pour over top of oysters. Cover with remaining crumbs. Bake at 400°F (205°C) for 30 minutes.
720 mL	3 c	Oyster liquor (or milk)	

Note: 2 c (480 mL) finely chopped, partially cooked celery may be added.

CREOLE SHRIMP WITH RICE

Yield: 50 portions
Portion: 4 oz (114 g) Creole Shrimp
4 oz (114 g) rice

Amount			
Metric	U.S.	Ingredient	Procedure
227 g	8 oz	Shortening	Cook onion, celery, and
284 g	10 oz	Onion, chopped fine	garlic in shortening
340 g	12 oz	Celery, chopped fine	until almost tender but
5 g	1 t	Garlic, minced	not brown.
170 g	6 oz	Flour, all-purpose	Add flour, salt, and red
28 g	1 oz (1½ T)	Salt	pepper. Stir until
1 g	½ t	Pepper, red	smooth. Cook 5 minutes.
480 mL	2 c	Tomato juice	Add tomato juice,
2.37 L	2½ qt	Tomatoes, canned, diced	tomatoes, and sugar.
14 g	1 T	Sugar, granulated	Cook 10 minutes.
2.72 kg	6 lb (EP)	Shrimp, cooked, peeled, and deveined	Add shrimp and green pepper to sauce. Heat to serving temperature.
227 g	8 oz	Green pepper, chopped	
1.59 kg	3 lb 8 oz	Rice, long-grain	Cook rice according to
4 L	4¼ qt	Water, boiling	directions on p. 358.
38 g	2 T	Salt	Serve shrimp with 4-oz
30 mL	2 T	Cooking oil	ladle over No. 10 dipper of rice.

Note: If raw shrimp are used, purchase 12–14 lb (5.44–6.35 kg). Cook as directed on p. 280.

SALMON LOAF

Oven: 325°F (165°C)
Bake: 1¼ hours

Yield: 50 portions
5 loaves 5 × 9 in.
Portion: 3½ oz (100 g)

Amount		Ingredient	Procedure
Metric	U.S.		
720 mL	3 c	Milk, scalded	Mix milk and bread cubes.
454 g	1 lb	Bread cubes, soft	
15 (737 g)	15 (1 lb 10 oz)	Eggs	Beat eggs. Add to milk and bread cubes.
3.63 kg	8 lb	Salmon, flaked	Add salmon and other ingredients. Mix lightly.
23 g	1½ T	Salt	
2 g	1 t	Paprika	Place in 5 greased 5 × 9-in. loaf pans, 2 lb 8 oz (1.14 kg) per pan. Set in pans of hot water to bake. Bake at 325°F (165°C) for 1–1¼ hours.
57 g	2 oz	Onions, chopped	
120 mL	½ c	Lemon juice	
1 g	½ t	Pepper, white	

Note: For a lighter-textured product, beat egg whites separately and fold into salmon mixture.

SALMON CROQUETTES

Deep-fat fryer: 375°F (190°C)
Fry: 4 minutes
Yield: 100 croquettes
Portion: 2 2½-oz (70-g) croquettes

Amount Metric	U.S.	Ingredient	Procedure
340 g	12 oz	Margarine or butter	Melt margarine. Add flour and salt. Stir until smooth. Add milk gradually, stirring constantly. Cook until thick. Cool.
255 g	9 oz	Flour, all-purpose	
6 g	1 t	Salt	
1.42 L	1½ qt	Milk	
3.63 kg	8 lb	Salmon	Drain salmon. Remove skin and bones. Flake salmon and add to white sauce.
170 g	6 oz	Cornflake crumbs	Add cornflakes, onions, and pimiento to salmon mixture. Mix carefully. Measure with No. 20 dipper onto greased baking sheets. Chill. Shape croquettes cylindrically.
28 g	3 T	Onion, finely chopped	
198 g	7 oz	Pimiento, chopped	
8 (397 g)	8 (14 oz)	Eggs, beaten	Combine eggs and milk. Dip croquettes in egg mixture, then roll in crumbs. Fry in deep fat for about 4 minutes. Serve with Egg Sauce (p. 471).
480 mL	2 c	Milk or water	
680 g	1 lb 8 oz	Bread crumbs	

Note: The croquettes may be baked about 30 minutes in a 400°F (205°C) oven.

Variations:
1. **Salmon Patties.** Measure with No. 8 dipper and flatten into 50 patties. Place on greased baking pans. Bake at 350°F (175°C) for 30 minutes. May be grilled on lightly greased grill preheated to 325°F (165°C).
2. **Tuna Patties.** Substitute tuna or flaked white fish for salmon.

SCALLOPED SALMON

Oven: 375°F (190°C)
Bake: 25 minutes

Yield: 50 portions
2 pans 12 × 20 × 2 in.
Portion: 6 oz (170 g)

Amount		Ingredient	Procedure
Metric	U.S.		
454 g	1 lb	Margarine or butter	Melt margarine. Add flour and seasonings and stir until smooth. Add milk gradually, stirring constantly. Continue cooking until thickened.
340 g	12 oz	Flour, all-purpose	
28 g	1 oz (1½ T)	Salt	
1 g	½ t	Pepper, white	
3.79 L	1 gal	Milk	
60 mL	¼ c	Parsley, chopped	Add to sauce.
114 g	4 oz	Onion, chopped	
5 g	1 t	Celery salt	
4.54 kg	10 lb	Salmon	Drain salmon. Remove skin and bones. Flake.
227 g	8 oz	Bread crumbs	Arrange salmon, sauce, and crumbs in layers in 2 greased 12 × 20 × 2-in. baking pans, 10 lb (4.54. kg) per pan.
114 g	4 oz	Bread crumbs	Sprinkle buttered crumbs over top. Bake at 375°F (190°C) for 25 minutes.
114 g	4 oz	Margarine or butter, melted	

Note: Diced hard-cooked eggs and frozen peas are good additions.

Variation: **Scalloped Tuna.** Substitute tuna for salmon.

SALMON AND POTATO CHIP CASSEROLE

Oven: 375°F (190°C)
Bake: 20 minutes

Yield: 48 portions
2 pans 12 × 20 × 2 in.
Portion: 7 oz (198 g)

Amount Metric	U.S.	Ingredient	Procedure
340 g	12 oz	Margarine or butter	Melt margarine. Add flour stir until blended. Add soup and cook until mixture is thickened.
227 g	8 oz	Flour, all-purpose	
3 cans	3 46-oz cans	Cream of mushroom soup	
5.44 kg	12 lb	Salmon	Drain salmon. Remove skin and bones. Flake.
1.7 kg	3 lb 12 oz	Potato chips, coarsely crushed	Arrange 6 lb (2.72 kg) salmon 1¾ lb (794 g) potato chips, and 5 lb (2.27 kg) sauce in layers in each of 2 greased 12 × 20 × 2-in. baking pans. Bake at 375°F (190°C) for 20 minutes.

Note: 1 can cream of celery soup may be substituted for 1 can of cream of mushroom soup.

Variation: **Tuna and Potato Chip Casserole.** Substitute tuna for salmon.

TUNA AND NOODLES

Oven: 350°F (175°C)
Bake: 45 minutes

Yield: 48 portions
2 pans 12 × 20 × 2 in.
Portion: 8 oz (227 g)

Amount		Ingredient	Procedure
Metric	U.S.		
1.36 kg	3 lb	Noodles	Cook noodles according to directions on p. 348. Drain.
11.36 L	3 gal	Water, boiling	
57 g	2 oz (3 T)	Salt	
30 mL	2 T	Oil (optional)	
3.4 kg	7 lb 8 oz	Tuna	Flake tuna and add to noodles.
340 g	12 oz	Margarine or butter	Melt margarine. Add onions and sauté until tender.
114 g	4 oz	Onion, chopped	
170 g	6 oz	Flour, all-purpose	Add flour and seasonings. Stir until smooth.
24 g	4 t	Salt	
12 g	2 t	Celery salt	
2.84 L	3 qt	Milk	Add milk gradually, stirring constantly. Cook until thickened. Add to tuna and noodles. Divide into 2 greased 12 × 20 × 2-in. baking pans, 12 lb 8 oz (5.67 kg) per pan. Bake at 350°F (175°C) for 30 minutes.
680 g	1 lb 8 oz	Cheddar cheese, shredded	Sprinkle cheese over the noodles. Bake 15 minutes longer.

Note: 2½ 46-oz cans cream of mushroom or cream of celery soup may be substituted for the white sauce.

Variation: **Tuna and Rice.** Substitute 1 lb 8 oz (608 g) rice for the noodles.

CREAMED TUNA

Yield: 50 portions
7½ qt (7.1 L)
Portion: 4 oz (114 g)

Amount		Ingredient	Procedure
Metric	U.S.		
9	9	Eggs, hard-cooked (p. 256)	Peel eggs and chop coarsely.
340 g	12 oz	Margarine or butter	Melt margarine. Add flour and salt. Stir until smooth.
170 g	6 oz	Flour, all-purpose	
19 g	1 T	Salt	
3.79 L	1 gal	Milk	Add milk gradually, stirring constantly. Cook until thickened.
170 g	6 oz	Green pepper, chopped	Add green pepper, pimiento and seasonings to sauce.
170 g	6 oz	Pimiento, chopped	
90 mL	6 T	Worcestershire sauce (optional)	
¼ t	¼ t	Cayenne	
2.27 kg	5 lb	Tuna, flaked	Add tuna and hard-cooked eggs. Reheat to serving temperature. Serve with 4-oz ladle on toast, biscuits, or cornbread.

Note: Other cooked fish may be substituted for tuna.

Variations:

1. **Creamed Salmon.** Substitute salmon for tuna.

2. **Creamed Tuna and Celery.** Delete hard-cooked eggs and green pepper. Add 1 lb (454 g) diced cooked celery, 3 oz (85 g) chopped onion sautéed in margarine, and 3 oz (85 g) chopped pimiento.

3. **Creamed Tuna and Peas.** Delete hard-cooked eggs and green pepper. Add 3 lb (1.26 kg) frozen peas, cooked until just tender and drained.

4. **Tuna Rarebit.** Delete hard-cooked eggs. Add 1½ lb (680 g) shredded Cheddar cheese.

Meat

PURCHASING AND STORAGE

The quality of cooked meat depends on the quality purchased, the storage and handling of meat after delivery, and cooking methods. All meats marketed in interstate commerce must meet federal inspection standards for wholesomeness. This includes all processed meat products and fresh and frozen meats. Meat slaughtered, processed, and sold within a given state may not necessarily be federally inspected but is subject to state inspection.

Federal grading is on a voluntary basis. Federal and packer brand grades of meat are based on quality of the flesh and the degree of marbling and fat cover. Beef and lamb, when federally graded, also must be given a yield grade that measures the amount of lean meat that can be cut from a carcass.

Meat for institution food service is available in wholesale cuts, fabricated roasts, and portion-ready items. The form in which meat is purchased depends on the policies and size of the institution, the type of service it offers, and its storage and meat-cutting facilities. Fabricated and portion-ready cuts require less storage space, eliminate skilled labor for cutting, and do away with waste. Costs are easily controlled, since the weight and price of each portion are predetermined and only the amount needed is ordered.

Fresh meat may be stored unwrapped or loosely covered with waxed paper on trays at a temperature of 35–40°F (1–4°C), with a relative humidity of 80–90%. It should be used as soon after purchase as possible. The temperature should not fall below freezing, unless frozen meat is being stored.

Frozen meat requires a uniform holding temperature of 0°F (−18°C) or below. It should be well wrapped to exclude air and to prevent drying. If the meat is to be frozen on the premises, the temperature should be even lower, with some air movement. If possible, meat should be frozen in a blast freezer set at −20 to −40°F (−29 to −40°C) with forced air convection.

Frozen meat should not be unwrapped before defrosting in the refrigerator at 30–35°F (−1 to 1°C). It is not necessary to defrost meat cuts before cooking, with the exception of steaks and chops that are to be coated for frying or baking.

Meat should be cooked soon after defrosting. Once thawed, it should not be refrozen unless in an emergency and then there will be some sacrifice in juiciness. Cooked meat may be frozen provided it is frozen immediately after cooking and cooling.

Cured, and cured and smoked, meats such as ham and bacon, sausages, and dried beef require refrigerator storage. The two principal types of ham used in institution food services are *fully cooked ham*, which has been cooked sufficiently that it may be served without further cooking or may be heated just enough to serve hot; fully cooked hams require storage at refrigerator temperature before and after heating. Most canned hams, which are also fully cooked, require refrigeration. *Cook-before-eating hams* are partially cooked in processing and must be kept under refrigeration. Commercially processed hams indicate on the label which type they are or to what degree they have been cooked. Although ham, bacon, and other cured meats can be frozen, it should be only for short periods, since undesirable flavor changes occur because of the salt and spices in them.

COOKING METHODS

Meat is cooked either by dry or moist heat. The method used will depend on the grade and location of the cut. Tender cuts of high-grade meat usually are cooked by dry heat (roasted, broiled, or fried). Moist heat (braised or cooked in liquid) is used for less tender cuts from the upper grades and for all lower-grade cuts. There are exceptions to this rule, however. Veal, lamb, and pork, all tender meats, often are cooked with moist heat to develop their flavor and to provide variety in menu items. Veal, because of its delicate flavor and low fat content, combines well with sauces and other foods.

Dry-heat cookery does not improve tenderness and, under some conditions, it reduces it. Cooking with moist heat tends to make meat tender. A low temperature, regardless of the method, is desirable. The degree of doneness affects losses. The percentage loss is smaller in rare meat than in medium- or well-done meat, provided other factors are the same.

ROASTING

In roasting, which is a dry-heat method, meat is cooked in an oven, in an open pan, with no moisture added. Meat cuts must be tender to be roasted. In beef these are the lesser used muscles, or those attached to the backbone. In veal, pork, and lamb practically any cut may be cooked by this method.

Meats may be completely or partially defrosted or frozen at the time the cooking process is begun. Research has shown that meat roasted from the frozen state will yield as much meat as roasts partially or completely thawed before cooking. However, when time is a factor, as it is in a food service, defrosting meat before cooking usually is the accepted method. The additional cooking time required for frozen roasts is from ⅓ to ½ again the amount of time recommended for cooking a similar cut from the chilled state. Steps in roasting are:

1. Place the meat, fat-side up, on a rack, in an open roasting pan.
2. Insert a meat thermometer in the roast so that the bulb rests in the center of the cut, but not in contact with bone or a pocket of fat. If the meat is frozen, the

thermometer is inserted toward the end of the cooking period after the meat has thawed.

3. Season the roast with salt, pepper, and/or other spices if desired. Salt penetrates less than an inch during cooking, so it may make little difference whether the roast is seasoned at the beginning, during, or end of cooking.

4. Do not add water and do not cover. If water is added to the pan, the cooking will be by moist heat.

5. Roast at a constant low oven temperature, 250–350°F (121–175°C), depending on the kind of meat and size of the roast. If cooking in a convection oven, the temperature should be reduced by 50°F (10°C) to minimize drying of the surface of the roast by moving air. Searing the roast initially at a high temperature does not hold in meat juices and may increase cooking losses. A constant low temperature reduces shrinkage and produces a more evenly done roast that is easier to carve and more attractive to serve.

6. Roast to the desired degree of doneness. The length of the cooking period depends on several factors: oven temperature, size and shape of roast, style of cut (boned or bone in), oven load, quality of meat, and degree of doneness desired. Approximate cooking times and temperatures are given in Tables 2.7, 2.8, and 2.9. Although approximate total cooking time can be used as a general guide, the interior temperature of the meat as measured by a meat thermometer is a more reliable indicator of doneness. Roasts will continue cooking for a period of time after removal from the oven, and the internal temperature of the roast may rise as much as 10°F.

The roast should be allowed to set in a warm place for 15–20 minutes before it is sliced. The roast becomes more firm, retains more of its juices, and is easier to slice. Refrigerating the roast for an extended period of time prior to slicing and service, however, results in loss of flavor. To ensure the highest quality, roasts should be served as soon as possible after cooking and slicing.

BROILING

Broiling is a dry-heat cookery method using direct or radiant heat. It is used for small individualized cuts such as steaks, chops, and patties. Broiling is most successful for cuts 1–2 in. thick. Veal should not be broiled unless it is fairly mature and well marbled with fat, and then only loin chops or steaks. Recent research has shown that broiling is an acceptable cookery method for pork chops, but because pork should be cooked to an internal temperature of 170°F (75°C), the temperature should be moderate so the chop does not become charred by the time it is cooked well done.

Frozen cuts may be successfully broiled, especially those 1½ in. thick or less. They should be broiled at a greater distance from the heat or at a lower temperature than unfrozen cuts to provide more uniform doneness. Although cooking times will vary, a general guideline is that frozen steaks will take nearly twice as long as unfrozen steaks.

TABLE 2.7 TIMETABLE FOR ROASTING BEEF[a]

Cut	Approximate Weight of Single Roast (lb)[b]	Oven Temperature[c]	Interior Temperature of Roast when Removed from Oven[c]	Minutes per Pound Based on One Roast	Minutes per Pound Based on Total Weight of Roasts in Oven	Approximate Total Cooking Time
Rib (7-rib)	20–25	250°F	130°F (rare) 140°F (medium) 150°F (well)	13–15 15–17 17–19		4½–5 hr 5–6 hr 6–6½ hr
Rib (7-rib)	20–25	300°F	130°F (rare) 140°F (medium) 150°F (well)	10–12 12–14 14–16		4–4½ hr 4½–5 hr 5–5½ hr
Rib (7-rib)	56 (2 roasts)	300°F	130°F (rare) 140°F (medium) 150°F (well)		5 to 6 6 7 to 8	5–5½ hr 6 hr 6–7 hr
Rib eye	4–6	350°F	140°F (rare) 160°F (medium) 170°F (well)	18–20 20–22 22–24		1¼–1⅔ hr 1½–2 hr 1⅔–2¼ hr
Tenderloin, whole	4–6	425°F	140°F (rare)			45–60 min
Top loin, boneless	10–12	325°F	140°F (rare)	10		1½–2 hr
Top sirloin butt	8	300°F	140°F (rare)	25		3½ hr
Rump	5–7	300°F	150°F–170°F	25–30		2–3 hr
Top round	10	300°F	140°F (rare) 150°F (medium)	18–19 22–23		3–3¼ hr 3½–4 hr
Top round	15	300°F	140°F (rare) 150°F (medium)	15 17		3½–4 hr 4–4½ hr
Round (rump and shank off)	50	250°F	140°F (medium) 155°F (well)	12 14		10 hr 11–12 hr

From *Meat in the Foodservice Industry*, copyright 1977, National Live Stock and Meat Board, Chicago, IL, p. 62, 1977, reviewed 1982.

Metric weight equivalents: see p. 32.

Metric temperature equivalents: see p. 34.

TABLE 2.8 TIMETABLE FOR ROASTING LAMB AND VEAL[a]

Cut	*Approximate Weight (lb)[b]*	*Oven Temperature[c]*	*Interior Temperature of Roast when Removed from Oven*	*Minutes per Pound Based on One Roast*	*Approximate Total Cooking Time*
LAMB					
Leg	5–9	325°F	140°F (rare) 160°F (medium) 170°F–180°F (well)	20–25 25–30 30–35	2–3 hr 2½–3¾ hr 3–4½ hr
Leg, boneless	4–7	325°F	140°F (rare) 160°F (medium) 170°F–180°F (well)	25–30 30–35 35–40	2–3 hr 2¼–3½ hr 2½–4 hr
Crown roast	2½–4	325°F	140°F (rare) 160°F (medium) 170°F–180°F (well)	30–35 35–40 40–45	1½–2 hr 1¾–2¼ hr 2–2¾ hr
Shoulder, boneless	3½–5	325°F	140°F (rare) 160°F (medium) 170°F–180°F (well)	30–35 35–40 40–45	2–2½ hr 2¼–3 hr 2½–3½ hr
Rib	1½–2	375°F	140°F (rare) 160°F (medium) 160°F–180°F (well)	30–35 35–40 40–45	¾–1 hr 1–1¼ hr 1–1½ hr
Rib	2–3	375°F	140°F (rare) 160°F (medium) 170°F–180°F (well)	25–30 30–35 35–40	1–1¼ hr 1¼–1½ hr 1½–1¾ hr
VEAL					
Leg, rump and shank off	5–8	325°F	170°F	25–35	3–3½ hr
Leg, rump and shank off, boneless	3½–7	325°F	170°F	25–30	2–3 hr
Loin	4–6	325°F	170°F	30–35	2½–3 hr
Rib (rack)	3–5	325°F	170°F	30–35	1½–2½ hr
Shoulder, boneless	4–6	325°F	170°F	40–45	3–3½ hr

[a] From *Meat in the Foodservice Industry*, copyright 1977, National Live Stock and Meat Board, Chicago, IL., p. 63 1977, reviewed 1982.

[b] Metric weight equivalents: see p. 32.

[c] Metric temperature equivalents: see p. 34.

TABLE 2.9 TIMETABLE FOR ROASTING FRESH AND CURED PORK[a]

Cut	Approximate Weight (lb)[b]	Oven Temperature[c]	Interior Temperature of Roast when Removed from Oven[c]	Minutes per Pound Based on One Roast	Approximate Total Cooking Time
Fresh Pork					
Loin, boneless, tied	8–10	325°F	170°F	30–35	4½–5½ hr
Center loin	3–5	325°F	170°F	30–35	1¾–2½ hr
Picnic (shoulder)	5–8	325°F	170°F	30–35	3–4 hr
Picnic shoulder, boneless	4–6	325°F	170°F	35–40	3–3½ hr
Boston shoulder, boneless	4–6	325°F	170°F	40–45	3–4 hr
Ham (leg)	12–16	325°F	170°F	22–26	5–6 hr
Ham (leg) boneless, tied	10–14	325°F	170°F	24–28	4½–5½ hr
Spareribs	2–3	325°F	Cooked well done		1½–2½ hr
Cured Pork[d]					
Whole ham[e]	10–14	325°F	160°F	18–20	3–4 hr
Half ham[e]	5–7	325°F	160°F	22–25	2–3 hr
Whole ham, fully cooked	8–10	325°F	140°F	15–18	
Half ham, fully cooked	4–5	325°F	140°F	18–24	
Shoulder roll (butt)	2–4	325°F	170°F	35–40	1–2 hr
Arm picnic shoulder	5–8	325°F	170°F	30–35	3–4 hr
Canadian-style bacon	2–4	325°F	160°F	35–40	1–1¾ hr

[a] Adapted from *Meat in the Foodservice Industry*, copyright 1977, National Live Stock and Meat Board, Chicago, IL, pp. 62, 63, 1977, reviewed 1982.

[b] Metric weight equivalents: see p. 32.

[c] Metric temperature equivalents: see p. 34.

[d] Cooking times for cook-before-eating products except those specified "fully cooked".

Meat may be broiled in an oven broiler or other type of heat-from-above gas or electric broiler, or on an open hearth, which is heated from below. In pan broiling or griddle broiling, the heat is transferred from the pan or grill to the meat being cooked.

OVEN BROILING
1. Preheat the broiler.
2. Place meat on the broiler rack or grid 3–5 in. from the heat, depending on the thickness of the meat, the type and size of the equipment, the source of heat, and whether the meat is frozen.
3. Broil on one side until meat is browned and approximately half done. Season browned side, then turn and brown on the opposite side and cook to the desired degree of doneness. (See Table 2.10 for time.) Season second side. The meat should be turned only once.

PAN BROILING AND GRIDDLE BROILING
1. Place meat on a preheated ungreased griddle or heavy frying pan.
2. Cook slowly, turning as necessary. Since the meat is in contact with the hot metal of the pan or griddle, turning more than once may be necessary for even cooking. If the steak is a thick one, reduce the temperature after browning. Griddle broiling requires more attention than true broiling, but is more rapid than cooking in some types of broilers.
3. Care should be taken not to puncture the meat with the fork while cooking. A long-handled tong or a spatula is better than a fork for turning the meat.
4. Neither water nor fat should be added. Excess fat should be scraped from the griddle as it accumulates.
5. Cook the meat to the desired degree of doneness. See Table 2.11 for approximate cooking times.

FRYING
Frying is cooking in fat and may be accomplished by pan frying or griddle frying in a small amount of fat or by deep-fat frying, which uses a large amount of fat.

Meat for frying generally is cut thinner than that for broiling and may be breaded or tenderized by scoring, cubing, or grinding. Cuts lacking fat such as veal cutlets and liver or other variety meats usually are fried.

Procedures for pan frying or griddle frying are similar to pan- or griddle broiling, but the meat may be dredged with seasoned flour, and a small amount of fat is used for cooking.

TABLE 2.10 TIMETABLE FOR BROILING MEAT[a]

Cut	Approximate Thickness	Approximate Total Cooking Time		
		Rare (min)	Medium (min)	Well done (min)
Rib, club, top loin, T-bone, Porterhouse, tenderloin, or individual servings of beef sirloin steak	1 in.	15	20	
	1½ in.	25	35	
	2 in.	35	50	
Beef sirloin steak	1 in.	20–25	30–35	
	1½ in.	30–35	40–45	
Ground beef patties	1 in. (4 oz)	15	20	
Pork chops (rib or loin)	¾–1 in.			20–25
Pork shoulder steaks	½–¾ in.			20–22
Smoked pork chops (rib or loin)	½–¾ in.			15–20
Lamb shoulder, rib, loin, and sirloin chops or leg chops (steaks)	1 in.		12–16	
	1½ in.		17–20	
	2 in.		20–25	
Ground lamb patties	1 in. (4 oz)		18–20	
Smoked ham slice (cook-before eating)[b]	½ in.			10–12
	1 in.			16–20
Bacon				4–5

[a] From *Meat in the Foodservice Industry*, National Live Stock and Meat Board, Chicago, IL, p. 66, 1977, reviewed 1982.

[b] Allow 8–10 min for broiling ½-in. thick "fully cooked" ham slice and 14–16 min for 1-in. thick "fully cooked" ham slice.

TABLE 2.11 TIMETABLE FOR GRIDDLE BROILING MEAT[a]

Cut	Approximate Thickness	Approximate Total Cooking Time		
		Rare (min)	Medium (min)	Well done (min)
Beef steaks	¾ in.	4	8	12
	1 in.	6	10	15
	1½ in.	10–12	15–18	20
Ground beef patties	¾ in.	4–5	8–10	12
	1 in. (4 oz)	6–8	10–12	15
Lamb chops	1 in.		10	15
	1½ in.		15	20–25
Ground lamb patties	¾ in.		10	12–15
	1 in. (4 oz)		10–15	15–20
Smoked ham slice	½ in.			6–10
Bacon				2–3

[a] From *Meat in the Foodservice Industry*, National Live Stock and Meat Board, Chicago, IL, p. 68, 1977, reviewed 1982.

302   MEAT

Procedures for deep-fat frying follow:

1. Coat or bread meat (see p. 37 for methods of preparing food for deep-fat frying). Portioned, prebreaded items may be cooked from a frozen state in the deep-fat fryer.
2. Heat the fat to approximately 350°F (175°C).
3. Place pieces of meat in the wire basket and carefully lower into the fryer. Do not fill the basket while holding over the fat, because crumbs could fall into the fat.
4. Do not overload the basket or the fryer. An overload drastically reduces the temperature of the fat, thereby increasing fat absorption and inhibiting browning. This is especially true when the product is frozen. A ratio of about 5 to 1 by weight of fat to product is the maximum effective load.
5. Continue cooking until the outside of the product is browned and crisp and the meat reaches the desired doneness.
6. Remove meat from the fat and let drain. Do not shake the basket over the fat if the product is coated; this will cause particles and crumbs to fall into the fat. The product should not be salted over the fat, either, because salt shortens the life of the fat.

BRAISING

Braising is a moist-cookery method adapted to the less tender cuts of meat, particularly the much used muscles and low grades of beef. Certain cuts of veal and thin cuts of pork such as chops and steaks are better if braised, although they are tender. The terms *pot roasting* or *fricasseeing* also are applied to this method of cooking. Steps in braising are:

1. Season meat with salt (¼ t per pound of meat) and pepper if desired. Meat may be dredged with flour to increase browning.
2. Brown meat in a small amount of fat in a heavy kettle, roasting pan, tilting frypan, or steam-jacketed kettle.
3. Add small amount of water or other liquid; use additional liquid as needed during the cooking. Braising or pot roasting in a steam-jacketed kettle will require more water than pot roasting in the oven. Other liquid, such as meat stock, tomato juice, or cultured sour cream, may be used.
4. Cover; simmer until tender or bake at 325°F (165°C). See Table 2.12 for approximate cooking times.

COOKING IN LIQUID

This method of moist cookery involves cooking meat covered with water or other liquid and is sometimes referred to as *simmering, boiling,* or *stewing.* This method is suitable for the least tender cuts such as shank, neck, and brisket, and for variety meats such as heart and tongue.

1. Brown meat if desired and cover with water.
2. Season with salt and pepper. Herbs and spices, used wisely, add to the variety and flavor of stewed meats. Suggested seasonings are carrots, celery, onions, bay leaves, thyme, marjoram, and parsley.
3. Cook below boiling point until tender in a steam-jacketed kettle, tilting fry pan, or in a tightly covered heavy utensil on top of the range. See Table 2.13 for approximate cooking times.

TABLE 2.12   TIMETABLE FOR BRAISING MEAT[a]

Cut	Average Weight or Thickness	Approximate Total Cooking Time
Pot roast	4–6 lb	3–4 hr
Swiss steak	1–2½ in.	2–3 hr.
Round steak	½ in. (pounded)	45 min–1 hr
Short ribs	pieces 2 × 2 × 2 in.	1½–2 hr
Lamb shanks	½ lb each	1–1½ hr
Lamb neck slices	½–¾ in.	1–1½ hr
Lamb riblets	¾ × 2½ × 3 in.	1½–2½ hr
Pork chops or steaks	¾–1 in.	45 min–1 hr
Spareribs	2–3 lb	1½ hr
Veal cutlets	½ × 3 × 5½ in.	45 min–1 hr
Veal steaks or chops	½–¾ in.	45 min–1 hr

[a] From *Meat in the Foodservice Industry*, National Live Stock and Meat Board, Chicago, IL, p. 73, 1977, reviewed 1982.

TABLE 2.13   TIMETABLE FOR COOKING MEAT IN LIQUID (LARGE CUTS AND STEWS)[a]

Cut	Average Size or Average Weight	Approximate Cooking Time Min per lb	Total hr
Fresh beef	4–8 lb	40–50	3–4
Corned beef	6–8 lb	40–50	4–6
Beef shank cross-cuts	¾–1 lb		2½–3½
Lamb or veal for stew	1 to 2-in. cubes		1½–2½
Beef for stew	1 to 2-in. cubes		2–3

[a] From *Meat in the Foodservice Industry*, National Live Stock and Meat Board, Chicago, IL, p. 75, 1977, reviewed 1982.

MEAT RECIPES

Beef

POT ROAST OF BEEF

Oven: 300°F (150°F)
Bake: 4–5 hours

Yield: 50 portions
Portion: 3 oz (85 g)

Amount Metric	U.S.	Ingredient	Procedure
8.16 kg	18 lb	Beef, boneless inside round	Season meat with salt and pepper. Place in roasting pan and brown at 450°F (230°C) about 30 minutes.
28 g	1 oz (1½ T)	Salt	
1 g	½ t	Pepper, black	
1.89 L	2 qt	Water	When meat is browned, add water. Reduce heat to 300°F (150°C). Cover and cook slowly until tender (3–5 hours). Add water as necessary. When meat is done, remove from pan. Let stand ½ hour before slicing.
170 g	6 oz	Flour, all-purpose	Mix flour and cold water, stirring with wire whip until smooth. Add to drippings in pan. Remove excess fat if necessary and add water to make 1 gal (3.79 L) gravy.
360 mL	1½ c	Water, cold	
28 g	1 oz (1½ T)	Salt	
1 g	½ t	Pepper, black	
		Water as necessary	

Notes:
1. Beef chuck may be used. Increase to 20 lb (9.08 kg) AP.
2. Meat may be cooked in a steam-jacketed kettle. Brown in a small amount of fat. Add water, salt, and pepper. Cover kettle and cook until tender. Add water as necessary.

Variations:

1. **Savory Pot Roast or Brisket.** Place meat in baking pan. Sprinkle with 5 oz (142 g) dry onion soup mix. Cover tightly with alumium foil. Bake at 300°F (150°C) for 5–6 hours. Remove foil and bake ½ hour longer. Use juice for gravy. If brisket is used, increase to 25 lb (11.34 kg). Cooked Barbecue Sauce (p. 477) may be added the last half hour of cooking.

2. **Smoked Beef Brisket.** Combine ⅔ c (60 mL) liquid smoke, 1 T (19 g) salt, 1 T (19 g) onion salt, 3 T (57 g) celery salt, 3 T (57 g) garlic salt, 3 T (45 mL) Worcestershire sauce, and 1 T (7 g) black pepper. Spread on brisket. Cover with aluminum foil. Seal. Refrigerate overnight. Bake at 300°F (150°C) for 4 hours covered. Uncover and spread with Barbecue Sauce (p. 477). Bake 1 hour longer. To serve, slice in thin slices across the grain of the meat.

3. **Yankee Pot Roast.** Add 1½ qt (1.42 L) tomato purée and 1 bay leaf to the water used in cooking pot roast.

SALISBURY STEAK

Oven: 325°F (165°C)
Bake: 25 minutes
Yield: 50 portions
Portion: 5 oz (142 g)

Amount Metric	U.S.	Ingredient	Procedure
5.67 kg	12 lb 8 oz	Ground beef	Combine and mix on low
680 g	1 lb 8 oz	Bread crumbs	speed until blended.
14	14	Eggs	Do not overmix.
(680 g)	(1 lb 8 oz)		Portion onto greased
227 g	8 oz	Onions, chopped	pans, using No. 8
70 g	2½ oz	Salt	dipper. Flatten slightly.
1 g	½ t	Pepper, black	Bake at 325°F (165°C) for
1.08 L	4½ c	Milk	25 minutes. Pour off grease. Place in counter pans for serving.

Note: Steaks may be browned on a grill.

Variation: **Bacon-Wrapped Beef.** To 15 lb (6.8 kg) ground beef, add 4 oz (114 g) chopped green pepper, 8 oz (227 g) chopped onion, 2½ c (600 mL) catsup, 2 T (38 g) salt, and 1 T (7 g) black pepper. Shape as above and wrap 1 slice bacon around each portion. Place on baking sheet. Bake at 350°F (175°F) for 30–45 minutes.

SWISS STEAK

Oven: 350°F (175°C)
Bake: 2–2½ hours

Yield: 50 portions
Portion: 5 oz (142 g)

Amount		Ingredient	Procedure
Metric	*U.S.*		
7.71 kg	17 lb AP	Beef round, sliced, ¾ in. thick	Cut meat into portions, 3 per lb (454 g).
454 g	1 lb	Flour, all-purpose	Mix flour, salt, and pepper. Pound into meat.
85 g	3 oz	Salt	
4 g	2 t	Pepper, black	
680 g	1 lb 8 oz	Shortening, hot	Brown meat in shortening. Place, slightly overlapping, in 2 12 × 20 × 2-in. baking or counter pans.
170 g	6 oz	Fat (meat drippings), hot	Make gravy according to directions on p. 476. Add 1½ qt (1.42 L) to each pan. Cover tightly with aluminum foil. Bake at 350°F (175°C) for 2–2½ hours.
170 g	6 oz	Flour, all-purpose	
12 g	2 t	Salt	
2 g	¾ t	Pepper, black	
2.84 L	3 qt	Water or beef stock	

Note: Portioned steaks, cut 3 per pound (454 g), may be substituted for beef round. Reduce cooking time to 1½ hours.

Variations:

1. **Chicken Fried Steak.** Dip portioned steaks or beef cutlets into mixture of 6 eggs and 3 c (720 mL) milk, then into crumb mixture (1 lb 4 oz/567 g bread crumbs, 12 oz/340 g flour, 3 oz/85 g salt, and 2 T/14 g pepper). Brown steaks in hot shortening. Arrange slightly overlapping in lined counter pans. Cover with aluminum foil. Bake at 275°F (135°C) 1½ hours or until tender.

2. **Country Fried Steak.** Use beef round cut 3/8 in. thick. Proceed as for Swiss Steak except for adding gravy. Place steaks on racks in roaster or counter pans. Cover bottom of pan with water, 2 c (480 mL) per pan. Cover with aluminum foil and bake. Make Cream Gravy (p. 476) to serve with steaks.

3. **Smothered Steak with Onions.** Proceed as for Swiss Steak. Add 3 lb (1.36 kg) sliced onions lightly browned.

4. **Spanish Steak.** Substitute Spanish Sauce (p. 478) for gravy.

5. **Baked Steak Teriyaki.** Combine 2 c (480 mL) pineapple juice, drained from canned sliced pineapple, 1 qt (0.95 L) water, 1½ c (360 mL) soy sauce, ½ t (1 g) garlic powder, ¼ t ginger, and ¼ c (60 mL) honey. Bring to a boil. Thicken with 1½ c (360 mL) water and ½ c (64 g) cornstarch, mixed. Pour 2 lb 8 oz (1.14 kg) mixture over each pan of browned steaks. Cover tightly. Bake at 325°F (165°C) for 1–1½ hours or until tender. Garnish with green pepper rings and pineapple slices.

6. **Swiss Steak with Tomatoes.** Substitute 1 No. 10 can tomatoes for the gravy. Add 8 oz (227 g) chopped onions.

PEPPER STEAK

Yield: 50 portions
Portion: 6 oz (170 g)

Amount Metric	U.S.	Ingredient	Procedure
5.9 kg	13 lb	Beef round or sirloin, cut into thin strips	Cook meat in shortening until lightly browned, about 10 minutes.
227 g	8 oz	Shortening	
1.89 L	2 qt	Beef Stock (p. 494)	Add stock, tomatoes, and seasonings.
1 No. 10 can	1 No. 10 can	Tomatoes, canned, diced	Simmer until tender, 1–1½ hours, stirring occasionally.
454 g	1 lb	Onions, chopped	
3 cloves	3 cloves	Garlic, cut in half	
38 g	2 T	Salt	
12	12	Green peppers, thinly sliced in rings	Add green pepper and cook until tender but firm.
85 g	3 oz	Cornstarch	Combine cornstarch, water, and soy sauce into a smooth paste. Add to meat–vegetable mixture. Cook 5 minutes.
600 mL	2½ c	Water, cold	
160 mL	⅔ c	Soy sauce	
1.59 kg	3 lb 8 oz	Rice, long-grain	Cook according to directions on p. 358. Serve 6 oz (170 g) meat mixture over 4 oz (114 g) rice.
4 L	4¼ qt	Water, boiling	
38 g	2 T	Salt	
30 mL	2 T	Cooking oil	

CHUCK WAGON STEAK

Oven: 400°F (205°C)
Bake: 10 minutes
Yield: 50 portions
Portion: 6 oz (170 g)

Amount Metric	Amount U.S.	Ingredient	Procedure
50	50	Ground beef patties, 3 per lb (454 g)	
6 (312 g)	6 (11 oz)	Eggs	Mix eggs and milk. Dip meat in egg mixture. Drain.
420 mL	1¾ c	Milk	
539 g	1 lb 3 oz	Bread crumbs, dry	Combine bread crumbs, flour, and seasonings. Dredge steaks in crumb mixture and place on greased baking sheets. Brown steaks in 400°F (205°C) oven for 10 minutes. Arrange baked steaks in counter pans to serve.
340 g	12 oz	Flour, all-purpose	
9 g	1½ t	Salt	
1 g	½ t	Pepper, black	

SWEDISH MEATBALLS

Oven: 300°F (150°C)
Bake: 1 hour
Yield: 50 portions
Portion: 2 2½-oz (70-g) meatballs

Amount		Ingredient	Procedure
Metric	U.S.		
1.14 kg	2 lb 8 oz	Bread	Soak bread in milk 1
1.42 L	1½ qt	Milk	hour.
1.36 kg	3 lb	Ground beef	Combine meat, potato,
1.14 kg	2 lb 8 oz	Ground veal	onion, and seasonings
1.14 kg	2 lb 8 oz	Ground pork	in mixer bowl.
567 g	1 lb 4 oz	Potato, raw, grated	Add bread. Mix to blend. Do not overmix.
340 g	12 oz	Onion, minced	Dip with No. 16 dipper.
57 g	3 T	Salt	Shape into balls. Place
4 g	2 t	Pepper, black	in baking pans in a single layer. Brown in hot oven (400°F/205°C). Transfer to 2 12 × 20 × 2-in. counter pans.
180 mL	6 oz (¾ c)	Meat drippings	Add flour to meat
170 g	6 oz	Flour, all-purpose	drippings and blend.
12 g	2 t	Salt	Add salt and pepper.
4 g	¾ t	Pepper, black	Add milk gradually,
2.84 L	3 qt	Milk	stirring constantly. Cook until smooth and thickened. Pour over meatballs. Bake at 300°F (150°C) for 1 hour.

Note: Beef may be substituted for veal and pork.

MEAT LOAF

Oven: 325°F (165°C)
Bake: 1½ hours

Yield: 50 portions
5 loaves 5 × 9 in.
Portion: 4 oz (114 g)

Amount		Ingredient	Procedure
Metric	U.S.		
4.54 kg	10 lb	Ground beef	Mix all ingredients on low speed until blended. DO NOT OVERMIX.
908 g	2 lb	Ground pork	
340 g	12 oz	Bread crumbs, soft	
0.95 L	1 qt	Milk	Press mixture into 5 5 × 9-in. pans, 3 lb 4 oz (1.47 kg) per pan.
12 (595 g)	12 (1 lb 5 oz)	Eggs	
38 g	2 T	Salt	Bake at 325°F (165°C) for 1½ hours.
114 g	4 oz	Onion, finely chopped	Meat loaf also may be made in a 12 × 20 × 4-in. counter pan. Press mixture into pan. Divide into 2 loaves (Fig. 2.17). Increase baking time to 2 hours.
2 g	1 t	Pepper, black	
f.g.	f.g.	Cayenne	

Note: Topping of 8 oz (227 g) brown sugar, 2 T (14 g) dry mustard, 1¼ c (300 mL) catsup, and 1 T (8 g) nutmeg may be spread over loaves the last half hour of cooking.

Variations:

1. **Barbecued Meatballs.** Measure with No. 8 dipper. Shape into balls. Cover with 1 gal (3.79 L) Barbecue Sauce (p. 477).

2. **Meatballs.** Measure with No. 8 dipper and shape into balls. Proceed as for Swedish Meatballs (p. 309) or Spaghetti with Meatballs (p. 350).

3. **Meat Loaf Sandwiches.** For *hot* sandwiches, serve one slice meat loaf on top of 1 slice bread. Ladle 2 oz (57 g) gravy over sandwich. If whipped potatoes are served, use 4 oz (114 g) gravy. For *cold* sandwich, serve thin slice meat loaf and lettuce leaf between 2 slices of bread.

4. **Vegetable Meat Loaf.** Add 2 c (480 mL) catsup, 8 oz (227 g) each raw carrots, onions, and celery, and 4 oz (114 g) green peppers. Grind vegetables. Pour a small amount of tomato juice over loaves before baking.

Figure 2.17 Shaping Meat Loaf. (a) Press mixture into counter pan, then smooth top. (b) Form into 2 loaves.

SPANISH MEATBALLS

Oven: 325°F (165°C)
Bake: 1½ hours
Yield: 50 portions
Portion: 2 3-oz (85 g) meatballs

Amount Metric	U.S.	Ingredient	Procedure
510 g	1 lb 2 oz	Rice	Cook rice (p. 358) until slightly underdone. Drain off excess liquid.
1.18 L	1¼ qt	Water	
3 g	1 t	Salt	
5.44 kg	12 lb	Ground beef	Place ground beef in mixer bowl. Add cooked rice and other ingredients. Measure with No. 12 dipper and form into balls. Place in 2 baking pans 12 × 20 × 2 in. Bake at 325°F (165°C) for 1 hour. Drain fat.
12 (595 g)	12 (1 lb 5 oz)	Eggs	
57 g	2 oz	Onion, grated	
38 g	2 T	Salt	
454 g	1 lb	Potatoes, cooked and mashed	
114 g	4 oz	Green peppers, chopped	
2.84 L	3 qt	Tomato purée	Mix purée and water. Pour over meatballs. Cover tightly and bake an additional 30 minutes. Add more liquid if necessary.
1.89 L	2 qt	Water	

Note: Spanish Sauce (p. 478) may be substituted for tomato purée.

BEEF STEW

Yield: 50 portions
Portion: 7 oz (198 g)

Amount		Ingredient	Procedure
Metric	U.S.		
5.67 kg	12 lb 8 oz	Beef, 1-in. cubes	Brown beef in kettle or oven.
2.84 L	3 qt	Water	Add water and seasonings to meat.
28 g	1 oz (1½ T)	Salt	Cover and simmer 2 hours. Add more water as necessary.
2 g	1 t	Pepper, black	
908 g	2 lb	Potatoes, cubed	Cook vegetables in steamer or in small amount of water in kettle or oven.
908 g	2 lb	Carrots, sliced or cubed	
454 g	1 lb	Onion, cubed	
680 g	1 lb 8 oz	Celery, diced	
28 g	1 oz (1½ T)	Salt	
2 g	1 t	Pepper, black	
142 g	5 oz	Flour, all-purpose	Mix flour and water until smooth. Add to meat and cook until thickened. Add vegetables.
300 mL	1¼ c	Water	

Variations:

1. **Beef Pot Pie.** Omit potatoes and add 1 40-oz (1.14 kg) pkg frozen peas. Place cooked stew in 2 12 × 20 × 2-in. counter pans, 11 lb (4.99 kg) per pan. Cover with Pastry (p. 199), 1 lb 8 oz (680 g) per pan. Bake at 425°F (230°C) for 20–25 minutes.
2. **Beef Stew with Batter Crust.** Scale hot stew into 2 12 × 20 × 2-in. pans, 11 lb (4.99 kg) per pan. Prepare 1 recipe Batter Crust (p. 382) and pour 3 qt (2.84 L) over each pan. Bake at 425°F (230°C) for 20–25 minutes.
3. **Beef Stew with Biscuits.** Place hot stew in 2 12 × 20 × 2-in. counter pans, 11 lb (4.99 kg) per pan. Prepare ¾ recipe of Baking Powder Biscuits (p. 84). Cut into 72 2-in. biscuits. Place on hot stew, 24 per pan. Bake at 425°F (230°C) for 15–20 minutes.
4. **Beef Stew with Dumplings.** Drop Dumplings (p. 108) on meat mixture and steam 15–18 minutes.

BEEF STROGANOFF

Yield: 50 portions
2 gal (7.57 L)
Portion: 6 oz (170 g) Stroganoff
4 oz (114 g) noodles

Amount Metric	U.S.	Ingredient	Procedure
4.54 kg	10 lb	Beef round, cut in ¼-in. strips	Brown meat in shortening.
227 g	8 oz	Shortening	Add onion and seasonings.
567 g	1 lb 4 oz	Onion, chopped	
38 g	2 T	Salt	
2 g	1 t	Pepper, black	
2.37 L	2½ qt	Beef stock, hot (p. 494)	Add stock. Simmer 35–40 minutes or until meat is tender.
1.14 kg	2 lb 8 oz	Mushrooms, fresh, sliced	Sauté mushrooms in margarine.
114 g	4 oz	Margarine or butter	Add to meat.
1.89 L	2 qt	Cultured sour cream	Blend sour cream with flour. Just before serving, add to meat mixture, stirring constantly. Cook and stir until thickened.
227 g	8 oz	Flour, all-purpose	
2.04 kg	4 lb 8 oz	Noodles	Cook noodles according to directions on p. 348. Serve 6 oz (170 g) Stroganoff over 4 oz (114 g) noodles.
17 L	4½ gal	Water	
76 g	¼ c	Salt	
60 mL	¼ c	Oil (optional)	

Note: May be served over rice. Cook 3 lb 8 oz (1.59 kg) rice in 4¼ qt (4 L) water, 2 T (38 g) salt, and 2 T (30 mL) oil. See p. 358.

Variation: **Ground Beef Stroganoff.** Substitute ground beef for beef round. Add 1½ lb (680 g) chopped celery, ¼ c (28 g) paprika, ¼ c (60 mL) Worcestershire sauce, and 2 t (4 g) dry mustard.

HUNGARIAN GOULASH

Yield: 50 portions
Portion: 6 oz (170 g) goulash
4 oz (114 g) noodles

Amount Metric	U.S.	Ingredient	Procedure
4.54 kg	10 lb	Beef, cubed	Brown beef and vegetables in shortening.
680 g	1 lb 8 oz	Onion, chopped	
1 clove	1 clove	Garlic, finely chopped	
227 g	8 oz	Shortening	
142 g	5 oz	Sugar, brown	Combine sugar, seasonings, and water. Add to browned meat. Cover container and simmer 2½–3 hours or until meat is tender.
7 g	1 T	Mustard, dry	
28 g	1 oz (¼ c)	Paprika	
⅛ t	⅛ t	Cayenne	
76 g	¼ c	Salt	
360 mL	1½ c	Worcestershire sauce	
30 mL	2 T	Vinegar	
0.95 L	1 qt	Catsup	
2.84 L	3 qt	Water	
567 g	1 lb 4 oz	Flour, all-purpose	Mix flour and water until smooth. Add to hot mixture and cook until thickened.
0.95 L	1 qt	Water, cold	
2.04 kg	4 lb 8 oz	Noodles	Cook noodles according to directions on p. 348. Serve 6 oz (170 g) goulash over 4 oz (114 g) noodles.
17 L	4½ gal	Water, boiling	
76 g	¼ c	Salt	
60 mL	¼ c	Oil (optional)	

Notes:

1. Beef may be browned in a roasting pan in 450°F (230°C) oven.
2. 3 lb 8 oz (1.59 kg) dry rice, cooked, may be substituted for the noodles. See p. 358 for directions for cooking.

BEEF, PORK, AND NOODLE CASSEROLE

Oven: 325°F (165°C)
Bake: 30 minutes

Yield: 50 portions
2 pans 12 × 20 × 2 in.
Portion: 6 oz (170 g)

Metric	U.S.	Ingredient	Procedure
1.81 kg	4 lb	Ground beef	Brown meat and onion. Drain excess fat.
1.81 kg	4 lb	Ground pork	
454 g	1 lb	Onion, finely chopped	
1.42 L	1½ qt	Tomato soup	Mix soup, water, and seasonings. Add to meat.
1.42 L	1½ qt	Water	
19 g	1 T	Salt	
2 g	1 t	Pepper, black	
794 g	1 lb 12 oz	Noodles	Cook noodles according to directions on p. 348. Drain.
4.73 L	1¼ gal	Water, boiling	
38 g	2 T	Salt	
30 mL	2 T	Oil (optional)	
908 g	2 lb	Cheddar cheese, grated or ground	Combine noodles, meat mixture, and cheese. Scale into 2 12 × 20 × 2-in. pans, 8 lb 4 oz (3.74 kg) per pan.
510 g	1 lb 2 oz	Bread crumbs	Combine crumbs and margarine. Sprinkle over meat and noodle mixture, 10 oz (284 g) per pan. Bake at 325°F (165°C) for 30 minutes.
142 g	5 oz	Margarine or butter, melted	

PASTA, BEEF, AND TOMATO CASSEROLE

Yield: 50 portions
Portion: 8 oz (227 g)

Amount		Ingredient	Procedure
Metric	U.S.		
4.54 kg	10 lb	Ground beef	Cook meat in kettle. Stir often to prevent lumps from forming. Drain off fat.
170 g	6 oz	Onions, chopped	Add onions and celery to meat. Cook until tender.
85 g	3 oz	Celery, chopped	
3.79 L	1 gal	Tomatoes, canned, diced	Add tomatoes and seasonings. Simmer 45–60 minutes.
300 mL	1¼ c	Tomato purée	
720 mL	3 c	Chili sauce	
56 g	2 oz (3 T)	Salt	
1 g	½ t	Pepper, black	
28 g	2 T	Sugar, granulated	
1.14 kg	2 lb 8 oz	Macaroni, elbow	Cook macaroni, according to directions on p. 348.
9.46 L	2½ gal	Water, boiling	
60 mL	¼ c	Oil (optional)	
			Fold cooked macaroni into tomato–meat mixture. Simmer until hot.

Note: Other pasta shapes may be substituted for macaroni.

CREOLE SPAGHETTI

Oven: 325°F (165°C)
Bake: 45 minutes

Yield: 50 portions
2 pans 12 × 20 × 2 in.
Portion: 8 oz (227 g)

Amount Metric	U.S.	Ingredient	Procedure
3.63 kg	8 lb	Ground beef	Brown beef, onion, and green pepper. Drain off excess fat.
170 g	6 oz	Onion, finely chopped	
454 g	1 lb	Green pepper, chopped	
1.89 L	2 qt	Tomatoes, canned, diced	Combine tomatoes and spices.
1.89 L	2 qt	Tomato purée	
6 g	1 t	Salt	
2 g	¼ t	Garlic powder	
1 g	½ t	Pepper, black	
1.36 kg	3 lb	Spaghetti	Cook spaghetti according to directions on p. 348. Drain.
11.36 L	3 gal	Water, boiling	
57 g	2 oz	Salt	
45 mL	3 T	Oil (optional)	
680 g	1 lb 8 oz	Cheddar cheese, ground	Combine sauce and cooked spaghetti. Pour into 2 12 × 20 × 2-in. baking pans, 12 lb 8 oz (5.67 kg) per pan. Sprinkle cheese over top. Bake at 325°F (165°C) for 45 minutes.

SPANISH RICE

Oven: 350°F (175°C)
Bake: 1 hour
Yield: 50 portions
2 pans 12 × 20 × 2 in.
Portion: 8 oz (227 g)

Amount		Ingredient	Procedure
Metric	U.S.		
1.14 kg	2 lb 8 oz	Rice, uncooked	Cook rice, according to directions on p. 358.
2.84 L	3 qt	Water, boiling	
28 g	1 oz (1½ T)	Salt	
23 mL	1½ T	Cooking oil	
3.18 kg	7 lb	Ground beef	Cook beef until meat loses pink color.
680 g	1 lb 8 oz	Onion, chopped	Add onion, peppers, and celery.
227 g	8 oz	Green pepper, chopped	Cook about 10 minutes.
227 g	8 oz	Celery, chopped	
1 No. 10 can	1 No. 10 can	Tomatoes, canned, diced	Add remaining ingredients to meat mixture.
720 mL	3 c	Chili sauce	Combine with cooked rice.
720 mL	3 c	Tomato paste	Scale into 2 12 × 20 × 2-in. pans, 15 lb (6.8 kg) per pan.
57 g	2 oz	Salt	
¼ t	¼ t	Pepper, black	
f.g.	f.g.	Cayenne	
28 g	2 T	Sugar, granulated	Bake at 350°F (175°C) for 1 hour.
480 mL	2 c	Water	

Notes:

1. 3 lb (1.36 kg) bacon, cooked, may be substituted for the ground beef.
2. Spanish Rice may be used as a filling for Stuffed Green Peppers.

CHOP SUEY

Yield: 50 portions
Portion: 5 oz (142 g) sauce
4 oz (114 g) rice

Amount		Ingredient	Procedure
Metric	U.S.		
2.27 kg	5 lb	Beef, julienne strips	Brown meat in steam-jacketed kettle or roaster.
908 g	2 lb	Pork, julienne strips.	
1.89 L	2 qt	Water	Add water and salt.
12 g	2 t	Salt	Simmer until tender.
227 g	8 oz	Cornstarch	Make a smooth paste of cornstarch and water. Pour slowly into meat and broth, stirring constantly while pouring. Cook until thickened.
300 mL	1¼ c	Water, cold	
240 mL	1 c	Soy sauce	Add soy sauce and Worcestershire sauce. Stir to blend.
240 mL	1 c	Worcestershire sauce	
114 g	4 oz	Green peppers, sliced	Steam vegetables until tender crisp.
454 g	1 lb	Onions, sliced	
908 g	2 lb	Celery, sliced	
1.36 kg	3 lb	Bean sprouts, canned	Do not drain bean sprouts. Add bean sprouts and vegetables to meat mixture just before serving.
1.59 kg	3 lb·8 oz	Rice, long-grained	Cook rice according to directions on p. 358.
4 L	4¼ qt	Water, boiling	
38 g	2 T	Salt	
30 mL	2 T	Cooking oil	
			Serve 5 oz (142 g) Chop Suey over 4 oz (114 g) rice.

Notes:
1. 8 oz (227 g) water chestnuts may be added.
2. May be served over 2 oz (57 g) chow mein noodles instead of rice.

Variation: **Chicken Chow Mein.** Substitute cubed, cooked chicken or turkey for beef and pork; and Chicken Stock (p. 495) for water. Delete green peppers and add 1 lb (454 g) sliced mushrooms. Serve over rice or chow mein noodles.

CHEESEBURGER PIE

Oven: 450°F (230°C); 350°F (175°C)
Bake: 10 minutes; 1 hour
Yield: 48 portions
2 pans 12 × 20 × 2 in.
Portion: 7 oz (198 g)

Amount		Ingredient	Procedure
Metric	U.S.		
680 g	1 lb 8 oz	Flour, all-purpose	Make pastry according to directions on p. 199. Divide dough in half. Roll to cover bottom and sides of 2 12 × 20 × 2-in. baking pans, 1½ lb (680 g) per pan. Bake at 450°F (230°C) for 10 minutes.
510 g	1 lb 2 oz	Shortening	
240–300 mL	1–1¼ c	Water, cold	
19 g	1 T	Salt	
5.44 kg	12 lb	Ground beef	Brown beef. Drain off excess fat.
38 g	2 T	Salt	Add seasonings and crumbs to ground beef. Spread mixture over baked crusts.
7 g	1 T	Pepper, black	
454 g	1 lb	Green pepper, chopped	
114 g	4 oz	Onion, chopped	
908 g	2 lb	Bread crumbs	
4 g	2 T	Oregano, leaf	
15 (737 g)	15 (1 lb 10 oz)	Eggs, beaten	Combine eggs and milk. Add seasonings and cheese. Spread evenly over meat mixture.
0.95 L	1 qt	Milk	
14 g	2 T	Mustard, dry	
30 mL	2 T	Worcestershire sauce	
1.59 kg	3 lb 8 oz	Cheese, shredded	
840 mL	3½ c	Tomato sauce	Distribute 1¾ c (420 mL) sauce unevenly over cheese mixture in each pan. Bake at 350°F (175°C) for 1 hour. Cut 4 × 6.

BEEF BISCUIT ROLL

Oven: 450°F (230°C)
Bake: 15 minutes
Yield: 50 portions
Portion: 5 oz (142 g)

Amount		Ingredient	Procedure
Metric	U.S.		
1.36 kg	3 lb	Flour, all-purpose	Mix ingredients as for Baking Powder Biscuits (p. 84). Divide dough into 4 portions. Roll each portion ¼ in. thick.
85 g	3 oz	Baking powder	
19 g	1 T	Salt	
340 g	12 oz	Shortening	
0.95 L	1 qt	Milk	
3.63 kg	8 lb	Beef, cooked, chopped	Combine meat, onion, and gravy. Season as needed. Mix well. Spread 2 lb (908 g) meat mixture over each dough portion. Roll as for jelly roll. Slice each roll into pieces 1 in. thick. Place on greased baking sheet. Bake at 450°F (230°C) for 15 minutes or until lightly browned.
454 g	1 lb	Onion, finely chopped	
19 g	1 T	Salt	
2 g	1 t	Pepper, black	
0.95 L	1 qt	Gravy, cold	
2.84 L	3 qt	Brown Gravy (p. 476) or Mushroom Sauce (p. 474)	Serve with gravy or mushroom sauce.

Variations:
1. **Chicken or Turkey Biscuit Roll.** Substitute cooked poultry for meat. Serve with Mushroom Sauce (p. 474).
2. **Ham Biscuit Roll.** Use ground cooked ham. Delete salt. Serve with Mushroom Sauce (p. 474) or Cheese Sauce (p. 471).
3. **Tuna or Salmon Biscuit Roll.** Substitute tuna or salmon for meat and combine with Thick White Sauce (p. 470). Serve with Cheese Sauce (p. 471).

STUFFED PEPPERS

Oven: 350°F (175°C)
Bake: 45–60 minutes

Yield: 50 portions
Portion: 5 oz (142 g)

Amount Metric	U.S.	Ingredient	Procedure
25	25	Green peppers, large	Wash peppers and remove stem end. Cut peppers in half, lengthwise. Remove seeds and tough white portion. Reserve pepper trimmings for filling. Place in baking pans and steam or parboil for 3–5 minutes.
454 g	1 lb	Rice, long-grain	Cook rice according to directions on p. 358.
1.18 L	1¼ qt	Water, boiling	
12 g	2 t	Salt	
10 mL	2 t	Cooking oil	
4.08 kg	9 lb	Ground beef	Cook meat until it loses pink color. Drain off excess fat.
227 g	8 oz	Onions, chopped	Add to meat. Sauté for 5 minutes.
340 g	12 oz	Celery, chopped	
114 g	4 oz	Green pepper trimmings, chopped	
340 g	12 oz	Bread crumbs	Add to meat mixture. Add rice. Mix only until blended. Place No. 8 dipper of meat mixture in each pepper half.
18 (908 g)	18 (2 lb)	Eggs, beaten	
720 mL	3 c	Tomato sauce	
38 g	2 T	Salt	
2 1.42-kg cans	2 50-oz cans	Tomato soup	Combine soup and sauce. Ladle 2 oz (57 g) over each pepper. Bake at 350 °F (175°C) for 45–60 minutes. Ladle extra sauce over peppers during baking.
1.89 L	2 qt	Tomato sauce	

BAKED HASH

Oven: 350°F (175°C)
Bake: 1 hour

Yield: 48 portions
2 pans 12 × 20 × 2 in.
Portion: 7 oz (198 g)

Amount Metric	U.S.	Ingredient	Procedure
4.54 kg	10 lb	Beef, cooked	Chop or grind meat and vegetables coarsely.
3.63 kg	8 lb	Potatoes, cooked	
454 g	1 lb	Onions	
76 g	¼ c	Salt	Add seasonings and liquid. Mix to blend. Pour into 2 greased 12 × 20 × 2-in. baking pans. Bake at 350°F (175°C) for 1 hour. Cut 4 × 6.
2 g	1 t	Pepper, black	
1.89 L	2 qt	Beef Stock (p. 494) or gravy	

Note: Raw potatoes, well chopped, or hashed brown potatoes may be used in place of cooked potatoes. Increase baking time to 1¼–1½ hours.

Variations:
1. **Corned Beef Hash.** Substitute cooked corned beef for the cooked beef and delete salt.
2. **Saucy Beef Hash.** Substitute 2 qt (1.89 L) condensed cream of celery soup for meat stock. Add 2 T (30 mL) Worcestershire sauce. Delete salt.

CHILI CON CARNE

Yield: 3 gal (11.36 L)
Portion: 1 c (8 oz/227 g)

Amount		Ingredient	Procedure
Metric	U.S.		
4.54 kg	10 lb	Ground beef	Cook beef, onions, and garlic in steam-jacketed kettle until meat loses pink color.
227 g	8 oz	Onions, chopped	
1 clove	1 clove	Garlic, minced	
2.37 L	2½ qt	Tomatoes, canned, diced	Mix tomato and seasonings. Add to beef. Cook until blended.
1.89 L	2 qt	Tomato purée	
57 g	2 oz	Chili powder	
10 g	1½ T	Cumin seed, ground	
57 g	2 oz (3 T)	Salt	
1 g	½ t	Pepper, black	
57 g	2 oz	Sugar, granulated	
4.31 kg	9 lb 8 oz	Beans, kidney or red, canned Water to make total volume of 3 gal (11.36 L)	Add beans and water. Simmer 1½ – 2 hours.

Notes:
1. If dried beans are used, substitute 3 lb (1.36 kg) for canned beans. Wash and prepare according to directions on p. 523.
2. If desired, thicken chili by mixing 5 oz (142 g) flour and 2 c (480 mL) cold water. Add to chili mixture and heat until flour is cooked.

Variations.
1. **Chili and Cheese.** Sprinkle grated Cheddar or Monterey jack cheese over chili, 1 T (15 mL) per bowl.
2. **Chili Spaghetti.** Use only 7 lb (3.18 kg) ground beef. Cook 1½ lb (680 g) spaghetti according to directions on p. 348. Add to chili mixture just before serving. Macaroni or other pasta shapes may be used also.

CREAMED BEEF

Yield: 6¼ qt (5.91 L)
Portion: ¾ c (6 oz/170 g)

Amount		Ingredient	Procedure
Metric	U.S.		
5.9 kg	13 lb	Ground beef	Brown beef and onion.
85 g	3 oz	Onions, chopped	Drain off excess fat. Use for making sauce.
454 g	1 lb	Fat from beef or margarine	Melt fat. Stir in flour and cook 3–4 minutes.
227 g	8 oz	Flour, all-purpose	Add beef stock and milk, while stirring. Cook until thickened.
1.89 L	2 qt	Beef Stock (p. 494)	
1.89 L	2 qt	Milk	
57 g	2 oz (3 T)	Salt	Add seasonings and meat. If beef soup base has been used for stock, salt may need to be reduced.
2 g	1½ t	Pepper, black	
			Serve 6 oz (170 g) meat over toast, biscuits, or baked potato.

Variation: **Sausage Gravy on Biscuits.** Substitute sausage for ground beef. Delete onions and pepper. Reduce salt to 1 T (19 g). Serve over hot Baking Powder Biscuits (p. 84).

CREAMED CHIPPED BEEF

Yield: 6¼ qt (5.91 L)
Portion: ½ c (4 oz/114 g)

Amount		Ingredient	Procedure
Metric	U.S.		
1.14 kg	2 lb 8 oz	Chipped beef	Chop beef coarsely.
454 g	1 lb	Margarine or butter	Sauté beef in margarine until edges curl.
567 g	1 lb 4 oz	Margarine or butter	Melt margarine. Stir in flour and pepper. Cook 3–4 minutes. Add milk, stirring constantly. Cook until thickened. Add chipped beef. Serve 4 oz (114 g) beef over toast, biscuit, or baked potato.
284 g	10 oz	Flour, all-purpose	
2 g	1 t	Pepper, white	
4.73 L	5 qt	Milk	

Variations:

1. **Chipped Beef and Eggs.** Add 2 doz hard-cooked eggs, sliced or coarsely chopped. Reduce white sauce to 1 gal (3.79 L).

2. **Chipped Beef and Noodles.** Add 2 lb (908 g) ground Cheddar cheese to white sauce. Combine with 2 lb (908 g) AP noodles, cooked. Top with buttered crumbs. Bake at 350°F (175°C) for 30 minutes.

3. **Creamed Chipped Beef and Peas.** Reduce beef to 2 lb (908 g) and add 1 40-oz (1.14 kg) package frozen peas, cooked until peas are tender before serving.

PIZZA

Oven: 400°F (205°C)
Bake: 15–20 minutes

Yield: 48 portions
3 pans 18 × 26 × 1 in.
Portion: 7 oz (198 g)

Amount Metric	U.S.	Ingredient	Procedure
2.5 kg	5 lb 8 oz	Flour, all-purpose	Place in mixer bowl. Mix thoroughly, using dough hook on low speed.
12 g	2 t	Salt	
57 g	2 oz (¼ c)	Sugar, granulated	
21 g	¾ oz	Yeast, active dry	Soften yeast in warm water.
0.95 L	1 qt	Water, warm (110°F/43°C)	
85 g	3 oz	Shortening	Add softened yeast and shortening to dry ingredients. Mix on low speed to form dough. Knead until smooth and elastic. Cover and let rise until double in bulk, about 2 hours. Punch down and let rest 45 minutes. Divide into 3 portions, 2 lb 8 oz (1.14 kg) each. Roll out very thin, stretching to fit 3 18 × 26 × 1-in. baking sheets, allowing ¼ in. to extend up sides of pan.
1.42 L	1½ qt	Tomato paste	Mix tomato and seasonings. Spread over dough, 1 qt (0.95 L) per pan.
1.42 L	1½ qt	Tomato purée	
2 g	1 T	Thyme or oregano	
24 g	4 t	Salt	
1 g	¾ t	Cumin, ground	
1 clove	1 clove	Garlic crushed	
21 g	3 T	Chili powder	

Amount		Ingredient	Procedure
Metric	U.S.		
1.7 kg	3 lb 12 oz	Sausage	Cook and drain meat.
1.7 kg	3 lb 12 oz	Ground beef	Add onions and cook
142 g	5 oz	Onion, chopped	until tender.
			Sprinkle evenly over tomato sauce, approximately 1 lb 8 oz (680 g) per pan.
1.7 kg	3 lb 12 oz	Mozzarella cheese, sliced or shredded	Top with 1 lb 4 oz (567 g) cheese per pan. Bake at 400°F (205°C) for 15–20 minutes. Cut each pan 2 × 4 and then each of the 8 pieces diagonally, yielding 16 portions per pan. (See Fig. 2.18, p. 330)

Notes:

1. Active dry yeast may be mixed with dry ingredients. See p. 110 for procedure.
2. Processed Cheddar cheese may be substituted for Mozzarella. Sweet basil (1 t) may be sprinkled over top of each pan.

Variations:

1. **Beef Pizza.** Delete sausage. Increase ground beef to 7 lb (3.18 kg).
2. **Cheese Pizza.** Delete meat. Top each pan with 2 lb 8 oz (1.14 kg) shredded Mozzarella cheese, 2 lb (908 g) shredded processed cheese, and 1 lb (454 g) Parmesan cheese, combined.
3. **Pepperoni Pizza.** Substitute sliced pepperoni for ground beef.

330 MEAT

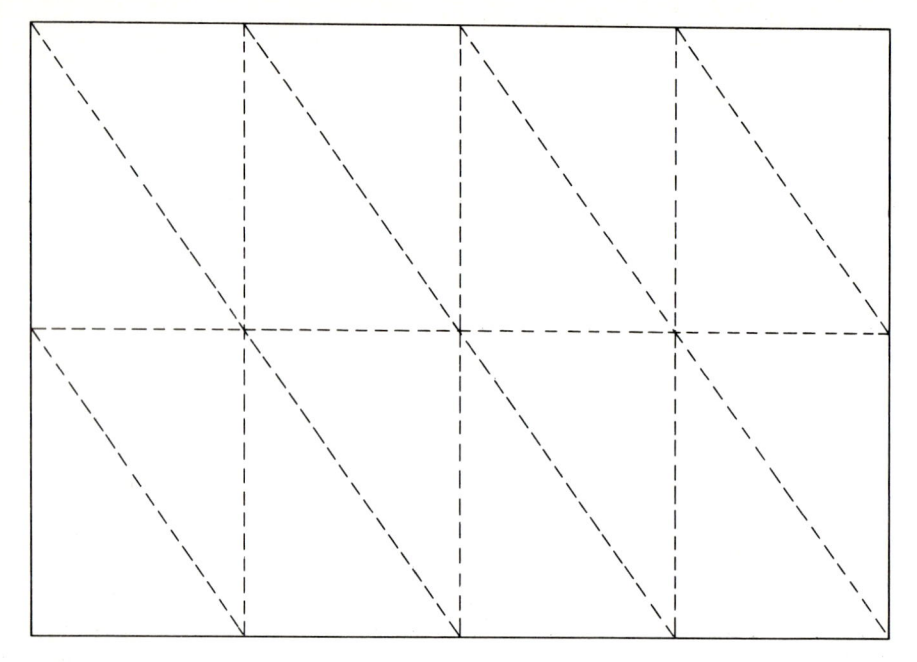

Figure 2.18 Cutting Pizza. For Pizza baked in 18 × 26 × 1-in. sheet pan. Cut lengthwise into 2 sections, then cut crosswise into 4 pieces. Cut each of the 8 pieces diagonally, yielding 16 portions.

TACO SALAD CASSEROLE

Yield: 48 portions
3 pans 12 × 20 × 2 in.
Portion: 8 oz (227 g)

Amount		Ingredient	Procedure
Metric	U.S.		
1.14 kg	2 lb 8 oz	Corn chips	Spread corn chips in bottoms of 3 12 × 20 × 2 in. counter pans, 14 oz (397 g) per pan.
3.63 kg	8 lb	Ground beef	Brown meat. Drain off excess fat.
227 g 3 cloves	8 oz 3 cloves	Onions, minced Garlic, minced	Add onions and garlic. Cook until tender.
85 g 1.18 L	3 oz 1¼ qt	Flour, all-purpose Tomato juice	Combine flour and tomato juice and add to meat mixture.

MEAT RECIPES 331

Amount Metric	U.S.	Ingredient	Procedure
30 mL	2 T	Vinegar	Add to meat mixture.
360 mL	1½ c	Catsup	Blend. Heat until very
240 mL	1 c	Chili sauce	hot.
28 g	2 T	Sugar, granulated	Scale 4 lb 5 oz (1.96 kg)
38 g	2 T	Salt	meat sauce over each
1 g	½ t	Pepper, black	pan of chips. Keep
3 g	1½ t	Chili powder	warm.
¼ t	¼ t	Cayenne	
3 mL	¾ t	Tabasco sauce	
5 mL	1 t	Worcestershire sauce	
1.7 kg	3 lb 12 oz	Beans, red, canned	
1.81 kg	4 lb	Lettuce, chopped	Combine vegetables. Mix gently.
340 g	12 oz	Green peppers, chopped	Sprinkle over hot meat mixture, 2 lb 8 oz (1.14 kg) per pan.
340 g	12 oz	Onions, finely chopped	
1.19 kg	2 lb 10 oz	Tomatoes, fresh, diced	
1.19 kg	2 lb 10 oz	Processed cheese, shredded	Sprinkle 14 oz (397 g) per pan. Cut 4 × 4. Serve immediately.

Notes:

1. Casserole may be assembled on each plate individually. Place ¾ oz (21 g) taco chips on plate. Ladle 4 oz (114 g) hot meat mixture over chips and top with 2½ oz (70 g) salad mixture and ¾ oz (21 g) shredded cheese.
2. Serve with Spicy Tomato Sauce (p. 479) or commercial salsa.

BEEF LIVER WITH SPANISH SAUCE

Oven: 350°F (175°C)
Bake: 1 hour

Yield: 50 portions
Portion: 3½ oz (100 g)

Amount Metric	U.S.	Ingredient	Procedure
4.54 kg	10 lb	Beef liver, sliced, cut 5 per lb	Dredge liver in seasoned flour.
227 g	8 oz	Flour, all-purpose	Brown in hot shortening.
57 g	2 oz (3 T)	Salt	
4 g	2 t	Pepper, black	
680 g	1 lb 8 oz	Shortening	
1 recipe	1 recipe	Spanish sauce (p. 478)	Place liver in 2 12 × 20 × 2-in. baking pans. Pour Spanish Sauce over liver, 5 c (1.18 L) per pan. Cover with aluminum foil. Bake at 350°F (175°C) until tender, about 1 hour.

Note: Liver may be soaked in milk before cooking.

Variations:
1. **Baked Liver and Onions.** Brown liver as above. Sauté 5 lb (2.27 kg) sliced onions in 8 oz (227 g) shortening. Arrange liver in 2 counter pans. Spread onions over liver. Cover pans with aluminum foil. Bake 30–40 minutes.
2. **Braised Liver.** Brown liver. Cover with sauce made of 10 oz (284 g) shortening, 5 oz (142 g) flour, 3 qt (2.84 L) beef stock, 2 oz (57 g) salt, and 2 t (4 g) pepper.
3. **Grilled Liver and Onions.** Have liver cut ⅜ in. thick. Preheat grill to 350°F (175°C). Oil grill slightly. Cook liver quickly, browning on one side, then turn and brown on other side. Serve immediately with steamed or grilled sliced onions.
4. **Liver and Bacon.** Dredge liver with seasoned flour and fry in bacon fat. Top each serving with 1 slice crisp bacon.

Veal

BREADED VEAL CUTLETS

Oven: 325°F (165°C)
Bake: 1 hour
Yield: 50 portions
Portion: 4 oz (114 g)

Amount Metric	U.S.	Ingredient	Procedure
5.67 kg	12 lb 8 oz	Veal cutlets, 4 oz (114 g)	Dredge cutlets in seasoned flour.
227 g	8 oz	Flour, all-purpose	
28 g	1 oz (1½ T)	Salt	
¼ t	¼ t	Pepper, black	
7 (340 g)	7 (12 oz)	Eggs, beaten	Combine eggs and milk.
360 mL	1½ c	Milk	Dip cutlets in egg mixture,
454 g	1 lb	Bread crumbs, fine	then roll in crumbs.
908 g	2 lb	Shortening	Brown meat in hot fat. Place, slightly overlapping in 2 12 × 20 × 2-in. counter pans. Add 2 c (480 mL) water to each pan. Cover with aluminum foil. Bake at 325°F (165°C) for 45–60 minutes.

Note: Veal round, sliced ¼-in. thick and cut into 5-oz (142-g) portions, may be used.

Variations:

1. **Veal Cacciatore.** Dredge cutlets in flour. Brown. Place in baking pans. Pour over sauce made of 1 lb (454 g) chopped peppers, 1 lb (454 g) chopped onions, ⅛ t minced garlic, simmered in margarine or butter for 10 minutes; 1½ lb (680 g) sautéed sliced mushrooms, 1½ qt (1.42 L) canned tomatoes, ¼ c (60 mL) vinegar, 2 qt (1.89 L) chicken stock, 1 oz (28 g) salt, and 1 t (2 g) pepper. Bake for 45 minutes.

2. **Veal New Orleans.** To 2 qt (1.89 L) Medium White Sauce (p. 470), add 8 oz (227 g) chopped onions, 12 oz (340 g) sliced mushrooms, 2 T (30 mL) Worcestershire sauce, ¼ t (1 g) salt, ¼ t pepper, ¼ t paprika, and 3½ c (840 mL) tomato soup. Arrange browned breaded cutlets in 2 12 × 20 × 2-in. counter pans. Pour 1¾ qt (1.66 L) sauce over each pan. Cover with aluminum foil and bake at 325°F (165°C) for 1 hour.

3. **Veal Parmesan.** Add 8 oz (227 g) grated Parmesan cheese to bread crumbs. After cutlets are browned and arranged in baking pans, pour 2 qt (1.89 L) Tomato Sauce (p. 478) over them. Top with 1½ lb (680 g) grated Mozzarella cheese. Bake 1 hour.

4. **Veal Piccata.** Flour cutlets and brown in hot shortening. Arrange in 2 12 × 20 × 2-in. counter pans. Sauté 1 lb (454 g) sliced mushrooms and 2 cloves garlic, minced, in 2 T (28 g) margarine. Add 2½ c (600 mL) beef stock and 2 T (30 mL) lemon juice. Bring to boil. Pour 2 c (480 mL) over each pan. Sprinkle ¼ c (60 mL) Parmesan cheese over each pan. Cover with foil. Bake at 325°F (165°C) for 1 hour.

5. **Veal Scallopini.** Dredge cutlets in seasoned flour and sauté in hot shortening. Arrange in baking pans. Sauté 3 lb (1.36 kg) fresh mushrooms, sliced, and 1 lb (454 g) chopped onion in 8 oz (227 g) margarine or butter. Add 2 qt (1.89 L) Chicken Stock (p. 495), 1½ c (360 mL) lemon juice or vinegar, and 1 t (5 mL) each of parsley, rosemary, and oregano or marjoram. Pour over cutlets. Bake 1 hour.

VEAL BIRDS

Oven: 300°F (150°C)
Bake: 2 hours
Yield: 50 portions
Portion: 4 oz (114 g)

Metric	U.S.	Ingredient	Procedure
170 g	6 oz	Margarine or butter	Sauté onion and celery in the margarine.
57 g	2 oz	Onions, finely chopped	
114 g	4 oz	Celery, finely chopped	
1.36 kg	3 lb	Bread, dry, cubed	Combine. Add onion.
12 g	2 t	Salt	
1 g	½ t	Pepper, black	
8 g	2 T	Sage, ground	
1.18 L	1¼ qt	Beef Stock (p. 494) or water.	
50	50	Veal cutlets, 4 oz (114 g)	Place No. 16 dipper of bread mixture on each piece of meat. Roll and fasten with a toothpick.
227 g	8 oz	Flour, all-purpose	Roll each bird in flour mixture. Brown in hot shortening. Place in 2 12 × 20 × 2-in. counter pans.
57 g	2 oz (3 T)	Salt	
1.14 kg	2 lb 8 oz	Shortening	
0.95 L	1 qt	Water	Add 2 c (480 mL) water to each pan. Cover with aluminum foil. Bake at 300°F (150°C) for 2 hours.

Note: Veal round, ¼-in. thick, cut into 4-oz (114-g) pieces, may be substituted for the cutlets.

Variations:
1. **Beef Birds.** Make with beef cubed or flank steaks.
2. **Pork Birds.** Make with pork cutlets.
3. **Veal Birds with Sausage Stuffing.** Reduce bread to 2½ lb (1.14 kg). Reduce salt to 1 t (6 g) and sage to 1 T (3 g). Add 2½ lb (1.14 kg) sausage, cooked and drained.

Pork

BREADED PORK CHOPS

Oven: 400°F (205°C); 325°F (165°C)
Bake: 1 hour 10 minutes
Yield: 50 chops
Portion: 5 oz (142 g)

Amount Metric	Amount U.S.	Ingredient	Procedure
7.71 kg	17 lb	Pork chops, cut 3 per lb (454 g)	Dredge chops in seasoned flour.
340 g	12 oz	Flour, all-purpose	
85 g	3 oz	Salt	
14 g	2 T	Pepper, black	
6 (284 g)	6 (10 oz)	Eggs, beaten	Combine eggs and milk. Dip chops in egg mixture.
840 mL	3½ c	Milk	Roll in crumbs. Place in single layer on greased sheet pans.
567 g	1 lb 4 oz	Bread crumbs	
227 g	8 oz	Shortening, melted	Pour melted shortening over top of chops. Bake at 400°F (205°C) until browned, about 10 minutes.
0.95 L	1 qt	Water	Remove from oven and arrange in partially overlapping rows in 2 12 × 20 × 2-in. counter pans. Add 2 c (480 mL) water to each pan. Cover pans. Bake at 325°F (165°C) until done, approximately 1 hour.

Variations:

1. **Baked Pork Chops.** Dredge chops in 8 oz (227 g) flour, 2 oz (57 g) shortening, and 2 oz (57 g) salt, mixed. Place on well-greased sheet pans. Bake at 350°F (175°C) until thoroughly cooked and browned, approximately 1¼ hours.

2. **Baked Pork Chops and Apples.** Brown chops as for Breaded Pork Chops. Place in 2 greased 12 × 20 × 2-in. baking pans. Pour over 1 qt (0.95 L) apple juice, 2 c (480 mL) per pan. Bake at 350°F (175°C) for 1 hour. Serve with Buttered Apples (p. 430)

DEVILED PORK CHOPS

Oven: 350°F (175°C)
Bake: 1½ hours

Yield: 50 chops
Portion: 5 oz (142 g)

Amount		Ingredient	Procedure
Metric	U.S.		
1.42 L	1½ qt	Chili sauce	Combine into a sauce.
720 mL	3 c	Water	
2 g	1 t	Mustard, dry	
45 mL	3 T	Worcestershire sauce	
45 mL	3 T	Lemon juice	
10 mL	2 t	Onion, grated	
7.71 kg	17 lb	Pork chops, cut 3 per lb	Dip each chop in sauce. Place in single layer on greased baking sheets. Bake at 350°F (175°C) for 1½ hours.

Note: Chops also may be placed on edge, close together, with fat side up in 12 × 20 × 2-in. counter pan. Bake 2–2½ hours.

Variations:

1. **Barbecued Pork Chops.** Place chops on greased baking sheets. Brush with melted fat. Sprinkle with salt. Brown chops in 450°F (230°C) oven for 12–15 minutes. Remove to counter pans. Pour Barbecue Sauce (p. 477) over chops. Bake at 325 °F (165°C) for 1½ hours or until chops are tender.

2. **Honey Glazed Pork Chops.** Marinate pork chops for 4 hours in a mixture of 2 c (480 mL) soy sauce, 6 oz (170 g) honey, 1 c (240 mL) applesauce, 1 oz (28 g) salt, and 4 oz (114 g) sugar. Place in single layer on greased baking sheets. Bake at 350°F (175°C) for 1 hour. Turn and brush with marinade as needed.

3. **Pork Chops Supreme.** Arrange chops in single layer in baking pans. Sprinkle with salt. Combine 1 lb (454 g) brown sugar, 3 c (720 mL) catsup, and 1 c (240 mL) lemon juice. Place about 2 T (30 mL), No. 30 dipper, on each chop. Cut 4 medium onions into thin slices. Place 1 slice on top of each chop. Cover and bake at 350°F (175°C) for 45 minutes. Uncover and bake 30 minutes longer.

PORK CHOPS WITH DRESSING

Oven: 350°F (175°C)
Bake: 1½ hours

Yield: 50 chops
Portion: 5 oz (142 g)

Amount Metric	U.S.	Ingredient	Procedure
7.71	17 lb	Pork chops, cut 3 per lb	Brown chops. Arrange in 2 12 × 20 × 2-in. baking or counter pans. Sprinkle with salt.
57 g	2 oz	Salt	
1.81 kg	4 lb	Bread, dry, cubed	Add seasonings to bread.
19 g	1 T	Salt	
1 g	¾ t	Pepper, black	
18 g	⅓ c	Sage or poultry seasoning	
284 g	10 oz	Margarine or butter	Sauté onion and celery in margarine. Add to bread mixture. Mix lightly.
85 g	3 oz	Onion, minced	
170 g	6 oz	Celery, chopped (optional)	
1.42 L	1½ qt	Chicken Stock (p. 495)	Add chicken stock and eggs to bread mixture. Toss lightly. Avoid overmixing.
4 (198 g)	4 (7 oz)	Eggs, beaten	
2.84 L	3 qt	Milk	Place 2 oz (57 g) dressing with No. 16 dipper on each chop. Pour milk over chops. Bake at 350°F (175°C) for 1½ hours. Baste frequently with milk.

Note: Dressing may be spread in pan and pork chops placed on top.

Variation: **Stuffed Pork Chops.** Use 6-oz (170-g) pork chops. Cut pocket in each chop. Fill with dressing and proceed as above. Use ¾ amount of dressing given in recipe. Apple Stuffing (p. 393), ½ recipe, is good with the chops.

BARBECUED SPARERIBS

Oven: 350°F (175°C)
Bake: 2½ hours

Yield: 50 portions
Portion: 8 oz (227 g) AP

Amount Metric	U.S.	Ingredient	Procedure
11.34 kg	25 lb	Pork spareribs or loin back ribs	Separate ribs into 8-oz (227-g) portions. Place in roasting pans. Brown uncovered in oven at 350°F (175°C) until browned lightly, about 30 minutes. Pour off excess fat.
2.84 L	3 qt	Barbeque Sauce (p. 477)	Pour barbecue sauce over ribs. Cover with aluminum foil. Bake at 350°F (175°C) until meat is tender, about 1½ hours. Uncover and bake an additional 20–30 minutes.

Note: For more generous portions, use 40 lb (18.14 kg) spareribs and 1 gal (3.79 L) barbecue sauce.

Variations:

1. **Baked Spareribs with Dressing.** Brown ribs as above. Pour off excess fat. Spread with mixture of 2 oz (57 g) salt, 2 t (4 g) pepper, 1½ t (2 g) ground sage, 1 lb (454 g) apples, chopped, 2 t (4 g) caraway seeds, 1 t (2 g) ground cloves, and 12 oz (340 g) brown sugar. Bake 1½ hours until tender. Baste to keep moist. Serve with Bread Dresssing (p. 392).
2. **Baked Spareribs with Sauerkraut.** Sprinkle ribs with 2 oz (57 g) seasoned salt. Brown lightly. Pour off excess fat. Remove from pan. Add 2 No. 10 cans sauerkraut to baking pan. Place ribs on top. Bake for 1 hour, basting frequently.
3. **Barbecued Shortribs.** Substitute beef shortribs for spareribs.
4. **Sweet-Sour Spareribs.** Brown spareribs for 30 minutes in 400 °F (205°C) oven, or simmer in water 1 hour. Drain and cover with Sweet-Sour Sauce (p. 481). Bake at 350°F (175°C) until meat is done. Serve with steamed rice or with Fried Rice with Almonds (p. 360).

SWEET–SOUR PORK

Yield: 50 portions
Portion: 5 oz (142 g) pork
4 oz (114 g) rice

Amount			
Metric	U.S.	Ingredient	Procedure
4.54 kg	10 lb	Pork, lean, 1-in. cubes	Pour soy sauce over meat. Mix lightly. Let stand at least 1 hour.
180 mL	¾ c	Soy sauce	
227 g	8 oz	Shortening	Drain soy sauce; save. Brown meat in hot shortening. Drain excess fat.
0.95 L	1 qt	Chicken Stock (p. 495)	Add stock and drained soy sauce to meat. Simmer until meat is tender, approximately 1 hour.
198 g	7 oz	Sugar, brown	Combine sugar, cornstarch, and salt.
57 g	2 oz	Cornstarch	
6 g	1 t	Salt	
240 mL	1 c	Pineapple juice	Add pineapple juice, vinegar, and soy sauce to sugar–cornstarch mixture. Mix until smooth. Add to meat while stirring. Cook slowly until thickened.
360 mL	1½ c	Vinegar	
120 mL	½ c	Soy sauce	
340 g	12 oz	Green peppers, cut into strips	15 minutes before serving, add green peppers and onions and cook gently.
454 g	1 lb	Onions, medium, cut into eighths	
908 g	2 lb	Tomatoes, fresh, medium, cut into wedges	Just before serving, add tomato wedges and pineapple chunks. Heat to serving temperature.
1 No. 10 can	1 No. 10 can	Pineapple chunks, well drained	
1.59 kg	3 lb 8 oz	Rice, long-grain	Cook rice according to directions on p. 358. Serve 5 oz (142 g) pork over 4 oz (114 g) rice.
4 L	4¼ qt	Water, boiling	
38 g	2 T	Salt	
30 mL	2 T	Oil (optional)	

Variation: **Sweet–Sour Chicken.** Substitute cooked chicken or turkey for the pork. Do not brown.

GLAZED BAKED HAM

Oven: 325°F (165°C)
Bake: 2–2½ hours
Yield: 50 portions
Portion: 3 oz (85 g)

Amount Metric	U.S.	Ingredient	Procedure
6.8 kg	15 lb	Ham, boneless, fully cooked	Place ham fat-side up on a rack in roasting pan. Do not cover. Bake at 325°F (165°C) for 2–2½ hours.
20 g	3 T	Cloves, whole	Remove ham from oven about 30 minutes before it is done. Drain off drippings. Score ham ¼ in. deep in diamond pattern. Stud with whole cloves. Cover with glaze.
Ham Glaze			
227 g	8 oz	Sugar, brown	Combine ingredients for glaze. Spoon over ham. Repeat if a heavier glaze is desired. Return ham to oven and bake until temperature reaches 140°F (60°C). See timetable, p. 299.
16 g	2 T	Cornstarch	
60 mL	¼ c	Corn syrup	
30 mL	2 T	Pineapple juice	

Note: If using a whole cured ham, not precooked, increase cooking time to 4–4½ hours; or simmer 3–4 hours in a kettle, then trim and glaze and complete cooking in the oven.

Variations:
1. **Apricot Glaze.** 1 c (240 mL) apricot jam and ¼ c (60 mL) fruit juice or enough to cover ham.
2. **Brown Sugar Glaze.** 6 oz (170 g) brown sugar, 1½ t (3 g) dry mustard (or 3 T/45 mL prepared mustard), and ¼ c (60 mL) vinegar.
3. **Cranberry Glaze.** 1¼ c (300 mL) strained cranberry sauce, or enough to cover.
4. **Honey Glaze.** 1 c (240 mL) honey, ½ c (120 mL) brown sugar, and ¼ c (60 mL) fruit juice. Baste with fruit juice or ginger ale.
5. **Orange Glaze.** 1 c (240 mL) orange marmalade and ¼ c (60 mL) spiced peach juice or orange juice.

HAM LOAF

Oven: 350°F (175°C)
Bake: 1–1½ hours

Yield: 50 portions
     5 pans 5 × 9 in.
Portion: 4 oz (114 g)

Amount		Ingredient	Procedure
Metric	U.S.		
2.27 kg	5 lb	Ground cured ham	Combine all ingredients.
1.81 kg	4 lb	Ground beef	Mix on low speed only
2.27 kg	5 lb	Ground fresh pork	until ingredients are
0.95 L	1 qt	Milk	blended. DO NOT
14	14	Eggs, beaten	OVERMIX.
(680 g)	(1 lb 8 oz)		Press mixture into 5
2 g	1 t	Pepper, black	5 × 9-in. loaf pans, 3 lb
454 g	1 lb	Bread crumbs	8 oz (1.59 kg) per pan.
			Bake at 350°F (175°C) for 1–1½ hours.
			Cover tops of loaves with glaze during last 30 minutes of cooking if desired. See Variation No. 2.
			Cut 10 slices per pan.

Notes:
1. Meat may be baked in 12 × 20 × 4-in. baking or counter pan. Press mixture into pan and divide into 2 loaves. Increase baking time to 1½–2 hours.
2. Beef may be omitted, using 9 lb (4.08 kg) ground cooked ham and 5 lb (2.27 kg) fresh pork.

Variations:
1. **Glazed Ham Balls.** Measure with No. 8 dipper and shape into balls. Place on baking sheets. Brush with glaze (Variation No. 2) and bake 1 hour.
2. **Glazed Ham Loaf.** Cover top of loaves with a mixture of 1½ lb (680 g) brown sugar, 1 c (240 mL) vinegar, and 1½ T (10 g) dry mustard.
3. **Ham Patties with Cranberries.** Measure with No. 8 dipper and shape into patties. Spread pan with Cranberry Sauce (p. 431). Place ham patties on sauce and bake 1 hour.
4. **Ham Patties with Pineapple.** Measure with No. 8 dipper and shape into patties. Top each with slice of pineapple and clove. Pour pineapple juice over patties and bake 1 hour.

CREAMED HAM

Yield: 50 portions
6¼ qt (5.91 L)
Portion: ½ c (4 oz/114 g)

Amount		Ingredient	Procedure
Metric	U.S.		
454 g	1 lb	Margarine or butter	Melt margarine. Add flour and stir until smooth.
170 g	6 oz	Flour, all-purpose	Add milk gradually, stirring constantly. Cook until thickened.
3.79 L	1 gal	Milk	
2.72 kg	6 lb	Ham, cooked	Cut ham in cubes or grind coarsely. Add to sauce and heat slowly for about 20 minutes. Add salt, if needed, and pepper. Serve 4 oz (114 g) ham over biscuits, toast, spoon bread, corn bread, or cheese soufflé.
To taste	To taste	Salt	
1 g	½ t	Pepper	

Note: 1 lb (454 g) chopped celery or sliced mushrooms or 1 doz chopped hard-cooked eggs may be added. Reduce ham to 5 lb (2.27 kg).

Variation: **Plantation Shortcake.** Substitute 3 lb (1.36 kg) cooked turkey for 3 lb (1.36 kg) cooked ham. Substitute chicken stock for half of milk in sauce. Add 1 lb (454 g) grated Cheddar cheese. Serve over hot corn bread.

OVEN-FRIED BACON

Oven: 375°F (190°C)
Bake: 6–8 minutes

Yield: 50 portions
Portion: 2 slices

Amount		Ingredient	Procedure
Metric	U.S.		
100 slices (2.27–2.72 kg)	100 slices (5–6 lb)	Bacon (17–20 slices per lb)	Arrange bacon slices on sheet pans. Bake at 375°F (190°C) without turning, until crisp, about 6–8 minutes. Pour off accumulating fat as necessary. Drain on paper towels or place in perforated pans for serving.

Note: Bacon may be purchased already laid out on parchment paper. Bake directly on paper after placing on pans.

SCRAPPLE

Yield: 50 portions
5 loaf pans 5 × 9 in.
Portion: 2 slices

Amount		Ingredient	Procedure
Metric	U.S.		
3.63 kg	8 lb	Sausage, bulk	Fry sausage until slightly brown. Do not overcook. Drain off fat.
3.79 L	1 gal	Water	Add salt to water. Bring to a boil.
28 g	1 oz (1½ T)	Salt	
1.36 kg	3 lb	Cornmeal	Mix cornmeal with cold water. Pour gradually into boiling water, stirring constantly. Cook until thick and smooth, about 10 minutes.
1.89 L	2 qt	Water, cold	
			Add cooked sausage to cornmeal mixture. Scale into 5 greased 5 × 9-in. loaf pans, 4 lb 5 oz (1.96 kg) per pan. Cover with waxed paper to prevent formation of crust. Chill for 24 hours.
			Cut into ½-in. slices. Cook on greased grill preheated to 350°F (175°C). Grill until browned and crisp on both sides. Serve hot with warm syrup.

Note: 8 lb (3.63 kg) fresh pork, simmered until done and chopped finely, may be used in place of the sausage. Increase salt to 2 oz (57 g).

Variation: **Fried Cornmeal Mush.** Delete sausage. Increase cornmeal to 4 lb (1.81 kg), boiling water to 1½ gal (5.68 L), and cold water to 2½ qt (2.37 L). Proceed as for Scrapple.

CHEESE-STUFFED FRANKFURTERS

Oven: 350°F (175°C)
Bake: 30 minutes

Yield: 100 frankfurters
Portion: 2 frankfurters

Amount Metric	U.S.	Ingredient	Procedure
4.54 kg	10 lb	Frankfurters, 10 per lb	Split frankfurters lengthwise, but do not cut completely through.
1.36 kg 0.95 L	3 lb 1 qt	Cheddar cheese Pickle relish	Cut cheese into strips about 3½ in. long. Place a strip of cheese and about ½ T relish in each frankfurter.
100 slices (1.8–2.27 kg)	100 slices (4–5 lb)	Bacon, 24–26 slices per lb	Wrap a slice of bacon around each frankfurter. Secure with a toothpick. Place on greased baking sheets. Bake at 350°F (175°C) for 30 minutes.

Note: 8 lb 4 oz (3.74 kg) wieners, 12 per lb, may be substituted for the frankfurters. With the wieners, 1 slice of bacon may be wrapped around 2 wieners.

Variations:
1. **Barbecued Frankfurters.** Place frankfurters in counter pans. Cover with Barbecue Sauce (p. 477). Bake at 400°F (205°C) for about 30 minutes. Add more sauce if necessary.
2. **Chili Dog.** Serve 2 oz (57 g) Chili con Carne (p. 325) over a frankfurter or wiener in a bun. Chili may be made with or without beans.
3. **Frankfurters and Sauerkraut.** Steam frankfurters or cook in boiling water. Serve with sauerkraut (2 No. 10 cans), which has been heated.
4. **Nacho Dog.** Serve 2 oz (57 g) Nacho Sauce (p. 274) over a frankfurter or wiener in a bun. Sprinkle over the top one or more of the following: chopped green chilies or jalapeño peppers, chopped tomatoes, chopped black olives, or chopped onion.

SAUSAGE ROLLS

Oven: 400°F (205°C)
Bake: 20 minutes

Yield: 50 rolls
Portion: 1 roll, 2 oz (57 g) gravy

Amount		Ingredient	Procedure
Metric	U.S.		
5.67 kg	12 lb 8 oz	Sausages, link	Partially cook sausages. Save fat for gravy.
1.14 kg	2 lb 8 oz	Flour, all-purpose	Make into biscuit dough, according to directions on p. 84. Divide dough into 2 portions. Roll each portion to ½-in. thickness and cut into 3 × 4 in. rectangles. Place 2 sausages in the center of each piece of dough and fold over. Bake at 400°F (205°C) for 20 minutes.
70 g	2½ oz	Baking powder	
19 g	1 T	Salt	
284 g	10 oz	Shortening	
720 mL	3 c	Milk	
170 g	6 oz	Sausage fat	Add flour to fat and blend. Add salt and pepper. Add water or stock gradually, stirring constantly. Cook until smooth and thickened. Serve 2-oz ladle of gravy over each sausage roll.
170 g	6 oz	Flour, all-purpose	
12 g	2 t	Salt	
1 g	½ t	Pepper, black	
2.84 L	3 qt	Water or chicken stock	

Variations:

1. **Pigs in Blankets.** Substitute wieners for link sausages. May serve with Cheese Sauce (p. 471).
2. **Pigs in Blankets with Cheese.** Wrap 1 oz (28 g) cheese around each wiener. Proceed as above.

Pasta, Rice, and Cereals

The cooking of pasta, rice, and cereals is similar. Water and heat are applied, and cooking is continued until gelatinization of the starch granules is completed.

PASTA

Pasta is a generic name for a basic dough mixture of durum or other high-protein hard wheat flour and water. With the exception of noodles, which contain eggs, the various pasta or macaroni foods are made of the same dough. Pasta comes in many different forms, and it is estimated that there are 150 different varieties. A few of the more popular types appear in Fig. 2.19. Flavor variations include whole wheat, herb, tomato, and spinach.

Dry pasta will approximately double in *volume* after cooking, except egg noodles which remain about the same. The *weight* of egg noodles and most pasta will triple when cooked. The thickness of the wall varies among pasta shapes, and the volume increase is directly related to this variation. Certain shapes such as ziti, lasagna, and rigatoni have more fluctuation in their volume increase than do spaghetti or macaroni.

A general rule for cooking pasta is to allow 1 gal (3.79 L) of water, 2 T (38 g) salt, and 1½ t (8 mL) cooking oil for every pound (454 g) of pasta. Directions for cooking are given on p. 348. Pasta should be cooked until it is tender but firm (al dente—"to the tooth").

RICE

Rice is cooked until all of the water is absorbed, so the key to properly cooked rice is the right proportion of rice to water and the correct cooking time. Converted (parboiled long-grain) white rice requires slightly more water and a longer cooking time than does regular long-grain or medium-grain rice. The cooking time for brown rice is almost double that of white rice. Rice may be cooked in a kettle, steamer, or oven. See p. 358 for cooking directions.

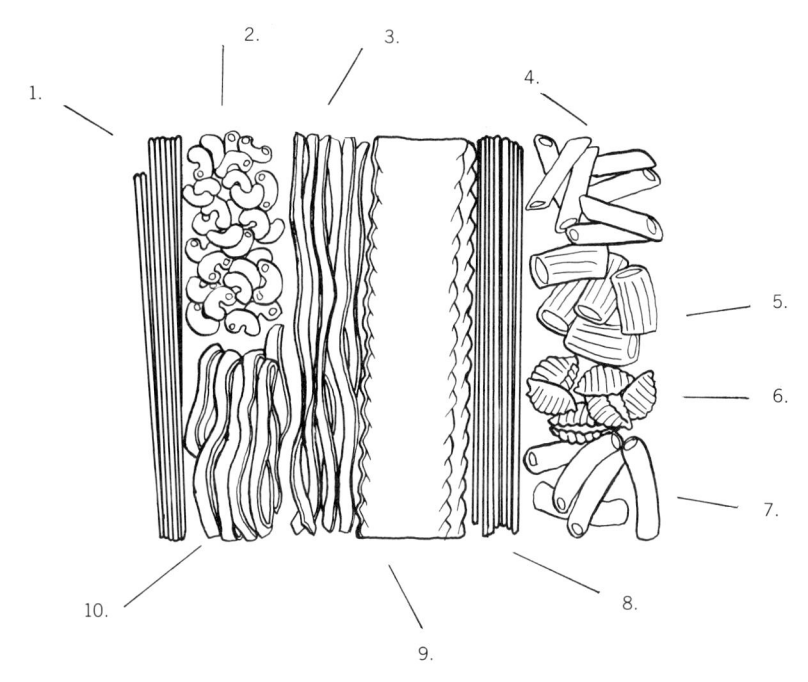

Figure 2.19 Frequently used pasta shapes. (1) Spaghetti. (2) Elbow macaroni. (3) Fettuccine. (4) Mostaccioli. (5) Rigatoni. (6) Shells. (7) Ziti. (8) Linguine. (9) Lasagne. (10) Egg Noodles.

CEREALS

Cereals may be whole, cracked, flaked or rolled, or granular. The amount of water used for cooking determines largely the volume of the finished product. Cereal swells to the extent of water used until the limit of the grain is reached. As a rule, granular cereals absorb more water than whole or flaked. The fineness of the grind of cereal and the amount of bran or cellulose are factors that determine the length of time a cereal needs to be cooked. Cereals in quantity usually are cooked in a steam-jacketed kettle or steamer but may be prepared in a heavy kettle on top of the range. Directions for cooking breakfast cereals are given on p. 362.

PASTA RECIPES

COOKING PASTA

Yield: 50 portions
Portion: 4 oz (114 g)

Amount		Ingredient	Procedure
Metric	U.S.		
2.27 kg	5 lb	Pasta (spaghetti, macaroni, or noodles)	Bring water to a boil. Add pasta gradually while stirring.
19 L	5 gal	Water	Reheat to boiling temperature. Cook uncovered at a fast boil until tender, about 10 minutes.
142 g	5 oz	Salt	Test for doneness. It should still be firm to the bite.
37 mL	2½ T	Oil (optional)	Stir occasionally to help prevent sticking. Drain. Rinse with hot water.

Notes:
1. Weight of cooked pasta will vary, depending on length of time cooked.
2. Additon of oil is optional. It helps prevent foaming and sticking.
3. Pasta is done when tender, but firm (al dente).
4. If pasta is to be used as part of a dish requiring further cooking, undercook slightly.
5. If product is not to be served immediately, drain and cover with cold water. Stir to aid in cooling. When pasta is cold, drain off water and toss lightly with a little salad oil. This will keep pasta from sticking or drying out. Cover tightly and store in the refrigerator. To reheat, put pasta in a colander and immerse in rapidly boiling water just long enough to heat through. *Do not continue to cook.* Or, reheat in a microwave oven.
6. Pasta can be refrigerated or frozen without any loss of product quality. Reheat to serving temperature.
7. Approximate reheating times for 1 8-oz portion are 15 seconds in boiling water or 3 minutes in a microwave (650 watts); for 4 8-oz portions, 15 seconds in boiling water or 10 minutes in a microwave (650 watts).
8. Yields for various pasta are

1 lb (454 g) dry yields	cooked weight	1 lb (454 g) dry yields	cooked weight
Spaghetti	2 lb 8 oz	Lasagne	2 lb 3 oz
Macaroni	2 lb 12 oz	Linguine	2 lb 8 oz
Noodles	2 lb 13 oz	Mostacciolo	2 lb 5 oz
Fettucini	2 lb 13 oz	Rigatoni	2 lb

SPAGHETTI WITH MEAT SAUCE

Yield: 50 portions
Portion: 6 oz (170 g) sauce
4 oz (114 g) spaghetti

Amount		Ingredient	Procedure
Metric	U.S.		
3.63 kg	8 lb	Ground beef	Brown beef. Pour off excess fat.
4.73 L	5 qt	Tomato purée (or tomatoes)	Add remaining sauce ingredients to cooked beef.
0.95 L	1 qt	Water	
1.66 L	1¾ qt	Catsup	Cook slowly, stirring frequently, until thickened, approximately ½ hour. Remove bay leaves before serving.
454 g	1 lb	Onions, chopped	
2	2	Bay leaves	
½ t	½ t	Thyme	
1 clove	1 clove	Garlic, minced	
3 g	1 T	Oregano	
1 t	1 t	Basil	
28 g	1 oz (2 T)	Sugar, granulated	
60 mL	¼ c	Worcestershire sauce	
4 g	2 t	Cayenne	
28 g	1 oz (1½ T)	Salt	
2.27 kg	5 lb	Spaghetti	Cook spaghetti according to directions on p. 348. Serve 6 oz (170 g) sauce over 4 oz (114 g) spaghetti.
19 L	5 gal	Water, boiling	
142 g	5 oz	Salt	
37 mL	2½ T	Cooking oil (optional)	

Note: Grated Parmesan cheese may be sprinkled over top of each serving.

SPAGHETTI WITH MEATBALLS

Oven: 400°F (205°C); 375°F (190°C)
Bake: 50 minutes

Yield: 50 portions
Portion: 2 meatballs
4 oz (114 g) spaghetti

Metric	U.S.	Ingredient	Procedure
3.63 kg	8 lb	Ground beef	Mix meat, bread, milk, and seasonings on low speed. DO NOT OVERMIX.
1.81 kg	4 lb	Ground pork	
6 slices	6 slices	Bread, crumbled	
480 mL	2 c	Milk	
38 g	2 T	Salt	Dip with No. 16 dipper onto baking sheets. Brown in 400°F (205°C) oven 15–20 minutes. Remove to 12 × 20 × 4-in. counter pan or roasting pan.
4 g	2 t	Pepper, black	
2.84 L	3 qt (2 50-oz cans)	Tomato soup	Make into sauce and simmer 1½ – 2 hours.
1.18 L	1¼ qt (1 46-oz can)	Tomato paste	Pour over browned meatballs.
3.31 L	3½ qt	Water, boiling	Cover and cook in 375°F (190°C) oven for about 30 minutes.
30 g	2 T	Mustard, prepared	
14 g	2 T	Paprika	
120 mL	½ c	Worcestershire sauce	
28 g	2 T	Sugar, granulated	
4 cloves	4 cloves	Garlic, minced	
227 g	8 oz	Onion, chopped	
2.27 kg	5 lb	Spaghetti	Cook spaghetti according to directions on p. 348. Serve 2 meatballs and 5 oz (142 g) sauce over 4 oz (114 g) spaghetti.
19 L	5 gal	Water, boiling	
142 g	5 oz	Salt	
37 mL	2½ T	Cooking oil	

Note: If desired, mix the cooked spaghetti with the tomato sauce. Place in 2 counter pans, arrange meatballs over top, and bake at 375°F (190°C) for 20–30 minutes.

SPAGHETTI WITH CHICKEN SAUCE

Yield: 50 portions
Portion: 6 oz (170 g) sauce
4 oz (114 g) spaghetti

Amount Metric	U.S.	Ingredient	Procedure
198 g	7 oz	Margarine or butter	Sauté vegetables in margarine until tender crisp.
680 g	1 lb 8 oz	Celery, chopped	
680 g	1 lb 8 oz	Onions, chopped	
57 g	2 oz	Green peppers, chopped	
57 g	2 oz	Pimiento, chopped	
284 g	10 oz	Flour, all-purpose	Stir in flour. Cook over low heat for 10 minutes.
4.5 L	4¾ qt	Chicken Stock (p. 495)	Add to vegetable mixture, stirring constantly. Cook until thickened.
12 g	2 t	Salt	Season with salt and pepper.
2 g	1 t	Pepper, white	
3.18 kg	7 lb	Chicken, cooked, cubed	Fold in chicken.
2.27 kg	5 lb	Spaghetti	Cook spaghetti according to directions on p. 348. Serve 6 oz (170 g) sauce over 4 oz (114 g) spaghetti.
19 L	5 gal	Water, boiling	
142 g	5 oz	Salt	
37 mL	2½ T	Cooking oil (optional)	

Note: Sauce may be combined with spaghetti and served as a casserole.

PASTA WITH VEGETABLE SAUCE

Yield: 50 portions
2½ gal (9.46 L)
Portion: 6 oz (170 g) sauce
4 oz (114 g) pasta

Amount Metric	U.S.	Ingredient	Procedure
240 mL	1 c	Olive oil	Sauté onion in oil until tender, using a steam-jacketed or other large kettle.
908 g	2 lb	Onions, chopped	
14 g	½ oz (½ c)	Oregano, leaf	Add spices to onion. Mix well.
14 g	½ oz (½ c)	Basil, dried	
85 g	3 oz (¾ c)	Garlic powder	
2 g	1 t	Pepper, black	
57 g	2 oz (3 T)	Salt	
2	2	Bay leaves	
5 1.36 L cans	5 46-oz cans	Tomato juice	Add to spices and onion. Heat to boiling. Reduce heat and simmer uncovered 3–4 hours. (See Note 2.) Taste and adjust seasonings if desired.
794 g	1 lb 12 oz	Tomato paste	
3.31 L	3½ qt	Water (See Note 1.)	
1.14 kg	2 lb 8 oz	Zucchini, sliced	Add zucchini and mushrooms just before serving. Cook only until zucchini is tender.
680 g	1 lb 8 oz	Mushrooms, sliced	
2.27 kg	5 lb	Pasta	Cook pasta according to directions on p. 348. Serve 6 oz (170 g) sauce over 4 oz (114 g) pasta.
19 L	5 gal	Water, boiling	
142 g	5 oz	Salt	
37 mL	2½ T	Oil (optional)	

Notes:
1. For a sauce that cooks in less time, delete water and cook 1–2 hours or until volume is reduced to 2 gal (7.57 L). Herb flavor may not be as pronounced as that in the longer cooking method.
2. Sauce must cook until thick and volume is reduced to 2 gal (7.57 L).
3. 2 c (480 mL) finely chopped fresh basil may be substituted for dry basil.

Variation: **Basic Tomato Sauce.** Delete zucchini and mushrooms. Use for any pasta or in lasagne.

VEGETARIAN SPAGHETTI

Yield: 50 portions
1 pan 12 × 20 × 4 in.
Portion: 8 oz (227 g)

Amount Metric	U.S.	Ingredient	Procedure
1.25 kg	2 lb 12 oz	Spaghetti	Cook spaghetti, according to directions on p. 348. Drain.
10.41 L	2¾ gal	Water, boiling	
85 g	3 oz	Salt	
8 mL	1½ t	Oil (optional)	
454 g	1 lb	Margarine or butter, melted	Combine margarine and flour in steam-jacketed kettle. Cook and stir until smooth. Cook 15–20 minutes. Stir frequently.
340 g	12 oz	Flour, all-purpose	
3.79 L	1 gal	Milk	Add milk gradually. Cook over low heat until thick, stirring constantly. Turn off heat.
19 g	1 T	Salt	Add salt and cheese. Stir until cheese melts.
624 g	1 lb 6 oz	Cheese, American, white	
794 g	1 lb 12 oz	Carrots, diced	Steam vegetables until tender. Drain. Combine with cheese sauce.
567 g	1 lb 4 oz	Green peppers, chopped	
567 g	1 lb 4 oz	Celery, chopped	
1.36 kg	3 lb	Mushrooms, pieces and stems, canned	Add mushrooms.
			Combine cooked spaghetti gently with cheese sauce.

Variation: **Spaghetti with Vegetarian Sauce.** Serve 4 oz (114 g) ladle of sauce over 4 oz (114 g) cooked spaghetti. Increase spaghetti to 5 lb (2.27 kg) AP for 50 servings.

PASTA WITH CLAM SAUCE

Yield: 50 portions
Portion: 6 oz (170 g) sauce
4 oz (114 g) pasta

Amount Metric	U.S.	Ingredient	Procedure
680 g	1 lb 8 oz	Margarine or butter	Melt margarine in a large kettle. Stir in flour and cook for 2 minutes.
454 g	1 lb	Flour, all-purpose	
6.15 L	6½ qt	Milk, hot	Add milk and seasonings to flour–margarine mixture. Heat to boiling.
57 g	2 oz	Salt	
1 g	½ t	Nutmeg	
1.42 L	1½ qt	Cream	Reduce heat. Add cream slowly and continue to cook until thick.
908 g	2 lb	Minced clams	Stir in clams.
2.27 kg	5 lb	Pasta	Cook pasta according to directions on p. 348. Serve 6 oz (170 g) sauce over 4 oz (114 g) pasta.
19 L	5 gal	Water, boiling	
142 g	5 oz	Salt	
37 mL	2½ T	Oil (optional)	

Notes:
1. Clam Sauce is excellent served on whole wheat pasta.
2. 2 oz (57 g) chopped green onion tops, 2 oz (57 g) chopped chives, or 6 oz (170 g) sliced mushrooms may be added for variety.

LASAGNE

Oven: 350°F (175°C)
Bake: 40–45 minutes

Yield: 48 portions
2 pans 12 × 20 × 2 in.
Portion: 6 oz (170 g)

Amount Metric	U.S.	Ingredient	Procedure
2.27 kg	5 lb	Ground beef	Cook together until meat has lost pink color. Drain off excess fat.
340 g	12 oz	Onion, finely chopped	
2 cloves	2 cloves	Garlic, minced	
2.84 L	3 qt	Tomato sauce	Add to meat. Continue cooking, about 30 minutes, stirring occasionally.
0.95 L	1 qt	Tomato paste	
2 g	1 t	Pepper, black	
2 g	1 t	Basil, crumbled	
7 g	1 T	Oregano, crumbled	
1.14 kg	2 lb 8 oz	Noodles, lasagne	Cook noodles according to directions on p. 348. Store in cold water to keep noodles from sticking. Drain when ready to use.
7.57 L	2 gal	Water, boiling	
38 g	2 T	Salt	
30 mL	2 T	Cooking oil	
1.14 kg	2 lb 8 oz	Mozzarella cheese, shredded	Combine cheeses. Arrange in 2 greased 12 × 20 × 2-in. counter pans in layers in the following order: Meat sauce (1 qt/0.95 L) Noodles, overlapping, (1 lb 12 oz/794 g) Cheeses (1 lb 4 oz/567 g) Repeat sauce, noodles, and cheeses. Spoon remainder of meat sauce on top. Bake at 350°F (175°C) for 40–45 minutes. Cut 4 × 6.
170 g	6 oz	Parmesan cheese, grated	
1.14 kg	2 lb 8 oz	Ricotta cheese or cottage cheese, dry or drained	

SPINACH LASAGNE (DEEP DISH)

Oven: 350°F (175°C)
Bake: 1½ – 2 hours

Yield: 64 portions
2 pans 12 × 20 × 4-in.
Portion: 10 oz (284 g)

Amount Metric	Amount U.S.	Ingredient	Procedure
850 g	1 lb 14 oz	Onions, chopped	Sauté vegetables in hot oil.
510 g	1 lb 2 oz	Green pepper, chopped	
57 g	2 oz	Garlic, minced	
240 mL	1 c	Cooking oil	
3.97 kg	8 lb 12 oz	Tomatoes, diced, canned	Stir into sautéed vegetables. Simmer uncovered about 20 minutes. Remove bay leaf.
3.31 L	3½ qt	Tomato juice	
1.25 kg	2 lb 12 oz	Tomato paste	
85 g	3 oz	Parsley, chopped	
2 g	1 T	Oregano, leaf	
2	2	Bay leaves	
1.36 kg	3 lb	Spinach, chopped	Cook spinach. Drain.
2.27 kg	5 lb	Cottage cheese	Mix. Add to spinach.
454 g	1 lb	Parmesan cheese	
5 (227 g)	5 (8 oz)	Eggs, beaten	
19 g	1 T	Salt	
2 g	2 t	Pepper, black	
2.27 kg	5 lb	Lasagne noodles, dry	
1.81 kg	4 lb	Mozzarella cheese, shredded	

Layer ingredients in each of 2 12 × 20 × 4-in. pans as follows:
1. Tomato sauce, 3 lb 10 oz (1.64 kg)
2. Dry noodles, 13 oz (369 g)
3. Spinach-cheese mixture, 2 lb 5 oz (1.05 kg)
4. Mozzarella cheese, 11 oz (312 g)
5. Repeat layers as above
6. Dry noodles, 13 oz (369 g)
7. Tomato sauce, 3 lb 10 oz (1.64 kg)
8. Mozzarella cheese, 8 oz (227 g)

Bake at 350°F (175°C) covered with aluminum foil for 1 hour. Remove foil and bake an additional 30–60 minutes or until hot and bubbly.

If browning too fast, cover again with foil.

Cut 4 × 8.

NOODLES ROMANOFF

Oven: 350°F (175°C)
Bake: 45 minutes

Yield: 50 portions
2 pans 12 × 20 × 2 in.
Portion: 5 oz (142 g)

Amount			
Metric	U.S.	Ingredient	Procedure
1.36 kg	3 lb	Noodles	Cook noodles according
11.36 L	3 gal	Water, boiling	to directions on p. 348.
85 g	3 oz	Salt	Drain.
19 g	1 T	Cooking Oil	
284 g	10 oz	Margarine or butter	Sauté onions in margarine
114 g	4 oz	Onions, chopped	until tender.
114 g	4 oz	Flour, all-purpose	Add flour and seasonings,
29 g	1½ T	Salt	stirring constantly.
¼ t	¼ t	Garlic powder	
1.18 L	1¼ qt	Milk	Add milk gradually, stirring constantly. Cook until thickened. Cool slightly.
114 g	4 oz	Parmesan cheese, grated	Add to sauce. Combine noodles and sauce. Scale into 2 12 × 20 × 2-in. counter pans, 8 lb (3.63 kg) per pan.
1.14 kg	2 lb 8 oz	Cottage cheese	
600 mL	2½ c	Cultured sour cream	
7 g	1 T	Paprika	
227 g	8 oz	Cheddar cheese, shredded	Sprinkle cheese over mixture, 4 oz (114 g) per pan. Bake at 350°F (175°C) for 45 minutes or until heated through.

RICE RECIPES

STEAMED OR BAKED RICE

Yield: 50 portions
Portion: 4 oz (114 g)

Amount		Ingredient	Procedure
Metric	U.S.		
1.59 kg	3 lb 8 oz	Rice, converted	**Steamer**
38 g	2 T	Salt	Weigh rice into 12 × 20 × 2-in. counter pan.
30 mL	2 T	Margarine or cooking oil (optional)	Add salt and margarine. Pour hot water over rice. Stir.
4 L	4¼ qt	Water, hot	Steam uncovered for 30–40 minutes. Fluff with fork.
			Oven
			Weigh rice into 12 × 20 × 2-in. counter pan.
			Add salt and margarine.
			Pour hot water over rice. Stir.
			Cover pans tightly with aluminum foil.
			Bake at 350°F (175°C) for 1 hour.
			Remove from oven and let stand covered for 5 minutes.
			Fluff with fork.

Notes:
1. If using regular white rice in place of converted rice, the cooking time may need to be reduced.
2. For brown rice, increase cooking time to 50–60 minutes for steamed rice, to 1½ hours for baked rice.
3. For buttered rice, add 5 oz (142 g) butter or margarine. Add to dry rice in counter pan. Add salt and hot water.
4. 1 lb (454 g) uncooked rice yields 2 qt (1.89 L) cooked rice.

BOILED RICE

Yield: 50 portions
Portion: 4 oz (114 g)

Amount		Ingredient	Procedure
Metric	U.S.		
4 L	4¼ qt	Water	Bring water to a boil in steam-jacketed kettle or large kettle.
38 g	2 T	Salt	
1.59 kg	3 lb 8 oz	Rice, converted	
30 mL	2 T	Cooking oil or margarine (optional)	Add salt and rice. Stir. Cover tightly. Cook on low heat until rice is tender and all water is absorbed, about 15–20 minutes. Remove from heat and let stand covered 5–10 minutes. Fluff with fork.

Notes:
1. If using regular white rice in place of converted rice, the cooking time may need to be reduced.
2. For brown rice, increase cooking time to 40–45 minutes.
3. 1 lb (454 g) uncooked rice yields 2 qt (1.89 L) cooked rice.

FRIED RICE

Yield: 50 portions
Portion: 4 oz (114 g)

Amount		Ingredient	Procedure
Metric	U.S.		
1.14 kg	2 lb 8 oz	Rice	Cook rice according to
2.84 L	3 qt	Water	directions on p. 358.
12 g	2 t	Salt	Do not overcook. Let cool.
680 g	1 lb 8 oz	Frozen peas	Cook peas and drain. Set aside.
6 (312 g)	6 (11 oz)	Eggs	Break eggs and mix. Add salt.
12 g	2 t	Salt	Sauté in oil. Stir to break
30 mL	2 T	Cooking Oil	into small pieces. Set aside.
454 g	1 lb	Onions, chopped	Sauté onions and carrots
227 g	8 oz	Carrots, shredded	in oil until tender.
180 mL	¾ c	Cooking oil	Add rice and cook until heated.
180 mL	¾ c	Soy sauce	Add soy sauce to rice mixture, stirring to mix evenly.
			Stir in cooked peas and eggs. Serve immediately.

Variations:

1. **Fried Rice with Almonds.** Cook 3 lb (1.36 kg) rice according to directions on p. 358. Sauté 4 oz (114 g) chopped onions and 4 oz (114 g) chopped green peppers in 1 c (240 mL) cooking oil. Add cooked rice, 1 T (7 g) pepper, 1 t (6 g) garlic salt, ½ c (120 mL) soy sauce, 2 lb (908 g) slivered almonds. Add salt if needed. Bake until thoroughly heated.
2. **Fried Rice with Ham.** Add 1 lb 8 oz (680 g) chopped ham.
3. **Green Rice.** To 2 lb (908 g) rice, cooked, add 4 lb (1.81 kg) finely chopped raw or frozen spinach, 2 T (30 mL) onion juice, and 1¼ qt (1.18 L) medium white sauce (p. 470). Place in 1 12 × 20 × 2-in. counter pan. Bake at 325°F (165°C) for 30–40 minutes.
4. **Pork Fried Rice.** Delete peas. Add 4 lb (1.81 kg) cubed, cooked pork. Fry 1 lb (454 g) bacon. Use grease for sautéing vegetables and rice. Crumble bacon and add.
5. **Shrimp Fried Rice.** Add 1 lb 8 oz (680 g) cooked shrimp.

RICE PILAF

Oven: 350°F (175°C)
Bake: 45 minutes

Yield: 50 portions
1 pan 12 × 20 × 4 in.
Portion: 4 oz (114 g)

Amount Metric	U.S.	Ingredient	Procedure
680 g	1 lb 8 oz	Onions, finely chopped	Sauté onion in margarine until it begins to soften.
227 g	8 oz	Margarine or butter, melted	Do not brown.
1.36 kg	3 lb	Rice, converted	Add rice. Stir over heat until completely coated with the margarine.
6 g	1 t	Salt	Place rice in 12 × 20 × 4-in. counter pan.
¼ t	¼ t	Pepper, white	Add seasonings and chicken stock. Stir to combine. Cover tightly with aluminum foil. Bake at 350°F (175°C) for 45 minutes; or steam uncovered for 30 minutes. Stir before serving.
1	1	Bay leaf	
3.79 L	1 gal	Chicken Stock (p. 495)	

Note: Chopped green pepper, pimiento, tomato, or nuts; sliced mushrooms, or water chestnuts; ground or diced ham may be added.

Variations:
1. **Curried Rice.** Add 3 T (21 g) curry powder.
2. **Mexican Rice.** Sauté 14 oz (397 g) chopped onion, 10 oz (284 g) chopped green pepper, and 3 oz (85 g) chopped celery in ⅓ c (80 mL) cooking oil. Add raw rice and stir 2–3 minutes until grains are coated with oil. Stir in 3 T (57 g) salt, 2 oz (57 g) chili powder, and 1 t (2 g) garlic powder. Place in 12 × 20 × 4-in. counter pan. Pour over a mixture of 2½ qt (2.37 L) tomato juice and 1¾ qt (1.66 L) Beef Stock (p. 494). Steam 25–35 minutes. Stir before serving.

CEREAL RECIPES

BREAKFAST CEREALS

Yield: 2 gal (7.57 L)
Portion: ⅔ c (160 ml)

Amount Metric	U.S.	Ingredient	Procedure
7.5–8.5 L	2–2¼ gal	Water	Measure water into steam-jacketed kettle or heavy stock pot.
57 g	2 oz (3 T)	Salt	Add salt and bring to a rolling boil.
908 g	2 lb	Cereal, flaked, granular, or cracked	Stir dry cereal gradually into boiling water, using wire whip. Stir until some thickening is apparent. Reduce heat and cook until cereal reaches desired consistency and raw starch taste has disappeared. Cereal should be thick and creamy but not sticky.

Notes:

1. Granular cereals may be mixed with cold water to separate particles and prevent formation of lumps.
2. Do not stir excessively; overstirring or overcooking produces a sticky, gummy product.
3. 1 lb (454 g) raisins may be added to cereal.

GRANOLA

Oven: 300°F (150°C)
Bake: 1 hour
Yield: 50 portions
Portion: 2¾ oz (78 g)

Metric	U.S.	Ingredient	Procedure
170 g	6 oz	Sugar, brown	Mix on medium speed.
397 g	14 oz	Almonds, slivered	
114 g	4 oz	Sesame seeds	
227 g	8 oz	Sunflower seeds, shelled	
28 g	1 oz	Bulgar	
1.25 kg	2 lb 12 oz	Coconut, shredded	
19 g	1 T	Salt	
10 mL	2 t	Vanilla	
10 mL	2 t	Almond extract	
240 mL	1 c	Water	
240 mL	1 c	Salad oil	
1.22 kg	2 lb 11 oz	Rolled oats, quick	Mix in rolled oats carefully so flakes are not broken.
			Spread mixture on sheet pans ½ in. deep. Bake at 300°F (150°C) for 1 hour or until golden brown and crispy. Stir every 15 minutes while baking. Cool and store in airtight container until served.

Note: Use for snacks, ice cream topping, or breakfast cereal.

BARLEY CASSEROLE

Oven: 350°F (175°C)
Bake: 1½ hours

Yield: 50 portions
Portion: 4 oz (114 g)

Amount		Ingredient	Procedure
Metric	U.S.		
170 g	6 oz	Margarine or butter	Sauté barley and vegetables.
1.08 kg	2 lb 6 oz	Pearl barley	
567 g	1 lb 4 oz	Onions, chopped	
765 g	1 lb 11 oz	Mushroom pieces and stems, canned	
3.31 L	3½ qt	Chicken Stock (p. 495)	Add chicken stock to vegetables and barley. Pour into 12 × 20 × 2-in. counter pan. Bake at 350°F (175°C) for 1½ hours. Serve with No. 10 dipper.

Poultry

PURCHASING AND STORAGE

Poultry is used extensively in all types of food services and is available in many different forms. It generally is purchased in the ready-to-cook state and may be fresh or frozen, whole or cut up, or a convenience product. Many food services find it advantageous to purchase chicken parts, although there is some price differential between custom-cut pieces and whole poultry. Each portion in the package is of identical weight; there is no waste, and the cost of each portion is easily determined.

Whole ready-to-cook turkeys range in size from 4 to 24 lb (1.81–10.9 kg), and some even higher. The larger birds yield more meat in proportion to bone weight than smaller ones, but their use may not be feasible because of equipment capacity and cooking time required. Many food service managers prefer to buy halves, quarters, or parts; or boneless turkey roasts and rolls, which are available either raw or cooked and which vary in ratio of dark to white meat.

Many other convenience poultry products are on the market. Frozen breaded chicken pieces, fillets, and patties are readily available. Nontraditional products such as turkey pastrami, turkey hot dogs, and other poultry cold cuts have increased in use over the past several years. Canned boned chicken and frozen diced chicken or turkey may be used satisfactorily in casseroles, salads, sandwiches, and soups.

All poultry is highly perishable, and extreme caution regarding cleanliness should be exercised in preparing, cooking, cooling, storing, and serving poultry products. Fresh-chilled poultry should be used within 1 to 2 days, and frozen poultry should be kept hard-frozen at 0°F (−18°C) until it is removed from storage for thawing and cooking.

Poultry should be defrosted in a refrigerator. Place wrapped birds on trays to catch any drippings and space on refrigerator shelves so that air can circulate around them. Allow 1 to 2 days for chickens, 2 to 4 days for larger birds.

If faster thawing is necessary, partially thaw in the original wrapper in the refrigerator and then place in cold water until completely thawed. *Change cold water often. Do not thaw in warm water.* Once thawed, poultry may be kept safely no longer than 24 hours at 38°F (3°C) before cooking. It should never be refrozen.

COOKING METHODS

Most frozen poultry, except prebreaded and precooked convenience products, is thawed prior to cooking. If cooking is started from the frozen state it will take approximately 1½ times the total allowance for thawed poultry.

Poultry should be cooked at moderate heat (325–350°F/165–175°C) for optimum tenderness and juiciness, and the cookery method chosen should be appropriate for the age of the bird. Dry-heat methods (broiling, frying, or roasting) are used for young, tender birds. Moist-heat methods (stewing, steaming, and braising or fricasseeing) are suitable for the older, more mature birds. Recommended cooking methods for various classes of poultry are given in Table 2.14.

BROILING

Only young tender chickens, 2½ lb (1.14 kg) or under, or 3- to 5-lb (1.36- to 2.27-kg) ready-to-cook turkeys should be broiled. Split each bird in half lengthwise or into quarters, depending on size. Fold wing tip back onto cut side with

TABLE 2.14 COOKING METHODS FOR POULTRY

Kind of Poultry	Class	Average Ready-to-Cook Weight lb	Average Ready-to-Cook Weight kg	Cookery Method	Per Capita Allowance Ready-to-Cook Weight oz	Per Capita Allowance Ready-to-Cook Weight g
Chicken	Broiler-fryer	2–3	0.9–1.4	Barbecue, fry, or broil	¼–½ bird	¼–½ bird
	Roaster	3–5	1.4–2.3	Roast	12–16	340–454
	Fowl or hen	3–5	1.4–2.3	Stew or fricassee	8–12	227–340
Turkey	Whole	8–24	3.6–10.9	Roast	12–16	340–454
	Roast, boned and tied	12	5.4	Roast	4–5	114–142
	Roast, cooked	8–10	3.6–4.5	Slice and heat in broth or heat in an uncovered pan	2½–3	70–85
	Roll, ready to cook	3–6	1.4–2.7	Roast	4–5	114–142
Duck		4–6	1.8–2.7	Roast	12–16	340–454
Goose		6–8	2.7–3.6	Roast	12–16	340–454

Note: For cooked yields for chicken and turkey, see p. 13

the thick part around the shoulder joint. Brush with melted fat. Season each piece with salt and pepper, and place, skin-side down, on broiler. Place broiler 7 in. below source of heat; chicken and turkey should broil slowly. Turn and brush with fat while broiling in order to brown and cook evenly. The time required to cook chicken varies from 50 to 60 minutes and 1 to 1¼ hours for turkey.

DEEP-FAT FRYING
Cut 1¾- to 2-lb (794- to 908-g) broiler-fryers into pieces of desired serving size. Roll chicken in seasoned flour; or dredge in flour, dip in egg and milk mixture, then roll in crumbs (Fig. 2.20); or, dip in batter (see Table 1.13). Fry in deep fat 12–15 minutes at no more than 325° (165°C). See recipe, p. 371.

PAN FRYING
Cut 13 2- to 2½-lb (0.908- to 1.14-kg) broiler-fryers into pieces. Roll chicken in seasoned flour (see recipe, p. 371) and brown in a skillet containing ½ in. of hot fat. Reduce heat and cook slowly until tender—usually about 45–60 minutes. Cooking time depends on size of pieces. Turn as necessary to assure even browning and doneness.

OVEN FRYING
Cut 13 2- to 2½-lb (0.908- to 1.14-kg) broiler-fryers into pieces. Dredge in seasoned flour, roll in melted fat, place on sheet pans, and bake 1–1½ hours at 350°F (175°C). This method should result in browning with no turning. See recipe, p. 372.

STEWING OR SIMMERING
Cover large fryers or hens with water and add 2 t (12 g) salt for each 4- to 5-lb (1.81- to 2.27-kg) bird. Cover kettle closely and simmer until tender, approximately 2½ hours. Do not boil. When meat is to be used in salads or creamed dishes, add to cooking water for additional flavor 1 carrot, 1 medium onion, 1 stalk of celery, 2 or 3 cloves, and 2 whole peppercorns for each bird. For cooking in a steamer, place whole or parts of birds in a solid steamer pan. Cook until tender, following instructions of the manufacturer.

If cooked poultry is to be held, it must be cooled immediately. Remove from broth and place on sheet pans. When poultry is cool enough to handle, remove meat from bones, place in shallow pans, and store in refrigerator at 38°F (3°C) or below. Cool broth rapidly, stirring frequently to hasten cooling, by placing container in cold running water or ice water. When broth is completely cooled, cover container and refrigerate. Cooked poultry should be used no later than the second day after it is cooked.

368 POULTRY

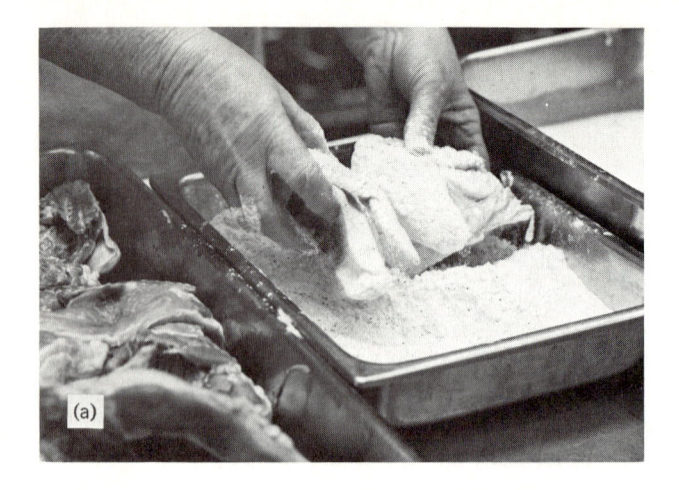

(a)

(b)

(c)

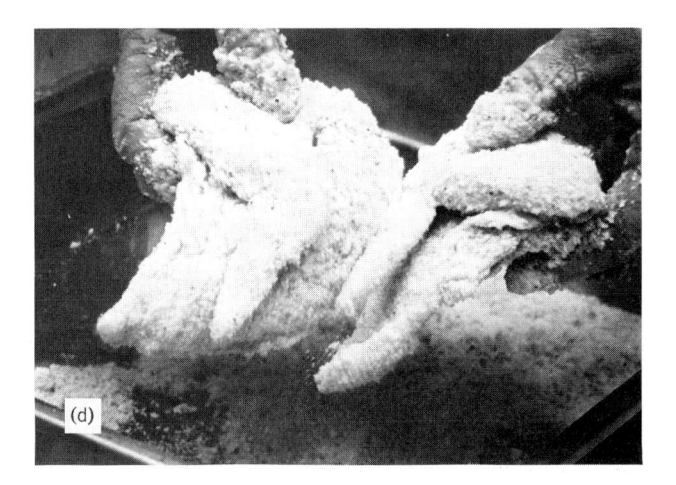

Figure 2.20 Breading chicken. Other foods may be breaded using this technique. Line up in a row the food to be breaded, flour, egg-milk mixture, pan for draining, bread crumbs, and baking sheet on which to place breaded product. See Table 1.13 for amounts of breading ingredients. (a) Dredge chicken in seasoned flour. (b) Dip in egg-milk mixture. (c) Drain. Picture shows how using a perforated pan set inside a solid counter pan. (d) Roll in bread crumbs. Place on baking sheet. If chicken is to be baked, line pan with parchment paper.

ROASTING

For large-quantity cookery, it usually is recommended that poultry be roasted unstuffed and that dressing be baked separately. If turkey is to be stuffed, *mix the stuffing just before it is needed.* Do not prepare dressing or stuff the bird in advance. Follow this order of procedure in preparing a roaster.

1. Prepare bird. Remove pin feathers if necessary. Wash well inside and out.
2. Salt inside and outside of bird.
3. Brush with soft fat or oil.
4. Place bird on a rack in a shallow baking pan, breast up. If not for show, bake breast down.
5. Baste with fat and hot water (4 oz/114 g fat to 1 qt/0.95 L hot water) if desired. Drippings also may be used for basting.
6. Roast at 325°F (165°C) to an internal temperature of 180°F (82°C). Insert meat thermometer in center of inside thigh muscle. Allow approximately 15–18 minutes per lb (454 g) for a 20-lb (9.08-kg) unstuffed turkey. Allow approximately 30 minutes per lb (454 g) for a 5-lb (2.27-kg) chicken. (See Table 2.15 for roasting guide.) If thermometer is not available, test doneness by moving drumstick. It moves easily at the thigh joint when done.
7. To roast turkey halves or quarters, place skin-side up in an open pan. Roast at 325°F (165°C) for 2–3 hours.

8. To roast a boneless turkey roast or roll, place on rack in an open pan. Roast at 325°F (165°C) until a meat thermometer inserted in the center registers 170–175°F (78–80°C), or follow cooking directions on package.

The yield of cooked meat from poultry is influenced by the size of the bird, the amount of bone, the method of preparation and service, and the size portions desired. Whole ready-to-cook turkey will yield approximately 42% edible cooked meat without skin, neck meat, or giblets; turkey roast or roll will yield about 66%. Ready-to-cook chickens (large fryers) will yield approximately 30–35% usable cooked meat for combination dishes.

TABLE 2.15   ROASTING GUIDE FOR POULTRY (DEFROSTED)

Kind	Ready-to-cook Weight lb	Ready-to-cook Weight kg	Approximate Total Roasting Time at 325°F (165°C) (hr)	Internal Temperature of Poultry When Done[a] °F	Internal Temperature of Poultry When Done[a] °C
Chicken, whole					
Roasters	2½–4½	1.1–2.0	2–3½		
Ducks	4–6	1.8–2.7	2–3		
Geese	6–8	2.7–3.6	3–3½		
	8–12	3.6–5.4	3½–4½		
Turkeys					
whole	6–8	2.7–3.6	3–3½	180–185	82–85
	8–12	3.6–5.4	3½–4½	180–185	82–85
	12–16	5.4–7.3	4½–5½	180–185	82–85
	16–20	7.3–9.1	5½–6½	180–185	82–85
	20–24	9.1–10.9	6½–7	180–185	82–85
Halves, quarters, and pieces	3–8	1.4–3.6	2–3		
	8–12	3.6–5.4	3–4		
Boneless turkey roasts	3–10	1.4–4.5	3–4	170–175	75–80

[a] Thermometer inserted in thigh of whole turkeys, in center of turkey roasts.

POULTRY RECIPES

PAN-FRIED CHICKEN

Yield: 50 portions
Portion: 8–12 oz (227–340 g) AP

Amount Metric	U.S.	Ingredient	Procedure
13	13	Fryers, 2–3 lb (0.9–1.4 kg)	Cut chickens into pieces of desired serving size.
454 g	1 lb	Flour, all purpose	Roll chicken pieces in seasoned flour.
38 g	2 T	Salt	
7 g	1 T	Paprika or poultry seasoning	
2 g	1 t	Pepper, black	
454 g	1 lb	Shortening	Brown chicken in hot shortening, ½ in. deep in pan. Reduce heat and cook slowly until tender, 45–60 minutes. Turn for even browning

Notes:
1. Chicken portions (quarters, thighs, or breasts) may be used.
2. Chicken may be browned in a skillet, then placed in counter pans or baking pans, skin-side up, and finished in the oven at 325°F (165°C) for 20–30 minutes.

Variations:
1. **Chicken Cantonese.** Flour chicken and brown as above. Place in 12 × 20 × 2-in. counter pans. Cover with aluminum foil. Bake at 350°F (175°C) for approximately 1 hour. Before serving, cover with sauce made of 3 qt (2.84 L) pineapple juice, 3 qt (2.84 L) orange juice, 12 oz (340 g) flour, 3 lb (1.36 kg) pineapple cubes, 12 oranges peeled and diced, 1¼ lb (567 g) almonds slivered and browned, 2 t (5 g) nutmeg, and 2 t (12 g) salt. Combine juice and flour; cook until thickened. Add seasonings, fruit, and almonds. Pour over chicken. Bake uncovered about 10 minutes. Serve with cooked rice (p. 358).
2. **Chicken Cacciatore.** Brown chicken as above. Arrange in 2 12 × 20 × 4-in. counter pans. Sauté 1 lb 8 oz (680 g) coarsely diced onions and 2 cloves garlic, minced, in 5 oz (142 g) margarine. Add 1 lb 8 oz (680 g) green peppers cut into strips, 2 lb (908 g) sliced mushrooms, 1 No. 10 can diced tomatoes with juice, ½ t oregano, ½ t thyme, and 1 qt (0.95 L) chicken stock. Thicken with 4 oz (114 g) flour mixed with 2 c (480 mL) cold water. Pour over chicken, 3½ qt (3.31 L) per pan. Cover with aluminum foil. Bake at 325°F (165°C) for 1 hour.
3. **Deep-Fat Fried Chicken.** Use 1¾- to 2-lb (794- to 908-g) broiler-fryers, cut in serving pieces, or chicken quarters. Dredge in seasoned flour as above; or dredge in flour, dip in egg and milk mixture (3 eggs to 1 c/240 mL milk), and roll in crumbs (12 oz/340 g); or dip in batter (p. 37). Fry in deep fat at 325°F (165°C) for 12–15 minutes or until golden brown and cooked through. For larger fryers, brown in deep fat, drain, then place in baking pans and finish in the oven at 325°F (165°C) for 20–30 minutes.

OVEN-FRIED CHICKEN

Oven: 350°F (175°C)
Bake: 1 hour

Yield: 50 portions
Portion: 1 chicken quarter, or 2 pieces

Amount Metric	U.S.	Ingredient	Procedure
50 or 100	50 or 100	Chicken quarters or Chicken breasts and thighs	Dredge chicken with seasoned flour.
454 g	1 lb	Flour, all-purpose	
227 g	8 oz	Nonfat dry milk	
38 g	2 T	Salt	
7 g	1 T	Paprika	
2 g	1 t	Pepper, white	
454 g	1 lb	Margarine or butter, melted	Place chicken pieces in single layer on greased or silicone paper-lined baking sheets. Brush each piece with melted margarine. Bake at 350°F (175°C) for 1 hour or until chicken is browned and tender.

Note: Chicken may be breaded. See Table 1.13 for coating and Fig. 2.20 for procedures.

Variations:
1. **Barbecued Chicken.** Brown chicken at 425°F (220°C) for 20–25 minutes. Reduce heat to 325°F (165°C). Pour 1½ gal (5.68 L) Cooked Barbecue Sauce (p. 477) over chicken. Bake 40–45 minutes.
2. **Chicken Parmesan.** Combine 1 lb (454 g) flour, 1 oz (28 g) salt, ½ t (1 g) pepper, and ¾ c (57 g) Parmesan cheese. Dredge chicken pieces in flour mixture, then dip in mixture of 12 (1 lb 5 oz/585 g) eggs and 1 qt (0.95 L) milk, then back into flour mixture. Arrange chicken on greased or silicone paper-lined baking sheets. Dribble lemon butter (8 oz/227 g melted margarine or butter and ¼ c/60 mL lemon or lime juice) over chicken. Bake at 325°F (165°C) for 1 hour. Use drippings from baking sheets for gravy.
3. **Chicken Teriyaki.** Marinate chicken overnight in a mixture of 3 c (720 mL) soy sauce, 10 oz (284 g) brown sugar, 1½ T (10 g) garlic powder, and 1½ T (10 g) ground ginger. Arrange chicken pieces in single layer on greased or silicone paper-lined baking sheets. Bake at 350°F (175°C) for 30 minutes. Remove from oven. Brush chicken with remaining marinade and bake until tender, about 30 minutes. 1 c (240 mL) orange juice or pineapple juice may be added to the marinade.

FRICASSEE OF CHICKEN

Oven: 325°F (165°C)
Bake: 1½–2 hours
Yield: 50 portions
Portion: 3 oz (85 g) cooked meat

Amount		Ingredient	Procedure
Metric	U.S.		
15.88 kg	35 lb AP	Chicken[a]	Cut chicken into desired pieces.
340 g	12 oz	Flour, all-purpose	Dip chicken in seasoned flour.
38 g	2 T	Salt	
2 g	1 t	Pepper, white	Brown in hot shortening.
454 g	1 lb	Shortening	Remove to roasting pan (or steam-jacketed kettle) and cover with boiling water. Cook slowly, adding more water if necessary, until tender, 1½ – 2 hours.
284 g	10 oz	Margarine	When tender, remove chicken from stock.
170 g	6 oz	Flour, all-purpose	Make gravy, using liquid in which chicken was cooked.
3.31 L	3½ qt	Chicken broth	Serve over chicken.

[a] 13 2½- to 3-lb (1.14- to 1.36-kg) fryers.

Variations:

1. **White Fricassee of Chicken.** Do not brown chicken. Simmer until tender. Remove from liquid. Boil liquid until concentrated. Add milk or cream to make 1½ gal (5.68 L), thicken to make a Medium White Sauce (p. 470). Beat constantly while pouring sauce gradually over 10 beaten egg yolks. Season to taste. Add chicken.

2. **Chicken with Black Olives.** Brown floured chicken. Place in baking pans. Cover with chicken gravy. Bake 1–1½ hours. Prior to serving, sprinkle with sliced ripe olives and sautéed fresh mushrooms.

CHICKEN TAHITIAN

Oven: 425°F (220°C); 325°F (165°C)
Bake: 65–70 minutes
Yield: 52 portions
Portion: 3 oz (85 g) cooked meat

Amount Metric	U.S.	Ingredient	Procedure
15.88 kg	35 lb AP	Chicken, cut into quarters[a]	Melt shortening in baking pans. Arrange chicken in pans in single layer. Brown in 425°F (220°C) oven for 30 minutes.
340 g	12 oz	Shortening	
2 355-mL cans	2 12-oz cans	Frozen orange juice, undiluted	Combine juice, margarine, ginger, and soy sauce.
454 g	1 lb	Margarine or butter, melted	Brush chicken with mixture.
14 g	2 T	Ginger	Bake at 325°F (165°C) for 30–40 minutes. Baste with orange mixture until chicken is glazed.
30 mL	2 T	Soy Sauce	Serve with Steamed Rice (p. 358) and garnish with slivered almonds and avocado wedges.

[a] 13 2½- to 3-lb (1.14- to 1.36-kg) fryers.

CHICKEN TURNOVERS

Oven: 400°F (205°C)
Bake: 25–30 minutes
Yield: 50 portions
Portion: 4 oz (114 g)

Metric	U.S.	Ingredient	Procedure
2.72 kg	6 lb	Cooked chicken	Dice or coarsely chop chicken.
170 g 114 g 28 g	6 oz 4 oz 1 oz (1½ T)	Margarine or butter Flour, all-purpose Salt	Melt margarine. Stir in flour and salt. Cook 3 minutes.
0.95 L	1 qt	Chicken Stock (p. 495)	Add chicken stock, stirring constantly. Cook until thickened. When thick, fold in chicken.
2.27 kg	5 lb	Pastry (p. 199)	Roll out pastry. Cut into 50 rounds with 6-in cutter. Place No. 20 dipper chicken mixture on each pastry round just below center. Fold rounds over and seal by pressing edges together with a fork. Bake at 400°F (205°C) for 25–30 minutes. Serve with chicken gravy or mushroom sauce (1 gal/3.79 L).

Note: 18-20 lb (8.16-9.08 kg) chickens AP will yield approximately 6 lb (2.72 kg) cooked meat.

Variations:
1. **Beef Turnovers.** Substitute coarsely chopped cooked beef for chicken and beef stock for chicken stock. Serve with beef gravy.
2. **Ham Turnovers.** Substitute ground ham for chicken. Delete salt. Serve with Mushroom Sauce (p. 474).

CREAMED CHICKEN

Yield: 50 portions
Portion: ¾ c (6 oz/170 g)

Amount		Ingredient	Procedure
Metric	U.S.		
2.72 kg	6 lb	Cooked chicken	Dice chicken.
794 g	1 lb 12 oz	Margarine or butter	Melt margarine. Add onions and sauté until tender.
114 g	4 oz	Onions, minced.	
567 g	1 lb 4 oz	Flour, all-purpose	Stir in flour and seasonings. Cook 3 minutes.
28 g	1 oz (1½ T)	Salt	
2 g	1 t	Pepper, white	
2.84 L	3 qt	Chicken Stock (p. 495)	Add stock and milk, stirring constantly. Cook until thickened. Carefully fold in chicken. Check for seasonings. Heat to serving temperature. Serve over biscuits, toast, or rice.
2.13 L	2¼ qt	Milk	

Note: 18-20 lb (8.16-9.08 kg) chickens AP will yield approximately 6 lb (2.72 kg) cooked meat.

Variations:

1. **Chicken à la King.** Add 4 oz (114 g) chopped green pepper, 4 oz (114 g) shredded pimiento, and 1 lb (454 g) sautéed sliced mushrooms.

2. **Tuna à la King.** Substitute tuna for chicken. Stir carefully to avoid breaking up tuna pieces.

3. **Turkey à la King.** Substitute turkey for chicken.

SCALLOPED CHICKEN

Oven: 350°F (175°C)
Bake: 30–40 minutes

Yield: 48 portions
2 pans 12 × 20 × 2 in.
Portion: 8 oz (227 g)

Amount Metric	U.S.	Ingredient	Procedure
2.72 kg	6 lb	Cooked chicken	Dice chicken.
454 g	1 lb	Margarine or butter	Melt margarine. Stir in flour.
227 g	8 oz	Flour, all-purpose	
3.79 L	1 gal	Chicken Stock (p. 495)	Add stock, while stirring. Cook until thickened.
28 g	1 oz (1½ t)	Salt (optional)	
12 (595 g)	12 (1 lb 5 oz)	Eggs, beaten	When sauce is thick add small amount of hot mixture to eggs, then stir into remainder of sauce.
1.81 kg	4 lb	Dry bread, cubed	Add seasonings to bread. Mix to distribute seasonings.
12 g	2 t	Salt	
1 g	½ t	Pepper, black	
20 g	⅓ c	Sage, ground, or poultry seasoning	
284 g	10 oz	Margarine or butter	Sauté celery and onion in melted margarine. Add to bread.
142 g	5 oz	Celery, chopped	
85 g	3 oz	Onion, chopped	
4 (198 g)	4 (7 oz)	Eggs, beaten	Add eggs and chicken stock to bread. Toss lightly. Do not overmix. Place dressing, sauce and chicken in 2 greased 12 × 20 × 2-in. counter pans, layered in each pan as follows: 4 lb 8 oz (2.04 kg) dressing 1¼ qt (1.18 L) sauce 3 lb (1.36 kg) chicken 1¼ qt (1.18 L) sauce
1.66 L	1¾ qt	Chicken Stock (p. 495)	
170 g	6 oz	Cracker crumbs, coarse	Mix and sprinkle on pans, 4 oz (114 g) each. Bake at 350°F (175°C) for 30–40 minutes. Cut 4 × 6.
85 g	3 oz	Margarine or butter, melted	

CHICKEN CRÊPES

Oven: 325°F (165°C)
Heat: 10 minutes

Yield: 50 portions
Portion: 2 crêpes

Amount Metric	U.S.	Ingredient	Procedure
680 g	1 lb 8 oz	Margarine or butter	Melt margarine. Add flour and salt. Blend.
340 g	12 oz	Flour, all-purpose	
38 g	2 T	Salt	
5.68 L	1½ gal	Chicken Stock (p. 495) or milk	Gradually add chicken stock, stirring constantly.
4.54 kg	10 lb	Cooked chicken, diced	Combine chicken, mushrooms, and seasonings. Add enough sauce to hold chicken together (approximately 2 qt/1.89 L). Reserve remaining sauce to pour over crepes.
2 227-g cans	2 8-oz cans	Mushrooms, chopped	
30 mL	2 T	Worcestershire sauce	
14 g	2 T	Curry powder	
		Salt to taste	
1 recipe	1 recipe	Crêpes (p. 106)	Make batter. Fry on lightly greased griddle, using 1 No. 30 dipper (1½ oz/43 g) batter. Brown lightly on one side. Turn and cook to set batter. Portion No. 20 dipper of chicken mixture onto each crepe; roll and place on baking sheets. Heat in 325°F (165°C) oven for 10 minutes. Serve with remaining sauce, with 2-oz ladle.

Variations:

1. **Fruit-Cheese Crêpes.** Fill crêpes (recipe, p. 106) with 1½ T (23 mL) of the following mixture: 2 lb (908 g) cream cheese, whipped and combined with 2 c (480 mL) cultured sour cream. Serve with frozen strawberries or raspberries, thickened slightly, or with prepared fruit pie filling, heated.

2. **Spinach Crêpes.** Omit chicken and sauce. Fill crêpes with cooked Spinach Soufflé (p. 558). Serve with Cheese Sauce (p. 471).

HOT CHICKEN SALAD

Oven: 350°F (175°C)
Bake: 25–30 minutes

Yield: 56 portions
2 pans 12 × 20 × 2 in.
or 50 individual casseroles
Portion: 5 oz (142 g)

Amount		Ingredient	Procedure
Metric	U.S.		
2.72 kg	6 lb	Cooked chicken	Dice chicken.
1.81 kg	4 lb	Celery, diced	Combine with chicken.
85 g	3 oz	Onion, chopped	Mix lightly.
454 g	1 lb	Almonds, browned and chopped coarsely	Place in 2 12 × 20 × 2-in. counter pans (or in individual casseroles, using No. 8 dipper).
180 mL	¾ c	Lemon juice	
18 g	3 T	Lemon rind, grated	
2 g	1 t	Pepper, white	
19 g	1 T	Salt	
1.42 L	1½ qt	Mayonnaise	
1.36 kg·	3 lb	Cheddar cheese, shredded	Sprinkle cheese over top of salad mixture.
340 g	12 oz	Potato chips, crushed	Distribute potato chips uniformly over cheese. Bake at 350°F (175°C) for 25–30 minutes, or until cheese is bubbly. Cut 4 × 7.

Note: 18-20 lb (8.16-9.08 kg) chickens AP will yield approximately 6 lb (2.72 kg) cooked meat.

Variation: **Hot Turkey Salad.** Substitute cooked turkey for chicken. A 16- to 18-lb (7.26- to 8.16-kg) turkey AP will yield approximately 6 lb (2.72 kg) cooked meat.

CHICKEN LOAF

Oven: 325°F (165°C)
Bake: 1½ hours

Yield: 50 portions
5 loaves 5 × 9 in.
Portion: 5 oz (142 g)

Amount Metric	U.S.	Ingredient	Procedure
340 g	12 oz	Rice, long-grain	Cook rice according to directions on p. 358.
0.95 L	1 qt	Water, boiling	
9 g	1½ t	Salt	
8 mL	1½ t	Cooking oil (optional)	
2.72 kg	6 lb	Cooked chicken	Dice chicken.
114 g	4 oz	Pimiento, chopped	Combine chicken, cooked rice, pimiento, and onion. Mix lightly.
57 g	2 oz	Onion, grated	
12 (595 g)	12 (1 lb 5 oz)	Eggs, beaten	Add remaining ingredients. Mix only until blended. Divide into 5 greased loaf pans, 3 lb 2 oz (1.42 kg) per pan. Bake at 325°F (165°C) for 1½ hours. Cut each pan in 10 slices. Serve with Chicken Gravy (p. 476) or Mushroom Sauce (p. 474).
19 g	1 T	Salt	
2 g	¾ t	Pepper, white	
1.42	1½ qt	Chicken Stock (p. 495)	
720 mL	3 c	Milk	
340 g	12 oz	Bread crumbs, soft	

Notes:
1. 18-20 lb (8.16-9.08 kg) chickens AP will yield approximately 6 lb (2.72 kg) cooked meat.
2. May be baked in 12 × 20 × 4-in. counter pan.
3. Turkey or tuna may be used in place of chicken.

BRUNSWICK STEW

Yield: 50 portions
3 gal (11.36 L)
Portion: 1 c (8 oz/227 g)

Amount			
Metric	U.S.	Ingredient	Procedure
908 g	2 lb	Pork AP, diced	Brown pork. Drain off excess fat.
3.4 kg	7 lb 8 oz	Cooked chicken	Cube chicken.
680 g 1.02 kg 908 g 284 g	1 lb 8 oz 2 lb 4 oz 2 lb 10 oz	Celery, diced Carrots, diced Potatoes, diced Onions, finely chopped	Cook vegetables until partially done.
227 g 227 g 3.79 L 19 g 3 g	8 oz 8 oz 1 gal 1 T 1½ t	Margarine or butter Flour, all-purpose Chicken Stock (p. 495) Salt Pepper, white	Melt margarine. Add flour and stir until smooth. Add chicken stock gradually, stirring constantly. Add salt and pepper. Add chicken, pork and vegetables. Simmer until vegetables are done. Do not overcook at this point.
454 g	1 lb	Frozen peas	Add peas. Cook an additional 5 minutes. Stew should be fairly thick. Serve in soup bowls or deep plates.

Note: If large fryers are used, cook 15 lb (6.8 kg) AP. Remove meat from bones and dice. Save broth for sauce.

BATTER CRUST FOR CHICKEN OR MEAT POT PIES

Oven: 400°F (205°C)   Yield: 6 qt (5.68 L)
Bake: 20–25 minutes   Portion: ½ c (120 mL) per individual pie

Amount		Ingredient	Procedure
Metric	U.S.		
1.02 kg	2 lb 4 oz	Flour, all-purpose	Combine dry ingredients.
49 g	1½ oz	Baking powder	
19 g	1 T	Salt	
57 g	2 oz	Sugar, granulated	
1.89 L	2 qt	Milk	Combine milk, egg yolks, and margarine.
18	18	Egg yolks, beaten	
(312 g)	(11 oz)		Add to dry ingredients.
114 g	4 oz	Margarine or butter, melted	Stir only enough to mix.
18	18	Egg whites	Beat egg whites until stiff.
(595 g)	(1 lb 5 oz)		Fold into batter.
			Pour ½ c (120 mL) batter over contents of each individual casserole. Pour around edges and then in center to form a thin covering over meat or chicken mixture.
			If using for 12 × 20 × 2-in. pans, pour 2 lb 3 oz/992 g (3 qt) batter over hot chicken mixture in each pan.

Note: Batter may be refrigerated until needed. Thin mixture with cold milk if too thick.

CHICKEN PIE WITH BATTER CRUST

Oven: 400°F (205°C)
Bake: 20–25 minutes

Yield: 50 portions
2 pans 12 × 20 × 2 in.
Portion: 8 oz (227 g)

Amount Metric	U.S.	Ingredient	Procedure
340 g	12 oz	Margarine or butter	Sauté onions in margarine.
397 g	14 oz	Onions, chopped	
624 g	1 lb 6 oz	Flour, all-purpose	Add flour and pepper. Stir until blended. Cook 30 minutes.
1 g	½ t	Pepper, black	
4.73 L	1¼ gal	Chicken Stock (p. 495)	Add chicken stock, stirring constantly. Cook until thickened, stirring often. Check for seasoning. Add salt if necessary.
2.72 kg	6 lb	Chicken, cooked	Cut chicken into ½–¾-in. pieces. Add to sauce.
680 g	1 lb 8 oz	Celery, sliced	Cook celery and carrots until partially done. Drain. Fold into sauce.
908 g	2 lb	Carrots, sliced	
908 g	2 lb	Peas, frozen	Add peas uncooked to chicken mixture. Mix carefully. Scale into 2 12 × 20 × 2-in. counter pans, 12 lb (5.44 kg) per pan.
5.68 L	6 qt	Batter Crust (p. 382)	Make 1 recipe Batter Crust. Pour 3 qt (2 lb 3 oz/992 g) batter over each pan. Bake at 400°F (205°C) for 20–25 minutes, or until batter crust is done.

Notes:
1. 18-20 lb (8-9 kg) chickens AP will yield approximately 6 lb (2.72 kg) cooked meat.
2. Pastry (p. 199) may be substituted for Batter Crust. Roll out 1 lb 8 oz (680 g) for each pan.
3. Chicken mixture may be topped with Baking Powder Biscuits (p. 84).
4. For individual pot pies, scale 8 oz (227 g) hot chicken pie mixture into each of 50 casseroles. Pour ½ c (4 oz/114 g) batter crust over each. Bake as above.

Variation: **Turkey Pie.** Substitute turkey for chicken.

CHICKEN SOUFFLÉ

Oven: 325°F (165°C)
Bake: 1 hour

Yield: 48 portions
2 pans 12 × 20 × 2 in.
Portion: 6 oz (170 g)

Amount		Ingredient	Procedure
Metric	U.S.		
2.72 kg	6 lb	Cooked chicken	Dice chicken.
454 g	1 lb	Margarine or butter	Melt margarine. Add flour and stir until smooth. Add chicken stock and milk gradually, stirring constantly. Cook until thickened.
114 g	4 oz	Flour, all-purpose	
28 g	1 oz (1½ T)	Salt	
2 g	1 t	Pepper, white	
600 mL	2½ c	Chicken Stock (p. 495)	
3.55 L	3¾ qt	Milk	
24 (425 g)	24 (15 oz)	Egg yolks, beaten	Add egg yolks and crumbs. Mix well.
454 g	1 lb	Bread crumbs	Add chicken. Mix lightly.
24 (794 g)	24 (1 lb 12 oz)	Egg whites	Beat egg whites until they form a rounded peak. Fold into chicken mixture. Scale into 2 greased 12 × 20 × 2-in. baking pans, 9 lb 12 oz (4.41 kg) per pan. Bake at 325°F (165°C) for 1 hour or until soufflé is set. Cut 4 × 6. Serve immediately. Serve with Bechamel Sauce (p. 473) or Mushroom Sauce (p. 474).

Note: 18-20 lb (8-9 kg) chickens AP will yield approximately 6 lb (2.72 kg) cooked meat.

Variations:
1. **Ham Soufflé.** Substitute coarsely ground cooked ham for chicken. Delete salt.
2. **Tuna Soufflé.** Substitute tuna for chicken.
3. **Turkey Soufflé.** Substitute turkey for chicken.

CHICKEN CROQUETTES

Deep-fat fryer: 375°F (190°C)   Yield: 50 portions
Fry: 3–4 minutes   Portion: 2 2½-oz (70-g) croquettes

____Amount____			
Metric	U.S.	Ingredient	Procedure
2.72 kg	6 lb	Cooked chicken	Chop chicken finely.
680 g	1 lb 8 oz	Rice	Cook rice in chicken stock,
2.84 L	3 qt	Chicken Stock (p. 495)	according to directions on p. 358.
57 g	2 oz	Salt	Add seasonings to rice and
6 g	1 t	Celery salt	mix lightly.
15 mL	1 T	Lemon juice	
30 mL	2 T	Onion juice	
170 g	6 oz	Flour, all-purpose	Make a smooth paste of
480 mL	2 c	Chicken Stock (p. 495), cold	flour and cold chicken stock.
480 mL	2 c	Chicken Stock (p. 495)	Bring stock to boiling point. Add flour paste. Stir and cook until thick. Combine sauce, chicken, and rice. Mix well. Measure with No. 16 dipper onto greased baking sheets. Chill.
6 (312 g)	6 (11 oz)	Eggs, beaten	Shape chicken mixture into croquettes.
480 mL	2 c	Milk or water	Mix eggs and milk. Dip
680 g	1 lb 8 oz	Bread crumbs	croquettes into egg–milk mixture, then roll in crumbs. Chill 2 hours. Fry in deep fat for 3–4 minutes.

Notes:
1. 18-20 lb (8.16-9.08 kg) chickens AP will yield approximately 6 lb (2.72 kg) cooked meat.
2. Croquettes may be baked at 350°F (175°C) for about 30 minutes.

Variations:
1. **Ham Croquettes.** Substitute ground cooked ham for chicken. Delete salt.
2. **Meat Croquettes.** Substitute cooked chopped meat for chicken and beef stock for chicken stock. Add 2 oz (57 g) finely chopped onion.

CHICKEN AND NOODLES

Oven: 350°F (175°C)
Bake: 30 minutes

Yield: 50 portions
2 pans 12 × 20 × 2 in.
Portion: 8 oz (227 g)

Amount Metric	U.S.	Ingredient	Procedure
3.4 kg	7 lb 8 oz	Cooked chicken	Dice chicken.
1.36 kg	3 lb	Noodles	Cook noodles according to directions on p. 348. Drain.
11.36 L	3 gal	Water, boiling	
114 g	4 oz	Salt	
15 mL	1 T	Cooking oil	
340 g	12 oz	Margarine or butter	Melt margarine. Add onions and sauté until tender.
57 g	2 oz	Onions, chopped	
198 g	7 oz	Flour, all-purpose	Add flour and salt. Stir until blended.
19 g	1 T	Salt	
3.31 L	3½ qt	Chicken Stock (p. 495) or milk	Add chicken stock or milk slowly, stirring constantly. Cook until thickened.
			Combine chicken, cooked noodles, and sauce. Scale into 2 12 × 20 × 2-in. counter pans, 11 lb 12 oz (5.33 kg) per pan. Bake at 350°F (175°C) for 30 minutes.

Note: 20-22 lb (9-10 kg) chickens AP will yield approximately 7 lb 8 oz (3.4 kg) cooked meat.

Variations:

1. **Chicken and Noodles with Mushrooms.** Add 2 lb (908 g) sliced mushrooms, sautéed with the onions.
2. **Pork and Noodle Casserole.** Substitute 10 lb (4.54 kg) pork, diced and cooked, for chicken.
3. **Turkey and Noodle Casserole.** Substitute cooked turkey for chicken (cook 18 to 20-lb/8 to 9-kg turkey).

CHICKEN TETRAZZINI

Oven: 350°F (175°C)
Bake: 35–40 minutes

Yield: 50 portions
2 pans 12 × 20 × 2 in.
Portion: 8 oz (227 g)

Amount Metric	U.S.	Ingredient	Procedure
2.72 kg	6 lb	Cooked chicken	Dice chicken. Add pimiento and parsley.
170 g	6 oz	Pimiento, chopped	
7 g	2 T	Parsley, chopped	
1.14 kg	2 lb 8 oz	Spaghetti	Cook spaghetti according to directions on p. 348. Drain.
9.46 L	2½ gal	Water, boiling	
28 g	1 oz (1½ T)	Salt	
30 mL	2 T	Cooking oil (optional)	
340 g	12 oz	Margarine or butter	Sauté onions and mushrooms in margarine.
227 g	8 oz	Onion, finely chopped	
680 g	1 lb 8 oz	Mushrooms, sliced	
170 g	6 oz	Flour, all-purpose	Blend flour and seasonings into sautéed vegetables.
28 g	1 oz (1½ T)	Salt	
2 g	1 t	Pepper, white	
1.89 L	2 qt	Milk	Add milk and chicken stock, stirring constantly. Cook until thickened.
0.95 L	1 qt	Chicken stock (p. 495)	
454 g	1 lb	Cheddar cheese, shredded	Combine cooked spaghetti, chicken, and sauce. Scale into 2 greased 12 × 20 × 2-in. baking pans, 12 lb (5.44 kg) per pan. Sprinkle 8 oz (227 g) cheese over top of each pan. Bake at 350°F (175°C) for 35–40 minutes or until heated through and cheese is bubbly.

Note: 18-20 lb (8.16-9.08 kg) chickens AP will yield approximately 6 lb (2.72 kg) cooked meat.

Variations:
1. **Tuna Tetrazzini.** Substitute tuna for chicken.
2. **Turkey Tetrazzini.** Substitute turkey for chicken.

CHICKEN AND RICE CASSEROLE

Oven: 350°F (175°C)
Bake: 1 hour

Yield: 50 portions
2 pans 12 × 20 × 2 in.
Portion: 8 oz (227 g)

Amount Metric	U.S.	Ingredient	Procedure
2.72 kg	6 lb	Cooked chicken	Dice chicken.
1.14 g	2 lb 8 oz	Rice	Cook rice according to directions on p. 358.
1.89 L	2 qt	Water, boiling	
38 g	2 T	Salt	
170 g	6 oz	Margarine or butter, melted	Sauté onions, celery, and mushrooms in margarine.
85 g	3 oz	Onion, chopped	
227 g	8 oz	Celery, chopped	
454 g	1 lb	Mushrooms, sliced	
227 g	8 oz	Flour, all-purpose	Add flour and stir to blend.
1.42 L	1½ qt	Milk	Add milk and chicken stock, stirring constantly. Cook until thickened. Check for seasonings. Add salt if needed.
1.89 L	2 qt	Chicken Stock (p. 495)	
170 g	6 oz	Almonds, slivered	Add almonds, pimiento, and chicken. Combine carefully. Scale into 2 lightly greased 12 × 20 × 2-in. baking pans, 10 lb 8 oz (4.76 kg) per pan.
85 g	3 oz	Pimiento, chopped	
255 g	9 oz	Bread crumbs	Combine bread crumbs, margarine, and shredded cheese. Sprinkle over mixture in pans, 9 oz (255 g) per pan. Bake at 350°F (175°C) for 1 hour or until heated through.
85 g	3 oz	Margarine or butter, melted	
170 g	6 oz	Cheddar cheese, shredded	

Notes:
1. 18-20 lb (8-9 kg) chickens AP will yield approximately 6 lb (2.72 kg) cooked meat.
2. Sliced water chestnuts may be substituted for almonds.
3. Chopped parsley may be sprinkled over the baked product just before serving.

TURKEY CASSEROLE

Oven: 350°F (175°C)
Bake: 25–30 minutes

Yield: 50 portions
2 pans 12 × 20 × 2 in.
Portion: 8 oz (227 g)

Amount Metric	U.S.	Ingredient	Procedure
2.72 kg	6 lb	Cooked turkey	Dice turkey.
454 g	1 lb	Margarine or butter	Melt margarine. Add onion and celery. Sauté for 3 minutes.
170 g	6 oz	Onion, chopped	
908 g	2 lb	Celery, chopped	
680 g	1 lb 8 oz	Flour, all-purpose	Add flour and stir until blended.
2.84 L	3 qt	Chicken Stock (p. 495)	Add chicken stock, stirring constantly. Cook until thickened.
2 1.42 kg cans	2 50-oz cans	Cream of mushroom soup	Add soup and blend.
908 g	2 lb	Almonds or cashews, toasted	Combine turkey, sauce, and nuts. Scale into 2 lightly greased 12 × 20 × 2-in. baking pans, 12 lb 8 oz (5.67 kg) per pan, or into individual casseroles, 8 oz (227 g) each. Bake at 350°F (175°C) for 25–30 minutes.
1 No. 10 can	1 No. 10 can	Mandarin oranges	To serve, garnish with mandarin oranges.

Note: A 16- to 18-lb (7- to 8-kg) turkey will yield approximately 6 lb (2.72 kg) cooked meat.

Variation: **Chicken Casserole.** Combine 6 lb (2.72 kg) cooked chicken, 1 lb (454 g) chopped onions, and 1 lb 4 oz (567 g) chopped celery sautéed in 8 oz (227 g) margarine or butter, and 12 oz (340 g) shredded Cheddar cheese. Place layers of chicken mixture, 3 qt (2.84 L) buttered bread cubes, and 1 gal (3.79 L) chicken gravy or cream of chicken soup (2 50-oz cans) thinned slightly with chicken broth. Bake at 300°F (150°C) for 1–1½ hours.

TURKEY DIVAN

Oven: 350°F (175°C)
Bake: 15 minutes

Yield: 50 portions
Portion: 3 oz (85 g) broccoli
2 oz (57 g) turkey

Amount Metric	U.S.	Ingredient	Procedure
4.54 kg	10 lb EP	Broccoli spears, fresh or frozen	Cook broccoli according to directions on p. 533. Arrange in 3-oz (85-g) portions in 2 12 × 20 × 2-in. counter pans.
227 g	8 oz	Margarine or butter	Melt margarine and pour over broccoli.
28 g 1 g 255 g	1 oz (1½ T) ½ t 9 oz	Salt Pepper, black Parmesan cheese, grated	Sprinkle broccoli with salt, pepper, and cheese.
3.18 kg	7 lb	Cooked turkey roll or breast	Slice turkey in 2-oz (57 g) portions. Arrange turkey slices over broccoli. Serving will be easier if edges of turkey slices are tucked under the broccoli portions.
340 g 170 g 28 g	12 oz 6 oz 1 oz (1½ T)	Margarine or butter Flour, all-purpose Salt	Melt margarine. Add flour and salt. Cook until blended.
2.84 L	3 qt	Milk	Add milk, stirring constantly. Cook until thickened.
240 mL	1 c	Egg yolks, slightly beaten	Add egg yolks. Stir until blended. Pour sauce over turkey and broccoli. Bake at 350°F (175°C) for 15 minutes or until bubbly and golden brown.

Note: Turkey or chicken stock may be substituted for part of milk in sauce; salt may then need to be reduced.

SINGAPORE CURRY

Yield: 50 portions
Portion: 8 oz (227 g) curry
6 oz (170 g) rice

Amount		Ingredient	Procedure
Metric	U.S.		
6.8 kg	15 lb	Cooked chicken	Dice chicken.
454 g	1 lb	Margarine or butter	Melt margarine. Add flour and stir until smooth.
567 g	1 lb 4 oz	Flour, all-purpose	
4.73 L	5 qt	Chicken stock	Add chicken stock, stirring. constantly. Cook until thickened.
to taste		Salt	
to taste		Pepper, white	
57 g	2 oz	Curry powder	Add salt and pepper. Stir in curry powder. Add chicken and stir gently. Taste and add more seasonings, as the chicken takes up the curry flavor. It should be quite yellow and have a distinct curry flavor.
2.27 kg	5 lb	Rice	Cook rice according to directions on p. 358. This will allow very generous servings.
85 g	3 oz	Salt	
5.91 L	6¼ qt	Water, boiling	
50 servings	50 servings	French fried onion rings	Serve curried chicken over rice, with accompaniments. See directions for serving in Note 2.
4.54 kg	10 lb	Tomatoes, fresh, sliced	
4.54 kg	10 lb	Bananas, sliced or cut in chunks	
1 No. 10 can	1 No. 10 can	Pineapple chunks, drained	
680 g	1 lb 8 oz	Coconut, shredded or flaked	
454 g	1 lb	Salted peanuts	
2 jars	2 1-lb jars	Chutney	

Notes:
1. Shrimp, veal, lamb, or a combination of chicken and pork may be used, allowing 6 oz (170 g) cooked meat per person.
2. For a Singapore Curry dinner, arrange foods on buffet table in the following order: rice, curried chicken or other meat, and accompaniments in order listed in recipe. Each guest serves rice in the center of the plate, dips a generous serving of curried meat over the rice, then adds accompaniments as desired.

391

BREAD DRESSING (OR STUFFING)

Oven: 350°F (175°C)
Bake: 30–45 minutes

Yield: 50 portions
1 pan 12 × 20 × 2 in.
Portion: 4 oz (114 g)

Amount Metric	U.S.	Ingredient	Procedure
2.72 kg	6 lb	Dry bread, cubed	Add seasonings to bread and mix to distribute.
28 g	1 oz (1½ T)	Salt	
2 g	1 t	Pepper, black	
28 g	1 oz	Sage or poultry seasoning	
114 g	4 oz	Onion, minced	Sauté onion and celery in margarine until tender. Add to bread mixture. Mix lightly.
227 g	8 oz	Celery, chopped (optional)	
454 g	1 lb	Margarine or butter	
2.37 L	2½ qt	Chicken Stock (p. 495)	Add chicken stock and eggs to bread mixture. Toss lightly. Avoid overmixing, which causes dressing to be soggy and solid. Place in 1 greased 12 × 20 × 2-in. counter pan. Bake at 350°F (175°C) for 30–45 minutes. Serve with No. 10 dipper.
6 (312 g)	6 (11 oz)	Eggs, beaten	

Notes:
1. The amount of liquid (water, stock, or milk) will depend on the dryness of the bread.
2. If chicken stock is made with soup base, salt may need to be reduced.

Variations:
1. **Apple Stuffing.** Add 1 lb (454 g) finely chopped apples. Reduce bread cubes to 5 lb 8 oz (2.5 kg). Add 4 oz (114 g) chopped celery.
2. **Chestnut Stuffing.** Add 1¼ lb (567 g) cooked chestnuts, chopped, and 8 oz (227 g) chopped celery. Reduce bread to 5 lb 8 oz (2.5 kg). Substitute milk for chicken stock.
3. **Corn Bread Stuffing.** Reduce bread cubes to 4 lb (1.81 kg). Increase onion to 8 oz (227 g). Add 2 lb (908 g) corn bread, crumbled (⅓ recipe, p. 94). Eggs may be hard-cooked, chopped and tossed lightly with bread.
4. **Mushroom Stuffing.** Substitute 2 lb (908 g) mushrooms, sautéed in margarine or butter, for 6 oz (170 g) bread cubes. Omit sage.
5. **Nut Stuffing.** Add 2 c (480 mL) chopped almonds or pecans that have been browned lightly in 4 oz (114 g) melted margarine or butter. Substitute 2 c (480 mL) milk for 2 c (480 mL) of other liquid.
6. **Oyster Stuffing.** Substitute 1½ lb (680 g) oysters for 6 oz (170 g) bread cubes. Add 1 lb (454 g) cooked ham, minced, and ½ bay leaf, minced.
7. **Raisin Stuffing.** Add 1 lb (454 g) seedless raisins.
8. **Sausage Stuffing.** Reduce bread cubes to 5 lb (2.27 kg). Add 2 lb (908 g) sausage, cooked and drained, and 1 lb (454 g) tart apples, peeled and chopped. Reduce sage to ½ oz (14 g).

Salads and Salad Dressings

SALADS

Salads continue to be popular menu items, either as an appetizer salad, as an accompaniment to a main course of a dinner or luncheon, or as an entrée. A salad served as a main course should be large and substantial. One served as an accompaniment to a meal may be smaller and should be an appropriate supplement to the entrée. A variety of salads, including mixed greens, fruit salads, gelatin salads, vegetable salads, and relishes generally are offered by cafeterias and on selective menus. The increased use of the salad bar has expanded the selection of items available in all types of food services.

SALAD PREPARATION
1. Use only clean, well-drained, cold, and crisp salad greens, broken or cut. If a mechanical salad cutter is used, be careful not to chop too fine. See p. 395 for preparation of greens.
2. Cut fruits and vegetables into generous wedges, slices, or cubes for an attractive salad. Each piece should retain its identity. See pp. 398–402 for preparation of fruits and vegetables.
3. Drain fruit or any ingredients surrounded by liquid if they are to be used for a placed salad. Self-serve salad items may be served with juice.
4. When desired, marinate each ingredient separately in a well-seasoned dressing.
5. Drain and toss ingredients together lightly, if a mixed salad. Add tomato sections or juicy fruits just before serving to avoid wilting salad greens.
6. Select a dressing that will enhance the flavor of the salad ingredients.

PLACED SALADS
1. For individual salads, arrange chilled plates or bowls on large trays or in rows on the table. Select dishes that will add to the attractiveness of the salad.
2. Place salad greens on plates. Place lettuce cups so that the curly edge is at the back and top of the salad. The leaf should not extend over the edge of the plate. Tossed green salads usually have no underliner.

3. Build from the back to the front, with the salad green as a base. To give height, place chopped lettuce in the lettuce cup under salad ingredients such as fruit or vegetable slices, asparagus tips, or gelatin ring molds.
4. Top salad lightly with some material that will give accent in color and flavor, if desired.
5. Refrigerate until service.
6. Add salad dressing just before serving (sprinkle, do not pour), or pass for individual service. If adding before service, use only enough to moisten the vegetables or fruits. For a green salad, 2–3 cups is an ample allowance for 50 servings.

SALAD BAR

A basic salad bar consists of salad greens, with a number of accompaniments and dressings. However, it may also include prepared salads, such as macaroni, potato, bean, fruit, or gelatin; and often includes cottage cheese, pickles, olives, relishes, and marinated vegetables. Lettuce usually is the basic salad ingredient, but spinach, endive, or other greens may be added.

Examples of accompaniments for the salad greens are sliced tomatoes, whole cherry tomatoes, sliced or chopped cucumbers, shredded or sliced carrots, green pepper rings, fresh sprouts, sliced radishes, sliced or chopped onions, partially defrosted frozen peas or corn, garbanzo beans, chopped hard-cooked egg, crumbled crisp bacon, French fried onions, croutons, and shredded cheese.

The salad bar should be attractively presented and the salad ingredients kept cold. Following is a suggested arrangement for a salad bar.

1. Salad plates or bowls that have been prechilled, if possible.
2. A large bowl (or two, if a double line is used) of torn or cut pieces of lettuce on a bed of ice or other cold surface. If other greens, such as spinach or endive, are to be used, place near the lettuce or mix with it.
3. Arrange accompaniments in a logical order for "building" a salad. These foods should be in containers that can be removed, cleaned, and replenished periodically throughout the serving period.
4. Prepared salads.
5. Garnishes.
6. Choice of salad dressing, usually oil and vinegar, French, mayonnaise, thousand island, Roquefort or blue cheese, or specialty of the food service.

PREPARATION OF SALAD INGREDIENTS

Salad Greens Greens should be clean, crisp, chilled, and well drained. It may be necessary to separate leaves for thorough washing. Wash in a spray of water or in a large container of water. Shake off excess water, drain thoroughly, and refrigerate. Draining in a colander or on a rack placed on a sheet pan will keep the greens from standing in water while chilling. Cover with a clean damp cloth or plastic to prevent dehydration.

When preparing head lettuce for garnish, remove stem end or core (Fig. 2.21). Hold inverted head under cold, running water to loosen tightly wrapped leaves. Do not soak. Turn heads open-side down to drain. Separate the leaves and stack 6 or 7 leaves in a nest. Invert and pack in a covered container or plastic bag. Refrigerate 2 hours or more to complete crisping. Leaf lettuce is convenient to use for salad liners. Wash lettuce thoroughly (Fig. 2.22). Cut stem end and place in perforated pan to drain. Chill 2 to 3 hours for crisping.

Spinach should be carefully examined, removing tough stems and discarding all dry, yellow, wilted, or decayed leaves. Wash first in tepid water, then in cold, as many times as necessary to remove sand.

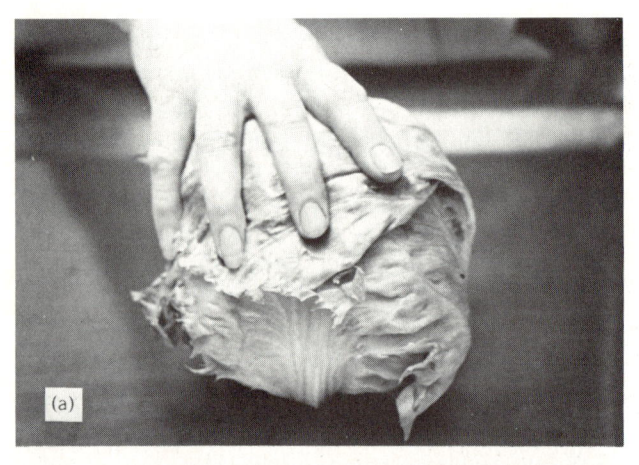

Figure 2.21 Coring head lettuce. (a) Hit stem end of lettuce sharply on flat surface. (b) Remove loosened core.

SALADS 397

Figure 2.22 Preparing leaf lettuce. (a) Wash under cold running water. (b) Remove stem end by cutting with a sharp knife. (c) Place leaf end up in a perforated pan to drain. Chill 2 to 3 hours to crisp.

Fresh Fruits

Apples. Wash, pare, core, remove bruises and spots. If the skins are tender and the desired color, do not pare.

To dice, cut into rings and dice with sectional cutter. Drop diced pieces into salad dressing, lemon, pineapple, or other acid fruit juice to prevent discoloration. If diced apple is placed in fruit juice, drain before using in a salad.

To section, cut into uniform pieces, so the widest part of the section is not more than 1/2 in. thick. Remove core from each section. If the peeling has not been removed, score it in several places to facilitate cutting when it is served. Prevent discoloration by the same method as for diced apples, only do not use salad dressing.

Apricots. Cut into halves or sections and remove seed. Remove skins if desired.

Avocados. If hard, ripen at room temperature. Peel shortly before serving, cut into halves or quarters, and remove seed. Slice, dice, or cut into balls. Dip into French dressing or lemon juice to prevent discoloration.

Bananas. Remove skins and soft or discolored parts. Cut into strips, sections, wedges, or slices. Dip each piece into pineapple, other acid fruit juice, or salad dressing to prevent discoloration.

Cantaloupes and Other Melons. Pare, dice, and cut into balls, or cut into uniform wedges or strips.

Cherries and Grapes. Wash, drain, halve, and remove seeds. To frost, brush with slightly beaten egg white. Sprinkle with sugar. Let dry before using.

Grapefruit. For sections, select large grapefruit, wash and dry. Cut off a thick layer of skin from the top and bottom. Place grapefruit on cutting board, start at the top, and cut toward the board (Fig. 2.23). Always cut with a downward stroke and deeply enough to remove all the white membrane. Turn grapefruit while cutting. When paring is completed and pulp is exposed, remove sections by cutting along the membrane of one section to the center of the fruit. Turn the knife and force the blade along the membrane of the next section to the exterior of the fruit. Repeat for each section.

Kiwi. Pare and slice crosswise.

Oranges. Pare, section as grapefruit, or slice or dice.

Peaches. Remove skins only a short time before using. Peel or submerge in boiling water for a few seconds and remove skins. Chill. Cut into halves, wedges, or slices. Drop into acid fruit juice to prevent discoloration.

Pears. Pare and remove core and seeds a short time before serving. Cut into halves, wedges, or slices. Dipping in lemon or other acid fruit juice will prevent discoloration.

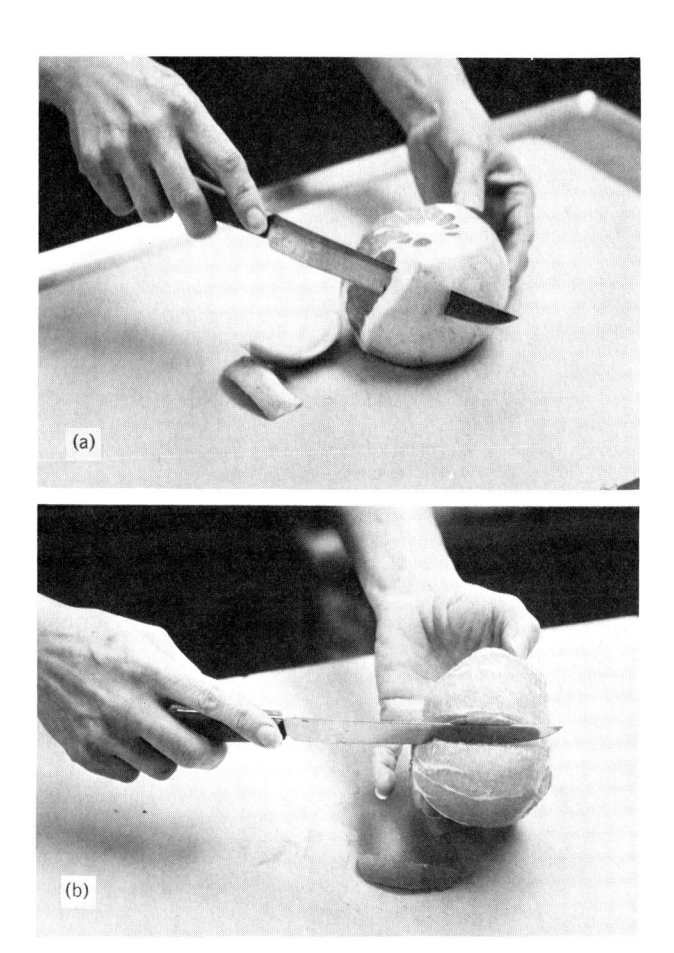

Figure 2.23 Peeling and sectioning grapefruit. (a) Cut layer of peel from top and bottom of grapefruit. Using a sharp knife, remove peel. Cut with a downward stroke and deeply enough to remove all the white membrane. (b) Section grapefruit by cutting along membrane of one section to the center of the fruit. Turn the knife and force the blade along the membrane of the next section.

Pineapple. Remove crown by holding pineapple in one hand and crown in the other, then twisting in opposite directions (Fig. 2.24). Trim top of pineapple and cut off base. Using a sharp knife, remove peel by using a downward cutting motion. Remove eyes by making narrow wedge-shaped grooves into the pineapple. Cut diagonally around the fruit, following the pattern of the eyes. Cut away as little of the fruit as possible. Cut pineapple vertically into eighths, then cut hard center core from each spear. To make pineapple chunks, cut each spear into pieces of the desired size.

Pomegranate. Cut open and remove seeds. Discard peeling and white membrane.

400 SALADS AND SALAD DRESSINGS

(a)

(b)

(c)

(d)

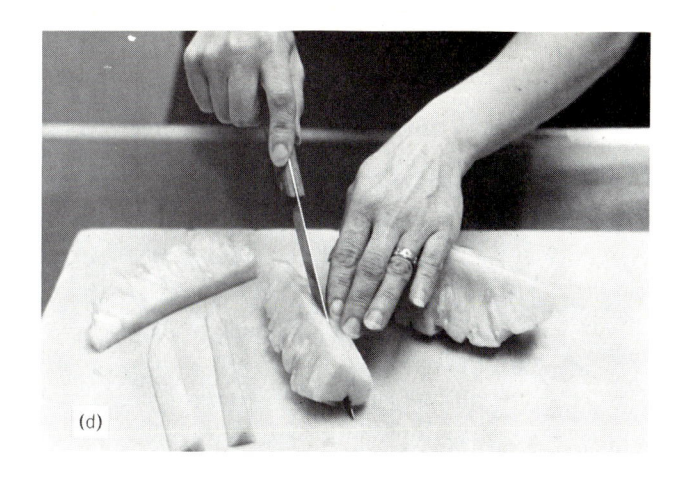

Figure 2.24 Preparing fresh pineapple. (a) Remove crown by holding pineapple in one hand and crown in the other, then twisting in opposite directions. (b) Trim top of pineapple and cut off base. Using a sharp knife, remove peel by using a downward cutting motion. (c) Remove eyes by making narrow wedge-shaped grooves into the pineapple. Cut diagonally around the fruit, following the pattern of the eyes. Cut away as little of the fruit as possible. (d) Cut pineapple vertically into eighths, then cut the hard center core from each spear. To make pineapple chunks, cut each spear into pieces of the desired size.

Canned Fruit

Select whole pieces uniform in size and shape and with a firm appearance. Drain. If cubes or sections are desired, cut into pieces uniform in size and shape with well-defined edges. Pieces should not be too small.

Vegetables

Whether used raw or cooked, strive to preserve shape, color, flavor, and crispness of vegetables. Marinating in a well-seasoned French dressing adds flavor.

Asparagus. Break or cut off tough part of stems. Thoroughly wash remaining portions. Cook and marinate in French dressing.

Beans, Dry. Cook, keeping beans whole (p. 523).

Beans, Green. Leave whole or cut lengthwise. Wash, cook, and marinate.

Beets. Wash, cook, peel, remove any blemishes. Cut into desired shape and marinate.

Cabbage. Remove outer leaves. Wash heads, cut into 4–6 pieces. Remove center stalk. Shred remaining portions as desired with a long sharp knife or shredder. Crisp in ice water 15–30 minutes.

Carrots. Pare and remove blemishes. Cut into wedges, rounds, or strips. Grind, shred, or cook; then cut into desired shapes and marinate. For carrot curls, see Relishes, p. 402.

Cauliflower. Remove all leaves and cut away dark spots. Separate into flowerets, leaving 1-in. stem. Soak in salt water (1 oz/28 g salt or ⅓ c/80 mL vinegar per gal). Cauliflower may be cooked and marinated, or it may be marinated and served raw.

Celery. Separate outer stalks from heart. (Outer stalks may be used for soup.) Wash, trim, and remove strings, bruised, and blemished parts. If necessary to sanitize, add 1 T (15 mL) household bleach to each gal (3.79 L) water. Submerge celery for 30 seconds. Rinse well. Air dry. Use within 8 hours. To dice, cut lengthwise. Several stalks may be cut at one time. Place on a board and cut crosswise with a French knife. For celery curls, see p. 402.

Celery Cabbage. Remove outer leaves and wash. Shred as lettuce or cut into 1- to 2-in. slices.

Chives. Remove roots and any objectionable portions. Wash. Drain. Cut leaves crosswise with a sharp knife or scissors.

Cucumbers. Wash and pare, or score lengthwise with a fork. Crisp and let stand in salted ice water 15 minutes. Cut into slices or wedges.

Green Peppers. Wash, remove seeds and stems. Cut into rings or strips; dice or chop.

Onions. Pour water over onions to cover. Under water, remove wilted leaves, outer layer of the bulb, firm root end, and all bruised or decayed parts. Cut as desired.

Potatoes. Pare. Remove eyes and bruised parts. Cut into ½-in. cubes and cook; or wash, cook with skins on, peel, and dice. Marinate 2 hours before using.

Tomatoes. Wash and peel. If skins are difficult to remove, place in a wire basket and dip in boiling water until skins begin to loosen. Dip in cold water and remove skins. Chill.

Turnips. Remove tops, wash, pare by hand. Shred or cut into fine strips.

Relishes

Carrot Curls. Cut long, paper-thin slices. Roll each strip around finger, fasten with toothpick, and chill in ice water for several hours.

Carrot Sticks. Cut carrots into thin strips. Chill in ice water for several hours.

Celery Curls or Fans. Cut celery into 2½-in. lengths. Make lengthwise cuts ⅛ in. apart about 1 in. in length on one or both ends of celery strips. Place in ice water about 2 hours before serving.

Celery Rings. Cut celery into 2-in. lengths and then into pieces ⅛ in. thick. Place in ice water for several hours. Each strip of celery will form a ring.

Green Pepper Rings. Remove stem and seeds. Cut into thin slices.

Green Pepper Sticks. Cut pepper lengthwise into narrow strips.

Radish Roses. Cut off root end of radish with sharp knife. Leave an inch or two of the green stem. Cut 4 or 5 petal-shaped slices around the radish from cut tip to center. Place radishes in ice water, and petals will open.

Radish Accordions. Cut long radishes not quite through into 10–12 narrow slices. Place in ice water. Slices will fan out accordion-style.

Other Foods

Almonds, Blanched. To blanch almonds, cover with boiling water and let stand until skins will slip. Drain. Cover with cold water and rub off skins. Place skinned almonds between dry clean towels to remove water.

Almonds, Toasted. Spread blanched almonds in a shallow pan in a thin layer. Heat at 250°F (121°C), stirring occasionally until nuts are light brown in color.

Cheese. Grate, shred, or cut in tiny cubes; or soften and put through a pastry tube.

Chicken or Turkey. Cook, remove skin, gristle, and bone. Cut into ⅓-in. cubes. Marinate if desired. Mix with dressing and other ingredients just before serving.

Eggs. Hard-cook (p. 256). Use whole, halved, sliced, or sectioned. Slice or mince whites. Force yolks through ricer.

Fish. Cook, remove skin and bones. Flake. Marinate if desired. Mix with dressing just before serving. See p. 281 for preparation of crab, lobster, and shrimp.

Meat. Cut cooked meat into ⅓-in. cubes. Marinate with French or Italian dressing. Mix just before serving.

Nuts. Heat in hot oven to freshen if desired. Use whole, shredded, or chopped.

SALAD DRESSINGS

The basic ingredients of a salad dressing are oil and vinegar, or other acid food such as lemon juice. To that are added emulsifiers, ingredients that bind together the oil and vinegar. They may be herbs, spices, sugar, or salt, which only emulsify temporarily as in French or Italian dressing. The emulsifier may be egg yolk, as in mayonnaise, or a starch paste/egg mixture as in a cooked dressing, which yield a permanent emulsion.

There are four basic types of salad dressings. *French Dressing* is a mixture of oil and vinegar plus seasonings, which must be stirred or shaken vigorously before serving for a good distribution of ingredients. This type of dressing is good on salad greens and should be added just before serving. A sweeter version (p. 445) often is used on fruit salads.

Mayonnaise is made from egg (preferably egg yolk), oil, and vinegar. Seasonings are mixed with the vinegar and egg, and the oil is added very slowly while beating on high speed. It will be smooth and creamy with a mild, slightly tart flavor. It should not separate, but if it does, it can be reemulsified. This type of dressing is good with meats, fish, poultry, and cooked vegetable salads. A recipe for mayonnaise and variations is given on p. 438 and for mayonnaise with a cooked base on p. 440. The starch base in this dressing provides a stable emulsion.

Cooked Salad Dressing (p. 441) uses a starch paste with egg mixture to which vinegar, seasonings, and margarine or butter are added. The oil content of this dressing is low, but the egg content is high and it should be fluffy and creamy with a zippy flavor. This type of dressing and a fruit salad dressing (which uses fruit juices instead of vinegar (p. 445)) are especially good with fruit.

A fourth type of salad dressing that is used extensively today because it costs less than mayonnaise is *Salad Dressing*, a blend of cooked dressing and mayonnaise. It contains less egg and oil than mayonnaise but is often used as a mayonnaise substitute. Salad dressings should be stored in glass, plastic, or stainless-steel containers with tight fitting lids at 40−50°F (4−10°C).

SALAD RECIPES

Vegetable and Pasta Salads

BASIC MIXED GREEN SALAD

Yield: 50 portions
10 lb (4.54 kg)
Portion: 3 oz (85 g)

Amount Metric	U.S.	Ingredient	Procedure
3.18 kg	7 lb	Head lettuce	Break or cut lettuce and other greens into bite-sized pieces.
1.36 kg	3 lb	Leaf lettuce, Bibb or Romaine	
1.18 L	1¼ qt	French dressing, Oil and Vinegar, or Italian dressing	Just before serving, toss lightly with dressing or portion greens into individual salad bowls, 3 oz (85 g) per bowl, and serve with choice of dressings.

Notes:
1. Any combination of salad greens may be used. See p. 406 for suggestions.
2. If serving on a salad bar, place greens in a large bowl and offer choice of dressings and garnishes (see p. 406).

Variations:
1. **Hawaiian Tossed Salad.** To 7 lb (3.18 kg) mixed greens, add sections from 8 grapefruit, 8 oranges, 4 avocados, and 1 fresh pineapple, cubed. Serve with Honey–Orange Dressing, p. 445.
2. **Salad Greens with Grapefruit.** Place 3 oz (85 g) greens in each bowl. Garnish each with 3 sections pink grapefruit. Serve with Poppy Seed Dressing (p. 444) or French Dressing (p. 442).
3. **Spinach Salad.** Use 4 lb (1.81 kg) lettuce and 6 lb (2.72 kg) fresh spinach, 2 bunches green onions, sliced, and 12 eggs hard-cooked and sliced. To serve, toss lightly with French Dressing and portion into bowls. Sprinkle with bacon (1 lb/454 g), which has been diced, cooked until crisp, and drained.
4. **Spinach–Mushroom Salad.** Use 10 lb (4.54 kg) fresh spinach (may be part lettuce), 4 lb (1.81 kg) fresh mushrooms, sliced, and 2 bunches green onions, sliced. Toss lightly with French Dressing just before serving. Sprinkle with cooked crumbled bacon if desired.

TOSSED VEGETABLE SALAD

Yield: 50 portions
10 lb (4.54 kg)
Portion: 3 oz (85 g)

Amount		Ingredient	Procedure
Metric	U.S.		
3.18 kg	7 lb	Salad greens[a]	Wash greens thoroughly and drain. Tear or cut into bite-sized pieces.
1.36 kg	3 lb	Salad ingredients[b]	Add to greens. Toss lightly. Portion into individual salad bowls or plates, 3 oz (85 g) per portion.
		Garnish[c]	Garnish salads if desired.
1.18 L	1¼ qt	Salad dressing[d]	Serve with choice of dressings. If preferred, French, Italian, or oil and vinegar dressing may be added to the salad just before serving.

[a] **Salad Greens.** Select one or more: head (iceberg) lettuce, romaine, leaf lettuce, bibb lettuce, Boston lettuce, endive, spinach, escarole, celery cabbage, watercress. See Fig. 2.25 for kinds of lettuce.

[b] **Salad Ingredients.** Select one or more: fresh tomato wedges, halved cherry tomatoes, sliced or diced cucumbers, sliced fresh mushrooms, chopped red cabbage, sliced cauliflower flowerets, sliced or diced celery, green and red pepper strips or rings, sliced zucchini, sliced Jerusalem artichokes, shredded carrots, sliced water chestnuts, bean sprouts, sliced green onions or scallions, sliced radishes, chopped broccoli, sliced avocado, cooked green peas, garbanzo beans, artichoke hearts.

[c] **Garnishes.** Sliced olives, coarsely chopped or sliced hard-cooked eggs, onion rings, seasoned croutons, cheese strips or cubes, crumbled crisp-cooked bacon, tomato wedge, cherry tomato, parsley sprig.

[d] **Salad Dressings.** French, Italian, Oil and Vinegar, Roquefort, Thousand Island.

Figure 2.25 Lettuce for green salads. Clockwise from bottom left: romaine, leaf, iceberg (head), red tipped leaf, curly endive, and Boston.

BROWN BEAN SALAD

Yield: 50 portions
6 qt (5.68 L)
Portion: ½ c (4 oz/142 g)

Amount			
Metric	U.S.	Ingredient	Procedure
12	12	Eggs, hard-cooked (p. 256)	Peel and dice eggs.
340 g	12 oz	Celery, diced	Mix all ingredients.
85 g	3 oz	Green pepper, chopped	
85 g	3 oz	Onion, minced	
284 g	10 oz	Pickle relish	
1½ No. 10 cans	1½ No. 10 cans	Beans, brown or kidney, drained and rinsed	
180 mL	¾ c	Vinegar	
38 g	2 T	Salt	
720 mL	3 c	Salad dressing	

Notes:
1. 4 lb (1.81 kg) dried beans, cooked according to directions on p. 523 may be substituted for canned beans.
2. Great Northern or pinto beans may be substituted for half of the kidney beans.

GARBANZO BEAN SALAD

Yield: 50 portions
4½ qt (4.26 L)
Portion: ⅓ c (3 oz/85 g)

Amount Metric	U.S.	Ingredient	Procedure
1.14 kg	2 lb 8 oz	Beans, garbanzo, canned	Rinse beans with cold water. Drain.
680 g	1 lb 8 oz	Beans, red, canned	
908 g	2 lb	Beans, pinto, canned	
454 g	1 lb	Celery, sliced	Combine with beans.
340 g	12 oz	Cucumbers, peeled and sliced	
142 g	5 oz	Onions, green, sliced	
227 g	8 oz	Radishes, sliced	
114 g	4 oz	Olives, black, sliced	
240 mL	1 c	French Dressing (Light), p. 442	Pour dressing over bean mixture. Toss lightly. Marinate 2 hours.

Notes:
1. Cooked Great Northern beans may be substituted for garbanzo beans.
2. Vegetable Marinade (p. 486) may be substituted for French Dressing.

Variation: **Garbanzo Pasta Salad.** Delete pinto beans. Cook 8 oz (227 g) shell macaroni al dente. Combine with other ingredients.

TRIPLE BEAN SALAD

Yield: 50 portions
6 qt (5.68 L)
Portion: ½ c (4 oz/114 g)

Amount Metric	U.S.	Ingredient	Procedure
1.59 kg	3 lb 8 oz (1 No. 10 can)	Green beans, French style or cut	Drain green and wax beans thoroughly.
1.14 kg	2 lb 8 oz	Wax beans, cut	Rinse kidney beans.
1.36 kg	3 lb	Kidney beans, canned	
680 g	1 lb 8 oz	Onion, thinly sliced	Add onion, green pepper, and seasonings to beans. Cover. Marinate overnight in refrigerator.
170 g	6 oz	Green pepper, diced	
720 mL	3 c	Vinegar	
680 g	1 lb 8 oz	Sugar, granulated	
60 mL	¼ c	Soy sauce	
76 g	¼ c	Celery salt	
12 g	2 t	Salt	
4 g	2 t	Pepper, black	
240 mL	1 c	Salad oil	Just before serving, drain vegetables well. Add oil and toss lightly. Serve with No. 12 dipper.

Variations:

1. **Cauliflower–Bean Salad.** Delete kidney beans and add 3 lb (1.36 kg) cauliflower flowerets, slightly cooked.
2. **Oriental Bean Salad.** Delete kidney beans. Add 1½ lb (680 g) cooked red beans, drained and rinsed, and 1½ lb (680 g) bean sprouts.

CARROT RAISIN SALAD

Yield: 50 portions
4¼ qt (4.02 L)
Portion: ⅓ c (2½ oz/70 g)

Amount Metric	U.S.	Ingredient	Procedure
227 g	8 oz	Raisins	Soften raisins in steamer or slow oven for about 3 minutes.
3.18 kg	7 lb AP	Carrots, raw	Pare carrots. Shred or grind coarsely. Combine with raisins.
480 mL	2 c	Mayonnaise	Mix mayonnaise, salad dressing, and salt. Add to carrot–raisin mixture. Mix lightly. Serve with No. 12 dipper.
480 mL	2 c	Salad dressing	
19 g	1 T	Salt	

Variations:

1. **Carrot–Celery Salad.** Omit raisins. Use 5 lb (2.27 kg) ground carrots. Add 2 lb (908 g) chopped celery and 2 oz (57 g) sugar.
2. **Carrot–Celery–Apple Salad.** Substitute 3 lb (1.36 kg) diced apples for 2 lb (908 g) carrots.
3. **Carrot–Celery–Cucumber Salad.** Use 4½ lb (2.04 kg) shredded carrots, 1½ lb (680 g) chopped celery, and 1½ lb (680 g) chopped cucumber.
4. **Carrot–Coconut Salad.** Substitute 1 lb (454 g) toasted coconut for raisins.
5. **Marinated Carrots.** Cook 5 lb (2.27 kg) sliced raw carrots until tender crisp. Drain. Combine 2 c (480 mL) canned tomato soup, 1 lb (454 g) sugar, ¾ c (180 mL) salad oil, 1½ c (360 mL) vinegar, 2 t (12 g) salt, 1 t (2 g) black pepper, 1 T (15 g) prepared mustard, 1 T (15 mL) Worcestershire sauce, 8 oz (227 g) chopped onions, and 3 oz (85 g) chopped green peppers. Stir in warm carrots. Marinate for several hours. Yield: 50 2-oz (57-g) portions.

CARRIFRUIT SALAD

Yield: 50 portions
4½ qt (4.26 L)
Portion: ⅓ c (2½ oz/70 g)

Amount		Ingredient	Procedure
Metric	U.S.		
2.04 kg	4 lb 8 oz	Carrots, shredded	Combine ingredients. Mix lightly.
1.25 kg	2 lb 12 oz	Pineapple tidbits, drained	
227 g	8 oz	Coconut, flaked	
255 g	9 oz	Marshmallows, miniature	
540 mL	2¼ c	Mayonnaise	Mix mayonnaise and cream.
180 mL	¾ c	Cream, half and half	Add to salad ingredients. Mix carefully. Serve with No. 12 dipper.

Note: 8 oz (227 g) raisins may be added.

COLE SLAW

Yield: 50 portions
4½ qt (4.26 L)
Portion: ⅓ c (3 oz/85 g)

Amount		Ingredient	Procedure
Metric	U.S.		
3.18 kg (4.08 kg AP)	7 lb EP (9 lb AP)	Cabbage	Shred or chop cabbage.
720 mL	3 c	Vinegar	Combine vinegar, sugar, and seasonings.
680 g	1 lb 8 oz	Sugar, granulated	
28 g	1 oz (1½ T)	Salt	Add to cabbage.
4 g	1 t	Celery seed (optional)	Mix lightly.

Note: Red cabbage may be substituted for part or all of green cabbage.

Variations:
1. **Cauliflower–Broccoli Salad.** Substitute 3½ lb (1.59 kg) EP each of cauliflower and broccoli for the cabbage. Add 3 oz (85 g) chopped onion.
2. **Green Pepper Slaw.** Add 4 oz (114 g) chopped green pepper, 2 oz (57 g) chopped onion, and 4 T (16 g) celery seed.

CREAMY COLE SLAW

Yield: 50 portions
4¼ qt (4.02 L)
Portion: ⅓ c (3 oz/85 g)

Amount Metric	U.S.	Ingredient	Procedure
3.18 kg (4.08 kg AP)	7 lb EP (9 lb AP)	Cabbage	Shred or chop cabbage.
480 mL	2 c	Mayonnaise or salad dressing	Combine and add to cabbage. Mix lightly. Serve with No. 12 dipper.
480 mL	2 c	Cream, half and half, or sour cream	
120 mL	½ c	Vinegar	
114 g	4 oz	Sugar, granulated	
28 g	1 oz (1½ T)	Salt	
1 g	½ t	Pepper, white	

Note: Whipped topping may be used in place of cream. Reduce sugar to 2 oz (57 g).

Variations:

1. **Cabbage–Apple Salad.** See p. 425.

2. **Cabbage–Carrot Slaw.** Reduce cabbage to 5 lb (2.27 kg) EP. Add 1 lb 12 oz (794 g) shredded or chopped carrots, 8 oz (227 g) chopped green pepper, and 4 oz (114 g) chopped onion.

3. **Cabbage–Pineapple–Marshmallow Salad.** To 4 lb (1.81 kg) shredded or chopped cabbage, add 2 lb (908 g) diced pineapple, 1 lb (454 g) miniature marshmallows, and a dressing made of 2 c (480 mL) mayonnaise or salad dressing and 2 c (480 mL) cream, whipped.

4. **Creamy Cauliflower–Broccoli Salad.** Substitute 3½ lb (1.59 kg) EP each of cauliflower and broccoli for the cabbage. Add 3 oz (85 g) chopped green onion.

SLICED CUCUMBER AND ONION IN SOUR CREAM

Yield: 50 portions
4¼ qt (4.02 mL)
Portion: ⅓ c (2½ oz/70 g)

Amount			
Metric	U.S.	Ingredient	Procedure
2.27 kg	5 lb	Cucumbers	Cut cucumbers and
227 g	8 oz	Onions	onions in thin slices.
720 mL	3 c	Cultured sour cream	Blend rest of ingredients
720 mL	3 c	Mayonnaise	to form a thin cream
9 g	1½ t	Salt	dressing.
42 g	3 T	Sugar, granulated	Pour over cucumbers and
180 mL	¾ c	Vinegar	onions. Mix lightly.

Note: This cream dressing may be used as a dressing for lettuce.

Variation: **German Cucumbers.** Reduce onions to 4 oz (114 g). Delete cream dressing. Pour mixture of 1 c (240 mL) vinegar, 1 c (240 mL) water, 2 T (38 g) salt, and 8 oz (227 g) sugar over cucumbers and onions. Marinate at least 1 hour.

MARINATED GARDEN SALAD

Yield: 50 portions
8 lb (3.63 kg)
Portion: ⅓ c (2½ oz/70 g)

Amount			
Metric	U.S.	Ingredient	Procedure
454 g	1 lb EP	Carrots, sliced	Steam carrots just until tender crisp. Drain.
908 g	2 lb EP	Cauliflower, fresh	Cut cauliflower into flowerets.
908 g	2 lb EP	Broccoli spears, frozen	Cut broccoli into flowerets and sliced stems.
454 g	1 lb	Mushrooms, fresh	Clean mushrooms. Cut large mushrooms in half. Combine all vegetables.
1.42 L	1½ qt	French Dressing (Light), p. 442	Combine dressing and seasonings.
7 g	¼ oz	Dill weed	Pour over vegetables.
4 g	1 T	Basil leaves	Marinate at least 2 hours.
1 g	1 t	Oregano leaves	

MARINATED MUSHROOMS

Yield: 50 portions
Portion: 2¾ oz (78 g)

Amount		Ingredient	Procedure
Metric	U.S.		
2.72 kg	6 lb	Mushrooms, fresh, small	Clean mushrooms and trim ends. Leave whole.
0.95 L	1 qt	Water	Combine water and lemon juice. Bring to a boil.
120 mL	½ c	Lemon juice	Add mushrooms. Cook 1–3 minutes. Drain.
1.42 mL	1½ qt	Vegetable Marinade (p. 486)	Pour over mushrooms. Refrigerate 2–3 hours. Drain off most of the marinade before serving.

Note: Before serving, mushrooms may be tossed with fresh minced parsley.

Variations:
1. **Marinated Asparagus.** Cook fresh or frozen asparagus spears until tender crisp. Marinate.
2. **Marinated Green Beans.** Cover whole green beans with marinade. If fresh green beans are used, cook until tender crisp.
3. **Vegetable Collage.** Pour 3 c (720 mL) Italian Salad Dressing (p. 442) or Vegetable Marinade (p. 486) over: 2 lb (908 g) broccoli flowerets, 2 lb (908 g) cauliflower flowerets, 12 oz (340 g) sliced celery, 1 lb 8 oz (680 g) cherry tomatoes cut in half, 2 lb (908 g) sliced zucchini, 1 lb (454 g) sliced green onions, 6 oz (170 g) sliced carrots, and 1 lb 8 oz (680 g) sliced ripe olives. Marinate in refrigerator for 4 hours or more. Before serving, add 1 lb (454 g) cooked crumbled bacon and toss.

SALAD RECIPES 415

ORIENTAL SALAD

Yield: 50 portions
Portion: 2½ oz (70 g)

Metric	U.S.	Ingredient	Procedure
1.14 kg	2 lb 8 oz	Bean sprouts, canned	Drain bean sprouts.
284 g	10 oz	Celery, sliced	Combine vegetables with bean sprouts. Toss lightly.
284 g	10 oz	Cucumbers, peeled and sliced	
85 g	3 oz	Green peppers, chopped	
2.27 kg	5 lb	Tomatoes, fresh, diced	
57 g	2 oz	Chives, chopped	
360 mL	1½ c	Tomato Dressing (p. 442)	Combine dressing, soy sauce and salt.
60 mL	¼ c	Soy sauce	Pour over vegetables and toss lightly.
3 g	½ t	Salt	

Note: 2 lb (908 g) fresh bean sprouts may be substituted for canned.

SPINACH CHEESE SALAD

Yield: 50 portions
Portion: 3 oz (85 g)

Metric	U.S.	Ingredient	Procedure
1.36 kg	3 lb	Spinach, chopped, frozen	Thaw spinach. Squeeze out excess moisture and drain.
10	10	Eggs, hard-cooked (p. 256)	Peel and chop eggs coarsely.
170 g	6 oz	Onion, chopped	Add onions, celery, cheese, and eggs to spinach. Mix lightly.
227 g	8 oz	Celery, chopped	
454 g	1 lb	Cheddar cheese, shredded	
1.18 L	1¼ qt	Mayonnaise or salad dressing	Combine mayonnaise and seasonings. Pour over spinach mixture. Mix lightly. Refrigerate for 2 hours. Serve with No. 12 dipper.
12 g	2 t	Salt	
10 mL	2 t	Tabasco sauce	
30 mL	2 T	Vinegar	
160 mL	⅔ c	Horseradish	

MACARONI SALAD

Yield: 50 portions
6 qt (5.68 L)
Portion: ½ c (4 oz/114 g)

Amount		Ingredient	Procedure
Metric	U.S.		
908 g	2 lb	Macaroni, elbow	Cook macaroni according
7.57 L	2 gal	Water, boiling	to directions on p. 348.
57 g	2 oz (3 T)	Salt	Rinse in cold water. Drain
15 mL	1 T	Cooking oil (optional)	well after rinsing.
680 g	1 lb 8 oz	Cheddar cheese, diced or shredded	Add remaining ingredients to macaroni. Mix lightly.
454 g	1 lb	Pickle relish	Chill.
14	14	Eggs, hard-cooked (p. 256), chopped	Serve with No. 12 dipper.
680 g	1 lb 8 oz	Celery, finely chopped	
28 g	1 oz	Onion, finely chopped	
85 g	3 oz	Pimiento, chopped	
19 g	1 T	Salt	
2 g	¾ t	Pepper, white	
720 mL	3 c	Mayonnaise	

Notes:
1. Other types of pasta may be substituted for elbow macaroni. (See p. 347.)
2. 8 oz (227 g) chopped green pepper may be substituted for 8 oz (227 g) celery.

Variations:
1. **Ham and Pasta Salad.** Delete eggs and reduce cheese to 1 lb (454 g). Add 2 lb (908 g) cooked ham, diced.
2. **Chicken and Pasta Salad.** Delete cheese, pickle relish, and eggs. Cook 2 lb 8 oz (1.14 kg) fettuccini or other type of pasta according to directions on p. 348. Add 3 lb (1.36 kg) cooked chicken, diced.

ITALIAN PASTA SALAD

Yield: 50 portions
Portion: 4 oz (114 g)

Amount Metric	U.S.	Ingredient	Procedure
908 g	2 lb	Rotini or other pasta	Cook pasta according to directions on p. 348. Rinse in cold water. Drain.
7.57 L	2 gal	Water, boiling	
38 g	2 T	Salt	
1.66 L	1¾ qt	Thousand Island Dressing (p. 439)	Combine dressing and seasonings. Pour over pasta. Mix gently. Chill.
3 g	1 T	Basil leaves	
19 g	1 T	Salt	
794 g	1 lb 12 oz	Beans, garbanzo, canned	Drain and rinse beans. Add to pasta mixture.
680 g	1 lb 8 oz	Tomatoes, fresh, cut in wedges	Add vegetables and olives to pasta mixture. Toss gently. Refrigerate until served.
454 g	1 lb	Cucumbers, peeled and sliced	
227 g	8 oz	Cauliflower, fresh, sliced	
114 g	4 oz	Olives, large ripe, pitted	

Note: An oil base dressing may be substituted for Thousand Island Dressing.

POTATO SALAD

Yield: 50 portions
7 qt (6.62 L)
Portion: 4 oz (114 g)

Amount Metric	U.S.	Ingredient	Procedure
4.54 kg EP (5.44 kg AP)	10 lb EP (12 lb AP)	Potatoes, pared	Cook potatoes until tender. Dice while warm.
120 mL	½ c	Salad oil	Make a marinade of oil, vinegar, lemon juice, and seasonings. Add to warm potatoes and mix gently. Marinate until cold.
120 mL	½ c	Vinegar	
15 mL	1 T	Lemon juice	
28 g	2 T	Mustard, prepared	
85 g	3 oz	Sugar, granulated	
19 g	1 T	Salt	
f.d.	f.d.	Tabasco sauce	
12	12	Eggs, hard-cooked (p. 256), diced	Add eggs, celery, onion, and pepper to marinated potatoes. Mix lightly.
454 g	1 lb	Celery, diced	
227 g	8 oz	Onion, finely chopped	
1 g	½ t	Pepper, black	
480 g	2 c	Mayonnaise	Add mayonnaise. Mix carefully to blend. Chill at least 1 hour before serving. Serve with No. 12 dipper.

Notes:

1. 2 c (480 mL) French Dressing (Light), p. 442, may be substituted for marinade given in recipe.
2. Sour cream or yogurt may be substituted for half of the mayonnaise.
3. Potatoes may be cooked with skins on, then peeled. Use 12 lb (5.44 kg) AP.
4. 4 oz (114 g) chopped green pepper, pimiento, or pickle may be added.

Variation: **Sour Cream Potato Salad.** Reduce eggs to 8 and mayonnaise to 1 c (240 mL). Add 2 c (480 mL) cultured sour cream, 1 t (1 g) celery seed, and 12 oz (340 g) peeled, sliced cucumbers.

HOT POTATO SALAD

Yield: 50 portions
Portion: ⅔ c (6 oz/170 g)

Amount		Ingredient	Procedure
Metric	U.S.		
5.44 kg EP (6.8 kg AP)	12 lb EP (15 lb AP)	Potatoes	Wash potatoes and trim as necessary. Steam until just tender, about 30 minutes. Peel and slice.
16	16	Eggs, hard-cooked (p. 256)	Peel and slice or dice eggs.
454 g	1 lb	Bacon	Dice bacon. Cook until crisp. Drain; reserve fat.
85 g	3 oz	Onions, chopped	Sauté onions in bacon fat.
114 g	4 oz	Flour, all-purpose	Add flour and stir until smooth.
567 g	1 lb 4 oz	Sugar, granulated	Mix sugar, salt, vinegar, and water. Boil 1 minute. Add to fat–flour mixture gradually while stirring. Cook until slightly thickened.
76 g	¼ c	Salt	
720 mL	3 c	Vinegar	
720 mL	3 c	Water	
			Add hot dressing to warm potatoes, bacon, and eggs. Mix lightly. Serve hot.

Notes:
1. 6 oz (170 g) chopped green pepper may be added.
2. Mayonnaise or a combination of mayonnaise and salad dressing may be used in place of the hot vinegar dressing. Add to potato mixture and heat to serving temperature.

Gelatin Salads
PERFECTION SALAD

Yield: 40 or 48 portions
1 pan 12 × 20 × 2 in.
Portion: 2¼ × 2½ or 2 × 2½ in.

Amount Metric	U.S.	Ingredient	Procedure
85 g	3 oz	Gelatin, unflavored	Sprinkle gelatin over cold water. Let stand 10 minutes.
480 mL	2 c	Water, cold	
2.84 L	3 qt	Water, boiling	Add boiling water. Stir until gelatin is dissolved.
240 mL	1 c	Vinegar	Add vinegar, lemon juice, salt, and sugar. Stir until sugar is dissolved. Chill.
240 mL	1 c	Lemon juice	
28 g	1 oz (1½ T)	Salt	
454 g	1 lb	Sugar, granulated	
680 g (EP)	1 lb 8 oz (EP)	Cabbage, chopped	When liquid begins to congeal, add vegetables. Pour into 12 × 20 × 2-in. counter pan. Place in refrigerator to congeal. Cut 5 × 8 for 40 portions. Cut 6 × 8 for 48 portions.
284 g	10 oz	Celery, chopped	
114 g	4 oz	Pimiento, chopped	
114 g	4 oz	Green pepper, chopped	
7 g	1 T	Paprika	

TOMATO ASPIC

Yield: 40 or 48 portions
1 pan 12 × 20 × 2 in.
Portion: 2¼ × 2½ in. or 2 × 2½ in.

Amount		Ingredient	Procedure
Metric	U.S.		
114 g	4 oz	Gelatin, unflavored	Sprinkle gelatin over cold water. Let stand 10 minutes.
0.95 L	1 qt	Water, cold	
3.79 L	1 gal	Tomato juice	Combine tomato juice and seasonings. Boil 5 minutes. Strain.
2	2	Onions, small, sliced	
1	1	Bay leaf	
4	4	Celery stalks	
8	8	Cloves, whole	
4 g	2 t	Mustard, dry	
397 g	14 oz	Sugar, granulated	
19 g	1 T	Salt	
			Add gelatin to hot juice. Stir until dissolved.
480 mL	2 c	Vinegar or lemon juice	Add vinegar or lemon juice. Pour into 12 × 20 × 2-in. counter pan. Place in refrigerator to congeal. Cut 5 × 8 for 40 portions. Cut 6 × 8 for 48 portions.

FRUIT GELATIN SALAD

Yield: 40 or 48 portions
1 pan 12 × 20 × 2 in.
Portion: 2¼ × 2½ or 2 × 2½ in.

Amount Metric	U.S.	Ingredient	Procedure
680 g	1 lb 8 oz	Gelatin, flavored	Pour boiling water over gelatin. Stir until dissolved.
1.89 L	2 qt	Water, boiling	
1.89 L	2 qt	Fruit juice or water, cold	Add juice or cold water. Chill.
1.36–1.81 kg	3–4 lb	Fruit, drained	Place fruit in counter pan. When gelatin begins to congeal, pour over fruit. Place in refrigerator to congeal.

Notes:
1. For quick preparation, dissolve 24 oz (680 g) flavored gelatin in 1½ qt (1.42 L) boiling water. Measure 2½ qt (2.37 L) chipped or finely crushed ice, then add enough cold water or fruit juice to cover ice. Add to gelatin and stir constantly until ice is melted. Gelatin will begin to congeal at once. Speed of congealing depends on proportion of ice to water and size of ice particles.
2. One or more canned, frozen, or fresh fruits, cut into desired shapes and sizes, may be used. Fresh or frozen pineapple must be cooked before adding to gelatin salad.
3. Fruit juice may be used for part or all of the liquid. Not more than 50% of heavy syrup, however, can be substituted for water.
4. If unflavored granulated gelatin is used, sprinkle 2½ oz (70 g) over 2 c (480 mL) cold water and let stand for 10 minutes. Add 3½ qt (3.31 L) boiling fruit juice and 1 lb (454 g) sugar.

Variations:
1. **Applesauce Gelatin Salad.** Add 24 oz (680 g) lime gelatin to 3 qt (2.84 L) boiling hot applesauce and stir until dissolved. Add 1 qt (0.95 L) ginger ale and pour into salad molds or 12 × 20 × 2-in. pan.
2. **Arabian Peach Salad.** Drain 1 No. 10 can sliced peaches, saving juice. Combine peach juice, 1½ c (360 mL) white vinegar, 1 lb 12 oz (794 g) sugar, 1 oz (28 g) stick cinnamon, and 2 t (4 g) whole cloves. Simmer 10 minutes. Strain, and add enough hot water to make 1 gal (3.79 L) liquid. Add to 24 oz (680 g) orange gelatin and stir until dissolved. When slightly thickened, add peaches. Apricot halves may be substituted for peaches.
3. **Autumn Salad.** Dissolve 24 oz (680 g) orange gelatin in 2 qt (1.89 L) hot water. Add 2 qt (1.89 L) cold liquid, 2½ lb (1.14 kg) sliced fresh peaches and 2½ lb (1.14 kg) fresh pears.

4. **Bing Cherry Salad.** Dissolve 24 oz (680 g) raspberry or cherry gelatin in 1 qt (0.95 L) boiling water. Add 3½ qt (3.31 L) cherry juice and cold water. Add 2 No. 2½ cans bing cherries, pitted, drained, 8 oz (227 g) chopped pecans, and 12 oz (340 g) sliced stuffed olives. 1 No. 10 can crushed pineapple may be substituted for the olives.

5. **Blueberry Gelatin Salad.** Make in two layers. First layer: 12 oz (340 g) raspberry gelatin dissolved in 1 qt (0.95 L) boiling water; add 1 qt (0.95 L) blueberry juice and 6 No. 303 cans blueberries, drained. Chill. Second layer: 12 oz (340 g) lemon gelatin, dissolved in 1 qt (0.95 L) hot pineapple juice; and 1 No. 10 can crushed pineapple, drained, and 1 qt (0.95 L) cultured sour cream. Cool. Pour over first layer.

6. **Cranberry Ring Mold.** Dissolve 24 oz (680 g) cherry or raspberry gelatin in 2 qt (1.89 L) hot water. Add 3 lb (1.36 kg) fresh or frozen cranberry relish, 1 lb (454 g) chopped apples, and 1 lb (454 g) crushed pineapple or 1 No. 10 can whole cranberry sauce and 6 oranges, ground. Pour into individual ring molds or 1 12 × 20 × 2-in. counter pan.

7. **Cucumber Soufflé Salad.** Dissolve 24 oz (680 g) lime or lemon gelatin in 1½ qt (1.42 L) hot water. Add 2 qt (1.89 L) ice and water. Chill until partially set. Whip until fluffy. Add 3 c (720 mL) mayonnaise and ⅓ c (80 mL) lemon juice. Fold in 5 lb (2.27 g) cucumbers (10–12), chopped.

8. **Frosted Cherry Salad.** Dissolve 24 oz (680 g) cherry gelatin in 2 qt (1.89 L) hot water. Add 2 qt (1.89 L) cold fruit juice, 3 lb (1.36 kg) drained, pitted red cherries, and 2 lb (908 g) crushed pineapple. When congealed, frost with whipped cream cheese and chopped toasted almonds.

9. **Frosted Lime Mold.** Dissolve 24 oz (680 g) lime gelatin in 2 qt (1.89 L) hot water. Add 2 qt (1.89 L) cold fruit juice and, when mixture begins to congeal, add 4 lb (1.81 kg) crushed pineapple, drained, 2½ lb (1.14 kg) cottage cheese, 8 oz (227 g) diced celery, 4 oz (114 g) chopped pimiento, and 4 oz (114 g) chopped nuts. When congealed, frost with mixture of 4 lb (1.81 kg) cream cheese blended with ½ c (120 mL) mayonnaise.

10. **Ginger Ale Fruit Salad.** Use lemon gelatin. Substitute 2 qt (1.89 L) ginger ale for 2 qt (1.89 L) cold water. Add 1 lb (454 g) grapes or white cherries, 12 oz (340 g) chopped celery, 1 lb (454 g) cubed apples, 2 lb (908 g) pineapple chunks, drained.

11. **Jellied Citrus Salad.** Dissolve 24 oz (680 g) lemon or orange gelatin in 2 qt (1.89 L) hot water. Add 2 qt (1.89 L) cold water, sections from 15 oranges and 8 grapefruit; or 4 No. 2 cans mandarin oranges and 3 lb (1.36 kg) frozen grapefruit sections.

12. **Jellied Waldorf Salad.** Dissolve 24 oz (680 g) raspberry or cherry gelatin in 2 qt (1.89 L) boiling water. Add 1 c (240 mL) red cinnamon candies and stir until dissolved. Add 2 qt (1.89 L) cold liquid. When mixture begins to congeal, add 2 lb (908 g) diced apple, 12 oz (340 g) finely diced celery, and 8 oz (227 g) chopped pecans or walnuts.

13. **Molded Pineapple–Cheese Salad.** Dissolve 24 oz (680 g) lemon gelatin in 2 qt (1.89 L) hot liquid. Add 2 qt (1.89 L) cold fruit juice, 1 lb (454 g) grated Cheddar cheese, 3 lb (1.36 kg) drained crushed pineapple, 3 oz (85 g) chopped green pepper or pimiento, and 4 oz (114 g) finely chopped celery.

14. **Ribbon Gelatin Salad.** Dissolve 24 oz (680 g) raspberry gelatin in 1 gal (3.79 L) hot water. Divide into 3 equal parts. Pour ⅓ into 1 12 × 20 × 2-in. pan and chill. Add 1 lb (454 g) cream cheese to another third and whip to blend; pour on the first part when it is congealed. Return to the refrigerator until it, too, is congealed, then top with remaining portion.

15. **Strawberry–Rhubarb Salad.** To 4 lb (1.81 kg) frozen rhubarb, add 2 lb (908 g) sugar and 1 qt (0.95 L) water. Cook 5 minutes. Add 4 lb (1.81 kg) frozen sliced strawberries and 24 oz (680 g) strawberry gelatin dissolved in juice from rhubarb and strawberries. Add enough hot water to make 1 gal (3.79 L) liquid.

16. **Sunshine Salad.** Dissolve 24 oz (680 g) lemon gelatin in 2 qt (1.89 L) hot liquid. Add 2 qt (1.89 L) cold fruit juice, 3 lb (1.36 kg) drained crushed pineapple, and 8 oz (227 g) grated raw carrot.

17. **Swedish Green-Top Salad.** Dissolve 12 oz (340 g) lime gelatin in 2 qt (1.89 L) boiling water. Pour into a 12 × 10 × 2-in. pan. Dissolve 12 oz (340 g) orange gelatin in 2 qt (1.89 L) boiling water and stir until dissolved. While mixture is still hot, add 1½ lb (680 g) marshmallows and stir until melted. When cool, add 12 oz (340 g) cream cheese, 1½ c (360 mL) mayonnaise, and ½ t (3 g) salt, blended together. Fold in 1 pt (475 mL) cream, whipped. Pour over congealed lime gelatin and return to refrigerator to chill.

18. **Under-the-Sea Salad.** Dissolve 24 oz (680 g) lime gelatin in 1 gal (3.79 L) hot water. Divide into 2 parts. Pour 1 part into a 12 × 20 × 2-in. pan and chill. When it begins to congeal, add 12 oz (340 g) sliced pears or drained crushed pineapple. To the remaining gelatin mixture, add 1 lb (454 g) cream cheese and whip until smooth. Pour over first portion.

Fruit Salads

WALDORF SALAD

Yield: 50 portions
6 qt (5.68 L)
Portion: ⅓ c (3 oz/85 g)

Amount Metric	U.S.	Ingredient	Procedure
120 mL	½ c	Cream, whipping (optional)	Whip cream. Combine with mayonnaise.
480 mL	2 c	Mayonnaise or salad dressing	
3.63 kg	8 lb EP	Apples, tart (peeled or unpeeled)	Dice apples into fruit juice to prevent apples from turning dark. Drain and stir into salad dressing.
908 g	2 lb EP	Celery, chopped	Add celery, seasonings, and nuts. Mix lightly until all ingredients are coated with dressing. Serve with No. 12 dipper.
28 g	1 oz (1½ T)	Salt	
170 g	6 oz	Sugar (optional)	
227 g	8 oz	Walnuts, coarsely chopped	

Note: Fruit Salad Dressing (p. 445) may be substituted for mayonnaise.

Variations:

1. **Apple–Cabbage Salad.** Use 6 lb (2.72 kg) diced apples and 4 lb (1.81 kg) crisp shredded cabbage. Omit celery. Sour cream or plain yogurt may be substituted for half the mayonnaise.
2. **Apple–Carrot Salad.** Use 6 lb (2.72 kg) diced apples, 3 lb (1.36 kg) shredded carrots, and only 1 lb (454 g) chopped celery.
3. **Apple–Celery Salad.** Delete walnuts. Add 8 oz (227 g) marshmallows.
4. **Apple–Date Salad.** Substitute 2 lb (908 g) cut dates for celery.
5. **Apple–Fruit Salad.** Substitute 4 lb (1.81 kg) fresh fruit in season for half of the apples.

SPICED APPLE SALAD

Yield: 50 portions
Portion: 1 apple

Amount		Ingredient	Procedure
Metric	U.S.		
50	50	Apples, fresh	Core and peel apples. Leave whole unless apples are large; then cut in half crosswise. Place apples in a flat pan.
2.72 kg	6 lb	Sugar, granulated	Combine sugar, water, and flavorings. Boil about 5 minutes to form a thin syrup. Pour over apples. Cook on top of range or in oven until tender. Turn while cooking. Cool.
1.89 L	2 qt	Water	
240 mL	1 c	Vinegar	
3 mL	½ t	Red coloring	
28 g	1 oz	Stick cinnamon or f.d. oil of cinnamon	
28 g	1 oz	Cloves, whole	
227 g	8 oz	Celery, chopped	Combine celery and nuts. Add mayonnaise and salt. Fill centers of cooked apples with this mixture.
114 g	4 oz	Nuts, chopped	
180 mL	¾ c	Mayonnaise	
3 g	½ t	Salt	

Notes:
1. Select apples that will hold their shape when cooked, such as Jonathan, Rome Beauty, or Winesap. Approximately 12 lb (5.44 kg) will be needed.
2. 8 oz (227 g) softened cream cheese may be substituted for mayonnaise.

CREAMY FRUIT SALAD

Yield: 50 portions
6½ qt (6.15 L)
Portion: ½ c (4 oz/114 g)

Amount Metric	U.S.	Ingredient	Procedure
2.37 L	2½ qt	Fruit Salad Dressing (p. 445)	Make salad dressing. Chill.
1.81 kg	4 lb	Pineapple chunks	Combine fruits. Drain.
1.81 kg	4 lb	Oranges, peeled and diced	Add salad dressing. Mix lightly.
1.36 kg	3 lb	Apples, tart (pared or unpared), diced	
908 g	2 lb	Bananas, peeled and sliced	

Notes:
1. Any combination of canned or fresh fruit in season may be substituted.
2. 8 oz (227 g) miniature marshmallows, chopped nuts, or coconut may be added.

GRAPEFRUIT–ORANGE SALAD

Yield: 50 portions
Portion: 2 orange, 3 grapefruit sections

Amount		Ingredient	Procedure
Metric	U.S.		
16	16	Grapefruit, medium	Pare and section fruit according to directions on p. 339. For each salad, arrange 3 sections of grapefruit and 2 sections of orange alternately on lettuce or other salad garnish. Serve with Celery Seed Fruit Dressing (p. 444) or Honey French Dressing (p. 445).
17	17	Oranges, large	

Variations:

1. **Citrus–Pomegranate Salad.** Arrange grapefruit and orange sections on curly endive. Sprinkle pomegranate seeds over fruit. Serve with Celery Seed Dressing (p. 443).
2. **Fresh Fruit Salad Bowl.** Place chopped lettuce or other salad greens in individual salad bowls (2 oz/57 g per bowl). Arrange wedges of cantaloupe, honeydew melon, and avocado, and sections of orange or grapefruit on the lettuce. Garnish with green grapes or bing cherries. Fresh pineapple, peaches, or apricots also are good in this salad. Serve with Celery Seed Fruit Dressing (p. 444) or Honey French Dressing (p. 445).
3. **Grapefruit–Apple Salad.** Substitute wedges of unpeeled red apples for oranges.
4. **Grapefruit–Orange–Avocado Salad.** Place avocado wedges between grapefruit and orange sections. Garnish with fresh strawberries.
5. **Grapefruit–Orange–Pear Salad.** Alternate slices of fresh pear with grapefruit and orange sections.

FROZEN FRUIT SALAD

Yield: 48 portions
1 pan 12 × 20 × 2 in.
Portion: 4 oz (114 g)

Amount Metric	U.S.	Ingredient	Procedure
28 g	1 oz	Gelatin, unflavored	Sprinkle gelatin over cold water. Let stand 10 minutes.
120 mL	½ c	Water, cold	
420 mL	1¾ c	Orange Juice	Combine juices and heat to boiling point. Add gelatin. Stir to dissolve. Cool until slightly congealed.
420 mL	1¾ c	Pineapple juice	
480 mL	2 c	Cream, whipping	Whip cream. Combine with mayonnaise. Fold into the slightly congealed gelatin mixture.
240 mL	1 c	Mayonnaise	
794 g	1 lb 12 oz	Pineapple chunks, drained	Fold fruit into gelatin mixture. Pour into 12 × 20 × 2-in. counter pan or into molds. Freeze. Cut 6 × 8.
680 g	1 lb 8 oz	Orange sections, cut in halves	
680 g	1 lb 8 oz	Peaches, sliced, drained	
908 g	2 lb	Bananas, diced	
340 g	12 oz	Pecans, chopped	
227 g	8 oz	Maraschino cherries	
227 g	8 oz	Marshmallows, miniature	

Notes:
1. Whipped topping may be used in place of whipped cream.
2. Other combinations of fruit (a total of 8 lb/3.6 kg) may be used.

Relishes

BUTTERED APPLES

Yield: 50 portions
7 qt (6.62 L)
Portion: ½ c (4 oz/114 g)

Amount Metric	Amount U.S.	Ingredient	Procedure
7.26 kg (5.9 kg)	16 lb (AP) (13 lb EP)	Apples, fresh	Wash apples and cut into sections. Remove cores. Arrange in pan.
227 g	8 oz	Margarine or butter, melted	Mix remaining ingredients and pour over apples. Cover and simmer until apples are tender, approximately 1 hour.
480 mL	2 c	Water, hot	
680 g	1 lb 8 oz	Sugar, granulated	
28 g	1½ T	Salt	

Notes:
1. Apple sections may be arranged in a counter pan and steamed until tender. Sprinkle margarine and sugar over the top and bake for 15–20 minutes.
2. Hot buttered apples often are served in place of a vegetable.
3. Frozen or canned apples may be used.

Variations:
1. **Apple Rings.** Cut rings of unpared apples, steam until tender. Add sugar and margarine or butter and bake 15 minutes.
2. **Cinnamon Apples.** Cut apples into rings. Add cinnamon drops (redhots) for flavor and color. Proceed as for Buttered Apples but reduce sugar to 12 oz (340 g).
3. **Fried Apples.** Melt 1 lb (454 g) margarine or butter in frypan. Add sliced apples. Add 8 oz (227 g) brown sugar, 1 t (6 g) salt, and 1 t (2 g) cinnamon. Cook apples, turning occasionally, until apples are lightly browned and just tender. Frozen apple slices, thawed and drained, may be used.

CRANBERRY RELISH (RAW)

Yield: 50 portions
5 qt (4.73 L)
Portion: ⅓ c (3 oz/85 g)

Amount		Ingredient	Procedure
Metric	U.S.		
3 (size 72)	3 (size 72)	Oranges, unpeeled	Wash and quarter oranges and apples.
2.27 kg	5 lb	Apples, cored	Sort and wash cranberries.
1.36 kg	3 lb	Cranberries, raw	Put fruit through chopper or grinder.
1.02 kg	2 lb 4 oz	Sugar, granulated	Add sugar and blend. Chill 24 hours. Serve with No. 16 dipper as a relish or salad.

Variation: **Cranberry–Orange Relish.** Delete apples. Increase oranges to 6 and sugar to 3 lb (1.36 kg); add ¼ c (60 mL) lemon juice.

CRANBERRY SAUCE

Yield: 50 portions
5 qt (4.73 L)
Portion: ⅓ c (3 oz/85 g)

Amount		Ingredient	Procedure
Metric	U.S.		
1.81 kg	4 lb (AP)	Cranberries	Wash cranberries. Discard soft berries.
1.81 kg	4 lb	Sugar, granulated	Combine sugar and water. Bring to a boil. Add cranberries and boil gently until skins burst. Do not overcook. Chill. Serve with No. 16 dipper.
0.95 L	1 qt	Water	

Note: Make sauce at least 24 hours before using.

Variations:
1. **Puréed Cranberry Sauce.** Add water to cranberries and cook until skins burst. Purée cranberries and add sugar. Cook until sugar is dissolved.
2. **Royal Cranberry Sauce.** Make half of cranberry sauce recipe. When cool add 3 oranges, chopped; 1 lb (454 g) apples, chopped; 1 lb (454 g) white grapes, seeded; 1 lb (454 g) pineapple, diced; and 4 oz (114 g) chopped pecans. Serve with No. 24 dipper as a relish. Yield: 1 gal (3.79 L).

PICKLED BEETS

Yield: 50 portions
2 gal (7.57 L)
Portion: 3 oz (85 g)

Amount Metric	U.S.	Ingredient	Procedure
1.89 L	2 qt	Vinegar, mild	Mix vinegar, sugar, and spices. Heat to boiling point. Boil 5 minutes.
454 g	1 lb	Sugar, brown	
227 g	8 oz	Sugar, granulated	
6 g	1 t	Salt	
1 g	½ t	Pepper, black	
2	2	Cinnamon, stick	
2 g	1 t	Cloves, whole	
2 g	1 t	Allspice	
4.54 kg	10 lb EP or 2 No. 10 cans	Beets, cooked, sliced	Pour hot, spiced vinegar over beets. Chill 24 hours before serving.

Notes:
1. Add onion rings if desired.
2. Whole baby beets may be used.

SAUERKRAUT RELISH

Yield: 50 portions
Portion: ⅓ c (3 oz/85 g)

Amount Metric	U.S.	Ingredient	Procedure
1 No. 10 can	1 No. 10 can	Sauerkraut	Combine all ingredients. Refrigerate for at least 12 hours.
454 g	1 lb	Carrots, grated	
340 g	12 oz	Celery, diced	
227 g	8 oz	Onion, chopped	
454 g	1 lb	Green pepper, chopped	
680 g	1 lb 8 oz	Sugar, granulated	

Note: Sauerkraut may be chopped before combining with other ingredients.

Entrée Salads

CHEF'S SALAD BOWL

Yield: 50 portions
Portion: 7 oz (198 g)

Amount			
Metric	U.S.	Ingredient	Procedure
5.44 kg	12 lb	Head lettuce or mixed greens	Break or cut lettuce into bite-sized pieces. Portion into individual salad bowls, 4 oz (114 g) per bowl.
2.72 kg	6 lb	Cooked turkey	Cut meat and cheese into thin strips. Arrange on top of lettuce, 2 oz (57 g) turkey and 1 oz (28 g) each of ham and cheese per bowl.
1.36 kg	3 lb	Cooked ham	
1.36 kg	3 lb	Cheddar cheese or Swiss cheese	
50 (3.63 kg)	50 (8 lb AP)	Green pepper rings	Garnish with 1 green pepper ring, 2 tomato wedges, and 2 egg quarters.
2.72 kg	6 lb AP	Tomatoes, cut into wedges	
25	25	Eggs, hard-cooked, quartered	
1.4–1.8 L	1½–2 qt	Salad dressing[a]	

[a] Suggested salad dressings: mayonnaise, Thousand Island, Roquefort, or creamy French.

Variations:

1. **Chicken and Bacon Salad.** Delete ham and cheese. Mix 6 lb (2.72 kg) chicken or turkey with salad greens. Sprinkle 4 lb (1.81 kg) chopped, crisply cooked bacon over top of salads, 1 oz (28 g) per salad.

2. **Seafood Chef Salad.** Delete turkey and ham. Substitute 1 oz (28 g) tuna or salmon, drained and broken into small chunks, 1 oz (28 g) shrimp pieces or 2 whole shrimp.

CHICKEN SALAD

Yield: 50 portions
6¼ qt (5.91 L)
Portion: ½ c (4 oz/114 g)

Amount		Ingredient	Procedure
Metric	U.S.		
3.63 kg	8 lb	Cooked chicken	Cut chicken into ½-in. cubes.
12	12	Eggs, hard-cooked (p. 256)	Peel and dice eggs.
1.36 kg	3 lb	Celery, diced	Combine all ingredients.
38 g	2 T	Salt	Mix lightly. Chill.
2 g	1 t	Pepper, white	Serve with No. 10 dipper.
0.95 L	1 qt	Mayonnaise	
20 mL	4 t	Lemon juice	
10 g	2 T	Onion, minced	

Notes:
1. 24-25 lb (10-11 kg) chickens AP will yield approximately 8 lb (3.63 kg) cooked meat.
2. Cubed chicken may be marinated in ⅔ c (160 mL) French dressing for 2 hours.

Variations:
1. **Chicken–Avocado–Orange Salad.** Delete eggs. Add 1 qt (0.95 L) diced orange segments, 12 oz (340 g) broken toasted almonds, and 6 oz (170 g) chopped pimiento. Just before serving, add 6 avocados, diced.
2. **Crunchy Chicken Salad.** Add 8 oz (227 g) sliced water chestnuts or coarsely chopped nuts.
3. **Curried Chicken Salad.** Add 1 T (7 g) curry powder to mayonnaise.
4. **Fruited Chicken Salad.** Just before serving add 2½ lb (1.14 kg) seedless grapes or pineapple chunks, drained, and 8 oz (227 g) sunflower seeds.
5. **Turkey Salad.** Substitute turkey for chicken.

COTTAGE CHEESE SALAD

Yield: 50 portions
6 qt (5.68 L)
Portion: ½ c (4 oz/114 g)

Amount Metric	U.S.	Ingredient	Procedure
1.36 kg	3 lb	Tomatoes, fresh, peeled and diced	Combine ingredients and mix lightly. Chill.
114 g	4 oz	Green peppers, chopped	Serve with No. 10 dipper.
454 g	1 lb	Celery, diced	
454 g	1 lb	Cucumber, diced	
227 g	8 oz	Radishes, sliced	
2.72 kg	6 lb	Cottage cheese, dry	
57 g	2 oz (3 T)	Salt	
720 mL	3 c	Mayonnaise (use less if cheese contains cream)	

SHRIMP–RICE SALAD

Yield: 50 portions
Portion: ½ c (4 oz/114 g)

Amount Metric	U.S.	Ingredient	Procedure
454 g	1 lb	Rice, long-grain	Cook rice according to directions on p. 358. Chill.
1.18 L	1¼ qt	Water	
19 g	1 T	Salt	
2.27 kg	5 lb	Cooked shrimp, chilled	Combine cooked rice, shrimp, celery, and green peppers.
680 g	1 lb 8 oz	Celery, sliced crosswise, thin	
454 g	1 lb	Green peppers, sliced in thin strips	
250 mL	1 c	Vinegar	Combine and pour over shrimp–rice mixture. Marinate at least 3 hours.
120 mL	½ c	Salad oil	
30 mL	2 T	Worcestershire sauce	
28 g	2 T	Sugar, granulated	
19 g	1 T	Salt	
4 g	2 t	Curry powder	
1 g	¾ t	Ginger	
1 g	½ t	Pepper, black	
1.36 kg	3 lb	Pineapple tidbits, drained	Just before serving, add pineapple. Serve with No. 8 dipper.

SHRIMP SALAD

Yield: 50 portions
6¼ qt (5.91 L)
Portion: ½ c (4 oz/114 g)

Amount Metric	U.S.	Ingredient	Procedure
2.72 kg	6 lb	Cooked shrimp[a]	Cut shrimp into ½-in. pieces. Place in bowl.
908 g	2 lb	Celery, diced	Add vegetables to shrimp.
454 g	1 lb	Cucumber, diced	
1 head	1 head	Lettuce, chopped (optional)	
0.95 L	1 qt	Mayonnaise	Combine mayonnaise and seasonings.
30 mL	2 T	Lemon juice	
12 g	2 t	Salt	Add to shrimp mixture.
2 g	1 t	Paprika	Mix lightly. Chill.
10 g	2 t	Mustard, prepared	Serve with No. 10 dipper.

[a] 10 lb (4.54 kg) raw, peeled, and deveined; or 12 lb (5.4 kg) raw shrimp in shell. Cook according to directions on p. 281.

Notes:
1. 1 doz hard-cooked eggs, coarsely chopped, may be added; reduce shrimp to 5 lb (2.27 kg).
2. May be garnished with tomato wedges or served in a tomato cup.

CRAB SALAD

Yield: 50 portions
6 qt (5.68 L)
Portion: ½ c (4 oz/114 g)

Amount Metric	U.S.	Ingredient	Procedure
30	30	Eggs, hard-cooked (p. 256)	Peel and chop eggs coarsely.
2.27 kg	5 lb	Crab meat	Flake crab meat coarsely.
454 g	1 lb	Almonds, blanched, slivered (optional)	Add eggs and other ingredients. Mix lightly. Chill.
454 g	1 lb	Ripe olives, sliced	Serve with No. 10 dipper.
80 mL	⅓ c	Lemon juice	
0.95 L	1 qt	Mayonnaise	

Notes:
1. Olives may be deleted and 1 lb (454 g) diced cucumbers added.
2. If desired, omit mayonnaise and marinate with French dressing.

Variation: **Lobster Salad.** Substitute lobster for crab.

TUNA SALAD

Yield: 50 portions
6¼ qt (5.91 L)
Portion: ½ c (4 oz/114 g)

Amount Metric	U.S.	Ingredient	Procedure
12	12	Eggs, hard-cooked (p. 256)	Peel and dice eggs.
3.18 kg	7 lb	Tuna, flaked	Add celery, cucumber, onion, relish, and eggs to tuna. Mix lightly.
454 g	1 lb	Celery, chopped	
454 g	1 lb	Cucumber, diced	
227 g	8 oz	Pickle relish, drained	
57 g	2 oz	Onion, minced	
0.95 L	1 qt	Mayonnaise	Add mayonnaise. Mix lightly to blend. Chill. Serve with No. 10 dipper.

Variations:
1. **Tuna–Apple Salad.** Substitute tart, diced apples for cucumbers. Omit pickle relish.
2. **Salmon Salad.** Substitute salmon for tuna.

STUFFED TOMATO SALAD

Yield: 50 portions
Portion: 1 tomato

Amount Metric	U.S.	Ingredient	Procedure
50	50	Tomatoes, medium size	Place tomatoes in a wire basket and dip in boiling water. Let stand 1 minute. Dip in cold water. Remove skins. Chill.
4.54 kg	10 lb	Chicken, crab, shrimp, tuna, or egg salad	Turn tomato stem-end down. Cut, not quite through, into fourths. Fill with No. 12 dipper of salad.

Note: 50 medium-sized tomatoes will weigh approximately 12 lb (5.44 kg).

Variations:
1. **Tomato–Cabbage Salad.** Stuff with No. 40 dipper of mixture: 1 lb (454 g) cabbage and 1 lb (454 g) celery, chopped fine; 1 T (19 g) salt, mixed with 1 c (240 mL) mayonnaise.
2. **Tomato–Cottage Cheese Salad.** Substitute 6 lb (2.72 kg) cottage cheese, seasoned, for salad mixture. Fill tomato cups, using No. 20 dipper.

SALAD DRESSING RECIPES

MAYONNAISE

Yield: 1 gal (3.79 L)

Amount Metric	U.S.	Ingredient	Procedure
8 (142 g)	8 (5 oz)	Egg yolks[a]	Place egg yolks and seasonings in mixer bowl. Mix thoroughly.
57 g	2 oz (3 T)	Salt	
4 g	2 t	Paprika	
14 g	2 T	Mustard, dry	
60 mL	¼ c	Vinegar	Add vinegar and blend.
1.89 L	2 qt	Salad oil	Add oil very slowly, beating steadily on high speed until an emulsion is formed. Oil may then be added, ½ c at a time and later 1 c at a time, beating well after each addition.
60 mL	¼ c	Vinegar	Add vinegar. Beat well.
1.89 L	2 qt	Salad oil	Continue beating and adding oil until all oil has been added and emulsified.

[a] 4 whole eggs (14 oz/397 g) may be used in place of egg yolks.

Note: The addition of oil too rapidly or insufficient beating may cause the oil to separate from the other ingredients, resulting in a curdled appearance. Curdled or broken mayonnaise may be reformed by adding it (a small amount at a time and beating well after each addition) to 2 well-beaten egg yolks or eggs. It also may be reformed by adding it to a small portion of uncurdled mayonnaise.

Variations for approximately 2 qt (1.89 L) dressing:

1. **Buttermilk Dressing.** To 1 qt (0.95 L) mayonnaise, add 1 qt (0.95 L) buttermilk, 2 t (2 g) basil, ½ t oregano, 1 T (2 g) finely chopped fresh parsley, 1 clove garlic, minced, 2 t (4 g) black pepper, 2 oz (57 g) chopped onion, and 1 t (1 g) tarragon.
2. **Campus Dressing.** Combine ⅓ c (20 g) chopped parsley, ¼ c (36 g) chopped green pepper, and ½ c (56 g) finely chopped celery with 2 qt (1.89 L) mayonnaise.
3. **Chantilly Dressing.** Whip 1½ c (360 mL) heavy cream and fold in 1½ qt (1.42 L) mayonnaise.
4. **Creamy Blue Cheese Dressing.** Add 2 c (480 mL) cultured sour cream, ¼ c (60 mL) lemon juice, 1 T (15 mL) grated onion, 1 t (6 g) salt, and 8 oz (227 g) blue cheese, crumbled fine, to 1 qt (0.95 L) mayonnaise.

5. **Dilly Dressing.** To 1½ qt (1.42 L) mayonnaise, add 2 c (480 mL) evaporated milk or buttermilk, 1 T (19 g) seasoned salt, 1 t (2 g) garlic powder, ¼ c (21 g) dill weed, chopped.
6. **Egg and Green Pepper Dressing.** Combine 12 chopped, hard-cooked eggs, ¼ c (56 g) finely chopped green pepper, 2 T (30 mL) onion juice, and a few grains cayenne with 1¾ qt (1.66 L) mayonnaise.
7. **Garden Dressing.** Combine 1½ qt (1.42 L) cultured sour cream and 3 c (720 mL) mayonnaise. Add 3 oz (85 g) sugar, 2 t (12 g) salt, and 1 t (2 g) black pepper. Fold in 12 oz (340 g) thinly sliced green onions, 8 oz (227 g) thinly sliced radishes, 8 oz (227 g) chopped cucumbers, and 8 oz (227 g) minced green pepper.
8. **Honey–Cream Dressing.** Blend 4 oz (114 g) cream cheese, 1⅓ c (320 mL) honey, 1 c (240 mL) lemon or pineapple juice, and ¼ t (1 g) salt. Fold in 1½ qt (1.42 L) mayonnaise.
9. **Roquefort Dressing.** Add 2 c (480 mL) French dressing, 8 oz (227 g) Roquefort cheese, crumbled, and 2 t (10 mL) Worcestershire sauce to 1½ qt (1.42 L) mayonnaise.
10. **Russian Dressing.** Add 2 c (480 mL) chili sauce, 2 T (30 mL) Worcestershire sauce, 2 t (10 mL) onion juice, and f.g. cayenne to 2 qt (1.89 L) mayonnaise.
11. **Thousand Island Dressing.** To 1½ qt (1.42 L) mayonnaise, add 1½ oz (43 g) minced onion, 3 oz (85 g) chopped pimiento, 1 c (240 mL) chili sauce, 8 chopped hard-cooked eggs, 1 t (6 g) salt, ¼ c (60 mL) pickle relish, and f.g. cayenne.

SOUR CREAM DRESSING

Yield: 2 qt (1.89 L)

Amount Metric	Amount U.S.	Ingredient	Procedure
16 (794 g) 0.95 L	16 (1 lb 12 oz) 1 qt	Eggs, beaten Cultured sour cream	Mix eggs and sour cream.
908 g 43 g 240 mL	2 lb 1½ oz 1 c	Sugar, granulated Flour, all-purpose Water	Combine sugar and flour. Add water and mix only until smooth. Add to the cream and egg mixture.
480 mL	2 c	Vinegar	Add vinegar. Cook until thick. Stir as necessary.

Note: 1 pt (480 mL) cream, whipped, may be added before serving.

MAYONNAISE WITH COOKED BASE

Yield: 3 gal (11.36 L)

Amount Metric	U.S.	Ingredient	Procedure
454 g	1 lb	Cornstarch	Mix cornstarch and water to a smooth paste.
480 mL	2 c	Water, cold	
1.89 L	2 qt	Water, boiling	Add boiling water, stirring vigorously with a wire whip. Cook until mixture is clear. Pour into mixer bowl. Beat on medium speed until cool.
20 (340 g)	20 (12 oz)	Egg yolks[a]	Add eggs, ¼ at a time, while beating on high speed.
57 g	2 oz (3 T)	Salt	Add seasonings. Mix well.
4 g	2 t	Paprika	
28 g	¼ c	Mustard, dry	
480 mL	2 c	Vinegar	Add vinegar. Blend.
3.79 L	1 gal	Salad oil	Gradually add oil, 1 c (240 mL) at a time. Beat well on high speed after each addition.
480 mL	2 c	Vinegar	Add vinegar, then add oil slowly, beating constantly.
3.79 L	1 gal	Salad oil	

[a] 12 whole eggs (1 lb 5 oz/595 g) may be used in place of egg yolks.

COOKED SALAD DRESSING

Yield: 3 gal (11.36 L)

Amount			
Metric	U.S.	Ingredient	Procedure
1.36 kg	3 lb	Sugar, granulated	Combine dry ingredients.
680 g	1 lb 8 oz	Flour, all-purpose	
170 g	6 oz	Salt	
85 g	3 oz	Mustard, dry	
0.95 L	1 qt	Water, cold	Add water and stir until a smooth paste is formed.
3.79 L	1 gal	Milk, hot	Add hot milk and water, stirring continuously while adding. Cook 20 minutes, or until thickened.
1.89 L	2 qt	Water, hot	
454 g	1 lb	Margarine or butter	Add margarine and vinegar.
2.84 L	3 qt	Vinegar, hot	
50 (908 g)	50 (2 lb)	Egg yolks, beaten	Add cooked mixture slowly to egg yolks, stirring briskly. Cook 7–10 minutes. Remove from heat and cool.

Note: 25 whole eggs may be substituted for egg yolks, and hot water for hot milk.

Variations:

1. **Chantilly Dressing.** Add 2 c (480 mL) cream, whipped, to 1 qt (0.95 L) cooked salad dressing.
2. **Combination Dressing.** Combine 1 qt (0.95 L) cooked salad dressing and 1 qt (0.95 L) mayonnaise.

FRENCH DRESSING (LIGHT)

Yield: 3 qt (2.84 L)

Amount Metric	U.S.	Ingredient	Procedure
57 g	3 T	Salt	Combine dry ingredients in mixer bowl.
14 g	2 T	Mustard, dry	
14 g	2 T	Paprika	
7 g	1 T	Pepper, black	
1.89 L	2 qt	Salad oil	Add oil, vinegar, and onion juice. Beat on high speed until thick and blended. This is a temporary emulsion that separates rapidly. Beat well or pour into a jar and shake vigorously just before serving.
0.95 L	1 qt	Vinegar	
20 mL	4 t	Onion juice	

Variations for approximately 2 qt (1.89 L) dressing:

1. **Chiffonade Dressing.** Add 3 T (12 g) chopped parsley, 2 oz (57 g) chopped onion, 3 oz (85 g) chopped green pepper, 2 oz (57 g) chopped red pepper or pimiento, and 8 chopped hard-cooked eggs to 1½ qt (1.42 L) French dressing.
2. **Italian Dressing.** Delete paprika. Add 2 t (2 g) oregano, ¼ t garlic powder, and 1 T basil.
3. **Mexican Dressing.** Add 5 oz (142 g) chopped green pepper, 1½ c (360 mL) chili sauce, and 2 oz (57 g) chopped onion to 1½ qt (1.42 L) French dressing.
4. **Oil and Vinegar.** Delete mustard, paprika, and onion juice.
5. **Piquante Dressing.** Add 1 T (15 mL) mustard, 1 t (5 mL) Worcestershire sauce, and 1 T (15 mL) onion juice to 2 qt (1.89 L) French dressing.
6. **Roquefort Cheese Dressing.** Add slowly 1½ qt (1.42 L) French dressing, while whipping, into 8 oz (227 g) finely crumbled Roquefort cheese. 2 c (480 mL) cream may be mixed with cheese before adding French dressing.
7. **Tarragon Dressing.** Use tarragon vinegar in place of cider vinegar.
8. **Tomato Dressing.** Add 8 oz (227 g) sugar, 2 t (10 mL) onion juice, and 3 c (720 mL) tomato soup to 1½ qt (1.42 L) French dressing. 2 T (30 mL) celery or poppy seed may be added.
9. **Vinaigrette Dressing.** Add 1½ c (360 mL) chopped pickle, 6 oz (170 g) chopped green olives, ⅓ c (20 g) chopped parsley, 2 t (10 mL) onion juice, and ¼ c (60 mL) capers to 1½ qt (1.42 L) French dressing.

FRENCH DRESSING (THICK)

Yield: 1½ qt (1.42 L)

Amount Metric	U.S.	Ingredient	Procedure
908 g	2 lb	Sugar, granulated	Combine sugar and seasonings in mixer bowl.
14 g	2 T	Paprika	
8 g	4 t	Mustard, dry	
38 g	2 T	Salt	
8 mL	1½ t	Onion juice	
320 mL	1⅓ c	Vinegar	Add vinegar. Mix well.
0.95 L	1 qt	Salad oil	Gradually add oil in small amounts. Beat well after each addition.

Variations:
1. **Celery Seed Dressing.** Add 2 oz (57 g) celery seed.
2. **Poppy Seed Dressing.** Add 1 oz (28 g) poppy seed.

FRENCH DRESSING (SEMIPERMANENT)

Yield: 1¼ qt (1.18 L)

Amount Metric	U.S.	Ingredient	Procedure
20 mL	4 t	Gelatin, unflavored	Sprinkle gelatin over cold water. Let stand 10 minutes.
60 mL	¼ c	Water, cold	
120 mL	½ c	Water, boiling	Add hot water. Stir until dissolved. Chill.
8 g	4 t	Mustard, dry	Combine dry ingredients in mixer bowl.
8 g	4 t	Paprika	
57 g	3 T	Sugar, granulated	
f.g.	f.g.	Red pepper	
38 g	2 T	Salt	
0.95 L	1 qt	Salad oil	Add oil slowly while beating on high speed.
240 mL	1 c	Vinegar	Add vinegar slowly. Beat on high speed for 5 minutes. Stir in gelatin.

BACON DRESSING

Yield: 2 qt (1.89 L)

Metric	U.S.	Ingredient	Procedure
340 g	12 oz	Bacon, cut into 1-in. pieces	Fry bacon until crisp. Remove from grease.
114 g	4 oz	Onions, finely chopped	Sauté onions in bacon grease.
227 g	8 oz	Sugar, granulated	Add sugar, vinegar, and water. Bring to boiling point. Cool.
60 mL	¼ c	Vinegar	
360 mL	1½ c	Water	
720 mL	3 c	Mayonnaise	Place mayonnaise in mixer bowl. Add cooled onion–vinegar mixture slowly, beating on low speed until smooth. Stir in bacon pieces.

CELERY SEED FRUIT DRESSING

Yield: 2 qt (1.89 L)

Metric	U.S.	Ingredient	Procedure
680 g	1 lb 8 oz	Sugar, granulated	Mix dry ingredients.
50 g	⅓ c	Cornstarch	
14 g	2 T	Mustard, dry	
38 g	2 T	Salt	
14 g	2 T	Paprika	
480 mL	2 c	Vinegar	Add vinegar. Cook until thickened and clear.
5 mL	1 t	Onion juice	Add onion juice. Cool to room temperature.
0.95 L	1 qt	Salad oil	Add oil slowly while beating on high speed.
14 g	2 T	Celery seed	Add celery seed. Serve with any fruit salad combination.

Variation: **Poppy Seed Dressing.** Add poppy seed in place of celery seed.

FRUIT SALAD DRESSING

Yield: 4½ qt (4.26 L)

Amount Metric	U.S.	Ingredient	Procedure
0.95 L	1 qt	Pineapple juice	Combine juices. Heat to boiling point.
720 mL	3 c	Orange juice	
480 mL	2 c	Lemon juice	
908 g	2 lb	Sugar, granulated	Mix sugar and cornstarch. Add to hot mixture while stirring with a wire whip.
142 g	5 oz	Cornstarch	
16 (794 g)	16 (1 lb 12 oz)	Eggs, beaten	Add eggs to hot mixture while stirring. Cook until thickened. Chill.
480 mL	2 c	Cream, whipping	Whip cream and fold in just before serving. Serve with fruit salads.

HONEY FRENCH DRESSING

Yield: 2 qt (1.89 L)

Amount Metric	U.S.	Ingredient	Procedure
8 g	4 t	Mustard, dry	Mix mustard, salt, and celery seed in large mixing bowl.
6 g	1 t	Salt	
9 g	4 t	Celery seed or poppy seed	
480 mL	2 c	Honey	While mixing, add remaining ingredients in order listed.
300 mL	1¼ c	Vinegar	
60 mL	¼ c	Lemon juice	
6 g	1 T	Grated onion	
0.95 L	1 qt	Salad oil	

CHILEAN DRESSING

Yield: 1½ qt (1.42 L)

Amount Metric	U.S.	Ingredient	Procedure
480 mL	2 c	Salad oil	Combine all ingredients.
240 mL	1 c	Vinegar	Beat on low speed until well blended.
114 g	4 oz	Sugar, granulated	
12 g	2 t	Salt	Store in covered container.
57 g	2 oz	Onion, finely chopped	Shake or beat well before serving.
480 mL	2 c	Chili sauce	
240 mL	1 c	Catsup	

Sandwiches

Sandwiches may be served hot or cold, closed or open-faced. A variety of breads and rolls are available that add variety in flavor, texture, size, and shape.

MAKING SANDWICHES

PREPARATION OF INGREDIENTS
1. Soften margarine or butter by letting it stand at room temperature. Allow 1 lb (454 g) to spread 100 slices, 1 t each. Margarine or butter helps to prevent fillings from soaking into the bread. If mayonnaise is used on one side, allow 1 c (240 mL). Margarine or butter may be whipped for easy spreading. See p. 451.
2. Cut foods such as cheese, tomatoes, and meat into even slices. Very thinly sliced meat, 1−2 oz (28−57 g) gives greater volume and may be more tender than one thick slice.
3. Prepare mixed fillings the day they are to be served. Prepare only in such quantities as will be used during one serving period. Avoid leftovers. For 50 sandwiches, allow 2½ qt (2.37 L), and portion with a No. 20 dipper.
4. Wash lettuce thoroughly; core, separate leaves, drain, and crisp. Allow 3 medium heads for 50 sandwiches.

CLOSED SANDWICHES
1. Prepare filling and spread.
2. Arrange fresh bread in rows, preferably 4 rows of 10 slices each.
3. Spread all bread slices out to the edges with softened margarine or butter.
4. Portion filling with dipper or spoon on alternate rows of bread and spread to the edges, or arrange sliced filling to fit sandwich.
5. If lettuce is used, arrange leaves on filling. Omit lettuce if sandwiches are to be held for some time.
6. Place plain buttered slices of bread on the filled slices.
7. Stack several sandwiches together and cut with a sharp knife.
8. To keep sandwiches fresh, place in sandwich bags or plastic wrap. Or place sandwiches in storage pans on damp towel covered with waxed paper and cover completely with more waxed paper and a damp towel. Avoid stack-

ing sandwiches more than 3 high, as this insulates the filling and prevents it from reaching the desired temperature as quickly as it should.

9. Refrigerate until serving time. If freezing sandwiches for later use, see precautions on p. 450.
10. Handle bread and fillings as little as possible during preparation. Avoid the use of hands in direct contact with foods if tools or equipment can do the job efficiently. Consider plastic gloves as necessary equipment.

GRILLED AND TOASTED SANDWICHES

1. For a grilled sandwich, place filling between two slices of bread. Fillings may be cheese, meat, fish, or poultry salads; or a combination of fillings as in Reuben Sandwiches (p. 464).
2. Brush the outside with melted margarine or butter. For large quantities, a paint roller dipped in the melted spread may be used. See Fig. 2.26.
3. Brown on the grill, in a hot oven, or under a broiler.
4. For a toasted sandwich, toast the bread before filling.

OPEN-FACED HOT SANDWICHES

1. Place buttered or unbuttered bread on a serving plate.
2. Cover with hot meat or other filling.
3. Top with gravy, sauce, or other topping.
4. For a hot sandwich that is to be broiled, arrange slices of bread on a baking pan. Cover with slices of cheese or other topping. Broil just before serving.

CANAPÉS

1. Remove crusts from bread.
2. Cut into desired shapes.
3. Spread with softened butter.
4. Cover with filling.
5. Decorate with parsley, sliced olives, sliced radishes, pimiento pieces, chopped hard-cooked eggs, or other garnish.

RIBBON SANDWICHES

1. Spread one or more fillings on slices of white and whole wheat bread.
2. Make stacks of 5 slices of bread, alternating whole wheat and white.
3. Press firmly together.
4. Cut off crusts.
5. Arrange stacks in shallow pan; cover with waxed paper and moist cloth.
6. Chill for several hours.
7. To serve, cut each slice into thirds, halves, or triangles.

MAKING SANDWICHES 449

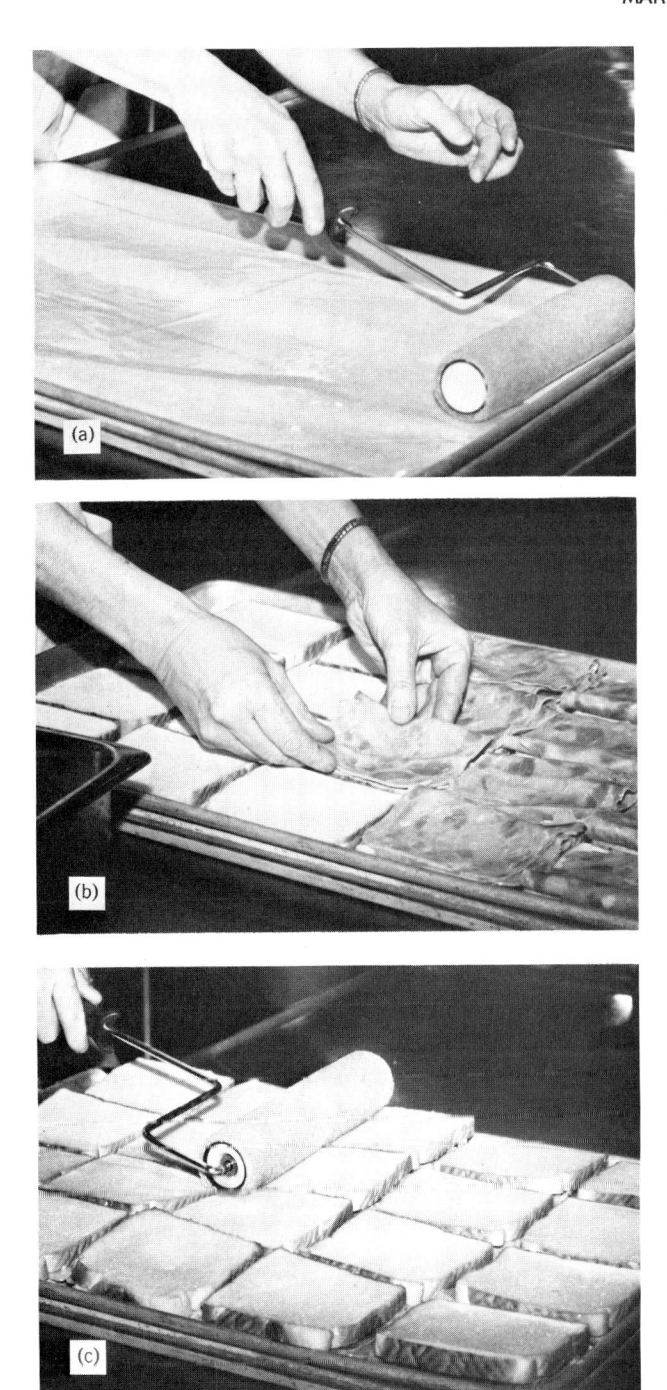

Figure 2.26 Preparing sandwiches for grilling. (a) Place parchment paper in bottom of sheet pan. Apply melted margarine or butter with brush, or with paint roller as shown in this picture. (b) Place bread slices directly on coated paper. Add filling to all slices in pan. (c) Top with slices of bread. Apply melted margarine or butter with brush or paint roller.

CHECKERBOARD SANDWICHES

1. Spread slices of white and whole wheat bread with desired filling.
2. Make stacks of ribbon sandwiches by alternating 2 slices of white and 2 slices of whole wheat bread. Trim and cut each stack into ½-in. slices.
3. Using butter or smooth spread as a filling, stack 3 slices together so that white and whole wheat squares alternate to give a checkerboard effect.
4. Chill for several hours.
5. Remove from refrigerator and, with sharp knife, slice into checkerboard slices, ½ in. thick.

ROLLED SANDWICHES

1. Remove crusts from 3 sides of unsliced bread.
2. With crust at left, cut loaf into lengthwise slices ⅛ – ¼ in. thick.
3. Run rolling pin the length of each slice to make it easier to handle.
4. Spread with softened margarine or butter.
5. Spread with desired smooth filling.
6. Place olives, watercress, or other foods across the end.
7. Starting at end with garnish, roll tightly, being careful to keep sides straight. Tight rolling makes for easier slicing.
8. Wrap rolls individually in waxed paper or aluminum foil, twisting ends securely.
9. Chill several hours or overnight. Rolls may be made ahead of time, then wrapped and frozen. Let thaw about 45 minutes before slicing.
10. Cut chilled rolls into ¼ – ½ in. slices.

FREEZING SANDWICHES

When making sandwiches to be frozen for later use, certain precautions should be taken.

1. Spread bread with margarine or butter instead of mayonnaise or salad dressing.
2. Do not use fillings containing mayonnaise, egg white, or some vegetables such as tomatoes and parsley. Chicken, meat, egg yolks, fish, cheese, or peanut butter freeze well.
3. Wrap large closed sandwiches individually in plastic or place each in a sandwich bag.

4. Pack tea-sized closed sandwiches in layers, separated by waxed paper or plastic wrap, in freezer boxes; or place in any suitable box and overwrap with moisture vapor-proof material.
5. Place open-faced sandwiches on cardboard or trays, wrap as for closed sandwiches.
6. Wrap ribbon, closed, or other loaf sandwiches uncut.
7. Allow 1 to 2 hours for sandwiches to thaw. Do not remove outer wrapping until sandwiches are partly thawed.
8. If sandwiches are not served immediately after thawing, refrigerate until serving time.

SANDWICH RECIPES

WHIPPED MARGARINE OR BUTTER

Yield: Spread for 50 sandwiches
Portion: 1 t (5 mL) per slice

Amount Metric	U.S.	Ingredient	Procedure
454 g	1 lb	Margarine or butter	Place in mixer bowl. Let stand at room temperature until soft enough to mix.
120 mL	½ c	Milk or boiling water (optional)	Add milk or water while whipping. Mix on low speed, gradually increasing to high speed. Whip until fluffy.

Variations.
1. **Honey Butter.** Cream 1 lb (454 g) margarine or butter until light and fluffy. Add 8 oz (227 g) honey gradually, beating on medium speed until mixture is light. Serve with hot biscuits or other hot bread.
2. **Lemon Butter.** Blend 1 lb (454 g) margarine or butter, 1 c (240 mL) lemon juice, and 2 T (30 mL) grated lemon rind. Use for seasoning vegetables or fish.
3. **Onion Butter.** Blend 1 oz (28 g) dry onion soup mix with 1 lb (454 g) margarine or butter. Use with baked potatoes or other vegetables.
4. **Savory Spread.** Add minced cucumber, onion, or pimiento; chopped chives or parsley; or horseradish or prepared mustard.

SANDWICH SPREAD

Yield: Spread for 100 sandwiches
Portion: 1 t (5 mL) per slice

Amount Metric	U.S.	Ingredient	Procedure
227 g	8 oz	Margarine or butter	Whip margarine on high speed until fluffy.
60 mL	¼ c	Cream, half and half	Add cream and mix.
7 mL	1½ t	Mustard, prepared	Fold in remaining ingredients.
720 mL	3 c	Mayonnaise	Use as a spread for meat or cheese sandwiches.
120 mL	½ c	Pickle relish	

EGG SALAD SANDWICH

Yield: 50 sandwiches
Portion: 2 oz (57 g) filling

Amount Metric	U.S.	Ingredient	Procedure
36	36	Eggs, hard-cooked (p. 256)	Peel eggs and chop coarsely.
480 mL	2 c	Mayonnaise or salad dressing	Combine and add to eggs. Mix lightly.
480 mL	2 c	Pickle relish	
12 g	2 t	Salt	
¼ t	¼ t	Pepper, white	
5 mL	1 t	Onion juice	
114 g	4 oz	Pimiento, chopped	
100 slices	100 slices	Bread	Assemble filling, bread, and lettuce (p. 447). Portion filling with No. 20 dipper.
2–3 heads	2–3 heads	Lettuce	

Notes:
1. 1 lb (454 g) chopped celery may be substituted for the pickle relish.
2. 2 T (28 g) prepared mustard may be added.

CHICKEN SALAD SANDWICH

Yield: 50 sandwiches
Portion: 2 oz (57 g) filling

Amount		Ingredient	Procedure
Metric	U.S.		
2.27 kg	5 lb	Cooked chicken	Chop chicken coarsely.
12 g	2 t	Salt	Add remaining ingredients.
1 g	½ t	Pepper, white	Mix to blend.
227 g	8 oz	Celery, finely chopped	
60 mL	¼ c	Lemon juice or vinegar	
480 mL	2 c	Mayonnaise or salad dressing	
100 slices	100 slices	Bread	Assemble filling, bread, and lettuce (p. 447). Portion filling with No. 20 dipper.
2 – 3 heads	2 – 3 heads	Lettuce	

Note: 4 oz (114 g) chopped, toasted almonds may be added.

HAM SALAD SANDWICH

Yield: 50 sandwiches
Portion: 2 oz (57 g) filling

Amount		Ingredient	Procedure
Metric	U.S.		
1.81 kg	4 lb	Cooked ham	Grind ham coarsely.
6	6	Eggs, hard-cooked (p. 256)	Peel eggs and chop coarsely.
227 g	8 oz	Pickle relish	Combine all ingredients.
480 mL	2 c	Mayonnaise or salad dressing	Mix lightly.
100 slices	100 slices	Bread	Assemble filling, bread, and lettuce (p. 447). Portion filling with No. 20 dipper.
2 – 3 heads	2 – 3 heads	Lettuce	

Variations:

1. **Ham and Cheese Salad Sandwich.** Delete eggs. Reduce ham to 3 lb (1.36 kg). Add 1 lb 8 oz (680 g) Cheddar or Swiss cheese, ground.
2. **Meat Salad Sandwich.** Substitute ground cooked beef or pork for ham. Add 4 oz (114 g) finely chopped celery. Check for seasoning. Add salt and pepper if needed.

TUNA SALAD SANDWICH

Yield: 50 sandwiches
Portion: 2 oz (57 g) filling

Amount Metric	Amount U.S.	Ingredient	Procedure
7	7	Eggs, hard-cooked (p. 256)	Peel eggs and chop coarsely.
1.81 kg	4 lb	Tuna, flaked	Combine all filling ingredients.
114 g	4 oz	Celery, chopped	
60 mL	¼ c	Lemon juice	
5 mL	1 t	Onion juice	
360 mL	1½ c	Mayonnaise or salad dressing	
100 slices	100 slices	Bread	Assemble filling, bread, and lettuce (p. 447). Portion filling with No. 20 dipper.
2–3 heads	2–3 heads	Lettuce	

Note: 1 c (240 mL) pickle relish may be substituted for celery.

Variations:
1. **Grilled Tuna Salad Sandwich.** Brush both sides of sandwiches with melted margarine or butter. Grill until golden brown.
2. **Salmon Salad Sandwich.** Substitute salmon for tuna.

HOT TUNA BUN

Oven: 350°F (175°C)
Bake: 15–20 minutes
Yield: 50 sandwiches
Portion: 2½ oz (70 g) filling

Amount Metric	U.S.	Ingredient	Procedure
12	12	Eggs, hard-cooked (p. 256)	Peel eggs and chop coarsely.
1.81 kg	4 lb	Tuna, drained	Combine all filling ingredients. Mix lightly.
454 g	1 lb	Cheddar cheese, shredded	
85 g	3 oz	Green pepper, chopped	
57 g	2 oz	Onion, chopped	
114 g	4 oz	Stuffed green olives, chopped	
170 g	6 oz	Pickle relish	
720 mL	3 c	Mayonnaise or salad dressing	
50	50	Buns, hamburger or coney	Fill buns using No. 16 dipper. Place in counter pans, cover with aluminum foil. Bake at 350°F (175°C) for 15–20 minutes or until cheese is melted.

Variation: **Hot Picnic Bun.** Grind coarsely 3 lb (1.36 kg) ham, bologna, or other luncheon meat. Add 2 lb (908 g) shredded cheese 2 c (480 mL) pickle relish, 1 c (240 mL) chili sauce, 1 c (240 mL) mayonnaise, ½ c (120 mL) prepared mustard, and ¼ c (60 mL) grated onion. Fill buns and heat as above.

BACON, LETTUCE, AND TOMATO SANDWICH

Yield: 50 sandwiches

Amount		Ingredient	Procedure
Metric	*U.S.*		
3.18 kg	7 lb	Tomatoes, fresh	Wash tomatoes. Peel, if desired, and cut into thin slices.
2–3 heads	2–3 heads	Lettuce	Wash lettuce and separate leaves. Drain.
150 slices (3.18 kg)	150 slices (7 lb)	Bacon	Cook bacon according to directions on p. 342. Drain.
100 slices 240 mL 227 g	100 slices 1 c 8 oz	Bread Mayonnaise Whipped margarine or butter (p. 451)	Spread 50 slices of bread with mayonnaise. Place 3 cooked bacon slices, 2 slices of tomato, and a lettuce leaf on each. Top with remaining 50 slices of bread, which have been spread with whipped margarine or butter.

Variation: **Club Sandwich.** Use 150 slices white bread toasted. Spread with mayonnaise. Place on first slice 1 lettuce leaf, 2 tomato slices, and 2 strips of bacon. Place second slice of toast on top, spread side down. Spread top with mayonnaise, then add 2 oz (57 g) thinly sliced turkey or chicken breast, and lettuce leaf. Top with third slice of toast, spread-side down. Secure with 4 picks. Cut in quarters to serve.

SUBMARINE SANDWICH

Yield: 50 sandwiches

Amount Metric	U.S.	Ingredient	Procedure
50	50	Buns, submarine or Vienna	Slice buns in half lengthwise.
1 recipe	1 recipe	Sandwich Spread (p. 452)	Spread both sides of bun with sandwich spread.
1.42 kg	3 lb 2 oz	Salami, 1-oz slices	Cut slices of meat and cheese in half.
1.42 kg	3 lb 2 oz	Luncheon meat, 1-oz slices	Arrange on bottom half of each bun 2 half-slices of each kind of meat and 4 half-slices of cheese. Alternate slices and arrange so that full length of each bun is covered.
1.42 kg	3 lb 2 oz	Ham, pullman, 1-oz slices	
1.42 kg	3 lb 2 oz	Cheese, processed, American or Swiss, 1-oz slices	
24	24	Tomatoes, fresh, sliced	Place 2 slices tomato, ½ oz (14 g) shredded lettuce, and 2 dill pickle slices on each sandwich. Cover with top half of bun.
0.95 L	1 qt	Dill pickle slices, well drained (optional)	
709 g	1 lb 9 oz	Shredded lettuce	To serve, cut each sandwich in half.

Notes:

1. Other meats such as turkey, corned beef, pastrami, or roast beef may be used.
2. Shredded red or green cabbage, alfalfa sprouts, or leaf lettuce may be substituted for shredded lettuce.

CHIMICHANGA

Deep-fat fryer: 325°F (165°C)

Yield: 50 portions
Portion: 4 oz (114 g)

Amount Metric	U.S.	Ingredient	Procedure
4.88 kg	10 lb 12 oz	Ground beef	Brown meat in steam-jacketed kettle. Drain.
737 g	1 lb 10 oz	Onions, chopped	Add onions and chili peppers. Cook until tender.
227 g	8 oz	Green chili peppers, chopped	
114 g	4 oz	Flour, all-purpose	Add flour and seasonings. Cook over medium heat 10 minutes. Stir often.
1 g	½ t	Garlic powder	
4 g	2 t	Cumin, ground	
7 g	1 T	Chili powder	
850 g	1 lb 14 oz	Salsa (see Note 1)	Add salsa and beef stock. Cook 15–20 minutes or until very thick. This may be done the day before and refrigerated.
0.95 L	1 qt	Beef Stock (p. 494)	
2.5 kg	5 lb 8 oz	Flour tortillas, 10-in.	Separate tortillas and place slightly overlapping in counter pans. Cover tightly and heat a few at a time about 5 minutes or just until soft.
540 mL	2¼ c	Water	Mix water and cornstarch.
57 g	2 oz	Cornstarch	

To assemble:
1. Brush edges of tortillas with water–cornstarch mixture (Fig. 2.27).
2. Place No. 12 dipper or 4 oz (114 g) meat mixture slightly below center of each tortilla.
3. Fold bottom edge over filling.
4. Fold sides in, then roll into a cylinder. If necessary, brush on more water–cornstarch mixture to help seal edges.
5. Place seam-side down on baking sheets until ready to fry. Cover.
6. Fry at 325°F (165°C) until golden brown and crisp. Internal temperature should be 160°F (70°C).
7. Place in counter pans with liners. Do not cover.
8. Serve with topping (recipe follows).

Topping			
1.59 kg	3 lb 8 oz	Lettuce, shredded	Serve each chimichanga with: 1 oz (28 g) each of shredded lettuce, chopped tomato, guacamole, sour cream, olives; and 2 oz (57 g) salsa or sauce. See Note 1.
1.59 kg	3 lb 8 oz	Tomato, chopped	
1.59 kg	3 lb 8 oz	Guacamole (p. 65)	
1.59 kg	3 lb 8 oz	Cultured sour cream	
1.59 kg	3 lb 8 oz	Black olives, chopped	
2.84 L	3 qt	Spicy Tomato Sauce (p. 479) or Spanish Sauce (p. 478)	

Notes:
1. Spicy Tomato Sauce (p. 479) can be substituted for salsa.
2. 7 lb (3.18 kg) shredded cooked beef may be substituted for ground beef. Omit browning the beef and sauté onions and peppers in a little shortening.

460 SANDWICHES

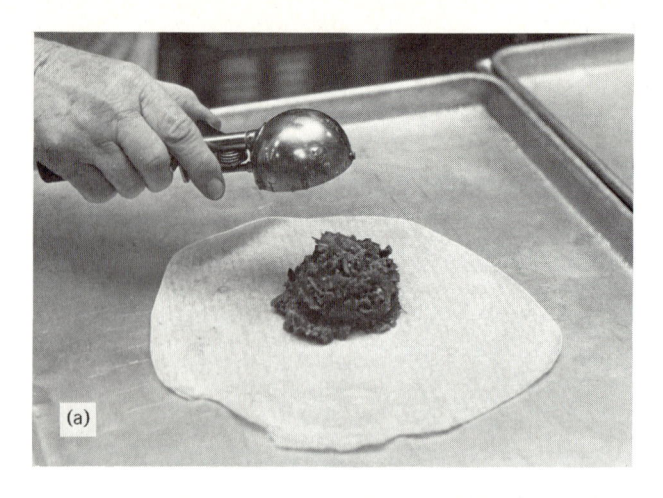

(a)

(b)

(c)

Figure 2.27 Making chimichangas. (a) Portion meat mixture onto flour tortilla. (b) Shape meat mixture into elongated form. Brush tortilla edges with water-cornstarch mixture. (c) Fold bottom edge over filling. (d) Fold in sides of tortilla. (e) Roll into a cylinder shape. (f) Brush water-cornstarch mixture on the top edge to help seal. Place seam side down on baking sheets and cover until ready to fry.

CHEESE SANDWICH

Yield: 50 sandwiches

Metric	U.S.	Ingredient	Procedure
1.59 kg	3 lb 8 oz	Cheddar cheese	Grind or shred cheese.
480 mL	2 c	Salad dressing or cream	Combine with cheese.
12 g	2 t	Salt	
f.g.	f.g.	Cayenne	
114 g	4 oz	Margarine or butter, softened	
100 slices	100 slices	Bread	Assemble filling and bread (p. 447). Portion filling with No. 20 dipper.

Variation: **Pimiento Cheese Sandwich.** Add 6 oz (170 g) chopped pimiento.

GRILLED CHEESE SANDWICH

Yield: 50 sandwiches

Metric	U.S.	Ingredient	Procedure
100 slices	100 slices	Bread	Place 2 slices cheese between 2 slices of bread.
2.84 kg	6 lb 4 oz	Cheese, processed, 1-oz (28-g) slices	
454 g	1 lb	Margarine or butter, melted	Brush sandwiches with melted margarine or butter. Preheat grill to 325°F (165°C). Grill sandwiches on both sides until golden brown and cheese begins to melt.

Notes:
1. Cheese may be ground and the following ingredients added to make a spread: 2 T (30 mL) prepared mustard, ½ c (120 mL) chili sauce, and 1 c (240 mL) mayonnaise.
2. Salad mixtures such as chicken, ham, tuna, and egg salad are satisfactory fillings for grilled sandwiches.
3. Rye bread and Swiss cheese filling may be used.

Variations:
1. **French Fried Cheese Sandwich.** Cut sandwiches into 2 triangles. Dip in batter (p. 37) and fry in deep fat at 375°F (190°C) for 1–2 minutes.
2. **Grilled Ham and Cheese Sandwich.** Use 1 oz (28 g) sliced cooked ham and 1 oz (28 g) sliced cheese.

OVEN-BAKED HAMBURGER

Oven: 400°F (205°C)
Bake: 15–20 minutes

Yield: 50 portions
Portion: 4 oz (114 g)

Amount		Ingredient	Procedure
Metric	U.S.		
5.44 kg	12 lb	Ground beef	Place meat in mixer bowl.
3 (142 g)	3 (5 oz)	Eggs, beaten	Combine eggs and milk and add to meat.
480 mL	2 c	Milk	
114 g	4 oz	Bread crumbs, soft	Add crumbs and seasonings.
114 g	4 oz	Onion, chopped	Blend on low speed for approximately 1 minute. Measure with No. 10 dipper onto lightly greased baking sheets. Flatten into patties. Bake at 400°F (205°C) for 15–20 minutes.
38 g	2 T	Salt	
4 g	2 t	Pepper, black	
50	50	Hamburger buns	Serve patties on warm buns.

Variation: **Barbecued Hamburger.** Place browned hamburgers in baking pans. Pour Barbecue Sauce (p. 477) over patties. Cover with aluminum foil and bake at 325°F (165°C) for 20–25 minutes.

REUBEN SANDWICH

Yield: 50 sandwiches
Portion: 3 oz (85 g) filling

Amount Metric	U.S.	Ingredient	Procedure
2.04 kg	4 lb 8 oz	Cooked corned beef	Cut corned beef into very thin slices.
100 slices	100 slices	Rye bread	Spread No. 100 dipper (scant 2 t/10 mL) dressing on bread.
480 mL	2 c	Mayonnaise or Sandwich Spread (p. 452)	
1.42 L	1½ qt	Sauerkraut, well drained	Place filling on bread, in order given:
1.42 kg	3 lb 2 oz	Swiss cheese, 1-oz (28-g) slices	1½ oz (43 g) corned beef 2 T (30 mL) sauerkraut 1 oz (28 g) cheese Cover with top slice of bread.
454 g	1 lb	Margarine or butter, melted	Brush sandwiches with melted margarine. Preheat grill to 325°F (165°C). Grill sandwiches on both sides until delicately browned.

HOT ROAST BEEF SANDWICH

Yield: 50 sandwiches
Portion: 3 oz (85 g) meat
¼ c (60 mL) gravy

Amount			
Metric	U.S.	Ingredient	Procedure
4.54 kg EP (6.8 kg AP)	10 lb EP (15 lb AP)	Beef roast	Roast beef according to directions on p. 295. Slice into 3-oz (85-g) portions. Place in 2 12 × 20 × 2-in. counter pans.
1.42 L	1½ qt	Beef Stock (p. 494)	Heat beef stock. Pour over meat. Cover with aluminum foil and place in oven to keep warm.
50 slices	50 slices	Bread	Place 3 oz (85 g) meat on each slice of bread.
5.67 kg	12 lb 8 oz	Mashed Potatoes (p. 551)	Serve with No. 12 dipper mashed potato beside bread.
3.79 L	1 gal	Gravy (p. 476)	Cover meat and potato with gravy, using 2-oz ladle.

Note: Meat may be covered with additional slice of bread if desired. Omit mashed potatoes. Cover entire sandwich with gravy.

Variations:

1. **Barbecued Beef Sandwich.** Place thinly sliced beef roast in 2 counter pans and keep warm. Heat 1½ qt (1.42 L) Barbecue Sauce (p. 477) and pour 3 c (720 mL) over each pan of meat. Toss together until sauce is evenly distributed. Serve in warm hamburger buns.
2. **French Dip Sandwich.** Slice roast beef wafer thin. Place in 12 × 20 × 2-in. counter pan. Pour 1 c (240 mL) Beef Stock (p. 494) over meat. Cover with aluminum foil and keep warm. To serve, place 3 oz (85 g) beef on hard roll bun. Serve with side cup of hot seasoned broth for dipping.
3. **Hot Roast Pork Sandwich.** Substitute roast pork for beef.
4. **Hot Turkey Sandwich.** Substitute roast turkey or turkey roll for beef.

RUNZA

Oven: 400°F (205°C)
Bake: 25–30 minutes
Yield: 50 sandwiches

Amount Metric	U.S.	Ingredient	Procedure
DOUGH			
35 g	1¼ oz	Yeast, active dry	Sprinkle yeast over water.
1.89 L	2 qt	Water, warm (110°F/43°C)	Let stand 5 minutes.
397 g	14 oz	Sugar, granulated	Add sugar, salt, and flour.
28 g	1 oz (1½ T)	Salt	Mix on medium speed, using dough hook or flat beater until mixture is smooth.
1.08 kg	2 lb 6 oz	Flour, all-purpose	
8 (397 g)	8 (14 oz)	Eggs	Add eggs and shortening. Continue beating.
142 g	5 oz	Shortening, melted	
2.5 kg	5 lb 8 oz	Flour, all-purpose	Add flour on low speed to make a soft dough. Knead 5 minutes. Cover and let rise until double in bulk. Punch down. Divide dough into 4–5 portions. Roll out. Cut into 4 × 6-in. rectangles (3 oz/85 g dough). Place on each piece of dough a No. 6 dipper of filling (recipe below). Fold lengthwise and pinch edges of dough securely to seal. Place on baking sheets with sealed edges down. Bake at 400°F (205°C) for 25–30 minutes.
1	1	Egg yolk	Brush with egg and water mixture. Return to oven for 5 minutes.
30 mL	2 T	Water	

Amount		Ingredient	Procedure
Metric	U.S.		
FILLING			
3.63 kg	8 lb	Ground beef	Brown and drain beef.
908 g	2 lb	Cabbage, chopped	Steam cabbage and onion until slightly underdone.
992 g	2 lb 3 oz	Onion, chopped	
60 mL	¼ c	Worcestershire sauce	Add seasonings and vegetables.
57 g	2 oz	Salt	
2 g	1 t	Pepper, black	
2 g	1 t	Savory	
2 g	1 t	Chili powder	

WESTERN SANDWICH

Yield: 50 sandwiches
Portion: 3 oz (85 g)

Amount		Ingredient	Procedure
Metric	U.S.		
4.54 kg	10 lb	Ground beef	Brown beef and onion. Drain off fat.
227 g	8 oz	Onion, chopped	
0.95 L	1 qt	Tomato purée	Add remaining filling ingredients. Simmer 20–30 minutes.
38 g	2 T	Salt	
4 g	2 t	Paprika	
4 g	2 t	Mustard, dry	
30 mL	2 T	Worcestershire sauce	
4 g	2 t	Chili powder	
50	50	Hamburger buns	Serve with No. 12 dipper of filling on buns.

TACOS

Yield: 50 portions
Portion: 2 tacos

Amount Metric	U.S.	Ingredient	Procedure
5.44 kg	12 lb	Ground beef	Brown beef and onion.
908 g	2 lb	Onion, chopped	Drain off fat.
720 mL	3 c	Spicy Tomato Sauce (p. 479)	Add to beef. Simmer 30 minutes.
120 mL	½ c	Worcestershire sauce	
57 g	2 oz	Chili powder	
38 g	2 T	Garlic salt	
8 g	2 T	Oregano, leaf	
14 g	2 T	Paprika	
4 g	1 T	Rosemary, crushed	
7 g	1 T	Cumin, ground	
2 g	1 t	Pepper, black	
f.d.	f.d.	Tabasco sauce	
100	100	Taco shells	Place shells in counter pans. Heat in oven until warm and crisp. To serve, fill each taco shell with No. 20 dipper meat mixture.
Topping			
1.81 kg	4 lb EP	Lettuce, chopped	Cover meat mixture with lettuce, then tomato, and top with shredded cheese.
1.36 kg	3 lb EP	Tomatoes, fresh, diced	
908 g	2 lb	Processed cheese, shredded	Serve with Spicy Tomato Sauce (p. 479) or commercial salsa to spoon on top.

Notes:
1. Commercial salsa may be substituted for Spicy Tomato Sauce.
2. Commercial taco seasoning mix may be substituted for spices. Follow manufacturer's directions for amount to use.

Variation: **Tostadas.** Fry 50 10-in. flour or corn tortillas in hot oil, 20–30 seconds on each side, until crisp and golden brown. Drain on paper towel. Keep warm. To serve, spread each tortilla with No. 20 dipper refried beans (p. 532). Top with 1 oz (28 g) chopped lettuce, 1 oz (28 g) chopped fresh tomatoes, and ½ oz (14 g) shredded cheese. Serve with Guacamole (p. 65), sour cream, and Spicy Tomato Sauce (p. 479) or commercial salsa.

Sauces

A sauce serves to complement an entrée, vegetable, or dessert. It may be used as a binding agent to hold foods together or as a topping. Sauces add richness, moistness, color, and form to foods and may enhance or offer contrast in flavor or color to foods they accompany. The appearance of food may be improved by the addition of a complementary sauce.

Basic to many sauces is a roux, which is a cooked mixture of fat and flour, usually equal parts by weight. A roux may range from white, in which the fat and flour are cooked only for a short time, to brown, cooked until it is light brown in color and has a nutty aroma.

Many meat and vegetable sauces are modifications of basic recipes, such as white sauce, bechamel sauce, and brown sauce. *White sauce* (p. 470), made with a roux of fat and flour and with milk as the liquid, has many uses in quantity food preparation, as a sauce with vegetables, eggs, and fish and as an ingredient in many casseroles. A white sauce mix (p. 472) in which flour, fat, and nonfat dry milk are combined may be made and stored in the refrigerator until needed. Water and seasonings are added when the mixture is to be used. *Bechamel sauce* (p. 473) and its variations use milk and chicken stock as the liquid and usually are served with poultry, seafood, eggs, or vegetables. *Brown sauce* (p. 475) is made with a well-browned roux and beef stock and is used mainly with meat.

Other sauces may have a butter, tomato, or mayonnaise base. A broth made with a high-quality commercial stock base can be substituted for the chicken or beef stock called for in sauces, but the salt in the recipe may need to be adjusted if the soup base is highly seasoned.

Sauces made from concentrated canned soups are time-saving and may be used effectively in many items. Undiluted canned cream soups such as chicken, mushroom, celery, cheese, and tomato may be used alone or in combination. If the soup is too thick, a small amount of milk or chicken or meat stock may be added. Two soups may be combined for a special flavor effect, or pimiento, green pepper, almonds, curry powder, or other ingredients may be added for variety.

Marinades are used to flavor and tenderize meats and poultry and to flavor raw or cooked vegetables. The less tender cuts of meat should be marinated at least 2 hours; pork, chicken, and the more tender cuts of beef often are basted before and during cooking but do not need to stand in the marinade.

MEAT AND VEGETABLE SAUCE RECIPES

WHITE SAUCE

Yield: 1 gal (3.79 L)

Consistency	Milk[a]	Flour (all-purpose)	Margarine or butter	Salt	Uses
Very thin	4 qt (3.79 L)	2 oz (57 g)	8 oz (227 g)	1 oz (1½ T) (28 g)	Cream soup made from starchy foods
Thin	4 qt (3.79 L)	4 oz (114 g)	8 oz (227 g)	1 oz (1½ T) (28 g)	Cream soup made from nonstarchy foods
Medium	4 qt (3.79 L)	8 oz (227 g)	1 lb[b] (454 g)	1 oz (1½ T) (28 g)	Creamed dishes, gravies
Thick	4 qt (3.79 L)	12–16 oz (340–454 g)	1 lb[b] (454 g)	1 oz (1½ T) (28 g)	Soufflés
Very thick	4 qt (3.79 L)	1 lb 4 oz (567 g)	1 lb 4 oz (567 g)	1 oz (1½) (28 g)	Croquettes

Method 1. Melt margarine, remove from heat. Add flour and stir until smooth. Add salt, then milk gradually, stirring constantly. Cook and stir as necessary, until smooth and thick, about 15 minutes.

Method 2. Combine flour with one fourth of the milk. Heat remaining milk. Add flour–milk paste, using wire whip. Cook to desired consistency, then add margarine and salt.

Method 3. This method is used for making quantities larger than 4 qt (3.79 L). Melt margarine. Add flour and stir until smooth. Add one fourth of the milk and beat with wire whip until smooth. Gradually add remaining milk while stirring. Cook until smooth and thickened, about 15 minutes.

Method 4. This method uses a steamer. Make a paste of flour and margarine. Add cold milk until mixture is the consistency of cream. Heat remaining milk; add flour and margarine mixture, stirring constantly with wire whip. Place in steamer until flour is cooked; if necessary, stir once during cooking.

[a] 1 lb (454 g) nonfat dry milk and 3¾ qt (3.55 L) cool water may be substituted for fluid milk. Combine dry milk and water. Whip until smooth. Heat to scalding. Add roux made of margarine and flour, while stirring. Cook on low heat, stirring as necessary, until thickened.

[b] Reduce margarine or butter to 8–10 oz (227–284 g) in medium, thick, and very thick white sauce when using Method 2.

Variations:
1. **à la King Sauce.** Add 12 oz (340 g) chopped green pepper and 12 oz (340 g) sliced mushrooms, sautéed, and 1 lb (454 g) chopped pimiento to 1 gal (3.79 L) Medium White Sauce. Combine with cubed cooked chicken, meats, seafood, vegetables, or eggs.
2. **Bacon Sauce.** Add 1½ lb (680 g) cooked chopped bacon to 1 gal (3.79 L) Medium White Sauce. Use bacon fat in making the sauce. Combine with eggs or vegetables in scalloped dishes.
3. **Cheese Sauce.** Add 3 lb (1.36 kg) sharp Cheddar cheese (shredded or ground), 2 T (30 mL) Worcestershire sauce, and f.g. cayenne to 1 gal (3.79 L) Medium White Sauce. Serve on fish, egg dishes, soufflés, and vegetables.
4. **Egg Sauce.** Add 20 chopped hard-cooked eggs and 2 T (30 mL) prepared mustard to 1 gal (3.79 L) Medium White Sauce. Serve over salmon loaf or croquettes.
5. **Golden Sauce.** Add 2 c (480 mL) slightly beaten egg yolks to 1 gal (3.79 L) Medium White Sauce. Serve on fish, chicken, or vegetables.
6. **Mushroom Sauce.** Add 1½ lb (680 g) sliced mushrooms and 4 oz (114 g) minced onion, sautéed in 4 oz (114 g) margarine or butter, to 1 gal (3.79 L) Medium White Sauce. Serve over egg, meat, or poultry dishes or vegetables.
7. **Pimiento Sauce.** Add 1¼ lb (567 g) finely chopped pimiento and 2 c (480 mL) finely chopped parsley to 1 gal (3.79 L) Medium White Sauce. Serve with poached fish, croquettes, or egg dishes.
8. **Shrimp Sauce.** Add 4 lb (1.81 kg) cooked shrimp, 2 T (30 mL) prepared mustard, and 2 T (30 mL) Worcestershire sauce to 1 gal (3.79 L) Medium White Sauce. Serve with fish, eggs, or cheese soufflé.

WHITE SAUCE MIX

Yield: 21 lb (9.53 kg) mix

Amount Metric	U.S.	Ingredient	Procedure
1.36 kg	3 lb	Flour, all-purpose	Blend flour and milk in large (60-qt) mixing bowl.
4.08 kg	9 lb	Nonfat dry milk	
2.04 kg	4 lb 8 oz	Shortening	Using pastry knife or flat beater, blend fats with dry ingredients until mixture is crumbly, scraping down bowl occasionally. Store in covered containers in the refrigerator.
2.04 kg	4 lb 8 oz	Margarine or butter	
To prepare 1 gal white sauce			
3.79 L	1 gal	Water	Heat water and salt to boiling point.
43 g	1½ oz	Salt	
Thin			Add mix for sauce of desired thickness. Stirring with a wire whip, continue cooking until thickened.
964 g	2 lb 2 oz	White sauce mix	
Medium			
1.30 kg	2 lb 14 oz	White sauce mix	
Thick			
1.59 kg	3 lb 8 oz	White sauce mix	

BECHAMEL SAUCE

Yield: 2 qt (1.89 L)
Portion: 3 T (1½ oz/43 g)

Amount			
Metric	U.S.	Ingredient	Procedure
1.42 L	1½ qt	Chicken Stock (p. 495)	Cook stock and seasonings together for 20 minutes.
4	4	Onion slices	Strain.
19 g	2 T	Peppercorns	Save liquid for preparation
85 g	3 oz	Carrots, chopped	of sauce. There should
1	1	Bay leaf	be 1 qt (0.95 L) liquid.
227 g	8 oz	Margarine or butter	Melt margarine. Add flour and stir until smooth.
114 g	4 oz	Flour, all-purpose	
0.95 L	1 qt	Seasoned stock (prepared above)	Add liquids gradually, stirring constantly.
0.95 L	1 qt	Milk, hot	Cook until smooth and thickened.
3 g	½ t	Salt	
1 g	½ t	Pepper, white	Add seasonings.
f.g.	f.g.	Cayenne	Serve with 2-oz ladle (scant) on chicken or meat entrées.

Variations:

1. **Mornay Sauce.** Add gradually to hot Bechamel Sauce 4 oz (114 g) each of grated Parmesan and Swiss cheese. Let sauce remain over heat until cheese is melted, then remove and gradually beat in 8 oz (227 g) margarine or butter. Serve with fish or egg entrées.

2. **Velouté Sauce.** Substitute chicken stock for milk. Serve on chicken turnovers or other chicken entrées.

FRESH MUSHROOM SAUCE

Yield: 1 gal (3.79 L)
Portion: 2½ oz (70 g)

Amount Metric	U.S.	Ingredient	Procedure
1.81 kg	4 lb	Mushrooms, fresh	Clean, trim, and slice mushrooms.
227 g	8 oz	Margarine or butter	Melt margarine. Sauté onions and mushrooms.
57 g	2 oz	Onions, minced	
114 g	4 oz	Flour, all-purpose	Add flour and blend.
1.89 L	2 qt	Chicken Stock (p. 495), hot	Add chicken stock and milk while stirring.
480 mL	2 c	Milk or cream	Taste for seasoning.
		Salt to taste	Add salt if needed.

Note: Canned, drained mushrooms may be substituted for fresh mushroms. Stir into prepared sauce.

Variations:
1. **Mushroom and Almond Sauce.** Add 1 lb (454 g) slivered almonds. Serve over rice as entrée.
2. **Mushroom and Cheese Sauce.** Add 1 lb (454 g) shredded Cheddar cheese. Serve over asparagus or broccoli.

MEUNIERE SAUCE

Yield: 3 c (720 mL)

Amount Metric	U.S.	Ingredient	Procedure
567 g	1 lb 4 oz	Margarine or butter	Heat margarine until lightly browned.
57 g	2 oz	Onion, minced	Add onion and brown slightly.
120 mL	½ c	Lemon juice	Add juice and seasonings.
15 mL	1 T	Worcestershire sauce	Serve hot over broccoli, Brussels sprouts,
6 g	1 T	Lemon rind, grated	green beans, spinach,
6 g	1 t	Salt	or cabbage.

Note: 3 oz (85 g) toasted sliced almonds may be sprinkled over top of vegetable.

BROWN SAUCE

Yield: 2 qt (1.89 L)
Portion: 3 T (1½ oz/43 g)

Amount		Ingredient	Procedure
Metric	U.S.		
1.89 L	2 qt	Beef Stock (p. 494)	Add onion and seasoning to meat stock. If soup base has been used to make stock, taste before adding salt. Simmer about 10 minutes. Strain.
114 g	4 oz	Onion, thinly sliced	
12 g	2 t	Salt	
¼ t	¼ t	Pepper, black	
227 g	8 oz	Shortening	Heat shortening and blend with flour. Cook until it becomes uniformly brown in color. Add hot stock while stirring. Cook until thickened.
142 g	5 oz	Flour, all-purpose	

Variations:

1. **Jelly Sauce.** Add 2 c (480 mL) currant jelly, beaten until melted, 2 T (30 mL) tarragon vinegar, and 4 oz (114 g) sautéed minced onions. Serve with lamb or game.

2. **Mushroom Sauce.** Add 1 lb (454 g) sliced mushrooms and 2 oz (57 g) minced onions, sautéed. Serve with steak.

3. **Olive Sauce.** Add 6 oz (170 g) chopped stuffed olives. Serve with meat or duck.

4. **Piquante Sauce.** Add 2 oz (57 g) minced onions, 2 oz (57 g) capers, ½ c (120 mL) vinegar, 4 oz (114 g) sugar, ¼ t salt, ¼ t paprika, and ½ c (120 mL) chili sauce or chopped sweet pickle. Serve with meats.

5. **Savory Mustard Sauce.** Add ½ c (120 mL) prepared mustard and ½ c (120 mL) horseradish. Serve with meats.

PAN GRAVY

Yield: 1 gal (3.79 L)
Portion: 1/3 c (2 1/2 oz/70 g)

Amount Metric	U.S.	Ingredient	Procedure
227 g	8 oz	Fat (meat drippings), hot	Add flour to fat and blend.
227 g	8 oz	Flour, all-purpose	
19 g	1 T	Salt	Add salt and pepper.
2 g	1 t	Pepper, black	
3.79 L	1 gal	Water or meat stock (pp. 494, 495)	Add water or stock gradually, stirring constantly with a wire whip. Cook until smooth and thickened.

Note: If soup base is used for stock, delete or reduce salt.

Variations:
1. **Brown Gravy.** Use 10 oz (284 g) flour and brown in the fat.
2. **Cream Gravy.** Substitute milk for water or stock.
3. **Giblet Gravy.** Use chicken drippings for fat and chicken stock for liquid. Add 1 qt (0.95 L) cooked giblets, chopped.
4. **Onion Gravy.** Lightly brown 1 lb (454 g) thinly sliced onions in fat before adding flour.
5. **Vegetable Gravy.** Add 1 lb (454 g) diced carrots, 4 oz (114 g) chopped celery, and 12 oz (340 g) chopped onion, cooked in water or meat stock.

UNCOOKED BARBECUE SAUCE

Yield: 1 gal (3.79 L)

Amount Metric	U.S.	Ingredient	Procedure
1 No. 10 can	1 No. 10 can	Catsup	Mix all ingredients.
720 mL	3 c	Vinegar	Pour over meat or chicken.
340 g	12 oz	Sugar, granulated	
114 g	4 oz	Salt	
114 g	4 oz	Onion, grated	

COOKED BARBECUE SAUCE

Yield: 1½ gal (5.68 L)

Amount		Ingredient	Procedure
Metric	U.S.		
1 No. 10 can	1 No. 10 can	Catsup	Combine all ingredients.
2.84 L	3 qt	Water	Simmer 10 minutes.
480 mL	2 c	Vinegar	Baste chicken or meat with
38 g	2 T	Salt	sauce during cooking.
2 g	1 t	Pepper, black	
114 g	4 oz	Sugar, granulated	
2 g	1 t	Chili powder	
60 mL	¼ c	Worcestershire sauce	
15 mL	1 T	Tabasco sauce	
114 g	4 oz	Onion, grated	
2	2	Lemons, sliced	

DRAWN BUTTER SAUCE

Yield: 2 qt (1.89 L)
Portion: 3 T (1½ oz/43 g)

Amount		Ingredient	Procedure
Metric	U.S.		
57 g	2 oz	Butter	Melt butter. Add flour
114 g	4 oz	Flour, all-purpose	and blend.
1.89 L	2 qt	Water, hot	Gradually add hot water while stirring. Cook 5 minutes.
6 g	1 t	Salt	When ready to serve, add
170 g	6 oz	Butter, cut into pieces	salt and butter. Beat until blended.

Note: Serve with green vegetables, fried or broiled fish, or egg dishes.

Variations:
1. **Almond Butter Sauce.** Add ¼ c (60 mL) lemon juice and 6 oz (170 g) toasted slivered almonds just before serving.
2. **Lemon Butter Sauce.** Add 1 T (6 g) grated lemon rind and ¼ c (60 mL) lemon juice just before serving. Serve with fish, new potatoes, broccoli, or asparagus.
3. **Maitre d'Hotel Sauce.** Add ¼ c (60 mL) lemon juice, ¼ c (7 g) chopped parsley, and 8 egg yolks, well beaten.
4. **Parsley Butter Sauce.** Add 1½ c (43 g) minced parsley just before servng. Serve with fish, potatoes, or other vegetables.

TOMATO SAUCE

Yield: 2 qt (1.89 L)
Portion: 2½ T (1½ oz/43 g)

Amount Metric	U.S.	Ingredient	Procedure
1.89 L	2 qt	Tomato juice	Combine tomato juice and seasonings. Simmer 20 minutes.
114 g	4 oz	Onion, finely chopped	
28 g	2 T	Sugar, granulated	
6 g	1 t	Salt	
¼ t	¼ t	Pepper, black	
5 mL	1 t	Worcestershire sauce	
170 g	6 oz	Margarine or butter	Melt margarine. Add flour and blend.
114 g	4 oz	Flour, all-purpose	Add hot tomato juice gradually while stirring. Cook until thickened.

SPANISH SAUCE

Yield: 3 qt (2.84 L)
Portion: 3 T (3 oz/85 g)

Amount Metric	U.S.	Ingredient	Procedure
114 g	4 oz	Onion, chopped	Sauté onions in shortening.
114 g	4 oz	Shortening, melted	
1.89 L	2 qt	Tomatoes, canned, diced	Add remaining ingredients. Simmer until vegetables are tender.
454 g	1 lb	Celery, diced	
227 g	8 oz	Green pepper, chopped	
170 g	6 oz	Pimiento, chopped	
19 g	1 T	Salt	
1 g	½ t	Pepper, black	
f.g.	f.g.	Cayenne	

Note: Serve with meat, fish, cheese, or Mexican entrées.

SPICY TOMATO SAUCE

Yield: 2 qt (1.89 L)

Metric	U.S.	Ingredient	Procedure
908 g	2 lb	Tomatoes, canned diced	Drain tomatoes. Reserve juice. Chop tomatoes until puréed. Place chopped tomatoes and reserved juice in kettle.
142 g	5 oz	Green pepper, chopped	Add to tomatoes. Simmer about 15 minutes or until of desired consistency.
142 g	5 oz	Onion, chopped	
½ t	½ t	Garlic, minced	
85 g	3 oz	Green chilies, chopped	
120 mL	½ c	Vinegar	
6 g	1 t	Salt	
5 g	1 t	Sugar, granulated	
720 mL	3 c	Tomato juice	
5 mL	1 t	Tabasco sauce	
16 g	2 T	Tapioca	
½ t	½ t	Oregano leaves	
¼ t	¼ t	Cayenne	
¼ t	¼ t	Cumin, ground	

Note: May be served as a condiment with tacos, tostadas, chimichangas, or other Mexican entrées.

RAISIN SAUCE

Yield: 1½ qt (1.42 L)
Portion: 2 T (1 oz/28 g)

Amount Metric	U.S.	Ingredient	Procedure
454 g	1 lb	Raisins, seedless	Steam raisins or simmer in small amount of water for 3–5 minutes.
114 g	4 oz	Sugar, granulated	Heat sugar and water to boiling point.
480 mL	2 c	Water	
454 g	1 lb	Currant jelly	Add cooked raisins, currant jelly, and remaining ingredients. Simmer 5 minutes or until jelly is dissolved.
80 mL	⅓ c	Vinegar	
57 g	2 oz	Margarine	
15 mL	1 T	Worcestershire sauce	
6 g	1 t	Salt	
¼ t	¼ t	Pepper, white	
½ t	½ t	Cloves	
⅛ t	⅛ t	Mace	
f.d.	f.d.	Red food coloring (optional)	

Note: Serve with baked ham.

MUSTARD SAUCE

Yield: 1 qt (0.95 L)
Portion: 1 T (15 mL)

Amount Metric	U.S.	Ingredient	Procedure
28 g	2 T	Sugar, granulated	Mix dry ingredients.
3 g	½ t	Salt	
4 g	2 t	Mustard, dry	
30 mL	2 T	Water	Add water, vinegar, and eggs. Cook until thick.
60 mL	¼ c	Vinegar	
2 (85 g)	2 (3 oz)	Eggs, beaten	
28 g	1 oz	Margarine or butter	Add margarine. Stir until melted. Cool.
480 mL	2 c	Cream, whipping	Whip cream and fold into cooked mixture.

Note: Serve cold with ham or with pork or beef roast.

MEAT AND VEGETABLE SAUCE RECIPES

HOT MUSTARD SAUCE

Yield: 2 qt (1.89 L)
Portion: 2 T (1 oz/28 g)

Amount			
Metric	U.S.	Ingredient	Procedure
1.89 L	2 qt	Beef Stock (p. 494)	Heat stock.
142 g	5 oz	Cornstarch	Blend dry ingredients
28 g	2 T	Sugar, granulated	with cold water.
12 g	2 t	Salt	Add gradually to hot
1 g	½ t	Pepper, white	stock. Cook and stir
120 mL	½ c	Water, cold	until thickened.
57 g	2 oz	Mustard, prepared	Add remaining ingre-
114 g	4 oz	Horseradish	dients.
30 mL	2 T	Vinegar	Stir until blended.
28 g	1 oz	Margarine or butter	

Note: Serve hot with boiled beef, fresh or cured ham, or fish.

SWEET-SOUR SAUCE

Yield: 5 qt (4.73 L)

Amount			
Metric	U.S.	Ingredient	Procedure
227 g	8 oz	Onion, chopped	Sauté vegetables in
170 g	6 oz	Celery, chopped	shortening for 5
170 g	6 oz	Green pepper, chopped	minutes. Set aside.
114 g	4 oz	Shortening	
480 mL	2 c	Vinegar	Combine vinegar, water,
480 mL	2 c	Water	sugar, soy sauce, and
227 g	8 oz	Sugar, granulated	salt. Bring to a boil.
60 mL	¼ c	Soy sauce	
19 g	1 T	Salt	
114 g	4 oz	Cornstarch	Mix cornstarch and water
240 mL	1 c	Water, cold	into a smooth paste. Add to hot liquid while stirring. Cook until clear.
1 No. 10 can	1 No. 10 can	Pineapple tidbits	Add vegetables and pineapple to sauce. Pour over spareribs or other pork cuts and bake.

Note: Onion celery, and green pepper may be cut in strips or chunks.

HORSERADISH SAUCE

Yield: 5 c (1.18 L)
Portion: 1½ T (½ oz/14 g)

Amount		Ingredient	Procedure
Metric	U.S.		
227 g	8 oz	Horseradish, drained	Combine.
28 g	2 T	Mustard, prepared	
6 g	1 t	Salt	
¼ t	¼ t	Paprika	
⅛ t	⅛ t	Cayenne	
80 mL	⅓ c	Vinegar	
480 mL	2 c	Cream, whipping	Whip cream. Fold in horseradish mixture. Chill.

Note: Serve with ham or roast beef.

APPLE-HORSERADISH SAUCE

Yield: 3 c (720 ml)
Portion: 1 T (½ oz/14 g)

Amount		Ingredient	Procedure
Metric	U.S.		
240 mL	1 c	Applesauce, sieved	Fold applesauce and horseradish into mayonnaise.
240 mL	1 c	Horseradish	
240 mL	1 c	Mayonnaise	

Notes:
1. Serve with ham.
2. Whipped cream may be substituted for mayonnaise if served at once.

COCKTAIL SAUCE

Yield: 2 qt (1.89 L)
Portion: 2½ T (1½ oz/43 g)

Amount			
Metric	U.S.	Ingredient	Procedure
0.95 L	1 qt	Chili sauce	Mix all ingredients.
480 mL	2 c	Catsup	Chill.
240 mL	1 c	Lemon juice	
30 mL	2 T	Onion juice	
284 g	10 oz	Celery, finely chopped	
25 mL	5 t	Worcestershire sauce	
85 g	3 oz	Horseradish	
f.d.	f.d.	Tabasco sauce	

Note: Serve over clam, crab, lobster, oyster, or shrimp.

TARTAR SAUCE

Yield: 1¾ qt (1.66 L)
Portion: 2 T (1 oz/28 g)

Amount			
Metric	U.S.	Ingredient	Procedure
0.95 L	1 qt	Mayonnaise	Mix all ingredients.
170 g	6 oz	Pickle relish	
43 g	¼ c	Green pepper, chopped	
7 g	¼ c	Parsley, chopped	
170 g	1 c	Green olives, chopped	
14 g	1 T	Onion, minced	
57 g	¼ c	Pimiento, chopped	
120 mL	½ c	Vinegar or lemon juice	
f.d.	f.d.	Worcestershire sauce	
f.d.	f.d.	Tabasco sauce	

Note: Serve with fish.

CUCUMBER SAUCE

Yield: 3 c (720 mL)
Portion: 1 T (½ oz/14 g)

Amount Metric	U.S.	Ingredient	Procedure
454 g	1 lb	Cucumbers	Peel cucumbers; remove seeds. Grate or chop finely.
240 mL	1 c	Cultured sour cream	Combine remaining ingredients and add to cucumber. Chill.
14 g	1 T	Onion, grated	
15 mL	1 T	Vinegar	
23 mL	1½ T	Lemon juice	
3 g	½ t	Salt	
Dash	Dash	Red pepper	

Note: Serve with fish.

HOLLANDAISE SAUCE

Yield: 12 portions
Portion: 1½ T (¾ oz/21 g)

Amount Metric	U.S.	Ingredient	Procedure
57 g	2 oz	Butter	Place butter, lemon juice, and egg yolks over hot (not boiling) water. Cook slowly, beating constantly.
23 mL	1½ T	Lemon juice	
3	3	Egg yolks	
57 g	2 oz	Butter	When first portion of butter is melted, add second portion and beat until mixture thickens.
57 g	2 oz	Butter	Add third portion of butter and seasonings. Beat until thickened. Serve immediately.
f.g.	f.g.	Salt	
f.g.	f.g.	Cayenne	

Notes:
1. Serve with fish or green vegetables such as asparagus or broccoli.
2. If sauce tends to curdle, add hot water, a teaspoon at a time, stirring vigorously.
3. It is recommended that this sauce be made only in small quantity.

MOCK HOLLANDAISE SAUCE

Yield: 2 qt (1.89 L)
Portion: 2½ T (1½ oz/43 g)

Amount Metric	U.S.	Ingredient	Procedure
170 g	6 oz	Butter or margarine	Melt butter. Add flour
85 g	3 oz	Flour, all-purpose	and stir until smooth.
1.42 L	1½ qt	Milk	Add milk gradually, stirring constantly. Cook until smooth and thickened.
6 g	1 t	Salt	Add seasonings.
1 g	½ t	Pepper, white	
f.g.	f.g.	Cayenne	
12 (227 g)	12 (8 oz)	Egg yolks, unbeaten	Add 1 egg yolk at a time, a little butter, and a little lemon juice until all are added.
454 g	1 lb	Butter, cut in pieces	
120 mL	½ c	Lemon juice	Beat well.

HOT BACON SAUCE

Yield: 2½ qt (2.37 L)

Amount Metric	U.S.	Ingredient	Procedure
454 g	1 lb	Bacon	Dice bacon. Fry until crisp.
114 g	4 oz	Flour, all-purpose	Add flour and stir until smooth.
567 g	1 lb 4 oz	Sugar, granulated	Mix sugar, salt, vinegar, and water. Boil 1 minute. Add to fat–flour mixture gradually while stirring. Cook until slightly thickened.
57 g	¼ c	Salt	
720 mL	3 c	Vinegar	
720 mL	3 c	Water	

Note: Use to wilt lettuce or spinach; or with hot potato salad or shredded cabbage.

MEAT MARINADE

Yield: 2 qt (1.89 L)

Amount Metric	U.S.	Ingredient	Procedure
0.95 L	1 qt	Salad oil	Combine ingredients, mixing well. Pour over meat. Marinate overnight.
60 mL	¼ c	Worcestershire sauce	
60 mL	¼ c	Liquid smoke	
480 mL	2 c	Soy sauce	
60 mL	¼ c	Vinegar	
4 cloves	4 cloves	Garlic, minced	
57 g	¼ c	Celery salt	
28 g	¼ c	Mustard, dry	
28 g	¼ c	Ginger, ground	
142 g	1 c	Sugar, brown	

Note: Use for chicken, pork, or beef.

VEGETABLE MARINADE

Yield: 1½ qt (1.42 L)

Amount Metric	U.S.	Ingredient	Procedure
37 mL	2½ T	Lemon juice	Combine.
80 mL	⅓ c	Vinegar, white	
240 mL	1 c	Salad oil	
15 mL	1 T	Worcestershire sauce	
80 mL	⅓ c	Water	
70 g	½ c	Onion, finely chopped	Add and mix.
2 cloves	2 cloves	Garlic, crushed	
57 g	¼ c	Pimiento, chopped	
60 mL	¼ c	Parsley, finely chopped	
28 g	1½ T	Salt	Blend in and mix. Pour over fresh vegetables and marinate.
⅛ t	⅛ t	Pepper, black	
4 g	1 T	Tarragon	
14 g	1 T	Sugar, granulated	

Note: May be used for fresh mushrooms and other fresh vegetables, or pasta.

DESSERT SAUCE RECIPES

BUTTERSCOTCH SAUCE

Yield: 1¼ qt (1.18 L)
Portion: 1½ T (1 oz/28 g)

Amount Metric	U.S.	Ingredient	Procedure
454 g	1 lb	Sugar, brown	Combine. Cook to soft-ball stage (240°F/115°C).
320 mL	1⅓ c	Corn syrup	
160 mL	⅔ c	Water	Remove from heat.
170 g	6 oz	Margarine or butter	Add margarine and marshmallows. Stir until melted. Cool.
57 g	2 oz	Marshmallows	
320 mL	1⅓ c	Evaporated milk	When cool, add milk.

CARAMEL SAUCE

Yield: 2 qt (1.89 L)
Portion: 2½ T (1½ oz/43 g)

Amount Metric	U.S.	Ingredient	Procedure
454 g	1 lb	Sugar, brown	Mix sugar, flour, and water.
454 g	1 lb	Sugar, granulated	
57 g	2 oz	Flour, all-purpose	Boil until slightly thick.
0.95 L	1 qt	Water	
227 g	8 oz	Margarine or butter	Stir in margarine and vanilla.
15 mL	1 T	Vanilla	

Note: Serve hot or cold over ice cream or apple desserts.

CHOCOLATE SAUCE

Yield: 1½ qt (1.42 L)
Portion: 2 T (1 oz/28 g)

Metric	U.S.	Ingredient	Procedure
340 g	12 oz	Sugar, granulated	Mix dry ingredients.
57 g	2 oz	Cornstarch	
6 g	1 t	Salt	
85 g	3 oz	Cocoa	
240 mL	1 c	Water, cold	Add cold water gradually to form a smooth paste.
840 mL	3½ c	Water, boiling	Add boiling water slowly while stirring. Boil for 5 minutes or until thickened. Remove from heat.
170 g	6 oz	Margarine or butter	Add margarine and vanilla. Stir to blend.
5 mL	1 t	Vanilla	

Note: Serve hot or cold on puddings, cake, or ice cream.

HOT FUDGE SAUCE

Yield: 1½ qt (1.42 L)
Portion: 2 T (1 oz/28 g)

Metric	U.S.	Ingredient	Procedure
227 g	8 oz	Margarine or butter, soft	Combine margarine, sugar, and milk over hot water.
680 g	1 lb 8 oz	Sugar, powdered	
1 can	1 13-oz can	Evaporated milk	Stir and cook slowly for 30 minutes.
227 g	8 oz	Chocolate, chipped or melted	Add chocolate. Stir until blended.

Notes:
1. Serve hot over ice cream.
2. This sauce may be stored in the refrigerator. Heat over hot water before serving. If too thick or grainy, add evaporated milk before heating.

CUSTARD SAUCE

Yield: 1 gal (3.79 L)
Portion: ⅓ c (2½ oz/70 g)

Amount		Ingredient	Procedure
Metric	U.S.		
397 g	14 oz	Sugar, granulated	Mix dry ingredients.
57 g	2 oz	Cornstarch	
3 g	½ t	Salt	
480 mL	2 c	Milk, cold	Add cold milk and mix until smooth.
2.84 L	3 qt	Milk, hot	Add cold mixture to hot milk gradually while stirring.
10 (170 g)	10 (6 oz)	Egg yolks, beaten	Add egg yolks. Cook over hot water until thickened, about 5 minutes.
30 mL	2 T	Vanilla	Remove from heat and add vanilla. Cool.

Note: Serve over cake-type puddings.

PEANUT BUTTER SAUCE

Yield: 2 qt (1.89 L)
Portion: 2½ T (1½ oz/43 g)

Amount		Ingredient	Procedure
Metric	U.S.		
340 g	12 oz	Sugar, granulated	Combine sugar, syrup, and water.
320 mL	1⅓ c	Syrup, white	Cook to 228°F (110°C)
180 mL	¾ c	Water, hot	and turn off heat.
170 g	6 oz	Margarine or butter	Add margarine and marshmallows. Stir until melted. Cool. Place in mixer bowl.
85 g	3 oz	Marshmallows, miniature	
340 g	12 oz	Evaporated milk	Add milk and peanut butter. Beat until well blended. Refrigerate.
227 g	8 oz	Peanut butter	

Note: Serve over ice cream.

LEMON SAUCE

Yield: 3 qt (2.84 L)
Portion: 3 T (2 oz/57 g)

Metric	U.S.	Ingredient	Procedure
908 g	2 lb	Sugar, granulated	Mix dry ingredients.
85 g	3 oz	Cornstarch	
3 g	½ t	Salt	
1.89 L	2 qt	Water, boiling	Add boiling water. Cook until clear.
160 mL	⅔ c	Lemon juice	Add lemon juice and margarine.
28 g	1 oz (2 T)	Margarine or butter	

Note: Serve hot with Steamed Pudding (p. 239), Bread Pudding (p. 238), or Rice Pudding (p. 238).

Variations:

1. **Nutmeg Sauce.** Omit lemon juice. Add 1 t (2 g) nutmeg. Increase margarine or butter to 4 oz (114 g).

2. **Orange Sauce.** Substitute orange juice for lemon juice. Add 1 t (3 g) freshly grated orange rind.

3. **Vanilla Sauce.** Omit lemon juice and reduce sugar to 1¼ lb (567 g). Add 2 T (30 mL) vanilla.

FLUFFY ORANGE SAUCE

Yield: 3 qt (2.84 L)
Portion: 3 T (1½ oz/43 g)

Metric	U.S.	Ingredient	Procedure
595 g	1 lb 5 oz	Margarine or butter	Melt margarine. Gradually add sugar. Beat with wire whip until like whipped cream.
964 g	2 lb 2 oz	Sugar, powdered	
10 (510 g)	10 (1 lb 2 oz)	Eggs, beaten	Add eggs slowly, beating constantly.
420 mL	1¾ c	Orange juice	Slowly blend in orange rind. Heat 10–15 minutes. Beat again.
9 g	1½ T	Orange rind, grated	

RASPBERRY SAUCE

Yield: 3 qt (2.84 L)
Portion: 3 T (2 oz/57 g)

Amount		Ingredient	Procedure
Metric	U.S.		
2.27 kg	5 lb	Red raspberries, frozen	Defrost berries. Do not drain.
57 g	¼ c	Sugar, granulated	Combine sugar and cornstarch and add to berries. Cook until clear.
28 g	1 oz (3½ T)	Cornstarch	
600 mL	2½ c	Currant jelly	Add jelly. Stir until melted. Cool.

Notes:
1. Serve over vanilla ice cream; raspberry, lemon, or lime sherbet.
2. Raspberries may be strained before thickening.

Variation: **Peach Melba.** Pour 3 T (45 mL) Raspberry Sauce over a scoop of vanilla ice cream placed in the center of a canned, fresh, or frozen peach half.

HARD SAUCE

Yield: 3⅓ c (800 mL)
Portion: 1 T (½ oz/14 g)

Amount		Ingredient	Procedure
Metric	U.S.		
227 g	8 oz	Butter	Cream butter on medium speed until soft and fluffy.
30 mL	2 T	Water, boiling	Add water and continue to cream until very light.
539 g	1 lb 3 oz	Sugar, powdered	Add sugar gradually. Continue creaming. Add lemon juice. Place in refrigerator to harden.
3 mL	½ t	Lemon juice	

Note: Serve with Christmas Pudding (p. 239), or Baked Apples (p. 248).

Variations:
1. **Cherry Hard Sauce.** Add ½ c (120 mL) chopped maraschino cherries.
2. **Strawberry Hard Sauce.** Omit lemon juice and water. Add ¾ c (180 mL) fresh or frozen strawberries, chopped.

BROWN SUGAR HARD SAUCE

Yield: 1 qt (0.95 L)
Portion: 1 T (½ oz/14 g)

Amount Metric	U.S.	Ingredient	Procedure
340 g	12 oz	Butter	Cream butter on medium speed until light.
567 g	1 lb 4 oz	Sugar, light brown	Add sugar gradually while creaming.
10 mL	2 t	Vanilla	Add vanilla. Cream until fluffy.
180 mL	¾ c	Cream, whipping	Whip cream. Fold into sugar mixture. Chill.

Note: Serve with Christmas Pudding (p. 239).

BROWN SUGAR SYRUP

Yield: 2 gal (7.57 L)

Amount Metric	U.S.	Ingredient	Procedure
2.27 kg	5 lb	Sugar, brown	Combine all ingredients.
2.5 kg	5 lb 8 oz	Sugar, granulated	Stir and heat until sugar is dissolved.
240 mL	1 c	Corn syrup	
2.37 L	2½ qt	Water	
114 g	4 oz	Margarine or butter	

Notes:
1. Serve hot or cold on pancakes, fritters, or waffles.
2. ½ t maple flavoring may be added.

Soups

Soups may be clear and light or thick and hearty. Most soups are at their best piping hot; others are served chilled.

Stock, the basic ingredient of many soups, is made by simmering meat, poultry, seafood, and/or vegetables in water to extract their flavor. *Brown stock*, made from beef that has been browned before simmering; and *white* or *light stock*, made from veal and/or chicken, are the stocks used most often. To prepare stock, cover the meat or poultry with cold water, bring to the boiling point, and simmer for 3–4 hours. Strain and cool the broth, and remove the fat. When cold, the fat will congeal on top and may be skimmed off. To clarify the stock after it has been chilled, add egg whites and crushed egg shells, boil for 15–20 minutes, then strain (p. 495). Stock is highly perishable. If it is not to be used immediately, it may be reduced in volume by boiling to one half or one fourth its volume and frozen for later use.

Bouillon is made from clarified beef broth, *consommé* from clarified white or light stock.

Cream soups are made with a thin white sauce combined with mashed, strained, or finely chopped vegetables, meat, chicken, or fish. Chicken stock may be used to replace part of the milk in the sauce to enhance the flavor.

Bisque is a mixture of chopped shellfish, stock, milk, and seasonings, usually thickened.

Purée is a thick soup made by pressing cooked vegetables or fish through a sieve into their own stock.

Chowder is an unstrained, heavy, thick soup prepared from meat, poultry, seafood, and/or vegetables. Most contain potatoes and milk or cream.

The preparation of soups, especially those made from stock, is time consuming, and many food services now use commercial food or soup bases. The amount of meat concentrate in commercial soup bases varies, so the choice of base should be made carefully to assure a desirable, full-flavored stock. A high-quality soup base is a concentrate of cooked meat, poultry, seafood, or vegetables, with the concentrated cooking juices and seasonings included. It has a purée-like consistency and may require refrigeration. One pound of soup base produces an average of 5 gal of ready-to-use stock. Soup bases can be used to prepare sauces, gravies, and stuffings also. Most granulated soup bases and some paste products consist of flavored salt as the primary ingredient, so when using these products the salt listed in the recipe should be deleted or reduced.

STOCK SOUP RECIPES

BEEF STOCK

Yield: 3 gal (11.36 L)

Amount Metric	U.S.	Ingredient	Procedure
6.8 kg	15 lb	Beef shank, lean	Pour water over beef shanks in large kettle or steam-jacketed kettle.
18.93 L	5 gal	Water, cold	
227 g	8 oz	Onions, quartered	Add vegetables and seasonings.
227 g	8 oz	Celery, with leaves, chopped	Bring to boiling point.
227 g	8 oz	Carrots, chopped	Reduce heat and simmer until meat leaves bone, about 4 hours.
9 g	1 T	Peppercorns	
2	2	Bay leaves	
85 g	3 oz	Salt	Remove meat, strain, and refrigerate for several hours. Fat will congeal on top. Skim off.

Variations:

1. **Beef Stock with Soup Base.** Add 8 oz (227 g) concentrated beef base to 2½ gal (9.46 L) water. Exact proportion may vary with different manufacturers. If using for sauces and casseroles, delete or reduce amount of salt specified in recipe.

2. **Brown Stock.** Allow 10 lb (4.54 kg) beef shank to stand 30 minutes in cold water. Heat slowly to boiling point. Simmer 2 hours. Add vegetables that have been browned with remaining meat. Add seasonings. Simmer 3 hours.

CHICKEN STOCK

Yield: 3 gal (11.36 L)

Amount Metric	U.S.	Ingredient	Procedure
9.08 kg	20 lb AP	Chicken	Cut up chicken. Place in large kettle or steam-jacketed kettle. Add water.
18.93 L	5 gal	Water, cold	
227 g	8 oz	Onions, quartered	Add vegetables and seasonings. Bring to boiling point.
227 g	8 oz	Celery, with leaves, chopped	
227 g	8 oz	Carrots, chopped	Reduce heat and simmer until chicken is tender.
85 g	3 oz	Salt	
9 g	1 T	Peppercorns	Remove chicken and strain broth. Refrigerate. Remove chicken from bones. Cut up for soup or reserve for later use.
2	2	Bay leaves	
2 g	2 t	Marjoram	
3	3	Egg shells, crushed	When broth is cold, fat will congeal on top. Skim off. If a clear broth is desired, clarify by adding egg shells and whites to broth. Bring to boiling point and simmer 15 minutes. Strain through cheesecloth or fine strainer.
3	3	Egg whites, beaten	

Variations:

1. **Chicken Stock with Soup Base.** Add 8 oz (227 g) concentrated chicken base to 2½ gal (9.46 L) water. Exact proportion may vary with different manufacturers. If using for sauces and casseroles, delete or reduce amount of salt specified in recipe.

2. **White Stock.** Substitute knuckle of veal for part of chicken.

BOUILLON

Yield: 3 gal (11.36 L)
Portion: 1 c (240 mL)

Amount		Ingredient	Procedure
Metric	U.S.		
3.63 kg	8 lb	Beef, lean	Sear beef. Add bone and water.
1.81 kg	4 lb	Bone, cracked	Simmer for 3–4 hours. Replace water as necessary.
15.14 L	4 gal	Water, cold	
227 g	8 oz	Carrots, diced	Add vegetables and seasonings.
227 g	8 oz	Celery, chopped	Cook 1 hour. Strain.
227 g	8 oz	Onions, quartered	Chill overnight.
1	1	Bay leaf	Remove fat.
9 g	1 T	Peppercorns	
76 g	¼ c	Salt	
3	3	Egg shells, crushed	Add egg shells and whites to clear the broth. Bring slowly to boiling point, stirring constantly. Boil 15–20 minutes without stirring. Strain through a cloth.
3	3	Egg whites, beaten	

Variations:

1. **Chicken Bouillon.** Substitute 20 lb (9.08 kg) chicken, cut up, for the beef and bone. Do not sear chicken.
2. **Tomato Bouillon.** To 1½ gal (5.68 L) bouillon, add 4 46-oz (1.36-L) cans tomato juice, 2 oz (57 g) chopped onion, 2 oz (57 g) sugar, 2 oz (57 g) salt (amount may vary), ½ t (1 g) pepper, and 2 bay leaves.

STOCK SOUP RECIPES 497

BEEF BARLEY SOUP

Yield: 50 portions
3 gal (11.36 L)
Portion: 1 c (8 oz/227 g)

Amount Metric	U.S.	Ingredient	Procedure
1.36 kg	3 lb	Beef, cubed	Brown beef cubes in kettle. Drain off fat.
624 g	1 lb 6 oz	Celery, chopped	Add celery and onions.
624 g	1 lb 6 oz	Onions, chopped	Sauté until tender.
11.36 L	3 gal	Beef Stock (p. 494)	Add remaining
21 g	3 T	Pepper, black	ingredients. Bring to
1	1	Bay leaf	a boil.
624 g	1 lb 6 oz	Carrots, diced	Lower heat and simmer
284 g	10 oz	Pearl barley	1 hour.

VEGETABLE BEEF SOUP

Yield: 50 portions
3 gal (11.36 L)
Portion: 1 c (8 oz/227 g)

Amount Metric	U.S.	Ingredient	Procedure
7.57 L	2 gal	Beef Stock (p. 494)	Heat stock in kettle.
227 g	8 oz	Carrots, cubed	Add vegetables and
454 g	1 lb	Celery, chopped	seasonings.
680 g	1 lb 8 oz	Onions, chopped	Cover and simmer about
454 g	1 lb	Potatoes, cubed	1 hour. Replace water
38 g	2 T	Salt	as necessary.
2 g	1 t	Pepper, black	
1 No. 10 can	1 No. 10 can	Tomatoes, diced, canned	
908 g	2 lb	Cooked beef, chopped	Add chopped beef. Heat to serving temperature.

Notes:
1. 8 oz (227 g) raw rice or 4 oz (114 g) dry noodles may be substituted for the potatoes.
2. Browned beef cubes may be substituted for cooked beef. Brown in kettle before stock is added.

Variations:
1. **Julienne Soup.** Cut carrots, celery, and potatoes in long, thin strips.
2. **Vegetable Soup.** Delete beef. Increase carrots and celery to 1½ lb (680 g) each.

HEARTY BEEF VEGETABLE SOUP

Yield: 50 portions
3 gal (11.36 L)
Portion: 1 c (8 oz/227 g)

Amount		Ingredient	Procedure
Metric	*U.S.*		
3.63 kg	8 lb	Ground beef	Brown meat. Drain off fat.
454 g	1 lb	Onions, chopped	Add onions and cook until tender.
255 g	9 oz	Margarine	Melt margarine and stir in flour. Cook 10 minutes.
255 g	9 oz	Flour, all-purpose	
4.73 L	1¼ gal	Beef Stock (p. 494)	Add beef stock and seasonings, stirring constantly. Cook until mixture boils and has thickened. Add browned meat and onions.
19 g	1 T	Salt	
1 g	½ t	Pepper, black	
340 g	12 oz	Carrots, fresh, diced	Cook vegetables until barely tender. Drain. (Vegetables should be crunchy.)
284 g	10 oz	Celery, sliced	
1.81 kg	4 lb	Mixed vegetables, frozen	Cook mixed vegetables until partially done. Add, with other vegetables, to the soup. Stir carefully to blend.
1.14 kg	2 lb 8 oz	Tomatoes, diced, canned	Add tomatoes. Heat to serving temperature.

BEEF NOODLE SOUP

Yield: 50 portions
3 gal (11.36 L)
Portion: 1 c (8 oz/227 g)

Amount		Ingredient	Procedure
Metric	U.S.		
908 g	2 lb	Beef, fresh, cubed	Heat oil in kettle. Add beef cubes and seasonings and cook until lightly browned. Drain off fat.
12 g	2 t	Salt	
1 g	½ t	Pepper, black	
120 mL	½ c	Cooking oil	
227 g	8 oz	Onions, chopped	Add onions and celery and sauté.
227 g	8 oz	Celery, chopped	
10.41 L	2¾ gal	Beef Stock (p. 494)	Add beef stock. Simmer 1 hour.
454 g	1 lb AP	Noodles	Add noodles and simmer until tender, 5–10 minutes. Add salt if needed.

Variations:

1. **Alphabet Soup.** Use alphabet noodles.
2. **Beef Rice Soup.** Substitute 1 lb 8 oz (1.36 kg) rice for noodles.
3. **Creole Soup.** Reduce beef stock to 2¼ gal (8.52 L). Add 1 No. 10 can tomatoes, 8 oz (227 g) shredded green peppers, 1 lb (454 g) sliced okra, and 4 bay leaves. Substitute rice for noodles.

CHICKEN NOODLE SOUP

Yield: 50 portions
3 gal (11.36 L)
Portion: 1 c (8 oz/227 g)

Amount Metric	U.S.	Ingredient	Procedure
11.36 L	3 gal	Chicken Stock (p. 495)	Bring stock to a boil. Add onion and celery. Cook until tender.
227 g	8 oz	Onion, chopped	
227 g	8 oz	Celery, chopped	
454 g	1 lb	Noodles	Add noodles. Cook for about 15 minutes or until noodles are done.
227 g	8 oz	Margarine, melted	Blend margarine and flour. Add to soup, stirring until slightly thickened.
114 g	4 oz	Flour, all-purpose	
680 g	1 lb 8 oz	Cooked chicken, diced	Add chicken and simmer for 5 minutes.

Variation: **Chicken Rice Soup.** Substitute 12 oz (340 g) rice for the noodles.

MINESTRONE SOUP

Yield: 50 portions
3 gal (11.36 L)
Portion: 1 c (8 oz/227 g)

Amount			
Metric	U.S.	Ingredient	Procedure
454 g	1 lb	Bacon, diced	Fry bacon until crisp. Drain.
340 g 2 cloves	12 oz 2 cloves	Onions, chopped Garlic, minced	Sauté onion and garlic in a little bacon fat until tender. Place, with bacon, in a large kettle.
7.57 L 2 2 g	2 gal 2 1 t	Beef Stock (p. 494) Bay leaves Pepper, black	Add stock and seasonings. Heat to boiling.
340 g 340 g 340 g 340 g 85 g 340 g 57 g 908 g 794 g	12 oz 12 oz 12 oz 12 oz 3 oz 12 oz 2 oz 2 lb 1 lb 12 oz	Cabbage, chopped Carrots, fresh, diced Potatoes, raw, chopped Celery, chopped Spinach, fresh, chopped Green beans, cut, canned Spaghetti, long Tomatoes, canned, diced Beans, red, canned	Add vegetables and spaghetti. Simmer 45 minutes.
85 g 240 mL	3 oz 1 c	Flour, all-purpose Water, cold	Make a smooth paste of the flour and water. Stir into soup. Cook 10 minutes longer.

MULLIGATAWNY SOUP

Yield: 50 portions
3 gal (11.36 L)
Portion: 1 c (8 oz/227 g)

Amount Metric	U.S.	Ingredient	Procedure
170 g	6 oz	Margarine	Melt margarine in steam-jacketed kettle or stock pot.
340 g	12 oz	Onions, finely chopped	
340 g	12 oz	Carrots, Julienne	Add vegetables and apples. Cook 5 minutes.
340 g	12 oz	Celery, thinly sliced	
454 g	1 lb	Green peppers, cut in thin strips	
908 g	2 lb	Apples, pared and chopped	
340 g	12 oz	Flour, all-purpose	Stir in flour and seasonings.
7 g	1 T	Curry powder	
19 g	1 T	Salt	
2 g	¾ t	Pepper, black	
7.57 L	2 gal	Chicken Stock (p. 495)	Slowly add chicken stock, tomatoes, and cloves.
1 No. 10 can	1 No. 10 can	Tomatoes, canned, diced, with juice	
8	8	Cloves, whole	
1.36 kg	3 lb	Cooked chicken, diced	Add chicken. Bring to a boil. Reduce heat and simmer until ingredients are tender, about 30 minutes.
15 g	¼ c	Parsley, chopped	Add parsley. Simmer 5 minutes.

PEPPER POT SOUP

Yield: 50 portions
3 gal (11.36 L)
Portion: 1 c (8 oz/227 g)

Amount		Ingredient	Procedure
Metric	U.S.		
340 g	12 oz	Margarine or butter	Sauté vegetables in margarine until lightly browned, about 15 minutes.
57 g	2 oz	Onion, finely chopped	
227 g	8 oz	Green peppers, finely chopped	
170 g	6 oz	Celery, chopped	
1.59 kg	3 lb 8 oz	Potatoes, diced	
142 g	5 oz	Flour, all-purpose	Add flour and stir until well blended.
8.52 L	2¼ gal	Beef or Chicken Stock (p. 494, 495)	Combine stock and milk. Add to vegetable mixture, while stirring.
0.95 L	1 qt	Milk, hot	If soup base is used for stock, taste before adding salt.
28 g	1 oz (1½ T)	Salt	
19 g	2 T	Red pepper or pimiento, chopped	Add red pepper. Keep just below boiling point for 30 minutes, stirring frequently.

Note: This soup is good served with Spaetzles (p. 108). Prepare 1 recipe for 50 servings.

RICE SOUP

Yield: 50 portions
3 gal (11.36 L)
Portion: 1 c (8 oz/227 g)

Amount Metric	U.S.	Ingredient	Procedure
4.73 L	5 qt	Beef or Chicken Stock (p. 494, 495)	Place in large kettle. Heat.
340 g	12 oz	Rice	Cook rice according to directions on p. 358. Add to hot stock.
900 mL	3¾ c	Water, boiling	
9 g	1½ t	Salt	
3.79 L	1 gal	Milk, hot	Add milk and seasonings to stock and rice. If soup base has been used for stock, taste before adding salt.
5 ml	1 t	Onion juice	
57 g	3 T	Salt	
2 g	1 t	Pepper, black	
15 g	¼ c	Parsley, chopped	

Note: To serve, garnish with toast rings sprinkled with chopped parsley and Parmesan cheese.

TOMATO RICE SOUP

Yield: 50 portions
3 gal (11.36 L)
Portion: 1 c (8 oz/227 g)

Amount Metric	U.S.	Ingredient	Procedure
7.57 L	2 gal	Beef or Chicken Stock (p. 494, 495)	Heat stock and purée to boiling point.
3.79 L	1 gal	Tomato purée	
57 g	2 oz	Onion, chopped	Add vegetables and rice. Cook until rice is tender.
114 g	4 oz	Green pepper, chopped	
227 g	8 oz	Rice	
170 g	6 oz	Margarine or butter	Melt margarine and add flour. Mix until smooth. Add to soup while stirring. Salt to taste.
85 g	3 oz	Flour, all-purpose	

Variation: **Tomato Barley Soup.** Add 1 lb (454 g) barley in place of rice.

FRENCH ONION SOUP

Yield: 50 portions
3 gal (11.36 L)
Portion: 1 c (8 oz/227 g)

Amount		Ingredient	Procedure
Metric	U.S.		
3.63 kg	8 lb	Onions, fresh	Cut onions in thin slices.
340 g	12 oz	Margarine or shortening	Sauté in margarine in large kettle.
85 g	3 oz	Flour, all-purpose	Add flour and seasonings.
	to taste	Salt	Cook 10 minutes.
	to taste	Pepper, black	
11.36 L	3 gal	Beef Stock (p. 494)	Add stock and Worcestershire sauce.
45 mL	3 T	Worcestershire sauce	Cook until onions are tender.
340 g	12 oz	Croutons	To serve, ladle soup over croutons or toasted bread.
57 g	2 oz	Parmesan cheese, grated, or Swiss cheese, shredded	Sprinkle with cheese.

NAVY BEAN SOUP

Yield: 50 portions
3 gal (11.36 L)
Portion: 1 c (8 oz/227 g)

Amount Metric	U.S.	Ingredient	Procedure
1.36 kg	3 lb	Navy beans, dry	Wash beans. Add boiling water. Cover and let stand 1 hour or longer. Simmer beans about 1 hour.
11.36 L	3 gal	Water, boiling	
1.36 kg	3 lb	Ham cubes	Add ham and seasonings. Cook until beans are tender, 1–1½ hours. Add water to make volume of 3¼ gal (12.3 L). Check seasoning. Add salt if needed. Heat to serving temperature.
114 g	4 oz	Onion, chopped	
227 g	8 oz	Celery, diced	
6 g	1 T	Pepper, black	
		Water	

Notes:

1. Great Northern beans may be substituted for navy beans.
2. Ham base may be substituted for part of the water.

SPLIT PEA SOUP

Yield: 50 portions
3 gal (11.36 L)
Portion: 1 c (8 oz/227 g)

Amount		Ingredient	Procedure
Metric	U.S.		
1.81 kg	4 lb	Split peas	Wash peas. Add boiling water, cover, and soak 1 hour or longer.
7.57 L	2 gal	Water, boiling	
908 g	2 lb	Ham cubes	Add ham and onion. Cook 1–2 hours or until peas are soft. Add water to make 2½ gal (9.46 L)
114 g	4 oz	Onion, chopped	
		Water	
114 g	4 oz	Margarine or butter	Melt margarine and add flour. Stir until smooth. Add stock while stirring and cook until thickened. Add to peas. Add salt if needed.
57 g	2 oz	Flour, all-purpose	
1.89 L	2 qt	Chicken Stock (p. 495)	
1 g	½ t	Pepper, black	

Note: If soup becomes too thick, add hot water to bring to desired consistency. If a smoother soup is desired, purée peas.

CORN CHOWDER

Yield: 50 portions
3 gal (11.36 L)
Portion: 1 c (8 oz/227 g)

Amount		Ingredient	Procedure
Metric	U.S.		
454 g	1 lb	Bacon or salt pork, diced	Fry bacon until crisp.
340 g	12 oz	Onion, chopped	Add onions and cook slowly for 5 minutes. Remove bacon and onions from fat.
114 g	4 oz	Bacon fat	Add flour and salt to bacon fat. Blend.
114 g	4 oz	Flour, all-purpose	
57 g	3 T	Salt	
7.57 L	2 gal	Milk	Add milk, stirring constantly.
2.27 kg	5 lb	Potatoes, cubed, cooked	Add potatoes, corn, bacon, and onions. Heat to serving temperature.
1 No. 10 can	1 No. 10 can	Corn, whole kernel	

Variation: **Potato Chowder.** Omit corn and increase potatoes to 8 lb (3.63 kg). Add 6 oz (170 g) celery, chopped. Use chicken stock for half the milk if desired.

HEARTY POTATO HAM CHOWDER

Yield: 50 portions
3 gal (11.36 L)
Portion: 1 c (8 oz/227 g)

Amount Metric	U.S.	Ingredient	Procedure
85 g	3 oz	Margarine or butter	In steam-jacketed or other large kettle, sauté onions and green pepper in margarine until tender.
227 g	8 oz	Onion, green, finely chopped	
340 g	12 oz	Green peppers, chopped	
85 g	3 oz	Flour, all-purpose	Add flour and seasonings. Stir until blended. Cook 10 minutes, stirring often.
1 g	½ t	Pepper, white	
2 g	1 t	Paprika	
2.84 L	3 qt	Chicken Stock (p. 495)	Add stock. Stir until smooth. Cook and stir until mixture begins to thicken.
1.14 kg	2 lb 8 oz	Ham, coarsely chopped	Add ham, potatoes, and corn. Heat.
2.5 kg	5 lb 8 oz	Potatoes, cooked, cubed	
1.7 kg	3 lb 12 oz	Corn, whole kernel	
2.6 L	2¾ qt	Milk	Add milk and mix well. Heat to serving temperature.
120 mL	½ c	Parsley, fresh, chopped	Sprinkle parsley over chowder before serving.

CREAM SOUP RECIPES

BASIC SAUCE FOR CREAM SOUP

Yield: 2½ gal (9.46 L) basic sauce

Amount		Ingredient	Procedure
Metric	U.S.		
340 g	12 oz	Margarine or butter	Melt margarine. Add
57 g	2 oz	Onions, finely chopped	onions and sauté until tender.
170 g	6 oz	Flour, all-purpose	Add flour and seasonings
57 g	2 oz (3 T)	Salt	and stir until blended.
1 g	½ t	Pepper, white	
8.52 L	2¼ gal	Milk, hot	Add milk while stirring. Cook until thickened. Add vegetables and seasonings as suggested below to make a variety of cream soups.

Suggestions for Cream Soups: One recipe Basic Sauce for Cream Soup plus additions suggested below will yield 3 gal (11.36 L) soup, 50 portions, 1 c (8 oz/227 g).

1. **Cream of Asparagus Soup.** Add 6½ lb (2.95 kg) cooked, chopped or puréed asparagus.
2. **Cream of Broccoli Soup.** Add 6 lb (2.72 kg) cooked, chopped broccoli.
3. **Cream of Celery Soup.** Add 1½ lb (680 g) cooked chopped celery and 8 oz (227 g) diced carrots.
4. **Cream of Mushroom Soup.** Increase onion to 4 oz (114 g). Decrease flour to 4 oz (114 g). Chicken stock may be substituted for part of the milk. Add 2 lb (908 g) mushrooms, sliced or chopped, sautéed with the onion in margarine.
5. **Cream of Potato Soup.** Increase onions to 6 oz (170 g). Add 12 lb (5.44 kg) cooked diced potatoes and 8 oz (227 g) chopped celery. Potatoes may be mashed or puréed if desired.
6. **Cream of Spinach Soup.** Add 3 qt (2.84 L) chopped, fresh or frozen spinach.
7. **Cream of Vegetable Soup.** Add 1 lb (454 g) chopped celery, 1 lb (454 g) diced carrots, and 2 lb (908 g) diced potatoes that have been cooked until tender. Increase onion to 4 oz (114 g).
8. **Vegetable Chowder.** Add 2 No. 2 cans whole kernel corn, 5 oz (142 g) green pepper, chopped, and 1 lb (454 g) diced cooked bacon.

CREAM OF CHICKEN SOUP

Yield: 50 portions
3 gal (11.36 L)
Portion: 1 c (8 oz/227 g)

Amount		Ingredient	Procedure
Metric	U.S.		
227 g	8 oz	Margarine or butter	Melt margarine. Add flour and salt and stir until blended. Cook for 3–4 minutes.
85 g	3 oz	Flour, all-purpose	
28 g	1 oz (1½ T)	Salt	
3.79 L	1 gal	Milk	Add milk while stirring. Cook over low heat until of consistency of thin white sauce.
7.57 L	2 gal	Chicken Stock	Add stock and seasonings. If soup base is used for stock, taste before adding celery salt.
5 g	2 t	Celery salt	
¼ t	¼ t	Pepper, white	
680 g	1 lb 8 oz	Cooked chicken, chopped	Add chicken. Heat to serving temperature.

Note: 1 lb (454 g) cooked rice or noodles may be added.

Variation: **Chicken Velvet Soup.** Substitute light cream or half and half for milk. Increase flour to 9 oz (255 g) and cooked chopped chicken to 2½ lb (1.14 kg). Add 6 oz (170 g) sliced celery and simmer until celery is of the desired doneness, about 10 minutes.

CREAM OF TOMATO SOUP

Yield: 50 portions
3 gal (11.36 L)
Portion: 1 c (8 oz/227 g)

Amount		Ingredient	Procedure
Metric	U.S.		
5.68 L	1½ gal	Tomato juice	Add onion and bay leaf to tomato juice. Heat to boiling point.
28 g	1 oz	Onion, finely chopped	
½	½	Bay leaf	
12 g	1 T	Baking soda	Add soda.
284 g	10 oz	Margarine or butter	Melt margarine and add flour and seasonings. Stir until blended.
85 g	3 oz	Flour, all-purpose	
57 g	2 oz (3 T)	Salt	
2 g	1 t	Pepper, white	
114 g	4 oz	Sugar, granulated	
5.68 L	1½ gal	Milk, hot	Add milk while stirring. Cook until thickened. Just before serving, add hot tomato mixture gradually, while stirring. Remove bay leaf before serving.

CHEESE SOUP

Yield: 50 portions
3 gal (11.36 L)
Portion: 1 c (8 oz/227 g)

Amount		Ingredient	Procedure
Metric	U.S.		
227 g	8 oz	Margarine or butter	Sauté onion in margarine until lightly browned.
227 g	8 oz	Onion, chopped	
114 g	4 oz	Flour, all-purpose	Add flour and cornstarch. Blend. Cook 3–4 minutes.
57 g	2 oz	Cornstarch	
5 mL	1 t	Paprika	Add seasonings and blend. Add milk and stock slowly, while stirring. Cook until thickened.
38 g	2 T	Salt	
2 g	1 t	Pepper, white	
3.79 L	1 gal	Milk	
5.68 L	1½ gal	Chicken Stock (p. 495)	
454 g	1 lb	Carrots, finely diced	Cook carrots and celery until tender but slightly crisp.
340 g	12 oz	Celery, finely diced	
454 g	1 lb	Cheddar cheese, sharp, shredded	Add cheese and blend at low temperature. Garnish with chopped parsley.

BROCCOLI AND CHEESE SOUP

Yield: 50 portions
3 gal (11.36 L)
Portion: 1 c (8 oz/227 g)

Amount Metric	U.S.	Ingredient	Procedure
284 g	10 oz	Onions, finely chopped	In steam-jacketed or other large kettle, sauté onions in melted margarine until tender.
284 g	10 oz	Margarine or butter	
369 g	13 oz	Flour, all-purpose	Add flour and seasonings. Stir until blended. Cook 10 minutes, stirring often.
19 g	1 T	Salt	
2 g	1 t	Pepper, black	
5.68 L	1½ gal	Milk	Add milk and stock. Stir until blended. Reduce heat and cook until thickened, stirring often.
2.37 L	2½ qt	Chicken Stock (p. 495)	
1.05 kg	2 lb 5 oz	Processed cheese, coarsely shredded	Add cheese. Stir until melted.
1.81 kg	4 lb	Broccoli cuts, frozen	Steam broccoli until just tender. Chop, if necessary. Add to cheese mixture and heat to serving temperature.

NEW ENGLAND CLAM CHOWDER

Yield: 50 portions
3 gal (11.36 L)
Portion: 1 c (8 oz/227 g)

Amount		Ingredient	Procedure
Metric	U.S.		
2.72 kg	6 lb	Potatoes, cubed	Cook potatoes until
0.95 L	1 qt	Water	tender. Do not drain.
19 g	1 T	Salt	Add in last step.
227 g	8 oz	Onion, chopped	Sauté onion and bacon in
114 g	4 oz	Bacon, finely diced	steam-jacketed or other large kettle for 5 minutes, or until lightly browned.
227 g	8 oz	Margarine or butter	Add margarine and melt.
85 g	3 oz	Flour, all-purpose	Add flour and seasonings.
2 g	1 t	Pepper, white	Stir until blended. Cook 5 minutes.
7.57 L	2 gal	Milk	Add milk gradually while stirring. Cook until thickened.
1.81 kg	4 lb	Clams, minced, undrained	Add clams, potatoes, and potato water. Heat to serving temperature.

Notes:

1. 1 gal (3.79 L) fresh clams may be used. Clean and steam until tender. Drain and chop. Save juice.

2. Garnish with fresh or frozen chives, chopped.

Variation: **Fish Chowder.** Delete clams. Add 1 t (1 g) thyme, 1 t (1 g) crushed rosemary, 1 lb (454 g) diced celery, 2 t (10 mL) Worcestershire sauce, ½ t (3 mL) Tabasco sauce, and 3 lb (1.36 kg) flaked white fish, or 1 lb (454 g) shrimp and 2 lb (908 g) minced clams.

MANHATTAN FISH OR CLAM CHOWDER

Yield: 50 portions
3 gal (11.36 L)
Portion: 1 c (8 oz/227 g)

Amount		Ingredient	Procedure
Metric	U.S.		
454 g	1 lb	Bacon, diced	Cook bacon until crisp. Drain off excess fat.
595 g	1 lb 5 oz	Onions, chopped	Add onions, Sauté until tender. Place onions and bacon in large kettle.
2.84 L	3 qt	Water	Add water, vegetables, and spices. Bring to a boil. Reduce heat. Simmer 40–45 minutes or until vegetables are tender
1 No. 10 can	1 No. 10 can	Tomatoes, diced	
1.36 kg	3 lb	Potatoes, chopped	
567 g	1 lb 4 oz	Carrots, fresh, diced	
567 g	1 lb 4 oz	Celery, chopped	
480 mL	2 c	Catsup	
80 mL	⅓ c	Worcestershire sauce	
38 g	2 T	Salt	
2 g	1 t	Pepper, black	
2	2	Bay leaves	
1 g	1 t	Thyme, powdered	
1.59 kg	3 lb 8 oz	Fish, boneless, cooked and flaked, or minced clams	Add fish. Cover and simmer 5–10 minutes.
14 g	¼ c	Parsley, fresh, chopped	Sprinkle parsley over soup before serving.

OYSTER STEW

Yield: 50 portions
3 gal (11.36 L)
Portion: 1 c (8 oz/227 g)

Amount			
Metric	U.S.	Ingredient	Procedure
9.46 L	2½ gal	Milk	Scald milk.
2.37 L	2½ qt	Oysters	Heat oysters and butter only until edges of oysters begin to curl.
227 g	8 oz	Butter or margarine	
57 g	2 oz (3 T)	Salt	About 10 minutes before serving, add oysters and oyster liquor and seasonings to scalded milk.
1 g	½ t	Pepper	
			Serve immediately to avoid curdling.

CHILLED SOUP RECIPES

GAZPACHO (SPANISH CHILLED SOUP)

Yield: 50 portions
1¾ gal (6.62 L)
Portion: ½ c (4 oz/114 g)

Amount Metric	U.S.	Ingredient	Procedure
114 g	4 oz	Mushrooms, fresh, chopped	Sauté mushrooms in olive oil until light brown.
120 mL	½ c	Olive oil	
3 cloves	3 cloves	Garlic	Crush garlic in salt.
38 g	2 T	Salt	
1.36 kg	3 lb	Tomatoes, fresh, finely chopped	Combine remaining ingredients in a stainless steel or glass container.
567 g	1 lb 4 oz	Green peppers, finely chopped	
340 g	12 oz	Celery, finely chopped	Add mushrooms and garlic.
454 g	1 lb	Cucumbers, finely chopped	If too thick, add more tomato juice.
680 g	1 lb 8 oz	Onion, finely chopped	Cover and chill.
30 mL	2 T	Chives, chopped	
7 g	3 T	Parsley, chopped	
7 g	1 T	Pepper, black	
15 mL	1 T	Worcestershire sauce	
360 mL	1½ c	Tarragon wine vinegar	
5 mL	1 t	Tabasco sauce	
2.37 L	2½ qt	Tomato juice	

Note: Serve chilled with croutons, crackers, or specialty breads.

VICHYSSOISE (CHILLED POTATO SOUP)

Yield: 50 portions
3 gal (11.36 L)
Portion: 1 c (8 oz/227 g)

Amount			
Metric	U.S.	Ingredient	Procedure
3.79 L	1 gal	Chicken Stock (p. 495)	Combine stock and onions and cook until onions are tender. Strain.
1.36 kg	3 lb	Onions, chopped	
2.72 kg	6 lb	Potatoes, diced	Steam potatoes until tender. Mash.
19 g	1 T	Salt	Add seasonings and chicken stock to potatoes.
12 g	2 t	Celery salt	
6 g	1 t	Garlic salt	
1 g	½ t	Pepper, white	
4.73 L	1¼ gal	Cream, half and half	Add cream and mix well. Chill thoroughly.
9 g	⅓ c	Parsley, chives, or green onion tops, chopped	Garnish chilled soup with parsley, chives, or green onion tops.

VEGETABLES

The use of vegetables in food services has increased over the past few years and today holds an important place on the menus of many food service establishments.

Vegetables are available as fresh, frozen, canned, or dried. Frozen and canned vegetables require less labor to prepare and have more predictable yields than do the fresh. Many dietitians and food service managers, however, like to use fresh vegetables when they are in season, and particularly the ones that are not excessively time consuming to prepare. Correct preparation and cooking methods are essential to preserving the nutritive value, color, and palatability of fresh vegetables.

The quantity of vegetables to buy depends on the desired portion size and the method of preparation. One No. 10 can or 5 lb (2.27 kg) of frozen vegetables yields 25 3-oz portions of most kinds. For fresh vegetables, the loss in preparation must be considered in determining the amount to purchase. Table 1.2 gives the approximate yield in the preparation of fresh vegetables.

FRESH AND FROZEN VEGETABLES

Fresh or frozen vegetables may be cooked by boiling, steaming, baking, or frying. The method used depends largely on the type of product, the amount to be cooked, and the equipment available.

A small, steam-jacketed kettle, if time and pressure are carefully controlled, is highly satisfactory for cooking both fresh and frozen vegetables. It usually is large enough to prevent crowding; it will bring water to a boil quickly after vegetables are added; and it will cook a large or small amount equally well. A tilting fry pan may be used successfully also.

Vegetables may be cooked with satisfactory results in a steamer under pressure if cooked in small quantities and arranged in thin layers in shallow pans. Here, too, the time and temperature must be carefully controlled. Quick cooking in a high-pressure or zero-pressure steamer is especially successful. One advantage of steam cooking is that vegetables may be weighed and placed in hot food inset pans as they are prepared, then cooked and served from the same pans, thus minimizing the breakage that results from transferring vegetables.

When steam equipment is not available, top-of-range or oven cooking may be used. Cook in as small an amount of water as is practicable and as quickly as possible.

FRESH AND FROZEN VEGETABLES

Whatever the method used, vegetables should be cooked only until tender. *Do not overcook*. Vegetables should be cooked in as small quantity at one time as is feasible for the type of service. The needs of most food services can be met by the continuous cooking of vegetables in small quantities. Vegetables should be served as soon as possible after cooking for optimum quality and should be handled carefully to prevent breaking or mashing. A variety of seasonings may be used to add interest to vegetables.

DIRECTIONS FOR BOILING

1. Prepare vegetables. See pp. 524–564 for directions for preparing fresh vegetables. Frozen vegetables should not be thawed before cooking except for solid pack frozen vegetables, which should be thawed only long enough to break apart easily.
2. Add prepared vegetables to boiling salted water in steam-jacketed kettle or stockpot. Cook in lots no larger than 10 lb (4.54 kg). Use 1 1/3 T (25 g) salt to amount of water specified in Table 2.16, except for corn. Add salt and/or sugar after cooking to prevent toughening and discoloring of corn kernels. The amount of water used in cooking all vegetables is important for retention of nutrients. The less water used, the more nutrients retained. Addition of baking soda to the water also causes loss of vitamins.

    Older root vegetables that need longer cooking will require more water than young, tender vegetables. Spinach and other greens need only the water clinging to their leaves from washing.
3. Cover and bring water quickly back to the boiling point. Green vegetables retain their color better if the lid is removed just before boiling begins; strong flavored vegetables, such as cabbage, cauliflower, and Brussels sprouts, should be cook uncovered to prevent development of unpleasant flavors.
4. Start timing when water returns to boiling point. Use Table 2.16 as a guide. Stir greens occasionally while boiling.
5. Drain cooked vegetables and place in serving pans. Add 4–8 oz (114–227 g) melted margarine or butter to each 50 portions.
6. Adjust seasonings.

DIRECTIONS FOR STEAMING

1. Place prepared vegetables not more than 3–4 in. deep in stainless-steel inset pans. Use perforated pans for best circulation. Use solid pans if cooking liquid needs to be retained. When cooking winter squash or sweet potatoes, cover with a lid or aluminum foil to prevent water from accumulating in the pan.
2. Steam, using Table 2.16 as a guide. Begin timing when steamer reaches proper cooking pressure.
3. Add 2–4 oz (57–114 g) melted margarine or butter and 2 t (12 g) salt to each 5 lb (2.27 kg) of drained cooked vegetables.

VEGETABLES

TABLE 2.16 TIMETABLE FOR BOILING OR STEAMING VEGETABLES

	Boiling[a]	*Steaming*[b,c]	
	Cooking Time (minutes)	Cooking Time (minutes)	
		5–6 lb psi	12–15 lb psi
Asparagus, fresh, frozen	15–20	7–10	1½
Beans, blackeyed beans or peas	30–45	20–30	10–15
Beans, green or wax, fresh	20	15–25	1
Beans, green or wax, frozen	10–12	10–15	1
Beans, lima, frozen	12–14	10–15	1½
Broccoli, cuts or spears, fresh, frozen	10–15	5–10	1
Brussels sprouts, fresh, frozen	10–15	5–10	3
Cabbage, cored, cut	10–20	10–15	1½
Carrots, fresh	25	18–25	2
Carrots, frozen	20	9–13	1½
Cauliflower, fresh, frozen	12	10–15	1
Celery, fresh	10	4	1
Corn, whole kernel, frozen	6–8	9–13	½
Corn on cob, fresh	15–20	10–15	4
Corn on cob, frozen	15–20	10–15	5–6
Eggplant, fresh	15–20	10–15	4–6
Greens, fresh, collard	30–40	10–15	8–10
Kale, fresh	15–20	10–15	8–10
Okra, fresh, frozen	10–12	5–8	4–5
Onions, fresh	15–20	15–20	5
Parsnips, fresh	20	15–20	4–6
Peas, green, fresh, frozen	15–20	6–9	1
Potatoes, fresh, whole	30–40	20–30	5–6
For dicing	25–30	20–30	4–6
For slicing	25–30	20–30	4–6
For mashing	30–40	20–30	4–6
Rutabagas, fresh	20	15–20	4–6
Spinach, fresh	8–10	4–6	1–3
Spinach, frozen, thawed	8–10	4–6	1–3
Squash, summer, fresh, frozen	10–15	3–6	2
Squash, winter, fresh	15–30	15–20	10–12
Sweet potatoes, fresh	30–40	20–30	5–6
Turnips, fresh	30–40	25–35	2
Vegetables, mixed, frozen	12–15	6–9	1

[a] Figures calculated for boiling 10–12 lb (4.54–5.44 kg) of vegetables in 1–3 qt (0.95–2.84 L) water. Greens require the addition of no extra water; the water clinging to their leaves is sufficient.

[b] Figures calculated for steaming 5–6 lb (2.27–2.72 kg) vegetables per batch. A steamer filled less than capacity will need the cooking time reduced slightly. An overloaded steamer may require a longer cooking time.

[c] Time required for cooking vegetables in atmospheric pressure steamers is slightly longer than 12–15 lb psi steamers but considerably less than 5–6 lb psi steamers.

DIRECTIONS FOR STIR-FRYING
1. Select vegetables for color, texture, shape, and flavor.
2. Cut or dice diagonally.
3. Heat oil in pan, steam-jacketed kettle, or tilting fry pan.
4. Stir in vegetables. Continue to stir 1 minute.
5. Add water or broth and seasonings, or sauce.
6. Stir quickly over high heat.
7. Cover and steam for 3 minutes or until vegetables are tender but crisp.

CANNED VEGETABLES

Schedule heating of canned vegetables so they will be served soon after heating. Prepare in lots of 2 No. 10 cans. This will make approximately 50 portions.

DIRECTIONS FOR HEATING IN STOCK POT OR IN STEAM-JACKETED KETTLE
1. Drain off half the liquid; use for soups, gravies, and sauces.
2. Heat vegetables and remaining liquid in a stock pot or steam-jacketed kettle. Heat only long enough to bring to serving temperature (140–160°F/60–70°C).
3. Drain vegetables and place in counter pans. Add 4–8 oz (114–227 g) melted margarine or butter.

DIRECTIONS FOR HEATING IN STEAMER OR OVEN
1. Drain off half the liquid; use for soups, gravies, and sauces.
2. Transfer vegetables and remaining liquid to steamer pans and cover. (A 12 × 20 × 2-in. pan will hold contents of 2 No. 10 cans.)
3. Heat in steamer at 5–6 lb pressure for about 3 minutes, at 12–15 lb pressure for 1 minute, or in a 350°F (175°C) oven until serving temperature is reached (140–160°F/60–70°C).
4. Drain vegetables and add 4–8 oz (114–227 g) melted margarine or butter for each lot of vegetables.

DRIED VEGETABLES

To cook dried beans, peas, or lentils:
1. Sort and wash.
2. Heat 1½ gal (5.68 L) water to boiling in steam-jacketed kettle.

3. Add vegetable and boil for 2 minutes.
4. Turn off steam and allow to stand for 1 hour.
5. Add salt and cook slowly until vegetables are tender (1–1½ hours).
6. Vegetable may be covered with cold water and soaked overnight, drained, then cooked.

VEGETABLE RECIPES

SEASONED FRESH ASPARAGUS

Yield: 50 portions
Portion: 3 oz (85 g)

Metric	U.S.	Ingredient	Procedure
8–9 kg (4.5 kg)	18–20 lb (AP) (10 lb EP)	Fresh asparagus	Break or cut off tough stems. Wash and thoroughly clean remaining portions.
24 g	4 t	Salt	Arrange spears in pans with tips in one direction *or* cut into 1-in. pieces. Boil or steam. See p. 521.
114 g	4 oz	Margarine or butter, melted	Pour margarine over cooked asparagus.

Notes:
1. For frozen asparagus, use 10 lb (4.54 kg). See p. 521 for cooking.
2. Seasonings for Asparagus: Sesame seed, lemon juice, browned butter, crumb butter.

Variations:
1. **Asparagus with Cheese Sauce.** Serve 5 or 6 stalks of cooked asparagus with 2 T (30 mL) Cheese Sauce. Make 2 qt (1.89 L) sauce (p. 471).
2. **Asparagus Vinaigrette.** Cook asparagus. Marinate in 1½ qt (1.42 L) Vinaigrette Dressing (p. 442) or Vegetable Marinade (p. 486).
3. **Creamed Asparagus.** Add 1 gal (3.79 L) Medium White Sauce (p. 470) to 10 lb (4.54 kg) EP asparagus cut in 2-in. lengths and cooked.
4. **Fresh Asparagus with Hollandaise Sauce.** Serve 1 T (15 mL) Hollandaise Sauce (p. 484) over cooked asparagus spears.

SEASONED FRESH GREEN OR WAX BEANS

Yield: 50 portions
Portion: 3 oz (85 g)

Amount		Ingredient	Procedure
Metric	U.S.		
4–5 kg (4.54 kg)	11–12 lb (AP) (10 lb EP)	Fresh green or wax beans	Wash beans. Trim ends. Cut or break beans into 1-in. pieces.
24 g	4 t	Salt	Boil or steam. See p. 521.
114 g	4 oz	Margarine or butter, melted	Pour margarine over cooked beans.

Notes:
1. For frozen beans, use 10 lb (4.54 kg). See p. 521 for cooking.
2. For canned beans, use 2 No. 10 cans. See p. 523 for heating.
3. Seasonings for green beans: basil, dill, marjoram, oregano, savory, tarragon, thyme, onion, chives, mushrooms, bacon.

Variations:
1. **French Green Beans.** Cook 10 lb (4.54 kg) frozen French cut green beans. Drain and season with 1 c (240 mL) mayonnaise, ¾ c (180 mL) cultured sour cream, 2 T (30 mL) vinegar, 2 oz (57 g) chopped onion sautéed in 2 oz (57 g) margarine or butter, and salt and pepper to taste.
2. **Green Beans Amandine.** Add 8 oz (227 g) slivered almonds lightly browned in 8 oz (227 g) margarine or butter.
3. **Green Beans and Mushrooms.** Add 2 lb (908 g) sliced mushrooms that have been sautéed in 8 oz (227 g) margarine or butter.
4. **Green Beans Provincial.** Season green beans with 8 oz (227 g) Onion Butter (p. 451), 2 cloves garlic, minced, 3 T (12 g) chopped parsley, and 2 t (2 g) thyme.
5. **Herbed Green Beans.** Season 10 lb (4.54 kg) frozen green beans, cooked, or 2 No. 10 cans green beans with 1 lb (454 g) chopped onions, 8 oz (227 g) chopped celery, and 1 t (5 mL) minced garlic sautéed in 8 oz (227 g) margarine or butter, 2 t (10 mL) basil, and 2 t (10 mL) rosemary.
6. **Southern-Style Green Beans.** Cut 1½ lb (680 g) bacon into small pieces. Add 6 oz (170 g) chopped onion and sauté until onion is lightly browned. Add to hot, drained green beans. Good served with ham and corn bread.

GREEN BEAN CASSEROLE

Oven: 350°F (175°C)
Bake: 30 minutes

Yield: 50 portions
1 pan 12 × 20 × 2 in.
Portion: 4 oz (114 g)

Amount Metric	U.S.	Ingredient	Procedure
3.4 kg	7 lb 8 oz	Green beans, frozen, French cut or cut	Cook green beans (p. 521). Drain.
284 g	10 oz	Mushrooms, fresh	Clean mushrooms and slice.
85 g	3 oz	Margarine or butter, melted	Sauté in margarine.
0.95 L	1 qt	Cream of mushroom soup, undiluted	Blend soup, milk, and seasonings.
240 mL	1 c	Milk	
1 g	½ t	Pepper, black	
15 mL	1 T	Soy sauce	
454 g	1 lb	Water chestnuts	Drain water chestnuts. Slice. Combine soup, mushrooms, and water chestnuts. Add to green beans. Mix lightly. Pour into 1 12 × 20 × 2-in. pan.
227 g	8 oz	Cheddar or Swiss cheese, shredded	Sprinkle cheese over beans. Bake at 350°F (175°C) for 25 minutes.
284 g	10 oz	French fried onions, canned	Sprinkle onions over bean mixture. Bake 5–10 minutes.

Note: 2 No. 10 cans cut green beans may be substituted for frozen beans. Drain before using.

SPANISH GREEN BEANS

Yield: 50 portions
Portion: 3 oz (85 g)

Amount Metric	U.S.	Ingredient	Procedure
227 g	8 oz	Bacon, diced	Sauté bacon, onion, and green pepper until lightly browned.
170 g	6 oz	Onion, chopped	
114 g	4 oz	Green pepper, chopped	
114 g	4 oz	Flour, all-purpose	Add flour and stir until smooth.
1.89 L	2 qt	Tomatoes, canned	Chop tomatoes and heat. Add salt. Add gradually to bacon/vegetable mixture. Stir and cook until thickened.
19 g	1 T	Salt	
2 No. 10 cans	2 No. 10 cans	Green beans, drained	Gently stir tomato sauce into the green beans. Simmer 20–30 minutes or until beans are heated to 160°F (70°C).

Note: 8 lb (3.63 kg) EP fresh or frozen green beans may be substituted for canned beans. Cook before combining with tomato sauce.

Variations:

1. **Creole Green Beans.** Omit bacon. Sauté onion, green pepper, and 8 oz (227 g) celery in 2 oz (57 g) margarine or butter. Add 2 oz (57 g) sugar to tomatoes.
2. **Green Beans with Dill.** Delete bacon and onion. Sauté the green pepper in 5 oz (142 g) margarine or butter. Add 1 t (2 g) pepper and 1 T (15 mL) dill seeds. Simmer slowly 10–15 minutes. Tomato may be increased to 1 No. 10 can.
3. **Hacienda Green Beans.** Add 1 oz (28 g) sugar, 1½ T (10 g) chili powder, and ½ t (2 g) garlic powder.

SEASONED LIMA BEANS

Yield: 50 portions
Portion: 3 oz (85 g)

Amount		Ingredient	Procedure
Metric	U.S.		
4.54 kg	10 lb	Frozen lima beans, baby or fordhook	Boil or steam beans (p. 521).
24 g	1⅓ T	Salt	
114 g	4 oz	Margarine or butter, melted	Pour margarine over beans.

Note: Seasonings for lima beans: basil, marjoram, oregano, sage, savory, tarragon, thyme, pimiento, mushrooms, onion butter, sour cream.

Variations:

1. **Baked Lima Beans and Peas.** Thaw 5 lb (2.27 kg) frozen baby lima beans and 5 lb (2.27 kg) frozen peas. Combine with 2 T (30 mL) basil, 1⅓ T (24 g) salt, ½ t cracked black pepper, and 16 green onions, sliced. Place in baking pan. Sprinkle with 1 c (240 mL) water and dot with 4–6 oz (114–170 g) margarine or butter. Cover and bake at 325°F (165°C) for 45 minutes. Stir occasionally.

2. **Succotash.** Use 5 lb (2.27 kg) lima beans and 5 lb (2.27 kg) frozen or canned whole kernel corn. Season with 4 oz (114 g) margarine or butter.

BAKED LIMA BEANS

Oven: 350°F (175°C)
Bake: 1 hour

Yield: 50 portions
2 pans 12 × 20 × 2 in.
Portion: 5 oz (142 g)

Amount		Ingredient	Procedure
Metric	U.S.		
2.72 kg	6 lb (AP)	Lima beans, dry, large	Wash beans. Add boiling water. Cover. Let stand 1 hour or longer. Cook beans in the same water until tender, about 1 hour.
3.79 L	1 gal	Water, boiling	
114 g	4 oz	Pimiento, chopped	Add seasonings. Pour into 2 12 × 20 × 2-in. pans, 8 lb 6 oz (3.8 kg) per pan.
227 g	8 oz	Bacon fat	
28 g	1 oz (1½ T)	Salt	
240 mL	1 c	Molasses	
680 g	1 lb 8 oz	Bacon	Place bacon on top of beans. Bake at 350°F (175°C) until top is brown, about 1 hour.

Variations:

1. **Baked Lima Beans and Sausage.** Omit bacon and bacon fat. Place 6 lb (2.72 kg) link sausages on top of beans.

2. **Boiled Lima Beans and Ham.** Omit bacon and seasonings. Add 5 lb (2.27 kg) diced ham to beans and simmer until tender.

BAKED BEANS

Oven: 350°F (175°C)
Bake: 5–6 hours

Yield: 50 portions
1 pan 12 × 20 × 4 in.
Portion: 5 oz (142 g)

Amount Metric	U.S.	Ingredient	Procedure
2.27 kg	5 lb AP	Beans, navy or Great Northern, dry	Wash beans. Add boiling water. Let stand 1 hour or longer.
5.68 L	1½ gal	Water, boiling	Cook in same water until tender, about 1 hour. Add more water as necessary.
114 g	4 oz	Salt	Add remaining ingredients.
170 g	6 oz	Sugar, brown	Pour into 1 12 × 20 × 4-in. baking pan.
2 g	1 t	Mustard, dry	Bake uncovered at 350°F (175°C) for 5–6 hours.
30 mL	2 T	Vinegar	
240 mL	1 c	Molasses	
600 mL	2½ c	Catsup (optional)	
454 g	1 lb	Bacon or salt pork, cubed	
85 g	3 oz	Onion, chopped	

Variations:

1. **Baked Pork and Beans.** Use 2 No. 10 cans pork and beans. Fry 1 lb (454 g) diced bacon until partially cooked. Add 4 oz (114 g) chopped onion and cook until onions are tender. Pour off bacon fat. Add bacon/onions to pork and beans. Stir in 1 c (240 mL) catsup, ¼ c (60 mL) vinegar, 4 oz (114 g) brown sugar, and 1 T (30 mL) prepared mustard. Bake at 350°F (175°C) for 1–2 hours.
2. **Boston Baked Beans.** Omit catsup.

RANCH STYLE BEANS

Oven: 300°F (150°C)
Bake: 6–8 hours

Yield: 50 portions
      1 pan 12 × 20 × 4 in.
Portion: 5 oz (142 g)

Amount			
Metric	U.S.	Ingredient	Procedure
2.27 kg	5 lb	Beans, dry, red or pinto	Wash beans. Add boiling water. Cover and let stand 1 hour or longer.
5.68 L	1½ gal	Water, boiling	
1.14 kg	2 lb 8 oz	Salt pork or bacon, 1-in. cubes	Add salt pork to beans. Add cold water to cover. Cook slowly until tender, about 1 hour.
		Water, cold	
3–4 pods	3–4 pods	Chili peppers	Soak chili peppers in warm water. Remove pulp from pods and add to beans.
1.89 L	2 qt	Tomatoes, canned	Add tomatoes and other seasonings. Cook slowly in kettle an additional 5 hours or pour into a 12 × 20 × 4-in. baking pan and bake at 300°F (150°C) for 5–6 hours.
227 g	8 oz	Onion, sliced	
28 g	1 oz (1½ T)	Salt	
7 g	1 T	Pepper, black	
f.g.	f.g.	Cayenne	
2 cloves	2 cloves	Garlic, chopped	

Notes:

1. If chili peppers are not available, 1 oz (28 g) chili powder may be substituted.

2. 2 No. 10 cans red beans may be substituted for dry beans. Reduce baking time to 1–2 hours.

REFRIED BEANS

Yield: 50 portions
Portion: 4 oz (114 g)

Amount		Ingredient	Procedure
Metric	U.S.		
4.54 kg	10 lb	Beans, pinto, canned	Drain beans. Reserve stock. Place beans in mixer bowl and mash thoroughly.
360 mL	1½ c	Cooking oil	Heat oil in fry pan.
170 g	6 oz	Onions, chopped	Add chopped onion. Cook until tender.
14 g	2 T	Chili powder	Add seasonings and mix thoroughly.
2 g	1 t	Garlic powder	
12 g	2 t	Salt	
f.d.	f.d.	Tabasco sauce	
0.95 L	1 qt	Beef Stock (p. 494)	Add beef stock and mix well. Add mashed beans, mixing until well blended. Turn mixture constantly to keep from burning. Small amounts of bean stock may be added if mixture becomes too thick. Cook bean mixture for 45–60 minutes or until dry.

Note: 5 lb (2.27 kg) dry pinto beans may be substituted for canned beans. Cook according to directions on p. 523.

SEASONED BROCCOLI

Yield: 50 portions
Portion: 3 oz (85 g)

Amount Metric	U.S.	Ingredient	Procedure
7–9 kg (4.5 kg)	16–20 lb (AP) (10 lb EP)	Broccoli, fresh	Trim off large leaves. Remove tough ends of lower stems. Wash. If stems are thicker than 1 in., make lengthwise gashes in each stem.
24 g	1 1/3 T	Salt	Boil or steam broccoli spears. See p. 521.
114 g	4 oz	Margarine or butter, melted	Pour margarine over cooked broccoli.

Notes:
1. For frozen broccoli, use 12 lb (5.44 kg) spears or 10 lb (4.54 kg) chopped.
2. Seasonings for broccoli: caraway seed, dill, mustard seed, or tarragon, lemon, almond, pimiento, onion butter.

Variations:
1. **Almond Buttered Broccoli.** Brown slivered almonds in margarine or butter and pour over cooked and drained broccoli.
2. **Broccoli with Cheese Sauce.** Prepare 2 qt (1.89 L) Cheese Sauce (p. 471). Serve 2 T (1 oz/28 g) sauce over each portion of cooked broccoli.
3. **Broccoli with Hollandaise Sauce or Lemon Butter.** Serve cooked spears or chopped broccoli with 1 T (15 mL) Hollandaise Sauce (p. 484) or 1 t (5 mL) lemon butter.

SEASONED FRESH BEETS

Yield: 50 portions
Portion: 3 oz (85 g)

Amount		Ingredient	Procedure
Metric	U.S.		
6.35 kg (4.99 kg)	14 lb (AP) (11 lb EP)	Beets, fresh	Cut off all but 2 in. of the beet tops. Wash beets and leave whole, with root ends attached. Boil or steam until tender. See p. 521. Drain. Run cold water over beets; slip off skins and remove root ends. Slice, dice, or cut into shoestring pieces.
114 g	4 oz	Margarine or butter, melted	Pour margarine over cooked beets. Sprinkle with salt. Heat to serving temperature.
24 g	1⅓ T	Salt	

Notes:
1. For canned beets, use 2 No. 10 cans. See p. 523 for heating directions.
2. Seasonings for beets: allspice, bay leaves, caraway seed, cloves, dill, ginger, mustard seed, basil, nutmeg, onion, sour cream, vinegar.

Variations:
1. **Beets in Sour Cream.** Grate fresh cooked beets and season with a mixture of 1½ c (360 mL) lemon juice, 1½ T (23 mL) onion juice, 2 t (12 g) salt, and 10 oz (284 g) sugar. Toss lightly. Serve with a spoonful of cultured sour cream on each portion.
2. **Julienne Beets.** Cut 8 lb (3.63 kg) cooked beets into julienne strips. Season with a mixture of 4 oz (114 g) margarine or butter, 4 oz (114 g) sugar, 4 t (24 g) salt, and 1 c (240 mL) lemon juice.
3. **Pickled Beets.** See p. 432.

HARVARD BEETS

Yield: 50 portions
Portion: 3 oz (85 g)

Amount		Ingredient	Procedure
Metric	U.S.		
2 No. 10 cans	2 No. 10 cans	Beets, sliced or diced	Drain beets. Reserve juice for sauce.
1.42 L	1½ qt	Beet juice	Add bay leaf and cloves to beet juice. Heat to boiling point.
1	1	Bay leaf	
2 g	1 t	Cloves, whole	
340 g	12 oz	Sugar, granulated	Combine dry ingredients. Add to beet juice while stirring briskly. Cook until thickened and clear.
28 g	1 oz	Salt	
170 g	6 oz	Cornstarch	
114 g	4 oz	Margarine or butter	Add margarine and vinegar. Stir until mixed and margarine is melted. Heat beets. Add sauce.
480 mL	2 c	Vinegar	

Note: For fresh beets, use 10 lb (4.54 kg) EP (5–6 kg AP). See p. 521 for cooking procedure.

Variations:

1. **Beets with Orange Sauce.** Omit bay leaf, cloves, and vinegar. Add 2 c (480 mL) orange juice and ½ c (120 mL) lemon juice.

2. **Hot Spiced Beets.** Drain juice from 2 No. 10 cans sliced beets and add 1 T (5 g) whole cloves, 1½ T (28 g) salt, ½ t (1 g) cinnamon, 1 lb (454 g) brown sugar, 8 oz (227 g) granulated sugar, and 1 qt (0.95 L) vinegar. Cook 10 minutes. Pour sauce over beets and heat to serving temperature.

SEASONED CABBAGE

Yield: 50 portions
Portion: 3 oz (85 g)

Amount		Ingredient	Procedure
Metric	U.S.		
6.35 kg (5.44 kg)	14 lb (AP) (12 lb EP)	Cabbage, fresh	Remove wilted outside leaves. Wash and core. Crisp in cold water, if wilted.
24 g	1⅓ T	Salt	Cut cabbage into wedges or shred coarsely. Cook until tender. See p. 521. Drain.
114 g	4 oz	Margarine or butter, melted	Pour margarine over cabbage.

Note: Seasonings for cabbage: basil, caraway seed, celery seed, curry powder, dill, nutmeg.

Variations:

1. **Cabbage au Gratin.** Reduce cabbage to 7 lb (3.18 kg). Alternate layers of cooked coarsely shredded cabbage, white sauce, and grated sharp cheese in a 12 × 20 × 2-in. baking pan. Use 2½ qt (2.37 L) white sauce, 1 lb (454 g) Cheddar cheese. Combine 6 oz (170 g) crumbs and 3 oz (85 g) melted margarine or butter and sprinkle on top. Bake at 350°F (175°C) about 25 minutes.

2. **Cabbage Polonnaise.** Arrange cabbage wedges, partially cooked, in baking pans. Cover with 3 qt (2.84 L) medium white sauce. Sprinkle with buttered bread crumbs. Bake at 350°F (175°C) about 25 minutes.

3. **Creamed Cabbage.** Omit margarine or butter. Pour 2 qt (1.89 L) medium white sauce over shredded, cooked, drained cabbage.

4. **Scalloped Cabbage.** Omit margarine or butter. Pour 2 qt (1.89 L) medium white sauce over chopped, cooked, drained cabbage. Cover with buttered crumbs. Bake at 400°F (205°C) for 15–20 minutes. Shredded cheese may be added.

HOT CABBAGE SLAW

Yield: 50 portions
1 ¼ gal (4.73 L)
Portion: 3 oz (85 g)

Amount		Ingredient	Procedure
Metric	U.S.		
3.4 kg (2.72 kg)	7 lb 8 oz (AP) (6 lb EP)	Cabbage, fresh	Remove outside leaves and wash cabbage. Shred.
340 g 12 g 85 g 2 g	12 oz 2 t 3 oz 1 t	Sugar, granulated Salt Flour, all-purpose Mustard, dry	Mix dry ingredients.
600 mL 720 mL	2½ c 3 c	Milk, hot Water, hot	Add milk and water while stirring. Cook until thickened.
5 (255 g)	5 (9 oz)	Eggs, beaten	Add eggs gradually while stirring briskly. Cook 2–3 minutes.
360 mL	1½ c	Vinegar, hot	Add vinegar.
4 g	2½ t	Celery seed	Pour hot sauce over cabbage just before serving. Add celery seed and mix lightly.

PARSLEY BUTTERED CARROTS

Yield: 50 portions
Portion: 3 oz (85 g)

Amount		Ingredient	Procedure
Metric	U.S.		
6.35 kg (4.5 kg)	14 lb (AP) (10 lb EP)	Carrots, fresh	Pare and cut carrots into desired shapes (slices, strips, or quarters).
24 g	1⅓ T	Salt	Steam or boil until just tender. See p. 521.
114 g	4 oz	Margarine or butter, melted	Pour margarine over carrots.
28 g	1 oz	Parsley, chopped	Sprinkle with chopped parsley.

Note: Seasonings for carrots: allspice, basil, caraway seed, dill, fennel, ginger, mace, marjoram, mint, nutmeg, thyme, parsley.

Variations:

1. **Candied Carrots.** Cut carrots into 1-in. pieces. Cook until tender but not soft. Melt 12 oz (340 g) margarine or butter. Add 9 oz (255 g) sugar and 1½ T (28 g) salt. Add to carrots. Bake at 400°F (205 °C) for 15–20 minutes. Turn frequently.

2. **Lyonnaise Carrots.** Arrange cooked carrot strips in baking pan. Add 3 lb (1.36 kg) chopped onion that has been cooked until tender in 4 oz (114 g) margarine or butter. Bake at 350°F (175°C) for 10–15 minutes or until vegetables are lightly browned. Just before serving sprinkle with chopped parsley.

3. **Marinated Carrots.** See p. 410.

4. **Mint-Glazed Carrots.** Cut carrots into quarters lengthwise. Cook until almost tender. Drain. Melt 8 oz (227 g) margarine or butter, 8 oz (227 g) sugar, 1½ T (28 g) salt, and 1 c (240 mL) mint jelly. Blend. Add carrots and simmer 5–10 minutes.

5. **Savory Carrots.** Cook carrots in beef or chicken stock. When done, season with 4 oz (114 g) melted margarine or butter, salt and pepper, and ¼ c (60 mL) lemon juice. Sprinkle with chopped parsley.

6. **Sweet–Sour Carrots.** Add to cooked carrots a sauce made of 1½ qt (1.42 L) vinegar, 2¼ lb (1.02 kg) sugar, 2 T (38 g) salt, and 12 oz (340 g) melted margarine or butter. Bake at 350°F (175°C) for 15–20 minutes, or simmer until carrots and sauce are thoroughly heated.

CELERY AND CARROTS AMANDINE

Yield: 50 portions
Portion: 3 oz (85 g)

Amount			
Metric	U.S.	Ingredient	Procedure
3.18 kg (2.27 kg) 12 g	7 lb (AP) (5 lb EP) 2 t	Celery Salt	Wash and trim celery. Cut into diagonal slices. Steam. See p. 521.
3.18 kg (2.27 kg) 12 g	7 lb (AP) (5 lb EP) 2 t	Carrots, fresh Salt	Wash and pare carrots. Cut into strips. Cook (p. 521) until tender but firm. Drain.
227 g 227 g	8 oz 8 oz	Margarine or butter Almonds, blanched, slivered	Heat margarine in fry pan. Add almonds and brown lightly.
80 mL	⅓ c	Lemon juice	Remove almonds from heat. Add lemon juice. Combine vegetables. Pour almond mixture over and stir carefully to mix seasoning with vegetables.

Variation: **Creole Celery.** Cook 5 lb (2.27 kg) diced celery until partially done. Add 1 lb (454 g) chopped onions and 4 oz (114 g) chopped green pepper that have been sautéed in 6 oz (170 g) margarine or butter. Add 2 No. 10 cans tomatoes and 1½ t (9 g) salt. Cook until tender.

SEASONED CAULIFLOWER

Yield: 50 portions
Portion: 3 oz (85 g)

Amount Metric	U.S.	Ingredient	Procedure
7.26 kg (4.5 kg)	16 lb (AP) (10 lb EP)	Cauliflower, fresh	Remove outer leaves and stalks. Break into flowerets. Wash.
24 g	1⅓ T	Salt	Steam or boil cauliflower. See p. 521.
114 g	4 oz	Margarine or butter, melted	Pour margarine over cooked cauliflower.

Note: Seasonings for cauliflower: caraway seed, celery salt, dill, mace, tarragon, buttered crumbs, cheese.

Variations:
1. **Cauliflower with Almond Butter.** Season freshly cooked cauliflower with 12 oz (340 g) slivered almonds that have been browned in 8 oz (227 g) margarine or butter.
2. **Cauliflower with Cheese Sauce.** Pour 3 qt (2.84 L) Cheese Sauce (p. 471) over cooked fresh cauliflower.
3. **Cauliflower with Peas.** Combine 6 lb (2.72 kg) freshly cooked cauliflower with 4 lb (1.81 kg) cooked frozen peas. Season with 4 oz (114 g) melted margarine or butter.
4. **Creamed Cauliflower.** Pour 3 qt (2.84 L) white sauce over cooked cauliflower.
5. **French Fried Cauliflower.** See p. 545.

SEASONED WHOLE KERNEL CORN

Yield: 50 portions
Portion: 3 oz (85 g)

Amount Metric	U.S.	Ingredient	Procedure
4.54 kg	10 lb	Whole kernel corn, frozen	Boil or steam corn (p. 521).
114 g	4 oz	Margarine or butter, melted	Pour margarine over corn. Stir in salt.
24 g	1⅓ T	Salt	

Note: For canned corn, use 2 No. 10 cans. See p. 523 for heating.

Variations:
1. **Corn in Cream.** Add 1¼ qt (1.18 L) light cream, 6 oz (170 g) margarine or butter, 1⅓ T (24 g) salt, and 1 T (15 mL) white pepper to cooked corn. Bring just to boiling point and serve immediately.
2. **Corn O'Brien.** Add 1 lb (454 g) chopped bacon, 12 oz (340 g) chopped green pepper, and 12 oz (340 g) chopped onion that have been cooked together. Just before serving, add 3 oz (85 g) chopped pimiento, salt, and pepper.

SCALLOPED CORN

Oven: 350°F (175°C)
Bake: 35–40 minutes
Yield: 50 portions
2 pans 12 × 20 × 2 in.
Portion: 4 oz (114 g)

Amount Metric	U.S.	Ingredient	Procedure
2 No. 10 cans	2 No. 10 cans	Corn, cream style	Mix corn, milk, and seasonings.
0.95 L	1 qt	Milk	
19 g	1 T	Salt	
1 g	½ t	Pepper, black	
397 g	14 oz	Cracker crumbs	Combine crumbs and margarine. Place alternate layers of buttered crumbs and corn mixture in 2 12 × 20 × 2-in. baking pans. Bake at 350°F (175°C) for 35–40 minutes.
340 g	12 oz	Margarine or butter, melted	

Note: 6 oz (170 g) chopped green pepper and 6 oz (170 g) chopped pimiento may be added.

CORN PUDDING

Oven: 325°F (165°C)
Bake: 40–45 minutes
Yield: 50 portions
2 pans 12 × 20 × 2 in.
Portion: 5 oz (142 g)

Amount Metric	U.S.	Ingredient	Procedure
4.08 kg	9 lb	Corn, whole kernel, frozen	Thaw corn.
24 (454 g)	24 (1 lb)	Egg yolks, beaten	Combine corn and all ingredients except egg whites.
2.84 L	3 qt	Milk	
170 g	6 oz	Margarine or butter, melted	
38 g	2 T	Salt	
2 g	1 t	Pepper	
24 (737 g)	24 (1 lb 10 oz)	Egg whites	Beat egg whites until stiff but not dry. Fold into corn mixture. Pour into 2 12 × 20 × 2-in. baking pans. Place in pans of hot water. Bake at 325°F (165°C) for 40–45 minutes.

BAKED EGGPLANT

Oven: 375°F (190°C)
Bake: 30 minutes

Yield: 50 portions
Portion: 3 oz (85 g)

Amount		Ingredient	Procedure
Metric	U.S.		
5.44 kg (4.54 kg)	12 lb AP (10 lb EP)	Eggplant	Pare and cut eggplant into ½-in. slices. Soak in salt water (1 T/19 g salt to 1 qt/0.95 L water) for 30 minutes.
454 g	1 lb	Flour, all-purpose	Drain eggplant slices.
6 (284 g)	6 (10 oz)	Eggs, beaten	Dip in flour, then in egg–milk mixture. Roll in crumbs. Place on greased baking sheets. Sprinkle with melted margarine. Bake at 375°F (190°C) for 30 minutes.
480 mL	2 c	Milk	
680 g	1 lb 8 oz	Bread crumbs	
227 g	8 oz	Margarine or butter, melted	

Note: Seasonings for eggplant: garlic, marjoram, onion, oregano, cheese, tomato.

Variations:

1. **Eggplant Casserole.** Pare and slice eggplant 1 in. thick. Steam or parboil until fork-tender. Place in 2 12 × 20 × 2-in. pans in a single layer. Sprinkle with salt and pepper. Cook 1 lb 8 oz (680 g) chopped onion and 4 cloves garlic, minced, in 1½ c (360 mL) cooking oil and 12 oz (340 g) margarine. Add to 5 lb (2.27 kg) peeled, chopped fresh tomatoes, 1 c (57 g) chopped parsley, ¼ t oregano, ½ t thyme, 1 t basil, and 1 lb (454 g) bread crumbs. Pile mixture on individual slices of eggplant. Sprinkle grated Swiss cheese (2 lb/908 g) over top. Bake at 350°F (175°C) until eggplant is hot and cheese is melted.

2. **French Fried Eggplant.** See p. 545.

3. **Sautéed Eggplant.** Prepare as above. Sauté in margarine or butter until tender.

CREOLE EGGPLANT

Oven: 350°F (175°C)   Yield: 50 portions
Bake: 30 minutes   Portion: 5 oz (142 g)

Amount		Ingredient	Procedure
Metric	*U.S.*		
4.54 kg	10 lb AP	Eggplant	Pare eggplant and cut into 1-in. cubes.
(3.63 kg)	(8 lb EP)		
5.68 L	1½ gal	Water, boiling	Cook in boiling salted water for 5 minutes or steam according to directions on p. 521.
38 g	2 T	Salt	
454 g	1 lb	Margarine or butter, melted	Cook onion, green pepper, and celery in margarine until tender.
680 g	1 lb 8 oz	Onion, chopped	
340 g	12 oz	Green pepper, coarsely chopped	
454 g	1 lb	Celery, coarsely chopped	
1 No. 10 can	1 No. 10 can	Tomatoes, diced	Combine tomatoes and seasonings with eggplant and other ingredients. Pour into 2 12 × 20 × 2-in baking pans.
38 g	2 T	Salt	
4 g	2 t	Pepper, black	
28 g	2 T	Sugar, granulated	
340 g	12 oz	Bread crumbs	Top with buttered crumbs. Bake at 350°F (175°C) for 30 minutes.
227 g	8 oz	Margarine or butter, melted	

BAKED ONIONS

Oven: 400°F (205°C)
Bake: 20–30 minutes

Yield: 50 portions
Portion: 1 4-oz (114-g) onion

Amount		Ingredient	Procedure
Metric	U.S.		
50 (6.8 kg)	50 (15 lb AP)	Onions, 4 oz, Bermuda or Spanish	Peel onions and steam (p. 521) until tender. Place in greased baking pans.
19 g	1 T	Salt	Sprinkle with salt and buttered crumbs.
227 g	8 oz	Bread crumbs	
227 g	8 oz	Margarine or butter, melted	
0.95 L	1 qt	Beef or chicken stock (p. 494, 495)	Pour stock around onions. Bake at 400°F (205 °C) for 20–30 minutes.

Notes:
1. Onions may be cut into thick slices.
2. Seasonings for onions: basil, caraway seed, marjoram, oregano, rosemary, sage, or thyme.

Variations:
1. **Creamed Pearl Onions.** Cook 12½ lb (5.67 kg) small unpeeled white onions (p. 521), then peel. Add 2 qt (1.89 L) Medium White Sauce (p. 470) to which 4 oz (114 g) additional margarine or butter has been added. Garnish with paprika.
2. **Glazed Onions.** Mix 1 lb 12 oz (794 g) brown sugar, 2 c (480 mL) water, 8 oz (227 g) margarine or butter, and ½ t (3 g) salt. Pour over cooked onions and bake.
3. **Onion Casserole.** Cook 10 lb (4.54 kg) cooked small pearl onions (p. 521). Combine with 10 oz (284 g) chopped walnuts, 8 oz (227 g) pimiento strips, and 8 10½-oz cans cream of mushroom or cream of chicken soup. Cover with 6 oz (170 g) shredded Cheddar or Swiss cheese. Bake approximately 30 minutes at 400°F (205°C).
4. **Stuffed Baked Onions.** Scoop out center of 50 large onions. Fill with mixture of 1½ qt (1.42 L) Medium White Sauce (p. 470), 8 oz (227 g) margarine or butter, 6 beaten egg yolks, and onion centers cooked and chopped. 12 oz (340 g) chopped toasted almonds may be added. Cover tops of onions with buttered crumbs. Bake at 400°F (205°C) for 30 minutes.

FRENCH FRIED ONION RINGS

Deep-fat fryer: 350°F (175°C)
Fry: 3–4 minutes

Yield: 50 portions
Portion: 3 oz (85 g)

Amount		Ingredient	Procedure
Metric	U.S.		
4.54 kg (3.63 kg)	10 lb AP (8 lb EP)	Onions	Peel onions and cut crosswise into ¼-in. slices. Separate into rings.
6 (284 g) 480 mL	6 (10 oz) 2 c	Eggs, beaten Milk	Combine eggs and milk.
340 g 12 g 9 g	12 oz 2 t 1½ t	Flour, all-purpose Baking powder Salt	Combine dry ingredients add to egg–milk mixture to make a batter. Dip onion rings in batter and fry in deep fat for 3–4 minutes. Drain.

Variations:

1. **French Fried Cauliflower.** Dip 10 lb (4.54 kg) cold cooked cauliflower into batter and fry at 370°F (185°C) for 3–4 minutes.

2. **French Fried Eggplant.** Pare and cut 13 lb (5.9 kg) AP eggplant as for French Fried Potatoes (p. 550). Dip in batter and fry at 370°F (185°C) for 5–7 minutes. Eggplant may be dipped in egg and crumb mixture (p. 37) and fried. Eggplant discolors quickly, so it should be placed in cold water if not breaded immediately.

3. **French Fried Mushrooms.** Clean mushrooms by brushing or trimming. Do not soak. Dip in batter and fry at 370°F (185°C) for 4–6 minutes.

4. **French Fried Zucchini Sticks.** Cut unpared zucchini lengthwise into strips about ½ in. thick. Dip in batter and fry at 370°F (185°C) for 4–6 minutes.

SEASONED PEAS

Yield: 50 portions
Portion: 3 oz (85 g)

Amount		Ingredient	Procedure
Metric	U.S.		
4.54 kg	10 lb	Peas, frozen	Steam or boil (p. 521).
24 g	1⅓ T	Salt	
114 g	4 oz	Margarine or butter, melted	Pour margarine over cooked peas.

Notes:
1. If using canned peas, heat 2 No. 10 cans. See p. 523.
2. For fresh peas, use 25 lb (11.34 kg) AP. Shell and rinse. Steam or boil (p. 521).
3. Seasonings for peas: basil, dill, marjoram, mint, oregano, rosemary, sage, savory, mushrooms, water chestnuts, onions.

Variations:
1. **Creamed Peas with New Potatoes.** Combine 7 lb (3.18 kg) freshly cooked new potatoes and 5 lb (2.27 kg) cooked frozen peas with 3 qt (2.84 L) Medium White Sauce (p. 470).
2. **Green Peas and Sliced New Turnips.** Combine 5 lb (2.27 kg) frozen peas, cooked, with 3 lb (1.36 kg) new turnips, sliced and cooked. Add 4 oz (114 g) melted margarine and salt to taste.
3. **Green Peas with Pearl Onions.** Combine 7½ lb (3.4 kg) frozen peas, cooked, and 3 lb (1.36 kg) pearl onions, cooked. Add 4 oz (114 g) melted margarine or butter or 2 qt (1.89 L) Medium White Sauce (p. 470).
4. **New Peas with Mushrooms.** Add 2 lb (908 g) fresh mushrooms, sliced, sautéed in 8 oz (227 g) margarine or butter, to 10 lb (4.54 kg) cooked frozen peas.
5. **Peas with Lemon–Mint Butter.** Cream 1 lb (454 g) margarine or butter, ¼ c (60 mL) lemon juice, and 1 t (3 g) grated lemon rind. Add ½ c (120 mL) finely chopped fresh mint. The lemon–mint butter can be made ahead and stored in the refrigerator. When ready to use, melt and pour over hot peas.

AU GRATIN POTATOES

Oven: 400°F (205°C)
Bake: 25 minutes

Yield: 50 portions
2 pans 12 × 20 × 2 in.
Portion: 5 oz (142 g)

Amount Metric	U.S.	Ingredient	Procedure
4.54 kg (3.63 kg)	10 lb AP (8 lb EP)	Potatoes	Pare potatoes. Boil or steam (p. 521) until just tender. Dice (or dice before cooking).
340 g 170 g 19 g	12 oz 6 oz 1 T	Margarine or butter Flour, all-purpose Salt	Melt margarine. Add flour and salt. Stir until smooth. Cook 2–3 minutes.
2.84 L	3 qt	Milk	Add milk gradually while stirring. Cook until thickened.
680 g	1 lb 8 oz	Cheddar cheese, shredded	Add cheese to white sauce and stir until cheese is melted. Pour over potatoes. Place in 2 12 × 20 × 2-in. baking pans, 8 lb (3.63 kg) per pan.
340 g 227 g	12 oz 8 oz	Bread crumbs Margarine or butter, melted	Combine crumbs and margarine and sprinkle over top of potatoes, 10 oz (284 g) per pan. Bake at 400°F (205°C) for 25 minutes.

Note: 1 lb 10 oz (737 g) sliced dehydrated potatoes, reconstituted in 5 qt (4.73 L) boiling water, and 1½ oz (43 g) salt may be substituted for fresh potatoes.

BAKED POTATOES

Oven: 400°F (205°C)
Bake: 1–1½ hours
Yield: 50 portions
Portion: 1 potato

Amount Metric	U.S.	Ingredient	Procedure
50	50	Baking potatoes, uniform size	Scrub potatoes and remove blemishes.
114 g	4 oz	Shortening	Rub or brush lightly with shortening. Place on baking pans. Bake at 400°F (205°C) for 1–1½ hours or until soft.

Variations:

1. **Fancy Top Potato.** Prepare potatoes as above. Serve with one of the following toppings and one or more of the accompaniments.

    Toppings: Cheese Sauce (p. 471), 3 oz/85 g
    Nacho Sauce (p. 274), 3 oz/85 g
    Guacamole (p. 65), 2 oz/57 g
    Sour cream, 1 oz/28 g
    Chili con Carne (p. 325), 3 oz/85 g
    Creamed Chicken (p. 376), Ham (p. 342), Salmon (p. 293), or Beef (p. 326), 3 oz/85 g

    Accompaniments: Chopped broccoli, shredded cheese, sliced mushrooms, chopped green onions, chopped chives, sliced black olives, chopped ham or chicken, chopped lettuce, chopped tomatoes, crumbled cooked bacon, slivered almonds.

2. **Stuffed Baked Potato.** Cut hot baked potatoes into halves lengthwise. If potatoes are small, cut a slice from one side. Scoop out contents. Mash, season with 2 T (38 g) salt, 1 t (2 g) white pepper, 8 oz (227 g) melted margarine or butter, and 3–4 c (720–950 mL) hot milk. Beat until light and fluffy. Pile lightly into shells, leaving tops rough. Sprinkle with paprika or parmesan cheese, if desired. Bake at 425°F (220°C) until potatoes are hot and lightly browned, about 30 minutes.

COTTAGE-FRIED POTATOES

Yield: 50 portions
Portion: 4 oz (114 g)

Amount Metric	U.S.	Ingredient	Procedure
8.16 kg (6.8 kg)	18 lb AP (15 lb EP)	Potatoes	Pare potatoes. Steam or boil until tender (p. 521).
28 g 2 g	As needed 1 oz (1½ T) 1 t	Fat, hot Salt Pepper, black	Slice cooked potatoes. Add to hot fat in frying pan. Add salt and pepper. Turn potatoes as needed and fry until browned.

Variations:

1. **American Fried Potatoes.** Add raw sliced potatoes to hot fat. Fry until brown and potatoes are tender. Add additional fat as needed.
2. **Hashed Brown Potatoes.** Add finely chopped boiled potatoes to hot fat in frying pan. Add salt and pepper. Stir occasionally and fry until browned.
3. **Lyonnaise Potatoes.** Cook 2 lb (908 g) chopped onion slowly in fat without browning. Add seasoned cut, boiled potatoes and cook until browned; *or* cut potatoes as for French fries. Steam until tender, place in greased baking pan. Cover top with fat and onions. Place in oven and bake until browned.
4. **O'Brien Potatoes.** Cook cubed potatoes in small amount of fat with chopped onion and pimiento.
5. **Oven-Fried Potatoes.** Prepare potatoes as for French fried potatoes. Place in greased shallow pans to make a thin layer and brush with melted fat, turning to cover all sides. Bake at 450°F (230°C) for 20–30 minutes, or until browned, turning occasionally. Drain on absorbent paper and sprinkle with salt.

FRENCH FRIED POTATOES

Deep-fat fryer: 365°F (182°C)
Fry: 6–8 minutes

Yield: 50 portions
Portion: 3 oz (85 g)

Amount		Ingredient	Procedure
Metric	U.S.		
8.16 kg (6.8 kg)	18 lb AP (15 lb EP)	Potatoes, white	Pare and cut potatoes into uniform strips from 3/8–1/4 in. thick. Cover with cold water to keep potatoes from darkening. Just before frying, drain well or dry with paper towels. Fill fryer basket about 1/3 full of potatoes. Fry according to Method 1 or 2.

Method 1. Half fill fryer with fat. Preheat fat to 365°F (182°C). Fry potatoes for 6–8 minutes. Drain. Sprinkle with salt. Serve immediately.

Method 2. **Blanching.** Heat fat to 360°F (180°C). Place drained potato strips in hot fat, using an 8 to 1 ratio of fat to potatoes, by weight, as a guide for filling fryer basket. Fry 3–5 minutes depending on thickness of potato. (The potatoes should not brown.) Drain. Turn out on sheet pans. Refrigerate for later browning. **Browning.** Reheat fat to 375°F (190°C). Place about twice as many potato strips in kettle as for first-stage frying. Fry 2–3 minutes or until golden brown. Drain; sprinkle with salt if desired. Serve immediately.

Notes:
1. Select a long, mealy type potato, such as a russett.
2. To cook frozen French fried potatoes, use 12 lb (5.44 kg) for 50 3-oz (85-g) portions. Fry at 375°F (190°C) for 3–5 minutes or until golden brown.

Variations:
1. **Deep-Fat Browned Potatoes.** Partially cook pared whole or half potatoes. Fry in deep fat at 365°F (182°C) for 5–7 minutes. Transfer to serving pan. Sprinkle with salt.
2. **Lattice Potatoes.** Cut potatoes with lattice slicer. Fry at 365°F (182°C) for 3–10 minutes. Transfer to serving pan. Sprinkle with salt.
3. **Potato Chips.** Cut potatoes into very thin slices. Fry at 365°F (182°C) 3–6 minutes. Transfer to serving pan, sprinkle with salt.
4. **Shoestring Potatoes.** Cut potatoes into 1/8-in. strips. Fry at 365°F (182°C) 3–6 minutes. Transfer to serving pan. Sprinkle with salt.

MASHED POTATOES

Yield: 50 portions
Portion: 5 oz (142 g)

Amount		Ingredient	Procedure
Metric	U.S.		
6.8 kg (5.44 kg)	15 lb AP (12 lb EP)	Potatoes, pared	Peel and eye potatoes and cut into uniform size pieces. Steam or boil (p. 521). When done, drain and place in mixer bowl. Mash, using whip attachment on low speed until there are no lumps. Whip on high speed about 2 minutes.
1.9–2.3 L 227 g 57 g	2–2½ qt 8 oz 2 oz (3 T)	Milk, hot Margarine or butter Salt	Add hot milk, margarine, and salt. Whip on high speed until light and creamy.

Notes:
1. Potato water may be substituted for part of the milk.
2. 8 oz (227 g) nonfat dry milk and 2–2½ qt (1.9–2.3 L) water may be substituted for the liquid milk. Sprinkle dry milk over potatoes before mashing.
3. 2–2½ lb (0.91–1.05 kg) dehydrated potatoes may be substituted for the raw potatoes. Follow processor's instructions for preparation.

Variations:
1. **Duchess Potatoes.** Add 18 eggs (2 lb/908 g), beaten, to mashed potatoes. Add additional milk if necessary. Pile lightly into baking pans. Bake at 350°F (175°C) for 20–30 minutes, or until set.
2. **Mashed Potato Casserole.** Add ¼ c (60 mL) chopped chives, ¼ c (60 mL) crisp bacon bits, 12 oz (340 g) cream cheese, and white pepper and garlic powder to taste. Mix until blended. Place in baking pans. Sprinkle lightly with grated parmesan cheese and paprika. Brush lightly with melted margarine or butter. Bake at 375°F (175°C) for 30 minutes or until light brown.
3. **Potato Croquettes.** Add 18 (12 oz/340 g) egg yolks, well beaten. Shape into croquettes and dip in egg–milk mixture and crumbs (p. 37). Chill. Fry in deep fat at 360°F (180 °C) 5–8 minutes.
4. **Potato Rosettes.** Force Duchess Potatoes through a pastry tube, forming rosettes or fancy shapes. Bake at 350°F (175°C) until lightly browned. Use as a garnish for planked steak.

OVEN-BROWNED OR RISSOLÉ POTATOES

Oven: 450°F (230°C)
Bake: 1 hour
Yield: 50 portions
Portion: 1 potato

Amount Metric	U.S.	Ingredient	Procedure
50	50	Potatoes, baking variety	Pare potatoes and partially cook, about 10 minutes.
454 g	1 lb	Margarine, melted	Place potatoes on well-greased baking sheets.
28 g	1 oz (1½ T)	Salt	Pour melted margarine over potatoes. Sprinkle with salt. Bake at 450°F (230°C) for 1 hour or until tender. Baste every 15 minutes with margarine from pan. Turn potatoes once during baking to ensure uniform browning.

Variations:

1. **Franconia Potatoes.** Cook pared uniform sized potatoes approximately 15 minutes. Drain and place in pan in which meat is roasting. Bake approximately 40 minutes or until tender and lightly browned, basting with drippings in pan or turning occasionally to brown all sides. Serve with roast.
2. **French Baked Potatoes.** Select small, uniform potatoes and pare. Roll potatoes in melted margarine or shortening, then in cracker crumbs or crushed cornflakes. Place in shallow pans and bake.
3. **Herbed Potato Bake.** Pare baking potatoes and cut into ½-in. slices. Place in greased baking pans. Salt. Cover with 1½ c (360 mL) melted margarine or butter, 3½ oz (100 g) dehydrated onion soup mix, and 2 T (30 mL) rosemary and toss lightly. Bake at 325°F (165°C) for 1½ hours or until potatoes are tender.

SCALLOPED POTATOES

Oven: 350°F (175°C)
Bake: 1½–2 hours

Yield: 50 portions
2 pans 12 × 20 × 2 in.
Portion: 6 oz (142 g)

Amount		Ingredient	Procedure
Metric	U.S.		
6.8 kg (5.44 kg)	15 lb AP (12 lb EP)	Potatoes	Peel and eye potatoes. Slice and place in 2 greased 12 × 20 × 2-in. pans, 10 lb 10 oz (5 kg) per pan. Sprinkle with salt.
57 g	2 oz (3 T)	Salt	
227 g	8 oz	Margarine or butter	Melt margarine. Add flour and salt. Stir until smooth. Cook 2 minutes.
114 g	4 oz	Flour, all-purpose	
28 g	1 oz (1½ T)	Salt	
3.79 L	1 gal	Milk	Add milk gradually, while stirring. Cook until thickened. Pour over potatoes.
170 g	6 oz	Bread crumbs	Sprinkle buttered crumbs over potatoes. Bake at 350°F (175°C) for 1½–2 hours.
57 g	2 oz	Margarine or butter, melted	

Notes:
1. Potatoes may be partially cooked and hot white sauce added to shorten baking time.
2. 2 lb 8 oz (1.14 kg) dehydrated sliced potatoes, reconstituted in 2 gal (7.57 L) boiling water, and 2 oz (57 g) salt may be substituted for the fresh potatoes.

Variations:
1. **Scalloped Potatoes with Ham.** Add 5 lb (2.27 kg) cubed ham to white sauce. Cut salt to 1 T (19 g).
2. **Scalloped Potatoes with Onions.** Before baking, cover potatoes with onion rings. About 5 minutes before removing from oven, cover potatoes with shredded cheese.
3. **Scalloped Potatoes with Pork Chops.** Brown chops, season, and place on top of potatoes before baking.

PARSLEY BUTTERED NEW POTATOES

Yield: 50 portions
Portion: 3 oz (85 g)

Amount Metric	U.S.	Ingredient	Procedure
6.8 kg (4.54 kg)	15 lb AP (10 lb EP)	New potatoes	Wash and pare potatoes, removing eyes.
24 g	1 1/3 T	Salt	Cut potatoes into 1 1/2-in. cubes, or leave whole. If whole potatoes, cut as necessary to be of uniform size. Steam or boil (p. 521) until tender.
227 g	8 oz	Margarine or butter, melted	Distribute margarine uniformly over cooked potatoes.
28 g	1 oz	Parsley, chopped	Sprinkle with parsley.

Variations:

1. **Creamed New Potatoes.** Add 3 qt (2.84 L) Medium White Sauce (p. 470) to cooked potatoes.
2. **Creamed New Potatoes and Peas.** See p. 546.
3. **New Potatoes Parmesan.** Scrub small uniform-sized potatoes. Take 1 in. of peeling off around center of potatoes. Steam or boil (p. 521) until just done. Roll potatoes in melted margarine or butter. Place in baking pans. Sprinkle with Parmesan cheese. Bake at 350°F (175°C) for 20–25 minutes. Canned small whole potatoes may be substituted for fresh potatoes.
4. **Persillade New Potatoes.** Peel and cook uniform, small, new potatoes. Pour over them a mixture of lemon juice and butter, then roll in minced parsley.
5. **Potatoes Continental.** Peel and cook small potatoes in meat stock with bay leaves until tender. Drain and season with chopped onion browned in margarine or butter. Garnish with minced parsley and paprika.
6. **Potatoes in Jackets.** Wash medium-sized potatoes and remove blemishes. Steam or boil until tender and serve without removing skins.

POTATO PANCAKES

Yield: 50 portions
100 cakes
Portion: 2 2-oz (57-g) cakes

Amount		Ingredient	Procedure
Metric	U.S.		
6.8 kg (5.44 kg)	15 lb AP (12 lb EP)	Potatoes	Peel potatoes and onions. Grind. Drain.
680 g	1 lb 8 oz	Onions	
8 (397 g)	8 (14 oz)	Eggs, beaten	Combine and add to potatoes and onion.
227 g	8 oz	Flour, all-purpose	
57 g	2 oz (3 T)	Salt	
5 g	1 t	Baking powder	
180 mL	¾ c	Milk	
			Drop potato mixture with No. 20 dipper on hot greased griddle. Fry, turning once, until golden brown on both sides. Serve with Applesauce (p. 249).

GLAZED OR CANDIED SWEET POTATOES

Oven: 400°F (205°C)
Bake: 20–30 minutes

Yield: 50 portions
Portion: 4 oz (114 g)

Amount		Ingredient	Procedure
Metric	U.S.		
7.26 kg (5.9 kg)	16 lb AP (13 lb EP)	Sweet potatoes or yams	Scrub potatoes. Steam or boil in skins until tender (p. 521). When cool enough to handle, peel and cut into halves lengthwise. Arrange in shallow pans.
794 g	1 lb 12 oz	Sugar, brown	Mix sugar, water, margarine and salt.
480 mL	2 c	Water	Heat to boiling point.
227 g	8 oz	Margarine or butter	Pour over potatoes.
3 g	½ t	Salt	Bake at 400°F (205°C) for 20–30 minutes.

Notes:
1. 3 No. 10 cans sweet potatoes may be substituted for fresh sweet potatoes.
2. Seasonings for sweet potatoes: allspice, cardamom, cinnamon, cloves, or nutmeg.

Variations:
1. **Baked Sweet Potatoes.** Select small even-sized sweet potatoes or yams. Scrub and bake 40–45 minutes, or until tender, at 425°F (220°C).
2. **Candied Sweet Potatoes with Almonds.** Proceed as for glazed sweet potatoes. Increase margarine or butter to 12 oz (340 g) and reduce brown sugar to 1½ lb (680 g). Add 1 c (240 mL) dark syrup and 2 t (10 mL) mace. When partially glazed, sprinkle top with chopped almonds and continue cooking until almonds are toasted.
3. **Glazed Sweet Potatoes with Orange Slices.** Add ¼ c (60 mL) grated orange rind to syrup. Cut 5 oranges into thin slices; add to sweet potatoes when syrup is added.
4. **Mashed Sweet Potatoes.** Cook and mash sweet potatoes or yams (p. 551). Reduce milk to 1½ qt (1.42 L). Add ¼ t nutmeg if desired.
5. **Sweet Potatoes and Apples.** Reduce sweet potatoes to 9 lb (4.08 kg), cooked, peeled, and sliced. Pare and slice 5 lb (2.27 kg) tart apples. Place alternate layers of sweet potatoes and apples in baking pans. Pour hot syrup (see recipe above) over potatoes and apples. Bake at 350°F (175°C) for 45 minutes.

SEASONED FRESH SPINACH AND OTHER GREENS

Yield: 50 portions
Portion: 3 oz (85 g)

Amount		Ingredient	Procedure
Metric	U.S.		
5.44 kg (4.54 kg)	12 lb AP (10 lb EP)	Fresh spinach or other greens	Sort and trim greens. Cut off coarse stems and roots.
24 g	1 ⅓ T	Salt	Wash leaves thoroughly, lifting out of water after each washing. Steam or boil. See p. 521.
114 g	4 oz	Margarine or butter, melted	Pour margarine over greens.

Notes:
1. Beet greens, chard, collards, kale, mustard greens, or turnip greens may be used. For kale, strip leaves from coarse stems.
2. For frozen spinach, use 10 lb (4.54 kg). See p. 521 for cooking.
3. Greens may be garnished with 12 hard-cooked eggs, chopped, and 1 ½ lb (680 g) crisp-cooked bacon, crumbled.
4. Seasonings for spinach: basil, mace, marjoram, nutmeg, oregano, mushrooms, bacon, cheese, hard-cooked eggs, vinegar.

Variations:
1. **Creamed Spinach.** Cook spinach. Drain. Chop coarsely. Add 2 qt (1.89 L) white sauce. Season with salt, pepper, and nutmeg.
2. **Wilted Spinach or Lettuce.** To 10 lb (4.54 kg) chopped raw spinach or lettuce, or a combination of the two, add 2 qt (1.89 L) Hot Bacon Sauce (p. 485) just before serving.

SPINACH SOUFFLÉ

Oven: 350°F (175°C)
Bake: 40 minutes

Yield: 48 portions
2 pans 12 × 20 × 2 in.
Portion: 4 oz (114 g)

Amount Metric	U.S.	Ingredient	Procedure
567 g	1 lb 4 oz	Margarine or butter	Melt margarine. Add flour and salt. Stir until smooth and cook 2 minutes.
227 g	8 oz	Flour, all-purpose	
48 g	2½ T	Salt	
1.18 L	1¼ qt	Milk	Add milk and sour cream. Blend over low heat until smooth, stirring constantly. Remove from heat.
1.18 L	1¼ qt	Cultured sour cream	
2.72 kg	6 lb	Frozen chopped spinach, thawed and drained	Add spinach, onion, nutmeg, and egg yolks. Mix.
227 g	8 oz	Onion, finely chopped	
12 g	1½ T	Nutmeg	
18 (340 g)	18 (12 oz)	Egg yolks, beaten	
18 (595 g)	18 (1 lb 5 oz)	Egg whites	Beat egg whites until stiff. Fold into spinach mixture. Scale into ungreased 12 × 20 × 2-in. counter pans, 7 lb 8 oz (3.4 kg) per pan. Set in pans of hot water. Bake at 350°F (175°C) for 40 minutes or until soufflé is set. Cut 4 × 6.

BAKED ACORN SQUASH

Oven: 350°F (175°C)
Bake: 30–40 minutes
Yield: 50 portions
Portion: ½ squash

Amount Metric	U.S.	Ingredient	Procedure
25	25	Acorn squash	Wash squash and cut in half lengthwise. Scrape out seeds. Place cut-side down in shallow pans with a small amount of water. Bake at 350°F (175°C) for 20–25 minutes, or until just tender.
227 g	8 oz	Margarine or butter, melted	Place squash hollow side up. Sprinkle cavities with margarine, salt, and brown sugar. Bake until sugar is melted, 10–15 minutes.
28 g	1 oz (1½ T)	Salt	
340 g	12 oz	Sugar, brown	

Variations:

1. **Acorn Squash with Sausage.** Place 4 oz (114 g) sausage patty or 2 link sausages, partially cooked, in each cooked squash half. Continue baking until meat is done.
2. **Stuffed Acorn Squash.** Fill cooked squash half with No. 12 dipper of the following mixture: 5 qt (4.73 L) cooked rice, 4 lb (1.81 kg) chopped cooked meat, and 4 oz (114 g) minced onion, sautéed in margarine and moistened with meat stock.

MASHED WINTER SQUASH

Yield: 50 portions
Portion: 3 oz (85 g)

Amount Metric	U.S.	Ingredient	Procedure
6.8 kg (4.54 kg)	15 lb AP (10 lb EP)	Winter squash	Pare squash and cut into pieces. Steam or boil until tender (p. 521).
1.42 L	1½ qt	Milk, hot	Mash and add milk and seasonings. Whip until light.
227 g	8 oz	Margarine or butter, melted	
38 g	2 T	Salt	May be garnished with toasted slivered almonds.
227 g	8 oz	Sugar, brown	

Notes:

1. Acorn, butternut, hubbard, or other winter squash variety may be used.
2. Seasonings for squash: allspice, basil, cinnamon, cloves, fennel, ginger, nutmeg, or rosemary.

Variation: **Butternut Squash–Apple Casserole.** Cook 8 lb (3.63 kg) pared, cored, and sliced apples, 12 oz (340 g) margarine or butter, and 12 oz (340 g) sugar until barely tender. Arrange in baking pans. Cover with mashed butternut squash (use 10 lb/4.54 kg squash). Top with mixture of crushed cornflakes, chopped pecans, melted margarine or butter, and brown sugar. Bake at 350°F (175°C) 30–40 minutes.

SEASONED ZUCCHINI OR SUMMER SQUASH

Yield: 50 portions
Portion: 3 oz (85 g)

Amount Metric	U.S.	Ingredient	Procedure
4.9–5.4 kg (4.54 kg)	11–12 lb AP (10 lb EP)	Zucchini or other summer squash	Wash zucchini and remove ends. Do not peel. Cut into slices or spears. Steam or simmer until tender (p. 521).
114 g	4 oz	Margarine or butter, melted	Pour margarine over zucchini. Season.
19 g	1 T	Salt	
2 g	1 t	Pepper, white	

Notes:
1. 1 t (6 g) garlic salt may be substituted for part of salt.
2. ½ c (43 g) Parmesan cheese may be sprinkled over zucchini before serving.

Variations:
1. **French Fried Zucchini.** See p. 545.
2. **Zucchini Casserole.** Steam or parboil 8 lb (3.63 kg) sliced zucchini until tender crisp. Drain. Combine 1 46-oz can cream of chicken soup, 3 c (720 mL) sour cream, 1 c (240 mL) chopped green onions, and 1 oz (28 g) shredded carrots. Combine with zucchini. Mix 1 lb 12 oz (794 g) herb-seasoned bread crumbs and 8 oz (227 g) melted margarine or butter and spread half in a 12 × 20 × 2-in. counter pan. Pour zucchini mixture over crumbs. Top with remaining crumbs. Bake at 350°F (175°C) for 30–40 minutes or until heated through. Other vegetables such as broccoli, asparagus, cauliflower, or French cut green beans may be used in this casserole.
3. **Zucchini and Summer Squash.** Wash and slice 5 lb (2.27 kg) zucchini and 5 lb (2.27 kg) yellow summer squash. Cook until just tender. Season with 8 oz (227 g) melted margarine or butter, salt and pepper to taste. Add 2 lb (908 g) cherry tomatoes just before serving.
4. **Zucchini and Tomato Casserole.** In 12 × 20 × 2-in. counter pan, layer 7 lb (3.18 kg) sliced zucchini, 3 lb (1.36 kg) fresh tomatoes, peeled and chopped, and 1 lb (454 g) chopped onion. Salt and pepper lightly. Sprinkle 1 lb (454 g) grated Cheddar cheese and 1 lb (454 g) bacon, cooked and crumbled, over top. Cover with buttered bread crumbs. Bake covered at 400°F (205°C) for about 1 hour, uncovered for the last 20 minutes.

BAKED TOMATOES

Oven: 400°F (205°C)
Bake: 10–12 minutes

Yield: 50 portions
Portion: ½ tomato

Metric	U.S.	Ingredient	Procedure
25	25	Tomatoes, fresh (5 oz/142 g each)	Wash tomatoes. Cut in halves.
6 g	1 t	Salt	Sprinkle each tomato with salt and pepper or seasoned salt.
2 g	1 t	Pepper, black	
170 g	6 oz	Margarine or butter, melted	Combine margarine, bread crumbs, and onion.
57 g	2 oz	Bread crumbs	Place 2 t mixture on each tomato half.
170 g	6 oz	Onion, finely chopped	Bake at 400°F (205°C) for 10–12 minutes.

Note: Seasonings for tomatoes: bay leaf, basil, garlic, oregano, thyme, rosemary, chili powder.

Variations:
1. **Mushroom-Stuffed Tomatoes.** Add 2 lb (908 g) sautéed, sliced, or chopped mushrooms to crumb mixture.
2. **Broiled Tomato Slices.** Cut tomatoes in ½-in. slices. Salt, dot with margarine or butter, and broil.
3. **Spinach-Stuffed Tomatoes.** Wash medium size fresh tomatoes. Remove core and part of the tomato pulp. Fill center with 2 oz (57 g) Spinach Soufflé (p. 558). Sprinkle with buttered crumbs and parmesan cheese. Bake at 350°F (175°C) for about 1 hour.

TOMATO VEGETABLE MEDLEY

Yield: 50 portions
Portion: 5 oz (142 g)

Amount		Ingredient	Procedure
Metric	U.S.		
908 g	2 lb EP	Celery, cut in strips	Steam celery and carrots for 15 mintues.
908 g	2 lb EP	Carrots, cut in 2-in. strips	
908 g	2 lb EP	Onions, sliced	Mix all ingredients and place in 2 12 × 20 × 2-in. pans.
454 g	1 lb EP	Green peppers, cut in strips	
1 No. 10 can	1 No. 10 can	Green beans, cut	Cover with aluminum foil and cook in steamer for 30 minutes.
1 No. 10 can	1 No. 10 can	Tomatoes	
38 g	2 T	Salt	
170 g	6 oz	Tapioca, minute	
284 g	10 oz	Margarine or butter, melted	
2 g	¾ t	Pepper, black	
170 g	6 oz	Sugar, granulated	

Note: Vegetables may be baked for 1–1½ hours at 350°F (175°C). Do not precook celery and carrots.

Variations:

1. **Breaded Tomatoes.** Add 1 lb (454 g) cubed bread, 8 oz (227 g) margarine or butter, and 6 oz (170 g) sugar to 2 No. 10 cans tomatoes. Bake at 350°F (175°C) for about 30 minutes.

2. **Creole Tomatoes.** Drain 2 No. 10 cans tomatoes. To the juice add 1 lb (454 g) celery, 4 oz (114 g) onion, and 8 oz (227 g) green pepper, coarsely chopped. Cook about 15 minutes. Add the tomatoes, 2 T (38 g) salt, and ¾ t (2 g) pepper, and place in baking pan. Cover with 2 qt (1.89 L) toasted bread cubes and bake at 350°F (175°C) for about 30 minutes.

3. **Tomatoes and Celery.** Combine 2 No. 10 cans tomatoes, 8 oz (227 g) celery, cut into ¾-in. lengths, 1 T (14 g) sugar, 1 l (19 g) salt, 2 oz (57 g) margarine or butter. Cover and simmer for 15 minutes or until celery is tender.

STIR-FRIED VEGETABLES

Yield: 50 portions
Portion: 3 oz (85 g)

Amount		Ingredient	Procedure
Metric	U.S.		
43 g	⅓ c	Cornstarch	Combine cornstarch and water. Set aside for last step.
240 mL	1 c	Water	
3.1–3.6 kg (2.95 kg)	7–8 lb AP (6 lb 8 oz EP)	Assorted vegetables (see below for suggestions)	Prepare vegetables. Cut into thin slices, strips, or diagonal slices.
240 mL	1 c	Cooking oil	Combine oil, garlic, and ginger root in fry pan. Heat to 350°F (175°C).
2 cloves	2 cloves	Garlic, minced	
½ t	½ t	Ginger root, fresh, minced.	
227 g	8 oz	Water chestnuts, sliced	Add water chestnuts and prepared vegetables to heated oil. Stir with long spatulas in a folding motion. Cook until vegetables are tender crisp.
720 mL	3 c	Chicken Stock (p. 495)	Combine stock and soy sauce.
120 mL	½ c	Soy sauce	Mix quickly into vegetables. Reduce heat. Pour cornstarch mixture over vegetables. Cook and stir just until sauce thickens and vegetables are glazed.

Notes:
1. Select vegetables for contrast in color, shape, texture, and flavor. At least three vegetables should be selected. Cut vegetables into small enough pieces to cook quickly. Frozen vegetables should be thawed before stir frying.
2. Suggested vegetables: cauliflower, broccoli, green beans, snow peas, carrots, celery, onions, zucchini squash, mushrooms.

VEGETABLE TIMBALE

Oven: 300°F (150°C)
Bake: 2 hours

Yield: 40 portions
1 pan 12 × 20 × 2 in.
Portion: 3 oz (85 g)

Amount		Ingredient	Procedure
Metric	U.S.		
16 (709 g)	16 (1 lb 9 oz)	Eggs	Beat eggs.
38 g	2 T	Salt	Add salt, margarine, and milk.
142 g	5 oz	Margarine or butter, melted	
1.42 L	1½ qt	Milk	
1.36 kg	3 lb	Spinach, chopped, frozen	Cook spinach (p. 521). Drain well. Add to egg mixture. Mix until well blended. Pour into greased 12 × 20 × 2-in. pan. Set into another pan with 3 c hot water in it. Bake at 300°F (150°C) for 2 hours. Test with a silver knife as for custard. Cut 5 × 8. Serve with 1 oz (28 g) Cheese Sauce (p. 471).

Note: Spinach, broccoli, Brussels sprouts, or asparagus or any combination of these vegetables may be used.

Variation: **Chicken Timbale.** Use 32 eggs (3 lb 8 oz/1.59 kg), 1 oz (28 g) salt, 1 lb (454 g) margarine or butter, melted, 1 t (2 g) white pepper, 12 oz (340 g) bread crumbs, and 6 lb (2.72 kg) chopped cooked chicken. Mix melted margarine, bread crumbs, and milk. Cook for 5 minutes. Add beaten eggs, seasonings, and chicken. Bake as for Vegetable Timbale. Cut 6 × 8. Serve with Béchamel Sauce (p. 473).

PART THREE

MENU
PLANNING

Menu Planning

Planning menus that are creative, exciting, and nutritious continues to be a challenge for persons responsible for food service operations. Because of the increased awareness of and exposure to a variety of foods, clientele have become more vocal in their dining preferences. The impact of the two-income family has caused menu planners to address the needs and desires of those eating over one third of their meals outside the home. Away-from-home dining facilities have become an integral part of the American lifestyle.

FACTORS AFFECTING MENU PLANNING

A well-planned menu is the cornerstone of a successful food service and is the focal point from which many functions and activities start. The menu must offer a selection of foods that is satisfying to the clientele, but it must be one that can be produced within the constraints of the physical facility and limitations dictated by management policies. Factors to consider when planning a menu include:

Clientele The menu planner must consider the makeup of the group to be served—age, sex, nutritional needs, food habits, and individual preferences. This is especially important in food services where a limited choice of food is offered, as in extended care facilities, child care centers, and retirement complexes. In this type of food service, meals must be planned to meet the complete nutritional needs of the group, offer enough variety to minimize monotony and, insofar as possible, satisfy their food preferences.

In food services offering a choice of menu items and in those having a transient clientele, the providing of nutritionally adequate meals is not necessarily a goal of the food service, but many do assume some responsibility for nutrition education. The public is becoming more aware of good nutrition and menus must offer choices reflecting this change in eating habits.

The public today is more knowledgeable about new and different foods and desire greater variety and a wider selection. Interest has grown, too, in ethnic, vegetarian, and regional foods, and many establishments have expanded their menus to meet these requests. Some food services include routinely one or more ethnic foods, while others may introduce an international food periodically through a special meal or day. Planning menus that are acceptable to a group requires that the menu planner be aware of the food preferences of the group and periodically evaluate the acceptance of the foods and food combinations offered.

Type of Food Service   The menu pattern is influenced by the type of food service. Cafeteria meals may be different from the menu offered in a full-service restaurant.

Number to be Served   Besides affecting the variety of food that can be included in the menu, the number to be served also influences the method of preparing it. For example, it may be difficult, under some institutional conditions, to prepare stuffed baked potatoes or individual placed salads for a large group.

The Food Budget   The amount of income allotted for raw food cost and labor is a determining factor in the type of menu that can be planned and served in a nonprofit institution. In a commercial food service, the selling price is calculated on the basis of raw food and labor costs plus a "markup," and the restaurant may restrict its menu items to those within a predetermined price range.

Available Equipment   Preparing suitable meals with the available equipment in a given length of time presents one of the major problems of those responsible for planning menus. Special attention should be given to oven capacity, refrigerator and freezer facilities, number and size of steam-jacketed kettles and steamers, and availability and capacity of mixers. Certain combinations of menu items often must be avoided because of lack of pans or dishes.

Number and Experience of Employees   The man-hours of labor available and the efficiency and skill of employees are important to the successful preparation of any meal.

Distribution of Work   The distribution of work among the various areas of preparation is of prime importance in meeting a time schedule and in maintaining the morale of the employees. In determining a day's work load, the menu planner should consider not only 1 day's menu but also any preparation necessary for meals for the following day. To introduce variety in the menu, a limited number of foods requiring time-consuming processes may be included if combined with other food items that require minimum preparation.

The many ready-to-cook frozen foods, prepared vegetables, and other convenience foods now make possible a less restricted menu than can be offered when all food preparation is done on the premises. Discrimination in the selection and use of many of the prepared foods, however, is needed to maintain high food standards and to preserve the individuality of the food service.

Some foods require last-minute cooking to assure products of high quality. To avoid confusion and delayed meal service, the menu should be so planned that there is a balance between items that may be prepared early and those that must be cooked just prior to serving.

Availability and Seasonability of Foods Availability of foods in the local markets exert a limited influence on the menu items. Although most foods are now available in fresh or frozen form in all sections of the country, fresh foods produced locally are often of better quality and less expensive during the growing season than those shipped from distant markets.

Cooked Foods on Hand Unused cooked foods more often are used to effect changes in a menu than as the basis of the original menu. However, the successful use of foods on hand requires careful thought and imagination to incorporate them in such a way that they will be acceptable. Foods should be used promptly and stored properly until used. Some foods may be offered in their original form as a choice on a selective menu; others may be incorporated into food combinations.

Recipes Menus should be based on recipes standardized to the requirements of the individual food service.

MENU PATTERNS AND CYCLES

MENU PATTERN
The menu pattern is the outline of food items to be included in each meal and the extent of the choices that will be offered must be decided before menus are planned.

The *nonselective* or *set* menu has a single item in each category. To assure nutritional adequacy, foods from each of the four basic food groups should be included. A general pattern for a nonselective menu is given below.

A nonselective menu may be modified to include a limited selection; for example, a choice of two vegetables may be given, or a soup and salad may be offered as an alternative to an entrée and vegetable for those who wish a lighter meal. In health care facilities, the dinner meal may be scheduled for noon with a lighter supper in the evening.

The *selective* menu offers 2 or more items within each menu category. The number of options varies with the type of food service. A commercial cafeteria, for example, may offer a wider selection than does a college or university cafeteria or a hospital. Some items may appear on the cafeteria counter every day, and often the pattern for lunch and dinner are identical. Foods from which the individual patron may choose a well-balanced meal should be provided. Hospitals use the selective menu extensively, as do most commercial and college food services. Following is a suggested pattern for a selective menu, using the same format for lunch and dinner.

MENU CYCLE
Menus should be planned well in advance of use and should include a minimum of one week's menus.

The *cycle menu*, which is a carefully planned set or sets of menus that are rotated at definite intervals, is used extensively and is particularly effective in food services having a frequent change of clientele. Cycle menus save time for the planner and are effective tools for food and labor cost control, forecasting, and purchasing. Repetition of the same or nearly the same menu helps standardize preparation procedures and gives the employees an opportunity to become more efficient through repeated use of familiar recipes. Menus can become monotonous and repetitious, though, if not carefully planned.

The length of the cycle depends on the type of food service. A 7- or 10- day cycle is appropriate for hospitals, where the average patient stay is 5 to 7 days. Schools may use 8-week, semester, or yearly cycles, while restaurants may prefer monthly or seasonal cycles or may use the same menu throughout the year. Many food services recognize seasonal changes by having spring, summer, autumn, and winter cycles.

Regardless of the length of the cycle, the menus should be constantly reviewed, updated, and improved. Each day's menus should be reviewed the day after service and any production problems or adverse reactions by the clientele noted and corrected before the next cycle. The menu planner must allow flexibility for changes due to holidays, special occasions, and inability to obtain specific food items for production.

MENU PLANNING PROCEDURES

Creative menu planning requires imagination, originality, an interest in food, and attention to detail. The menu maker should set aside prejudices and food likes and dislikes. The menu maker must be aware of the needs of the clientele being served and must understand the food service operation.

If at all possible, the menu should be planned during uninterrupted time in a place away from noise and confusion and at a desk or table large enough to accommodate menu planning materials. These materials include:

1. Menu forms as dictated by type and needs of the food service.
2. Standardized recipe file.
3. Cookbooks for large and small quantity cooking.
4. Menu suggestion lists, as shown on p. 582.
5. File of previous menus.
6. Summaries of food preference surveys of clientele.
7. Periodicals containing recipe and menu suggestions.
8. Idea file.

KEY POINTS IN MENU PLANNING
- Plan for variety
  1. Include a wide variety of foods from day to day. Unless you provide a choice, avoid the same form of food on consecutive days; for example, meat loaf on Monday and spaghetti and meat balls on Tuesday.
  2. Avoid repeating the same food on the same day of the week. For this reason, the 7-day cycle may be undesirable.
  3. Vary method of preparation. For example, serve vegetables raw or cooked, buttered, stir fried, marinated, or with a sauce.
  4. Introduce new foods occasionally and, on a selective menu, pair a new food with a well-liked food.
- Plan for eye appeal
  1. Try to visualize the appearance of the food on the plate or on the cafeteria counter.
  2. Use at least 1 or 2 colorful foods on each menu.
  3. Use colorful foods in combination with foods having little or no color.
- Plan for contrast in texture and flavor
  1. Offer crisp foods with soft, creamy foods.
  2. Use strong and mild flavored foods together.
  3. Balance light and heavy foods; for example, in a nonselective menu use light desserts with hearty entrées.
- Plan for consumer acceptance
  1. Include food combinations most acceptable to the clientele.
  2. The completed menu should, if possible, have a predominance of familiar and well-accepted menu items, with the introduction of new and less well-liked foods spaced throughout the menu period.
  3. In nonselective menus, it is important that the less popular foods be accompanied by some that are well liked by the majority of the clientele.
  4. Periodically assess the food preferences of the consumers.

STEPS IN MENU PLANNING
- Determine a time period
  1. Plan menus for at least a week, preferably longer.
  2. If a cycle menu is being planned, decide on length of the cycle.
- Select menu items systematically, about in the following order:
  1. **Entrées.** Select meat and other entrées for the entire cycle or length of time for which menus are being planned. If planning a week's menus only, choose entrées for a month or longer, then complete the menus as needed. In this way, an entrée cycle can be developed that would simplify planning each week's menus.

On a selective menu, offer at least 1 meat and a meatless entrée, along with poultry, fish, and meat extenders to complete the number of entrées required.

Be specific about method of preparation when recording the menu; for example, show pork chops as baked, stuffed, barbecued, breaded, or whatever method of preparation is desired.

2. **Soups and Sandwiches.** Plan with entrées if they are to be offered as a main dish in lieu of meat or other entrée. On a selective menu, offer a cream soup and a stock soup. In a cafeteria, a variety of sandwiches may be offered, and these may not change from day to day.

3. **Vegetables.** Select vegetables that are compatible with the entrées. Potatoes, rice, or pasta may be included as one choice. On a selective menu, pair a popular vegetable with one that is less well-liked.

4. **Salads.** If only one salad is to be offered, select one that complements or is a contrast in texture to the other menu items. On a selective menu, include a green salad; fruit, vegetable, and gelatin salads to complete the desired number. Certain salad items may be offered daily such as tossed salad, cottage cheese, or cabbage slaw; or a salad bar may be a standard menu feature.

5. **Breads.** Vary the kinds of breads offered or provide a choice of white or whole grain bread and a hot bread.

6. **Desserts.** If no choice is offered, plan a light dessert with a hearty meal and a rich dessert when the rest of the meal is not too heavy. On a selective menu, include a two-crust pie, a soft pie, cake, pudding, and gelatin dessert. Ice cream, yogurt, baked custard, and fruit may be offered daily.

7. **Breakfast Items.** Certain breakfast foods such as cooked and cold cereal, toast, and fruit may be standard. Variety may be introduced through a choice of entrées, hot breads, fresh fruits, and fruit juices.

8. **Beverages.** A choice of beverages usually is provided. Coffee, decaffeinated coffee, tea, and milk, including lowfat, usually are offered each day. Lemonade, fruit punch, and a variety of juices may be included also.

- Evaluate the completed menu

After the menu has been planned, check carefully to see if it has met the established criteria. Evaluate the menu again after the meals have been served. Make notations of satisfactory menus and difficulties encountered in production and service of the meals. If the cycle is to be repeated, desired alterations should be noted.

The responsibility of the menu planner does not end with the writing of the menu. The task is completed only when the food has been prepared and served and the reaction of the consumer noted.

MENU PLANNING FOR DIFFERENT TYPES OF FOOD SERVICES

ELEMENTARY AND SECONDARY SCHOOLS

The school lunch program is designed to provide nutritious, reasonably priced lunches to school children and children in residential child care institutions, to contribute to a better understanding of good nutrition, and to foster good food habits. School food service has become a basic part of the nutrition and education program of the nation's schools. The growing School Breakfast Program has further expanded this role.

The nutrition goal for school lunches is to provide approximately one third of the Recommended Dietary Allowances (RDA) by age categories. In the years since passage of the School Lunch Act, the implementation of its provisions has been changed to permit more choice and greater flexibility in menu patterns and adjustment in portion sizes for various age groups. School lunch patterns for various age groups are given on p. 580. To qualify for reimbursement, a school is required to use this framework, but other foods may be added to help improve acceptability and to satisfy students' appetites.

An "offer versus serve" provision allows students to choose less than all of the food items within the lunch pattern. Students must be offered all 5 food items of the school lunch, and the student must choose at least 3 of these items for their lunch to be reimbursed. Schools are required to implement the "offer versus serve" provision for senior high school students. The implementation of this provision in middle and junior high schools is left to the descretion of local school food authorities, but it is not allowed in elementary schools.

The cycle menu is used to some extent in school food services, and many schools are using selective menus in which students may select from two items of comparable nutritional value for part of the menu; for example, a student may have a choice of two vegetables and two or more desserts. Some schools offer multiple menus in which more than one complete menu is offered, such as a soup and sandwich meal that meets federal requirements and a plate lunch. Some junior and senior high schools offer à la carte menus.

Many foods on the Menu Planning Suggestions listed on p. 582 are suitable for school lunches, keeping in mind the nutritional requirements, cost, labor and equipment restraints, and food preferences of the age group to be served. Many schools include a salad bar, and most schools introduce ethnic and international foods through special promotions.

An amendment to the National School Lunch Act provides assistance to eligible food services for preschool and school-age children in day care centers, settlement houses, recreation centers, and summer day camps. In planning food for children in these centers, the total daily food requirements of children should be considered. The combination of meals and snacks will vary according to the age group, their time of arrival at the center, and their length of stay. It is important that the planner consider the nutritional needs of the children, their food preferences, regional food habits, and equipment, personnel, and other management functions.

Young children need nutritious foods at frequent intervals, but it is important to schedule the service of food to allow sufficient time between meals and supplements. Young children enjoy food they can handle easily. Finger food, snacks, and bite-sized pieces are most popular. Apple wedges, banana slices, berries, dried peaches or pears, fresh peach, pear, or pineapple wedges, grapefruit or orange sections, pitted plums and prunes, raisins, cabbage wedges, carrot and celery sticks, cauliflowerets, tomato wedges, cheese cubes, crackers or rusks with peanut butter or cheese, and small sandwiches are examples of finger foods.

Those responsible for food service in child care centers should provide the opportunity for children to learn to eat and enjoy a variety of nutritious foods.

COLLEGES AND UNIVERSITIES

Meals in most college and university residence halls today are served cafeteria style. Although many have meal plans entitling students to a set number of meals per week for a stated cost, some offer cash cafeterias and specialty shops to meet the needs and preferences of the students more adequately.

Planning cafeteria menus for students is similar to that for a commercial cafeteria except that the choices may be more limited. There is a responsibility also to provide foods that are adequate to meet the nutritional requirements of the residents.

Usually a choice of two or more items in each menu category is provided. The selective menu pattern on p. 579 is appropriate for college and university food services. Certain salad items, such as tossed salad, cottage cheese, fruit and gelatin, may be offered each day on a salad bar. Likewise, fruit, yogurt, and ice cream may be served each meal, with other desserts added for variety. Fast food lines that serve soups and salads, milk shakes, hamburgers and French fries, submarine sandwiches, or pizza are well liked by students and make it possible for them to eat in a short span of time. Special meals depicting certain themes, such as Hawaiian, Oriental, or German, regional specialties, and ethnic foods are popular in many university settings.

HOSPITALS

Although often more complex, the principles of meal planning in a hospital are the same as those in other types of institutions. For one service period foods must be provided for many kinds of diets. These may range from liquid, ground, soft, or regular to bland, low sodium, carbohydrate, protein, or fat restricted, with a wide range in caloric requirements.

Food for hospital personnel, usually served cafeteria style, must be planned. The menu may be a modification of the patient menu, with a few additions to offer a wider selection than is desirable for the patients. Often foods must be available 24 hours a day.

When developing a hospital meal pattern, the first step is to plan a regular or normal diet that will supply all food essentials necessary for good nutrition. This pattern then becomes the foundation for most diets required for therapeutic purposes and is the core of all meal planning in a hospital of any type or size. Patients requiring other than a normal diet will receive various modifications of the regular diet to fit their particular needs.

In planning a normal or regular diet, meals should be planned for each day as a unit. Each day's menu then may be checked to be sure that all essential foods have been included. A suggested 3-meal-a-day menu pattern for a normal diet follows.

The selective menu adds much to the satisfaction of patients and also helps to prevent waste. Choices that appeal to various patients usually can be made available with little extra work, if careful planning is used in pairing items on the menu. The main items on the selective menu are the same as those on the general menu. Some items, such as the choice of meat and vegetables, may be the same as foods prepared for one of the modified diets or for the cafeteria. Other choices may be soup or fruit juice, or fruit or ice cream in place of a prepared dessert. On the dinner menu, choices of light or heavy items may do much to promote patient satiety. Some hospitals have adopted a selective menu similar to the table d'hôte menu of the commercial field. A varied selection of foods is listed and offered each day. Patients may order any food item on the menu unless it is restricted on his diet.

Some hospitals find it advantageous to use a 5-meal plan. Patients like eating smaller meals and more often. Dietitians who use the 5-meal plan claim the cost of food and labor are somewhat reduced because all food requiring skilled cooks can be prepared during one work shift. An outline menu pattern for the 5-meal plan follows:

7 A.M.	Coffee, with toast or sweet roll.
10 A.M.	Breakfast: fruit or juice, cereal with milk, egg or other entrée, toast, coffee, milk, or both.
1 P.M.	Soup, crackers. Cheese, fruit or juice, and melba toast.
4 P.M.	Dinner: fruit juice, meat, potato and other vegetable, dessert, coffee, or milk.
8 P.M.	Sandwich, milk, custard, or ice cream.

EXTENDED CARE FACILITIES AND RETIREMENT COMMUNITIES

For people residing in extended health care facilities and retirement communities, food satisfies a basic emotional and physical need.

Those persons planning meals for older adults should be aware of the problems peculiar to this age group. Their fixed habits and food preferences developed through many years may influence but should not determine entirely the meals planned for them. Healthy adults regardless of age need a well-balanced diet and, in planning the day's food, the basic pattern for the normal diet should be followed. Individual problems of the group members, such as difficulty in chewing solid food, special diet requirements, and their limited mobility and activity, must also be of concern.

At least 3 well-planned meals should be served daily, with a hot food at each meal. The menu pattern is similar to that of the regular hospital diet (p. 579), with adjustments in portions and some modification for residents with individual eating problems. The caloric intake or quantity of food eaten usually is smaller because of lessened activity.

The daily food plan should include (1) at least 1 food of good quality protein at each meal—eggs, lean meat, fish, poultry, or cheese; (2) milk offered at mealtime, with at least 2 c a day for each person; (3) 4 or more servings of fruits and vegetables, including a green leafy or yellow vegetable and a citrus fruit, such as grapefruit, orange, or some other high source of vitamin C; and although chewing may be difficult for some, raw vegetables or fruits should be included; (4) 4 or more servings from the bread—cereal group, which includes in addition to bread and breakfast cereals rice, macaroni, spaghetti, noodles, and baked goods made with whole grain or enriched flour. Additional foods containing fat, sweets, and flavoring add to the acceptance of meals.

If a nonselective menu is used, some modification will add to the residents' acceptance of the food. Choice may be provided by offering certain menu items daily in addition to a set menu or through a choice of two items in each menu category for the dinner meal. Food service in this type of long-range facility offers opportunity for use of the 8-week or longer cycle.

COMMERCIAL FOOD SERVICES

Menu planning for commercial food services varies according to the size and type of operation, its goals, and the expected check average. Menus range from the fast food chain's limited menu for high volume and speedy service to the elaborate table d'hôte menu of a formal seated-service restaurant.

Planning the menu for the commercial food service has much in common with that for the institution food service. Consideration must be given to the basic rules of successful meal planning and food combination and the specific requirements of the clientele. As in any other food service, labor is one of the largest items of expense and one of the most difficult to control. The use of preportioned foods, portion-ready entrées, ready-to-cook foods, and other labor-saving items are of major importance in effecting economies of time and cost.

Some restaurants have a fixed menu with daily specials featured, others have found the use of cycle menus to be valuable in reducing the time spent in planning and as an aid in the equitable distribution of labor and food. In commercial cafeterias, the noon and evening meals may be essentially the same with a wide selection of entrées, sandwiches, and desserts. It is not uncommon to have 5–6 entrées, 8–10 salads, and 8–10 desserts. Cafeteria operations may offer special food items on individual days or serve a unique soup, salad, or dessert as their specialty.

NONSELECTIVE MENU PATTERN

Breakfast	Lunch	Dinner
Fruit	Soup (optional)	Soup (optional)
Cereal	Entrée	Entrée
Protein dish	Salad and/or vegetable	Two vegetables (one may be potato or starchy food)
Bread, butter, or margarine	Bread, butter or margarine	Salad
Beverage	Fruit or other light dessert	Bread, butter or margarine
	Beverage	Dessert
		Beverage

SELECTIVE MENU PATTERN[a]

Breakfast	Lunch and Dinner
Fruits: 2 or more juices, fresh fruit in season	Soups: 1 cream, 1 broth
Cereals: cooked, choice of cold cereals	Entrées: at least 1 meat, 1 meatless, 1 meat extender, poultry or fish, and a cold plate.
Entrées: eggs, bacon, ham, or sausage	Sandwiches: 1 hot, 1 or more cold
Breads: toast, white and whole grain; one or more hot breads	Rice or Pasta: in addition to or as alternative to potatoes
Beverages: coffee, decaffeinated coffee; tea; milk, whole and lowfat	Vegetables: 3 or 4, including potatoes in some form
	Salads: 4 to 10, including entrée, tossed green, vegetable, gelatin, fruit, cottage cheese, relishes
	Breads: 2 to 3, including white and whole grain, 1 hot bread
	Desserts: 4 to 8, including 2-crust pie, soft pie, cake and/or cookies, pudding, yogurt, ice cream or sherbet, fruit
	Beverages: coffee, decaffeinated coffee; tea; milk, whole and lowfat; fruit juice or fruit flavored drinks.

[a]Menu variety may be increased or decreased to fit the demands of the food service.

MENU PATTERN FOR A NORMAL HOSPITAL DIET

Breakfast	Lunch	Dinner
Fruit or juice	Cream soup *or*	Soup (optional)
Cereal with milk	Main dish (made with meat, fish, poultry, egg, or cheese)	Meat, poultry, or fish
Egg		Potato or alternate starchy vegetable
Bread or toast	Vegetable or salad	
Butter or margarine	Bread with butter or margarine	Green or yellow vegetable
Beverage	Fruit or other simple dessert	Salad: fruit or vegetable
	Beverage	Bread with butter or margarine
		Dessert
		Beverage

SCHOOL LUNCH PATTERNS FOR VARIOUS AGE/GRADE GROUPS

U.S. Department of Agriculture, National School Lunch Program

USDA recommends, but does not require, that you adjust portions by age/grade group to better meet the food and nutritional needs of children according to their ages. If you adjust portions, Groups I–V are minimum requirements for the age/grade groups specified. If you do not adjust portions, the Group IV portions in the shaded column are the portions to serve all children.

MINIMUM QUANTITIES

COMPONENTS		Preschool ages 1–2 (Group I)	Preschool ages 3–4 (Group II)	Grades K–3 ages 5–8 (Group III)
MEAT OR MEAT ALTERNATE	A serving of one of the following or a combination to give an equivalent quantity:			
	Lean meat, poultry, or fish (edible portion as served)	1 oz	1½ oz	1½ oz
	Cheese	1 oz	1½ oz	1½ oz
	Large egg(s)	1	1½	1½
	Cooked dry beans or peas	½ c	¾ c	¾ c
	Peanut butter	2 T	3 T	3 T
VEGETABLE AND/OR FRUIT	Two or more servings of vegetable or fruit or both to total	½ c	½ c	½ c
BREAD OR BREAD ALTERNATE	Servings of bread or bread alternate A serving is: • 1 slice of whole grain or enriched bread • A whole grain or enriched biscuit, roll, muffin, etc. • ½ cup of cooked whole grain or enriched rice, macaroni, noodles, whole grain or enriched pasta products, or other cereal grains such as bulgur or corn grits • A combination of any of the above	5 per week	8 per week	8 per week
MILK	A serving of fluid milk	¾ c (6 fl. oz)	¾ c (6 fl. oz)	½ pt (8 fl. oz)

[a] From *Menu Planning Guide for School Food Service*, USDA Food and Nutrition Service, PA 1260, 1980.

[b] Group IV is the one meal pattern which will satisfy all requirements if no portion size adjustments are made.

[c] Group V specified recommended, not required, quantitites for students 12 years and older. These students may request smaller portions, but not smaller than those specified in Group IV.

RECOMMENDED QUANTITIES[2]

Grades 4–12[a] ages 9 & over (*Group IV*)	*Grades 7–12* ages 12 & over (*Group V*)	**SPECIFIC REQUIREMENTS**
		• Must be served in the main dish or the main dish and one other menu item.
2 oz	3 oz	• Textured vegetable protein products, cheese alternate products, and enriched macaroni with fortified protein may be used to meet part of the meat/meat alternate requirement. Fact sheets on each of these alternate foods give detailed instructions for use.
2 oz	3 oz	
2	3	NOTE: The amount you must serve of a single meat alternate may seem too large for the particular age group you are serving. To make the quantity of that meat alternate more reasonable, use a smaller amount to meet part of the requirement and supplement with another meat or meat alternate to meet the full requirement.
1 c	1½ c	
4 T	6 T	
¾ c	¾ c	• No more than one-half of the total requirmeent may be met with full-strength fruit or vegetable juice. • Cooked dry beans or peas may be used as a meat alternate or as a vegetable but not as both in the same meal.
8 per week	10 per week	• At least ½ serving of bread or an equivalent quantity of bread alternate for Group I, and 1 serving for Groups II–V must be served daily. • Enriched macaroni with fortified protein may be used as a meat alternate or as a bread alternate but not as both in the same meal. NOTE: *Food Buying Guide for School Food Service*, PA-1257 (1980) provides the information for the minimum weight of a serving.
½ pt (8 fl. oz)	½ pt (8 fl. oz)	At least one of the following forms of milk must be offered: • Unflavored lowfat milk • Unflavored skim milk • Unflavored buttermilk NOTE: This requirement does not prohibit offering other milks, such as whole milk, or flavored milk along with one or more of the above.

Menu-Planning Suggestions

Entrées

MEAT
Beef
Pot Roast
Smoked Beef Brisket
Swiss Steak
Chicken Fried Steak
Country Fried Steak
Baked Steak Teriyaki
Spanish Steak
Pepper Steak
Salisbury Steak
Bacon-Wrapped Beef
Chuck Wagon Steak
Meat Loaf
Meatballs, Swedish
   Spanish
   With Spaghetti
Beef Liver, Braised
   With Onions
   With Bacon
Beef Birds
Corned Beef
Roast Round
Chuck Roast
Standing Rib Roast
Rolled Rib Roast
Broiled Steak, T-Bone
   Sirloin
   Filet Mignon
   Club
Kabobs

Veal
Breaded Veal Cutlets
Veal Cacciatori
Veal Scallopini
Veal Piccata
Veal New Orleans
Veal Birds
Veal in Sour Cream
Roast Leg of Veal
Roast Veal Shoulder

Pork
Pork Chops, Breaded
   Baked
   Deviled
   Barbecued
   With Dressing
   Stuffed
   With Scalloped Potatoes
Spareribs, Barbecued
   Sweet—Sour
   With Dressing
Glazed Baked Ham
Grilled Ham Slices
Ham Loaf
Ham Patties
Ham Balls
Bacon
Roast Fresh Ham
Roast Pork Loin
Roast Pork Shoulder
Roast Pork with Dressing
Breaded Pork Cutlets

Lamb
Roast Leg of Lamb
Roast Lamb Shoulder
Broiled Lamb Chops
Lamb Stew
Curried Lamb with Rice

MEAT EXTENDERS
Beef Stew with
   Vegetables
   With Biscuits
Beef Pot Pie
Beef Stroganoff
Hungarian Goulash
Beef, Pork, and Noodle
   Casserole
Pasta, Beef, and Tomato
   Casserole
Creole Spaghetti
Spanish Rice
Chop Suey
Cheeseburger Pie
Beef Biscuit Roll
Stuffed Peppers
Baked Hash
Creamed Beef
Creamed Chipped Beef
Chipped Beef and Noodles
Chili con Carne
Taco Salad Casserole
Pizza
Lasagne

Frankfurters,
  Cheese-Stuffed
  With Sauerkraut
Meat Turnovers
See also Pasta Entrées
Sweet−Sour Pork
Pork and Noodle Casserole
Creamed Ham on
  Spoonbread or Biscuits
Plantation Shortcake
Ham à la King
Ham Croquettes
Ham Soufflé
Ham Timbales
Ham and Egg Scallop
Ham Biscuit Roll
Ham Turnovers with
  Cheese Sauce
Ham and Cheese Quiche
Sausage Rolls
Sausage Gravy on Biscuits
Sausage Cakes
Baked Acorn Squash
  with Sausage
Fried Scrapple

POULTRY

Chicken Cutlets
Pan Fried Chicken
Chicken Cantonese
Chicken Cacciatore
Oven-Fried Chicken
Chicken Parmesan
Barbecued Chicken
Chicken Fricassee
Chicken Tahitian
Broiled Chicken
Breast of Chicken with
  Ham Slice
Chicken Teriyaki
Chicken with Dumplings
Sweet−Sour Chicken
Chicken Turnovers
Creamed Chicken on
  Biscuits
    On Chow Mein Noodles
    On Spoon Bread

In Patty Shell
In Toast Cups
Chicken à la King
Scalloped Chicken
Chicken Crepes
Hot Chicken Salad
Chicken Loaf
Chicken Pie with
  Batter Crust
Brunswick Stew
Chicken Soufflé
Chicken Croquettes
Chicken and Noodles
Chicken Rice Casserole
Singapore Curry
Chicken Chow Mein
Chicken Biscuit Roll
Chicken Fried Rice
Spaghetti with Chicken
  Sauce
Roast Turkey with Dressing
Turkey Divan
Turkey Casserole
Turkey Tetrazzini
Turkey à la King
See Entrée Salads

FISH

Baked Fish Fillets
Lemon Baked Fish
Breaded Fish Fillets
Fillet of Sole Amandine
Salmon Loaf
Salmon Croquettes
Salmon Patties
Scalloped Salmon
Scalloped Tuna
Tuna and Noodles
Creamed Tuna
  With Peas
Tuna à la King
Tuna Soufflé
Tuna Patties
Scalloped Oysters
Creole Shrimp
Deviled Crab
Seafood Quiche

ENTRÉES   583

Shrimp Fried Rice
See Entrée Salads

EGGS AND CHEESE

Egg and Sausage Bake
Creamed Eggs
Curried Eggs
Eggs à la King
Scotch Woodcock
Goldenrod Eggs
Scrambled Eggs
Omelets
Quiche
Egg Cutlets
Egg Foo Yung
Hot Stuffed Eggs
Scalloped Eggs and Cheese
Welsh Rarebit
Cheese Balls on Pineapple
  Slice
Cheese Croquettes
Cheese Soufflé
  With Shrimp Sauce
Cheese Fondue
Macaroni and Cheese
Cheese and Broccoli Strata
Nachos
Spinach Lasagne
Spinach Cheese Crepes

PASTA

Macaroni and Cheese
  with Ham
Creole Spaghetti
Spaghetti with Meat Sauce
  With Meat Balls
  With Chicken Sauce
Pasta with Clam Sauce
  With Vegetable Sauce
Vegetarian Spaghetti
Lasagne
Spinach Lasagne
Noodles Romanoff
Chicken Tetrazzini
Chicken and Noodles
Beef and Noodles

Pasta, continued
Pasta, Beef, Tomato
   Casserole
Ravioli

SANDWICH ENTRÉES
Meat Loaf
Hamburger
   Barbecued
   With Cheese
Hot Roast Beef
Barbecued Beef
Submarine
Reuben
Chimichanga
Runza
Tacos
Nacho Dog
Chili Dog
Western Sandwich
Deep Sea Dandy on Bun
Chicken Salad
Club Sandwich

Sliced Turkey
Hot Turkey
Chicken Cutlet
Ham Salad
Ham and Cheese
Baked Ham
Bacon, Lettuce, and
   Tomato
Bacon and Tomato on Bun
   with Cheese Sauce
Hot Roast Pork
Egg Salad
Tuna Salad
Cheese
Pimiento Cheese
Grilled Cheese
French Fried Cheese
Grilled Tuna and Cheese
Hot Tuna Buns

SALAD ENTRÉES
Taco Salad

Chef's Salad Bowl
Seafood Chef Salad
Cottage Cheese Salad
Chicken Salad
Chicken–Orange–
   Avocado Salad
Fruited Turkey Salad
Crab Salad
Shrimp Salad
Shrimp–Rice Salad
Tuna Salad
Salmon Salad
Stuffed Tomato Salad
Tomato Cottage Cheese
   Salad
Pasta and Chicken Salad
Fruit and Nutbread Salad
   Plate
Ham Salad and Tomato
   Herb Bun Salad Plate
Antipasto Salad Plate

Vegetables

POTATOES
White
Au Gratin
Baked
   Fancy Topped
   Stuffed Baked
   French Baked
   Herbed Potato
   Lyonnaise Baked
Browned
Chips
Creamed
Croquettes
Duchess
Fried
French Fried
Hashed Brown
Lyonnaise
Mashed

New, Buttered
   Creamed
   Creamed with Peas
   Parmesan
   Persillade
   Continental
   In Jackets
O'Brien
Potato Cakes
Potato Pancakes with
   Applesauce
Potato Salad, Hot or Cold
Rissole
Rosettes
Shoestring
Scalloped

Sweet
Baked

Candied or Glazed
Croquettes
   With Apples

PASTA AND RICE
Macaroni and Cheese
Macaroni Salad
Spaghetti
   With Tomato Sauce
Buttered Noodles
Noodles Romanoff
Buttered Rice
Curried Rice
Fried Rice
   With Almonds
Green Rice
Rice Pilaff
Mexican Rice

STARCHY VEGETABLES
Corn
Buttered
In Cream
On Cob
With Tomato
Corn Pudding
O'Brien
Scalloped
Succotash

Lima Beans
Buttered
In Cream
With Bacon
With Mushrooms
With Almonds

Parsnips
Buttered
Browned
Glazed

Squash
Baked Acorn
Baked Hubbard
Mashed Butternut
Mashed Hubbard
Stuffed Acorn

GREEN VEGETABLES
Asparagus
Buttered or Creamed
With Cheese or
 Hollandaise Sauce

Beans, Green
Buttered
Casserole
Creole
Herbed
With Almonds or
 Mushrooms
With Dill
Southern Style

Broccoli
Almond Buttered
Buttered
With Cheese Sauce
With Lemon Butter
With Hollandaise Sauce
With Crumb Butter

Brussels Sprouts
Buttered

Cabbage
Au Gratin
Buttered or Creamed
Creole
Hot Slaw
Polanaise
Scalloped

Celery
Buttered or Creamed
Creamed with Almonds
Creole
With Carrots Amandine

Peas
Buttered or in Cream
With Carrots, Cauliflower,
 Onions, or Turnips
With Mushrooms,
 Almonds, Mint,
 Lemon

Spinach
Buttered
Creamed
Wilted
With Egg or Bacon
With New Beets
Soufflé

Squash, Zucchini
Fried
Buttered
Baked
Casserole

Stir-Fried

OTHER VEGETABLES
Beets
Buttered
Harvard
Julienne
In Sour Cream
With Orange Sauce
Hot Spiced
Pickled

Carrots
Buttered or Creamed
Candied or Glazed
Mint Glazed
Lyonnaise
Marinated
Savory
With Celery
With Peas
Parsley Buttered
Sweet−Sour

Cauliflower
Buttered or Creamed
French Fried
With Almond Butter
With Cheese Sauce
With Peas

Eggplant
Creole
Casserole
Baked
Fried or French Fried

Mushrooms
Broiled
Sautéed
French Fried

Onions
Au Gratin
Baked
Buttered or Creamed
French Fried
Stuffed

Rutabagas
Buttered
Mashed

Squash, Summer
Buttered
With Zucchini
Creole

Tomatoes
Baked
Breaded
Broiled Tomato Slices
Creole
Scalloped
Stewed
With Celery
Tomato Vegetable Medley
Stuffed

Turnips
Buttered
In Cream
Mashed
With New Peas

FRUITS SERVED AS VEGETABLES
Apples
Buttered
Fried
Hot Baked

Bananas
Baked
French Fried

Grapefruit
Broiled

Peaches
Broiled
With Chutney

Pineapple Ring
Broiled
Sautéed
Glazed
With Chutney

Salads and Relishes

VEGETABLE SALADS
Mixed Green
Tossed Vegetable
Hawaiian Tossed
Brown Bean
Garbanzo Bean
Triple Bean
Cauliflower Bean
Oriental Bean
Carrifruit
Carrot Raisin
Carrot Celery
Marinated Carrots
Cole Slaw
Creamy Cole Slaw
Green Pepper Slaw
Cauliflower–Broccoli
Creamy Cauliflower
Sliced Cucumbers and
   Onions
German Cucumbers
Marinated Garden Salad
Marinated Asparagus
Marinated Green Beans
Vegetable Collage
Oriental
Spinach–Cheese
Spinach–Mushroom

Potato Salad
Sour Cream Potato Salad
Hot Potato Salad

FRUIT SALADS
Waldorf
Apple–Cabbage
Apple–Carrot
Creamy Fruit
Grapefruit Orange
   with Avocado
   with Apple
Frozen Fruit
Banana Log
Melon Ball
Mixed Fruit
Peach Half with
   Cream Cheese
Blushing Pear
Pineapple Ring

GELATIN SALADS
Perfection
Tomato Aspic
Applesauce Mold
Arabian Peach

Autumn Salad
Bing Cherry Salad
Blueberry Gelatin
Cranberry Molded Salad
Cucumber Soufflé
Frosted Cherry
Jellied Waldorf
Ribbon Gelatin
Strawberry Rhubarb
Sunshine
Swedish Green Top
Under-the-Sea

PROTEIN SALADS
Tuna
Chicken or Turkey
Ham
Cottage Cheese
Chicken and Bacon
Chicken and Pasta
Ham and Pasta

PASTA AND RICE SALADS
Garbanzo and Pasta
Dilled Rice

Macaroni
Italian Pasta
Chicken and Pasta
Ham and Pasta

SHERBET AS SALAD
Cranberry
Lemon
Lime
Mint
Orange
Pineapple
Raspberry

RELISHES
Marinated Mushrooms
Spiced Apples
Buttered Apples
Cranberry Relish
Cranberry Sauce
Pickled Beets
Sauerkraut Relish
Sweet Pickles
Dill Pickles
Carrot Curls or Sticks
Celery Sticks
Cauliflowerets

Cherry Tomatoes
Green Pepper Rings
Olives, Green, Ripe, Stuffed
Radishes
Spiced Pear
Spiced Peach
Spiced Crabapples
Stuffed Celery
Tomato Slices or Wedges
Turnip Sticks or Slices
Watermelon Pickles
Zucchini Sticks or Slices

Soups

STOCK SOUPS
Chicken Bouillon
Chicken Gumbo
Chicken Noodle
Chicken Rice
Mulligatawny
French Onion
Julienne
Tomato Barley
Tomato Bouillon
Tomato Rice
Vegetable
Beef Alphabet
Beef Barley
Beef Noodle
Beef Rice
Creole Beef
Hearty Beef Vegetable
Pepper Pot
Vegetable Beef
Minestrone
Manhattan Fish Chowder

CREAM SOUPS
Chicken Velvet
Cream of Chicken
Corn Chowder
Fish Chowder
Clam Chowder
Potato Chowder
Vegetable Chowder
Cream of
  Asparagus
  Broccoli
  Celery
  Corn
  Mushroom
  Potato
  Spinach
  Tomato
  Vegetable

ENTRÉE SOUPS
Chicken with Spaetzles

Brunswick Stew
Beef Stew
Chili con Carne
Chili Spaghetti
Hearty Beef Vegetable
Hearty Potato Ham
  Chowder
See Cream Soups
Split Pea
Navy Bean
Broccoli Cheese
Cheese
Clam or Fish Chowder
Oyster Stew

CHILLED SOUPS
Gazpacho
Vichyssoise

Desserts

CAKES
Angel Food
  Chocolate

Frozen Filled
Yellow
Orange Chiffon

Walnut Chiffon
Boston Cream Pie
Dutch Apple

Cakes, continued
Lazy Daisy
Marble
Praline
Pineapple Upside Down
White, with variations
Lady Baltimore
Applesauce
Banana
Burnt Sugar
Carrot
Fudge
German Chocolate
Pineapple Cashew
Jelly Roll
Chocolate Roll
Ice Cream Roll
Gingerbread
Fruit Cake
Cupcakes

COOKIES
Butter Tea
Thimble
Butterscotch Drop
Chocolate Drop
Butterscotch Pecan
Butterscotch Refrigerator
Chocolate Chip
Chocolate Tea
Coconut Macaroons
Crisp Ginger
Molasses Drop
Oatmeal Crispies
Oatmeal Drop
Peanut Cookies
Peanut Butter Cookies
Sandies
Snickerdoodles
Sugar, Rolled
  Drop
  Whole Wheat
Brownies
Butterscotch Squares
Coconut Pecan Bars
Dreamland Bars
Date Bars
Oatmeal Bars
Marshmallow Squares

PIES
Fruit
Apple
  Sour Cream
  Crumb
Apricot
Berry
Cherry
Gooseberry
Peach
Pineapple
Raisin
  Sour Cream
Rhubarb
  Custard

Soft Pies
Cream
  Banana
  Butterscotch
  Chocolate
  Date
  Pineapple
Chiffon
  Apricot
  Lemon
  Chocolate
  Strawberry
Custard
  Coconut
Pumpkin
  Praline
Pecan
Lemon
Eggnog
Black Bottom
Frozen Mocha Almond
Ice Cream Pie

FROZEN DESSERTS
Sundaes and Parfaits
Hot Fudge Sundae
Peanut Butter Sundae
Caramel Sundae
Strawberry Sundae
Chocolate Parfait
Strawberry Parfait

Ice Cream
Butter Brickle
Chocolate
Chocolate Chip
Chocolate Almond
Coffee
Lemon Custard
Peach
Pecan
Peppermint
Pistachio
Strawberry
Toffee
Vanilla

Sherbet
Cranberry
Lemon
Lime
Orange
Pineapple
Raspberry

PUDDINGS
Cream
  Banana
  Butterscotch
  Chocolate
  Coconut
  Pineapple
  Tapioca
  Vanilla
Custard, Baked
  Caramel
  Rice
Floating Island
Bread Pudding
Date Pudding
Fudge Pudding
Lemon Cake Pudding
Christmas Pudding
Steamed Pudding
Royal Rice Pudding
Russian Cream

MISCELLANEOUS DESSERTS
Cheese Cake
Cream Puffs

Apricot Whip
English Toffee
Lemon Snow
Strawberry Bavarian Cream
Pineapple Refrigerator
   Dessert

Jellied Fruit
Apple Brown Betty
Apple Crisp
Fruit Crisp
Fruit Cobbler
Baked Apples

Apple Dumplings
Strawberry Shortcake

Garnishes

YELLOW-ORANGE
Cheese and Eggs
Balls, Grated, Strips
Rosettes
Egg, Hard-Cooked or
   Sections
Deviled Egg Halves
Riced Egg Yolk

Fruit
Apricot Halves, Sections
Cantaloupe Balls
Lemon Sections, Slices
Orange Sections, Slices
Peach Slices
Peach Halves with Jelly
Spiced Peaches
Tangerines

Sweets
Apricot Preserves
Orange Marmalade
Peanut Brittle, Crushed
Sugar, Yellow or Orange

Vegetables
Carrots, Rings,
   Shredded, Strips

Miscellaneous
Butter Balls
Coconut, Tinted
Gelatin Cubes
Mayonnaise

RED
Fruit
Cherries
Cinnamon Apples
Cranberries
Plums
Pomegranate Seeds
Red Raspberries
Maraschino Cherries
Strawberries
Watermelon Cubes, Balls

Sweets
Red Jelly
   Apple, Cherry, Currant,
   Loganberry, Raspberry
Cranberry Glacé, Jelly
Gelatin Cubes
Red Sugar
Beets, Pickled, Julienne
Beet Relish
Red Cabbage
Peppers, Red, Rings, Strips,
   Shredded
Pimiento, Chopped, Strips
Radishes, Red, Sliced,
   Roses
Stuffed Olives, Sliced
Tomato, Aspic, Catsup,
   Chili Sauce, Cups,
   Sections, Slices,
   Broiled

Miscellaneous
Paprika
Tinted Coconut

Cinnamon Drops
   "Red Hots"

GREEN
Fruit
Avocado
Cherries
Frosted Grapes
Green Plums
Honeydew Melon
Lime Wedges

Sweets
Citron
Green Sugar
Gelatin Cubes
Mint Jelly
Mint Pineapple
Mints

Vegetables
Endive
Green Pepper, Strips,
   Chopped
Green Onions
Lettuce Cups
Lettuce, Shredded
Mint Leaves
Olives
Parsley, Sprig, Chopped
Pickles
   Burr Gherkins
   Strips, Fans, Rings
Spinach Leaves

Miscellaneous
Coconut, Tinted
Sunflower seeds
Pistachios

WHITE
Fruit
Apple Rings
Apple Balls
Grapefruit Sections
Gingered Apple
White Raisins
Pear Balls
Pear Sections

Vegetables
Cauliflowerets
Celery Cabbage
Celery Curls, Hearts, Strips
Cucumber Rings, Strips, Wedges, Cups
Mashed Potato Rosettes
Onion Rings
Onions, Pickled
Radishes, White

Miscellaneous
Cream Cheese Frosting
Sliced Hard-cooked Egg White
Shredded Coconut
Marshmallows
Almonds
Mints
Whipped Cream
Powdered Sugar

BROWN-TAN
Breads
Crustades
Croutons
Cheese Straws
Fritters, Tiny
Noodle Rings
Toast, Cubès, Points, Strips, Rings

Miscellaneous
Cinnamon
Dates
French Fried Cauliflower
French Fried Onions
Mushrooms
Nutmeats
Nut-covered Cheese Balls
Potato Chips
Rosettes
Toasted Coconut

BLACK
Caviar
Chocolate-covered mints
Chocolate Sprill
Chocolate, Shredded
Chocolate Sauce
Olives, Ripe
Prunes
Prunes, Spiced
Pickled Walnuts
Raisins, Currants
Truffles

PART FOUR

SPECIAL MEALS AND RECEPTIONS

Planning Special Meals and Receptions

Food service personnel in schools, hospitals, and other organizations often are asked to provide meals or refreshments for special occasions. Service for these functions may be requested by the administration, another department in the institution, or a community organization; or it may be considered a social and educational responsibility of the food service to the people it serves. Examples of this are holiday meals and the introduction of ethnic and international foods through special dinners. A decision to serve meals for outside groups should be made in accordance with institutional policies.

The type of function may vary from a morning coffee or a reception to a seated service luncheon or dinner. Although some food services are equipped to provide plate service for these meals, many will serve the meals buffet or cafeteria style, made festive by the choice of food and decorations.

In commercial food services, the scheduling of banquets, luncheons, and receptions on the premises or the catering of food to another location may be routine. Menu selections, with prices for each, are established, and preparation and service procedures are well defined and standardized. Qualified service personnel are available, either as regular fulltime employees or part-time employees who are on call. In other types of food services, providing food for special occasions may necessitate a temporary change in normal schedules and procedures.

PLANNING RESPONSIBILITIES

Careful advance planning is important to the success of any special function. If the food is to be prepared by regular employees, some prepreparation should be scheduled for 1 or 2 days in advance. Many foods, especially those for receptions, may be prepared ahead and frozen. The other meals on the day of the special function may need to be simplified to avoid work overloads. Extra service personnel, if needed and if inexperienced, should be provided with detailed instructions.

The major responsibilities of the food service staff in charge of a special meal or other function are:

1. Confer with representatives of the group to be served to determine the type of function, time and place, number to be served, service desired, and financial arrangements. Program arrangements and responsibility for table decorations should be discussed also.
2. Plan menu with the organization representative. Duplicate copies of the menu plans should be signed and kept by the group's representative and the food director. This confirms the agreement and may prevent a misunderstanding of details and avoid last-minute changes.
3. Determine quantity and estimated cost of food to be served.
4. Place food order. It is important that orders for special or unusual foods be made early enough to ensure delivery.
5. Check dishes and equipment on hand and make arrangements for obtaining any additional items needed. A list including the amount and kind of linen, dishes, silver, glassware, and serving utensils required should be compiled by the manager and arrangements made for assembling these at least 1 day before they are to be used.
6. Prepare work schedules. A detailed work schedule includes prepreparation, cooking, serving, and cleanup assignments. If workers are inexperienced, the schedule should indicate time for each task, detailed procedures, and other special instructions. For a seated service luncheon or dinner, assign cooks and other personnel to the serving counter from which the plates will be filled. Assign and instruct waiters or waitresses for dining room service. See pp. 602–604 for directions for table setting and service.
7. Supervise the preparation and service of food.
8. Supervise the dishwashing and cleanup of preparation and service areas.
9. Prepare, and keep on file, a detailed report including information concerning menu, numbers served, income and expenses, and useful comments for service of similar meals in the future.

RECEPTIONS AND TEAS

Receptions and teas may vary in degree of formality and may accommodate a few or a large number of guests. The menu may be simple or elaborate and should be planned according to the type of event, time of day, the number to be served, and the money and labor available.

One or two beverages usually are offered, coffee and tea or coffee and punch. The menu may be limited to an attractive dessert, with nuts and mints; or may include several kinds of sandwiches, cookies, or cakes. Suggested choices for a reception or tea follow.

Beverages	Coffee, tea, hot spiced tea or cider, punch.
Breads	Open-face sandwiches spread with a variety of fillings and decorated attractively; rolled, ribbon, checkerboard, or pinwheel sandwiches; nut bread or fruit bread sandwiches with cream cheese filling, cut in squares, triangles, round, or oblong shapes; cheese wafers or cheese straws; miniature cream puffs filled with chicken or fish salad.
Dips	Dips with cheese, cream cheese, or sour cream base, served with crisp raw vegetables, fruits, and/or crackers and chips.
Cakes, Cookies, and Tarts	Petits fours, small decorated cupcakes, meringue shells with whipped cream and fruit fillings, small pecan or fruit tarts, small tea cookies that offer a variety of shapes, flavors, and colors.
Nuts and Candies	Salted, toasted, or spiced nuts; candied orange or grapefruit peel; mints in pastel colors.

Figure 4.1 suggests a table arrangement for a reception or tea, using 2 lines of service and set up so that a guest may start with a plate and beverage, then select food items, and pick up silverware and napkin last. The table covering, centerpiece, tea service, silver, and serving dishes should be the best available, and the food should be colorful, attractive, and interestingly arranged. To prevent a crowded appearance, there should be a limited amount of silver, china, napkins, and food on the table when the serving begins. A small serving table with extra china and silver near the tea table is a convenience. Replacements of small dishes and appointments are brought on trays from the kitchen. If two beverages are served, they are placed at either end of the table. Cookies, sandwiches, and other foods should be arranged so they do not appear crowded. It is best to use small serving plates and replace them frequently so there is an assortment of food at all times. Arrangements should be made for 1 or 2 persons to pour the beverages, and employees or hostesses should be assigned to replenish the tea table and to remove empty plates from guests.

COFFEES AND BRUNCHES

Food service personnel frequently are asked to provide food for a morning coffee hour or a brunch. Both are easy and popular ways to entertain a few or many guests.

An ample supply of hot fresh coffee is necessary, and an alternate choice of tea and/or decaffeinated coffee may be offered. One or more hot breads are served, and the menu may be expanded to include fresh fruit or juice. A fruit tray, with

598 PLANNING SPECIAL MEALS AND RECEPTIONS

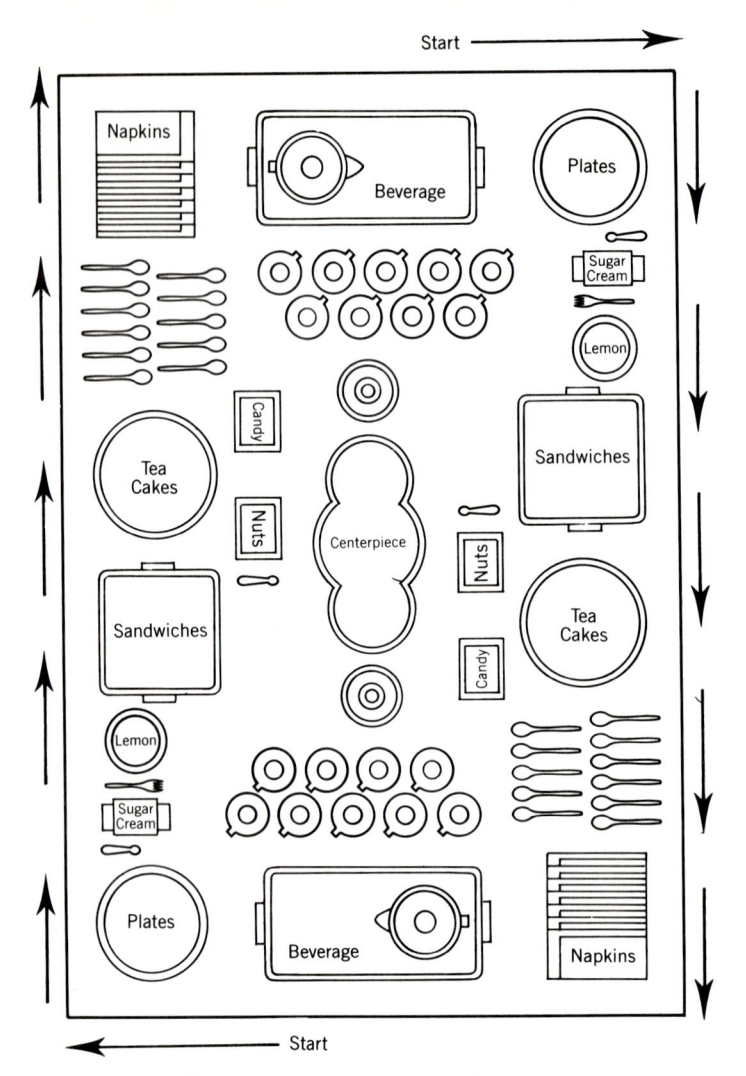

Figure 4.1 Table arrangement for a reception or tea.

bite-sized pieces of fresh fruit arranged on a silver or other appropriate tray, is an attractive centerpiece and an interesting addition to a coffee hour or brunch.

Brunch, a cross between breakfast and lunch, usually includes a wider variety of food than does a coffee hour. The menu may be made up of foods normally served at breakfast or may resemble a luncheon menu, depending partly on the hour of service. It may be quite simple, consisting of fruits, hot breads, and coffee, or it may be a more substantial meal that will replace lunch. The food usually is placed on a buffet table for self-service but may be served to guests seated at tables. Brunch often starts with fruit juice served to guests from a punch bowl before they go to the buffet table. The main dish may be one or more typical breakfast entrées, such as eggs in some form, bacon, ham, or sausage; or a luncheon-type entrée of chicken, turkey, or fish. An assortment of breads usually is offered. A dessert may be served if the meal is scheduled late in the morning, but it should be light. Suggested foods for coffee hours and brunches follow.

Fruits and Juices	Orange juice, pineapple juice, tomato juice, fresh fruit cup, fresh strawberries, cantaloupe and honeydew wedges, fruit kebobs.
Fruit Trays	Fresh pineapple chunks, banana wedges, orange sections, and fresh strawberries; apple slices, honeydew melon wedges, kiwi fruit, and frosted grapes; plums or bing cherries, pear slices, cantaloupe wedges, green grapes, and cheese cubes.
Entrées	Canadian bacon, grilled ham, sausage patties on apple rings, small biscuits with ham slice, scrambled eggs, egg cutlets, egg and sausage casserole, cheese and broccoli strata, quiche, chicken and mushroom crepes, chicken à la king in patty shells or on rice, cheese soufflé.
Breads	Small pecan or orange rolls, coffee cake, scones, kolaches, Danish pastry, toasted English muffins with marmalade, small doughnuts or doughnut holes, cinnamon puffs, small nut or fruit bread sandwiches.
Desserts	Strawberry—sour cream crepes, fresh pineapple and strawberries, ambrosia, sherbet, cookies, or small cakes.

BUFFET DINNERS AND LUNCHEONS

Buffet dinners and luncheons provide a means of serving relatively large groups of people with a minimum of service personnel. In general, the buffet meal is limited to 2 courses, but an assortment of hors d'oeuvres and a beverage may be served to guests before they go to the buffet.

A greater variety of food generally is included in a buffet menu than can be offered at table d'hôte meals, although the extent of the variety will depend on preparation time and space on the buffet table, among other factors. The menu may be built around 1 entrée, with 1 or 2 vegetables, a salad or salad bar, relishes, hot bread, dessert, and beverage. The menu may consist of a more elaborate offering of entrées, such as sliced cold meats, a chicken or fish casserole, and a hot meat, with accompanying vegetables, a variety of salads and relishes, bread, and dessert. In planning a buffet menu, consideration should be given to contrasts in colors, shapes, and sizes of food and to ease of serving and eating, as well as to pleasing flavor combinations. An assortment of breads adds interest and variety to the buffet table. Desserts usually are "finger foods" such as cookies, small cakes or tarts, or a fresh fruit and cheese tray. If the dessert is to be served to the guests, however, only one is planned, and it might be pie, cake, ice cream, or a baked dessert. Foods appropriate for buffets may be selected from Menu-Planning Suggestions, pp. 582 to 590. In planning a buffet meal, certain precautions should be observed.

1. Keep the service as simple as possible (i.e., avoid foods difficult to serve or that are soft or "soupy" on the plate). Foods that require extra silverware, such as bread and butter spreaders and salad or cocktail forks, should be avoided. If the guests will be eating from a tray, plan entrées that can be cut with a fork.
2. Include a few attractively decorated foods, assorted salads, and an assortment of relishes. Attractive garnishing is important.
3. Plan hot foods that can be prepared ahead and served easily. A hot counter, chafing dishes, or heated trays are essential if hot food is to be served.
4. Plan the arrangement of the table at the same time the menu is planned to be sure of adequate table space and suitable serving dishes.
5. Plan enough food so that the last person in the buffet line will have a choice and will see an attractive display. This can be accomplished partly by having the serving dishes or pans not too large and replenished often. The amount of each food to prepare will depend to a great extent on the variety of foods being offered. Unless there is a limited choice, most people will take smaller servings than normal, and some may select only a few items.

The success of a buffet meal depends not only on the quality of food, but also on the attractiveness of the buffet table. Interesting colors may be introduced in the table covering, the serving dishes, the food, or the decorations.

Food in a buffet service is arranged in the order in which it usually is served: meats or other entrées, potato or substitute, vegetables, salads, and relishes. Figure 4.2 illustrates a typical buffet arrangement with a single service line. A double line, as shown in Fig. 4.3 will speed service but requires more space and duplicate serving dishes.

Desserts may be placed on a separate table from which the guests will later serve themselves. If the guests are seated, dishes from the first course usually are removed and the desserts brought to the guests by service personnel.

The type of service depends largely on the equipment available. If ample table space is provided, places may be set with covers, rolls, and water, and provisions may be made for the beverage to be served by employees. If table room for all is not available, each guest may be given an individual tray on which to place silver, napkin, water glass, and the plate containing the assembled food. Hot beverages and rolls are served by a food service worker. When the group is too large or the food service does not have suitable buffet tables, the food may be served from the regular cafeteria line, or a combination of the two may be used. A first course of beverage and accompaniments might be served in the reception area, hot entrées, vegetables, and breads from the cafeteria line, and special salad and dessert tables set up in the dining area.

BUFFET DINNERS AND LUNCHEONS 601

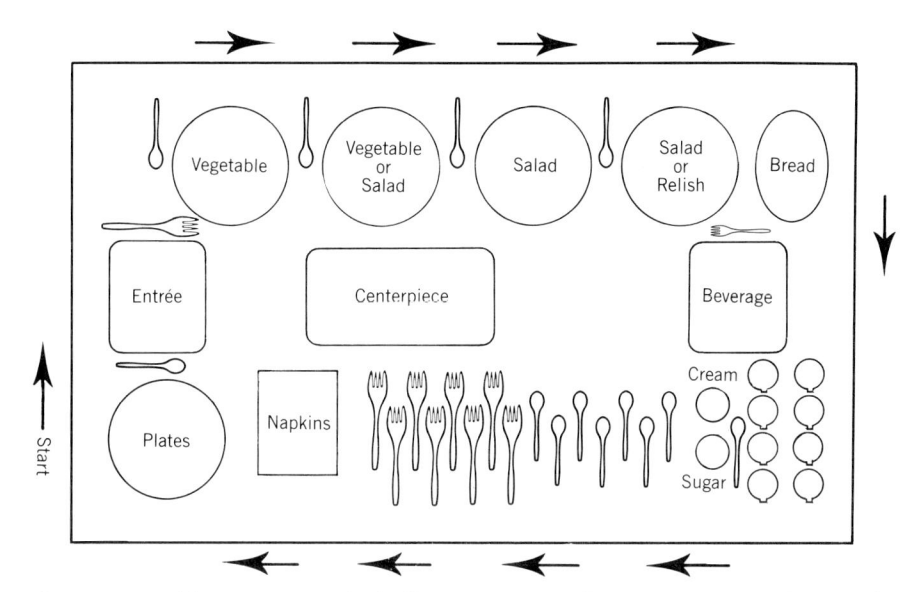

Figure 4.2 Table arrangement for buffet service, single line. Beverages may be served at tables.

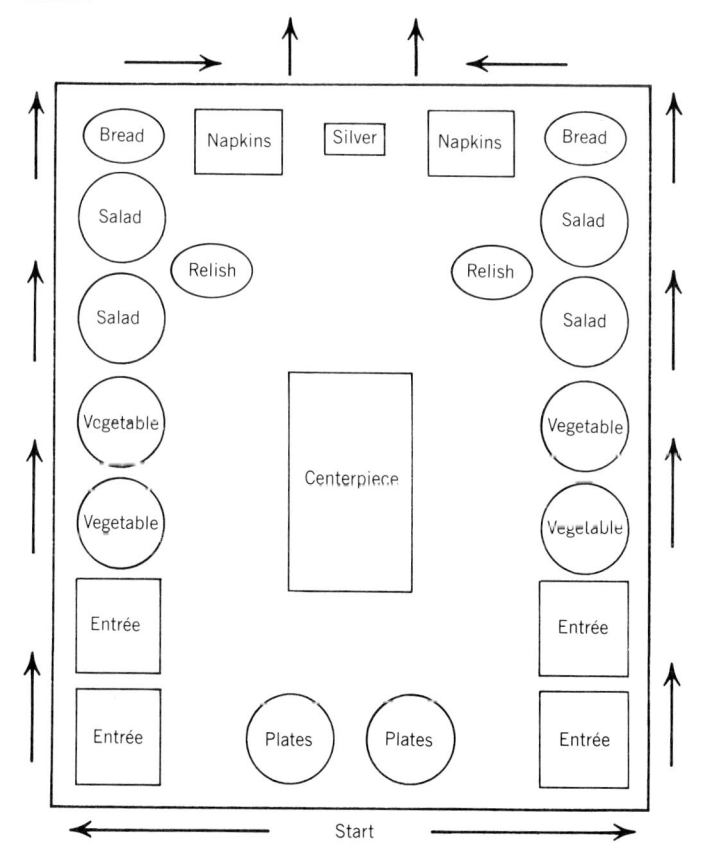

Figure 4.3 Table arrangement for buffet service, double line. Beverages may be served at tables.

BANQUET SERVICE

Although table service for banquets in hotels and many other commercial food services may be elaborate, a simplified service may be the most practical for institutions in which only an occasional banquet is served. The discussion of table setting and plate service that follows is intended primarily for this type of facility.

PREPARATION OF THE DINING ROOM

Arrangement of tables and chairs should provide adequate space for serving after the guests are seated. Chairs should be placed so that the front edge of each touches or is just below the tablecloth. If there is to be a head table, it should be placed so that it is easily seen by the guests, with a podium and microphone available for the program. Audiovisual equipment, if needed, should be properly placed and adjusted. Serving stands, conveniently placed, facilitate service. Such provision is especially important when the distance to the kitchen is great.

SETTING THE TABLES

1. **Tablecloth.** Tablecloths generally are used for banquets, although place mats make an attractive table setting when the finish of the table top permits and are appropriate for informal meals. Place the cloth on the table so that the center lengthwise fold comes exactly in the middle of the table and the 4 corners are an equal distance from the floor. The cloth should extend over the table top 6–12 in. and should not touch the chair bottom.

2. **The Cover.** The plate, silver, glasses, and napkin to be used by each is called a "cover" (see Fig. 4.4). Consider 20 in. of table space as the smallest permissible allowance for each cover; 25–30 in. is better. Place all silver and dishes required for 1 cover as close together as possible without crowding.

3. **Silver.** Place knives, forks, and spoons about 1 in. from the edge of the table and in the order of their use. (see Fig. 4.4). Some prefer to place the salad or dessert fork next to the plate as the menu dictates. The trend is away from the use of salad forks when salad is not served as a separate course. If the menu requires no knife, omit it from the cover. When cocktail forks are used, they are placed at the extreme right of the cover. If a butter spreader is used, lay it across the upper right-hand side of the bread and butter plate, with the cutting edge toward the center of the plate. It may be placed straight across the top of the plate or with the handle at a convenient angle. Dessert silver often is not placed on the table when the cover is laid, except when the amount of silver required for the entire meal is small or if it is necessary to simplify the service. If a dessert fork is used, it is sometimes placed in the area above the dinner plate, so the guest will use it for the final course.

BANQUET SERVICE 603

Figure 4.4 Cover for a served meal. (1) Bread and butter plate. (2) Water glass. (3) Wine glass. (4) Napkin. (5) Salad fork. (6) Dinner fork. (7) Knife. (8) Teaspoon.

4. **Napkin.** Place the napkin at the left of the fork with the loose corner at lower right and the open edges next to the edge of the table and the plate. It may be placed between the knife and fork if space is limited, and it may be folded into an accordion shape and placed upright.

5. **Glasses.** Place the water glass at the tip of the knife or slightly to the right. Goblets and footed tumblers often are preferred for luncheon or dinner and should be used for a formal dinner. Wine glasses are placed to the right and slightly below the water glass.

6. **Bread and Butter Plate.** Place the bread and butter plate at the tip of the fork or slightly to the left.

7. **Salt and Pepper.** Salt and pepper shakers should be provided for every 6 covers. They should be placed parallel to the edge of the table and in line with sugar bowls and creamers.

8. **Decorations.** Some attractive decorations should be provided for the center of the table. A centerpiece should be low so the view across the table will not be obstructed. Candles should not be used in the daytime unless the lighting is inadequate or the day is dark. When used, they should be the sole source of light. Do not mix candlelight and daylight or candlelight and electric light. Tall candles in low holders should be high enough so that the flame is not on a level with the eyes of the guests. If place cards are used, they are set on the napkin or above the cover.

SEATING ARRANGEMENT

The guest of honor, if a woman, usually is seated at the right of the host; if a man, at the right of the hostess. At banquets and public dinners, a woman is seated at the right of her partner.

PLATE SERVICE

Food should be served from hot counters or, if these are unavailable, the utensils containing food should be placed in hot water. Some provision must be made also for keeping plates and cups hot. For serving 50 plates or less, the plan should provide 1 person to serve each food item. Such an arrangement for serving may be termed a "setup." For 60–100 persons, two setups should be provided in order to hasten service. For more than 100 persons, it is well to provide additional setups.

Food is placed on the hot counter in the following order: meat, potato or substitute, vegetables, sauces, and garnish. The supervisor should demonstrate the size of portions to be given and their arrangement on the plate. There should be a checker at the end of the line to remove with a damp cloth any food spots from the plate and to check the plate for completeness, arrangement, and uniformity of servings. The importance of standardized servings can hardly be overemphasized; on this may depend the enjoyment of the guests and the financial success or failure of a meal.

TABLE SERVICE

1. Service personnel should report to the supervisor to receive final instructions at least 15 minutes before the time set for serving the banquet.
2. If the salad is to be on the table when the guests arrive, it should be placed there by the service personnel not more than 15 minutes before serving time. It should be placed at the left of the fork (Fig. 4.5). If space does not permit this arrangement, place the salad plate at the tip of the fork and the bread and butter plate, if used, directly above the dinner plate between the water glass and the salad plate. If the salad is to be served as a separate course, it is placed between the knife and the fork, then removed before the main course is served.
3. Place creamers at the right of sugar bowls.
4. Place relishes on the table, if desired.
5. For small dinners, the first course may be placed on the table before dinner is announced. For large banquets, however, it is best to wait until the guests are seated. Hot soups or plated appetizers are served after the guests are seated. A first course of beverages and appetizers may be offered as the guests arrive in the reception area.
6. Place butter on the right side of the bread and butter plate. If no bread and butter plate is used and the salad is to be on the table when guests arrive, place the butter on the side of the salad plate. This is often necessary where dishes and table space are limited.
7. Place glasses filled with ice water on the table just before guests are seated.
8. When the guests are seated, service personnel line up in the kitchen for trays containing the first course. It is helpful if 2 persons work together, 1 carrying

Figure 4.5 Placement of food and cover for a served meal. (1) Bread and butter plate. (2) Water glass. (3) Wine glass. (4) Salad plate. (5) Dinner plate. (6) Cup and saucer. The salad is placed at the left of the fork when salad and beverage are both served with the main course. If space does not permit, place salad plate at tip of fork and bread and butter plate above the dinner plate.

the tray and the other placing the food. Place the cocktail glasses, soup dishes, or canapé plates on the service plates, which are already on the table.

9. Place and remove all dishes from the left with the left hand, except those containing beverages, which are placed and removed from the right with the right hand.
10. Serve the head table first, progressing from there to the right. It is preferable to have the head table the one farthest from the kitchen entrance.
11. When the guests have finished the first course, service personnel remove the dishes. Follow the same order used in serving.
12. For the main course, plates may be brought to the dining room on plate carriers or on large trays holding several plates and set on tray stands. Each worker serves the plates to a specified group of guests.

    An alternate method often is used in serving large groups. A tray of filled plates is brought from the kitchen by bus personnel to a particular station in the dining room, from which the plates are served. The dining room service personnel remain at their stations during the serving period.
13. Place the plate 1 in. from the edge of the table with the meat nearest the guest.
14. As soon as a table has been served with dinner plates and salad, specially appointed workers should follow immediately with rolls and coffee.
15. Place the coffee cups at the right of the spoons with the handles toward the right. If the coffee is served with the main course, the cup and saucer may be placed on the table with the rest of the cover. If it is served with the dessert only, the cups are not placed on the table until the dessert is served.

16. An ice or sorbet served with the dinner course is placed directly above the plate.
17. Serve rolls at least twice. Offer them from the left at a convenient height and distance. Plates or baskets of rolls may be placed on the table to be passed by the guests.
18. Refill water glasses as necessary. If the tables are crowded, it may be necessary to remove the glasses from the table to fill them. Handle the glass near the base.
19. Refill coffee cups as necessary. Do not remove cups from table when filling.
20. At the end of the course, remove all dishes and food belonging to that course. Remove dishes from the left of the guest.
21. If the silver for the dessert was not placed on the table when the table was set, take in on a tray and place at the right of the cover.
22. Serve desserts two at a time and in the same order that the plates were served. When pie is served, place it with the point toward the guest.
23. If possible, the table should be cleared except for decorations before the program begins.
24. The handling of dishes should cease before the program begins. Rattling dishes has ruined many banquets and is an unnecessary offense to the guest.

Appendix

Use of Herbs and Spices in Cooking

Herb or Spice	Use[a]
Allspice (ground or whole)	Pot roast, baked products, fruits, puddings, squash, sweet potatoes
Basil	Roasted meat and poultry, stews, fish, pasta, green salads, salad dressings, vegetables
Bay leaf	Beef, fish, chicken, soups, stews, marinades
Caraway seed	Rye bread, apples, beets, cabbage, cheese spreads
Cardamom	Coffee cakes, Danish pastry, curries, soups
Cayenne (red pepper)	Meats, fish, sauces, Mexican dishes
Celery salt, seeds, flakes	Meat, poultry, eggs, soups, salads. If celery salt is used, reduce amount of salt in recipe
Chili powder	Chili, Mexican dishes, eggs, meat sauces, dips
Cilantro	Guacamole, chili, dips, salsa
Cinnamon (ground or stick)	Baked products, apples, peaches, beverages, squash
Cloves (ground or whole)	Pork, lamb, marinades, squash, sweet potatoes. Use whole to stud ham, fruit, glazed pork, or onions
Coriander (ground or whole)	Curries, baked products
Cumin	Chili, curries, stews
Curry powder	Chicken, lamb, pork, fish, eggs, rice
Dill (seed or weed)	Lamb, eggs, salads, vegetables
Fennel seed	Italian and Swedish cookery
Ginger (fresh, ground, candied)	Meats, poultry, oriental dishes, fruits, baked products, carrots, squash, sweet potatoes
Mace	Meats, poultry, fish, baked products
Marjoram	Meats, poultry, fish, soups, stews, tomato dishes, vegetables
Mint leaves	Lamb, veal, iced tea, sauces, carrots, peas
Mustard (ground or seed)	Meat, poultry, eggs, cheese, salad dressings, cheese spreads, sauces
Nutmeg	Meatballs, veal, chicken, seafood, baked products, carrots, spinach, sweet potatoes, eggnog, custards

Herb or Spice	Use[a]
Oregano	Meat, poultry, seafood, eggs, cheese, soups, stews, pizza, chili, pasta sauces, barbecue sauce, tomatoes
Paprika	Veal, chicken, fish, salad dressings, garnish
Parsley	Meat, poultry, fish, soups, eggs, cheese, cheese spreads, vegetables, garnish
Poppy seed	Cakes, cookies, bread toppings, fruit salad dressing, sprinkled on noodles, sweet roll fillings
Rosemary	Roasted meat and poultry, baked or broiled fish, eggs, soups, stews, vegetables
Saffron	Veal, poultry, rice, soups
Sage (leaf or ground)	Meats, poultry, stuffings, chowders
Savory	Meats, poultry, fish, eggs, soups, stews, green vegetable salads, rice
Sesame seeds	Bread, rolls, salads, oriental cooking
Tarragon	Poultry, seafood, eggs, tomatoes, green salads, salad dressings
Thyme	Meat, poultry, fish, eggs, soups, stews, vegetables
Turmeric, ground	Ingredient of curry powder, coloring for condiments

[a] Spices and herbs can be creatively combined to enhance the flavor of foods. The art of skillfully adding the right amount of seasonings is basic to successful cookery. Both low-sodium and low-calorie foods can be made more interesting by the addition of spices and herbs. Experimentation, using this chart, may add to patron satisfaction.

Glossary of Menu and Cooking Terms

à la (ah lah), French. In the manner of.

à la carte (ah lah cart), French. On the menu, but not part of a meal, usually prepared as ordered and individually priced.

à la king, French. Served in cream sauce containing green pepper, pimiento, and mushrooms.

à la mode (ah lah mohd), French. When applied to desserts, means with ice cream. *à la mode, boeuf,* a well-larded piece of beef cooked slowly in water with vegetables, similar to braised beef.

al dente (al den' tay), Italian. The point in cooking pasta at which it is still fairly firm to the bite.

allemande (ahl mahnd'), French. A smooth yellow sauce consisting of white sauce with the addition of cream, egg yolk, and lemon juice.

amandine. Served with almonds.

antipasto (ahn tee pahs' toe), Italian. Appetizer; a course consisting of relishes, vegetables, fish, or cold cuts.

aspic. A jellied meat juice or liquid held together with gelatin.

au gratin (oh grah' ton), French. Made with crumbs, scalloped. Often refers to dishes made with cheese sauce.

au jus (oh zhu), French. Meat served in its natural juices or gravy.

bake. To cook in the oven by dry heat.

barbecue. To cook on a grill or spit over hot coals, or in an oven, basting intermittently with a highly seasoned sauce.

bar-le-Duc (bahr luh dük'), French. A preserve made of currants and honey. It frequently forms a part of the cheese course.

baron. Double sirloin of beef.

baste. To moisten meat while roasting to add flavor and to prevent drying of the surface. Melted fat, meat drippings, water, or water and fat may be used for basting.

batter. Flour and liquid mixture, usually combined with other ingredients, thin enough to pour or drop from a spoon.

bearnoise (bay ar nayz'), French. Sauce of melted butter, egg yolks, vinegar, onion, and spices.

beat. To mix ingredients with a rotating motion, using spoon, wire whip, or paddle attachment to mixer.

béchamel (bay sha mel'), French. A cream sauce made with equal parts of chicken stock and cream or milk.

beurre (buhr), French. Butter. *Au beurre noire* (oh buhr nwor), with butter sauce browned in a pan. *beurre manie* (buhr mah nee), French. Well-blended mixture of butter and flour used to add thickening to hot soups.

bisque (bisk), French. A thick soup usually made from fish or shellfish. Also a frozen dessert. Sometimes defined as ice cream to which finely chopped nuts are added.

blanch. To dip briefly in boiling water.

blanquette (blang ket'), French. A white stew usually made with veal, lamb, or chicken.

blend. To thoroughly mix two or more ingredients.

bleu (bluh), French. Blue.

boeuf (buff), French. Beef. *Boeuf à la jardinière* (buff a lah zhar de nyoyr), braised beef with vegetables; *boeuf koti* (buff kotee), roast beef.

boil. To cook foods in water or a liquid in which the bubbles are breaking on the surface and steam is given off.

bombe (bahm), French. A frozen dessert made of a combination of 2 or more frozen mixtures packed in a round or melon-shaped mold.

bordelaise (bor d'layz'), French. Of Bordeaux. *Sauce bordelaise*, a sauce with Bordeaux wine as its foundation, with various seasonings added.

borsch (borsch), Russian. A soup made with beets and served with thick sour cream.

bouillabaisse (boo yah bes'), French. A highly seasoned fish soup made with two or more kinds of fish.

bouillon (boo ee yon'), French. Clear, white meat stock.

bouquet (boo kay'). Volatile oils that give aroma.

bouquet garni (boo kay' garnee'), French. Herbs and spices tied in a cloth bag, used for flavoring soups, stews, and sauces, then removed after cooking is completed.

bourguignon (bohr ghee n'yang), French. In the Burgundy style, especially a beef stew made with red wine (for which Burgundy is noted), mushrooms, salt pork, and onions.

braise (brays), French. To brown in a small amount of fat, cover, add a small amount of liquid, and cook slowly.

GLOSSARY OF MENU AND COOKING TERMS 611

bread. To coat food with an egg–milk mixture and then bread crumbs before frying.

brew. To cook in liquid to extract flavor, as with beverages.

brioche (bree ohsh'), French. A slightly sweetened rich bread used for rolls or babas.

brochette, à la (bro shet'), French. Food arranged on a skewer and broiled.

broil. To cook over or under direct heat, as in a broiler or over live coals.

broth. A thin soup or water in which meat or vegetables have been cooked.

brunoise (broo noyz), French. Finely shredded vegetables, such as celery, carrots, leeks, and turnips for soups and sauces.

buffet (boo fay'), French. A table displaying a variety of foods.

cacciatore (ca chi a tor' ee), Italian. Stewed with tomatoes, onion, and garlic.

café au lait (caw fay' oh lay'), French. Coffee with hot milk.

café noir (caw fay' nwar), French. Black coffee, after-dinner coffee.

canapé (can ah pay'), French. An appetizer of meat, fish, egg, or cheese arranged on a bread base.

candy. To preserve or cook with heavy syrup.

caper (kay' per). Small pickled bud from wild caper bush; used in salads and sauces.

caramelize. To heat sugar until a brown color and a characteristic flavor develops.

carte au jour (kart o zhur'), French. Bill of fare or menu for the day.

caviar (cav ee ar'), French. Salted roe of sturgeon or other large fish. May be black or red.

chantilly (shang te' ye), French. Foods containing whipped cream.

charlotte (shar' lot), French. Dessert with gelatin, whipped cream, fruit, or other flavoring, in a mold, garnished with lady fingers.

chiffonade (shee' fahn ahd), French. With minced or shredded vegetables, as in salad dressing.

chill. To refrigerate until thoroughly cold.

chop. To cut food into fairly fine pieces with a knife or other chopping device.

choux paste (shoo paste), French. Cream puff batter.

chowder. A thick soup of fish or vegetables and milk.

chutney (chut-ni). A spicy relish made from several fruits and vegetables.

clarify. Make clear by skimming or adding egg white and straining.

clarified butter. Butter that has been melted and chilled. The solid is then lifted away from the liquid and discarded. Clarification heightens the smoke point of butter.

cloche (klosh), French. Bell, dish cover. *Sous cloche* (soo klosh), under cover.

coat. To cover entire surface with flour, fine crumbs, sauce, batter, or other food as required.

cocktail. An appetizer, either a beverage or a light, highly seasoned food, served before a meal.

coddle. To simmer gently in liquid for a short time.

compote (kom' poht), French. Mixed fruit, either raw or stewed in syrup; a stemmed serving dish.

consommé (kon so may'), French. A clear soup usually made from 2 or 3 kinds of meat.

court bouillon (cort boo e yon'), French. Seasoned broth in which fish, meat, or vegetables are cooked.

cream. To mix fat and sugar until soft and creamy.

creole (kre' ohl), French. Foods containing meat or vegetables with tomatoes, peppers, onions, and other seasonings.

crepe (krayp), French. Thin, delicate pancake, often rolled and stuffed, served as appetizers, entrée or dessert. *Crépe suzette*, a small, very thin and crisp pancake served for tea or as dessert.

crisp. To make foods firm and brittle, as in chilling vegetables or heating cereals or crackers in the oven to remove excessive moisture.

croissant (krwa sang'), French. Crescent; applied to rolls and confectionary of crescent shape.

croquette (crow ket'). Mixture of chopped, cooked meat, poultry, fish, or vegetables bound with thick cream sauce, shaped, breaded, and fried.

croustade (krus tad'). A toasted case or shell of bread.

croutons (kroo tons'). Bread cubes, toasted, for use in garnishing soups and salads.

crudites (croo dee tays'), French. Raw vegetables.

cube. To cut into ½-in. squares.

curry (kur' ee). Highly spaced condiment from India; a stew seasoned with curry.

cut in. To cut a solid fat into flour with knives or mixer until fat particles are of desired size.

cutlet. Thin slice of meat, usually breaded, for frying; also croquette mixture made in a flat shape.

GLOSSARY OF MENU AND COOKING TERMS 613

deep fry. To cook in fat deep enough for food to float.

deglaze. To dilute and wash down pan juices by adding liquid.

de la maison (de lah mayzon), French. Specialty of the house.

demitasse (deh mee tahss'), French. Small cup of black coffee served after dinner.

dice. To cut into ¼-in. cubes.

dot. To scatter small bits of butter or margarine over surface of food.

dough. A mixture of flour, liquid, and other ingredients, thick enough to roll or knead.

drawn butter. Melted butter.

dredge. To thoroughly coat a food with flour or other fine substance.

drippings. Fat and liquid residue from frying or roasting meat or poultry.

du jour (doo zhoor'), French. Of the day, such as soup of the day.

dust. To sprinkle lightly with flour.

eau (oh), French. Water.

eclair (ay klair'), French. Finger-shaped cream puff paste filled with whipped cream or custard.

egg and crumb. To dip a food into diluted, slightly beaten egg and dredge with crumbs. This treatment is used to prevent soaking of the food with fat or to form a surface easily browned.

enchilada (en chee lah' dah), Mexican. Tortillas filled and rolled, served with sauce.

en cocotte (ahn ko cot'), French. In individual casserole.

entrée (ahn' tray), French. The main course of a meal or a single dish served before the main course of an elaborate meal.

espagnole (ays pah nyol), French. Spanish; brown sauce.

farci (far' see), French. Stuffed.

fillet (fee lay'), French. Flat slice of lean meat or fish, without bone.

flake. To break into small pieces, usually with a fork.

flan. In France, a filled pastry; in Spain, a custard.

flambé (flam bay'), French. To flame, using alcohol as the burning agent.

fold in. To blend ingredient into a batter by cutting vertically through the mixture, and turning over and over by sliding the implement across the bottom of the mixing bowl with each turn.

frappé (fra pay'), French. Mixture of fruit juices frozen to a mush.

French fry. To cook in deep fat.

fricassee (frik a see'). To cook by browning in a small amount of fat, then stewing or steaming; most often applied to fowl or veal cut into pieces.

frijoles (free hol' ays), Mexican. Beans cooked with fat and seasonings.

fritter. A deep-fat fried batter containing meat, vegetables, or fruit.

frizzle. To pan fry in a small amount of fat until edges curl.

florentine. A food containing or placed upon spinach.

froid (frwä), French. Cold.

fry. To cook in hot fat. The food may be cooked in a small amount of fat (also called sauté or pan fry), or in a deep layer of fat (also called deep-fat fry).

glacé (glah say'), French. Iced, frozen; or coated with sugar syrup.

glaze. To make a shiny surface. In meat preparation, a jellied broth applied to meat surface; in breads and pastries, a wash of egg or syrup; for doughnuts and cakes, a coating with a sugar preparation.

goulash (goo' lash), Hungarian. Thick beef or veal stew with vegetables and seasoned with paprika.

grate. To rub food against grater to form small particles.

gratinée (grah teen ay´), French. To brown a food sprinkled with cheese or bread crumbs; or a food covered with a sauce that turns brown under a broiler flame or intense oven heat.

grease. To rub lightly with fat.

grill. To cook by direct heat.

grind. To change a food to small particles by putting through grinder or food chopper.

grits. Coarsely ground corn, served either boiled or boiled and then fried.

gumbo. A rich, thick Creole soup containing okra or filé.

herbs. Aromatic plants used for seasoning and garnishing of foods.

hollandaise (hol'ahn days), French, of Dutch origin. Sauce of eggs, butter, lemon juice, and seasonings; served hot with fish or vegetables.

hors d'oeuvre (oh durv'), French. Small portions of food served as appetizers.

Italienne (e tal yen'), French. Italian style.

jardinière (zhar de nyayr'), French. Mixed vegetables in a savory sauce or soup.

julienne (zhu lee en'), French. Vegetables or other foods cut into fine strips or shreds.

jus (zhoo), French. Juice or gravy.

kebobs. Marinated meat and vegetables cooked on skewers.

kippered. Lightly salted and smoked fish.

knead. To work dough with a pressing motion accompanied by folding and stretching.

kolachy (ko lahch 'ee), Bohemian. Fruit-filled bun.

kosher (ko' sher). Food handled in accordance with the Jewish religious customs.

kuchen (koo' ken), German. Cake, not necessarily sweet.

lait (lay), French. Milk.

lard. To insert small strips of fat into or on top of uncooked lean meat or fish to give flavor or prevent dryness.

lebkuchen (lab koo' ckhen), German. Famous German cake; sweet cake or honey cake.

leek. Seasoning vegetable resembling a large spring onion with wide leaves, always cooked.

limpa. Swedish rye bread.

lox. Jewish. Smoked salmon.

lyonnaise (lee' oh nayz), French. Seasoned with onions and parsley, as lyonnaise potatoes.

macédoine (mah say dwan'), French. Mixture or medley of cut vegetables or fruits cut in uniform pieces.

maitre d'hotel (mai tre doh tel'), French. Steward. *maitre d'hotel butter,* a well-seasoned mixture of butter, minced parsley, and lemon juice.

marinade (mah ree nahd'), French. Mixture of oil, acid, and seasonings used to flavor and tenderize meats and vegetables; French dressings often used as marinades.

marinate. To steep a food in a marinade long enough to modify its flavor.

marzipan (mahr' zi pan). Powdered sugar and almond paste colored and formed into fruit and vegetable shapes.

mask. To coat a food with a thick sauce before it is served. Cold foods may be masked with a mayonnaise mixture or white sauce, which gels after chilling.

melt. To liquify by the application of heat.

meringue (mah rang'). Stiffly beaten egg white and sugar mixture used as a topping for pies or other desserts; or formed into small cakes or cases and browned in the oven.

mèunière, à la (meh nyair'), French. Floured, sautéed in butter and served with butter sauce and lemon and sprinkled with chopped parsley; usually refers to fish.

milanaise (me lan ayz'), French. Food cooked in a style developed in Milan, Italy. Implies the use of pasta and cheese with a suitable sauce, often Bechamel.

mince. To chop food into very small pieces—not so fine and regular as grinding, yet finer than those produced by chopping.

minestrone (mee ne stroh' nay), Italian. Thick vegetable soup with beans and pasta.

mirepoix (meer' pwa), French. Mixture of chopped vegetables used in flavoring soup stock.

mix. To combine two or more ingredients by stirring.

mocha (moh' ka). Coffee flavor or combination of coffee and chocolate.

mornay (mohr nay'), French. Sauce of thick cream, eggs, cheese, and seasonings.

monosodium glutemate (MSG). White crystalline material made from vegetable protein, used to enhance natural flavor of food.

mousse (moose), French. Frozen dessert with fruit or other flavors, whipped cream and sugar; also a cold dish of puréed chicken or fish with egg whites, gelatin, and unsweetened whipped cream.

mulligatawny (mul i ga taw' ni). A highly seasoned thick soup, of Indian origin, flavored with curry powder and other spices.

napoleans. Puff pastry kept together in layers with a custard filling, cut into portion-size rectangles, and iced.

neopolitan. (also harlequin and panachée). Molded dessert of 2 to 4 kinds of ice cream or ices arranged in layers.

nesselrode pudding. Frozen dessert with a custard foundation to which chestnut purée, fruit, and cream have been added.

newburg, à la. Creamed dish with egg yolk added, flavored with sherry; most often applied to lobster, but may be used with other foods.

noisette (nooa zet´), French. Nut-brown color; may imply nut-shaped. A small round piece of lean meat. *Potatoes noisette*, potatoes cut into the shape and size of hazelnuts and browned in fat.

oeuf (oof), French. Egg.

paella (pä ay' yah), Spanish. Dish with rice, seafood, chicken, and vegetables, usually served in a wide shallow pan in which it is cooked.

pan broil. To cook, uncovered, on hot metal, such as a fry pan, pouring off the fat as it accumulates. Liquid is never added.

pan fry. To cook in a skillet in a small amount of fat.

papillote (pah pe yote'), French. Meat, chicken, or fish cooked in a closed paper container.

parboil. To boil until partially cooked, the cooking being completed by another method.

parch. To cook in dry heat until slightly browned.

pare. To cut off the outside covering, usually with a knife.

parfait (par fay'), French. A mixture containing whipped cream, egg, and syrup that is frozen without stirring. May be ice cream layered with fruit or syrup in parfait glasses.

parmigiana (par mee zhan' ah), Italian. Parma style, particularly veal, chicken, or eggplant covered with tomato sauce, mozarella cheese, Parmesan cheese, and browned under the broiler or in the oven.

pasta, Italian. Any of a large family of flour paste products, such as macaroni, spaghetti, and noodles.

paste. Soft, smooth mixture of a dry ingredient and a liquid.

pastrami (pahs tram' ee), Italian. Boneless meat cured with spices and smoked.

paté (pah tay'), French. Paste, dough; highly seasoned meat paste used as an appetizer.

paté de foie gras (pah tay d'fwah grah'), French. Paste of fat goose livers.

patty shell. Shell or case of pastry or puff paste used for individual portions of creamed mixtures.

peel. To strip off the outside covering.

persillade (payr se yad'), French. Served with or containing parsley.

petit pois (puh tee pooá), French. A fine grade of very small peas with a delicate flavor.

petits fours (pe teet foor'), French. Small fancy cakes frosted and decorated.

pilauf or pilau (pih lahf' or pih low), Turkish. Dish of rice cooked with meat, fish, or poultry, and seasoned with spices.

piquant (pee kahnt'), French. Sharp, highly seasoned.

pizza (peet' zah), Italian. Flat yeast bread covered with tomato, cheese, and meat, or other toppings.

plank. Hardwood board used for cooking and serving broiled meat or fish. *Planked steak,* a broiled steak served on a plank and garnished with a border of suitable vegetables.

poach. To cook gently in a hot liquid, held just below the boiling point, the original shape of the food being retained.

polenta (poh lent'ah), Italian. Thick cornmeal mush; cheese is usually added before serving.

polonaise (po lo nays'), French. Dishes prepared with bread crumbs, chopped eggs, browned butter, and chopped parsley.

pomme de terre (pom de tare'), French. Potato; literally, apple of the earth.

pot-au-feu (poh toh fu'), French. Meat and vegetables boiled together in broth.

pot roast. To cook large cuts of meat by braising.

618 GLOSSARY OF MENU AND COOKING TERMS

potage (po tazh'), French. Soup, usually of a thick type.

prawn. Large shrimp.

preheat. To heat oven or other cooking equipment to desired temperature before putting in the food.

prosciutto (pro shoot' toh), Italian. Ham, usually thinly sliced and served as an appetizer or as a component in veal dishes.

puff paste. Rich dough, made flaky by repeated folding and rolling.

purée (pu ray'), French. Foods rubbed through a sieve; also a nutritious vegetable soup in which milk or cream is seldom used.

quiche (keesh). Custard, cheese, and seasonings baked in a pie shell and served warm.

ragout (ra goo'), French. A thick, well-seasoned stew containing meat.

ramekin (ram'e kin). Small baking dish for individual portions.

rarebit. Mixture of white sauce, cheese, and seasonings.

ravioli (rav vee oh' lee), Italian. Bite-sized cases of pasta dough filled with finely ground meat, cheese, and spinach; served with a highly seasoned tomato sauce.

reconstitute. To restore concentrated foods to their normal state, usually by adding water, as in fruit juice and milk.

reduce. To boil down, evaporating liquid from a cooked dish.

rehydrate. To cook or soak dehydrated foods or restore water lost during drying.

remoulade (ray moo lad'), French. Pungent sauce made of hard-cooked eggs, mustard, oil, vinegar, and seasonings. Served with cold dishes.

ricotta (ri cot' toh), Italian. Rice dish with meat, vegetables, seafood, cheese, or other accompaniments.

rissolé (ree sall'), French. Savory meat mixture encased in rich pastry and fried in deep fat.

roast. To cook uncovered in oven by dry heat, usually meat or poultry.

roe. Eggs of fish.

rosette (roh zet'), French. Thin, rich batter made into fancy shape with special iron and fried in deep fat.

roulade (roo lahd'), French. Rolled thin piece of meat, usually stuffed and roasted or braised.

roux (roo), French. Browned flour and fat used for thickening sauces, stews, and soups.

sabayon (sa by on'), French. Custard sauce with wine added.

saurbraten (sour brah' ten), German. Beef marinated in spiced vinegar, pot-roasted, and served with gingersnap gravy.

sauté (soh tay'), French. To cook in a small amount of fat.

scald. To heat a liquid to a point just below boiling; pour boiling water over or dip food briefly into boiling water.

scallion. An onion that has not developed a bulb.

scallop. To bake food, cut into pieces and cover with a liquid or sauce and crumbs. The food and sauce may be mixed together or arranged in alternate layers in a baking dish, with or without crumbs. *Escalloped* is a synonymous term.

scallopine (skol a pee' nee), Italian. Small flat pieces of meat, usually veal, sautéed and served in a sauce.

scone (scahn). Scottish quick bread containing currants.

score. To make shallow lengthwise and crosswise slits on the surface of meat.

sear. To brown the surface of meat quickly at high temperatures.

set. Allow to stand until congealed, as in gelatin and puddings.

shallot. Onion having a stronger but more mellow flavor than the common variety.

shirr. To break eggs into dish, cover with cream and crumbs, and bake.

shortening. Fat suitable for baking or frying.

simmer. To cook in a liquid in which bubbles form slowly and break just below the surface.

skewer. Pin of metal or wood used for fastening meat or poultry while cooking; or long pins used for holding bits of food for broiling or roasting.

skim. To remove surface fat or foam from liquid mixture.

sliver. To cut into long, slender pieces, as in slivered almonds.

smorgåsbord (smor gas bohrd'), Swedish. Arrangement of appetizers and other foods on a table in attractive assortment.

sorbet (sor bay'), French. Sherbet made of several kinds of fruits.

soubise (soo' bees), French. White sauce containing onion and sometimes parsley.

soufflé (soo flay'), French. A light fluffy baked dish with beaten egg whites; may be sweet or savory.

soy sauce. Chinese sauce made from fermented soy beans.

spaetzle (spet'zel), Austrian. Fine noodles made by pressing batter through colander into boiling water or broth.

spoon bread. Southern corn bread baked in a casserole and served with a spoon.

springerle (spring'er le), German. A Christmas cookie. The dough is rolled into a sheet and pressed with a springerle mold before baking.

spumoni (spoo moh' nee), Italian. Rich ice cream made in different layers, usually containing fruit and nuts.

steam. To cook in steam with or without pressure. Steam may be applied directly to the food, as in a steamer, or to the vessel, as in a double boiler.

steep. To cover with boiling water and let stand to extract flavors and colors.

stew. To simmer in a small amount of liquid.

stir. To mix food materials with a circular motion.

stir-fry. To cook quickly in oil over high heat, using light tossing and stirring motion to preserve shape of food.

stock. Liquid in which meat, fish, poultry or vegetables have been cooked.

stroganoff (stro' gan off), Russian. Sautéed beef in sauce of sour cream, with mushrooms and onions.

strudel (stroo'dl), German. Pastry of flaky, paper-thin dough filled with fruit.

tabasco (tah bas'koh), Mexican. Hot red pepper sauce.

table d'hôte (tabl doht'), French. Meal at a fixed price.

tacos (tah' cos), Mexican. Rolled sandwiches of tortillas filled with meat, onions, lettuce, and hot sauce.

tamale (ta mah' lee), Mexican. Highly seasoned meat mixture rolled in cornmeal mush, wrapped in corn husks, and steamed.

tart. Small pie or pastry.

tartar sauce. Mayonnaise to which chopped pickles, onions, and other seasonings have been added; usually served with fish.

terrine (tay reen´), French. Tureen, an earthenware pot resembling a casserole. *Chicken en terrine*, chicken cooked and served in a tureen.

timbale. Thin fried case for holding creamed mixtures; or unsweetened baked custard with meat, poultry, or vegetables.

toast. To apply direct heat until the surface of the food is browned.

torte (tor'te), German. Rich cake made from crumbs, eggs, and nuts; or meringue in the form of a cake.

tortilla (tohr tee'yah), Mexican. A round thin unleavened flour or cornmeal cake baked on a griddle.

toss. To mix ingredients lightly without crushing.

tournedos, Spanish. Small round fillets of beef.

trifle, English. Dessert made with sponge cake soaked in fruit juice and wine and covered with jam, custard, almonds, and whipped cream.

truffle. A dark mushroom-like fungus, found chiefly in France. Used mainly for garnishing and flavor.

truss. To tie or skewer poultry or meat so that it will hold its shape while cooking.

turnover. Food encased in pastry and baked.

tutti frutti. Mixed fruit.

veloute (ve loo tay'), French. A rich white sauce, usually made of chicken or veal broth.

vinaigrette (vee nay groit'), French. French dressing with chopped eggs, capers, and herbs.

whip. To beat rapidly to increase volume by the incorporation of air.

wienerschnitzel (ve'ner schnit sel), German. Breaded cutlets, frequently served with tomato sauce or lemon.

won ton. Stuffed dumplings cooked in chicken broth.

Yorkshire pudding, English. Accompaniment for roast beef, a popover-like mixture baked in drippings of the roast.

zeste, French. Peel of citrus fruits, such as orange or lemon, which contains aromatic oil.

zwieback (tsvee' bahk), German. Toasted bread, crisp and slightly sweet.

Index

Abbreviations used in recipes, 61
Acidulated water for fish, 278
Acorn Squash, Baked, 559
  with Sausage, 559
  Stuffed, 559
Adjusting recipes, see Recipe Adjustment
à la King Sauce, 471
All-Bran Muffins, 89
Almond Butter Sauce, 477
Almond Filling for Rolls, 131
Almond Meringue Gingerbread, 162
Almond Mushroom Sauce, 474
Almonds; Blanched, 403
  Toasted, 403
Alphabet Soup, 499
Amounts of food to serve 50, 4–19
Angel Food Cake and variations, 140
Angel Pie, 205
Appetizers, 62–66
  Canapé spreads and fillings, 65
  Cocktails, fruit and seafood, 66
  Dips, 64
  Hors d'oeuvres, 62, 63
  Soups, 66
Apple Brown Betty, 246
Apple Compote, 249
Apple Crisp, 247
  Cheese, 247
Apple Crumb Pie, 210
Apple Dumplings, 248, 249
Apple Fritters, 109
Apple-Horseradish Sauce, 482
Apple Nut Muffins, 88
Apple Pancakes, 105
Apple Pie, 206, 208
  Fresh, 210
  Sour Cream Nut, 211
Apple Rings, 430
Apple Salad (Waldorf), 425
  variations, 425
Apple Stuffing, 393

Apples: Baked, 248
  Buttered, 430
  Cinnamon, 430
  Fried, 430
  preparation for salad, 398
Applesauce, 249
Applesauce Cake, 160
Applesauce Gelatin Salad, 422
Apricot Bavarian Cream, 242
Apricot Filling, 172, 173
Apricot Glaze for Ham, 340
Apricot Muffins, 87
Apricot Pie, 212
Apricot-Pineapple Punch, 76
Apricot Roll, 157
Arabian Peach Salad, 422
Asparagus: with Cheese Sauce, 524
  cooking of, 524
  Creamed, 524
  with Hollandaise Sauce, 524
  Marinated, 414
  preparation for salads, 401
  Seasoned, 524
  seasonings for, 524
  Soup, Cream of, 510
  Vinaigrette, 524
Autumn Salad, 422
Avocado Dip, 64
Avocado-Shrimp Spread, 65
Avocados, preparation for salad, 398

Bacon, Lettuce and Tomato Sandwiches, 456
Bacon Muffins, 87
Bacon Omelet, 264
Bacon, Oven-fried, 342
Bacon Salad Dressing, 444
Bacon Sauce, Hot, 485
Bacon Waffles, 103
Bacon-Wrapped Beef, 305
Baked Apples, 248
Baked Beans, 530
Baked Fish Fillets, 282
  Lemon Baked, 282
Baked Ham, Glazed, 340
Baked Hash, 324

Baked Lima Beans, 529
Baking temperatures, 33
  metric equivalents, 34
Banana Cake, 150
Banana Cream Pie, 217
Banana Cream Pudding, 232
Banana Fritters, 109
Banana Nut Bread, 97
Banana Punch, 77
Bananas, deep-fat fried, 109
  preparation for salad, 398
Banquet Service, 602
  plate service, 604
  preparation of dining room, 602
  seating arrangement, 603
  setting tables, 602
  table service, 604
Barbecue Sauce, 476, 477
Barley Casserole, 364
Batter Crust for Pot Pies, 382
Batter for Deep-Fat Frying, 37
Bavarian Cream: Apricot, 242
  Pineapple, 242
  Strawberry, 242
Bean Soup, Navy, 506
Beans: Baked, 530
  Boston Baked, 530
  dry, preparation of, 523
  with Pork, 530
  Ranch Style, 531
  Refried, 532
Beans, Green: Amandine, 525
  Casserole, 526
  cooking of, 525
  Creole, 527
  with Dill, 527
  French, 525
  Hacienda, 527
  Herbed, 525
  Marinated, 410
  with Mushrooms, 525
  preparation for salad, 401
  Provincial, 525
  Seasoned, 525
  seasonings for, 525
  Southern Style, 525
  Spanish, 527

623

INDEX

Beans, Lima: Baked, 529
  Baked with Peas, 528
  Baked with Sausage, 529
  Boiled with Ham, 529
  cooking of, 523, 528
  Seasoned, 528
  seasonings for, 528
Beans, Ranch Style, 531
Bechamel Sauce, 473
Beef: amounts to serve 50, 10
  cooking methods, 295
  timetable for braising, 303
    broiling, 301, 303
    cooking in liquid, 303
    roasting, 297
Beef recipes, 304–332
  Bacon-Wrapped Beef, 305
  Baked Hash, 324
    Saucy Beef, 32
  Barbecued Shortribs, 338
  Beef Birds, 334
  Beef Biscuit Roll, 322
  Beef Brisket, Savory, 305
    Smoked, 305
  Beef, Pork and Noodle Casserole, 316
  Beef Stew, 313
    with Batter Crust, 313
    with Biscuits, 313
    with Dumplings, 313
  Beef Turnovers, 375
  Cheeseburger Pie, 321
  Chili Con Carne, 325
  Chili Spaghetti, 325
  Chipped Beef, Creamed, 327
  Chop Suey, 320
  Corned Beef Hash, 324
  Creamed Beef, 326
  Creole Spaghetti, 318
  Croquettes, 385
  Hungarian Goulash, 315
  Lasagne, 355
  Liver: with Bacon, 332
    Baked, with Onions, 332
    Braised, 332
    Grilled with Onions, 332
    with Spanish Sauce, 332
  Meatballs, 310
    Barbecued, 310
    with Spaghetti, 350
    Spanish, 312
    Swedish, 309
  Meat Loaf, 310
    Vegetable, 310
  Pasta, Beef, and Tomato Casserole, 317

Pizza, and variations, 328
Pot Pie, 313
Pot Roast, 304
  Savory, 305
  Yankee, 305
Sandwiches, see Sandwiches
Spaghetti with Meat Sauce, 349
Spanish Rice, 319
Steak: Chicken Fried, 306
  Chuck Wagon, 308
  Country Fried, 306
  Pepper, 307
  Salisbury, 305
  Smothered with Onions, 306
  Spanish, 306
  Swiss, 306
  Teriyaki, 306
Stroganoff, Beef, 314
Stuffed Peppers, 323
Taco Salad Casserole, 330
Turnovers, 375
Beef Barley Soup, 497
Beef Noodle Soup, 499
Beef Rice Soup, 499
Beef Stock, 494
  with Soup Base, 494
Beef Vegetable Soup, Hearty, 498
Beet Greens, see Spinach
Beets: cooking of, 534
  Harvard, 535
  Hot Spiced, 535
  Julienne, 534
  with Orange Sauce, 535
  Pickled, 432
  Seasoned, 534
  seasonings for, 534
  in Sour Cream, 534
Berry Pie, 206
Beverages, 67–79
  amounts to serve 50, 4
  Cocoa, 72, 73
  Coffee, 67, 69
  Punch, 68, 74–79
  Tea, 68, 70, 71
Bing Cherry Salad, 423
Biscuit Roll: Beef, 322
  Chicken or Turkey, 322
  Ham, 322
  Tuna or Salmon, 322
Biscuits: Baking Powder, 84
  Buttermilk, 85
  Butterscotch, 85
  Cheese, 85

Cinnamon, 85
Drop, 85
Orange, 85
Raisin, 85
Whole Wheat, 85
Bishop's Bread, 93
Bittersweet Frosting, 164
Blackeyed Peas, cooking of, 522
Blueberry Coffee Cake, 90
Blueberry Gelatin Salad, 423
Blueberry Muffins, 87
Blueberry Pancakes, 105
Blueberry Pie, 206, 208
Blue Cheese Salad Dressing, 438
Boiled Frosting, 163
Boston Baked Beans, 530
Boston Brown Bread, 96
Boston Cream Pie, 145
Bouillon, 496
  Chicken, 496
  Court, 278
  Tomato, 496
Bowknot Rolls, 120
Braids, Rolls, 120
Braising, timetable for, 303
Bread Dressing, and variations, 392
Bread Pudding, 238
Breads, 80–134
  amounts to serve 50, 4
  Quick Breads, mixing methods, 80
  Yeast Breads: ingredients, 81
    freezing, shaping and baking, 83
    mixing dough, fermentation, 82
Breads, Quick, recipes, 84–109
  All-Bran Muffins, 89
  Baking Powder Biscuits, 84
    variations, see Biscuits
  Banana Nut Bread, 97
  Bishop's Bread, 93
  Boston Brown Bread, 96
  Coffee Cake, 92
    Blueberry, 90
  Corn Bread, 94
  Cranberry Nut Bread, 98
  Crepes, 106
  Date Nut Bread, 99
  Doughnuts, Cake, 102
    Chocolate, 102
  Dumplings, 108
  French Breakfast Puffs, 88

INDEX 625

Fritters, and variations, 109
Nut Bread, 100
Oatmeal Muffins, 90
Pancakes, and variations, 105
   mix for, 104
Plain Muffins, 86
   variations, see Muffins
Pumpkin Bread, 101
Scotch Scones, 85
Spaetzles, 108
Spoon Bread, 95
Waffles, and variations, 103
Breads, Yeast, recipes, 110–134
   Basic Roll Dough, 120
      variations, see Rolls
   Buns, see Buns
   Butter Buns, 125
   Butter Slices, 113
   Caramel Crowns, 121
   Caraway Rye Bread, 117
   Cinnamon Bread, 113
   Cinnamon Rolls, 131
      variations, see Rolls
   Coffee Cake, 129
   Crullers, 129
   Danish Pastry, 129
   English Muffin Bread, 116
   French Bread, 113
   Fruit Coffee Rings, 132
   Kolaches, 129
   Long Johns, 129
   Norwegian Christmas Bread, 118
   Oatmeal Bread, 114
   Quick Roll Dough, 119
   Raised Muffins, 126
   Raisin Bread, 113
   Refrigerator Rolls, 124
   Swedish Braids, 129
   Swedish Rye Bread, 117
   Sweet Roll Dough, Basic, 128
      variations, see Rolls
   White Bread, 110
   Whole Wheat Bread, 113
Broccoli: Almond-Buttered, 533
   with Cheese Sauce, 533
   cooking of, 533
   with Hollandaise Sauce, 533
   with Lemon Butter, 533
   Seasoned, 533
   seasonings for, 533
Broccoli-Cauliflower Salad, 411
   Creamy, 412

Broccoli and Cheese Strata, 272
Broccoli Soup, Cream of, 510
   -Cheese, 514
Broiling, timetables for, 280, 300, 301
Brown Bean Salad, 407
Brown Bread, Boston, 96
Brownies, 193
Brown Sauce, 475
Brown Stock, 494
Brown Sugar Frosting, 165
Brown Sugar Glaze for Ham, 340
Brown Sugar Hard Sauce, 492
Brown Sugar Syrup, 492
Brunches, foods for, 599
   planning, 595
Brunswick Stew, 381
Brussels Sprouts, cooking of, 522
Buffet Dinners and Luncheons, 599
   planning, 595
   table arrangement, 601
Buns: Butter, 125
   Double Cinnamon, 132
   Hamburger, 122
   Herbed Tomato, 127
   Hot Cross, 122, 129
   Hot Dog, 122
Burnt Butter Frosting, 165
Burnt Sugar Cake, 151
Burnt Sugar Syrup (Caramel Flavoring), 151
Butter Buns, 125
Butter Cinnamon Topping, 133
Butter Crunch Topping, 133
Butterflake Rolls, 121
Butterfly Rolls, 131
Butterhorn Rolls, 121
Buttermilk Biscuits, 85
Buttermilk Pancakes, 105
   mix for, 104
Buttermilk Salad Dressing, 438
Butternut Squash, Mashed, 560
   with Apples, 560
Butterscotch Biscuits, 85
Butterscotch Chocolate Chip Brownies, 194
Butterscotch Cookies: Drop, 177
   Pecan, 179
   Refrigerator, 178
Butterscotch Cream Pie, 218
Butterscotch Cream Puffs, 240
Butterscotch Pudding, 229

Butterscotch Rolls, 131
Butterscotch Sauce, 487
Butterscotch Squares, 177, 194
Butter Slices, 113
Butter Tea Cookies, 176
Butter: Honey, 451
   Lemon, 451
   Onion, 451
   Whipped, 451

Cabbage: au Gratin, 536
   cooking of, 536
   Creamed, 536
   Hot Slaw, 537
   Polonnaise, 536
   preparation for salad, 401
   Scalloped, 536
   Seasoned, 536
   seasonings for, 536
Cabbage Salad (Cole Slaw), 411
   -Apple, 425
   -Carrot, 412
   -Pineapple-Marshallow, 412
Cake Frostings and Fillings, 163–174
   scaling weights, 138
Cakes, 135–162
   amounts to serve 50, 6
   Angel Food, 440
      Chocolate, 440
      Frozen Filled, 440
      Orange-Filled, 440
      Yellow (Sponge), 441
   Applesauce, 160
   Apricot Roll, 157
   Banana, 150
   Boston Cream Pie, 145
   Burnt Sugar, 151
   Carrot, 152
   Chiffon, Cocoa, 142
      Orange, 142
      Walnut, 142
   Chocolate, 147
      Chip, 149
      Roll, 156
      Sheet Cake, 154
   Coconut-Lime, 149
   Cup Cakes, Chocolate, 154
      Orange, 143
      White, 149
   Dutch Apple, 145
   Fruit, 161
   Fudge, 154
   German Sweet Chocolate, 155
   Gingerbread, and variations, 162

INDEX

Ice Cream Roll, 156
Jelly Roll, 157
Lady Baltimore, 149
Lazy Daisy, 145
Marble, 145
Master Mix, 146
methods of mixing, 135
Pineapple Cashew, 153
Pineapple Upside Down, 145
Plain, 144
  using mix, 147
Poppy Seed, 149
Praline, 145
scaling weights for batter, 138
Silver White, 149
Spice, 148
Sponge, 441
Starburst, 149
White, 148
Campus Salad Dressing, 438
Canapés, making, 448
  spreads and fillings, 65
Candies, temperature and tests for, 35
Can sizes, substitution of, 38
Cantonese Chicken, 371
Caramel Crowns, 121
Caramel Custard, 238
Caramel Flavoring (Burnt Sugar Syrup), 151
Caramelized Sugar, 151
Caramel Sauce, 487
Carrifruit Salad, 411
Carrot Cake, 152
Carrot Curls, 63, 402
Carrot Raisin Salad, and variations, 410
Carrots: Candied, 538
  and Celery Amandine, 539
  cooking of, 538
  Lyonnaise, 538
  Marinated, 410
  Mint-Glazed, 538
  Parsley Buttered, 538
  preparation for salad, 402
  Savory, 538
  seasonings for, 538
  Sweet-Sour, 538
Carrot Sticks, 402
Cauliflower: with Almond Butter, 540
  with Cheese Sauce, 540
  cooking of, 540
  Creamed, 540
  French-Fried, 545
  with Peas, 540
  preparation for salad, 402
  Seasoned, 540
  seasonings for, 540
Cauliflower-Bean Salad, 409
Cauliflower-Broccoli Salad, 411
  Creamy, 412
Celery: and Carrots Amandine, 539
  cooking of, 539
  Creole, 539
  Curls, Fans, Rings, 402
  preparation for salad, 402
  Stuffed, 64
Celery Cabbage, preparation for salad, 402
Celery Seed Dressing, 443, 444
Celery Soup, Cream of, 510
Cereals, 347
  amounts to serve 50, 5
  Breakfast Cereals, cooking of, 347, 362
  Granola, 363
Chantilly Salad Dressing, 438, 441
Chard, see Spinach
Checkerboard Sandwiches, 450
Cheese: Balls, 269
  Biscuits, 85
  and Broccoli Strata, 272
  Cake, 236
  cookery, 253
  Dip, Cheddar, 64
  Cream, 65
  Fondue, 270
  Ginger Cheese Balls, 63
  Guide to Natural Cheeses, 254
  Macaroni and, 273
    with Ham, 273
  Nachos, 274
  Olive Puffs, 62
  Omelet, 264
  Party Cheese Ball, 63
  Pizza, 329
  Sandwiches, 462
    French-Fried, 462
    Grilled, 462
    and Ham Grilled, 462
    Pimiento, 462
  Sauce, 471
  Soufflé, 271
  Soup, 513
  Spread, Mushroom, 65
  Wafers, 65
  Welsh Rarebit, 275
Cheeseburger Pie, 321
Cheese-Stuffed Frankfurters, 344
Chef's Salad Bowl, 433
  Seafood, 433
Cherry Crisp, 247
Cherry Hard Sauce, 491
Cherry Muffins, 87
Cherry-Nut Rolls, 129
Cherry Pie, 206, 208
Cherry Salad, Frosted, 423
Chestnut Stuffing, 393
Chicken: amount to serve 50, 13
  cooking methods, 366
  defrosting, 365
  preparation for salads, 403
  purchasing and storage, 365
Chicken, recipes, 371–388
  à la King, 376
  and Noodles, 386
    with Mushrooms, 386
  Barbecued, 372
  Biscuit Roll, 32
  with Black Olives, 373
  Bouillon, 496
  Broiled, 366
  Brunswick Stew, 381
  Cacciatore, 371
  Canapé Spread, 65
  Cantonese, 371
  Casserole, 389
  Chow Mein, 320
  Creamed, 376
  Crepes, 378
  Croquettes, 385
  Curried, for Singapore Curry, 391
  Cutlets, 266
  Deep-Fat Fried, 371
  Fricassee, 373
    White, 373
  Loaf, 380
  Oven-Fried, 372
  Pan-Fried, 371
  Parmesan, 372
  Pie, 383
    Batter Crust for, 382
  Rice Casserole, 388
  Salad, 434
    Avocado Orange, 434
    with Bacon, 433
    Crunchy, 434
    Curried, 434
    Fruited, 434

INDEX

Hot, 379
  with Pasta, 416
  Sandwiches, 453
  Sauce for Pasta, 351
Scalloped, 377
Singapore Curry, 391
Soufflé, 384
Soup, see Soups
Stewed, 367
Stock, 495
  with Soup Base, 495
Sweet-Sour, 339
Tahitian, 374
Teriyaki, 372
Tetrazzini, 387
Timbale, 565
Turnovers, 375
Chicken-Fried Steak, 306
Chiffonade Salad Dressing, 442
Chiffon Cakes, see Cakes
Chilean Salad Dressing, 446
Chili Con Carne, 325
  with Cheese, 325
Chili Con Queso, 64
Chili Dog, 344
Chili Spaghetti, 325
Chimichanga, 458
Chinese Omelet, 262
Chipped Beef, Creamed, 327
  and Eggs, 327
  and Noodles, 327
  and Peas, 327
  and Scrambled Eggs, 259
Chives, preparation of, 401
Chocolate: equivalent of cocoa, 39
  French, 73
  Hot, 72
Chocolate, Angel Food Cake, 440
  Butter Cream Frosting, 166
  Cake, 147
    Chip Chocolate, 149
    German Sweet Chocolate, 155
    Sheet, 154
  Chiffon Pie, 222
    Frozen, 222
    Peppermint, 222
  Cookies, Chip, 180
    Drop, 177
    Tea, 181
  Cream Filling, 171
  Cream Pie, 217
  Cream Pudding, 232
  Cup Cakes, 154

Doughnuts, 102
Frosting, 164
Glaze, 169
Marshmallow Squares, 198
Mousse, 171
Pudding, 230
Refrigerator Dessert, 222
Roll, 156
Sauce, 488
  Hot, 488
Chop Suey, 320
Chow Mein, Chicken, 320
Christmas Pudding, 239
  Flaming, 239
Christmas Wreath Cookies, 191
Chuck Wagon Steak, 308
Cider, Spiced, 79
Cinnamon Apples, 430
Cinnamon Biscuits, 85
Cinnamon Bread, 113
Cinnamon Buns, 131
Cinnamon-Raisin Rolls, 131
Cinnamon Rolls, 130
Citrus-Pomegranate Salad, 428
Citrus Salad, Jellied, 423
Clam Chowder, Manhattan, 516
  New England, 515
Clam Dip, 64
  -Cheese, Hot, 64
Clams, selection and cooking, 276, 280, 281
Clam Sauce for Pasta, 354
Clarifying broth, 495
Cloverleaf Rolls, 121
Club Sandwich, 456
Coating for baking pans, 139
Coatings for deep-fat fried foods, 37
Cobbler, Fruit, 250
  frozen fruit guide, 207
  Peach with Hard Sauce, 250
Cocktails, fruit, 66
  Sauerkraut Juice, 78
  Seafood, 66
  Tomato Juice, 78
    Hot Spiced, 79
Cocktail Sauce, 483
Cocoa 72
  amounts to serve 50, 4
  equivalent of chocolate, 39
  instant, 72
Cocoa Chiffon Cake, 142
Cocoa Frosting, 167
Coconut Cookies, 191
Coconut Cream Pie, 217

Coconut Cream Pudding, 232
Coconut Custard Pie, 219
Coconut Frosting, 166
Coconut Lime Cake, 149
Coconut Macaroons, 179
Coconut Pecan Bars, 195
Coconut Pecan Frosting, 166
Coffee: amounts to serve 50, 4
  Hot, 69
  Iced, 70
  Instant, 69
  preparation of, 67
  Steeped, 69
Coffee Cake, 92
  Blueberry, 90
  Yeast, 129
Coffees and Brunches, 596
  foods for, 599
  planning, 598
Cole Slaw, 411
  Creamy, 412
  Hot, 537
Collards, see Spinach
College and University Food Services, menu planning for, 576
Combination Salad Dressing, 441
Commercial Food Services, menu planning for, 578
Consommé, 493
Conventional method, cakes, 135
Conversion, weight to measure, 42
  U.S. to metric, 32, 34, 60
Cooked Salad Dressing, 441
Cookies, 175–198
  Brownies, 193
  Butterscotch Chocolate Chip, 194
  Butterscotch Drop, 177
  Butterscotch Pecan, 179
  Butterscotch Refrigerator, 178
  Butterscotch Squares, 177, 194
  Butter Tea, 176
  Chocolate Chip, 180
  Chocolate Drop, 177
  Chocolate Tea, 181
  Christmas Wreath, 191
  Coconut, 191
  Coconut Macaroons, 179
  Coconut Pecan Bars, 195
  Crisp Ginger, 182

628 INDEX

Cookies (Continued)
  Date Bars, 196
  dough, portioning, 175
  Dreamland Bars, 195
  Filled, 191
  Frosty Date Balls, 188
  Marshallow Squares, 198
    Chocolate, 198
    Peanut Butter, 198
  Molasses, Drop, 183
  Oatmeal Coconut Crispies, 184
  Oatmeal Crispies, 184
  Oatmeal Date Bars, 197
  Oatmeal Drop, 185
  Peanut, 186
  Peanut Butter, 187
  Pinwheel, 191
  Sandies, 188
  Snickerdoodles, 189
  Sugar, Drop, 190
    Rolled, 191
    Whole Wheat, 192
  Thimble, 176
Cooking Terms, Glossary, 609
Corn: Chowder, 508
  cooking of, 540
  in Cream, 540
  Fritters, 109
  O'Brien, 540
  Pudding, 541
  Scalloped, 541
  Seasoned, 540
Corn Bread, 94
Corn Bread Stuffing, 393
Corned Beef Hash, 324
Cornmeal Muffins, 87
Cornmeal Mush, Fried, 343
Cornmeal Waffles, 103
Cottage Cheese Salad, 435
  Tomato, 437
Cottage Pudding, 145
Country Fried Steak, 306
Court Bouillon, 278
Cover for a served meal, 605
Crab, Deviled, 285
Crabs, selection and cooking, 281
Crab Salad, 436
Cranberry Glaze for Ham, 340
Cranberry Muffins, 87
Cranberry Nut Bread, 98
Cranberry Punch, 77
Cranberry Relish, Raw, 431
  with Orange, 431
Cranberry Ring Mold, 423
Cranberry Sauce, 431

Puréed, 431
Royal, 431
Cream, equivalent substitutions, 39
Cream Cheese Dip, 65
Cream Cheese Frosting, 167
  Orange, 167
Cream Pie, and variations, 216. See also Pies
Cream Pudding, and variations, 232. See also Puddings and Other Desserts
Cream Puffs, and variations, 240
Cream Soup, Basic Sauce for, 510
  suggestions for, 510
Creamy Blue Cheese Dressing, 438
Creamy Cauliflower-Broccoli Salad, 412
Creamy Cole Slaw, 412
Creamy Frosting, 167
Creamy Fruit Salad, 427
Creole Soup, 499
Creole Spaghetti, 325
Creole Tomatoes, 563
Crepes, 106
  Chicken, 378
  Fruit-Cheese, 378
  Spinach, 378
Crescents, Rolls, 121
Croquettes: Chicken, 385
  Ham, 385
  Meat, 385
  Potato, 551
  Salmon, 289
Crullers, 129
Crumb Crusts, 204
Crumb Topping, 133
Cucumber and Onion in Sour Cream, 413
Cucumbers: German, 413
  preparation for salads, 401
Cucumber Sauce, 484
Cucumber Soufflé Salad, 423
Cup Cakes: Chocolate, 154
  Orange, 143
  White, 149
Currant Muffins, 87
Curry, Singapore, 391
Custard, Baked, 238
  Caramel, 238
  Rice, 238
Custard Filling, 171
Custard Pie, 219

Coconut, 219
Rhubarb, 215
Custard Sauce, 489
Cycle Menus, 571

Dairy Products, amount to serve 50, 5
Danish Pastry, 129
Date Bars, 196
  Oatmeal, 197
Date Cream Pie, 217
Date Filling, 173
Date Muffins, 87
Date Nut Bread, 99
Date Prune Filling, 172
Date Pudding, 233
Decimal equivalents of pounds, 45
Decreasing and increasing recipes, 42
Deep-Fat Frying, coatings for, 37
  temperatures for, 36
Defrosting: fish, 277
  meat, 294
  poultry, 365
Desserts: amounts to serve 50, 6. See also Cakes, Cookies, Pies, Puddings and Other Desserts
Dessert Sauces, 487–492
Deviled Crab, 285
Deviled Eggs, 268
Deviled Fish, 285
Deviled Pork Chops, 336
Dilly Salad Dressing, 439
Dinner Rolls, 121
Dipper Equivalents, 37
Dips, 64
Direct reading tables for adjusting recipes, 46
  home size recipes, 53
  in volume measurement, 50
  in weight, 47
Dishers, see Dippers
Dough: Basic Roll, 120
  Basic Sweet Roll, 128
  Quick Roll, 119
  Refrigerator Roll, 124
Dough-Batter method, cakes, 135
Doughnuts, Cake, 102
  Chocolate, 102
Drawn Butter Sauce, 477
Dreamland Bars, 195
Dressing or Stuffing, Bread, 392

INDEX 629

variations, see Stuffing
Dressings, Salad, 438–446. See also Salad Dressings
Dried vegetables, cooking of, 523
Duck, roasting, 369, 370
Dumplings, 108
  Apple, 248, 249
Dutch Apple Cake, 145

Eclairs, 240
Egg and Crumb, Deep-Fat Frying, 37
Egg Cutlets, 266
Egg Dumplings (Spaetzles), 108
Egg and Green Pepper Salad Dressing, 439
Eggplant: Baked, 542
  Casserole, 542
  cooking of, 542
  Creole, 543
  French-Fried, 545
  Sautéed, 542
  seasonings for, 542
Eggs: amount to serve 50, 7
  cookery, 253
  market forms, 252
  preparation for salad, 403
  procedure for cooking, 256
  processed, 252
  thickening agent, 41
Eggs, Recipes, 256–268
  à la King, 261
  Creamed, 261
  Curried, 261
  Cutlets, 266
  Deviled, 268
  Foo Yung, 267
  Goldenrod, 261
  Hot Stuffed, 268
  Omelet, and variations, 264
  Quiche, and variations, 265
  and Sausage Bake, 260
  Scotch Woodcock, 261
  Scrambled, and variations, 259
Egg Salad Sandwiches, 452
Egg Sauce, 471
Eggs and Cheese, 252–275
Endive, preparation of, 401
English Muffin Bread, 116
English Toffee Dessert, 241
Entrée salads, 433–437
Equivalents: can sizes, 38
  chocolate and cocoa, 39
  cream, 39

  dipper, 37
  flour, 39
  ladle, 38
  leavening agent, 39
  metric: temperature, 34
    volume, 32
    weight, 32
  milk and cream, 40
  ounces and decimals, 45
  shortening agents, 39
  thickening agents, 39
  weights and measures, 21, 29
    for commonly used foods, 30
Escarole, preparation of, 401
Extended Care Facilities, Menu Planning for, 577

Fan Tan Rolls, 121
Fig Filling, 172
Filled Cookies, 191
Fillet of Sole, Amandine, 284
Fillings, Cake: Apricot, 172, 173
  Chocolate Cream, 171
  Custard, 171
  Date, 173
  Fig, 172
  Lemon, 174
  Lime, 174
  Orange, 174
  Prune, 173
  Prune Date, 172
  scaling weights, 139
Fillings and Toppings: bread and rolls, 133
  Almond Filling, 133
  Butter Cinnamon Topping, 133
  Butter Crunch Topping, 133
  Cranberry Filling, 172
  Crumb Topping, 133
  Honey Filling, 132
  Prune Date Filling, 172
  Prune Filling, 173
Fish: 276–293
  amounts to serve 50, 7
  buying and cooking guide, 279
  cooking methods, fish, 277
    Baking, 278
    Broiling, 278
    Deep-Fat Frying, 36, 37
    Frying, 278
    Poaching or steaming, 278
    table for, 280

  cooking methods, shellfish, 280, 281
  defrosting, 277
  market forms, fish, 276
    shellfish, 276
  preparation for salads, 403
  purchasing and storage, 276
Fish, Recipes, 282–293
  Baked Fillets, 282
  Breaded Fillets, 283
  Chowder, Manhattan, 516
    New England, 515
  Creamed Salmon, 293
  Creamed Tuna, 293
    and Celery, 293
    and Peas, 293
  Creole Shrimp, 287
  Deviled Crab, 285
  Deviled Fish, 285
  Fillet of Sole, Amandine, 284
  Lemon Baked, 282
  Lemon Butter for, 451
  Salmon Croquettes, 289
  Salmon Loaf, 288
  Salmon Patties, 289
  Salmon and Potato Chip Casserole, 291
  Scalloped Oysters, 286
  Scalloped Salmon, 290
  Scalloped Tuna, 290
  Tuna and Noodles, 292
  Tuna Patties, 289
  Tuna and Potato Chip Casserole, 291
  Tuna Rarebit, 293
  Tuna and Rice, 292
  Tuna Soufflé, 384
  Tuna Tetrazzini, 387
Five Meal Plan for Hospitals, 577
Flaming Pudding, 239
Floating Island Pudding, 237
Flour, equivalent substitutions, 39
  thickening agent, 41
Fluffy Frosting, 165
  Brown Sugar, 165
Fondue, Cheese, 270
Foods, amounts to serve 50, 4–19
Food Terms, Glossary of, 609–621
Food Weights and Equivalents in Measure, 21
Foundation Fruit Punch, 75
Frankfurters, Barbecued, 344

INDEX

Frankfurters (*Continued*)
  Cheese-Stuffed, 344
  with Sauerkraut, 344
Freezing sandwiches, 450
French Bread, 113
French Breakfast Puffs, 88
French Dip Sandwiches, 465
French Dressing, 442, 443, 445. *See also* Salad Dressings
French Green Beans, 525
French Onion Soup, 505
French Toast, 107
  Cinnamon, 107
Fricassee of Chicken, 373
Fried Apples, 430
Fried Rice, and variations, 360
Fritters, 109
  Apple, 109
  Banana, 109
  Corn, 109
  Fruit, 109
Frosted Cherry Salad, 423
Frosted Lime Mold, 423
Frostings, 163–170
  Bittersweet, 164
  Boiled, 163
  Brown Sugar, 165
  Burnt Butter, 165
  Candied Fruit, 164
  Chocolate, 164
    Butter Cream, 166
    Glaze, 169
  Cocoa, 167
  Coconut, 164
  Coconut Pecan, 166
  Cream Cheese, 167
    Orange, 167
  Creamy, 167
  Fluffy, 165
  Ice Cream, 164
  Lemon Butter, 167
  Maple Nut, 164
  Maraschino Cherry, 164
  Mocha, 167, 169
  Orange, 168
  Orange Butter, 167
  Ornamental, 170
  Peppermint, 164
  Pineapple Butter, 168
  Powdered Sugar Glaze, 170
  scaling weights, 139
Frosty Date Balls, 188
Frozen Filled Angel Food Cake, 440
Frozen Fruit for Pies and Cobblers, guide for using, 207

Frozen Fruit Salad, 429
Fruit Cake, 161
Fruit Cobbler, 250
Fruit Cocktails, suggestions for, 66
Fruit Coffee Rings, and fillings, 132
Fruit Crisp, Fresh, 247
Fruit Cup, Jellied, 245
  suggested combinations, 245
Fruit Gelatin Salad, and variations, 422
Fruit Glazed Pie, 217
Fruit Juice, amount to serve 50, 10
Fruit Pies: with canned fruit, 208
  with frozen fruit, 206
Fruit Punch, Foundation, 75
Fruits, amounts to serve 50, 7
  preparation for salad, 398, 401
  yield in preparation, 20
Fruit Salad, Creamy, 427
Fruit Salad Bowl, Fresh, 428
Fruit Salad Dressing, 445
  Celery Seed, 444
Fruit Salads, 425–429
Fruit Slices, 250
Fruit Tarts, 217
Fudge Cake, 154
Fudge Pudding, 235
Fudge Sauce, Hot, 488

Garbanzo Bean Salad, 408
  with Pasta, 408
Garden Salad, Marinated, 413
Garden Salad Dressing, 439
Gazpacho (Spanish Chilled Soup), 518
Gelatin: Fruit Cup, 245
  Fruit Salad, and variations, 422
  preparation for salad, 422
  proportion as thickening agent, 41
  Salads, 420–424
German Cucumbers, 413
German Sweet Chocolate Cake, 155
Giblet Gravy, 476
Ginger Ale Fruit Punch, 74
Ginger Ale Fruit Salad, 423
Gingerbread, 162
  Almond Meringue, 162
  Praline, 162
Ginger Cheese Balls, 63

Ginger Cookies, Crisp, 182
Ginger Muffins, 162
Glaze, Powdered Sugar, 170
  Chocolate, 169
Glazes for Ham, 340
Glossary of Menu and Cooking Terms, 609
Golden Punch, 75
Goldenrod Eggs, 261
Golden Sauce, 471
Goose, roasting, 369, 370
Gooseberry Pie, 207
Goulash, Hungarian, 315
Graham Cracker Crust, 204
Granola, 363
Grapefruit: Broiled, 66
  with Salad Greens, 405
  sectioning of, 339
Grapefruit-Orange Salad, and variations, 428
Grape Punch, Sparkling, 75
Gravy, Brown, 476
  Cream, 476
  Giblet, 476
  Onion, 476
  Pan, 476
  Sausage, 326
  Vegetable, 476
Green Beans, *see* Beans, Green
Green Peppers: preparation of, 402
  Rings, Sticks, 403
Green Pepper and Egg Dressing, 439
Green Pepper Slaw, 411
Green Rice, 360
Greens, preparation of fresh, 395
Green Salad, Basic Mixed, 405
Greens, with Grapefruit, 405
Green-top Salad, Swedish, 424
Griddle Broiling, meat, 301
  timetable for, 301
Ground Beef Stroganoff, 314
Guacamole Dip, 65

Half and Half Rolls, 122
Ham: Baked Glazed, and variations, 340
  Balls, Glazed, 341
  Biscuit Roll, 322
  and Cheese Sandwiches, Grilled, 462
  Creamed, 342
  Croquettes, 385
  Glazes for, 340
  Loaf, 341

INDEX

Glazed, 341
Omelet, 264
and Pasta Salad, 416
Patties, 341
  with Cranberries, 341
  with Pineapple, 341
Plantation Shortcake, 342
Salad Sandwiches, 453
  and Cheese, 453
  with Scalloped Potatoes, 553
  with Scrambled Eggs, 259
Soufflé, 384
timetable for broiling, 301
timetable for roasting, 299
Turnovers, 375
Hamburger Buns, 122
Hamburgers, Barbecued, 463
  Oven-Baked with Bun, 463
Hard Sauce, 491
  Brown Sugar, 492
  Cherry, 491
  Strawberry, 491
Hash, Baked, 324
  Corned Beef, 324
  Saucy Beef, 324
Hawaiian Tossed Salad, 405
Hearty Beef Vegetable Soup, 498
Hearty Potato Ham Chowder, 509
Herbed Tomato Buns, 127
Herbs and Spices, Use of, 607
Hollandaise Sauce, 484
  Mock, 485
Home-size recipes, increasing, 54
Honey Butter, 451
  Filling, 133
  French Dressing, 445
  Rolls, 131
Hors d'Oeuvres, Cold, 63
  Hot, 62
Horseradish Sauce, 482
  with Apples, 482
Hospitals, Menu Planning for, 576, 579
  Five Meal Plan, 577
Hot Bacon Sauce, 485
Hot Cabbage Slaw, 537
Hot Chocolate, 72
Hot Cross Buns, 122, 129
Hot Dog Buns, 122
Hot Fudge Sauce, 488
Hot Mustard Sauce, 481
Hot Potato Salad, 419
Hubbard Squash, Mashed, 560
Hungarian Goulash, 315

Ice Cream, amount to serve 50, 6
Ice Cream Frosting, 164
Ice Cream Pie, 228
Ice Cream Puffs, 240
Ice Cream Roll, 156
Icings, see Frostings
Increasing and decreasing recipe yields, 42
Ingredients: used in standardizing recipes, 59
  proportion of, 41
  substitutions, 39
Italian Pasta Salad, 417
Italian Salad Dressing, 442

Jellied Fruit Cup, 245
Jellied Waldorf Salad, 423
Jelly Muffins, 87
Jelly Roll, 157
Jelly Sauce, 475
Juices, amount to serve 50, 10
Julienne Vegetable Soup, 497

Kale, see Spinach
Kolaches, 129

Ladle equivalents, 38
Lady Baltimore Cake, 149
Lamb, amounts to serve 50, 11
  timetables: for braising, 303
  broiling, 301
  cooking in liquid, 303
  roasting, 298
Lasagne, 355
  Spinach, 356
Lazy Daisy Cake, 145
Leavening agents, substitutions, 39
  proportions, 41
Lemonade, 74
Lemon Baked Fish, 282
Lemon Butter, 451
Lemon Butter Frosting, 167
Lemon Butter Sauce, 477
Lemon Cake Pudding, 234
Lemon Chiffon Pie, 225
  Frozen, 225
Lemon Filling, 174
Lemon Pie, 220
Lemon Refrigerator Dessert, 225
Lemon Sauce, 490
Lettuce, preparation for salads, 395
  Wilted, 557
Lima Beans, see Beans, Lima

Lime Filling, 174
Lime Mold, Frosted, 423
Liver, with Bacon, 332
  Baked with Onions, 332
  Braised, 332
  Grilled, 332
  with Spanish Sauce, 332
Liver Paté, 65
Lobsters, selection and cooking of, 276, 280, 281
Lobster Salad, 436
Long Johns, Rolls, 129
Luncheon Meats, amounts to serve 50, 12
Lunches for Schools, 580

Macaroni, directions for cooking, 348
Macaroni and Cheese, 273
  with Ham, 273
Macaroni Salad, 416
Macaroons, Coconut, 179
Maitre d'Hotel Sauce, 477
Manhattan Clam Chowder, 516
Manhattan Fish Chowder, 516
Maple Nut Frosting, 164
Maraschino Cherry Frosting, 164
Marble Cake, 145
Marinade, Meat, 486
Marinade, Vegetable, 486
Marinated Asparagus, 414
Marinated Carrots, 410
Marinated Garden Salad, 413
Marinated Green Beans, 410
Marinated Mushrooms, 414
Marmalade Rolls, Glazed, 131
Marshmallow Squares, 198
  Chocolate, 198
  Peanut Butter, 198
Mayonnaise, and variations, 438
  with Cooked Base, 440
  see also Salad Dressings
Meat, 304–345
  amount to serve 50: Beef, 10
  Lamb, 11
  Pork, cured, 11
  Pork, fresh, 12
  Variety and Luncheon Meats, 12
  Veal, 12
  cooking methods, 295
  preparation for salads, 403
  purchasing and storage, 294
  timetable: for braising, 303
  broiling, 301

Meat (*Continued*)
   cooking in liquid, 303
   griddle broiling, 301
   roasting beef, 297
   roasting fresh and cured pork, 299
   roasting lamb and veal, 298
   see also Beef; Ham; Lamb; Pork; Veal
Meatballs, 310
   Barbecued, 310
   with Spaghetti, 350
   Spanish, 312
   Swedish, 309
Meat Croquettes, 385
Meat Loaf, 310
   Sandwiches, 310
   Vegetable, 310
Meat Marinade, 486
Meat Salad Sandwiches, 453
Meat and Vegetable Sauces, 470–486
Melons, preparation for salads, 398
Menu Planning, 569–590
   cycle, 571
   for different types of food services, 575
      Child Care Centers, 576
      Colleges and Universities, 576
      Commercial, 576
      Extended Care and Retirement Facilities, 577
      Hospitals, 576, 579
      Schools, 575
   factors affecting, 569
   key points, 573
   pattern, 571
      hospitals, 579
      nonselective, 579
      school lunch, 580
      selective, 579
   procedures, 572
   steps in, 573
   suggestions, 582–590
      desserts, 587
      entrées, 582
      garnishes, 589
      salads and relishes, 586
      sandwiches, 584
      soups, 587
      vegetables, 584
Menu Terms, Glossary of, 609
Meringue, for Pies, 204
   amount to serve 50, 6

Shells, 205
Sticks, 205
Torte, 205
Metric: conversion from U.S. weights and measures, 32, 34, 60
   equivalents, temperature, 34
   volume, 32
   weight, 32
Meuniere Sauce, 474
Mexican Rice, 361
Mexican Salad Dressing, 442
Milk, cookery, 255
   dry solids, 255
Milk and cream, substitutions, 39
Minestrone Soup, 501
Mix, Cake, 146
   Pancake, 104
   White Sauce, 472
Mocha Almond Pie, Frozen, 227
Mocha Frosting, 167, 169
Molasses Cookies, Drop, 183
Mornay Sauce, 473
Morning Coffee, suggested foods for, 599
Mousse, Chocolate, 171
Muffins, All-Bran, 89
   Apple Nut, 88
   Apricot, 87
   Bacon, 87
   Blueberry, 87
   Cake, 88
   Cherry, 87
   Cornmeal, 87
   Cranberry, 87
   Currant, 87
   Date, 87
   Ginger, 162
   Jelly, 87
   Nut, 87
   Oatmeal, 90
   Plain, 86
   Raised, 126
   Raisin Nut, 87
   Spiced, 87
   Whole Wheat, 87
Mulligatawny Soup, 502
Mushrooms: French-Fried, 545
   Marinated, 414
Mushroom Sauce, 471, 475
   and Almond, 474
   and Cheese, 474
   Fresh, 474
Mushroom Soufflé, 271

Mushroom Soup, Cream of, 510
Mushroom Stuffing, 393
Mustard Greens, *see* Spinach
Mustard Sauce, 480
   Hot, 481
   Savory, 475

Nacho Dog, 344
Nachos, 274
Navy Bean Soup, 506
Nonselective Menu Pattern, 579
Noodles, with Beef and Pork, 316
   and Chicken, 386
   and Chipped Beef, 327
   and Pork Casserole, 386
   and Tuna, 292
   and Turkey, 386
   directions for cooking, 348
   Romanoff, 357
   see also Pasta
Norwegian Christmas Bread, 118
Nut Bread, 100
Nut Cream Pie, 217
Nutmeg Sauce, 490
Nut Muffins, 87
Nuts, amount to serve 50, 15
Nut Stuffing, 393

Oatmeal Bread, 114
Oatmeal Crispies, 184
Oatmeal Coconut Crispies, 184
Oatmeal Date Bars, 197
Oatmeal Drop Cookies, 185
Oatmeal Muffins, 90
Oil and Vinegar Dressing, 442
Okra, cooking of, 522
Olive Sauce, 475
Omelet, Bacon, 264
   Baked, 264
   Cheese, 264
   Chinese, 262
   Ham, 264
   Jelly, 264
   Mushroom and Cheese, 264
   Potato, 263
   Potato Ham, 263
   Spanish, 264
Onion Butter, 451
Onion Gravy, 476
Onions, Baked, 544
   Casserole, 544
   cooking of, 544

Creamed Pearl, 544
French-Fried, 545
Glazed, 544
  preparation for salads, 402
  seasonings for, 544
  Stuffed Baked, 544
Onion Soup, French, 505
Open-Faced Hot Sandwiches, 448
Orange Biscuits, 85
Orange Butter Frosting, 167
Orange Cheese Frosting, 167
Orange Chiffon Cake, 142
Orange Chiffon Pie, 225
Orange Cream Puffs, Chocolate Filling, 240
Orange Cup Cakes, 143
Orange-filled Angel Food Cake, 440
Orange Filling, 174
Orange Frosting, 168
Orange Glaze for Ham, 340
Orange Juice, amount to serve 50, 9
Orange Rolls, 131
Orange Sauce, 490
  Fluffy, 490
Oriental Bean Salad, 409
Oriental Salad, 415
Ornamental Frosting, 170
Ounces and Decimal Equivalents, 45
Oven temperatures, terms for, 34
Oysters, Scalloped, 280
  selection and cooking, 276, 280, 281
Oyster Stew, 517
Oyster Stuffing, 393

Pancakes, 105
  Apple, 105
  Blueberry, 105
  Buttermilk, 105
  mix and table for use, 104
  Pecan, 105
  Potato, 555
Pan Coating, 139
Pan Gravy, 476
Pan Rolls, 121
Parkerhouse Rolls, 123
Parsley Butter Sauce, 477
Parsnips, cooking of, 522
Party Cheese Ball, 63
Pasta, Rice, and Cereals, 346–364

Pasta: amount to serve 50, 13
  cooking of, 346
  directions for cooking, 348
  shapes, 347
  yields, 348
Pasta, Recipes, 348–357
  with Chicken Sauce, 351
  with Clam Sauce, 354
  Lasagne, 355
    Spinach, 356
  Noodles Romanoff, 357
  Pasta, Beef and Tomato Casserole, 317
  Spaghetti with Chicken Sauce, 351
  with Vegetable Sauce, 352
  Vegetarian Spaghetti, 353
  see also Macaroni, Noodles, Spaghetti
Pastry: amount to serve 50, 6
  Danish, 129
  Graham Cracker Crust, 204
  for One-Crust Pies, 200
  for Two-Crust Pies, 201
  preparation of, 199
  Vanilla Wafer Crust, 204
Peach Cobbler with Hard Sauce, 250
Peach Crisp, 247
Peach Melba, 491
Peach Pie, 206, 207, 208
Peanut Butter Cookies, 187
Peanut Butter Marshmallow Squares, 198
Peanut Butter Sauce, 489
Peanut Cookies, 186
Peas, cooking of, 546
  Creamed with New Potatoes, 546
  with Lemon-Mint Butter, 546
  with Mushrooms, 546
  with New Turnips, 546
  with Pearl Onions, 546
  Seasoned, 546
  seasonings for, 546
Pecan Pancakes, 105
Pecan Pie, 222
Pecan Rolls, 131
Pecan Waffles, 103
Peppermint Frosting, 164
Pepper Pot Soup, 503
Peppers, Green, preparation for salad, 402
  Stuffed, 323
Pepper Steak, 307
Perfection Salad, 420

Pickled Beets, 432
Picnic Buns, Hot, 455
Pie Crust, see Pastry
Pies, 199–228
  amount to serve 50, 6
  Angel, 205
  Apple, Fresh, 210
  Apple Crumb, 210
  Apple, Sour Cream Nut,
  Apricot, 212
  Banana Cream, 217
  Berry, 206, 208
  Blueberry, 206, 208
  Boston Cream, 145
  Butterscotch Cream, 218
  with Canned Fruit, 208
  Cherry, 206, 208
  Chocolate Chiffon, 222
    Frozen, 222
    Peppermint, 222
  Chocolate Cream, 217
  Coconut Cream, 217
  Coconut Custard, 219
  Cream, 216
  Crumb Crusts, 204
  Custard, 219
  Date Cream, 217
  Frozen Fruit Pie, 206
    Guide for, 207
  Fruit Glazed, 217
  Fruit Tarts, 217
  Gooseberry, 207
  Ice Cream, 228
  Lemon, 220
  Lemon Chiffon, 225
    Frozen, 225
  Meringue for Pies, 204
  Mocha Almond, Frozen, 227
  Nut Cream, 217
  Pastry for One-Crust Pies, 200
    for Two-Crust Pies, 201
    preparation of, 199
  Orange Chiffon, 225
  Peach, 206, 208
  Pecan, 222
  Pineapple, 206, 208
  Pineapple Cream, 217
  Pumpkin, 221
  Pumpkin, Praline, 221
  Raisin, 212
    Sour Cream, 213
  Raspberry Alaska, 228
  Rhubarb, 214
    Custard, 215
  Strawberry Chiffon, 226

634 INDEX

Pigs in Blankets, 345
  with Cheese, 345
Pilaf, Rice, 361
Pimiento Sauce, 471
Pineapple-Apricot Punch, 76
Pineapple Bavarian Cream, 242
Pineapple Butter Frosting, 168
Pineapple Cashew Cake, 153
Pineapple-Cheese Salad, Molded, 423
Pineapple Cream Pie, 217
Pineapple Cream Pudding, 232
Pineapple fresh, coring and peeling, 400, 401
Pineapple Pie, 206, 208
Pineapple Refrigerator Dessert, 243
Pineapple Upside Down Cake, 145
Pinwheel Cookies, 191
Piquante Salad Dressing, 442
Piquante Sauce, 475
Pizza, 328
  Beef, 329
  Cheese, 329
  Pepperoni, 329
Placement, food and cover, served meal, 603
Planning Special Meals and Receptions, 595
Plantation Shortcake, 342
Plate Service for Banquet, 604
Popcorn Rolls, 123
Poppy Seed Cake, 149
Poppy Seed French Dressing, 443
Poppy Seed Fruit Dressing, 444
Poppy Seed Rolls, 123
Pork: amounts to serve 50, 11
  Bacon, Oven-Fried, 342
  Birds, 334
  and Beans, Baked, 530
  Chops, Baked, 335
    Baked with Apples, 335
    Barbecued, 336
    Breaded, 335
    Deviled, 336
    with Dressing, 337
    Honey-Glazed, 336
    with Scalloped Potatoes, 553
    Stuffed, 337
    Supreme, 336
  cooking methods, 295
  and Noodle Casserole, 386
  Pigs in Blankets, 345
    with Cheese, 345

Roast, 295, 299
Sandwiches, *see* Sandwiches
Sausage Gravy on Biscuits, 326
Sausage Rolls, 345
Scrapple, 343
Spareribs: Barbecued, 338
  with Dressing, 338
  with Sauerkraut, 338
  Sweet Sour, 338
Sweet Sour, 339
timetable for: braising, 303
  broiling, 301
  roasting, 299
see also Bacon, Ham, Frankfurters
Pork Fried Rice, 360
Potato Chips, 550
Potato Chowder, 508
  Ham, 509
Potato Croquettes, 551
Potato Omelet, 263
  Ham, 263
Potato Pancakes, 555
Potato Rosettes, 551
Potatoes: American Fried, 549
  au Gratin, 547
  Baked, 548
  Continental, 554
  cooking of, 551
  Cottage Fried, 549
  Deep-Fat Browned, 550
  Duchess, 551
  Fancy Top Baked, 548
  Franconia, 552
  French Baked, 552
  French-Fried, 550
  Hashed Brown, 549
  Herbed Potato Bake, 552
  in Jackets, 554
  Lattice, 550
  Lyonnaise, 549
  Mashed, 551
    Casserole, 551
  New, Creamed, 554
    with Peas, 554
  O'Brien, 549
  Oven-Browned, 552
  Oven-Fried, 549
  Parmesan New, 554
  Parsley Buttered, 554
  Persillade, New, 554
  preparation of, 551
  Rissolé, 552
  Scalloped, 553
    with Ham, 553

    with Onions, 553
    with Pork Chops, 553
  Shoestring, 550
  Stuffed Baked, 548
  Sweet, *see* Sweet Potatoes
Potato Salad, 418
  Hot, 418
  Sour Cream, 418
Potato Soup, Cream of, 510
Pot Pie, Beef, 313
  Chicken, 383
Pot Roast of Beef, 304
  Savory, 305
  Yankee, 305
Poultry, 365–393
  amounts to serve 50, 13
  broiling, 366
  cooking methods, 366
    table for, 366
  deep-fat frying, 367
  defrosting, 365
  oven-frying, 367
  pan-frying, 367
  purchasing and storage, 365
  roasting, 369
    guide for, 370
  stewing or simmering, 367
  yields of cooked meat, 10–12
  see also Chicken; Duck; Goose; Turkey
Powdered Sugar Glaze, 170
Praline Cake, 145
Praline Gingerbread, 162
Praline Pumpkin Pie, 221
Preparation and Serving Guides, 33–41
Preparing food for deep-fat frying, 37
  batter, 37
  egg and crumb, 37
  light coating, 37
Processed Eggs, 252
Prune Date Filling, 172
Prune Filling, 173
Puddings and Other Desserts, 229–251
  amounts to serve 50, 7
  Apple Brown Betty, 246
  Apple Compote, 249
  Apple Crisp, 247
    with Cheese, 247
  Apple Dumplings, 248
    with Hot Butter Sauce, 249
  Applesauce, 249
  Apricot Bavarian Cream, 242
  Baked Apples, 248

INDEX

Banana Cream Pudding, 232
Bread Pudding, 238
Butterscotch Pudding, 229
Cheese Cake, 236
　with Fruit Glaze, 236
Cherry Crisp, 247
Chocolate Cream Pudding, 232
Chocolate Mousse, 171
Chocolate Pudding, 230
Chocolate Refrigerator Dessert, 222
Christmas Pudding, 239
　Flaming, 239
Cobblers, guide for frozen fruit, 207
Coconut Cream Pudding, 232
Cottage Pudding, 145
Cream Pudding, Vanilla, 232
Cream Puffs, 240
　Butterscotch, 240
　Ice Cream, 240
　Orange with Chocolate Filling, 240
Custard, Baked, 238
　Caramel, 238
　Rice, 238
Date Pudding, 233
Eclairs, 240
English Toffee Dessert, 241
Floating Island, 237
Fresh Fruit Crisp, 247
Fresh Peach Cobbler, 250
Fruit Cobbler, 250
Fruit Slices, 250
Fudge Pudding, 235
Ice Cream Puffs, 240
Jellied Fruit Cup, 245
Lemon Cake Pudding, 234
Lemon Refrigerator Dessert, 225
Meringue Shells, 205
Peach Crisp, 247
Peach Melba, 491
Pineapple Bavarian Cream, 242
Pineapple Cream Pudding, 232
Pineapple Refrigerator Dessert, 243
Russian Cream, 244
Strawberry Bavarian Cream, 242
Strawberry Shortcake, 251
Tapioca Cream, 231

Fruit, 231
　Puff Shells, 240
　Vanilla Cream Pudding, 232
Pumpkin Bread, 101
Pumpkin Pie, 221
　Praline, 221
Punch, 74–79
　amounts to serve 50, 4
　Apricot-Pineapple, 76
　Banana, 77
　Banana Slush, 77
　Cider, 79
　　Spiced, 79
　Cranberry, 77
　Foundation Fruit, 75
　Ginger Ale Fruit, 74
　Golden, 75
　Grape, Sparkling, 75
　Lemonade, 74
　preparation of, 68
　Rhubarb, 76
　Sauerkraut Juice Cocktail, 78
　Tomato Juice, Hot Spiced, 79
　Tomato Juice Cocktail, 78
　Wassail Bowl, 78

Quiche, 265
　Mushroom, 265
　Seafood, 265
　Swiss Spinach, 265
Quick Breads, see Breads, Quick

Radishes, Accordions, Roses, 403
Raised Muffins, 126
Raisin Biscuits, 85
Raisin Bread, 113
Raisin-Nut Muffins, 87
Raisin Pie, 212
　Sour Cream, 213
Raisin Sauce, 480
Raisin Stuffing, 393
Ranch Style Beans, 531
Raspberry Alaska Pie, 228
Raspberry Sauce, 491
Receptions and Teas, 596
Recipe Adjustment, 42
　converting to metric, 60
　converting from weight to measure, 42
　direct reading tables, 47, 50, 54
　factor method, 42
　increasing and decreasing yields, 42

　percentage method, 43
Recipe Information, 59
　abbreviations used, 61
　cooking time and temperature, 60
　ingredients used in standardizing, 59
　weights and measures, 60
　　metric, 60
　yield, 59
Refried Beans, 532
Relishes, 430–432
　amounts to serve 50, 14
　Apple Rings, 430
　Beet Pickles, 432
　Buttered Apples, 430
　Carrot Curls, Sticks, 402
　Celery Curls, 402
　Cinnamon Apples, 430
　Cranberry Relish, Raw, 431
　　-Orange, 431
　Cranberry Sauce, 431
　　Puréed, 431
　　Royal, 431
　Fried Apples, 430
　preparation of, 402
　Radish Accordions, Roses, 403
　Sauerkraut Relish, 432
Residence Halls, Menu Planning for, 576
Restaurants, Menu Planning for, 576
Reuben Sandwich, 464
Rhubarb Pie, 214
　Custard, 215
Rhubarb Punch, 76
Ribbon Gelatin Salad, 424
Ribbon Rolls, 123
Ribbon Sandwiches, 448
Rice: Baked, 358
　Boiled, 359
　and Chicken Casserole, 389
　cooking of, 346, 358
　Curried, 36
　Custard, 238
　Fried, 360
　　with Almonds, 360
　　with Ham, 360
　　with Pork, 360
　　with Shrimp, 360
　Green, 360
　Mexican, 361
　Pilaf, 361
　Soup, 504
　Spanish, 319

INDEX

Rice (*Continued*)
  Steamed, 358
Roast Beef Sandwiches, Barbecued, 465
  French Dip, 465
  Hot, 465
Roasting, timetables for, 297, 370
Roast Pork Sandwiches, Hot, 465
Rolls: amount to serve 50, 5
  Basic Dough, 120
  Bowknots, 120
  Braids, 120
  Butter Buns, 125
  Butterflake, 121
  Butterfly, 130
  Butterhorns, 121
  Butterscotch, 131
  Caramel Crowns, 121
  Cherry Nut, 129
  Cinnamon, 130
    Double, 131
    Raisin, 131
  Cloverleaf, 121
  Crescent, 121
  Dinner, 121
  Fan Tan, 121
  Glazed Marmalade, 131
  Half and Half, 122
  Hamburger Buns, 122
  Herbed Tomato Buns, 127
  Honey, 131
  Hot Cross Buns, 122, 129
  Hot Dog Buns, 122
  Kolaches, 129
  Long Johns, 129
  Orange, 132
  Pan, 121
  Parkerhouse, 123
  Pecan, 131
  Popcorn, 123
  Poppy Seed, 123
  Quick Roll Dough, 119
  Raised Muffins, 126
  Refrigerator, 124
  Ribbon, 123
  Rosettes, 123
  Rye, 117
  Sesame, 123
  Sugared Snails, 131
  Sweet Roll Dough, Basic, 128
  Twin, 123
  Twists, 123
  Whole Wheat, 123
  see also Breads, Yeast; Buns
Romaine, preparation of, 395

Roquefort Dressing, 439
  Creamy Blue, 438
  French, 442
Rosettes, Rolls, 123
Rounding off weights and measures, 44
Roux, 469
Runza, 466
Russian Cream, 244
Russian Salad Dressing, 439
Russian Tea, 70
Rutabagas, cooking of, 522
Rye Bread, Swedish, 117
  Caraway, 117
Rye Rolls, 117

Salad Dressings, 438–446
  amounts to serve 50, 14
  Bacon, 444
  Buttermilk, 438
  Campus, 438
  Celery Seed French, 443
  Celery Seed Fruit, 444
  Chantilly, 438, 441
  Chiffonade, 442
  Chilean, 446
  Combination, 441
  Cooked, 441
  Creamy Blue Cheese, 438
  Dilly, 439
  Egg and Green Pepper, 439
  French, Light, 442
    Semipermanent, 443
    Thick, 443
  Fruit, 445
  Garden, 439
  Honey-Cream, 439
  Honey French, 445
  Italian, 442
  Mayonnaise, 438
    with Cooked Base, 440
  Mexican, 442
  Oil and Vinegar, 442
  Piquante, 442
  Poppy Seed, 443
  Poppy Seed Fruit, 444
  Roquefort, 439
  Roquefort Cheese French, 442
  Russian, 439
  Sour Cream, 439
  Tarragon, 442
  Thousand Island, 439
  Tomato French, 442
  Vinaigrette, 442
Salads, 394-429

amounts to serve 50, 14
placed, 394
preparation, 394
  of ingredients, 395
recipes, 435–437
salad bar, 395
Salads, entrée, 433–437
  Chef's Salad Bowl, 433
  Chicken, 434
    –Avocado-Orange, 434
    with Bacon, 433
    Crunchy, 434
    Curried, 434
    Fruited, 434
    Hot, 379
    Pasta, 416
  Cottage Cheese, 435
  Crab, 436
  Deviled Eggs, 268
  Ham and Pasta, 416
  Lobster, 436
  Salmon, 437
  Seafood Chef, 433
  Shrimp, 436
  Shrimp-Rice, 435
  Tomato, Stuffed, 437
  Tomato-Cabbage, 437
  Tomato-Cottage Cheese, 437
  Tuna, 437
  Tuna-Apple, 437
  Turkey, 434
Salads, Fruit, 425–429
  Apple (Waldorf), and variations, 425
  Apple Spiced, 426
  Citrus-Pomegranate, 428
  Fresh Fruit Salad Bowl, 428
  Frozen Fruit, 429
  Fruit, Creamy, 427
  Grapefruit-Apple, 428
    -Orange, 428
    -Orange-Avocado, 428
    -Orange-Pear, 428
  Waldorf, 425
Salads, Gelatin, 420–424
  Applesauce, 422
  Arabian Peach, 422
  Autumn, 422
  Bing Cherry, 423
  Blueberry, 423
  Cranberry Ring Mold, 423
  Cucumber Soufflé, 423
  Frosted Cherry, 423
  Frosted Lime Mold, 423
  Fruit Gelatin, and variations, 422
  Ginger Ale Fruit, 423

INDEX

Jellied Citrus, 423
Jellied Waldorf, 423
Molded Pineapple-Cheese, 423
Perfection, 420
Ribbon, 424
Strawberry Rhubarb, 424
Sunshine, 424
Swedish Green-Top, 424
Tomato Aspic, 421
Under-the-Sea, 424
Salads, Vegetable and Pasta, 405–419
Brown Bean, 407
Cabbage-Apple, 425
Cabbage-Carrot Slaw, 412
Cabbage-Pineapple-Marshmallow, 412
Carrifruit, 411
Carrot-Raisin, and variations, 410
Cauliflower-Bean, 409
Cauliflower-Broccoli, 411
Creamy, 412
Cole Slaw, 411
Creamy, 412
Cucumber and Onion in Sour Cream, 413
Garbanzo Bean, 408
with Pasta, 408
German Cucumbers, 413
Green Mixed Salad, Basic, 405
Green Pepper Slaw, 411
Hawaiian Tossed, 405
Italian Pasta, 417
Macaroni, 416
Marinated Asparagus, 414
Marinated Carrots, 410
Marinated Garden Salad, 413
Marinated Green Beans, 414
Marinated Mushrooms, 414
Oriental, 415
Oriental Bean, 409
Potato, 418
Hot, 419
Sour Cream, 418
Salad Greens with Grapefruit, 405
Spinach, 405
Spinach-Cheese, 415
Spinach-Mushroom, 405
Tossed Vegetable, 406
Triple Bean, 409
Vegetable Collage, 414
Salisbury Steak, 305

Salmon Biscuit Roll, 322
Salmon, Creamed, 293
Salmon, Scalloped, 290
Salmon Biscuit Roll, 322
Salmon Croquettes, 289
Salmon Loaf, 288
Salmon Patties, 289
Salmon Potato Chip Casserole, 491
Salmon Salad, 437
Salmon Salad Sandwiches, 454
Sandies, 188
Sandwiches, 447–468
canapés, 448
checkerboard, 450
closed, 447
freezing, 450
grilled and toasted, 448
making, 447
open-faced, hot, 448
preparation of ingredients, 447
ribbon, 448
rolled, 450
Sandwiches, Recipes, 451–468
Bacon, Lettuce, and Tomato, 456
Barbecued Beef, 465
Cheese, 462
French-Fried, 462
Grilled, with Ham, 462
Chicken Salad, 453
Chili Dog, 344
Chimichanga, 458
Club, 456
Egg Salad, 452
French Dip, 465
Hamburgers: Barbecued, 463
Oven-Baked, 463
Ham Salad, 453
and Cheese, 453
Meat Loaf, 310
Meat Salad, 453
Nacho Dog, 344
Picnic Bun, Hot, 455
Pimiento Cheese, 462
Reuben, 464
Roast Beef, Hot, 465
Roast Pork, Hot, 465
Runza, 466
Salmon Salad, 454
Sandwich Spread, 452
Savory, 451
Submarine, 457
Tacos, 468

Tostados, 468
Tuna Buns, Hot, 455
Tuna Salad, 454
Grilled, 454
Turkey, Hot, 465
Western, 467
Whipped Margarine or Butter for, 451
Sauces, 469–492
amounts to serve 50, 14
uses of, 469
White Sauce, methods of preparing, 470
Sauces, Dessert, 487–492
Butterscotch, 487
Caramel, 487
Chocolate, 488
Hot, 488
Custard, 489
Fluffy Orange, 490
Hard, 491
Brown Sugar, 492
Cherry, 491
Strawberry, 491
Hot Fudge, 488
Lemon, 490
Nutmeg, 490
Orange, 490
Peanut Butter, 489
Raspberry, 491
Syrup, Brown Sugar, 492
Vanilla, 490
Sauces, Meat and Vegetable, 470–486
à la King, 471
Almond Butter, 477
Bacon, 471
Hot, 485
Barbecue, 476, 477
Bechamel, 473
Brown, 475
Cheese, 471
Chicken, for Pasta, 351
Clam for Pasta, 354
Cocktail, 483
Cranberry, 431
Cucumber, 484
Drawn Butter, 477
Egg, 471
Golden, 471
Gravy, 476
variations, see Gravy
Hollandaise, 484
Mock 485
Horseradish, 482
Apple, 482
Jelly, 475

INDEX

Sauces, Meat and Vegetable (*Continued*)
  Lemon Butter, 477
  Maitre d'Hotel, 477
  Meat Marinade, 486
  Meuniere, 474
  Mornay, 473
  Mushroom, 471, 475
    and Almond, 474
    and Cheese, 474
    Fresh, 474
  Mustard, 480
    Hot, 481
    Savory, 475
  Nacho, 274
  Olive, 475
  Parsley Butter, 477
  Pimiento, 471
  Piquante, 475
  Raisin, 480
  Shrimp, 471
  Spanish, 478
  Sweet-Sour, 481
  Tartar, 483
  Tomato, 478
    Basic, 352
    Spicy, 479
  Vegetable, for Pasta, 352
  Vegetable Marinade, 486
  Velouté, 473
  White Sauce, 470
    methods of preparing, 470
    Mix, 472
Sauerkraut Balls, 63
Sauerkraut Juice Cocktail, 78
Sauerkraut Relish, 432
Sausage Balls, 62
Sausage and Egg Bake, 260
Sausage Gravy, 326
Sausage Rolls, 345
Sausage Stuffing, 393
Savory Mustard Sauce, 475
Savory Spread, for Sandwiches, 451
Scaling weights, Cakes, 138
  Frostings and Fillings, 139
Scallops, selection and cooking of, 276, 281
Schools, menu planning for, 575
  lunch patterns, 580
Scones, Scotch, 85
Scoops, *see* Dippers
Scotch Woodcock, 261
Scrambled Eggs, 259
  and Cheese, 259

  and Chipped Beef, 259
  and Ham, 259
  oven method for cooking, 259
  steamer method for cooking, 259
Scrapple, 343
Seafood Chef Salad, 433
Seafood cocktails, suggestions for, 66
Seafood Quiche, 265
Seasonings, proportions of, 41
Selective Menu Pattern, 579
Sesame Rolls, 123
Shellfish, 276
  amount to serve 50, 7
  cooking methods, 281
  purchasing and storage, 276
Shortcake, Biscuit, 85
  Old-Fashioned Strawberry, 251
Shortening agents, substitutions, 39
Shortribs, Barbecued, 338
Shrimp, Creole, 287
Shrimp, Deep-Fat Fried, 36
Shrimp, selection and cooking of, 277, 281
Shrimp Fried Rice, 360
Shrimp Salad, 436
  with Rice, 435
Shrimp Sauce, 471
Silver White Cake, 149
Singapore Curry, 391
Smothered Steak with Onions, 306
Snickerdoodles, 189
Soufflé: Cheese, 271
  Chicken, 384
  Ham, 384
  Mushroom, 271
  Spinach, 558
  Tuna, 384
  Turkey, 384
Soups, 493–519
  amounts to serve 50, 15
  classification of, 493
  stock, preparation of, 494, 495
Soups, Recipes, 494–519
  Alphabet, 499
  Asparagus, Cream of, 510
  Basic Sauce for Cream Soup, 510
  Bean, Navy, 506
  Beef Barley, 497
  Beef Noodle, 499

  Beef Rice, 499
  Beef Stock, 494
    Brown, 494
    with Soup Base, 494
  Beef Vegetable, Hearty, 498
  Bouillon, and variations, 496
  Broccoli, Cream of, 510
  Broccoli and Cheese, 514
  Celery, Cream of, 510
  Cheese, 513
    and Broccoli, 514
  Chicken, Cream of, 511
  Chicken Noodle, 500
  Chicken Rice, 500
  Chicken Stock, 495
    with Soup Base, 495
  Chicken Velvet, 511
  Chili Con Carne, 325
  Chilled: Gazpacho, 518
    Vichyssoise, 519
  Clam Chowder, Manhattan, 516
    New England, 515
  Corn Chowder, 508
  Cream Soups, 510–517
    Basic Sauce for, 510
  Creole, 499
  Fish Chowder, Manhattan, 516
    New England, 515
  French Onion, 505
  Gazpacho, 518
  Julienne, 497
  Minestrone, 501
  Mulligatawny, 502
  Mushroom, Cream of, 510
  Oyster Stew, 517
  Pepper Pot, 503
  Potato, Cream of, 510
  Potato Chowder, 508
  Potato Ham Chowder, Hearty, 509
  Rice, 504
  Spinach, Cream of, 510
  Split Pea, 507
  Stock Soups, 494–509
  Stock: Beef, 494
    Brown, 494
    Chicken, 495
    White, 495
  Tomato, Cream of, 512
  Tomato Barley, 504
  Tomato Bouillon, 496
  Tomato Rice, 504
  Vegetable, 497
  Vegetable, Cream of, 510

Vegetable Beef, 497
Vegetable Chowder, 510
Vichyssoise, 519
Sour Cream Apple Nut Pie, 211
Sour Cream Potato Salad, 418
Sour Cream Raisin Pie, 213
Sour Cream Salad Dressing, 439
Spaetzles (Egg Dumplings), 108
Spaghetti: Chili, 325
  with Chicken Sauce, 351
  with Clam Sauce, 354
  Creole, 325
  directions for cooking, 348
  with Meatballs, 350
  with Meat Sauce, 349
  with Vegetable Sauce, 352
  Vegetarian, 353
  see also Pasta
Spanish Rice, 319
Spanish Sauce, 478
Spanish Steak, 306
Spareribs: Baked with Dressing, 338
  Barbecued, 338
  with Sauerkraut, 338
  Sweet Sour, 338
Special Meals and Receptions, 595–606
  Banquet Service, 602
  Buffet Dinners and Luncheons, 599
  Coffees and Brunches, 596
  Planning, 595
  Receptions and Teas, 596
Spice Cake, 148
Spiced Apple Salad, 426
Spiced Muffins, 87
Spiced Tomato Juice, Hot, 79
Spices and Herbs, use of, 607
Spinach: cooking of, 557
  Creamed, 557
  Crepes, 378
  Lasagne, 356
  Quiche, 265
  Salad, 405
    with Cheese, 415
    with Mushrooms, 405
  Seasoned, 557
  seasonings for, 557
  Soufflé, 558
  Soup, Cream of, 510
  Stuffed Tomatoes, 562
  Wilted, 557
Split Pea Soup, 507
Sponge Cake, 441

Spoon Bread, 95
Spread, Sandwich, 452
Squash, Winter: cooking of, 560
  Acorn, Baked, 559
    with Sausage, 559
    Stuffed, 559
  Butternut, Mashed, 560
  Butternut-Apple Casserole, 560
Squash, Zucchini or Summer: Casserole, 561
  French-Fried, 545
  Seasoned, 561
  and Tomato Casserole, 561
Starburst Cake, 149
Steak, see Beef
Steaming or boiling vegetables, 521
  timetable for, 522
Stew, Beef, and variations, 313
Stir-Fried Vegetables, 564
Stir-Frying, directions for, 523
Stock, Beef, 494
  Brown, 494
  Chicken, 495
Strawberry Bavarian Cream, 242
Strawberry Chiffon Pie, 226
Strawberry Hard Sauce, 491
Strawberry Rhubarb Salad, 424
Strawberry Shortcake, 251
Streusel Topping, 210
Stroganoff, Beef, 314
Stuffed Eggs, Hot, 268
Stuffed Peppers, 323
Stuffing or Dressing, Apple, 393
  Bread, 392
  Chestnut, 393
  Corn Bread, 393
  Mushroom, 393
  Nut, 393
  Oyster, 393
  Raisin, 393
  Sausage, 393
Submarine Sandwich, 457
Substitutions, can sizes, 38
Substitutions, ingredient, 39
Succotash, 528
Sugar, Caramelized, 151
Sugar Cookies: Drop, 190
  Rolled, 191
  Whole Wheat, 192
Sugared Snails, 131
Sunshine Salad, 424
Swedish Braids, 129

Swedish Green-Top Salad, 424
Sweet Potatoes: and Apples, 556
  Baked, 556
  cooking of, 556
  Glazed or Candied, 556
    with Almonds, 556
    with Orange Slices, 556
  Mashed, 556
  seasonings for, 556
Sweet Roll Dough, Basic, 128
  variations of, 129
Sweet-Sour Sauce, 481
Swiss Steak, 306
Syrup, Brown Sugar, 492
Syrup, Simple, 75
Syrups and Candies, temperatures and tests for, 35

Table arrangement, buffets, 601
  receptions and teas, 598
Table cover for served meal, 603
Tables and guides, use of, 3
Table service for banquets, 604
Tacos, 468
Taco Salad Casserole, 330
Tahitian Chicken, 374
Tapioca Cream, 231
  Fruit, 231
Tarragon French Dressing, 442
Tartar Sauce, 483
Tarts, Fruit, 217
Tea: amounts to serve 50, 4
  Hot, 70
  Iced, 71
  preparation of, 68
  Russian, 70
  Spiced, 70
Tea Cookies, Butter, 176
  Chocolate, 181
Teas, 596
Tea Sandwiches: canapés, 448
  checkerboard, 450
  ribbon, 448
  rolled, 450
Temperatures: baking, 33
  deep-fat frying, 36
  metric equivalents, 34
  oven, 34
  roasting meats, 297–299
  poultry, 370
  syrups and candies, 35
Teriyaki Chicken, 372
Teriyaki Steak, 306
Thickening agents, proportions, 41

640 INDEX

Thickening Agents (*Continued*)
  substitutions, 39
Thimble Cookies, 176
Thousand Island Dressing, 439
Timbales, Chicken, 565
  Vegetable, 565
Tomato Aspic, 421
Tomato Bouillon, 496
Tomato Cabbage Salad, 437
Tomato Cottage Cheese Salad, 437
Tomatoes: Baked, 562
  Breaded, 563
  Broiled Slices, 562
  and Celery, 563
  Creole, 563
  Mushroom-Stuffed, 562
  preparation for salads, 402
  seasonings for, 562
  Spinach-Stuffed, 562
Tomato French Dressing, 442
Tomato Juice: amounts to serve, 50, 4
  Cocktail, 78
  Hot Spiced, 79
Tomato Salad, Stuffed, and variations, 437
Tomato Sauce, 478
  Basic, 352
  Spicy, 479
Tomato Soup, with Barley, 504
  Cream of, 512
  with Rice, 504
Tomato Vegetable Medley, 563
Toppings, *see* Fillings
Tossed Vegetable Salad, 406
Tostados, 468
Triple Bean Salad, 409
Tuna, Creamed, 293
  with Celery, 293
  with Peas, 293
Tuna, Scalloped, 290
Tuna à la King, 376
Tuna Biscuit Roll, 322
Tuna Buns, Hot, 455
Tuna Casserole: with Noodles, 292
  with Potato Chips, 291
  with Rice, 292
Tuna Loaf, 380
Tuna Patties, 289
Tuna Rarebit, 293
Tuna Salad, 437
  with Apples, 437
Tuna Salad Sandwiches, 454

  Grilled, 454
Tuna Soufflé, 384
Tuna Tetrazzini, 387
Turkey: à la King, 376
  amounts to serve 50, 13
  Biscuit Roll, 322
  Casserole, 389
  cooking methods, 366
  Divan, 390
  Loaf, 380
  and Noodle Casserole, 386
  Pie, 383
  roasting guide, 370
  Salad, 434
  Salad, Hot, 379
  Sandwich, Hot, 465
  Scalloped, 377
  Soufflé, 384
  Tetrazzini, 387
Turnip Greens, *see* Spinach
Turnips with Peas, 546
Turnovers: Beef, 375
  Chicken, 375
  Ham, 375
Twin Rolls, 123
Twists, Rolls, 123

Under-the-Sea Salad, 424

Vanilla Cream Pudding, 232
Vanilla Sauce, 490
Vanilla Wafer Crust, 204
Veal: amounts to serve 50, 12
  cooking methods, 295
  timetable: for braising, 303
    cooking in liquid, 303
    roasting, 298
Veal, Recipes, 333–334
  Birds, 334
    with Sausage Stuffing, 334
  Breaded Cutlets, 333
  Cacciatore, 333
  New Orleans, 333
  Parmesan, 333
  Piccata, 333
  Scallopini, 334
Vegetable Beef Soup, 494
Vegetable Chowder, 510
Vegetable Collage, 414
Vegetable Marinade, 486
Vegetable and Pasta Salads, 405–419
Vegetables: 520–565
  amounts to serve 50, 15
  canned: can sizes, 38

  directions for heating, 523
  dried, cooking, 523
  fresh and frozen, cooking, 520
    boiling, 521
    steaming, 521
    stir-frying, 523
  preparation for salads, 401
  Stir-Fried, 564
  stir-frying, directions for, 523
  timetable for boiling or steaming, 522
  yield in preparation, 20
  see also individual vegetables
Vegetable Salad, Tossed, 406
Vegetable Soup, Cream of, 510
Vegetable Timbale, 565
Vegetarian Spaghetti, 350
Velouté Sauce, 473
Vichyssoise, 519
Vinaigrette Dressing, 442

Waffles, 103
  Bacon, 103
  Cornmeal, 103
  Pecan, 103
Waldorf Salad and variations, 425
  Jellied, 423
Walnut Chiffon Cake, 142
Wassail Bowl, 78
Wax Beans, cooking of, 525
  Seasoned, 525
Weights and measures, rounding off, 44
  tables of, 21
  used in recipes, 60
Welsh Rarebit, 275
Western Sandwich, 467
Whipped Margarine or Butter, 451
White Bread, 110
White Cake, 148
White Sauce, 470
  methods for making, 470
  Mix, 472
  variations of, 471
White Stock, 495
Whole Wheat Biscuits, 85
Whole Wheat Bread, 113
Whole Wheat Muffins, 87
Whole Wheat Rolls, 123
Whole Wheat Sugar Cookies, 192

Wieners, *see* Frankfurters
Wilted Lettuce or Spinach, 557
Yeast Bread, *see* Breads, Yeast

Yellow Angel Food Cake, 441
Yield, fresh fruits and vegetables, 20
Yield of recipes, 59

Zucchini Squash: Casserole, 561
French-Fried, 545
Seasoned, 561
and Summer Squash, 561